1/18

LINCOLN

&

CHURCHILL

Statesmen at War

LEWIS E. LEHRMAN

STACKPOLE BOOKS

Guilford, Connecticut

Published by Stackpole Books
An imprint of Globe Pequot
Trade Division of The Rowman & Littlefield Publishing Group, Inc.
4501 Forbes Boulevard, Suite 200, Lanham, Maryland 20706
www.rowman.com

Distributed by
NATIONAL BOOK NETWORK
800-462-6420

British Library Cataloguing in Publication Information Available

Library of Congress Cataloging-in-Publication Data

Names: Lehrman, Lewis E., author.
Title: Lincoln & Churchill : statesmen at war / Lewis E. Lehrman.
Description: Guilford, Connecticut : Stackpole Books, 2018. | Includes
  bibliographical references and index.
Identifiers: LCCN 2017037477 (print) | LCCN 2017037899 (ebook) | ISBN
  9780811767453 (e-book) | ISBN 9780811719674 (hardback : alk. paper) |
  ISBN 9780811767453 (ebook)
Subjects: LCSH: Lincoln, Abraham, 1809-1865—Military leadership. |
  Churchill, Winston, 1874-1965—Military leadership. | United States—
  History—Civil War, 1861-1865—Biography. | World War, 1939-1945—
  Biography. | Lincoln, Abraham, 1809-1865—Influence. | Churchill, Winston,
  1874-1965—Influence.
Classification: LCC E457.2 (ebook) | LCC E457.2 .L443 2018 (print) | DDC
  973.7092 [B] —dc23
LC record available at https://lccn.loc.gov/2017037477

First Edition

Printed in the United States of America

♾™ The paper used in this publication meets the minimum requirements of American National Standard for Information Sciences—Permanence of Paper for Printed Library Materials, ANSI/NISO Z39.48-1992.

"And some there be, which have no memorial; who are perished, as though they had never been . . ."

Ecclesiasticus (44:9)

For Louise, always.

For my children and their spouses: Leland and Vera, John and Jenifer, Thomas and Mara, Eliza and Filip, Peter and Eve.

For my grandchildren: Cree, Kestrel, Berenika, Peter Lewis, Rose, Isabel, Jasmine, James, Forest, Eleanor, Lawrence, Reed, Caroline, Sadie Louise.

In War: Resolution,
In Defeat: Defiance,
In Victory: Magnanimity,
In Peace: Good Will.

WINSTON S. CHURCHILL
inserted these phrases at the beginning of each volume of his
World War II memoirs (probably drafted in 1919 as a
possible inscription on a French war memorial).

With malice toward none; with charity for all; with
firmness in the right, as God gives us to see the right, let
us strive on to finish the work we are in; to bind up the
nation's wounds; to care for him who shall have borne
the battle, and for his widow, and his orphan—to do
all which may achieve and cherish a just, and a lasting
peace, among ourselves, and with all nations.

ABRAHAM LINCOLN
Second Inaugural Address
March 4, 1865

CONTENTS

PREFACE:
WARS OF NATIONAL SURVIVAL

Still in his teens, Winston Churchill took the entrance examination for the Royal Military Academy at Sandhurst. He chose to write his essay on the American Civil War. The topic fascinated him. As an adolescent, the future prime minister had seen British cartoons on slavery, published in the journal *Punch*. He exclaimed: "I was all for the slave." At first, young Churchill was not as sympathetic to President Lincoln as Churchill would become. Churchill would become an admirer of Ulysses S. Grant after reading the general's memoirs.[1]

During World War II, Churchill would meet many of the same challenges that Lincoln had faced eight decades earlier. Raised in very different social, economic, and professional environments, the harsh reality of wars of national survival would challenge them immediately upon becoming president and prime minister. Lincoln came to the presidency inexperienced in war—not well known, but well respected by those who knew him. Churchill became prime minister well experienced, very well known, but doubted by members of his Conservative Party. Like President Lincoln during his continental civil war, Churchill embraced the political and military leadership of his country in a global war that imperiled his country's survival.

Before taking supreme command of their nations' armed forces, both unconventional men had lived their lives at the edge of respectability—not so far "outside" as to affront those who knew them, but not so far "inside" as to limit their flexibility when events would require unconventional decisions. Lincoln's character and conduct gave rise to few permanent enemies. From early maturity, he would stick primarily to fixed goals and principles. Strategic principles gave him freedom to take prudent tactical action to attain his goals. Churchill's goals and ambition had caused him to change political parties twice. But on issues of principle, he stood fast, even while adapting to changed circumstances during a sixty-year political career. On the issue of Hitler's mortal threat to European and Christian civilization, the prime minister would establish his uncompromising opposition before he took office in 1940.

Neither the United States in 1860 nor Britain in 1939 had been well prepared for the cataclysms that would overtake them. Nothing could have made Lincoln or Churchill entirely ready for the challenges each would have to overcome. About three weeks after assuming office, both supreme commanders would prevail in crucial cabinet divisions on national strategy. In so doing, Lincoln and Churchill would thereafter set bold and heroic standards that defined their wartime leadership.

Shortly after the inauguration, on March 28, 1861, after a diplomatic dinner at the White House, the Lincoln Cabinet gathered to discuss secession and the military situation. General Winfield Scott could not attend, but he sent a strategy memo that proposed abandoning both Fort Sumter in South Carolina and Fort Pickens in Florida to the Confederates. Scott biographer Charles Winslow Elliott wrote: "The chair reserved at the table for the General-in-Chief being withdrawn, the dinner proceeded without him, and at its conclusion, when all the guests except the Cabinet members had taken their leave, Mr. Lincoln disclosed to his astonished advisers the fact that Scott had formally [in his memo] counseled the abandonment of the two beleaguered fortresses."[2] Scott's memorandum recommended appeasement of the seceding states: "Our Southern friends, however, are clear that the evacuation of both the forts would instantly soothe and give confidence to the eight remaining slave-holding States, and render their cordial adherence to this Union perpetual."[3]

President Lincoln rejected this advice despite the worries of his cabinet. Acting to the contrary, Lincoln took command: "I am directed by the President," wrote Lincoln aide John G. Nicolay, to General Scott, "to say that he [the president] desires you to exercise all vigilance for the maintenance of all the places within the military department of the United States."[4] The commander in chief made clear to the general-in-chief that the Federal forts would not be abandoned to the rebels. About two weeks later, the Confederate attack on Fort Sumter would trigger four years of bloody civil war, on a scale without precedent.

Nearly four score years later, during nine meetings of the War Cabinet held May 26–28, 1940—after the onset of the Nazi blitzkrieg—Churchill

Abraham Lincoln, November 1863
Gilder Lehrman Collection, GLC00245

Winston S. Churchill, ca. 1941
Library of Congress, LC-USZ62-64419

would encounter a major cabinet division over whether to approach Italy as an intermediary to bring about peace negotiations with Hitler's Germany. The British Foreign Secretary, Lord Halifax, favored such an approach. Frustrated by Churchill, he threatened to resign.[5] As discussions dragged on in the War Cabinet, Churchill—in his third week as prime minister—decided to speak with his junior cabinet ministers: "Every man of you would rise up and tear me down from my place if I were for one moment to contemplate parley or surrender," the prime minister told them. "If this long island story of ours is to end at last, let it end only when each one of us lies choking in his own blood upon the ground."[6] Churchill wrote of this critical meeting in his memoirs: "Quite a number seemed to jump up from the table and come running to my chair, shouting and patting me on the back. I was sure that every minister was ready to be killed quite soon, and have all his family and possessions destroyed, rather than give in. In this they represented the House of Commons and almost all the people."[7] For the prime minister, there would be no negotiations with Hitler—only war until Nazi Germany surrendered.

Facing senior cabinet opposition, Churchill and Lincoln stood fast against the appeasement policies embraced by their predecessors. Lincoln would reserve all the prerogatives of the constitutional commander in chief. For example, in August 1861, General John C. Frémont issued orders freeing slaves in his Missouri command. Lincoln first suggested to Frémont that the orders be withdrawn. When the general did not do so voluntarily, Lincoln ordered him to do so. Lincoln again rejected the slave-emancipation orders of General David Hunter in May 1862. Lincoln wrote emphatically to the general that the subject was one "I reserve to myself, and I can not feel justified in leaving to the decision of commanders in the field." Churchill himself would write of Lincoln: "Strength was certainly given him. It is sometimes necessary at the summit of authority to bear the intrigues of disloyal colleagues, to remain calm when others panic, and to withstand misguided popular outcries. All this Lincoln did."[8]

Both war leaders did have blind spots. Lincoln underestimated the Southern determination to secede, and then to make war to secure its independence as a slave republic. Both endured moments of humiliating defeat. For Lincoln, major defeats included the First and Second Battles of Bull Run, the Battles of Fredericksburg, and of Chancellorsville—among others. For Churchill, similar setbacks included the sinking of the *Prince of Wales* and the *Repulse* in 1941, the humiliating fall of Singapore, and the capture in 1942 of Tobruk in Tunisia. In his memoirs, Churchill recalled the news of December 1941, that the Japanese had sunk the *Prince of Wales* and the *Repulse*—two ships he himself had ordered to the Far East. "I put the telephone down. I was thankful to be alone. In all the war I never received a more direct shock. . . . There were no British or American capital ships in the Indian Ocean or the Pacific except the American survivors of Pearl Harbour, who were hastening back to California. Over all this vast expanse of waters Japan was supreme, and we were everywhere weak and naked."[9]

Bleak outcomes would often set off melancholy moments for Churchill and Lincoln. They recovered quickly, always to instill in subordinates and countrymen the will to persevere. "The President's faith in the Union cause was never dimmed by disappointments," wrote Churchill in his *History of the English-Speaking Peoples*. It is true that Lincoln "was beset by anxieties, which led him to crossexamine his commanders as if he were still a prosecuting attorney. . . . Lincoln's popularity with the troops stood high. They put their trust in him. They could have no knowledge of the relentless political pressures in Washington to which he was subjected. They had a sense however of his natural resolution and generosity of character. He had to draw deeply on these qualities in his work at the White House."[10] During World War II, such a description could have fit Prime Minister Churchill at 10 Downing Street.

In the spring of 1865 and in the spring of 1945, each statesman understood that the victory for which he had fought was imminent. On April 11, 1865, three nights before his assassination, Lincoln spoke to a crowd outside the White House: "The evacuation of Petersburg and Richmond, and the surrender of the principal insurgent army, give hope of a righteous and speedy peace whose joyous expression can not be restrained." Before recognizing the heroism of the country's soldiers and sailors, Lincoln declared: "He, from Whom all blessings flow, must not be forgotten. A call for a national thanksgiving is being prepared, and will be duly promulgated."[11] The surrender of Nazi Germany complete, Churchill would reflect on May 13, 1945, on the past and on the continuing conflict with Japan: "I told you hard things at the beginning of these last five years; you did not shrink, and I should be unworthy of your confidence and generosity if I did not still cry: Forward, unflinching, unswerving, indomitable, till the whole task is done and the whole world is safe and clean."[12]

Masters of their common language, these two great English-speaking statesmen would play out heroic roles on the world stage. There was an unimpeachable integrity to what they believed, what they said, what they did. Inspired by principles of honor, duty, and freedom, they would write, speak, and act not only for their times, but for generations unborn.

This book examines the crucial qualities of character and leadership in the lives of Lincoln and Churchill at war. Of course, there is much more to their comparative stories, but many fascinating aspects, for reasons of space, have been excluded. More may be found at the website www.LincolnandChurchill.org, where about thirty important topics are reviewed in depth. *Lincoln & Churchill: Statesmen at War* maintains its focus throughout on the character and leadership of Abraham Lincoln and Winston Churchill—the former in the American Civil War, the latter in World War II.

Indeed, war would characterize the life of Churchill (1874–1965). From 1854 to 1865, the life of Lincoln (1809–1865) would be absorbed first by the political war against the extension of slavery, then by the Civil War and the abolition of slavery. My aim in this study is simple and straightforward—to consider both great men in an intimate comparison of their roles of supreme command at the summit of human endurance—namely, wars of national survival.

Lewis E. Lehrman

Note on names and titles

If a British public official were elevated to the peerage before World War II—as in the cases of Lord Beaverbrook and Lord Halifax—then this book generally refers to him by that honorific. If a British official were raised to the peerage during or after the war—e.g., Frederick Lindemann became Lord Cherwell in 1941, John Maynard Keynes became Lord Keynes in 1942, and Dr. Charles Wilson became Lord Moran in 1943—then they are generally referred to by their pre-peerage names. Similarly, many top British generals were named field marshals as a result of their leadership during World War II—Harold Alexander (1944), Claude Auchinleck (1946), Alan Brooke (1944), John Dill (1941), Bernard Montgomery (1944), Archibald Wavell (1943), and Henry Maitland Wilson (1944). In this book they are generally not referred to by that title. For simplicity's sake, references to knighthood are generally omitted; "Sir" Winston Churchill was not knighted until 1953.

Note on quotations and endnotes

Because of the book's structure, there is occasional, necessary repetition. Moreover, I use many actual quotations of the principal leaders in the Civil War and in World War II, drawn from the primary and secondary sources of these periods (such as diaries) and from historians of both periods. These quotations, some of them quite long, tell a more intimate story than mere paraphrasing of quotations. In this practice, I follow Mr. Churchill, who wrote: "In telling a tale, the words written in the circumstances of the moment are of far greater significance than any paraphrase of them or subsequent composition." The endnotes, and their narrative content, are integral parts of the story. This book does not pretend to be a history of the Civil War, nor of World War II. Neither does it aim at the biography of the two great English-speaking statesmen. My hope is that other historians in the future will complete this first comparative history of Lincoln and Churchill as commanders in chief in wars of national survival—and improve upon it.

I do hope my books will be read and judged by scholars, but I should emphasize that they are written primarily for the literate general public.

It is not merely for to-day, but for all time to come that we should perpetuate for our children's children this great and free government, which we have enjoyed all our lives. I beg you to remember this, not merely for my sake, but for yours. I happen temporarily to occupy this big White House. I am a living witness that any one of your children may look to come here as my father's child has. It is in order that each of you may have through this free government which we have enjoyed, an open field and a fair chance for your industry, enterprise and intelligence; that you may all have equal privileges in the race of life, with all its desirable human aspirations. It is for this the struggle should be maintained, that we may not lose our birthright.[1]

ABRAHAM LINCOLN
Remarks to 166th Ohio Regiment
August 22, 1864

There is no room now for the dilettante, the weakling, for the shirker, or the sluggard. The mine, the factory, the dockyard, the salt sea waves, the fields to till, the home, the hospital, the chair of the scientist, the pulpit of the preacher—from the highest to the humblest tasks, all are of equal honour, all have their part to play.[2]

WINSTON CHURCHILL
Speech to Canadian Parliament
December 30, 1941

PROLOGUE

Abraham Lincoln and Winston Churchill made themselves great war leaders, never to be forgotten. *Lincoln & Churchill* tells the story of their war leadership. It is a story of character and statecraft in war. These remarkable men operated roughly eight decades apart, in colossal struggles that threatened their nations with extinction. The urgency of war concentrated the character of their leadership and tested the wisdom of their statecraft. One of Churchill's aides told a colleague in June 1940, as France fell to Hitler, that the new prime minister "had sobered down . . . becoming less violent, less wild and less impetuous." Eric Seal, then Churchill's principal private secretary, observed that Winston "believes in his mission to extricate this country from the present troubles, and he will certainly kill himself if necessary in order to achieve his object."[3]

War severed Lincoln and Churchill from their homes. Lincoln never returned to Springfield except in death. Churchill shut down his beloved home, Chartwell. War absorbed each man's life for many years of unrelenting toil. Springfield lawyer Thomas Lewis recalled being told by President Lincoln when he visited the White House in 1862: "You see the fix I am in. I am kept here every night until nine to twelve o'clock, and never know when I can leave."[4] Fortified by a late afternoon nap, Churchill often labored until 2 or 3 A.M.—keeping his colleagues up as well. The prime minister's work habits divided the day into two shifts—one before and one following his afternoon nap. Each working shift exhausted his key civilian and military staff. In bed at 2 A.M. or later, Churchill awakened to a big English breakfast in bed, where he might work in his nightgown until noon—interviewing generals and cabinet officers and staff—with a cigar and a very diluted glass of whiskey in hand. His later work, following a big lunch and a nap, was filled with appointments, speeches, or questions to answer in Parliament.

1

Churchill's sleeping habits disrupted the customary schedules not only of his military and civilian aides. Eleanor Roosevelt recalled Churchill's visits to the White House: "The prime minister took a long nap every afternoon, so was refreshed for hard work in the evening and far into the night. While he was sleeping, Franklin had to catch up on all of his regular work. . . . It always took him several days to catch up on sleep after Mr. Churchill left."[5] The prime minister could hold the president, cabinet officers, and military chiefs in session until the early hours of the morning. His schedule would have taxed a young man. Churchill was 65 when he became prime minister. He would be 70 at war's end (80 in 1955, after his second prime ministry).

War leadership totally commandeered the lives of both men, to the exclusion of much they cherished, but neither man devoted himself exclusively to fighting the war. Politics and patronage often distracted President Lincoln—a founder and builder of the new Republican Party, of which he was the first president. His obligation to act as the final arbiter of military justice, to choose candidates for the military and naval academies, to approve officers' commissions, to choose and dismiss generals and admirals, and to listen to the urgent pleas of mothers, wives, and widows on matters high and low—all preoccupied the working day of the president. Lincoln's White House opened the door to an aggressive press and an aggrieved citizenry. In Churchill's case, wrote historian Andrew Roberts, "Surprisingly large amounts of time had to be spent honing his speeches, attending Commons debates, lunching with newspaper editors, visiting bomb sites, factories and military encampments, watching weapons-testing, briefing the King, soothing the Tory Party (which he always feared secretly hated him), meeting ambassadors and foreign leaders, and . . . involving himself in military tactics at a far lower level than grand strategy."[6] But for briefing the King, this is but a partial description of Lincoln's duties. Churchill surrounded himself with a large and experienced staff, much of it inherited from Neville Chamberlain, which the prime minister personally organized and directed; whereas President Lincoln's immediate staff consisted of three young secretaries he brought from Illinois.

In the prime minister's case, this book focuses on Churchill's leadership in the European theater of the war—always his priority and the priority of the Anglo-American alliance he inspired. Indeed, the prime minister worked ceaselessly to make sure that defeating Hitler was

America's top priority, and that sufficient Allied resources were devoted to the defeat of the Nazis. Some American admirals and generals preferred to focus on the destruction of the Japanese Empire in the Pacific. The prime minister well understood global British interests, for he had been a member of Parliament since 1900 and had served in nine cabinet positions. Thus, Churchill seldom lost sight of British interests at home or in Central Asia, India, Southeast Asia, and Australia.

But Britain never had the financial and material resources to implement his plans in all these theaters. The fall of France was followed in 1940–1942 by serious military reverses in the Mediterranean and the Pacific. Indeed, Britain was technically insolvent by the end of 1940. As the prime minister said at the time of Yalta in 1945, the problems of the Pacific war with Japan were "remote and secondary" for him.[7] Indeed, Churchill's proposals for military campaigns in Southeast Asia led to fierce arguments with his top military commanders, who refused to approve them. To his credit, Churchill never overruled his military chiefs, but fight and argue with them he did. (In the Allied total war against the Nazis, the indispensable role of the Russian army should not be underestimated. Joseph Stalin could be occasionally charming, always cynical and shrewd, often well informed by spies about Anglo-American affairs. The Soviet dictator was in the mold of Adolf Hitler, but with fewer delusions and affectations.)

Lincoln and Churchill embraced a total commitment to victory. Unconditional surrender of the enemy became their goal—no matter the personal cost or occasional humiliation. "I will hold [George] McClellan's horse, if he will only bring us success," declared President Lincoln in November 1861.[8] General Dwight D. Eisenhower recalled an incident from 1943: "Just before I left England, Mr. Churchill had earnestly remarked, 'If I could meet [Admiral François] Darlan, much as I hate him, I would cheerfully crawl on my hands and knees for a mile if by doing so I could get him to bring that [French] fleet of his into the circle of Allied forces."[9]

As government chief executives and military commanders in chief, Lincoln and Churchill developed shrewd insights and strong convictions about the military strategy necessary for victory. Historian Correlli Barnett noted that Lincoln showed "he could learn better [about strategy] than the supposed professionals."[10] One Lincoln aide observed in November 1861: "The President is himself a man of great aptitude for military studies."[11] Many experienced generals in America and in Britain scoffed at the military strategy and tactics of Lincoln and Churchill. In the end, their strategy—an anaconda-like embrace of the enemy to squeeze the life from it—proved victorious. Military subordinates chafed at urgent suggestions from Lincoln and Churchill. But it was the prime minister and the president who had to grapple with two crucial problems in the first two years of war—the character and quality of their subordinate officer corps, and the recruitment, training, and fighting ability of their soldiers.

Despite their very different social origins and political experiences, both Lincoln and Churchill were driven by extraordinary ambition. Lincoln's law partner wrote that Lincoln's ambition was "a little engine that knew no rest." The same can be said of Churchill. In different ways, their fathers were skeptical of their talents, and unsympathetic to, even uninterested in, their goals as young men. Historian Robert Rhodes James wrote that the well-born Churchill "had immense application and capacity for work. He was not a natural speaker, with an inability to pronounce the letter S [Churchill lisped] but which he turned to advantage. Nor was he really a natural writer—if such a thing exists. It was all hard work. . . . Nothing came easily to him. Those glorious speeches and those marvelous books were the result of much toil. This is too often ill-appreciated, but it was a triumph of character in itself."[12]

Lincoln began the race of life in poverty, bound by the limits of the rural frontier. Like Churchill, he charted the direction of his own life. At 22, legally emancipated, Lincoln moved away from his farming family, seeking new skills, often failing, but acquiring vital knowledge and self-confidence. His nature and his early trials inclined him toward study and achievement in different vocations. Even as a child and later as a young man, Lincoln reached out for the stranger who might possess useful knowledge. Isolated as he was as a boy on the Indiana frontier, he sought books and experiences that might lead to honorable work. Like Churchill, Lincoln possessed a restless mind—his reflective, Churchill's more martial and literary in his early mature years. Worlds apart at birth, Mr. Lincoln was the son of a dirt farmer and carpenter, Churchill a grandson of the Duke of Marlborough.

Leadership in war may be the most demanding vocation of all. Lincoln and Churchill proved tireless at the task. General Hastings Ismay, the prime minister's top military aide, wrote: "His most fervent admirers would not say that he was considerate, but neither could his fiercest critics deny that, so far as waging war was concerned, he was more inconsiderate of himself than he was of others. Even when he was really ill, perhaps running a high temperature, he insisted on continuing to work."[13] The prime minister and the president had exceptional physical constitutions that, when combined with ambition and hard work, made them nearly inexhaustible.

Lincoln and Churchill, on the surface, were very different men with equally different backgrounds and leadership styles, but they lived through comparable challenges. Both put their country's interests ahead of their own and those of their families. Both developed strong wills and resilient characters that they brought to bear on overwhelming problems. As war leaders, they were generally decisive, but they searched for agreement among allies and staff, both military and civilian. Charles Portal, the head of the Royal Air Force, noted of Churchill: "For all his ardent advocacy of his own point of view he was at heart always a compromiser and he was most thoroughgoing in his search for advice and expert opinion . . . He knew his own weaknesses, and knew that he needed to have around him men who from their experience and their expert training could keep his imagination in check."[14] Churchill had learned well from his failures and humiliation in World War I. Lincoln had learned similar lessons through failure and humiliation when seeking political office in the 1840s and 1850s. Whatever their private doubts, Lincoln and Churchill showed optimism in public. Historian Geoffrey Best wrote: "Self-respect, courage, self-control, the classic qualities he [Churchill] had learned in study of great commanders like Marlborough, Wellington and Nelson, ensured that his public face would always be resolute and optimistic; and he demanded that everyone else's public face should be the same."[15] Such a public face was necessary to maintain the public will to fight a long and bloody war, until decisive victory was obtained.

In some respects, Lincoln and Churchill were unlikely leaders. The tall, awkward Lincoln and the short, heavy-set Churchill did not represent the conventional image of a commander in chief as exemplified by General Washington or the Duke of Wellington. In his 1858 debates with perennial presidential hopeful Stephen A. Douglas, Lincoln pointed out that "nobody has ever expected me to be President. In my poor, lean, lank face, nobody has ever seen that any cabbages were sprouting out."[16] In the 1930s, Churchill's willful, often contrarian judgments were so severely questioned that he was considered by some to be politically untouchable. Prime Minister Stanley Baldwin said in 1936 that Churchill had been given a multitude of gifts, including "imagination, eloquence, industry," but he lacked "judgement and wisdom."[17] On May 3, 1940, Britain's top general, Edmund Ironside, commented on the movement to oust Prime Minister Neville Chamberlain: "Naturally the only man who can succeed is Winston and he is too unstable, though he has the genius to bring the war to an end."[18]

Lincoln and Churchill had earned the same reputation upon taking office. After a decade of resistance to the appeasement of slavery by Lincoln in the 1850s and Churchill's resistance to the appeasement of Hitler in the 1930s—each was widely recognized as a man of principle. Churchill implied his attitude toward Germany in the 1930s, when he wrote as early as August 1918: "To set out to redress an intolerable wrong, to grapple with a cruel butcher [Germany], & then after a bit to find him so warlike that upon the whole it is better to treat him as a good hearted fellow & sit down & see if we can't be friends after all, may conceivably be a form of prudence but that is the best that can be said of it."[19]

After World War II, British philosopher Isaiah Berlin wrote that Churchill "knows with an unshakable certainty what he considers to be big, handsome, noble, and worthy of pursuit by someone in high station. . . . Tacking and bending and timid compromise may commend themselves to those sound men of sense whose hopes of preserving the world they defend are shot through with an often unconscious pessimism; but if the policy they pursue is likely to slow the tempo, to diminish the forces of life, to lower the 'vital and vibrant energy' which he admires, say, in Lord Beaverbrook, Mr. Churchill is ready for attack."[20]

**Winston S. Churchill at the Royal Albert Hall on
American Thanksgiving Day, November 1944**

Richard Langworth Collection

ABRAHAM LINCOLN
BEFORE THE CIVIL WAR

February 12, 1809 Abraham Lincoln born in impoverished Hardin County, Kentucky.

October 5, 1818 Lincoln's mother, Nancy, died.

December 2, 1819 Lincoln's father, Thomas, remarried to widow Sarah Bush Johnston.

1831 Lincoln settled in New Salem on Illinois frontier.

1832 Served in the Black Hawk War, elected militia captain.

August 6, 1832 Defeated in first race for Illinois House of Representatives.

August 4, 1834 Won first of four races for Illinois House of Representatives.

1836–1837 Admitted to the practice of law, self-prepared.

November–December 1839 First debates with Stephen A. Douglas.

November 4, 1842 At age 33, married Mary Todd.

1844 Began legal partnership with William H. Herndon, which continued until Lincoln's assassination.

August 3, 1846 Elected to Congress over Democrat Peter Cartwright.

1847–1849 Served in Congress. Voted repeatedly for Wilmot Proviso, prohibiting slavery in new territories acquired from Mexico. Opposed the Mexican-American War as unjust, but supported funding for the troops.

1849	Returned to Springfield and the practice of law.
January 17, 1851	Lincoln's father, Thomas, died.
1854	Campaigned against the Kansas-Nebraska Act, sponsored by Senator Stephen A. Douglas. Debated Douglas regarding his proslavery legislation, which could open the vast territory to slavery. Gave his seminal anti-slavery speech at Peoria.
February 1855	Lost state legislative vote for U.S. Senate.
June 19, 1856	Lost Republican nomination for vice president.
June 26, 1857	Delivered uncompromising speech against *Dred Scott* pro-slavery decision of the Supreme Court.
June 16, 1858	Nominated by Illinois Republicans for U.S. Senate seat occupied by Stephen A. Douglas. Delivered "House Divided" speech.
August–October 1858	Lincoln and Douglas debated in seven congressional districts. Narrowly lost Senate election to Douglas. Drew national attention.
February 27, 1860	Delivered Cooper Union Address.
May 18, 1860	Nominated on third ballot for president by Republican National Convention in Chicago.
November 6, 1860	Elected first Republican president over Democrat Stephen Douglas and two other candidates. Secession began.
March 4, 1861	Inaugurated president.
April 12, 1861	Civil War began with the Confederate attack on Fort Sumter.

WINSTON CHURCHILL
BEFORE WORLD WAR II

November 30, 1874	Winston Leonard Spencer-Churchill born at Blenheim Palace, grandson of Duke of Marlborough. (Hyphen in Spencer-Churchill is later dropped; Leonard dropped too.) Educated early at boarding schools and the elite Harrow School.
1893	Enrolled in the Royal Military Academy, Sandhurst.
January 1895	Commissioned a cavalry subaltern in the Fourth Hussars.
January 24, 1895	Churchill's father, Lord Randolph Churchill, died.
1896–1897	Served in India and saw battle in Northwest India.
1898	Served in Sudan. Saw action against Dervishes. Participated in last significant cavalry charge of British army at Omdurman.
1899	Lost election at Oldham to House of Commons.
1899–1900	Served as soldier and journalist in South Africa during the Boer War. Escaped from prison and became a national hero.
1900	Elected to Parliament as a Conservative MP for Oldham.
May 31, 1904	Switched from Conservative to Liberal Party.

1905	Named Under-Secretary of State for the Colonies.
1906	Published biography of his father, *Lord Randolph Churchill*, a former chancellor of the exchequer. Several books published previously.
May 1, 1907	Named Privy Councillor.
April 1908	Named President of the Board of Trade.
September 12, 1908	At age 33, married Clementine Hozier, age 23.
1910	Named Home Secretary.
October 1911	Named First Lord of the Admiralty.
August 1914	World War I began.
1915	Following controversial Dardanelles defeat, Churchill accepted responsibility and resigned from Cabinet.
1916	Commanded for six months the 6th Battalion Royal Scots Fusiliers in the trenches of Ploegsteert, Belgium. Subsequently resumed his political career.
July 1917	Named Minister of Munitions (1917–1919) by Prime Minister David Lloyd George.
October 1917	Bolshevik Revolution in Russia. Civil war followed, lasting until 1922. Churchill supported anti-Bolshevik military opposition.
November 1918	Armistice ended World War I.
January 1919	Named Secretary of State for War (1919–1921).
February 1921	Named Secretary of State for the Colonies (1921–1922).
1922	Defeated for reelection by Dundee.

1924	Reelected to Parliament, endorsed by local Conservative Party in Epping.
November 1924	Named Chancellor of the Exchequer (1924–1929 by Prime Minister Stanley Baldwin).
1925	Fateful decision to restore pre–World War I sterling–gold parity.
1930s	Spent much of "Wilderness Years" at his Chartwell estate. Published *My Early Life* and multivolume *Marlborough: His Life and Times*, a biography of John Churchill, first Duke of Marlborough, and other books and essays.
September 1, 1939	World War II began; Germany invaded Poland. Britain, bound by recent treaty with Poland, declared war on Germany.
September 3, 1939	For the second time, named First Lord of the Admiralty (1939–1940), this time by Prime Minister Neville Chamberlain.
May 10, 1940	Named Prime Minister on same day as Germany invaded France.

THE LINCOLN TEAM

Generals-in-Chief
Winfield Scott (1841–1861)
George B. McClellan (1861–1862)
Henry W. Halleck (1862–1864)
Ulysses S. Grant (1864–1868)

Commanders, Army of the Potomac
Irvin McDowell (1861)
George B. McClellan (1861–1862)
Ambrose Burnside (1862–1863)
Joseph Hooker (1863)
George Meade (1863–1865)

Leading Naval Officers
David Farragut
David Dixon Porter
Samuel Du Pont

Military Advisers
Quartermaster General Montgomery Meigs
General James Wadsworth
Naval Officer John Dahlgren
Assistant Secretary of War Charles Dana
Assistant Secretary of the Navy Gustavus V. Fox

Key Associates/Advisers

Noah Brooks, journalist

Orville H. Browning, Illinois Senator (1861–1863)

David Davis, U.S. Supreme Court Associate Justice (1863–1877)

Major Thomas T. Eckert, Superintendent, War Telegraph Office

Henry J. Raymond, editor, *New York Times*

Leonard Swett, Illinois attorney

Thurlow Weed, editor, *Albany Times*

Cabinet

Secretary of State: William H. Seward (1861–1869)

Secretary of War: Simon Cameron (1861–1862), Edwin M. Stanton (1862–1868)

Secretary of the Navy: Gideon Welles (1861–1869)

Secretary of the Treasury: Salmon P. Chase (1861–1864), William P. Fessenden (1864–1865), Hugh McCulloch (1865–1869)

Attorney General: Edward Bates (1861–1864), James Speed (1864–1866)

Secretary of the Interior: Caleb Smith (1861–1862), John Palmer Usher (1862–1865)

Postmaster General: Montgomery Blair (1861–1864), William Dennison (1864–1866)

Bodyguards

Ward Hill Lamon, U.S. Marshal

William Crook

White House Aides

John Hay

John G. Nicolay

William O. Stoddard

Edward D. Neill

White House staff

William Johnson, valet

William Slade, valet

THE CHURCHILL TEAM

Military Aides

Chief Staff Officer to the Minister of Defence and Secretary of the Committee of Imperial Defence: General Hastings "Pug" Ismay (Assistant: General Ian Jacob; Special Assistant and in charge of Special Information Centre: Joan Bright Astley)

Air Commander in Chief, SHAEF (17 January 1944): Arthur Tedder

Secretary to the Chief of Staff and Assistant Secretary to the War Cabinet: Leslie "Jo" C. Hollis

Supervisor of Defence Map Room: Richard Pike Pim

Director of Military Operations: John Kennedy

Director of Plans, War Office: D. G. Stewart

Military aide to Prime Minister: Charles Ralfe "Tommy" Thompson

Imperial General Staff

Chairman, Chiefs of Staff (COS) Committee: Dudley Pound (1939–1942), Alan Brooke (1942–1946)

Chief of the Imperial General Staff: Edmund Ironside (1939–1940), John Dill (1940–1941), Alan Brooke (1941–1945)

Air Chief Marshal/Chief of Air Staff: Cyril Newall (1937–1940), Charles Portal (1940–1945)

Admiral of the Fleet/First Sea Lord: Dudley Pound (1939–1943), Andrew Browne "ABC" Cunningham (1943–1946)

Chief of Combined Operations: Roger Keyes (1940), Louis Francis Albert Victor Nicholas "Dickie" Mountbatten (1940–1943), Robert Laycock (1943–1947)

Key British Commanders, Mediterranean
Archibald Wavell (1939–1941)
Claude Auchinleck (1941–1942)
Harold Alexander (1942–1945)
Bernard Montgomery (1942–1943)
Henry "Jumbo" Maitland Wilson (1943–1944)

Key Associates
Frederick "The Prof" Lindemann, scientific adviser and Paymaster
  General (1942–1945)
Brendan Bracken, Minister of Information (1941–1945), First Lord
  of the Admiralty (1945)
Lord Beaverbrook (Max Aitken), Minister of Aircraft Production
  (1940–1941), later Minister of Supply (1941–1942), Minister of
  War Production (1942), Lord Privy Seal (1943–1945)
Alexander Cadogan, Permanent Under-Secretary at the Foreign
  Office (1938–1946)
Duff Cooper, Minister of Information (1940–1941), diplomat (1944–
  1948)
Jan Christian Smuts, Prime Minister of South Africa (1939–1948)
Marshal Hugh Dowding, RAF Fighter Commander (1936–1940)

War Cabinet (1940–1942)
Neville Chamberlain, Lord President of the Council (1940,
  Conservative)
Clement Attlee, Lord Privy Seal (1940–1942, Labour)
Lord Halifax, Foreign Secretary (1938–1940, Conservative)
Anthony Eden, Foreign Secretary (1941–1945, Conservative)
Arthur Greenwood, Minister without Portfolio (1940–1942, Labour)

War Cabinet (1942–1945)
Clement Attlee, Deputy Prime Minister and Secretary of State for
  Dominion Affairs (1942–1945, Labour)
Stafford Cripps, Lord Privy Seal and Leader of the House of
  Commons (1942, independent). Cripps was later Minister of
  Aircraft Production (1942–1945), a position not in the War
  Cabinet.
Max Beaverbrook, Lord Privy Seal (1942–1945, Conservative)

Kingsley Wood, Chancellor of Exchequer (1940–1943, Conservative)

John Anderson, Chancellor of Exchequer (1943–1945, independent)

Anthony Eden, Foreign Secretary (1941–1945, Conservative). Also Leader of the House of Commons (1942–1945)

Oliver Lyttelton, Minister of Production (1942-1945, Conservative)

Ernest Bevin, Minister of Labour and National Service (1940–1945, Labour)

Herbert Morrison, Home Secretary (1940–1945, Labour)

Aides

Charles Barker, chief clerk (1941–1945)

Anthony Bevir, private secretary (1941–1945)

Edward Bridges, secretary to the War Cabinet (1938–1946)

Norman Brook, deputy secretary to the War Cabinet (1942)

John Rupert "Jock" Colville, assistant principal secretary (1940–1941, 1943–1945)

Kathleen Hill, confidential secretary (1936–1945)

W. I. Hughes, bodyguard

Marian Lumley-Holmes, secretary (1938–1945)

Peter Kinna, traveling secretary, clerk

John Miller Martin, principal private secretary (1941–1945)

Elizabeth Layton Nel, secretary (1940–1945)

John Peck, assistant private secretary (1939–1946)

Leslie Rowan, private secretary (1941–1945)

Frank Sawyers, butler-valet

Eric Seal, principal private secretary (1940–1941)

Margaret "Mags" Stenhouse, secretary

Cecil Syers, private secretary (1940–1941)

Mary Shearburn, personal private secretary (later wife of W. H. Thompson)

Nina Edith "Jo" Sturdee, secretary

Walter H. "Tommy" Thompson, retired detective inspector, body guard

Elizabeth M. Watson, correspondence secretary

Dr. Charles Wilson, personal physician

Abraham Lincoln, 1864
Gilder Lehrman Collection, GLC05111.02.0018

LINCOLN AT WAR:
A FEW KEY BATTLES OF THE CIVIL WAR

Fort Sumter, South Carolina. April 12–13, 1861.

First Battle of Bull Run. July 21, 1861.

Fort Donelson, Tennessee. February 12–16, 1862.

Seven Days Battle, Virginia. June 25–July 1, 1862.

Second Battle of Bull Run, Virginia. August 29–30, 1862.

Battle of Perryville, Kentucky. October 8, 1862.

First Battles of the Ironclads, Virginia. March 8–9, 1862.

Battle of Shiloh. April 6–7, 1862.

Battle of Antietam. September 17, 1862.

Battle of Fredericksburg. December 13, 1862.

Campaign for Vicksburg. 1863–1864.

Battle of Chancellorsville. May 3–4, 1863.

Battle of Gettysburg. July 1–3, 1863.

Surrender of Vicksburg. July 4, 1863

Battle of Chickamauga. September 19, 1863.

Battle of Chattanooga. October 27–28, 1863.

Battle of the Wilderness, May 5–7, 1864.

Battle of Spotsylvania. May 8–19, 1864.

Battle of Cold Harbor. June 3–12, 1864.

Capture of Petersburg and Richmond. April 2–3, 1865.

Surrender at Appomattox. April 9, 1865.

CHURCHILL AT WAR:
A FEW KEY MILITARY OPERATIONS IN EUROPE DURING WORLD WAR II

Operation Fall Weiss (1939). German invasion of Poland.

Operation Fall Gelb (1940). German invasion of Belgium, the Netherlands, and Luxembourg.

Operation DYNAMO (1940). Dunkirk evacuation.

Operation Seelöwe ("Sea lion") (1940). Planned German invasion of Britain.

Operation COMPASS (1940). British counteroffensive in North Africa.

Operation LUSTRE (1941). Allied reinforcement of Greece.

Operation DEMON (1941). Evacuation of Allied troops from Greece.

Operation Barbarossa (1941). German invasion of Russia.

Operation BATTLEAXE (1941). Unsuccessful British attack on Axis forces in North Africa to relieve Tobruk.

Operation ARCHERY (1941). British commando raid on Vågsøy, Norway.

Operation RUTTER: (August 1942). Planned British seaborne invasion of Dieppe, France.

Operation SUPERCHARGE (1942). British and Commonwealth attack on El Alamein, Egypt.

Operation GYMNAST (1942). Early name for Operation TORCH— Allied landings in Morocco and Algeria.

Operation SLEDGEHAMMER (1942–1943). First name for delayed cross-channel invasion of France.

Operation VULCAN (1943). Final Allied assault on Axis forces trapped around Tunis, Tunisia.

Operation HUSKY (1943). Allied invasion of Sicily, Italy.

Operation AVALANCHE (1943). Allied landings near Salerno, Italy.

Operation BOLERO (1943–1944). Buildup of American forces in Britain for Allied invasion of France.

Operation SHINGLE (1944). Allied landings at Anzio, Italy.

Operation OVERLORD (earlier named ROUNDUP) (1944). Allied invasion of Normandy, France (Operation NEPTUNE).

Operation ANVIL (1944). Allied invasion of Southern France. Name later changed to DRAGOON.

Operation MARKET GARDEN (1944). Unsuccessful Allied attempt to secure bridges over the main rivers of the Netherlands.

Operation PLUNDER (1945). Allied crossing of the Rhine.

Victory in Europe (VE) Day (May 8, 1945).

Victory in Japan (VJ) Day (August 15, 1945).

Adhere to your purpose and you will soon feel as well as you ever did. On the contrary, if you falter, and give up, you will lose the power of keeping any resolution, and will regret it all your life.[1]

ABRAHAM LINCOLN
to Cadet Quintin Campbell
June 28, 1862

Never give in. Never give in. Never, never, never, in nothing, great or small, large or petty—never give in, except to convictions of honour and good sense. Never yield to force; never yield to the apparently overwhelming might of the enemy.[2]

WINSTON CHURCHILL
Speech at Harrow School
October 29, 1941

A COMPARISON

Abraham Lincoln became president on March 4, 1861. Then a relatively unknown "railsplitter" from Illinois, his nomination and election had surprised the nation. His background frightened, even scandalized, the elites—especially in Washington. He had been merely a four-term state legislator on the frontier. His single term in Congress had come to an end in 1849, more than a decade before he entered the White House. In Congress, he had held firmly to his unpopular opposition to the Mexican-American War, which he believed unjust. During the Antebellum era, Democrat slaveowners and their continental expansion plans dominated the Washington establishment. Lincoln's opposition to the expansion of slavery and to the Mexican-American War had sent him into the political wilderness, not least because Illinois was probably the most racist Northern free state. Much of its population was composed of white settlers from the South. Southern Illinois was known as "little Egypt."

Some historians have asserted that Lincoln had almost no important political experience as preparation for the presidency. This judgment overlooks the facts and circumstances of Mr. Lincoln's life in the 1850s. From 1854 to 1860, in speeches and debates, he helped to define the principles and policy of the Republican Party in opposition to the spread of slavery. In contests for the U.S. Senate, he challenged the senior national Democrat, Senator Stephen A. Douglas. In unsurpassed antislavery speeches at Peoria, Illinois, in 1854, and at Cooper Union, New York, in 1860, he recovered the fundamental principles of the American Founding, based as they were on the equality proposition and inalienable rights of the Declaration of Independence. With these speeches, he became a national figure. With them, Lincoln mobilized a new Republican Party in Illinois and the nation, to vindicate the Founders' intent to prohibit the expansion of slavery into new American territory. The future president spelled out Republican antislavery policy in compelling but prudent arguments—despite the massed political power of the slave-owning South. He defiantly insisted on putting slavery in the course of ultimate extinction. In sum, Lincoln's political experience had been tested in public debate by the most divisive national issue of American history. He had gained political self-confidence by mastering the antislavery principles and policies with which he might lead the nation—if opportunity struck. His intimacy with public sentiment, his adherence to principle, and his genius for argument informed his vision and his ambition—without the approval of Washington elites.

Winston Churchill became prime minister on May 10, 1940—on the very day two million German soldiers began their well-prepared invasion of the Low Countries and France. Like Lincoln, Churchill had been "in the wilderness," effectively out of office for more than a decade. But his political biography, both as a Tory and a Liberal member of the House of Commons, covered almost four decades in Parliament, and nine distinguished appointments to the British Cabinet—including President of the Board of Trade, Home Secretary, Secretary of Munitions, First Lord of the Admiralty, Secretary of the Colonies, Secretary of State for War, and Chancellor of the Exchequer. Churchill once told the House of Commons: "My knowledge . . . has been bought, not taught"—bought in one case at the terrible price of total war from 1914 to 1918.[3] In 1900, Churchill had entered Parliament an ambitious, callow youth of 25. As a proven soldier and cavalry officer, brave and ambitious, he had aimed at a seat in the House of Commons. Fourteen years later, the First World War had supplied the Sandhurst graduate, well-read in military history, with a bloody postgraduate education in strategy, logistics, front-line operations, military technology, manufacturing, and relations among military and civilian leaders during wartime. Historian Raymond Callahan wrote: "Out of the searing experience between 1914 and 1918, Churchill learned much about the formulation and execution of strategy; about the mechanism for central direction of a national war effort; and about concentrating the manpower, production, and ingenuity of a nation in support of a total war effort."[4] Long before World War II, Churchill had directly experienced warfare in India, Afghanistan, Cuba, Sudan, South Africa, France, and in the World War I trenches of Belgium.

Unlike Lincoln, Churchill had wide and deep experience in high office. He knew firsthand that war was hell. He was ingenious and resourceful, but not always a deliberate and disciplined listener. Nor did he possess an equable temperament; on the contrary, he could be impetuous, emotional, romantic, and self-centered. By 1940, his critics, doubters, and supporters knew his strengths and weaknesses. Both Lincoln and Churchill had long experience as outstanding debaters on the key issues of their day. As war leaders, their challenges were different. However, both faced a similar challenge: how to mobilize ill-prepared nations, and how to organize and lead talented teams in wars of national survival. Churchill aide Edward Bridges noted that "arguing with Churchill could be very difficult uphill work, and that it was no use arguing with him unless you had a very good case indeed." Churchill's competitive ego and rhetorical genius were almost always present. To be effective, added Bridges, one could not simply disagree: "You had to make Churchill feel that you were on his side, that you sympathised with his general views, and that any criticism you made was genuinely intended to be helpful. Once convinced of this, he would listen to what you had to say, and you became, so to speak, a licensed critic." Bridges noted that "when the matters on the Agenda were less important or pressing, Churchill's love of argument, and his enjoyment in following up some point raised in the discussion which interested him, could lead to a far longer meeting than was necessary."[5]

President Lincoln was made from a different mold. He was not only the master of his ego, but he was also a good listener. His self-confidence and self-discipline enabled him to avoid time lost in aimless debate. Colleagues sometimes thought he wasted time telling stories.[6] Occasionally, President Lincoln used them to divert discussion from sensitive topics. "Mr. Churchill was not very sympathetic to stories of the 'Have you heard this one?' kind," recalled military aide Leslie Hollis. "When asked whether he knew such and such a story, his usual rejoinder was, 'Pray proceed.' But Mr Churchill was always ready to hear tales of valour or achievement, whether on the field of battle or elsewhere."[7] Lincoln's modest military experience had been gained in 1832, when he enlisted for three months in the Black Hawk War. His war service on the Indian frontier included elements of farce such as Lincoln himself would suggest. Unlike Lincoln, Churchill, only 5 feet 6 inches tall, was by vocation a warrior—in his early years an intrepid soldier of fortune. Forty years in politics and Parliament, joined to the writing and study of history, prepared him to be a statesman. Lincoln, nearly 6 feet 4 inches, was everywhere respected in frontier Illinois as a leader, even more as a gifted debater, a natural politician, self-taught but one of the most successful lawyers in the state. His judgment and mastery of American history had matured in the slavery debates of the 1850s. During the Civil War, he would acquit himself as a great statesman. Early in life, Lincoln had recognized his superior intelligence and his abiding ambition. Gradually he had left behind his humble origins, without losing his unfailing common touch. The family farm and the tiny village of New Salem did not fit the man who understood that he was not made for the plow.[8]

By temperament, Lincoln and Churchill were unorthodox professionals. Lincoln, as supreme warlord, was an untutored amateur, with none of Churchill's executive or military experience. Like Churchill, Lincoln was enterprising, a quick study who would master the military arts by reading, keen observation, and good judgment. Despite many professional and political reversals, each of them rose to power at the very moment his nation faced the prospect of dissolution in war. Lincoln would have agreed with Churchill's dictum: "The only answer for defeat is victory."[9]

"Every man is said to have his peculiar ambition," Lincoln, then 23, announced in his first political candidacy of 1832. "Whether it be true or not, I can say for one that I have no other so great as that of being truly esteemed of my fellow men, by rendering myself worthy of their esteem. How far I shall succeed in gratifying this ambition is yet to be developed."[10] Whereas Lincoln's ego came clearly under his control as he matured in his 40s, Churchill's ego would often burst its bounds throughout his life. Boyish good humor often followed an angry Churchillian display.[11] "I believe in personality," declared Churchill at 26, in a speech at a Liverpool dinner on November 21, 1901. "We live in an age of great events and little men, and if we are not to become the slaves of our own systems or sink oppressed among the mechanism we ourselves created, it will only be by the bold efforts of originality, by repeated experiment, and by the dispassionate consideration of the results of sustained and unflinching thought."[12] The hero in history was his model. His attitude never changed. As a young subaltern in India, Churchill "knew what he wanted to do in life. He confessed that from the beginning 'personal distinction' was his goal."[13] Historian Robert Rhodes James observed that young Churchill "was brash, egocentric, wholly absorbed

Abraham Lincoln, ca. 1846–1847
Library of Congress, LC USZC4 2439

in his political career, and unashamedly on the make."[14] In the political establishment, those qualities were held against him. However, his well-placed mother could open doors at the top. Thus, Churchill's aristocratic eccentricity was regularly—but not always—indulged.

Churchill's unrequited ambition to be number one—combined with his vast government and military experience—prepared him emotionally and professionally for the prime ministership. In September 1939, World War II would engulf much of Europe, and eventually almost the whole world. Appointed First Lord of the Admiralty September 3, 1939, he had time to prepare for the prime ministership he assumed in May 1940. "The job was made for him, he reveled in it," wrote Dr. Charles Wilson, his physician. "Winston in reckless delight doubled the weight he had to carry by his approach to the duties of the office. He had never done anything in moderation. Now his appetite for work was more voracious. He turned night into day."[15] In Lincoln's case, secession and dissolution of the union came as a great trial of honor and duty. Indeed, his election was itself a primary cause of secession, pledged as he was "to put slavery in the course of ultimate extinction."[16] Lincoln, to some extent, misread the South in 1861. Slaveowners' persistent threats to dissolve the Union over the slavery issue had become a fixture of antebellum politics; those threats so far had not materialized. Like most Northerners and many Southerners, Lincoln doubted they would become reality.

Unlike Churchill's move in London from Admiralty House to Downing Street, President Lincoln could not merely move his belongings around the corner. He must travel by rail halfway across the American continent to Washington, there to work with a cabinet he had appointed from afar, and to deal with a Congress he barely knew. There also he would meet the challenge of a war of national rebellion on an unprecedented scale. The senior partner of a two-person law firm in small-town Springfield, Illinois, had been elected to take charge of the federal government, the army, and the navy of the United States—in Washington, DC, a capital city dominated from its beginning, socially and politically, by slaveholding gentry. In order to restore the Union as commander in chief, he could mobilize at the beginning only a 16,000-man army spread across the continent. Ultimately Lincoln would transform the military into a fighting force of two million men in arms, more fighting men in the field than in any previous war of history.[17]

Though the president had been born in Kentucky, his only visits to the deep South, the slave-based cotton kingdom, had been two raft trips down the Mississippi as a very young man. When Lincoln became commander in chief of the army and navy, he had brought with him the few weeks' experience as an Illinois militia captain during the Black Hawk War of 1832. During four years of hard war (1861–1865), his supple intelligence, his physical strength, his iron will, deliberate good judgment would lead him—with few preconceptions and many mistakes—to mastery of battlefield strategy and the politics of war. In part, the president would compensate for his lack of military training by mastering the works of experienced military strategists like Antoine Henri de Jomini.

In contrast to Lincoln, Churchill was the more martial personality. As a young man, he was unselfconscious in his pursuit of glory. Churchill had some personality traits very different from Lincoln. "In his judgements about military commanders," wrote Correlli Barnett, "Churchill reveals himself as a romantic, a man of emotion, rather than a cool appraiser of talent. He responded well to military men who could express themselves with the fluency of a politician."[18] Churchill, a man of unimpeachable courage, had compiled a record as a proven soldier, an inspired historian of war, well prepared by leadership experience for supreme command in 1940. Like Lincoln, Churchill would look for generals who could fight and win. Both the president and the prime minister sought victory at all costs.

"I feel very lonely without a war," Churchill said in 1945.[19] Lincoln had been a peacemaker throughout his pre-presidential life. Churchill at 65 in 1940, and Lincoln at 52 in 1861, inherited a citizenry that, though aware of the threat of war, was not psychologically prepared for the scale it would take on. Britain had been exhausted by World War I and, until the eve of war in 1939, embraced appeasement of Hitler and Mussolini. The majority of Americans accepted the status quo of a nation half slave and half free—until the Confederate assault on Fort Sumter in April 1861. But at first the North would fight for reunion, not abolition of slavery. By 1940, the British people were ready for Churchill's war leadership, with Parliament following more gradually. "I doubt whether any of the Dictators had as much effective power throughout his whole nation as the British War Cabinet," wrote Churchill in his memoirs. "When we expressed our desires we were sustained by the people's representatives, and cheerfully obeyed by all."[20] Even in a total war of national survival, Churchill would defer to cabinet and parliamentary government.

Churchill and Lincoln possessed an indispensable character trait for exercising sustained leadership in war—indomitable will to win, maintained through persistent defeats. Both were resilient. Lincoln was more physically fit in his early fifties than Churchill in his late sixties. Churchill's eating habits were almost gluttonous; Lincoln's austere. The prime minister had carefully studied the Civil War president. The American president's "faith in the Union cause was never dimmed by disappointments," wrote Churchill.[21] President Lincoln's will to victory, reunion, and eventually slavery's abolition would overcome doubters. "I expect to maintain this contest until successful, or till I die, or am conquered, or my term expires, or Congress or the country forsakes me," he observed in June 1862.[22] Massachusetts Congressman John B. Alley recalled: "In small and unimportant matters, Mr. Lincoln was so yielding that many thought his excessive amiability was born of weakness." (Lincoln disarmingly said he was glad he was not born a woman, for he would yield too quickly.[23] Opponents who were deceived by this modest conceit did not prevail.) Alley added: "But, in matters of vital importance, he was as firm as a rock."[24] As a litigator in the courtroom, Lincoln's strategy would yield small points to win victory on decisive issues.

Churchill and Lincoln, unlike most politicians, were fundamentally guided by steadfast principle. Colleagues noticed they often became lost in their private thoughts as they reasoned through the evidence and the logic of a problem. Civil War journalist Noah Brooks wrote: "Lincoln was accustomed to fits of abstraction from which no ordinary call could rouse him. At such times his eyes had a far-away look . . . deaf to the voice of any caller."[25] Churchill had, with immense effort, made himself a proud master of rhetoric and the art of writing for a living. Except when sleeping, he surrounded himself with interesting people. He was at his most eloquent at dinner among peers and friends, energized by their admiration, especially happy luxuriating in champagne, brandy, wine, and cigars. Lincoln cultivated a greater capacity for making deep friendships—even among his political enemies. Churchill could alienate or ignore political allies and patrons—such as former Prime Minister David Lloyd George—sometimes with good reason. Tory Prime Minister Stanley Baldwin quipped in 1937 that Lloyd George "was born a cad and never forgot it; Winston

Winston S. Churchill, ca. 1900

Library of Congress, LC-DIG-ggbain-04739

was born a gentleman and never remembered it."[26] Lincoln was not so self-absorbed as Churchill. He was more detached, self-contained even when surrounded by people. Attorney Henry Clay Whitney concluded that Lincoln "had the greatest faculty for abstraction of any man I ever knew . . . I have, often, seen him in the midst of a busy scene, but entirely oblivious of all that was passing before his very eyes."[27] Lincoln, unlike the garrulous Churchill, was "the most shut-mouthed man" his law partner of sixteen years ever encountered. From detachment, concentration, and study emerged Lincoln's orderly decision-making, first in his mind, then in his actions. According to the Marquis de Chambrun, a French writer who came to know Lincoln in 1865, "Anyone hearing him express his ideas, or think aloud, either upon one of the great topics which absorbed him, or on an incidental question, was not long in finding out the marvelous rectitude of his mind, [and] the accuracy of his judgment. I have heard him give his opinion on statesmen, argue political problems, always with astounding precision and justness."[28]

Both men worked hard to cultivate extraordinary mastery of the English language and to develop the mental precision by which to define disputes clearly—Lincoln as president in few words, Churchill as prime minister in more. In his First Inaugural Address, Lincoln would succinctly define the major cause of civil war: "One section of our country believes slavery is *right*, and ought to be extended, while the other believes it is *wrong*, and ought not to be extended. This is the only substantial dispute."[29] In his Second Inaugural Address, the president observed: "Both parties deprecated war, but one of them would *make* war rather than let the nation survive, and the other would *accept* war rather than let it perish. And the war came." Lincoln never doubted the ultimate cause of civil war, declaring in his Second Inaugural Address that "slaves constituted a peculiar and powerful interest" for the South. "All knew that this interest was somehow the cause of the war."[30] Lincoln dismissed the rhetoric of so-called states' rights—which he defined as the right to make slaves of human beings.

Churchill's rhetoric was a heroic language of his own making. On September 3, 1939—two days after the Germans invaded Poland—he declared that "[w]e are fighting to save the whole world from the pestilence of Nazi tyranny and in defence of all that is most sacred to man."[31] Churchill gave no quarter to Englishmen, Europeans, and Americans

who suggested that Germany rightfully sought its place in the sun—
"lebensraum"—after the disaster of World War I, reparations, losses
of territory, and economic collapse. Churchill dismissed such rational-
izations as falsehoods meant to extenuate unacceptable Nazi military
enslavement of peoples and the destruction of independent nations.
Still, he acknowledged Germany's place in European and world affairs,
both before and after the war.

The steely determination shared by Churchill and Lincoln was
forged on the anvil of political defeat. Strength of character and force
of personality fueled their will to win in a just cause. "Politicians rise by
toils and struggles," wrote Churchill in 1931. "They expect to fall; they
hope to rise again."[32] Both were among the few successful war leaders
who would rise to ascendancy in modern wars of national survival. Each
was unique in his own way. On July 3, 1940, John Kennedy, Churchill's
chief of military operations who occasionally clashed with the prime
minister, observed that there was "no one else with the personality for
the job."[33] The prime minister and the president proved they had the
character, stamina, communication skills, and ruthless intensity required
for supreme command in war. "The figure of Lincoln is *sui generis* in the
annals of history. No initiative, no idealistic eloquence, no buskin, no
history drapery," noted Karl Marx from afar.[34]

Henry C. Whitney, a friend and fellow litigator, who traveled the
Eighth Judicial District of Illinois with Lincoln, concluded that Lincoln
"was one of the most uneven, eccentric, and heterogeneous characters,
probably, that ever played a part in the great drama of history; and it was
for that reason that he was so greatly misjudged and misunderstood."[35]
Some historians conclude the same about Winston Churchill.[36] Both men
inspired deep loyalty. Churchill ally Brendan Bracken observed: "Being
friendly with him is like being in love with a beautiful woman who drives
you mad with her demands until you can bear it not a moment longer and
fling out of the house swearing never to see her again. But next day she
smiles at you and you know there's nothing you wouldn't do for her and
she crooks her little finger and you come running."[37]

*At what point shall we expect the approach of danger? By
what means shall we fortify against it? Shall we expect
some transatlantic military giant, to step the Ocean, and
crush us at a blow? Never! All the armies of Europe, Asia
and Africa combined, with all the treasure of the earth (our
own excepted) in their military chest; with a Buonaparte
for a commander, could not by force, take a drink from the
Ohio, or make a track on the Blue Ridge, in a trial of a
thousand years. . . . I answer, if it ever reach us, it must
spring up amongst us. It cannot come from abroad. If
destruction be our lot, we must ourselves be its author and
finisher. As a nation of freemen, we must live through all
time, or die by suicide.*[1]

ABRAHAM LINCOLN
age 29, Young Men's Lyceum of Springfield, Illinois
January 27, 1838

*This is no war of chieftains or of princes, of dynasties or
national ambition; it is a war of peoples and of causes.
There are vast numbers, not only in this island but in
every land, who will render faithful service in this war but
whose names will never be known, whose deeds will never
be recorded. This is a War of the Unknown Warriors; but
let all strive without failing in faith or in duty, and the
dark curse of Hitler will be lifted from our age.*[2]

WINSTON S. CHURCHILL
age 65, BBC Broadcast
July 14, 1940

Men of Character:
Quintessential Leaders with Different Personalities

Abraham Lincoln and Winston Churchill differed in so very many ways. The president was tall, lean, and muscular. The prime minister was short, round, and inexhaustible. (As a young man he was lean and short.) Churchill cherished champagne, whiskey, and cigars, even indulging in his beloved hot baths while serving in the trenches of 1916.[3] Like his ally Franklin D. Roosevelt, Churchill had developed theatrical gestures. FDR's jauntily upturned cigarette holder paralleled Churchill's firmly clenched cigar. "He likes to smoke a cigar, but he realises that the public like to see him doing so even more," recalled his bodyguard. "He, therefore, takes good care to ensure that a cigar is in his mouth on all special occasions!"[4] Historian John Keegan wrote: "His intake of cigar smoke and whiskey, though it sustained him, would already have damaged a weaker man. Their effects are exaggerated, however. His whiskey-and-soda, as intimates testify, was more soda than whiskey, and most of his ten daily cigars were chewed rather than smoked."[5] Churchill's consumption of alcohol rarely impaired his mental agility. "Winston's whiskey was very much a whiskey and *soda*," reported one aide. "It was really a mouthwash. He used to get frightfully cross if it was too strong."[6]

Lincoln, a teetotaler, never smoked. When his neighbors offered to provide him with liquor for the Republican delegation announcing his presidential nomination in May 1860, he responded: "I shall provide cold water—nothing else."[7] His personal austerity was a perennial character trait, but Lincoln was no prude. Indifferent to what he ate, he lived in the White House as he had modestly lived before. Joseph Gillespie wrote that Lincoln "never knew what he did eat. He said to me once that he never felt his own utter unworthiness so much as when in the presence of a hotel clerk or waiter."[8] Churchill cherished elegant cuisine. In some respects, he was a Francophile. Lincoln, raised in the abolitionist Baptist church on the frontier, grew up where food was scarce. For him, hunting animals in the wild as a boy was a necessity. Churchill inherited privilege, but little money.[9] He was a tireless writer for a living.

The prime minister had very defined tastes—soup, for example, must be clear, not creamy. His friend F.E. Smith quipped that Churchill was "easily satisfied with the best."[10] Lincoln was a man of simple tastes who, through self-discipline and hard experience, would come to practice the virtue of humility.[11] For example, the president sometimes left the White House alone to hail a newspaper boy on Pennsylvania Avenue. A cabinet member criticized him for shining his own boots. The president queried whose boots the cabinet grandee would have him shine. It was different with the prime minister. Churchill's sister-in-law described him as "a pasha" at home, servants and secretaries catering to his every whim.[12] And when his wishes went unserved, Churchill could be morose.[13] His unstinting labors to make a rich living made him jealous of his earned prerogatives.

In and out of public office, Lincoln supported himself by the practice of law. Churchill supported himself by writing books and articles. Both men were very successful in these vocations—Lincoln in Illinois, Churchill a world-renowned author. As a writer, Lincoln would research a speech with the part-time help of Herndon, his law partner. Churchill would often draw on the best advice of the most knowledgeable experts, as well as that of paid researchers. Historian David Reynolds wrote: "Churchill's earnings as an author helped fund his political career and his self-indulgent lifestyle. . . . His bills for food, cigars, and drink were substantial; he ran a London apartment and an expensive country house, and all his domestic needs were provided by servants."[14] Clementine, his devoted wife, acted as head of household. She proved herself an indispensable partner. The prime minister had a loyal valet who freed him from most sartorial details. Lincoln could not have been more indifferent to the conventional privileges of the White House. Aide John Hay wrote of Lincoln's routine: "At noon the President took a little lunch—a biscuit, a glass of milk in winter, some fruit or grapes in summer. . . . He was very abstemious—ate less than any one I know. Drank nothing but water—not from principle, but because he did not like wine or spirits."[15] Churchill could be impulsive, more excitable and irritable than the steady Lincoln. Winston "is extraordinarily obstinate. He is like a child that has set his mind on some forbidden toy. It is no good explaining that it will cut his fingers or burn him. The more you explain, the more fixed he becomes in his idea," remarked the army chief of staff, General Alan Brooke, in December 1942. "Very often he seems to be quite immovable on some impossible project, but often that only means that he will not give way at that particular moment."[16] Biographer William Manchester observed that Churchill "was about as sound as the Maid of Orleans, a comparison he himself once made—'It's when I'm Joan of Arc that I get excited.'"[17] The prime minister did not like to be told "no." Neither did President Lincoln like to hear what could not be done. Steady calm was often Lincoln's public reaction to adversity. Churchill, too, was intrepid, uncommonly brave, yet so emotional and unselfconscious at times that tears were evoked in the presence of colleagues, staff, and generals, even the entire Parliament.[18] There lived in Churchill a childlike presence, even unto his mature later years. As Lincoln matured, he became less emotional, more reserved, more considerate, more self-disciplined.

Abraham Lincoln held to more regular hours. Early in the morning or late at night, seldom did Lincoln disturb others. White House visitors of all ranks, even those unannounced from the street, might have access to him. On occasion, he would join his private secretaries late at night. Lincoln aide William O. Stoddard wrote: "Towards his immediate subordinates, private secretaries, messengers, and other officials or servants, it may almost be said that he had no manner at all, he took their presence and the performance of their duties so utterly for granted. No one of them was ever made to feel, unpleasantly, the fact of his inferior position by reason of any look or word of the President."[19] Lincoln was sensitive to the feelings of others; Churchill, less so. Churchill aide John Colville wrote:

> Lovable though he was, and indeed an object of affection to everybody who came in close contact with him, he was at the same time curiously inconsiderate. In the war years, when feeding was difficult, he thought nothing of keeping the Cabinet in their seats until, for them, all hope of getting any food had

passed, because he himself had only to walk upstairs to lunch
or dinner. Equally, it never occurred to him to suppose that
anybody might be tired or overworked. He thought nothing of
sending for one in the temporary sanctuary of one's bath about
some trivial point which could well have waited until one was
dressed.[20]

Churchill could be generous with praise for others, but it was not
commonplace. President Lincoln was generous without excess. He kept
his own counsel. He was independent of his staff, whereas a vast and
devoted entourage surrounded Churchill.[21] When Lincoln decided to
attend a crucial meeting with Confederate peace commissioners in early
February 1865, he quietly left the White House without even informing his secretaries. The Lincoln-Churchill character difference may be
suggested by a Churchill-Roosevelt comparison. Max Hastings wrote:
"If Churchill's outbursts of ill temper sometimes irked colleagues, Roosevelt's associates were made uneasy by his bland geniality, his reluctance to display anger, or indeed to reveal any frank sentiment at all."[22]
Churchill could be genial, charming, and accommodating to Roosevelt
because he was a shrewd supplicant and dependent upon Roosevelt's support. Lincoln was not dependent on another chief-of-state of a foreign
country. He was dependent entirely on his own generals and armies in
the field. This difference in circumstances influenced the conduct in war
of Churchill and Lincoln.
    President Lincoln seldom indulged his anger. But his temper could
be triggered by incompetence—such as the canal boat debacle in February 1862, when costly army boats were built too wide to permit passage through canals for which they were made. "Why in hell didn't he
measure first!" complained the president of General George B. McClellan.[23] Lincoln went to great lengths to placate McClellan, his first
general-in-chief, but occasionally Lincoln would lose his temper with
him. When McClellan forwarded a report about the fatigue of the army's
horses a full month after the battle of Antietam, Lincoln became exas-
perated with the general's inactivity: "I have just read your dispatch
about sore-tongued and fatigued horses. Will you pardon me for asking
what the horses of your army have done since the battle of Antietam that
fatigue anything?"[24]
    Lincoln enjoyed listening to others sing. Churchill, always perform-
ing, liked to sing himself—especially at moments of happiness or joy.

Both loved animals. Lincoln especially liked dogs and cats. Churchill loved his poodle Rufus, the fish and geese at his pond, his cats, and his large pet collection, his open affection extending even to pigs.[25] The "British bulldog" would say: "Dogs look up to you, cats look down on you. Give me a pig. He just looks you in the eye and treats you as an equal."[26] Churchill once refused to prepare a goose for dinner, telling his wife: "You'll have to carve it, Clemmie. He was my friend."[27] Churchill, both a classical liberal in trade and a progressive in domestic policy, did retain some aristocratic impulses of his Marlborough bloodline. He loved remodeling his beloved and grand Chartwell estate, which he financed not with inherited wealth, but with a lifetime of work—writing to earn money to maintain his lifestyle.[28] If his expenses exceeded his earnings, he believed it was a goad to earn more money—not to cut expenses. Lincoln could not be bothered with property matters. He was not acquisitive. He worked to live and to rise. He delegated property duties to his wife and others. Lincoln clothed himself in his rarely cleaned linen "duster" and soiled top hat, elevating his profile to almost seven feet.[29] He carried a broken green umbrella and a carpetbag, paying little attention to what others thought of his unconventional appearance. However, in photographs, Lincoln did his best to appear the successful litigator and politician he had become.[30] Churchill—in his bowler, bow tie, and three-piece suit, with watch fob and cane—was very aware of his appearance and its impact on others.[31] In the class-based society of England, Churchill would dress the part. Of course, Lincoln had been raised on the rural frontier of Indiana, poor and obscure. The heritage of Lincoln's mother and grandmother was shrouded in plausible suggestions of illegitimate birth. Churchill had been born into one of England's ducal families. On his mother's side, he descended from a French Huguenot immigrant to America.[32] Her father, Leonard Jerome, was a prominent financier in New York.

Both war leaders had experienced difficult relationships with their fathers. Winston's father, Lord Randolph, believed his son was neither smart enough nor disciplined enough to go to Oxford, as he did, nor to succeed at a worldly profession.[33] Lincoln's father worried that his son was unwisely distracted by books and study, unwilling to attend full-time to the manual work of farming. Late in life, Churchill told his daughter, Mary Soames: "I should have liked my father to have lived long enough to see that I made something of my life."[34] Troubled families defined both Lincoln and Churchill—including unconventional marriages in which spouses spent long periods separated from their husbands.[35] Churchill had to cope with the knowledge that his father had died young, probably of a brain tumor.[36] Lincoln decided not to attend his father's funeral, so weak had the blood tie become.

Both statesmen had braved the struggles typical of ambitious men with unorthodox and independent views. Like Lincoln, Churchill wandered more than a decade in the political wilderness before he became prime minister. Both had been knocked down often, but they bounced back with the resilience that marks most men of strong character and intense ambition. Most importantly, they foresaw the future better than most conventional politicians. In the 1850s, Lincoln saw clearly that the controversial institution of slavery might spread and become national—making America a slave nation. Churchill in the 1930s foresaw the ultimate threat of Nazism—even beyond Europe, were it not to be stopped by diplomatic or military force. Both rising statesmen were prepared to fight rather than to accommodate the expansion of slavery—of either the Nazi variety or that of the American South.

That Nazism must be contained, Churchill believed long before the onset of war in September 1939. Appeasement, he believed, availed nothing but probable defeat. In 1932, Hitler was on the rise but not yet chancellor. During that year, in a debate on disarmament in the House of Commons, Churchill issued what he would call "my first formal warning of approaching war." He said: "I should very much regret to see any approximation in military strength between Germany and France. Those who speak of that as though it were right, or even a question of fair dealing, altogether underrate the gravity of the European situation. I would say to those who would like to see Germany and France on an equal footing in armaments: 'Do you wish for war?' For my part, I earnestly hope that no such approximation will take place during my lifetime or that of my children."[37] In a 1933 speech to the House of Commons, Churchill declared: "Our first supreme object is not to go to war. To that end we must do our best to prevent others from going to war. But we must be very careful that, in so doing, we do not increase the risk to ourselves of being involved in a war if, unfortunately, our well-meant efforts fail to prevent a quarrel between other Powers." He would dramatize the ominous threat: "When we read about Germany, when we watch with surprise and distress the tumultuous insurgency of ferocity and war spirit, the pitiless ill-treatment of minorities, the denial of the

Abraham Lincoln, 1865

Gilder Lehrman Collection, GLC05111.02.0025

normal protections of civilized society to large numbers of individuals solely on the ground of race—when we see that occurring in one of the most gifted, learned, scientific and formidable nations in the world, one cannot help feeling glad that the fierce passions that are now raging in Germany have not found, as yet, any other outlet but upon Germans."[38] German passions would spread outward into international politics. Hitler became chancellor of Germany in 1933. The post–World War I consensus would be destroyed by his ruthless expansionist strategy.

Churchill's conservative view of human nature—both good and evil—enabled him to recognize early that neither great learning and scientific distinction nor international institutions were guarantees of moral conduct or liberalism. In a private conversation at a French villa in September 1935, Churchill shared his conception of world affairs with a fellow guest:

> We have endeavoured, by means of the League of Nations and the whole fabric of international law, to make it impossible for nations nowadays to infringe upon each other's rights. In trying to upset the empire of Ethiopia, Mussolini is making a most dangerous and foolhardy attack upon the whole established structure, and the results of such an attack are quite incalculable. Who is to say what will come of it in a year, or two, or three? With Germany arming at breakneck speed, England lost in a pacifist dream, France corrupt and torn by dissension, America remote and indifferent—Madame, my dear lady, do you not tremble for your children?[39]

Churchill's mind grasped, during peacetime, in an era of pacifism, that the vectors of war had started in motion.

Churchill was combative and farseeing regarding Nazi aggression. Lincoln tended to be politic under different circumstances; there was no external threat. Always affirming the perpetual union, he appeared to minimize the threat of secession in the decade before the Civil War. Nevertheless, in July 1856, Lincoln would declare, in a stiff-necked speech addressed to the South, that "the Union, in any event, won't be dissolved. We don't want to dissolve it, and if you attempt it, *we won't let you*." Lincoln repeated lines he had directed at the slaveholding South earlier in Bloomington, when under his leadership the Illinois Republican Party was organized: "All this talk about the dissolution of the Union is humbug—nothing but folly. *We* WON'T dissolve the Union, and you SHAN'T."[40]

In the winter of 1860–1861, Lincoln continued to downplay secession publicly. Privately he was irreconcilably opposed to any further spread of slavery in the United States or its territories: "The tug has to come, & better now, than any time hereafter."[41] As to the potential fall of Fort Sumter and other federal military installations, Lincoln confided: "If the forts fall, my judgment is that they are to be retaken."[42] If necessary, the new president would not be afraid to oppose secession with his constitutional powers. On the way to Washington, Lincoln told the New Jersey State Senate on February 21, 1861: "The man does not live who is more devoted to peace than I am. None who would do more to preserve it. But it may be necessary to put the foot down firmly."[43] Lincoln would use this homely metaphor to suggest that he had considered the necessity of force to prevent secession, not least because it was treason against the oath of all government officials to uphold the Constitution.

As President Lincoln would say in his First Inaugural Address: "I hold, that in contemplation of universal law, and of the Constitution, the Union of these States is perpetual." He added: "Physically speaking, we cannot separate. We cannot remove our respective sections from each other, nor build an impassable wall between them. A husband and wife may be divorced, and go out of the presence, and beyond the reach of each other; but the different parts of our country cannot do this."[44] He stood firm in his Proclamation of April 15, 1861, mobilizing the militia to oppose the Confederacy: "I appeal to all loyal citizens to favor, facilitate and aid this effort to maintain the honor, the integrity, and the existence of our National Union, and the perpetuity of popular government; and to redress wrongs already long enough endured."[45] When a delegation headed by the mayor of Baltimore protested against the passage of Union soldiers through that city, Lincoln declared: "You, gentlemen, come here to me and ask for peace on any terms, and yet have no word of condemnation for those who are making war on us. You express great horror of bloodshed, and yet would not lay a straw in the way of those who are organizing in Virginia and elsewhere [e.g., Maryland] to capture this city [Washington]."[46] President Lincoln would send a special message to Congress on July 4, 1861, wherein he defined the historic secession issue: "And this issue embraces more than the fate of these United States. It presents to the whole family of man, the question, whether a constitutional republic, or a democracy—a government of the people, by the same people—can, or cannot, maintain its territorial integrity, against its own domestic foes."[47] When Lincoln delivered his First Annual Message to Congress in December 1861, he declared "that the insurrection is largely, if not exclusively, a war upon the first principle of popular government—the rights of the people."[48] Given that officers of the Confederacy had previously sworn an oath of loyalty to the Constitution and its union, the new president made clear again that the rebel war of insurrection was treason.

Accommodation of tyrannous evil was anathema for Lincoln and Churchill. After Prime Minister Neville Chamberlain signed the Munich Agreement with Hitler, partitioning Czechoslovakia in September 1938, in order to achieve "peace in our time," Churchill told Parliament:

> Czechoslovakia recedes into the darkness. She has suffered in every respect by her association with the Western democracies and with the League of Nations, of which she has always been an obedient servant. . . . When I think of the fair hopes of a long peace which still lay before Europe at the beginning of 1933 when Herr Hitler first obtained power, and of all the opportunities of arresting the growth of the Nazi power which have been thrown away, when I think of the immense combinations and resources which have been neglected or squandered, I cannot believe that a parallel exists in the whole course of history. So far as this country is concerned the responsibility must rest with those who have the undisputed control of our political affairs. They neither prevented Germany from rearming, nor did they rearm ourselves in time . . . They neglected to make alliances and combinations which might have repaired previous errors, and thus they left us in the hour of trial without adequate national defense or effective international security.

He would conclude: "And do not suppose that this is the end. This is only the beginning of the reckoning."[49]

His lonely speech in opposition did not enhance his popularity with the ruling Conservative Party, then bewitched by appeasement rather than the spirit of resistance.[50] First a Tory in 1900, then a Liberal in 1904, again a Tory in 1925, Churchill knew no welcome in 1938 among the incumbent Tory leaders. Furthermore, the British people, and those who dwelt throughout the Empire, were not yet with him in 1938. Only two short decades separated them from the suffering and destruction of World War I.

Neither Lincoln nor Churchill harbored illusions about the nature of evil. They were not moral relativists. In the years preceding war, by arguments from principle, both men tried to awaken their countrymen to the objective moral and physical dangers they faced. Lincoln had nothing but contempt for so-called Northern doughfaces—that is, Northern men with Southern principles—who collaborated with Southern slavemasters. Churchill spoke with contempt for those who appeased the Nazi dictatorship. Both men drew a bright red line between *opposition* to and *appeasement* of evil. Both gave notice they would stand upon the red line with armed force. One year before declaration of war, in a speech to the House of Commons on October 5, 1938, Churchill declared: "You must have diplomatic and correct relations, but there can never be friendship between the British democracy and the Nazi Power, that Power which spurns Christian ethics, which cheers its onward course by a barbarous paganism, which vaunts the spirit of aggression and conquest, which derives strength and perverted pleasure from persecution, and uses, as we have seen, with pitiless brutality the threat of murderous forces." He added: "An effort at rearmament the like of which has not been seen ought to be made forthwith, and all the resources of this country and all its united strength should be bent to that task."[51] Only such a vast rearmament might be sufficient to cope with the evil and scale of Nazi Germany.

Lincoln's situation was not so different. He had been a vocal adversary of the slave power of the South and its drive to extend slavery to new American territories—but he also faced a powerful political opponent who was willing to accept the extension of slavery, the senior senator of Illinois, Stephen A. Douglas.[52] The "declared indifference" of Douglas toward the spread of slavery in America provoked the Lincoln-Douglas debates of 1854 and of 1858. Both years Lincoln would campaign unsuccessfully for the Senate. Douglas's Kansas-Nebraska Act had passed Congress in May 1854, permitting slavery to spread to millions of acres where it had been prohibited by the Missouri Compromise of 1820. In response to this new act of Congress, Lincoln declared at Peoria on October 16, 1854: "I particularly object to the NEW position which the avowed principle of this [Kansas-] Nebraska law gives to slavery in the body politic. I object to it because it assumes that there CAN be a MORAL RIGHT in the enslaving of one man by another. I object to it as a dangerous dalliance for a [free] people—a sad evidence that, feeling prosperity we forget right—that liberty, as a principle, we have ceased to revere. I object to it because the fathers of the republic eschewed, and rejected it."[53] Lincoln's formidable adversaries included not only the institution of slavery and the famous Stephen Douglas, but also slave-power dominance of the federal government since the birth of the republic. Similarly, Churchill's historic personal adversary was Hitler, but the mortal threat to Britain in Europe was the expanding institution of Nazism, and its proposed enslavement of subject peoples.

In 1858, at the Alton debate with Senator Douglas, Lincoln minced no words. Slavery "is the real issue. That is the issue that will continue in this country when these poor tongues of Judge Douglas and myself shall be silent. It is the eternal struggle between these two principles—right and wrong—throughout the world."[54] In April 1864, President Lincoln would affirm his long-held conviction: "I am naturally anti slavery. If slavery is not wrong, nothing is wrong. I can not remember when I did not so think, and feel."[55] Moreover, Lincoln had not overlooked earlier slavery debates in England. In notes he wrote in 1858 for a campaign speech, Lincoln observed:

I have never failed—do not now fail—to remember that in the republican cause there is a higher aim than that of mere office—I have not allowed myself to forget that the abolition of the Slave-trade by Great Brittain [sic], was agitated a hundred years before it was a final success . . . School-boys know that [William] Wilbe[r]force, and Granville Sharpe [sic], helped that cause forward; but who can now name a single man who labored to retard it? Remembering these things I can not but regard it as possible that the higher object of this contest may not be completely attained within the term of my natural life. But I can not doubt either that it will come in due time. Even in this view, I am proud, in my passing speck of time, to contribute an humble mite to that glorious consummation, which my own poor eyes may not last to see.[56]

Winston S. Churchill, 1940

© National Portrait Gallery, London

In maturity Churchill might have been headstrong and Lincoln more deliberate, but both had thought deeply about how to apply ethical principles to public policy—given changing facts and circumstances. They listened to others, but they made up their own minds. John Colville argued that Churchill "always retained unswerving independence of thought. He approached a problem as he himself saw it and of all the men I have ever known he was the least liable to be swayed by the views of even his most intimate counsellors. Many people made the mistake of thinking that somebody—it might be General [Hastings] Ismay or Professor [Frederick] Lindemann—for whom the Prime Minister had the utmost respect and affection, would be able to 'get something through.'" Colville noted that Churchill, like Lincoln, "digested the more important of his decisions slowly. Sometimes it took him weeks of cogitation before he reached an answer which satisfied him."[57] Still, Lincoln was the more patient. The measured processes of President Lincoln's mind acted on firm principles and aimed at sensible policies. In his 40s, Lincoln had mastered the books of Euclidean logic. Reasoning from ethical axioms and postulates to their most plausible applications, amidst changing facts and circumstances, would characterize Lincoln's mature thought. "Lincoln's work as a legal draftsman doubtless contributed to his ability to write terse, precise prose and to think through such difficult legal subjects as emancipation and *habeas corpus*," observed historian Michael Burlingame.[58] "I have always regarded him . . . as one of the most conscientious men I have ever known," recalled Illinois Senator Orville H. Browning, a close friend of Lincoln for three decades. "I have never in our intercourse known him to swerve one hair's breadth from what he considered the strict line of duty."[59] In July 1864, shortly before Lincoln vetoed the punitive Wade-Davis bill for reconstruction of the defeated South, President Lincoln told aide John Hay: "At all events, I must keep some consciousness of being somewhere near right: I must keep some standard of principle fixed within myself."[60] Longtime best friend, Joshua Speed, wrote: "Unlike all other men there was entire harmony between his public and private life—He must believe that he was right and that he had truth and justice with him or he was a weak man—But no man could be stronger if he thought he was right."[61] Churchill could be equally strong, grounded as his thought was in decency and in right principle. Both leaders had severe critics in the officer corps, but for different reasons. American officers often questioned Lincoln's leadership and strategy. Two decades after the Battle of Britain, former Air Chief Marshal Hugh Dowding, who was forced out in late 1940, bitterly observed of Churchill's claims in *Their Finest Hour*, "You must remember that the foundation of all Churchill's writings is 'I was never wrong.'"[62] Dowding had reacted to the prime minister's self-assurance in his memoirs.

Churchill and Lincoln were students of history, Churchill the more learned.[63] Both had mastered the English language. Lincoln's mature prose tended toward spare, single-syllable Anglo-Saxon forms in preference to the Latinate. Churchill used both, but was more inclined to use ornate formulations and Latinate derivatives.[64] They were hardheaded but softhearted men who loved poetry. Lincoln once used a line from Thomas Gray's "Elegy Written in a Country Church-Yard" to describe his early life to a would-be biographer: "The short and simple annals of the poor." Lincoln added: "That's my life and that's all you or anyone can make of it."[65] Early in life, Churchill committed favorite poems to memory. At Harrow School, where the teenage Churchill had been educated, he won the school award for memorizing and declaiming 1,200 lines from Thomas Babington Macaulay's *Lays of Ancient Rome.* Lincoln seldom tired of reciting his more modest but favorite poem, "Mortality," by William Knox. "Oh, why should the spirit of mortal be proud?" he would exclaim in a melancholy mood. Congressman Isaac N. Arnold, an early Lincoln biographer, recalled that "his memory was so retentive and so ready, that in history, poetry, and in general literature, few, if any, marked any deficiency."[66] Churchill's memory was even more prodigious. "Without effort he could recall the potentialities of every weapon in current use, the calibre of shells, the performance of aircraft, and the detailed construction of warships," wrote historian Gerald Pawle.[67]

Lincoln had fewer than 12 months of formal education, but he would develop a shrewd understanding of a few masters of the English language. From childhood, Lincoln adapted to his rural circumstances, but he was never content with them. As a boy, he developed a thirst for knowledge—general knowledge that he narrowed down to useful knowledge—mastering the Bible, Blackstone's commentaries, Euclid's geometry, and during his presidency, books on military strategy. Shakespeare and Burns were constant English teachers of Lincoln. Poetic cadences of his favorite books influenced the rhythm of Lincoln's mature rhetoric, turning his most famous speeches into unforgettable prose poems.[68] His mastery of the King James Bible echoed throughout his great speeches.

Churchill was the more prolific. He wrote (and dictated) over 15 million words, while Lincoln's *Collected Works* can be found in a mere 10 volumes. Both statesmen were persuasive debaters, powerful speakers, and gifted writers. Throughout his life, Churchill was a very well-paid writer. Major compensation for his published writings made possible his expensive lifestyle. When not writing histories and biographies, he wrote articles for newspapers and magazines at home and abroad, which made him a world-famous writer. Lincoln wrote for the local press—but he did so anonymously, without pay. Lincoln's much more modest publications focused on politics and economics in the 1830s and 1840s, then slavery in the 1850s. Almost every word Lincoln wrote aimed at a public target; most were prepared for campaigns, for speeches, and for state papers.

Lincoln wrote not only for the eye, but especially for the ear. He composed all his speeches and letters in a clear, manly script. Churchill dictated to his many secretaries and stenographers letters, essays, and books. After the age of 50, he would dictate almost all his publications and war minutes to a round-the-clock staff of typists and stenographers. Churchill did acknowledge that he worked from "mouth to hand."[69] One Churchill secretary wrote: "To watch him compose some telegram or minute [memo] for dictation is to make one feel that one is present at the birth of a child, so tense is his expression, so restless his turnings from side to side, so curious the noises he emits under his breath. Then out comes some masterly sentence."[70] Churchill was a master of the memo (or "minute"), especially important in war. "The combination of intense thought and consultation, followed by a clear instruction for action, enabled the war machinery to advance," wrote his official biographer Martin Gilbert.[71] Churchill's clarity of mind during the chaos of war informed the clarity of his written orders and instructions.

Both men wrote and spoke with compelling imagery. Churchill, too, wrote for the ear. Speaking to the Canadian Parliament in December 1941, Churchill minced no words: "When I warned [the French] that Britain would fight on alone whatever they did, their [French] generals told their Prime Minister and his divided Cabinet: 'In three weeks England will have her neck wrung like a chicken.' Some chicken! Some neck!"[72] The Canadian Parliament roared with laughter. Broadcasting to Britain, fighting Hitler alone in June 1941, Churchill concluded his speech with an image of the British Empire: "And now, the old lion with her lion cubs at her side stands alone against hunters who are armed with deadly weapons and impelled by desperate and destructive rage."[73] Lincoln was also a master of the fit metaphor, telling General Ulysses S. Grant, stalled in his campaign outside Richmond in June 1864, to "[h]old on with bull-dog grip, and chew & choke, as much as possible."[74] The Union president used the same canine metaphor to describe the Union commander: "The great thing about Grant, I take it, is his perfect coolness and persistency of purpose. I judge he is not easily excited— which is a great element in an officer, and he has the *grit* of a bull-dog! Once let him get his 'teeth' *in* and nothing can shake him off."[75] Churchill used similar images to arrest one's attention: "I had hoped that we were hurling a wild cat on to the shore," said Churchill of the Allied landing at Anzio, Italy, in February 1944. He added that "all we got was an old stranded whale."[76]

Churchill's literary subjects were as varied as the world he and his imagination inhabited. The volume of his writing is astonishing—even considering that much was dictated. During his wilderness years in the 1930s, he spent much time on writing projects—including a four-volume biography of his famed ancestor, John Churchill, the First Duke of Marlborough. The last project of the decade was a multivolume *History of the English-Speaking Peoples.* The Civil War and President Lincoln were much on Churchill's mind with the approach of World War II, the onset of which delayed the publication. The rewriting and release of Churchill's epic history would wait until he had completed his six volumes of World War II memoirs.

By the time his *History of the English-Speaking Peoples* was published in the 1950s, Churchill's appreciation for America's Civil War president had deepened: "Lincoln's political foes, gazing upon him, did not know vigour when they saw it. These were hard conditions under which to wage a war to the death."[77] The defiant, indomitable Churchill of World War II recognized the defiant, indomitable Lincoln of the Civil War. Writing of Lincoln in the secession winter of 1860–1861, Churchill said, "Lincoln was inflexible. He would not repudiate the platform on which he had been elected. He could not countenance the extension of slavery to the Territories. This was the nub on which all turned."[78] Writing of Europeans at the time of the Civil War, Churchill noted: "None understood the strength of Abraham Lincoln or the resources of the United States."[79] It was as if Churchill had just read the imperative lines of Lincoln's last public address: "Important principles may, and must, be inflexible."[80]

Both leaders had foreseen the primal conflicts over which they might preside—Churchill with more clarity than Lincoln. In 1932, Churchill told the House of Commons: "All these bands of sturdy Teutonic youths, marching through the streets and roads of Germany, with the light of desire in their eyes to suffer for the Fatherland, are not looking for status. They are looking for weapons, and, when they have the weapons, believe me they will then ask for the return of lost territories and lost colonies."[81] Lincoln's forebodings were logical and based on the evidence. In his House Divided speech of June 1858, Lincoln warned that slavery threatened the Union:

> I believe this government cannot endure, permanently half *slave* and half *free*.
>
> I do not expect the Union to be dissolved—I do not expect the house to fall—but I do expect it will cease to be divided.
>
> It will become *all* one thing, or *all* the other.
>
> Either the *opponents* of slavery, will arrest the further spread of it, and place it where the public mind shall rest in the belief that it is in course of ultimate extinction; or its *advocates* will push it forward, till it shall become alike lawful in all the States, *old* as well as *new—North* as well as *South*.[82]

The prime minister reasoned similarly. Conservative MP Leslie Hore-Belisha, who had been Secretary of War under the Chamberlain government, sometimes opposed Churchill, but he appreciated Churchill's style of argument: "With care and patience he builds up a case. First he reads every document to be found on the subject, and with Churchill to read is to remember. Few men have a greater capacity for assimilating facts. I have never known him to go into a conference with an ill-prepared or half-digested case. He knows when he enters a Cabinet or committee meeting what he wants done. He has a scheme, a plan, a solution. Not for him the patient hearing while others sort out their views."[83]

Neither Churchill nor Lincoln permitted fear of war to deter them from plain speech describing the threats to their countries. Both men mobilized the English language, each in his own idiom, to unparalleled effect. For them, war rhetoric was a sword of victory. Their state papers, military orders, public letters, and speeches moved citizens to fight and to sacrifice; above all, they moved soldiers to give their last full measure. Prime Minister Churchill deployed the English language as a rapier with which to destroy Hitler and to save Britain. President Lincoln martialed his unique rhetoric to destroy slavery and to preserve the American Union.

This is a world of compensations; and he who would be no slave must consent to have no slave. Those who deny freedom to others deserve it not for themselves; and, under a just God, cannot long retain it.[1]

ABRAHAM LINCOLN
Letter to Henry L. Pierce
April 6, 1859

It is only in the twentieth century that this hateful conception of inducing nations to surrender by terrorising the helpless civil population, by massacring the women and children, has gained acceptance and countenance among men. This is not the cause of any one nation. Every country would feel safer if once it were found that the bombing aeroplane was at the mercy of appliances directed from the earth, and the haunting fears and suspicions which are leading nations nearer and nearer to another catastrophe would be abated.[2]

WINSTON S. CHURCHILL
Speech to the House of Commons
June 7, 1935

II.

The Unlikely Emergence of Lincoln and Churchill

Abraham Lincoln and Winston Churchill had little patience for government leaders who, through timidity and appeasement, lost the confidence of their countrymen. Most historians, with compelling evidence, have criticized President James Buchanan and Prime Minister Neville Chamberlain, who acted as if war must be avoided at the cost of national peril, even at the risk of national survival. During the failed Buchanan presidency (1857–1861), Lincoln seemed neither the logical nor the likely Republican successor to Buchanan. New York Senator William H. Seward was the frontrunner for the Republican nomination in 1860. He was eminently "available"—the contemporary term for appearing to be electable. But Lincoln, the master builder of the new Republican Party of Illinois, deployed his allies to Chicago, where they out-organized the well-financed throng imported by Seward's managers to work in and around the cavernous Wigwam, built specially for the convention. On May 18, 1860, after three ballots and clever negotiations by Lincoln's managers, the "Railsplitter" amassed enough delegate votes to be nominated. Lincoln was not at the convention; he was at home in Springfield. Lincoln would soon be inaugurated the first Republican President of the United States.

Churchill was neither the logical nor the likely Tory successor to Chamberlain's failed prime ministership.[3] "In the depths of that dusty soul there is nothing but abject surrender," Churchill had said of Chamberlain.[4] Lord Halifax was Chamberlain's likely successor—his loyal foreign minister who had held a variety of high ministerial posts for 15 years. Unlike Churchill, Halifax was a Tory party loyalist whom

Chamberlain, the party faithful, and King George VI preferred. In one of those unlikely rhymes of history, the outgoing prime minister summoned Churchill and Halifax to 10 Downing Street on the afternoon of May 10, 1940—the very same day German armies and tanks hurtled toward France. Earlier that morning, Randolph Churchill called his father and asked about the possibility that he might be named prime minister: "Oh, I don't know about that," replied Churchill, who was with guests at Admiralty House where he then lived. "Nothing matters now except beating the enemy."[5]

In his World War II memoirs, Churchill reported: "I have had many important interviews in my public life, and this was certainly the most important. Usually I talk a great deal, but on this occasion I was silent." Rare was such restraint for the talkative First Lord of the Admiralty, but he chose the effective strategy for the occasion. The tall, urbane Halifax finally declared "that he felt that his position as a peer, out of the House of Commons, would make it very difficult for him to discharge the duties of Prime Minister in a war like this. . . . He spoke for some minutes in this sense, and by the time he had finished, it was clear that the duty would fall upon me—had in fact fallen upon me."[6] Halifax had clearly thought out in advance the difficulties presented by assuming the prime minister's office. Halifax wrote in his diary:

> The PM [Chamberlain], Winston, David Margesson and I sat down to it. The PM recapitulated the position, and said that he had made up his mind that he must go, and that it must either be Winston or me. He would serve under either. I thought for all the reasons given the PM must probably go, but that I had no doubt at all in my own mind that for me to take it would create a quite impossible position. Quite apart from Winston's qualities as compared with my own at this particular juncture, what would in fact be my position? Winston would be running Defence, and in this connection one could not but remember how rapidly the position had become impossible between [Herbert] Asquith and Lloyd George [in World War I], and I should have no access to the House of Commons. The inevitable result would be that being outside both these vital points of contact I should speedily become a more or less honorary Prime Minister, living in a kind of twilight just outside the things that really mattered. Winston, with suitable expressions of regard and humility, said that he

could not but feel the force of what I had said, and the PM reluctantly, and Winston evidently with much less reluctance, finished by accepting my point of view.[7]

The ever-ambitious Churchill—the 65-year-old descendant of one of England's dukedoms, itself born of great wars two centuries past—had reached the pinnacle of British power. In an exquisite irony, the prime ministry fell to him because he had no title of nobility. After decades of striving and waiting, fortune would yield to Churchill's embrace. As the nineteenth-century Prime Minister Benjamin Disraeli had remarked, he had "reached the top of the greasy pole."[8] Returning from the palace, Churchill told his bodyguard of his new job: "God alone knows how great it is. I hope that it is not too late. I am very much afraid that it is. We can only do our best."[9] His 1930s prophecy of the mortal Nazi threat had been realized in a gale-force blitzkrieg that battered England's ally, France, into abject surrender. Churchill himself could not have estimated correctly the scale, the preparations, and the astounding power and strategy brought to bear by Hitler's *Wehrmacht*. When France fell, Churchill declared:

> The news from France is very bad and I grieve for the gallant French people who have fallen into this terrible misfortune. Nothing will alter our feelings towards them or our faith that the genius of France will rise again. What has happened in France makes no difference to our actions and purpose.
>
> We have become the sole champions now in arms to defend the world cause. We shall do our best to be worthy of this high honour. We shall defend our island home and with the British Empire we shall fight on unconquerable until the curse of Hitler is lifted from the brows of mankind.
>
> We are sure that in the end all will come right.[10]

Not unlike Churchill's selection as prime minister, the 1860 Republican presidential nomination had fallen to Lincoln because Seward was not so "available" as conventional wisdom believed. Seward, no matter his fame, was not a likely victor, given his enemies and the political circumstances. Despite the fact that Seward had been governor of New York and its senior senator, he was likely to lose moderate antislavery states like New Jersey, Pennsylvania, Indiana, and Illinois. Seward had inaccurately been tagged with the radical brand.[11] To win, the new Republican Party had to aim at the moderate free states, with the entire South going to the Democrats. Lincoln, as radical as Seward on slavery, was little known. Thus, he became the compromise nominee. Lincoln and Churchill would gain supreme command somewhat by default. But because his was a coalition government, the prime minister would not face a national election during the war. Lincoln would in 1864.

As they took office, there was widespread skepticism about the leadership capabilities of both. Lincoln was despised in the South for his antislavery views, and doubted in the North as unready for the crisis. Churchill was thought too unsteady. "In May 1940, the mere thought of Churchill as Prime Minister sent a cold chill down the spines of the staff at 10 Downing Street," recalled John Colville, who had worked there as an aide to Neville Chamberlain. "Seldom can a Prime Minister have taken office with 'the Establishment', as it would now be called, so dubious of the choice and so prepared to find its doubts justified."[12] Another important Churchill aide, General Ian Jacob, recalled: "I well remember the misgivings of many of us in the War Cabinet Office. We had not the experience or the imagination to realise the difference between a human dynamo when humming on the periphery and when driving at the centre."[13] Churchill and Lincoln would lead governments in which key leaders of their parties had grave doubts about them, their past political experience, their judgment, and their character. The doubts resolved themselves into one basic attitude: Churchill and Lincoln could not handle the monumental challenges. In London and Washington, the political and media establishments exhibited deep anxiety and relentless backbiting.

As politicians, Churchill and Lincoln were convivial men who did enjoy company. But in different ways, both were loners, much more secure in their own judgments than in the opinions of conventional experts. Churchill was egotistical, brilliant, unpredictable. Lincoln was publicly modest, more self-contained, equally self-confident. Churchill colleague Oliver Lyttelton recalled: "He knows when small things are likely to become big. Early the red light starts winking in the control room. Judgment must be exercised."[14] Throughout his life, Lincoln made loyal friends, but he was known to withdraw into his own thoughts, even while in conversation. Historian Allan Nevins wrote that Lincoln "was almost abnormally gregarious in the sense that he loved small social gatherings (not crowds, which he avoided), [and] was an unmatchable funmaker though never without a certain reserve of dignity." However, for major speeches, Lincoln longed for large crowds. He "felt instantly at home with men of all sorts—preachers, lawyers, politicians, farmers, boatmen, mechanics, newspapermen, anybody with a touch of comradeship in his disposition."[15] Judge David Davis, who for years traveled the Eighth Judicial Circuit of Illinois with Lincoln, often demanded that Lincoln entertain fellow lawyers. But Davis claimed that "Lincoln was not a social man by any means" and had "no Strong Emotional feelings for any person."[16]

Circumstances had changed in November 1860. As president, Lincoln knew he must connect with the influential Northern public opinion in order to deal with secession. Thus, he paid special attention to New York opinion leaders—including *New York Herald* publisher James Gordon Bennett, *Tribune* editor Horace Greeley, *New York Times* editor Henry Raymond, New York State Republican boss Thurlow Weed, Plymouth Church pastor Henry Ward Beecher, and U.S. Sanitary Commission Chairman Henry Bellows—who represented a wide range of opinion. These men would come to recognize Lincoln's ability and commitments. Both the president and the prime minister were moved by deep emotional and principled bonds to their homelands, especially to the causes of liberty and opportunity animating their national histories. An informed patriotism inspired their words and sustained their struggle toward victory. Intense ambitions for success would amplify the tenacious character of Lincoln and Churchill.

John Colville wrote that "Churchill was, indeed, interested in detail, but he seldom persisted for long in interference [with colleagues] except in relation to broad strategic designs." The prime minister emphasized the point: "Those who are charged with the direction of supreme affairs must sit on the mountain-tops of control: they must never descend into the valleys of direct physical and personal action."[17] He tended to abide by this dictum, but not always. Lincoln assistant William Stoddard observed that the president had "a provoking way of stepping over or across unessential things, with an instinctive perception of their lack of value. Some things that he [Lincoln] stepped over seemed vastly important to those who had them in hand, but at the same time he discovered real importances where others failed to see them."[18] The president would grasp better than anyone the world-historical importance of reunion and emancipation. "As our case is new, so we must think anew, and act anew," Lincoln announced in his Second Annual Message to Congress. "In times like the present, men should utter nothing for which they would not willingly be responsible through time and in eternity."[19]

After his election victory in November 1860, Lincoln was immobilized for four months as he waited for inauguration on March 4, 1861. By contrast, Churchill went into action immediately. He assumed office on May 10, 1940, the same day that King George VI asked him to form a government. Earlier that day, German panzer divisions had attacked the Low Countries. The new prime minister remembered that "as I went to bed at about 3 A.M., I was conscious of a profound sense of relief. At last I had the authority to give directions over the whole scene. I felt as if I were walking with Destiny, and that all my past life had been but a preparation for this hour and for this trial."[20] The president and the prime minister each had a strong sense of high personal destiny. Supreme power having been gained in the midst of a grave national crisis, neither man was willing to contemplate defeat. In his special war message to Congress of July 4, 1861, Lincoln argued that

> believing it to be an imperative duty upon the incoming Executive, to prevent, if possible, the consummation of such attempt to destroy the Federal Union, a choice of means to that end became indispensable. This choice was made; and was declared in the Inaugural address. The policy chosen looked to the exhaustion of all peaceful measures, before a resort to any stronger ones. It sought only to hold the public places and property, not already wrested from the Government, and to collect the revenue; relying for the rest, on time, discussion, and the ballotbox. It promised a continuance of the mails, at government expense, to the very people who were resisting the government; and it gave repeated pledges against any disturbance to any of the people, or any of their rights. Of all that which a president might constitutionally, and justifiably, do in such a case, everything was foreborne, without which, it was believed possible to keep the government on foot.[21]

The president's constitutional power as commander in chief of the army and the navy, and its use in the event of insurrection, had been foreborne, but not forgone. Lincoln would not prematurely strike the first, nor a major blow.

Abraham Lincoln, ca. 1858

Gilder Lehrman Collection, GLC07094.03

The hour of Churchill's trial, according to Correlli Barnett, "was the grimmest legacy ever inherited by an English Prime Minister."[22] Churchill did not have the luxury of time to prepare for supreme command. He must immediately form his Cabinet. The British government had been at war since September 1939. In contrast, Lincoln had four months to analyze the situation between election and inauguration—then another six weeks before military hostilities commenced at Fort Sumter. Another three months passed before the first battle of Bull Run—a limited, chaotic military engagement.

Both Seward and Halifax would remain important factors in the new administrations. Lincoln appointed Seward as secretary of state. The famous and self-important Seward initially tried to steer Lincoln toward accommodation with the South. Seward thought himself the presumptive prime minister for the inexperienced frontier president. Before the war, Halifax had tried to steer the British government toward accommodation with Germany. (For his part, Halifax thought the militant Churchill "an odd creature."[23]) Under the new prime minister, Halifax would continue his appeasement argument, but Churchill would ship him off in December 1940 to Washington as Britain's new ambassador. Anthony Eden would replace Halifax as foreign minister.

The prime minister knew he must deal with an important segment of the British political elite—those who continued to favor appeasement. As France collapsed in June 1940, Halifax would support negotiations with Hitler. But the new prime minister told the War Cabinet, "It was impossible to imagine that Herr Hitler would be so foolish as to let us continue our re-armament. In effect, his terms would put us completely at his mercy. We should get no worse terms if we went on fighting, even if we were beaten, than were open to us now."[24] On May 28, Churchill circumvented the foreign minister by making his case directly to 25 junior cabinet ministers—in the absence of Halifax and the War Cabinet. The prime minister exhorted the 25 to "fight on." They would agree. This special meeting of junior ministers was a bravura performance that secured Churchill's authority over the government. "If this long island story of ours is to end at last," the prime minister reportedly told them, "let it end only when each one of us lies choking in his own blood upon the ground."[25]

With Chamberlain's help, Churchill outmaneuvered Halifax to take command of British war policy, setting the precedent that he would govern this cabinet. Only the day before the prime minister's stirring comments to junior ministers, Halifax had confided to his diary: "I thought Winston talked the most frightful rot, also [Arthur] Greenwood, and after bearing it for some time I said exactly what I thought of them, adding that, if that was really their view, and if it came to the point, our ways must separate. . . . I despair when he [Churchill] works himself up to a passion of emotion when he ought to make his brain think and reason."[26] Still, the prime minister would provide the passionate leadership that the British Cabinet and the British public desperately needed, despite mixed opinions about his character and his past decisions in war and peace. Geoffrey Best observed: "In later May and early June [1940] the British public was so battered and bewildered by shocks and disaster that if a different leader—Lord Halifax, for example—had told it that there was no point in going on with the war, it would have followed him."[27] Had that happened, the British public would have been irreconcilably divided in defeat. Labourite Hugh Dalton, recently added to the Cabinet, got it right when he wrote that Churchill is "the man, and the only man we have, for this hour."[28]

At their best, Churchill and Lincoln were decisive in the midst of controversy, bringing to bear compelling arguments to carry the day. In his inaugural address of March 1861, the Southern slave states having already seceded, President Lincoln stubbornly insisted: "I therefore consider that the Union is unbroken; and, to the extent of my ability, I shall take care, that the laws of the Union be faithfully executed in all the States."[29] Churchill was equally determined that the integrity and the laws of the British Empire would be sustained by his government and its armed forces. The president and the prime minister focused on the paramount issue of national unity in order to mobilize the unconditional support of loyalists and soldiers.[30] "I take up my tasks with buoyance and hope," said Churchill on May 13, 1940. "I feel sure that our cause will not be suffered to fail among men. At this time I feel entitled to claim the aid of all, and I say, 'Come then, let us go forward together with our united strength.'"[31] The prime minister well understood the ominous moment in British history. He noted in his memoirs, "For the first time [since Napoleon] in a hundred and twenty-five years a powerful enemy was now established across the narrow waters of the English Channel."[32]

Early on as prime minister, Churchill made very tough decisions—for example, limiting the aid, especially fighter planes, he was willing to provide France, as German tanks headed toward Paris in June 1940. When Hitler erred in not destroying the British army at Dunkirk, the prime minister seized the opportunity to organize the evacuation of the devastated British and French army holed up at the coast.[33] After the collapse of France, he astounded the combatants when, on July 3, he attacked and destroyed the French fleet at Oran in order to keep it out of German hands. Churchill admitted it was "a hateful decision, the most unnatural and painful decision in which I have ever been concerned."[34] The prime minister wept before the members, after announcing his decision in Parliament.

His was a controversial action, even in England. Admiral Andrew Cunningham later called the operation "almost inept in its unwisdom."[35] Then came the Battle of Britain, a relentless air struggle with the *Luftwaffe* over English territory, in which the British RAF prevailed.[36] London, the capital of the British Empire, had been menaced by German arms from the air, just as Washington would be menaced by Confederate ground forces in every year of the Civil War except 1865. When the Nazi onslaught was at its peak, Churchill noted on September 15, 1940, that "our Bomber Command attacked in strength the shipping in the ports from Boulogne to Antwerp."[37] One month earlier, after observing RAF operations at the peak intensity of the Battle of Britain on August 16, Churchill told General Ismay: "Never in the field of human conflict was so much owed by so many to so few."[38] Although *Luftwaffe* attacks on London continued until the end of October 1940, RAF pilots had prevailed, establishing air superiority over Britain and the English Channel—a crucial strategic factor of D-Day success more than three years hence.

By his confident presence and with his bold speeches, Churchill rallied cabinet ministers, the parliament, the armed forces. He rallied the British people, extending his reach and rhetoric to the nations of the British Commonwealth. Then he rallied Franklin Roosevelt and America to the war against fascism. This last task, he believed, was the indispensable strategy for victory. With sincere empathy, he sought the advice and support of the cancer-ridden Chamberlain, keeping him a member of the War Cabinet until a few weeks before the former prime minister died in November 1940. Then Churchill would say of Chamberlain: "When, contrary to all his hopes, beliefs and exertions, the war came upon him, and when, as he himself said, all that he had worked for was shattered, there was no man more resolved to pursue the unsought quarrel to the death. The same qualities which made him one of the last to enter the war, made him one of the last who would quit it until the full victory of a righteous cause was won."[39]

Winston S. Churchill, 1904

© Imperial War Museum

Churchill became the round-the-clock leader. The prime minister, noted historian Paul Johnson, "set a personal example of furious and productive activity at Ten Downing Street. He was sixty-five but looked, seemed—was indeed—the embodiment of energy."[40] Attended to by his personal physician, Dr. Charles Wilson, Churchill worked from morning into the late night, requiring two shifts of assistants to keep up with him. He exhausted and infuriated civilian and military colleagues, forcing those at his beck and call to keep late hours. The aggravation, especially of the war command, was understandable; they had to rise early every day while the prime minister worked from bed.

Lincoln and Churchill themselves set the work ethic and the standards of excellence for their civilian and military officials. "Work, work, work is the main thing," Lincoln had advised a would-be lawyer in 1860.[41] By his example, he sustained that advice for all around him. His leadership schedule did preoccupy the president from dawn to midnight—his work as commander in chief necessary not only for Union victory, but also for Union morale. "The lady—bearer of this—says she has two sons who want to work," wrote President Lincoln in October 1861. "Set them at it, if possible. Wanting to work is so rare a merit, that it should be encouraged."[42] White House aide William O. Stoddard noted: "Lincoln's characteristic as a worker was his persistency, his tirelessness; and for this he was endowed with rare toughness of bodily and mental fibre. There was not a weak spot in his whole animal organism, and his brain was thoroughly healthy; his White House life, therefore, was a continual stepping from one duty to another."[43] Lincoln, a young president by previous standards, cared little for the Washington social establishment, nothing for the pomp and circumstance that the pretentious slaveholding and free-state elites had stamped on social life in the nation's capital.

Hard work did not disturb Lincoln's equanimity. Kentucky Congressman George Yeaman recalled an occasion when

I called and found the usually genial, sparkling, anecdote-telling president the most serious, intent and melancholy looking man that I ever beheld. His appearance gave me positive pain. He was alone, at his desk, hard at work, and I promptly offered to retire and call again. . . . Disasters had come in the field, and it was not all harmony among his supporters. While waiting, his barber entered the room. I again offered to retire. "No, just excuse me one moment;" and he rose, quickly threw off his coat, seated himself in one chair and stretched his long legs across another. The barber lathered his face and commenced stropping a razor, when that tired, overburdened president of the United States turned his face towards me and gently asked, "Now what can we do?" I told my mission. I was answered promptly, kindly, decided correctly, and I, wondering, went my way.[44]

A War Department official wrote that Lincoln "had immense physical endurance. Night after night he would work late and hard without being wilted by it, and he always seemed ready for the next day's work as though he had done nothing the day before."[45]

Churchill, much older than Lincoln, worked in different ways and places through a 24-hour day—from bed in the morning, with a nap in the late afternoon. He was attended at all times by staff and secretaries who took down his every word on silent typewriters—allowing Churchill to follow his dictum to his government that all of his decisions and orders must be committed promptly to writing during the war; thus, no one could pretend to represent his directive without a written Churchill instruction.[46] Second, he insisted upon a written record when possible because he knew he would write the history of the era. He often said, only half joking, that he would be well-treated by history because he would write it.[47] The nature of Churchill's demands, often excessive, enraged some government officials. John Colville recalled that working with Churchill "was sometimes wearisome and sometimes exasperating; but it was the most exhilarating of all experiences to serve, at close quarters and in war, that wayward, romantic, expansive and explosive genius, with the inspirational qualities of an Old Testament Prophet."[48] Future British Prime Minister Harold Macmillan wrote: "He is really a remarkable man. Although he can be so tiresome and pig-headed, there is no one like him. His devotion to work and duty is quite extraordinary."[49]

Churchill's devotion to the cause inspired those who feared for his life. Especially under wartime circumstances, leaders conjure up super-loyal protectors. U.S. Marshal Ward Hill Lamon, an old Lincoln friend from Illinois, occasionally lay down outside the president's bedroom to protect him from assassination. Bodyguard Walter Thompson occasionally remained outside No. 10 Downing Street to make sure Churchill did not sneak out in the middle of the night to visit bombed-out London.

Lincoln's staff, merely two or three aide-secretaries, had a hard time establishing a presidential routine in the secession crisis of March

1861—an effort made more difficult by the rush of Republican patronage seekers besieging the White House—at the same time the siege at
Fort Sumter neared its climax. Lincoln's decision on war strategy came
promptly after his inauguration. He would unite his Cabinet behind a
controversial tactic to resupply Fort Sumter with food and to prepare
for war. A Lincoln Cabinet meeting in late March found only one member, Montgomery Blair, strongly in favor of defending the fort. A hero
of the Mexican-American War and the army's commanding general in
1861, General Winfield Scott was too sick to attend, but he sent a memorandum favoring appeasement and capitulation to the Confederacy
in the Sumter crisis.[50] At the time, Lincoln was trying desperately to
keep Virginia and other border slave states from joining the Confederacy. The president would take no action to cause these states to secede,
but he would not accept any advice from his cabinet, accommodating
the legitimacy of secession. Lincoln's secretaries, later his biographers,
recalled the effect of the president's influence: "Without any formal vote,
there was a unanimous expression of dissent from Scott's suggestion [to
appease the Confederacy on Fort Sumter], and under the President's
request to meet in formal council next day, the Cabinet retired. That
night, Lincoln's eyes did not close in sleep. It was apparent that the time
had come when he must meet the nation's crisis."[51]

Neither generals nor cabinet members were much help to Lincoln in
this crisis. Navy Secretary Gideon Welles believed General Scott too much
influenced by Secretary of State Seward, who in early 1861 had advocated
compromise with the seceding states. Welles later wrote: "It was not surprising that General Scott viewed [Seward] as the coming man, and as
Mr. Seward was a man of expedients more than principle, he soon made
it obvious that he intended to have no war, but was ready to yield anything—the Constitution itself if necessary—to satisfy the Secessionists.
The General under this influence abandoned his early recommendations and ultimately advised surrendering all the forts."[52] Lincoln deftly
steered the Cabinet away from doing so. In the final Fort Sumter crisis, he
also assured the South that the soldiers in the island fortress at Charleston would be provided only with food, if the Confederate artillery laying siege to Fort Sumter forbore to attack the resupply ship. On April 12,
the Southern batteries in Charleston Harbor received orders to bombard
the Union fort. The rebels had fired the first shot. Talk of treason and
insurrection against the Union reverberated throughout the North. The
Union fort under Major Robert Anderson surrendered. The slavemasters

had declared war. The president's subtle, peaceful tactics tempted the impatient rebels to attack, galvanizing the North to defend the Union by accepting a war begun by the secessionist slave states.[53]

Both the president and the prime minister prevailed in similar cabinet crises at the onset of their administrations. The immediate challenge—for Lincoln in April 1861 and for Churchill in May 1940—was to mobilize their countries for war, the duration of which no one could foresee. Leonard Swett, Lincoln's friend from Illinois, noted that the president called out only 75,000 men because the government did not have the resources, even the uniforms, to handle more recruits at the beginning of the war. Recalling his efforts to get resources for an Illinois regiment, Swett noted:

> The government did not call for 500,000 men, simply because it could not utilize them. The time of which I speak was the spring and summer of 1861. . . . The industries of the nation had all to be changed. All the wool on the sheep's backs in the country, and all that could be bought, had to be diverted to uniforms, and the manufacturing capacity of the country had to be increased, and Mr. Lincoln might have added with equal truth that the ore with which to make the swords and the carbines was still in its native mountains. All the manufactories in the country had to be set in operation to make arms. New factories had to be built and new industries created, and even then whole regiments had to wait for their turn to be uniformed and armed.[54]

Many well-informed men on both sides believed the American Civil War would be a short one. Four years of all-out war ensued, causing more than 700,000 soldiers to perish in battle.[55] The slave states would be ravaged by war. The free states would prosper in war, despite great losses. Most of the rebel army would surrender in April 1865. Lincoln would be assassinated in the same month. By the end of 1865, ratification of the Thirteenth Amendment would abolish slavery. The Union army would remain in the South until 1877 to enforce the laws of reform and reconstruction. As the president suggested in his Second Inaugural Address, no one could have predicted such an astounding outcome on the eve of the Fort Sumter crisis in 1861.

Neither party expected for the war, the magnitude, or the duration, which it has already attained. Neither antici-pated that the cause *of the conflict might cease with, or even before, the conflict itself should cease. Each looked for an easier triumph, and a result less fundamental and astounding. Both read the same Bible, and pray to the same God; and each invokes His aid against the other. It may seem strange that any men should dare to ask a just God's assistance in wringing their bread from the sweat of other men's faces; but let us judge not, that we be not judged. The prayers of both could not be answered; that of neither has been answered fully.*[1]

ABRAHAM LINCOLN
Second Inaugural Address
March 4, 1865

We ask no favours of the enemy. . . . On the contrary, if tonight the people of London were asked to cast their vote whether a convention should be entered into to stop the bombing of all cities, the overwhelming majority would cry, "No, we will mete out to the Germans the measure, and more than the measure, that they have meted out to us." The people of London with one voice would say to Hitler: "You have committed every crime under the sun. Where you have been the least resisted there you have been the most brutal. It was you who began the indiscriminate bombing. . . . We will have no truce or parley with you, or the grisly gang who work your wicked will. You do your worst and we will do our best."[2]

WINSTON S. CHURCHILL
July 14, 1941

III.

The Rhetoric of Leadership

Winston Churchill's remarkable prose was inspired by the ambition he acknowledged as a young man—driven as well by the resolute principles he upheld as prime minister.[3] Abraham Lincoln's mature rhetoric was spare and austere, Euclidean in its logic, terse in its Anglo-Saxon single-syllable form. Churchill's politics, like his prose, exhibited the boldness of Prometheus unbound, and the wiliness of Odysseus to persevere. MP Harold Nicolson, himself a writer, observed in 1940: "I think that one of the reasons why one is stirred by his Elizabethan phrases is that one feels the whole massive backing of power and resolve behind them, like a great fortress: they are never words for words' sake."[4] John Colville wrote: "Among Churchill's most powerful armaments was simplicity. Simplicity of aim, simplicity of thought, simplicity of expression. There are some benighted, and seldom very impressive, people who think that you must be complicated in order to prove you are intelligent. . . . He did not seek to dazzle an audience with sophistries."[5]

Churchill's spirit exulted in defiance of what others might think overwhelming obstacles. The tenacity of the warrior bent on victory proved to be one of his greatest contributions to the Allied war effort. William Manchester and Paul Reid observed: "Everything about Churchill's speeches was extraordinary, not least the speed with which they were scrawled in longhand or dictated straight into the typewriter in odd moments before pressing duties."[6] Correlli Barnett commented that "the British nation recognised that Churchill was a born warrior: a pugilist who itched to land the heaviest possible punches on Hitler and his chum Mussolini. And so the nation gave him their trust, believing that his leadership would bring them safely through the storm."[7] British civil servant Oliver Franks observed: "Winston embodied the soul of the nation. He

71

succeeded in being the nation, for that is what he was. In the simplified conditions of war he could be that, whereas in the more complex days of peace, he never was, never could be."[8]

Churchill and Lincoln, both great writers and speakers, prepared carefully for public appearances. Although they could be good extemporaneous speakers, they respected the hard work required of the orator's art. They devoted hours, even days, to major speeches.[9] For the prime minister, the writer's task was made easier. In and out of government, he employed a large, skilled staff, including PhDs, to help him with his research and writing. But Churchill's speeches were his own laborious work. Lincoln worked alone. Sometimes his younger law partner, Billy Herndon, was asked to help. But usually—as was the case with Lincoln's unsurpassed, three-hour Peoria speech of 1854 and his 1860 Cooper Union speech at New York—it was Mr. Lincoln who did the work mostly on his own. He alone would walk from his office to the State Library in Springfield, there to spend days, sometimes weeks, researching the facts of early American history. When tired, distracted, or ill-prepared, Lincoln and Churchill could give ineffective speeches. But at key moments, they rose to the occasion well prepared. Their leadership would often hang on these moments.

Years of study and hard work had made them ready. Indeed, they were inspired students of history—Churchill encyclopedic, Lincoln focused on American history. They developed vast memory banks on which to draw. They had mastered the natural rhythms of their native tongue. They would practice its poetic cadences aloud. They would experiment with word order, refining it to their purpose. Their reading dwelt on masterpieces of English prose and poetry upon which they would draw for their writing and speeches. Elements of the Gettysburg Address of November 19, 1863, may be found in previous comments of Boston preacher Theodore Parker, but also in Lincoln's own response to a serenade of July 7, just after the Battle of Gettysburg, July 1–3.[10] Churchill would stockpile the building blocks of future speeches. Historian Andrew Roberts wrote: "When Churchill found a vivid phrase it often lodged in his brain to be called forth for later use; 'fight them on the beaches' first appears in relation to seal pups in Rudyard Kipling's *Kim*."[11] Both listened to the sound of their words as they practiced speeches. They would write for the ear. Churchill sometimes mumbled incoherently before he dictated important phrases to a waiting secretary.

In his office, Lincoln even read newspapers aloud. But he would tell William O. Stoddard: "What I want is an audience. Nothing sounds the same when there isn't anybody to hear it and find fault with it."[12]

On May 10, 1940, as news reached London of the German invasion of the Low Countries, Churchill met with two of Britain's civilian leaders of the war effort. "Churchill, whose spirit, so far from being shaken by failure or disaster, gathered strength in a crisis, was ready as always with his confident advice," recalled then Secretary for Air Samuel Hoare, a Chamberlain ally soon to be named ambassador to Spain. "I shall never forget the breakfast we had with him. It was six o'clock in the morning, after a fierce House of Commons debate and a late sitting. We had had little or no sleep, and the news could not have been worse. [The German invasion was under way.] Yet there he was, smoking his large cigar and eating fried eggs and bacon, as if he had just returned from an early morning ride."[13] He had dealt with great crises for decades. Churchill had been in Parliament from 1900—when at age 25 he was already one of England's most famous citizens. Now in World War II, his vast experience, including the painful instruction of World War I, had merged with his lifelong ambition. Having become the King's first minister, he took charge immediately. Speaking to Parliament on May 19—and later that night to the nation on the BBC—Churchill declared:

> I speak to you for the first time as Prime Minister in a solemn hour for the life of our country, of our empire, of our allies, and, above all, of the cause of Freedom. A tremendous battle is raging in France and Flanders. The Germans, by a remarkable combination of air bombing and heavily armored tanks, have broken through the French defenses north of the Maginot Line, and strong columns of their armored vehicles are ravaging the open country, which for the first day or two was without defenders. They have penetrated deeply and spread alarm and confusion in their track. Behind them there are now appearing infantry in lorries, and behind them, again, the large masses are moving forward. The regroupment of the French armies to make head against, and also to strike at, this intruding wedge has been proceeding for several days, largely assisted by the magnificent efforts of the Royal Air Force.

Churchill concluded his remarks: "Today is Trinity Sunday. Centuries ago words were written to be a call and a spur to the faithful servants of Truth and Justice: 'Arm yourselves, and be ye men of valour, and be in readiness for the conflict; for it is better for us to perish in battle than to look upon the outrage of our nation and our altar. As the Will of God is in Heaven, even so let it be.'"[14] Private Secretary John Martin recalled: "It was as if a great bell tolled. This sudden and unexpected reminder of our Faith and its most mysterious doctrine had a strange and moving effect."[15] In the words of American diplomat Dean Acheson, Churchill's "speeches were not only wise and right in context, but were prepared with that infinite capacity for taking pains that is said to be genius."[16]

During World War II, the prime minister gave fewer major BBC speeches than one might think. His most famous were given from May 1940 to the end of 1941—seven the first year and eighteen the second. "Once the tide had turned in the autumn of 1942," noted historian D. J. Wenden, "the need for such impassioned broadcasts diminished. Good news carries its own inspiration."[17] The quality of his radio broadcasts, which Churchill did not enjoy doing, was uneven in the eyes of those who had heard a more rested and energized prime minister deliver the same material in Parliament.[18] Churchill friend Violet Bonham Carter described his speech to the House in early June 1940 as "the greatest speech in my memory—one of the greatest speeches in history. Its candour & its courage were alike admirable."[19] However, on March 26, 1944, she wrote: "Winston broadcast for 3/4 of an hour—the worst I have ever heard him do. The war-part with which it opened was not inspiring—& the second part he slanged his critics over Planning."[20] The immediate broadcast audience is the microphone; in Parliament hundreds of MPs wait on the words of a successful prime minister.

On the morrow of his inauguration in 1861, Lincoln took charge. The president had no less an ambition than Churchill—to unite his countrymen, to save the nation. His manner was less dramatic, but his will and intellect were equally focused. Lincoln had none of the prime minister's executive and war experience. By nature, he was more deliberate and patient than Churchill. He sent his Cabinet nominations to the Senate. He met with state delegations. He conferred with incoming Secretary of State Seward on the evening of his first day as president. Ominously, outgoing Secretary of War Joseph Holt, ensnared by the

Abraham Lincoln, 1863

Gilder Lehrman Collection, GLC05111.02.0012

Fort Sumter crisis, informed Lincoln that "an expedition has been quietly prepared, and is ready to sail from New York on a few hours' notice,
for transporting troops and supplies [to Fort Sumter]."[21] Lincoln hoped
to avoid a collision with the rebels besieging the fort. He would give no
occasion for war. Nor would he begin one. To a Massachusetts delegation at the onset of the crisis, Lincoln was generous in his disposition
toward the South: "As President, in the administration of the Government, I hope to be man enough not to know one citizen of the United
States from another, nor one section from another."[22] In principle,
Southerners, Northerners, Westerners were his common countrymen.
He would not rush to war, even though urged by some to act against
the seven Southern states that had formally seceded from the Union—
actions tantamount to treason. No newly inaugurated president could
have been fully prepared for the unprecedented events of secession and
the potential dissolution of the United States. But Lincoln's steady temperament, natural prudence, and cautious language compensated for
his inexperience.

Churchill had gained extensive practical experience at the pinnacle
of power in the largest empire of world history—a fifth of the world's
population and almost one quarter of the earth's land mass.[23] He wrote
in his World War II memoirs, *Their Finest Hour*:

> In my long political experience I had held most of the great
> offices of State, but I readily admit that the post which had now
> fallen to me was the one I liked the best. Power, for the sake of
> lording it over fellow-creatures, or adding to personal pomp, is
> rightly judged base. But power in a national crisis, when a man
> believes he knows what orders should be given, is a blessing. In
> my sphere of action there can be no comparison between the
> positions of number one and numbers two, three, or four.[24]

Even before he became prime minister in May of 1940, Churchill as
First Lord of the Admiralty had rallied the nation with inspired speeches
on BBC radio. Geoffrey Best wrote that "these broadcasts before he
became Prime Minister had an overconfident, even boastful air which
displeased the fastidious. But he was fulfilling an immensely important
function. No other public figure had come forward with a convincing
explanation of why the war was being fought, through these months

when nothing seemed to be happening and the Poles were in danger of falling into the same memory hole as the Czechs."[25] September 1939 to May 1940 was known as "the phony war." Some sober Englishmen still believed that great issues could be resolved without bloodshed. Churchill, like Lincoln before him, understood that the rationale for war—violent death in battle—must be explained to the public. As prime minister, Churchill would again use BBC broadcasts to inform and to inspire his countrymen. The rhythms of Shakespeare and English poetry—of which he was a master—resonated in his speeches. In April 1941, he would invoke his greatest hope and desperate need of American intervention in the war.

> Last time I spoke to you I quoted the lines of Longfellow which President Roosevelt had written out for me in his own hand. I have some other lines which are less well known but which seem apt and appropriate to our fortunes tonight, and I believe they will be so judged wherever the English language is spoken or the flag of freedom flies:

> > . . . When daylight comes, comes in the light;
> > In front the sun climbs slow, how slowly!
> > But westward, look, the land is bright.[26]

In April 1941, Britain and its Empire stood alone against the might of German arms. It was not well known, but Britain was insolvent. Churchill would not despair. Look westward . . . to America, he urged his countrymen. To quicken Britain's courage for the struggle, to keep its manpower and industries working full-time, until America was drawn into the war, the prime minister deployed the last of British resources—including his pen as a battle-axe, his voice as a trumpet: "The battle of France is over," Churchill told the House of Commons on June 18, 1940. "Let us therefore brace ourselves to our duty and so bear ourselves that if the British Commonwealth and Empire lasts for a thousand years, men will still say, 'This was their finest hour.'"[27] The prime minister would often hearken to the language of Shakespeare's *Henry V*—the Saint Crispin Day speech before the Battle of Agincourt.[28] Churchill had the romantic imagination to feel himself an heir to King Henry V. As a young cavalry officer he had been no less bold, no less brave.

Lincoln, too, was a devoted, self-taught master of Shakespeare's tragedies and histories. In his 1862 presidential message to Congress, Lincoln also summoned the spirit of *Henry V*:

> Fellow-citizens, we cannot escape history. We of this Congress
> and this administration, will be remembered in spite of our-
> selves. No personal significance, or insignificance, can spare one
> or another of us. The fiery trial through which we pass, will light
> us down, in honor or dishonor, to the latest generation. We say
> we are for the Union. The world will not forget that we say this.
> We know how to save the Union. The world knows we do know
> how to save it. We—*even we here*—hold the power, and bear the
> responsibility. In *giving* freedom to the *slave*, we *assure* freedom
> to the *free*—honorable alike in what we give, and what we pre-
> serve. We shall nobly save, or meanly lose, the last best hope of
> earth. Other means may succeed; this could not fail. The way
> is plain, peaceful, generous, just—a way which, if followed, the
> world will forever applaud, and God must forever bless.[29]

It was not only the simple beauty of his prose, but it was also Lincoln's principles which ennoble his writings, which, as scholar Paul Angle
wrote, "fuse sincerity and sympathy, logical directness, a severity of style
almost classic, and homely plainness."[30]

As a parliamentary leader, Churchill appeared repeatedly in debate
at Westminster. Unlike America's presidential system, the parliamentary
system gave greater opportunities for the prime minister to make mem-
orable public comments. "I am a child of the House of Commons," he
once told the American Congress.[31] So he had been since 1900. "I am
expressing my opinion," Churchill told a Commons critic during World
War II. "When my hon. and gallant Friend is called, he will express his
opinion. That is the process which we call Debate."[32] During World War
II, despite the permanent crisis, the prime minister regularly reported
to the House of Commons. He submitted himself to the rigor of Prime
Minister's Questions. "We shall go on to the end," Churchill had told the
House of Commons on June 4, 1940. "We shall fight in France, we shall
fight on the seas and oceans, we shall fight with growing confidence and
growing strength in the air, we shall defend our island, whatever the cost
may be."[33] With France defeated, Britain was alone at war with Hitler.

The reality was grim. But Churchill reportedly remarked in an aside at the time, "And we'll fight them with the butt ends of broken beer bottles because that's bloody well all we've got!"[34]

Neither war leader believed in false optimism. Churchill might go to excess in public to reassure his countrymen, but Lincoln was careful at every public encounter. With well-chosen words the president and the prime minister would attempt to steel the home front against many defeats. Of the prime minister's appearance in the House of Commons in November 1940, MP Labour intellectual Harold Nicolson wrote: "He is rather grim. He brings home to the House as never before the gravity of our shipping losses and the danger of our position in the Eastern Mediterranean. It has good effect. By putting the grim side foremost he impresses us with his ability to face the worst. He rubs the palms of his hands with five fingers extended up and down the front of his coat, searching for the right phrase, indicating cautious selection, conveying almost medicinal poise."[35] He would speak often. Churchill would remark: "Asking me not to make a speech is like asking a centipede to get along and not to put a foot on the ground."[36] Lincoln never addressed the Congress; it was not customary then for the president to do so. (Thomas Jefferson set the American tradition in December 1801, when, as president, he decided not to address Congress in person. Jefferson was not an effective speaker. Lincoln, effective as he would have been, followed Jefferson's precedent.)

Churchill cherished his opportunity to speak to the U.S. Congress— the first time on December 26, 1941, after Pearl Harbor, when America had entered World War II. "I can not help reflecting that if my father had been American and my mother British," the prime minister told Congress, "instead of the other way round, I might have got here on my own. In that case, this would not have been the first time you would have heard my voice."[37] The congress roared with approval. On May 19, 1943, he spoke to America's lawmakers again: "War is full of mysteries and surprises. A false step, a wrong direction, an error in strategy, discord or lassitude among the Allies, might soon give the common enemy power to confront us with new and hideous facts. We have surmounted many serious dangers, but there is one grave danger which will go along with us till the end; that danger is the undue prolongation of the war."[38] War impoverished Britain, now utterly dependent on United States financing and supplies. The longer the war, the more certain became the complete collapse of British power, the decline of the British standard of living, and the demise of the British Empire. The prime minister felt this threat to the marrow of his bones.

Churchill's speeches and conversations were amusing not least because his idiosyncratic individualism caused him to make up words—creating words included in no dictionary. He would anglicize foreign words in his unique diction, in a sometimes parochial and patronizing pronunciation. In his mouth, "monty-vid-ee-oh" became the capital of Uruguay.[39] Lincoln's spelling, learned on his own, to some extent by ear, was often unorthodox. He was delighted to discover that "maintainance" was, in fact, spelled "maintenance."[40] Lincoln's Hoosier pronunciation sometimes grated on sophisticated Eastern ears. Although initially critical of Lincoln, the cosmopolitan Frederick L. Olmsted, executive director of the Sanitary Commission during the Civil War, wrote after a meeting in October 1861: "He was very awkward & ill at ease in attitude, but spoke readily, with a good vocabulary, & with directness and point. Not elegantly. 'I heerd of that' he said, but it did not seem very wrong from him, & his frankness & courageous directness overcame all critical disposition."[41]

Every public word "fitly chosen" was a matter of great moment to both war leaders. Max Hastings wrote that the prime minister "was hostile to the use of the word *invasion* in the context of D-Day: 'Our object is the liberation of Europe from German tyranny . . . we 'enter' the oppressed countries rather than 'invade' them and . . . the word 'invasion' must be reserved for the time when we cross the German frontier. There is no need for us to make a present to Hitler of the idea that he is the defender of a Europe we are seeking to invade."[42]

Similarly, in July 1863, General Robert E. Lee and the Confederate armies advancing into the North met defeat at Gettysburg in the heartland of the Union. After the battle, the commander of the Army of the Potomac, General Meade, announced that he intended to "drive from our soil every vestige of the presence of the invader." Lincoln recoiled in anger at Meade's usage. "Drive the invaders from our soil! My God!" exclaimed Lincoln.[43] "The whole country is *our* soil."[44]

Words mattered. Lincoln and Churchill would use vocabulary as strategy. "In times like the present," said the American president, "men should utter nothing for which they would not willingly be responsible through time and in eternity."[45] Over a year before he joined the

Winston S. Churchill, 1943
Library of Congress, LC USE6 D 009043

Chamberlain government in 1939, Churchill wrote: "Words are the only things that last for ever. . . . The Pyramids moulder, the bridges rust, the canals fill up, grass covers the railway track, but words spoken two or three thousand years ago remain with us now, not as mere relics of the past, but with all their pristine vital force."[46] He focused on choosing the best words. "He was intolerant of sloppiness and jargon in official letters," observed John Martin. "'Appreciate *that* . . . ' was a *bête noire*: again and again the substitution of 'recognise that' was the only amendment in a departmental draft of policy submitted for his approval."[47] Leslie Hollis, the top aide to General Hastings Ismay, recalled:

> During the height of the war, when we were working at the fullest pressure for anything up to eighteen hours a day, on a seven-day week, I recall that I submitted to the Prime Minister a rather loosely phrased minute. I opened a sentence with the words: "Having regard to the fact that . . . " It was sent back to me with a stern comment: "Colonel Hollis, you have used six words, where one word of two letters—namely 'as'—would have sufficed. Pray remember that in an efficient Administration small things count as well as great."[48]

"Pray," a Victorian commonplace with which to begin a sentence, followed Churchill into the mid-twentieth century, evoking the archaic courtesies of a bygone era.

Churchill's voice, a famous growl, contrasted with Lincoln's high-pitched tenor. One of the prime minister's secretaries, Elizabeth Layton Nel, described a speech at the war-damaged Guildhall in London:

> Mr. Churchill spoke very much as he always did on the radio— slowly but not too slowly, clearly and emphatically, so that one wondered why one had found it difficult to understand him when one first knew him. He made use of every pause, his sense of timing was perfect—he might not have been reading from his notes but speaking his thoughts as they came to him. His hands gestured in the well-known fashion; sometimes he would hold the front of his black coat, fingers tucked in, sometimes his hands would be clasped in front of him, sometimes a forefinger would be uplifted.[49]

From boyhood Churchill had a slight lisp that he tried to purge, but could not.

By the time Lincoln and Churchill had reached their nations' highest elected offices, they were practiced speakers and writers. The courtrooms of the Eighth Judicial District and the lower house of the Illinois legislature had served as Lincoln's classrooms for learning the art of public speaking and persuasion. Making a case to local juries helped Lincoln the litigator to understand the relationship between audience and speaker. Robert A. Ferguson, a scholar of rhetoric, argued that the effectiveness of Lincoln's presidential rhetoric was in part based on lessons he learned as a courtroom lawyer: "Forensic debate refined four essential sources of rhetorical power: first, equanimity in the face of conflict; second, an instinct for the root of a matter that tended to concede nonessentials; third, a gift for plain expression against the ornate style required of nineteenth-century orators; and fourth, a legal identity that encouraged religious thought away from the dogmatism of his day."[50] Lincoln biographer James G. Randall observed that Lincoln's "addresses seized the understanding of the man in the street. He had his own style, his special tang. . . . Some of his statements have that unerring quality of hitting the target that stamps them as proverbs or aphorisms."[51]

Lincoln's respect for public opinion was linked itself to his respect for public language. In his political maturity he was a careful speaker who seldom made idle public comments for the sake of gratifying his listeners. As president, he practiced the art of conciliatory language. Committed to victory over the rebels, but above all, to eventual reunion, he would rarely demonize his Confederate opposition. In his mind and in law, the territory of the country was one and indivisible, never lawfully divided into North and South. Churchill's antagonists were warlike foreigners, not fellow countrymen. The Nazis were demonic, Hitler a monster.[52] In his comments about the "wicked men" who were his German, Italian, and Japanese enemies, his language was bitter, blunt, and intemperate. The master of language became the master of invective. His ability to demonize was finely tuned, especially in the case of Benito Mussolini. "Tonight I speak to the Italian people," Churchill declared in a 1940 radio broadcast to Italy. "We have never been your foes till now. . . . How has all this come about, and what is it all for? Italians, I will tell you the truth. It is because one man, and one man alone, has ranged the Italian people in deadly struggle against the British Empire." Two years later in another radio broadcast, Churchill declared of Mussolini: "The hyena in his nature broke all bounds of decency and even commonsense."[53]

Churchill mangled names, sometimes deliberately—referring to Yugoslavia's Josip "Tito" Broz as "Toty." When the prime minister visited Cairo in 1942, he was pressed to visit with Panagiotis Kanellopoulos, the defense minister of the Greek government-in-exile, whose name Churchill pronounced as "Can't-ellopoulos."[54] Lincoln remembered names. His was a glue-like memory. An Illinois editor, Paul Selby, recalled:

> Lincoln never forgot anyone or anything. At one of the afternoon receptions at the White House a stranger shook hands with him, and, as he did so, remarked casually, that he was elected to Congress about the time Mr. Lincoln's term as representative expired, which happened many years before. "Yes," said the President, "you are from—(mentioning the State). I remember reading of your election in a newspaper one morning on a steamboat going down to Mount Vernon." At another time a gentleman addressed him, saying, "I presume, Mr. President, you have forgotten me?" "No," was the prompt reply; "your name is Flood. I saw you last, twelve years ago, at —."[55]

Lincoln was not only a founder, but the builder and organizer of the Illinois Republican Party. He had mastered the major as well as the minor skills of an entrepreneurial American politician: concentrate, never forget a name. He had also learned the political importance of wise patronage in 1849, when the Whig administration of President Zachary Taylor denied Lincoln—a loyal, hardworking Whig—a post he had earned and sought, giving it instead to a political adversary of President Taylor. The well-considered exchange of patronage was important in nineteenth-century politics. Lincoln was building a new party. A dutiful leader must reward faithful workers. As party leader, President Lincoln proved much superior to Churchill, not least because by nature he was less self-centered, thus enabling him to divine and satisfy the needs of minor loyalists who sustained his party and his armies in the field.

The president and the prime minister would embrace their duty to educate, to persuade, to rally the public, by demonstrating steadfastness in crisis.[56] President Lincoln concluded his special address to Congress of July 4, 1861: "And having thus chosen our course, without guile, and with pure purpose, let us renew our trust in God, and go forward without fear, and with manly hearts."[57] Lincoln's answers to questions were often simple and unselfconscious. A Union army officer reported the story of a "gentleman [who] was conversing with the President at a time during the war when things looked very dark. On taking leave, he asked the President what he should say to their friends in [slaveholding] Kentucky." The officer recalled: "'Tell my friends,' said Mr. Lincoln, drawing himself up to his full height, 'there is a man in here!'"[58]

In World War II, there lived a man without fear at 10 Downing Street. "No doubt at the beginning we shall have to suffer," Churchill argued, "because of having too long wished to lead a peaceful life. Our reluctance to fight was mocked as cowardice. Our desire to see an unarmed world was proclaimed [by the enemy] as the proof of our decay. Now we have begun. Now we are going on. Now, with the help of God, and with the conviction that we are the defenders of civilization and freedom, we are going to persevere to the end."[59] The prime minister's courage—proven as a young cavalry subaltern in three imperial battles of the late 1890s—intensified as crises threatened. "Danger, the evocation of battle, invariably acted as a tonic and a stimulant to Winston Churchill," noted Major-General Edward Spears, who served as the prime minister's personal representative in France as that nation collapsed before the German invasion.[60] Of Prime Minister Churchill, Joseph Stalin said it best at the Yalta Conference: "There have been few cases in history where the courage of one man has been so important to the future of the world."[61]

*Circumstances, to some of which you kindly allude,
induced me especially to expect that if justice and good
faith should be practiced by the United States, they would
encounter no hostile influence on the part of Great Britain. It is now a pleasant duty to acknowledge the demon-
stration you have given of your desire that a spirit of peace
and amity towards this country may prevail in the councils of your Queen, who is respected and esteemed in your
own country only more than she is by the kindred nation
which has its home on this side of the Atlantic.*[1]

ABRAHAM LINCOLN
Letter to Workingmen of Manchester
January 19, 1863

*It is not given to us to peer into the mysteries of the future.
Still, I avow my hope and faith, sure and inviolate, that
in the days to come the British and American peoples will
for their own safety and for the good of all walk together
side by side in majesty, in justice, and in peace.*[2]

WINSTON S. CHURCHILL
Speech to Congress
December 26, 1941

IV.

Anglo-American Relations

President-elect Abraham Lincoln arrived by train at Washington in February 1861, having begun his journey in frontier Illinois. There, he had been an accomplished Springfield lawyer, a four-term state legislator, a one-term U.S. congressman—modest experience for a president facing the most profound national crisis since the Revolutionary War. Twelve years had gone by since he last held public office. By every standard, the 52-year-old President Lincoln would find the Union government more unprepared for war than the First Lord of the Admiralty, Winston Churchill, found Britain in 1939.

In early 1941, the prime minister, then 66, knew that Hitler had abandoned any intention to invade England. Britain had no strong allies remaining. Bolshevik Russia—impoverished by civil war, vast purges, show trials, and famine in the Ukraine—had been eliminated as a possible co-belligerent by the Nazi-Soviet pact of 1939. Hitler would abide by this cynical pact until June 1941, when 150 German divisions and at least three million soldiers would storm into Russia. Although England was very much alone in early 1941, it was free of the Nazi invasion threat, which on June 22 would turn eastward into the Soviet Union.

It was in the fall of 1861 that Lincoln would send abroad prominent emissaries—including the Catholic archbishop of New York and the former Union general-in-chief—to keep Europe out of the American Civil War. European recognition of the rebel Confederate government would have been a crucial setback in the first year of the Civil War. Under different circumstances in January 1941, Churchill would welcome FDR-confidant Harry Hopkins to London, desperate as the prime minister was for American intervention into World War II. Hopkins would report back to Roosevelt: "Your 'former Naval person' is not only the

Prime Minister, he is the directing force behind the strategy and the conduct of the war in all its essentials. He has an amazing hold on the British people of all classes and groups."[3] This was exactly what Churchill wanted Roosevelt to know—that the prime minister and the British people would hold out.

During 1940 and 1941, after British victory in the air battle over England, Churchill would continue to foster belief in the potential Nazi invasion. Meanwhile, Churchill moved key military resources to the Middle East, to combat Italy and Germany in the eastern Mediterranean. He emphasized the invasion threat and demonstrated Britain's determination to persist and prevail against Hitler. In a memo to top military aides, Churchill wrote that "a note of invasion alarm should be struck, and everybody set to work with redoubled energy."[4] The prime minister's sense of urgency permeated his entire body politic. He did not disguise his hope that Germany would provoke the United States into war through some incident on the high seas, not unlike World War I. By the time FDR-envoy Hopkins departed England for the United States in February 1941, he was convinced "that most of the cabinet and all of the military leaders here believe that invasion is imminent. They believe it may come at any moment, but not later than May 1."[5] The prime minister had attained two objectives with Hopkins: convincing FDR's emissary that Britain could hold out; and convincing him that an unlikely Nazi invasion imperiled British survival without U.S. help. Thus would the Lend-Lease program be born—in order to provide needed supplies to Britain. Many isolationist obstacles in Congress had to be overcome so that Lend-Lease legislation would become law in March 1941.

The Japanese attack on Pearl Harbor of December 7, 1941, would echo the rebel attack on Fort Sumter in April 1861. The Confederate artillery bombardment and the Union surrender of Fort Sumter had mobilized reluctant free-state opinion—including that of loyal Northern Democrats—behind President Lincoln and a patriotic war of reunion. The president's determination to preserve the Union inspired the Northern war cry. Churchill in late 1941 was preoccupied with his Anglo-American diplomacy—convinced as he was that only American entry into the conflict could turn the tide against Hitler. "I don't know what will happen if England is fighting alone when 1942 comes," he told Hopkins in August 1941.[6] At that time Nazi Germany had betrayed and invaded Russia in June of 1941. The prime minister and many Americans expected a Russian collapse. Then, five months hence, on December 7, 1941, after dinner at Chequers with American Ambassador John G. Winant and Lend-Lease supervisor Averell Harriman, Churchill would hear the news on his portable radio of Japan's attack on Pearl Harbor. Churchill's valet, Frank Sawyers, confirmed the news: "The Japanese have attacked the Americans."[7]

Ambassador Winant promptly called FDR, putting the prime minister on the phone. "We are all in the same boat now," Roosevelt told Churchill.[8] The prime minister thought privately that Britain has "won after all!" Churchill, knowing that FDR seemed to require unequivocal *casus belli* to enter the war, believed Pearl Harbor "a blessing" for the United Kingdom. "Greater good fortune had never happened to the British Empire," wrote Churchill.[9] Indeed, on December 11, Hitler declared war on America, though no treaty obliged him to do so. America was now Great Britain's ally in war against both Nazi Germany and imperial Japan.

As early as 1939, First Lord of the Admiralty Churchill had begun cultivating President Roosevelt, after FDR had shrewdly reached out to him by letter to open a channel of communication. The president had confided to Churchill: "It is because you and I occupied similar positions in the World War that I want you to know how glad I am that you are back again in the Admiralty. Your problems are, I realize, complicated by new factors, but the essential is not very different. What I want you and the Prime Minister to know is that I shall at all times welcome it if you will keep me in touch personally with anything you want me to know about."[10] To gain Roosevelt's trust, Churchill would supply confidential information to FDR.

After Pearl Harbor, the prime minister insisted that he should go to Washington to plot strategy. Roosevelt resisted; Churchill prevailed. On December 13, 1941, he sailed into dangerous waters, patrolled by German submarines—arriving at Hampton Roads, Virginia, nine days later. Of the prime minister's mission to Washington, Dr. Wilson wrote: "The P.M. knows, of course, that there will be stupid people who will say that he ought to stay in London at the centre of things, but he scarcely gives them a thought. His plan is simple. First, he decides what he would like to do, and then he experiences no difficulty in finding good reasons for doing it."[11] Of the stormy Atlantic voyage aboard the battleship *Duke of York*, Commander "Tommy" Thompson observed: "Of all the journeys which the Prime Minister was destined to make during the war few rivalled this first voyage to America for sheer discomfort."[12] Going directly to the White House after disembarking at Hampton Roads, Churchill declined Roosevelt's invitation to stay in the Lincoln Bedroom (Lincoln's office during his presidency). The prime minister did not like the bed.[13] He quickly became the diplomatic master of political Washington. Asked at a press conference if British-held Singapore was not "the key to the whole situation out there" in the Pacific, Churchill replied: "The key to the whole situation is the resolute manner in which the British and American Democracies are going to throw themselves into the conflict."[14]

The Anglo-American relationship—both before and after the Japanese attack on Pearl Harbor—was not without great strain. American leaders had serious doubts about the ability of cash-strapped Britain to finance its defense against the Nazi onslaught. Britain had almost exhausted its financial reserves by early 1941. Indeed, Britain had never regained full economic strength after World War I. By customary standards, Britain was insolvent—a de facto bankruptcy in 1941. The financial issue between the Allies was only one major problem. There were considerable differences on economic and military issues at all levels of the Anglo-American relationship. But the prime minister would flatter and persuade FDR in order to win the president to his purpose. During the next four years, Churchill would make the alliance with Roosevelt his personal project.

The prime minister would combine pleas and praise in a stream of communications with his fellow "Former Naval Person"—in all, over two thousand communications between the president and the prime minister. Churchill's strategy was relentlessly pursued because he knew: 1) Britain could neither fight nor survive without American aid; 2) Britain could not win unless America entered the war; 3) FDR must be convinced to prosecute the war in Europe ahead of the war against Japan. "I shall drag the United States in," Churchill said to his son shortly after he became prime minister.[15] On June 14, 1940, he wrote Roosevelt: "If we go down, you may have a United States of Europe under the Nazi command, far more numerous, far stronger, far better armed than the new [world]."[16] Eleven months later, in May 1941, he warned America: "I have never said that the British Empire cannot make its way out of this war without American belligerence, but no peace that is any use to you or which will liberate Europe can be obtained without American belligerence."[17]

The prime minister not only courted Roosevelt; he would captivate Ambassador Winant and FDR's special envoys, Hopkins and Averell Harriman. They became the British prime minister's willing band of American brothers. Churchill would regularly play cards with Harriman.[18] Hopkins, whose code name was "Sancho Panza" (to Roosevelt's "Don Quixote"), became a key, sympathetic link to FDR. Churchill attended personally to Hopkins when he was in London, and directly by telegraph when Hopkins was elsewhere. The British prime minister pressed unstintingly for whatever assistance he could get from the American president—with modest success, such as Lend-Lease, until the Japanese destroyed much of the U.S. Pacific fleet at Pearl Harbor.[19] Only then would the U.S. production and financial capability be fully mobilized as the "arsenal of democracy," and ultimately as the arsenal of the Anglo-American-Russian war machine.

In 1940, Churchill had suggested to Roosevelt that if Britain was defeated, Germany might gain control of the British navy, using it to threaten the United States. FDR got the point. Churchill and Roosevelt would work together, sometimes circumventing American law, in order to provide food and munitions to Britain. Churchill capitalized on every opportunity to influence Roosevelt—especially when they were alone, away from the restraints of other American officials, whereupon the prime minister's superior knowledge and force of personality could be decisive.[20] Churchill's strategic courtship, enhanced by his respect and affection for Roosevelt, became a key weapon in the prime minister's war policy. "If anything happened to that man, I couldn't stand it," said Churchill in January 1943, after seeing FDR off on his plane from North Africa. "He is the truest friend; he has the farthest vision; he is the greatest man I have ever known."[21] Attitudes would change as FDR would gravitate in late 1943 and thereafter toward Stalin.

In Anglo-American relations, one thorny issue arose over Churchill's official responsibility for the British Empire, compounded by his personal devotion to its history and his belief in its contribution to civilization. Churchill's war aims included "victory at all costs," not only to preserve the United Kingdom, but also to maintain the British Empire and Commonwealth. "Imperial rhetoric came easily to Churchill," noted historian Richard Toye, but such language grated on American ears, including those of FDR. "We should all get on much better if you British would stop talking about the British Empire," an American senator told

Churchill.[22] During World War I and World War II, Britain relied upon its overseas colonies and the Commonwealth countries of Canada, Australia, New Zealand, and South Africa for loyalty, manpower, and war materials. The prime minister made his imperial policy clear in a memo of December 31, 1944: "There must be no question of our being hustled or seduced into declarations affecting British sovereignty in any of the Dominions or Colonies. Pray remember my declaration against liquidating the British Empire."[23] Few of Churchill's colleagues and allies had been born under Queen Victoria; fewer still had served in the cabinet under King Edward before World War I.

Americans—led by President Roosevelt—disdained Churchill's imperialism. It was an historic American attitude, born of the Revolutionary War. "Twisting the lion's tail" had a long history among the American people. The prime minister was infuriated in April 1942 when Roosevelt interfered in British negotiations with Indian nationalists. FDR wrote: "The feeling is almost universally held here that the deadlock has been caused by the unwillingness of the British government to concede to the Indians the right of self-government. . . . I feel I must place this issue before you very frankly and I know you will understand my reasons for doing so."[24] Churchill indulged neither Roosevelt nor the American attitude. On the contrary, "the string of [Churchill's] cuss words [regarding U.S. interference in India] lasted two hours into the night," according to Harry Hopkins.[25] Biographers William Manchester and Paul Reid wrote: "After regaining (some) of his composure, he voiced his long-held belief that any imposition of political will by the Hindus upon one hundred million Indian Muslims would result in a total breakdown of order, and large-scale bloodshed, and this at the very moment the Japanese were waiting in the wings, with Gandhi and his 'Quit India' cohorts ready to accept the enemy peacefully, thereby easing a Japanese passage to the Middle East."[26] When Churchill had received the seals of the prime minister's office from the King, he had also embraced his duty to preside over the Empire.

Churchill remained intransigent on the issue of independence for India. Although he was ever loyal to his allies in war, his first loyalty was to the Crown. His vision of the British Empire, however, clashed with the reality of American dominance of the alliance, especially after 1943. But the prime minister's policy toward India hardened nevertheless. From his cavalry experience when stationed in India, and from his knowledge

William H. Seward, ca. 1861
Gilder Lehrman Collection, GLC05111.02.0094

of the history of Hindu-Muslim relations, Churchill feared that India's Hindus and Muslims would be engulfed in civil war without British governance. Still, British power was transparently on the wane—much to Churchill's chagrin. In November 1943, there were "new feelings of spitefulness which had been apparently building up fast and exceeding ours," wrote General Alan Brooke about some of the allies. The prime minister "hated having to give up the position of the dominant partner which we had held at the start."[27] Churchill's son-in-law, Christopher Soames, later observed: "The winds of change had begun to blow . . . but Churchill had yet to see them."[28] Churchill felt the winds of change, but the prime minister inhaled deeply and stubbornly blew up his own storm of resistance.

Lincoln, too, worked carefully, craftily, patiently on Anglo-American relations during the Civil War. Lincoln's humor was often ironic, a match for Churchill's clever wit. In May 1863, the British Minister in Washington visited Lincoln to announce that the Prince of Wales "is about to contract a matrimonial alliance with her Royal Highness the Princess Alexandra of Denmark." Tongue-in-cheek, the president gave a friendly but direct order to the English bachelor: "Lord Lyons, go thou and do likewise."[29] Churchill wrote of Lincoln's visitors: "Most of them clamoured for quick victory, with no conception of the hazards of war. Many of them cherished their own amateur plans of operation which they confidently urged upon their leader. Many of them too had favourite Generals for whom they canvassed. Lincoln treated all his visitors with patience and firmness. His homely humour stood him in good stead. A sense of irony helped to lighten his burdens."[30]

Aide Edward Duffield Neill commented on the special open-door policy at Lincoln's White House: "President Lincoln's accessibility won the hearts of the people. No one was too poor to be received. When more important business was attended to, on some days, between two and three o'clock in the afternoon, he would have his door thrown open, and all in the hall were allowed to enter and prefer their requests. He playfully called it 'the Beggars' Opera.'"[31] Even those on the streets of Washington knew where to find Lincoln. They poured into the open White House, crowded the second floor, beseeching personal visits— so many that Lincoln had a private passage built so he could reach his office from the family quarters unhindered by supplicants. Such petitions beleaguered the president, who told a man who waylaid him outside the White House that he wasn't going to set up shop on the street.[32]

An immodest Churchill displayed few inhibitions when he appeared half-naked in the presence of generals, ministers, and secretaries. FDR apologized when he surprised the naked prime minister in his White House bedroom, Churchill having just finished his bath. He quickly declared that the prime minister of the British Empire had nothing to hide from the president of the United States.[33] For the president and the prime minister, words were gifts to win hearts and minds, even as they were weapons to win wars. In 1863, President Lincoln wrote to an English girl who said she supported his Civil War leadership: "We have a good deal of salt water between us. When you feel kindly towards us we cannot, unfortunately, be always aware of it. But it cuts both ways. When you, in England, are cross with us, we don't feel it quite so badly."[34]

During the Civil War, Anglo-American relations became tense to the cusp of war. From the outset, there were conflicts of interest between London and Washington—fueled by the dependency of England's dominant textile industry on slave-based Southern cotton.[35] Economic self-interest was compounded by sympathy among much of the British aristocratic elite for the pretentious planter class of Southern slaveholders. Many of the English nobility and mercantile upper class, joined by prominent institutions like the London *Times*, supported the slaveholding "cotton kingdom."[36] It was Lincoln's good fortune to have the competent, if humorless, Charles Francis Adams as his envoy in London.[37] Secretary of State Seward pushed Congressman Adams into the office, once held in the 1780s by his illustrious grandfather John Adams. The envoy, contemptuous of Lincoln's lack of sophistication in foreign affairs, later wrote that the Lincoln administration was virtually without diplomatic experience: "The Republican party had been so generally in opposition that but few of its prominent members had had any advantages or experience in office. And, in the foreign service especially, experience is almost indispensable to usefulness. Mr. Seward himself came into the State Department with no acquaintance with the forms of business other than that obtained incidentally through his service in the Senate. He had not had the benefit of official presence abroad, an advantage by no means trifling in conducting the foreign affairs."[38] Adams was correct on the facts. It is all the more remarkable that diplomatic historians rate the unschooled Lincoln as a master of diplomacy and international relations.[39]

Lord Lyons, the British minister at Washington, was very skeptical of the Lincoln administration. He would encourage grave doubts, held by the London government, about the probability of a Union victory. Lyons wrote home: "Mr. Lincoln has not hitherto given proof of his possessing any natural talents to compensate for his ignorance of everything but Illinois village politics."[40] Much of the Washington establishment held the same view. But the president was not intimidated by the self-appointed elites. Nor did he defer to them. Lincoln and his administration determined at the outset to prevent foreign diplomatic recognition of the Confederate government, a potentially war-losing event. This diplomatic tug-of-war led to bellicose exchanges between the United States and Britain. Historian Gordon H. Warren noted: "Unfortunately for relations between the two countries, Lyons's dispatches produced deep unrest and a sense of impending disaster within the London cabinet, and persuaded high civilian and military officials [especially after the *Trent* Affair] that war with the United States was almost a certainty."[41] War loomed large as the friction of events gave rise to seeming *casus belli* between the Union and its mother country. No one in Washington had forgotten the humiliations of the War of 1812. Nor had London forgotten its outcome.

Lord Lyons's diplomatic posture was, however, understandable. At the outset of the Civil War, Seward took a hard and belligerent attitude toward Britain, which had declared its neutrality on May 13, 1861—a policy that in Seward's view implied recognition of Confederate independence. Seward invited English journalist William Howard Russell to dinner. At that early moment in the Lincoln presidency, the presumptuous secretary of state thought himself Lincoln's prime minister. Seward read Russell a proposed dispatch to the British government. Russell wrote in his diary:

> At all the stronger passages Mr. Seward raised his voice, and made a pause at their conclusion as if to challenge remark or approval. At length I could not help saying, that the dispatch would, no doubt, have an excellent effect when it came to light in congress, and that the Americans would think highly of the writer; but I ventured to express an opinion that it would not be quite so acceptable to the Government and people of Great Britain. This Mr. Seward, as an American statesman, had a right to make but a secondary consideration. By affecting to regard Secession as a mere political heresy which can be easily

confuted, and by forbidding foreign countries alluding to it, Mr. Seward thinks he can establish the supremacy of his own Government, and at the same time gratify the vanity of the people. Even war with us may not be out of the list of those means which would be available for re-fusing the broken Union into a mass once more. However, the Secretary is quite confident in what he calls "re-action." "When the Southern States," he [Seward] says, "see that we mean them no wrong—that we intend no violence to persons, rights, or things—that the Federal Government seeks only to fulfill obligations imposed on it in respect to the national property, they will see their mistake, and one after another they will come back into the Union." Mr. Seward anticipates this process will at once begin, and that Secession will all be done and over in three months—at least, so he says. It was after midnight ere our conversation was over.[42]

The more belligerent passages in Seward's dispatches to Adams in London were tempered by the prudent edit of President Lincoln. Lincoln's diplomacy was crucial in the spring of 1861, when the impulsive, indeed irresponsible, Seward thought a conflict with Europe would be a useful diversion from domestic insurrection. Seward thereafter usually read his dispatches to Lincoln before sending them abroad. The patient Lincoln edited and mellowed Seward's hostile drafts. Seward would learn that Lincoln had a more discriminating judgment of not only the language of diplomacy, but also Union war strategy. The president did have a back channel into British politics through the ongoing correspondence between Massachusetts Senator Charles Sumner and prominent English liberals such as Richard Cobden and John Bright, admirers of Lincoln. The English middle class, influenced by men like Cobden and Bright, served as a checkmate to the Southern sympathies of British aristocrats and bankers.

In the final weeks of 1861, Lincoln became distracted by Anglo-American relations. In early November, an aggressive U.S. naval captain acted without authorization to intercept the RMS *Trent*, a British mail packet. In violation of maritime law and neutrality—often an occasion for war—the American officer removed and detained two Confederate diplomats, James Mason and John Slidell, appointed to head up Confederate missions to England and France. As a result, America and England careened toward hostilities. Cooler heads prevailed. One belonged to John Bright. Another was Queen Victoria's husband, the mortally ill Prince Albert, who wisely refined a British government dispatch to the American government charging—correctly—that the seizure of the *Trent* had been a violation of international law. Secretary of State Seward now became the diplomat, urging permission for the two Confederates to go to Europe as planned. In his response, he suggested that Britain had thereby acknowledged long-held American doctrines regarding freedom of the seas, and praised Britain for embracing U.S. policy. It worked—a potential third British-American war was averted. Seward's son later commented: "Presidents and kings are not apt to see flaws in their own arguments. But fortunately for the Union, it had a President at this time who combined a logical intellect with an unselfish heart."[43]

As the Civil War wore on, three major factors complicated Lincoln administration relations with London. First was the Union blockade of Southern cotton exports to British factories, weakening the rebels, but causing unemployment and shuttered factories in England. Second, Lincoln rhetorically mobilized British and foreign support of emancipation to block Britain and other European countries from intervening in the conflict. Lincoln made it clear there would be no European mediation on the issue of reunion. The Union and its president would resolve the issue of war and reunion without intervention from abroad. Third, Lincoln's diplomacy aimed to stop British construction of Confederate privateers, such as the commerce raider *Alabama*. On this issue, Seward and Adams cajoled, even threatened, England during this period.[44] Historian Burton J. Hendrick wrote that Seward had matured into a useful diplomat: "In addition to knowing when to threaten, when to bluster, when to prod, to hint, to instill suspicions and fears, Seward had another gift equally serviceable in diplomacy. He knew when to conciliate and when, without any loss in dignity, to yield."[45] Given Seward's inexperience and his early impetuosity, it is fair to say that the secretary of state had been instructed by the remarkable patience, tact and the firm, inner-directed character of the president, whose judgment compensated for his inexperience.

Seward, a former senator and governor, could also be innovative. In the fall of 1863, he took Washington diplomats, including the British ambassador, on a tour of upstate New York, to show the immense economic vitality of the country despite the ongoing Civil War. Seward's son recalled that during the tour, "every day's ride was a volume of

Anthony Eden, ca. 1941

Glasshouse Images / Alamy Stock Photo

instruction. Hundreds of factories with whirring wheels, thousands of acres of golden harvest fields, miles of railway trains laden with freight, busy fleets on rivers, lakes, and canals, all showed a period of unexampled commercial activity and prosperity."[46] The robust Union war economy, unconstrained by price controls and rationing, was operating at full capacity. The diplomats were impressed. Ultimately, Seward and Lincoln did find common cause with much of English opinion on the issue of slavery. Lincoln had long been an admirer of the heroic agitation by William Wilberforce and his parliamentary allies to abolish the international slave trade in 1808, by an act of Parliament. In 1808, the very first year permitted by the Constitution, the American Congress also abolished the international slave trade. Cooperation of the British and American navies to enforce this prohibition on the high seas, by penalty of death, was one of the many steps leading away from the historic British-American hostility that originated in the Revolution, compounded by the War of 1812. The "special" British-American relationship would await the twentieth century and its most unstinting advocate, Winston Churchill.

Before the Civil War and World War II, Lincoln and Churchill labored to raise their countrymen's consciousness of mortal threats by defining the vital issues and principles at stake. Preceding war, they had been effective debaters, even agitators. Once in office and at war, they inspired their citizens to believe the war could be won. On June 16, 1941, Churchill broadcast his speech upon accepting an honorary degree at the University of Rochester in New York: "For more than a year we British have stood alone, uplifted by your sympathy and respect and sustained by our own unconquerable will power, and by the increasing growth and hopes of your massive aid. In these British Islands that look so small upon the map we stand, the faithful guardians of the rights and dearest hopes of a dozen States and nations now gripped and tormented in a base and crude servitude."[47] Britain did face Nazi Germany alone, but FDR would not yet provide "massive aid." At that moment, the Germans had not yet invaded Russia. FDR would not go to war until after the Japanese bombed the fleet at Pearl Harbor on December 7, 1941. In private, Churchill's confidence could slip. Despairing again of getting President Roosevelt to see his way in 1943, a frustrated Churchill told a secretary: "The difficulty is not in winning the war; it is in persuading people to let you win it—persuading fools."[48] Despite doubts of the American and British general staffs, the prime minister rarely lost confidence in his own war strategy.

Lincoln and Churchill believed public sentiment in a democracy to be essential to victory. They would by word and action mobilize the people and resources of their countries to fight a relentless struggle for unconditional surrender of the enemy. Defeat was unthinkable. "You ask, what is our aim?" Churchill said on May 13, 1940, shortly after he took office. "I can answer in one word: it is victory, victory at all costs, victory in spite of all terror, victory, however long and hard the road may be; for without victory, there is no survival. Let that be realized; no survival for the British Empire, no survival for all that the British Empire has stood for, no survival for the urge and impulse of the ages, that mankind will move forward towards its goal."[49] At Harvard on September 6, 1943, Churchill preached perseverance: "[T]o the youth of America, as to the youth of Britain, I say, 'You cannot stop.' There is no halting-place at this point. We have now reached a stage in the journey where there can be no pause. We must go on. It must be world anarchy or world order."[50] To that end, Lincoln and Churchill (and Roosevelt) would settle for nothing less than unconditional surrender.

Roosevelt and Churchill had met briefly at the end of World War I —a lamentable introduction since the future president thought the future prime minister to be rude.[51] Churchill had forgotten his encounter with FDR. Their first substantive meeting during World War II came before Pearl Harbor, during the secret rendezvous at Placentia Bay, Newfoundland, in August of 1941. The prime minister worked hard to develop a personal relationship with Roosevelt. In Churchill's imagination, friendship would contribute to a speedy American entry into the war. Meeting aboard warships at Placentia Bay, the leaders quickly developed personal chemistry. It was more than a year after the collapse of France, but American entry into the war remained elusive. The prime minister never stopped nurturing his growing friendship with FDR, which was finally consummated with military alliance after the Japanese attack at Pearl Harbor. Churchill wrote in his memoirs of his reaction to the news of Pearl Harbor, "I had studied the American Civil War, fought out to the last desperate inch. American blood flowed in my veins. I thought of a remark which Edward Grey had made to me more than thirty years before—that the United States is like 'a gigantic boiler. Once the fire is lighted under it there is no limit to the power it can generate.' Being saturated and satiated with emotion and sensation, I went to bed and slept the sleep of the saved and thankful."[52] Churchill recalled:

"My relations with the President gradually became so close that the chief business between our two countries was virtually conducted by these personal interchanges between him and me."[53]

Before Pearl Harbor, Churchill persisted in his American alliance strategy despite British resentment of American isolationism and some American indifference to the fascist threat.[54] British General Hastings Ismay wrote: "Churchill, least patient of men, displayed almost unfailing public forbearance toward the United States, flattering its president and people, addressing with supreme skill both American principles and self-interest."[55] Churchill successfully wooed FDR's trusted lieutenants, Averell Harriman, Harry Hopkins, and Dwight Eisenhower—channels of American decision and command. He entertained and flattered them at 10 Downing Street and during weekend visits to Chequers. As always, he brought his mastery of the English language to bear for the purpose of uniting the two countries. On December 26, 1941, less than three weeks after Pearl Harbor, Churchill exhorted the American Congress:

> Prodigious hammer-strokes have been needed to bring us together again, or if you will allow me to use other language, I will say that he must indeed have a blind soul who cannot see that some great purpose and design is being worked out here below, of which we have the honor to be the faithful servants. It is not given to us to peer into the mysteries of the future. Still, I avow my hope and faith, sure and inviolate, that in the days to come the British and American peoples will for their own safety and for the good of all walk together side by side in majesty, in justice, and in peace.[56]

The special relationship, now an alliance, had quickened the prime minister's spirit and his strategy. It emboldened his language. In 1940, CBS broadcaster Edwin R. Murrow, stationed in London, had remarked that Churchill had "mobilized the English language, and sent it into battle."[57]

The prime minister and the president grew ever closer after Pearl Harbor.[58] "Their companionship grew, I think, with their respect for each other's ability," wrote Eleanor Roosevelt. "They did not agree on all things; I heard my husband make remarks which were sometimes inspired by annoyance and occasionally by a realistic facing of facts."

Increasingly from 1943 onward, the Americans would find Churchill difficult and British arms less important. After the U.S.-led invasion of North Africa in November 1942, and after Russia had decisively turned back the German eastern front in 1943, American military confidence and mobilization began to overshadow Britain's military preeminence. One source of continuing friction continued because of Churchill's insistence on the integrity of the British Empire. Mrs. Roosevelt recalled that the prime minister "acknowledged to me in casual conversation that he knew the world could never be the same. He once even said that all he wanted to do was to stay in office until he had seen the men come home from the war and until they had places in which to live." Roosevelt, an anti-imperial scold, thought Churchill had hardened his mind to obvious changes in the world. FDR vainly told his wife: "I am sure that in some ways it will be easier to make Mr. Stalin understand certain things after the war is over."[59] At Yalta in February 1945, FDR's presumption would not alter Stalin's cynical Imperial strategy.

Both the American president and the British prime minister overestimated their abilities to manipulate or to charm the taciturn, better-informed Soviet dictator, who cleverly alternated between amiability and hostility. Stalin shrewdly pitted the interests of the United States against those of the United Kingdom. The impressionable Harry Hopkins, miscalculating future events, declared at the end of the Teheran conference in November 1943: "The President knows now that Stalin is 'get-atable' and that we are going to get along fine in the future."[60] At this Teheran conference, FDR had put Churchill aside, trusting in his charm to corral Stalin—to little effect. Toward the end of the war, the Americans—including President Roosevelt—tended to ignore the warning counsel of the prime minister as his doubts about Stalin increased. However, Churchill himself could still be deceived by Stalin, even after Yalta.

Among FDR's pet peeves was the vanity of France's imperious Charles de Gaulle, far less likable than the stubborn but charming Churchill.[61] De Gaulle was disagreeable; Churchill would respond in kind. As the French resistance to the Nazis collapsed in June 1940, de Gaulle had pretended to see off, from the French airport, the departing British representative, General Edward Spears. Instead, de Gaulle climbed aboard the plane and took off before allies of Marshal Henri-Philippe Pétain could arrest him for treason. Churchill observed that de Gaulle had "carried with him, in this small aeroplane, the honor of France."[62] Churchill would write in his memoirs: "I preserved the impression, in contact with this very tall, phlegmatic man: 'Here is the Constable of France.'"[63]

As self-proclaimed leader of the Free French, de Gaulle managed to annoy his Anglo-American allies.[64] At Casablanca in January 1943, after finally meeting the imperious General Henri Giraud and Free-French leader Charles de Gaulle, FDR told his wife: "General Giraud is the type of French military man who loves his country and is not in any way a politician, but a good soldier. General de Gaulle is a soldier, patriotic, yes, devoted to his country; but on the other hand, he is a politician and a fanatic and there are, I think, in him almost the makings of a dictator." Eleanor Roosevelt later emphasized the obvious: "I do not think that between them [FDR and de Gaulle] there was any real understanding."[65] At one point in January 1944, Churchill became frustrated with de Gaulle and said: "Look here! I am the leader of a strong, unbeaten nation. Yet every morning when I wake my first thought is how can I please President Roosevelt, and my second is how can I conciliate Marshal Stalin. Your situation is very different. Why then should your first waking thought be how you can snap your fingers at the British and Americans?"[66] On one occasion, de Gaulle had been so rude to Churchill that the prime minister declared: "I won't see that chap again." The general recognized his mistake and asked to come to Chequers to apologize. "Mr. Churchill, who was wearing his siren suit and well-known dragon dressing-gown, walked into the office," recalled secretary Elizabeth Layton Nel, "and said, 'All right, all right, I'll be good. I'll be sweet. I'll kiss him on both cheeks—all four if you'd prefer it.'"[67] The prime minister "had to put up with a lot from [de Gaulle's] tantrums, but treated him like a boy who has had an unfortunate background and needed both encouragement and the occasional stick," recalled Leslie Hollis.[68]

FDR's contempt for the stiff-necked French leader expressed itself in an April 1943 note to Churchill: "I do not have any information which leads me to believe that de Gaulle and his Committee of National Liberation have as yet given any helpful assistance to our allied war effort."[69] The prime minister tried to keep de Gaulle on a tight leash. Foreign Secretary Anthony Eden thought de Gaulle would be more manageable under looser restraints. In the late summer of 1942, Eden went to see the general: "I have been charged by the War Cabinet to give you this message: 'We have ten times more trouble with the Committee of the

Free French than with all the allies put together." With a straight face, de Gaulle responded: "I have always maintained that France was a very great country."[70]

Thus could de Gaulle be maddening.[71] Francophile Churchill had a shrewd eye for de Gaulle's utility and heroism. In early 1943, Churchill said: "England's grievous offense in de Gaulle's eyes is that she has helped France. He cannot bear to think that she needed help. He will not relax his vigilance in guarding her honor for a single instant."[72] Despite his annoyance with de Gaulle, Churchill pressed the United States to accept reality and to treat him as the de facto leader of France. Roosevelt and American leaders awaited the emergence of someone more tractable and popular. The British were more realistic. With the help of General Dwight Eisenhower, recognition of de Gaulle's role in French civil administration was grudgingly granted in mid-1944.[73]

The dogmas of the quiet past are inadequate to the stormy present. The occasion is piled high with difficulty, and we must rise with the occasion. As our case is new, so we must think anew, and act anew. We must disenthrall ourselves, and then we shall save our country.[1]

ABRAHAM LINCOLN
Second Annual Message to Congress
December 1, 1862

Let us then address ourselves to our task, not in any way underrating its tremendous difficulties and perils, but in good heart and sober confidence, resolved that, whatever the cost, whatever the suffering, we shall stand by one another, true and faithful comrades, and do our duty, God helping us, to the end.[2]

WINSTON S. CHURCHILL
Canadian Parliament
December 30, 1941

V.

Virtues of Great War Leaders

Pesident Lincoln could only influence the American people at large by the written and spoken word—primarily through the press. Prime Minister Churchill commandeered the radio, the cinema news programs, the world press, and his dinner guests. For Lincoln, the written word became a weapon of persuasion. His use of stories or parables forced his listeners to think about the meaning of his arguments.[3] He mastered during the 1850s the subtle relationship between speaker and audience. Lincoln's exquisitely crafted annual messages to Congress were by tradition written, not oral. Occasionally, he would address the American people in the form of public letters—masterful briefs of persuasion. Brilliantly argued in his classic, simple prose, they were always carefully edited by him, intended to persuade a national readership.

During the Civil War, there were no grand occasions for Lincoln to deliver the unsurpassed one-hour and three-hour speeches for which he was famous prior to his election—such as the Peoria speech of 1854, the House Divided speech of 1858, and the Cooper Union speech of 1860. The president occasionally made brief comments to serenades by well-wishers outside the White House. He sometimes made short speeches to military regiments passing through Washington. On very rare occasions—Gettysburg (November 1863), Baltimore (May 1864), Philadelphia (June 1864)—Lincoln left the capital to make a speech. When he did so, he generally used a prepared text so that he might be quoted exactly. He would not be misunderstood by giving extemporaneous comments that might be misquoted. So, too, with his first and second inaugurals. Lincoln's mental self-discipline regulated his magnificent command of the English language. Churchill had less self-discipline in conversation—dominating almost every group, almost every cabinet meeting, most parliamentary sessions he attended as prime minister, taking every opportunity to speak publicly and at summit meetings. The prime minister, too, was a master of the English language. He had spent a lifetime in love with his native tongue. But Churchill's prose style could be noticeably different from the president's—more adjectives and adverbs, more subordinate clauses.

In the decade before he became president, Lincoln went to great efforts to edit his major antislavery speeches for printing, publication, and wide distribution. On the night he delivered the Cooper Union address in February 1860, he even went to the offices of the *New-York Tribune* to read galleys of the newspaper text. Lincoln believed the speech could influence the presidential nominating convention at Chicago in May, and he was right. As a dark horse candidate, he would be nominated on the third ballot. In the summer of 1863, he became annoyed when the text of the "Conkling Letter"—a public paper that he had carefully prepared for a rally in Springfield, Illinois—was prematurely and inaccurately published. Ohio Senator John Sherman, often a Lincoln critic, wrote that the president "possessed all the qualities required to inspire confidence and to unite all the loyal elements of our much-divided people in the great conflict of our civil war, when the possibility of Republican institutions, in a wide extended country, was on trial. At first I thought him slow, but he was fast enough to be abreast with the body of his countrymen, and his heart beat steadily and hopefully with them."[4] Indeed, Lincoln's self-confidence caused him to avoid unseemly self-promotion and the appearance of hurry—so typical of most politicians.

Lincoln, like Churchill, would persuade public opinion successfully. He not only learned to read the law; early on he learned to read personalities. As a young man, he understood that to coexist with the Clary Grove Boys, the neighborhood bullies at frontier New Salem, he would have to wrestle their leader for mastery. From these confrontations, Lincoln's goodwill would gain allies and supporters, not enemies. He "had an abiding faith in the good sense and intuitions of the people," recalled his best friend, Joshua F. Speed.[5] "Lincoln never attempted to propose what was more than one step ahead of the great body of political public opinion. But he always led the way," according to Lincoln scholar Harry V. Jaffa.[6] "Lincoln was serious about his bully pulpit," noted historian Phillip S. Paludan. "He was the nation's propagandist (persuader)-in-chief. He molded public opinion and provided the guidance that people needed."[7] His habits of attending to detail, his sensitivity to public sentiment, had been developed in his early mature years, first as a surveyor, then as a very successful trial lawyer, often arguing before the Illinois Supreme Court.[8] As Lincoln himself emphasized: "[p]ublic sentiment is everything. With public sentiment, nothing can fail; without it nothing can succeed."[9]

At war, Churchill and Lincoln publicly rejected the very notion of defeat—no matter their inner doubts. In the underground cabinet war rooms in London, a card in front of Churchill's seat quoted Queen Victoria: "Please understand that there is no depression in this House and we are not interested in the possibilities of defeat. They do not exist."[10] Historian Carlo D'Este wrote: "Whatever Churchill thought privately, not for an instant did he exhibit the slightest sign that Britain would ever give in to Hitler."[11] In order to keep faith with their countrymen, the prime minister and the president were keenly aware of the necessity to prepare public opinion for the worst. Both statesmen publicly displayed optimism—even while experiencing moments of personal despair.[12] Churchill "hated looking on the worst side of things; he felt that even to speak of failure was half-way to bringing it about," wrote a key British general.[13] "While Winston might at times express his doubts in the close confines of an intimate meeting," observed General Eisenhower, "he would never show pessimism or hesitancy in public." Eisenhower wrote of the D-Day preparations: "Among ourselves, the Prime Minister would add, following his expression of doubt, 'We are committed to this operation of war. And we must all, as loyal Allies, do our very best to make it a success.'"[14]

Before November 1942, despair hovered about the Allied war efforts, as defeats in Europe, the Middle East, and Asia came in rapid succession. In a brilliant campaign, the Japanese would capture Singapore, the British garrison surrendering without a fight on February 15, 1942. The capture of Singapore pained Churchill and General Alan Brooke because the British defenders outnumbered the Japanese attackers. Similarly, when the fortress of Tobruk surrendered in June 1942, the 33,000 British defenders outnumbered the Germans who surrounded the British stronghold in Libya.[15] General Alan Brooke confided to his diary: "Burma news now bad. Cannot work out why troops are not fighting better. If the army cannot fight better than it is doing at present we shall deserve to lose our Empire!"[16] After the fall of Singapore, bodyguard Walter Thompson noted that Churchill "was downcast. He was overtired, exhausted and sleeping little. He was more worried [than] I have ever known him. Realising that rest was essential if the Prime Minister was to avoid a complete breakdown, strict instructions were given that the house was to be kept completely quiet while he tried to rest." When an errant telephone interrupted his sleep, he said: "Sleep for me is finished. I shall do some work."[17]

Living with so many defeats early in their great wars of national survival, Lincoln and Churchill could not help but worry, mostly in silence, about the effectiveness of their soldiers. "There remained one great unmentionable, even in those newspapers most critical of Britain's military performance: the notion that man for man, the British soldier might be a less determined fighter than his German adversary," wrote Max Hastings. "The 'tommy' was perceived—sometimes rightly—as the victim of his superior's incompetence, rather than as the bearer of any personal responsibility for failures of British arms."[18] Officers in command bore much of the blame. Serious and ongoing questions arose about whether the armies of Lincoln and Churchill could measure up to their opponents in battle. The fall of strategic Singapore in February 1942 occasioned in England the same hand-wringing as the repeated loss of strategic Harpers Ferry on the Potomac River brought about in the Union. Both Harpers Ferry and Singapore were critical transportation junctures, vital threats in enemy hands. Churchill tried to find light in desperately dark circumstances, declaring in a speech to the British people: "We are in the midst of a great company. Three-quarters of the human race are now moving with us. The whole future of mankind may depend upon our action and upon our conduct. So far we have not failed. We shall not fail now. Let us move forward steadfastly together into the storm and through the storm."[19] Publicly, Churchill would suppress any loss of nerve or fear of defeat.

Although Lincoln and Churchill would buoy up the confidence of their supporters, they remained circumspect. They wanted realistic citizens to maintain vigilance. Fighting alone in February 1941, the prime minister told a BBC audience:

> I must drop one word of caution; for next to cowardice and treachery, over-confidence, leading to neglect or slothfulness, is the worst of martial crimes. Therefore, I drop one word of caution. A Nazi invasion of Great Britain last autumn would have been a more or less improvised affair. Hitler took it for granted that when France gave in we should give in; but we did not give in. And he had to think again. An invasion now will be

supported by a much more carefully prepared tackle and equipment of landing craft and other apparatus, all of which will have been planned and manufactured in the winter months. We must all be prepared to meet gas attacks, parachute attacks, and glider attacks, with constancy, forethought and practised skill.[20]

The prime minister would prepare his countrymen for the worst even if, at that moment, he doubted the likelihood of a Nazi invasion.

Many images of Lincoln suggest his serious demeanor, although he clearly smiled often when not (as the existing technology required) freezing his face for the camera. But his friends told intimate stories of his melancholy moments—stories to match Churchill's self-described "black dog."[21] Dr. Charles Wilson, never far from the prime minister on his travels during the war, asserted in 1943: "Winston has never been at all like other people. . . . Five out of the last seven Dukes of Marlborough suffered from melancholia."[22] Neither Churchill's "black dog" nor Lincoln's melancholy should be exaggerated. Leaders fighting wars of national survival, given the consequences of defeat, must suffer profound disappointments.

Churchill and Lincoln did enjoy merry moments of joy. Children in particular delighted Lincoln. So could a helpless kitten. His laughter resounded when he and friends were exchanging stories—frequently off-color. Churchill had a childlike, even childish, quality. Paul Johnson wrote: "His face could light up in the most extraordinarily attractive way as it became suffused with pleasure at an unexpected and welcome event. . . . He liked to share his joy, and give joy."[23] Clement Attlee once said of his wartime colleague and predecessor as prime minister: "We who worked with him know how quickly he could change from the great man to the naughty child."[24] Churchill's spontaneous language could be childlike too. Trying vainly to confuse the spies and to disguise his method of train travel in early 1942, Churchill told FDR by phone: "I can't tell you how we are coming, but we are coming by puff-puff, got it? *Puff-puff.*"[25] Churchill's tales were different from Lincoln's. "His stories are borrowed from the smoke-room, and are richly flavoured," wrote Churchill's physician. "Nevertheless, it is not, I think, unfair to Winston to say that he has more wit than humour. . . . Nor, when things go wrong, does he find relief in that particular brand of self-mockery to which the English soldier turns in adversity. Humour has never protected him from the bruises of political life."[26] But tears could. Churchill could cry, even in public places.

The wit of both war leaders could be sharp and devastating. Churchill would say of Prime Minister Stanley Baldwin: "Occasionally he stumbled over the truth, but hastily picked himself up and hurried on as if nothing had happened."[27] The president and the prime minister were accomplished storytellers. Lincoln's stories were frequently short parables to illustrate an argument. As a young man, he had mastered the stories of the Bible and Aesop's fables.[28] He did not claim to originate his tales, but some certainly came from his personal experience. Churchill preferred to reminisce. He "made no attempt at small talk." His "conversation often tended to monologue," wrote John Martin.[29] As Jock Colville described the prime minister's conversation after dinner, he dominated, but

> welcomed interruptions, however contradictory or irreverent, provided they were short, witty and did not stem the flow or divert the theme. . . . I remember on one occasion he saw us yawn, and he looked benignly at Commander Thompson, the "Flag Commander," saying: "You must admit, Tommy, that at least I do not repeat my stories as frequently as our dear friend, the President of the United States."[30]

Still, Martin noted, "At table the outpouring from a rich and fertile mind often dazzled and overwhelmed his audience."[31] Lincoln was more taciturn, but when moved by ideas, events, or the works of Shakespeare, he could become reflective and talkative, especially with his aides and longtime friends.

Whatever his private anguish and torment, Churchill exhibited a grim confidence in public, using his cigar as an exclamation point. "Everything felt the touch of his art," observed American diplomat Dean Acheson, "his appearance and gestures, the siren suit, the indomitable V sign for victory, the cigar for imperturbability. He used all the artifices to get his way, from wooing and cajolery through powerful advocacy to bluff bullying."[32] As First Lord of the Admiralty, in his first wartime speech on the BBC of October 1, 1939, Churchill struck the needed optimistic note in a sea of pessimism:

> Here I am in the same post as I was twenty-five years ago. Rough times lie ahead; but how different is the scene from that of October 1914! Then the French front, with the British army fighting in

Abraham Lincoln, 1864
Gilder Lehrman Collection, GLC05111.02.0016

the line, seemed to be about to break under the terrible impact of German Imperialism. Then Russia had been laid low at Tannenberg; then the whole might of the Austro-Hungarian Empire was in battle against us; then the brave, warlike Turks were about to join our enemies. Then we had to be ready night and day to fight a decisive sea battle with a formidable German fleet almost, in many respects, the equal of our own. We faced those adverse conditions then; we have nothing worse to face tonight.[33]

Churchill could not foresee that the military humiliations of 1940, 1941, and 1942 would be considerably worse, both in Europe and in the Pacific.

The prime minister realized that pessimism was among Britain's most potent enemies. On July 3 1940, he moved to stamp out defeatism with a memo to top British officials: "The Prime Minister expects all His Majesty's Servants in high places to set an example of steadiness and resolution. They should check and rebuke expressions of loose and ill-digested opinion in their circles, or by their subordinates."[34] In public, Churchill often suppressed his bulldog look with a smile. "I displayed the smiling countenance and confident air which are thought suitable when things are very bad," he said of his visits to a defeated France in June 1940.[35] Biographer Geoffrey Best wrote: "Self-respect, courage, self-control, the classic qualities he had learned in study of great commanders like Marlborough, Wellington and Nelson, ensured that his public face would always be resolute and optimistic; and he demanded that everyone else's public face should be the same."[36] Similarly, Lincoln's study of George Washington's character and appearance—a model of composure and self-control, especially under fire—was the standard by which he measured himself. In an address nearly two decades before the Civil War, Lincoln had declared: "Washington is the mightiest name of earth—*long since* mightiest in the cause of civil liberty; *still* mightiest in moral reformation."[37]

The president and the prime minister embraced work, duty, sacrifice—virtues necessary for supreme warlords. Lincoln's character sprang from attitudes formed early in life—grounded in love of country, his ambition to succeed, his sense of honor. Later as president, he would define his duty by loyalty to his sworn constitutional oath of office—to preserve, protect, and defend the constitution and the Union. Addressing the U.S. Sanitary Commission Fair in Philadelphia in June 1864, after fierce and bloody fighting in Virginia, Lincoln emphasized: "We *accepted* this war; we did not *begin* it. We accepted this war for an object, a worthy object, and the war will end when the object is attained."[38] That object was re-Union. Faced in the spring of 1863 with opposition to his administration's restrictions on civil liberties in wartime, Lincoln explained his reasoning:

> If I be wrong on this question of constitutional power, my error lies in believing that certain proceedings are constitutional when, in cases of rebellion or Invasion, the public Safety does not require them—in other words, that the constitution is not in it's [*sic*] application in all respects the same, in cases of Rebellion or invasion, involving the public Safety, as it is in times of profound peace and public security. The constitution itself makes the distinction; and I can no more be persuaded that the government can constitutionally take no strong measure in time of rebellion, because it can be shown that the same could not be lawfully taken in time of peace, than I can be persuaded that a particular drug is not good medicine for a sick man, because it can be shown to not be good food for a well one.[39]

Over a year later in August 1864, the president told an Ohio regiment passing the White House that "the constitutional administration of our government must be sustained, and I beg of you not to allow your minds or your hearts to be diverted from the support of all necessary measures for that purpose, by any miserable picayune arguments addressed to your pockets, or inflammatory appeals made to your passions or your prejudices."[40] President Lincoln was tough, immovable, irreconcilable on the issue of restoring the Union. He waged war on the insurrection, led as he said by traitors who had betrayed their solemn oaths of loyalty to the United States of America.

The president's idea of public service in America entailed austere obedience to law and constitutional authority. Ending a letter to Ohio Democrats protesting the arrest of Democrat Clement L. Vallandigham, a Copperhead Southern sympathizer in the North thought to be a traitor, Lincoln insisted that "in regard to Mr. V[allandigham] and all others, I must hereafter, as heretofore, do so much as the public service may seem to require."[41] Prudently, he would banish Vallandigham to the South with which he sympathized—a fitting punishment. The president would not make of him a martyr to a treasonous minority. In August 1864, Illinois Lieutenant Governor William Bross visited the White House to report on traitorous activities surrounding Camp Douglas in Chicago. "Well," Lincoln told Bross, "they want success and they haven't got it; but we are all doing the best we can. For my part, I shall stay right here and do my duty."[42] Duty, loyalty to the Constitutional Union were Lincoln's watchwords. General Oliver O. Howard and Congressman James F. Wilson reported a June 1862 meeting, in which one senator said: "I believe that, if we could only do right as a people, the Lord would help us, and we should have decided success in this terrible struggle." Lincoln replied: "My faith is greater than yours. I am confident that God will make us do sufficiently right to give us the victory."[43] An apocryphal story makes a different point: the president was told God was on his side. He supposedly answered: "I hope to have God on my side, but I must have Kentucky," a border state whose loyalty was critical to Union victory.[44]

Churchill believed it Britain's duty to help save Europe from tyranny. Speaking to the House of Commons on June 18, 1940, shortly before the French formally surrendered to Germany, Churchill spoke of the future of Britain and the continent: "I expect that the Battle of Britain is about to begin. Upon this battle depends the survival of Christian civilization. Upon it depends our own British life, and the long continuity of our institutions and our Empire. The whole fury and might of the enemy must very soon be turned on us." He continued:

> Hitler knows that he will have to break us in this Island or lose the war. If we can stand up to him, all Europe may be free and the life of the world may move forward into broad, sunlit uplands. But if we fail, then the whole world, including the United States, including all that we have known and cared for, will sink into the abyss of a new Dark Age made more sinister, and perhaps more protracted, by the lights of perverted science. Let us therefore brace ourselves to our duties, and so bear ourselves that if the British Empire and its Commonwealth last for a thousand years, men will still say, "This was their finest hour."[45]

The prime minister was no orthodox Christian, but he was unselfconscious in his embrace of Christendom, a synonym in his language for the Europe of faith, family, liberty, and civilization. The British prime minister knew well the speeches of Lincoln, holding them up as one of the great landmarks of the English-speaking peoples, the history of which he was writing. The American president had exclaimed in his Second Annual Message to Congress: "We shall nobly save, or meanly lose, the last, best hope of earth."[46] In the war to save the Union and to emancipate the slaves, Lincoln would appeal to the justice of the "living God."[47] Lincoln, too, was no orthodox Christian, but he and Churchill felt the hand of Providence at work.

To make his case rhetorically, Churchill was considerably more mobile than Lincoln. By air, boat, and rail, Churchill extended his campaign throughout the world. Lincoln made his way by horse, by carriage, later by rail, by military ambulance, sometimes by riverboat. Travel by rail was limited in the war-torn area surrounding Washington. The president could generally be found at the White House or, during summer, at the Soldiers' Cottage perched on a cooler high point at the outskirts of Washington. During all of the Civil War, Lincoln traveled north of Philadelphia only once, never home to Illinois, but he was often with his soldier boys at the battlefront to consult with generals, to inspire his fighting men, and to visit wounded men in the hospitals. Churchill could be found almost anywhere—at 10 Downing Street, in his underground bunker in the "Annexe," prowling the streets of London after an air raid, at the prime minister's weekend residence at Chequers, or at Ditchley Park when the moon made Chequers too tempting a target for German planes. By air and sea, he made many dangerous trips to the Middle East, the Near East, and North America. His war travels were so arduous, so risky, that General Douglas MacArthur remarked that the prime minister should receive the Victoria Cross (the British medal of honor) for extraordinary bravery.[48] All his life, Churchill harbored the wanderlust—which World War II accentuated. When France was falling to the Germans in May–June 1940, Churchill undertook five dangerous missions there to encourage its leaders to hold out. Later, when key generals and world leaders could not come to him, Churchill would go to them. Health problems were often the reason for the reluctance of FDR to travel—an excuse in the case of Stalin, fearful of a coup. Older than both, the prime minister himself had serious health problems. No matter, he went anyway—leaving Washington for Ottawa in December 1941, just days after a mild heart attack in the White House. He often crisscrossed the Atlantic and the Mediterranean. Thus, it would be Churchill—not FDR or Stalin—who stitched together the grand alliance to defeat Hitler despite the fact that during the war, the prime minister would suffer three bouts of pneumonia, repeated colds, influenza, and severe fevers in addition to minor heart attacks and strokes.

In late summer 1944, Churchill's associates had to conspire to keep him in bed, away from work. Longtime confidante Brendan Bracken was called in to confront the pneumonia-racked Churchill. Bracken asked if the prime minister had told King George that a new prime minister would have to be appointed. "Why should I? I am not going to die," responded the prime minister. "That is exactly where you are wrong. If you go on playing the fool [overworking] like this, you are certain to die," said Bracken.[49] But Churchill's indomitable constitution always recovered. In fact, his immense appetite—for huge breakfasts, multi-course luncheons, champagne, and rich dinners—rarely faltered. He would outlive many contemporaries, dying at 90.

On a sea voyage to Canada in September 1944, General Alan Brooke wrote that the prime minister looked "old, unwell, and depressed. Evidently he found it hard to concentrate and kept holding his head between his hands. He was quite impossible to work with, began by accusing us of framing up against him and of opposing him in his wishes."[50] One explanation of his behavior may have been the antimalarial pills he was taking. Churchill had recently returned from Italy where he had recovered from another bout of pneumonia. Colville wrote of that trip: "The P.M. had a slight temperature again and was highly irascible. Lord Moran does not think seriously of it—probably it is the heat—but he told me that he does not give him a long life and he thinks that when he goes it will be either a stroke or the heart trouble which first showed itself [seriously] at Carthage [in North Africa] last winter."[51] First Sea Lord Andrew Cunningham had written in his August 29 diary: "[I]t would be a tragedy if anything were to happen to him now. With all his faults & he is the most infuriating man; he has done a great job for the country & besides there is no one else."[52]

In the days before the HMS *Queen Mary* landed at Halifax on September 10, Churchill had infuriated his chiefs of staff. Ismay aide Joan Bright recalled:

> The Chiefs of Staff told General Ismay that if, as it seemed to them, the prime minister had lost confidence in them as a committee, they would proffer their resignations. General Ismay replied that this was not at all a good idea, that at this stage of

Winston S. Churchill, 1941

© Yousuf Karsh

the war it would destroy public confidence and would be a fatal step. A better way, he said, was for him to resign; he was not a public figure, but the effect on the Prime Minister might help to improve the strained relationships. He sent in his letter of resignation. It gave him a lot of distress to do so and his action was typical of his unselfish and honourable sense of duty. Mr. Churchill was horrified and left him in no doubt as to his feelings, telling him in some many words "not to write such rubbish again."[53]

President Lincoln and Prime Minister Churchill could set off to the war front on a moment's notice. Both preferred to meet commanding officers face-to-face to discuss strategy and tactics. In October 1861, Secretary of the Navy Gideon Welles wrote in his diary: "Called this morning at the White House, but learned the President had left the city. The porter said he made no mention whither he was going, nor when he would return. I have no doubt he is on a visit to McClellan and the army. None of his Cabinet can have been aware of this journey."[54] Transport limited Lincoln's travel to the nearby theater in which the Army of the Potomac operated, but the president felt compelled to visit the front. Churchill roamed the world. "No matter the circumstances—whether in the dining room at Chartwell or on a picnic chair in the desert—Churchill's profound belief in the importance of face-to-face meetings, and his unshakeable confidence in his ability to get his own way in such intimate encounters, never wavered," wrote Cita Stelzer. "It is summed up in a telegram to Roosevelt, sent shortly before he headed to Moscow in October 1944: 'I feel sure that personal contact is most necessary.'"[55]

Although he cherished comfort, especially piping hot baths, he deliberately put himself in positions of danger and discomfort, flying great distances to meetings with military and civilian leaders.[56] John Keegan wrote: "The necessity for him was to meet the others of the Big Three face-to-face, as often as possible, so that Britain's importance as a combatant, diminishing as it was, might be sustained by treaty or diplomacy. Altogether he met Roosevelt eleven times during the war, always—except at Casablanca, Cairo, Teheran, and Yalta—in North America."[57] While Roosevelt and Stalin preferred to stay home, Churchill would undertake punishing and dangerous missions. The prospect of seeing combat enticed Churchill; Stalin in contrast stayed far away from gunfire. The prime minister could change plans abruptly. On January 25, 1943, after an extensive military planning conference with FDR and Allied generals,

Churchill announced he was leaving Casablanca. When Brooke sought to dissuade him, Churchill responded brusquely: "We are off at six." Brooke asked "To where?" The enigmatic prime minister responded: "I have not decided yet."[58]

The prime minister preferred to be near the action—whether in London or abroad. Churchill reveled in a command position. He recalled a trip to Cairo in 1942: "Now for a short spell I became 'the man on the spot.' Instead of sitting at home waiting for the news from the front I could send it myself. This was exhilarating."[59] Some of his many luxuries traveled with him, but such trips were exhausting and hazardous. His August 1942 first trip to Moscow via Teheran was especially harrowing.

It was King George VI who prevented the prime minister from executing his plan to witness on the spot the D-Day landings of June 1944. To deter Churchill, the King threatened to go with the prime minister, writing him: "I don't think I need emphasize what it would mean to me personally, and to the whole Allied cause, if at this juncture a chance bomb, torpedo, or even a mine, should remove you from the scene; equally a change of Sovereign at this moment would be a serious matter for the country and Empire. We should both, I know, love to be there, but in all seriousness I would ask you to reconsider your plan."[60] In his memoirs, Churchill explained: "A man who has to play an effective part in taking, with the highest responsibility, grave and terrible decisions of war may need the refreshment of adventure. He may need also the comfort that when sending so many others to their death he may share in a small way their risks."[61] The prime minister fretted about a failed cross-channel Allied invasion, but he was not fearful for his own safety. The evening before D-Day, Winston asked Clementine: "Do you realise that by the time you wake up in the morning twenty thousand men may have been killed?"[62] Only one week after D-Day, the prime minister alighted in Normandy. "I had a jolly day on Monday on the beaches and inland," he wrote Roosevelt on June 14.[63]

"Thank God that I have lived to see this," said Lincoln of the fall of the Confederate capital of Richmond in April 1865. "It seems to me that I have been dreaming a horrid dream for four years and now the nightmare is gone. I want to see Richmond."[64] So, off to Richmond he went, just one day after Union troops had invested the Confederate capital on April 4. Secretary of War Edwin M. Stanton warned the president in a telegram on April 3: "Allow me respectfully to ask you to consider whether you ought to expose the nation to the consequences of any disaster to yourself in the pursuit of a treacherous and dangerous enemy like the rebel army. If it was a question concerning yourself only, I should not presume to say a word. Commanding Generals are in the line of their duty in running such risks. But is the political head of a nation in the same condition[?]"[65] Lincoln quickly responded: "Yours received. Thanks for your caution; but I have already been to Petersburg, staid [sic] with Gen. Grant an hour & a half and returned here. It is certain now that Richmond is in our hands, and I think I will go there [by boat] to-morrow. I will take care of myself."[66] The intrepid president was casual about his safety. He arrived in Richmond by boat on Tuesday, April 4, accompanied by twelve sailors. Naval officer John S. Barnes wrote that

> not a soldier was to be seen, and the street along the riverside in which we were, at first free from people, became densely thronged, and every moment became more and more packed with them. With one of my officers, the surgeon, I pushed my way through the crowd endeavoring to reach the side of the President, whose tall form and high beaver hat towered above the crowd. In vain I struggled to get nearer to him. In some way they had learned that the man in the high hat was President Lincoln, and the constantly increasing crowd, particularly the negroes, became frantic with excitement.[67]

The speaker of the U.S. House of Representatives subsequently complained to the president how anxious this trip made many Americans. "Why, if anyone else had been president and had gone to Richmond, I would have been alarmed too," replied Lincoln, "but I was not scared about myself a bit."[68]

President Lincoln was a fatalist about his own security. In Philadelphia, on the way to his first inauguration, the president-elect had declared at Independence Hall: "I would rather be assassinated on this spot than to surrender" the liberty proclaimed in the Declaration of Independence.[69] William Crook, who served as Lincoln's regular bodyguard, recalled that the president "hated being on his guard, and the fact that it was necessary to distrust his fellow Americans saddened him."[70] The president told one friendly journalist: "I long ago made up my mind that if anybody wants to kill me, he will do it. If I wore a shirt and mail, and kept myself surrounded by a body-guard, it would be all the same. There are a thousand ways of getting at a man if it is desirable that he should be killed." The president then suggested that his enemies might find Vice President Hannibal Hamlin an objectionable substitute.[71]

Churchill's trips often entailed very long journeys away from London. In November 1943, for example, the prime minister traveled to Cairo and Teheran to meet with FDR, Chiang Kai-shek, and Stalin. He returned to England two months later. Churchill believed that there were few issues that he himself could not resolve by a personal meeting. In some cases, his larger-than-life ego, his self-confidence that he might persuade anyone of his viewpoint, bordered on fantasy. It did make him the great practitioner of personal diplomacy and summitry—sometimes to his despair when ineffective. In person, he hoped he could persuade FDR and Stalin against their considered national interests. Compounding his desire for summitry, Churchill had an "almost obsessive love of travel," according to biographer Roy Jenkins.[72]

Lincoln had an abiding realism about the irreconcilable aims of North and South. The self-confident president had his ego well under control. He understood the persuasive power of his prose and his person. But his was a more limited and realistic ambition for personal diplomacy. Often implored to seek peace with Jefferson Davis, Lincoln declared in his Fourth Annual Message to Congress in December 1864:

> The national resources, then, are unexhausted, and, as we believe, inexhaustible. The public purpose to reestablish and maintain the national authority is unchanged, and, as we believe, unchangeable. . . . On careful consideration of all the evidence accessible it seems to me that no attempt at negotiation with the insurgent leader could result in any good. He would accept nothing short of severance of the Union—precisely what we will not and cannot give. His declarations to this effect are explicit and oftrepeated. He does not attempt to deceive us. He affords us no excuse to deceive ourselves. He cannot voluntarily reaccept the Union; we cannot voluntarily yield it. Between him and us the issue is distinct, simple, and inflexible. It is an issue which can only be tried by war, and decided by victory.[73]

In this, his final Annual Message to Congress, the clarity of Lincoln's analysis, the succinctness of his prose, and the precision of his vocabulary would compel his readers to yield to the force of evidence and logic in his arguments.

Your resignation of the office of Secretary of the Treasury, sent me yesterday, is accepted. Of all I have said in commendation of your ability and fidelity, I have nothing to unsay; and yet you and I have reached a point of mutual embarrassment in our official relation which it seems can not be overcome, or longer sustained, consistently with public service.[1]

ABRAHAM LINCOLN
to Salmon P. Chase
June 30, 1864

I am convinced that every man of you would rise up and tear me down from my place if I were for one moment to contemplate parley or surrender. If this long island story of ours is to end at last, let it end only when each one of us lies choking in his own blood upon the ground.[2]

WINSTON S. CHURCHILL
Meeting with Cabinet
May 28, 1940

VI.

Managing Ministers and Legislators

During the last five months of 1861, Union General George B. McClellan marshaled and drilled the Army of the Potomac. President Lincoln wanted action. With the rebel army but a short distance away in northern Virginia, McClellan would not fight. In December, Congressmen Schuyler Colfax and Reuben Fenton met with Lincoln to discuss growing public agitation about McClellan's inactivity. Colfax recalled the president

> said Providence, with favoring sky and earth, seemed to beckon the army on, but General [George B.] McClellan, he supposed, knew his business and had his reasons for disregarding these hints of Providence. "And," said Mr. Lincoln, "as we have got to stand by the General, I think a good way to do it may be for Congress to take a recess for several weeks, and by the time you get together again, if McClellan is not off with the army, Providence is very likely to step in with hard roads and force us to say, the army can't move." He continued: "You know [Charles] Dickens said of a certain man that if he would always follow his nose he would never stick fast in the mud. Well, when the rains set in it will be impossible for ever our eager and gallant soldiers to keep their noses so high that their feet will not stick in the clay mud of Old Virginia."[3]

By January 1862, the president understood he was saddled with a backstabbing, bedridden general who showed no signs of moving his army into battle.

The Union government, effectively insolvent by the end of 1861, struggled to obtain the credit to finance its growing war machine. Immobilized by military and financial stalemates, the president lamented to Secretary of War Simon Cameron: "It is exceedingly discouraging. As everywhere else, nothing can be done."[4] A few days later, the president confided to General Montgomery Meigs: "The people are impatient; [Treasury Secretary] Chase has no money, and he tells me he can raise no more; the General of the Army has typhoid fever. The bottom is out of the tub. What shall I do?"[5] Convertibility of the dollar to gold had been suspended, and the Union government would issue Treasury notes ("greenbacks") to finance government purchases. The Union treasury had found the means—paper money—to pay for the war, but the government did not impose rationing and comprehensive wage and price controls, as it would in World War II. Paper money led to inflation, a war boom, and a postwar bust, and as with most wars, the enrichment of well-placed elites.

Early in the wars, Lincoln and Churchill rearranged their cabinets. In January 1862, the president sent Simon Cameron, his corrupt and incompetent secretary of war, to Moscow as the American ambassador. In January 1942, Churchill did the opposite—welcoming home Stafford Cripps, the British ambassador to Moscow.[6] A BBC radio speech swiftly raised Cripps's stature and popularity, but when the prime minister offered Cripps a cabinet post, he declined, holding out for a position in the War Cabinet, which included only the most important ministers concerned with military issues. Before the war, Cripps, a socialist sympathetic to communism, had opposed Chamberlain's policy of appeasement, urging a union of left-wing parties, including the Communists.[7] Staunchly anti-Communist, the Labour Party had expelled him. In early 1942, Cripps suddenly loomed as a possible successor to a weakened Churchill, were he to be forced from office. The prime minister rejected Cripps's suggestion that Churchill give up his dual role as prime minister and Minister of Defence. "I was entirely resolved to keep my full power of war-direction," he recalled in his memoirs. In May 1940, Churchill had invented the senior cabinet office of minister of defence to replace his chairmanship of the Military Coordination Committee of the War Cabinet.[8] As Defence Minister, Churchill consolidated his direct leadership of the military.

By training, both Lincoln and Churchill were creatures of the legislature—Churchill in Parliament for half a century, Lincoln a four-term state legislator and one-term congressman. In an August 1939 speech on the eve of war with Nazi Germany, Churchill had protested the luxury of a two-month adjournment of Parliament: "This House is sometimes disparaged in this country, but abroad it counts. Abroad, the House of Commons is counted, and especially in Dictator countries, as a most formidable expression of the British national will and an instrument of that will in resistance to aggression."[9] More than two years later, he concluded a speech to the House of Commons on April 23, 1942: "As the war rises remorselessly to its climax, the House of Commons, which is the foundation of the British life struggle—this House of Commons which has especial responsibilities—will have the opportunity once again of proving to the world that the firmness of spirit, sense of proportion, steadfastness of purpose which have gained it renown in former days, will now once again carry great peoples and a greater cause to a victorious deliverance."[10] In May 1945, the prime minister would end his speech to Parliament announcing the surrender of Germany: "I have only two or three sentences to add. They will convey to the House my deep gratitude to this House of Commons, which has proved itself the strongest foundation for waging war that has ever been seen in the whole of our long history. We have all of us made our mistakes, but the strength of the Parliamentary institution has been shown to enable it at the same moment to preserve all the title deeds of democracy while waging war in the most stern and protracted form."[11]

Churchill's constitutional relationship with Parliament differed profoundly from Lincoln's with Congress. The prime minister is a creature of Parliament; the president is constitutionally independent of Congress. In the fall of 1861, Congress would set up a Joint Committee on the Conduct of the War, dominated by Radical Republicans such as Michigan's Zachariah Chandler and Ohio's Benjamin F. Wade. They aimed to constrain the constitutional powers of the president as commander in chief. They mounted postbattle investigations, interrogated generals, and bedeviled President Lincoln about his conduct of the war. Wade wrote in October 1861: "I begin to despair of ever putting down this rebellion through the instrumentality of this administration. They are blundering, cowardly, and inefficient." He complained that Lincoln's attitudes "could only come of one, born of poor white trash, and educated in a slave state [Kentucky]."[12] In 1862, when Lincoln started to tell a story during a meeting with Wade, the senator erupted: "Bother your stories, Mr. President. That is the way it is with you, sir. It is all story—story. You are the father of every military blunder that has been made during the war. You are on the road to hell, sir, with this Government, and you are not a mile off this minute." President Lincoln coolly replied: "Wade, that is about the distance from here to the Capitol."[13] The senator had come to urge the replacement of General McClellan. The president, as he often did, changed the topic.

Radical Republicans in Congress could be an irritable, self-righteous claque. Lincoln needed every bit of his humor and patience to deal with them. In 1864, Mr. Lincoln described Radical Republican leaders as "almost *fiendish*."[14] Generally, they complained about the sluggish war effort, lack of action to effect emancipation, the speed of Reconstruction, and the doubtful political allegiances of West Point–trained generals. "The Radicals credited Lincoln with limited political courage," wrote historian David Long, "and whenever he refused to accommodate them, they assumed it was because of conservative advice" from Secretary Seward, editor Thurlow Weed, and Postmaster General Montgomery Blair.[15]

In December 1862, Lincoln's difficult relations with Congress boiled over in a full-fledged revolt by Senate Republicans, unnerved by the disastrous Union defeat at the Battle of Fredericksburg. Barring congressional impeachment, only the American people could unseat Lincoln at a regularly scheduled election. The political status of Churchill, whose first parliamentary revolt came at the beginning of 1942, was quite different. Members of Parliament could, by a no-confidence vote, cause the fall of the prime minister. As historian David Reynolds noted, "The successive defeats of 1941 and 1942 saw sustained if muffled criticism about 'midnight follies' and 'cigar-stump diplomacy.'"[16] The "follies" often took place on weekends at Chequers, where British officials gathered in close quarters and listened to new Churchill schemes, which many thought harebrained.[17] The threat to the prime minister was real.

Led by Labour MP Aneurin Bevan, questions arose in January 1942 about Churchill's war leadership, in the wake of mortifying defeats of British arms in Greece, Crete, and the Far East. Storied ships of the British fleet had been sunk by German and Japanese airplanes, submarines, and ships. Key British positions in Hong Kong, Singapore, and Burma fell to the Japanese in the first few months of 1942. On January 27, MP Harold Nicolson witnessed the back-and-forth shift of sentiment in the House regarding Churchill's continuation in office: "Winston speaks for an hour and a half and justifies his demand for a vote of confidence. One can actually feel the wind of opposition [to Churchill] dropping sentence by sentence, and by the time he finishes it is clear that there is really no opposition at all—only a certain uneasiness."[18] Still, Bevan's rhetoric stung: "The question is beginning to arise in the minds of many: is he as good a war maker as he is a speech maker?"[19] Churchill did not flinch: "I make no apologies. I offer no excuses. I make no promises. In no way have I mitigated the . . . impending misfortunes that hang over us."[20] The prime minister suggested that one of his opponents was a "silly bastard. There are about half a dozen of them; they make a noise out of all proportion to their importance. The House knows this, but unfortunately people abroad take them too seriously; they do a lot of harm."[21] In his beloved House of Commons, the prime minister relished debates with his foes, taking on all adversaries with wit, scorn, and argument. Churchill would prevail in the vote of confidence, 464–1.

The prime minister's political position had nevertheless weakened, his leadership having been openly questioned. British politicians like Cripps and Max Beaverbrook maneuvered to replace Churchill. "However tempting it may be to some, when trouble lies ahead, to step aside adroitly and put someone else up to take the blows, the heavy and repeated blows—which are coming," the prime minister told Parliament on February 24, "I do not intend . . . to adopt that cowardly course."[22] Dr. Wilson wrote: "The P.M. somehow made them [the British people] feel that they were partners in that heroic struggle, though taking, himself, the fullest personal responsibility for whatever went wrong."[23]

In the late summer of 1942, Cripps put forward a series of proposals to reorganize war management. "With some of these I found myself in full sympathy, and initiated action to give effect to them," wrote Churchill in his memoirs. "But on the main question of the technical direction of the war I was profoundly at variance with the views expressed by the Lord Privy Seal [Cripps]. He did not, it is true, suggest that I should be superseded or displaced from my position; he proposed instead that as Minister of Defence I should have associated with me, as advisers, three persons of the calibre of the Chiefs of Staff who would supervise the Joint Planning Staffs and would be free to devote the whole of their time to military planning in its broadest sense." The prime minister rejected this "War Planning Directorate" as unworkable, writing: "It was a delusion to suppose that there was a large supply of officers 'of equal calibre' to [those] whom I had chosen to discharge the heavy responsibilities of Chiefs of Staff." Cripps recognized that his continuance in the War Cabinet was now untenable, but he agreed to remain until the initiation in November of Operation TORCH in North Africa.[24] By late November 1942, Cripps was no longer a member of the War Cabinet—nor was he any longer a threat to the prime minister's leadership. As Bevan biographer Michael Foot observed, "Churchill had shown much persuasive skill in warding off the political uproar which would undoubtedly have followed a Cripps resignation, and by the same stroke he had succeeded in putting Cripps as a political figure in cold storage for the rest of the war."[25]

Not unlike the Cripps challenge to Churchill, it was at the beginning of the Civil War that Secretary of State Seward thought himself Lincoln's "prime minister."[26] On April 1, 1861, Seward had written to the president a bold, presumptuous letter, stating that "further delay to adopt and prosecute our policies for both domestic and foreign affairs would not only bring scandal on the Administration, but danger upon the country." After spelling out his proposals, Seward continued: "For this purpose it must be somebody's business to pursue and direct it [our policies] incessantly. Either the President must do it himself, and be all the while active in it; or Devolve it on some member of his Cabinet." Seward, a former New York governor and senator, had made it clear that he was the required prime minister to stand in for the village lawyer from pioneer Illinois. Lincoln's response was direct and firm: "If this must be done, I must do it." He wrote: "When a general line of policy is adopted, I apprehend there is no danger of its being changed without good reason, or continuing to be a subject of unnecessary debate; still, upon points arising in its progress, I wish, and suppose I am entitled to have the advice of all the cabinet."[27] Lack of experience did not diminish the grittiness of Lincoln's intelligence, character, and judgment, nor would his self-confidence allow him to yield command. Neither would he be intimidated by Washington's patronizing elites.

Republican Party issues compounded the problems of Lincoln's cabinet. Though he and Churchill were party leaders, Lincoln remained

Salmon P. Chase, ca. 1861
Gilder Lehrman Collection, GLC05111.02.079

fully engaged as a founder and head of the Republican Party. In Britain's coalition government, Churchill was less engaged and less interested in grassroots politics (except when by-election defeats set off alarms). Many strong men of the British Tories and of the American Republicans held deep and jealous doubts about their prime minister and their president. The vehicle of dissent for Radical Republicans was the Joint Congressional Committee on the Conduct of the War. Periodically, its members arrived at the White House to criticize the president's war strategy. In the summer of 1862, the leader of the committee suggested that Union General McClellan should be replaced. The president then asked with whom McClellan should be replaced. The senator replied: "Why, anybody." The commander in chief artfully responded that "*anybody*" might do for the senator, but that the commander in chief must have "*somebody*."[28] Lincoln was generally patient and politic in these circumstances. As president, he would act with supreme self-confidence in his constitutional authority as chief executive and commander in chief of the army and the navy.

Churchill and Lincoln used their cabinets as sounding boards for discussion of strategy—the prime minister more, the president less. Under the parliamentary-cabinet system and traditions of the British constitution, the prime minister was bound to consult the cabinet.[29] Lincoln was at liberty to ignore his cabinet. The president prudently solicited cabinet advice, listening carefully at cabinet meetings. Lincoln encouraged discussion—sometimes general, sometimes very specific, on a problem he alone must resolve. Churchill, on the other hand, tended to dominate cabinet meetings in which he participated. The prime minister, given to monologues, often irritated his colleagues like Brooke, who noted that the prime minister would later use "the arguments which have been put to him as his own—even to those who have originally produced them—and as if they were something quite new."[30]

One of the prime minister's problems stemmed from the fact that Churchill had switched party allegiance from the Tories to the Liberals in 1904, then back to the Tories in 1925. As a result, Tory loyalists distrusted him. He bore the burden of the convert. In February 1942, he remarked that "the bulk of the Tories hated him." On this issue, the prime minister was insouciant. "Anyone can rat, but it takes a certain amount of ingenuity to rerat," Churchill cavalierly joked.[31] Still, he managed to maintain a fragile peace not only with skeptical Tories, but also with leaders of the Labour Party, not least because Labour had supported him over Lord Halifax as the replacement for Neville Chamberlain. By shrewdly appointing Labour leaders to key positions in his coalition government, Churchill strengthened his cabinet in a prolonged war of survival. During his frequent and long absences from London, Labour's prime-minister-in-waiting, Clement Attlee, became acting prime minister.

Congressional and parliamentary nightmares developed in the early years of the American Civil War and of World War II. Lincoln and Churchill had to put down serious revolts. Parliamentary dissatisfaction with the prime minister came first in January, and then again in June 1942. During the siege of Tobruk and its humiliating surrender in June, Churchill was in Washington with FDR. After an exhausting flight to London, Churchill faced a second no-confidence motion in the House of Commons, which in principle could force him from office. Labour dissident Aneurin Bevan quipped that Churchill "wins debate after debate and loses battle after battle. The Country is beginning to say that he fights debates like a war and the war like a debate."[32] Bevan even suggested that a Polish or Czech general might better command the British army (a proposal reminiscent of the 1862 proposal that Lincoln import the Italian nationalist Giuseppe Garibaldi to lead the Union army). Bevan carried on his criticism of Churchill. At the beginning of July, he declared in Parliament: "The Prime Minister has qualities of greatness—everybody knows that—but the trouble is that he has too much to do. He has not around him colleagues to whom he can delegate any of this matter concerning the central direction of the war. The result is that all these defects which he possesses are made dangerous, because the Prime Minister, among all his other qualities, has a gift of expression which is exceedingly dangerous. He very often mistakes verbal felicities for verbal inspiration."[33] Bevan believed that Churchill's powers of persuasion worked their effect not only on his constituents, but also on the prime minister's own perceptions, sometimes causing his judgment to be refractory in the face of great danger.

Lincoln's cabinet crisis came in December 1862, after the calamitous defeat and slaughter of Union troops at Fredericksburg. Northern despair was reflected in a diary entry by Ohio Congressman William P. Cutler: "We are at sea & [have] no pilot or captain. God alone can take care of us & all his ways *seem* to be against us & to favor the rebels & their allies—the Democrats. Truly it is a *day of darkness and of gloominess.*"[34]

President Lincoln rose to the occasion; he reorganized the Army of the Potomac and its leadership, simultaneously disarming those seeking to dismantle his cabinet.[35] Lincoln later told aide John Hay about the change in October 1863: "I do not now see how it could have been done better. I am sure it was right. If I had yielded to that storm [in the Senate] & dismissed Seward the thing would all have slumped over one way & we should have been left with a scanty handful of supporters. When Chase sent in his resignation I saw that the game was in my own hands & I put it through."[36] Republican mid-term electoral defeats in November 1862 had come before the Fredericksburg disaster. Secretary of the Treasury Salmon P. Chase—a brilliant, ambitious, abolitionist politician from Ohio who had lost the Republican nomination to Lincoln—spread plausible gossip among Republican senators, undermining Lincoln's administration. The jealous Chase had encouraged senatorial criticism of Seward, Chase's longtime rival. In the presence of the treasury secretary, the president finessed a Senate delegation seeking Seward's dismissal. Chase's private criticisms of Seward fell apart in front of the senators.

By 1862, Seward had become a Lincoln stalwart and an able adviser. Lincoln brushed aside the secretary of state's desire to resign: "Ah yes, Governor, that will do very well for you, but I am like the starling in [Laurence] Sterne's story, 'I can't get out.'"[37] Turning the tables, he obtained written resignations from both Seward and Chase. He pocketed the notes and declared to one senator: "Now I can ride; I have a pumpkin in each end of my bag."[38] The president was wilier and stronger than his more experienced cabinet members, and more clever than the imperious and skeptical members of the Senate establishment. A Massachusetts congressman later wrote of this incident: "He gave no heed to [the senators'] request, but afterwards remarked, that he could take care of a secret enemy in his Cabinet, if he had one, a great deal easier than he could take care of an open enemy, if he was a man of power, outside of the Cabinet."[39] Holding Chase close, Lincoln would wait to deal with him decisively.

Chase, a nationally prominent former governor and senator, thinking himself indispensable, repeatedly overplayed his hand. Eventually, he would bring about his own downfall. Fellow Ohio politician and future president Rutherford B. Hayes reported that Chase was "cold, selfish and unscrupulous," adding that "political intrigue, love of power and a selfish and boundless ambition were the striking features of his life and character."[40] Chase failed in February 1864 to rally support to replace Lincoln as the Republican presidential candidate. Lincoln had rejected Chase's written resignation. In managing his cabinet, as with handling his generals, Lincoln awaited the right moment to deal with difficult appointees. Then he would act decisively. In the spring of 1864, a clash over a key New York patronage position led to new conflict between Lincoln and Chase. Understanding that Radical Republicans controlled much of the city's patronage, Lincoln, as leader of the party, aimed to satisfy more moderate Republicans with the appointment of a new assistant secretary of the treasury for New York. The president knew that balance in the division of political spoils in New York was politically critical—especially when charges and countercharges of corruption were regularly exchanged. As Lincoln recalled:

Finally, as I was sitting here at my desk one morning, with the room full of people, a letter from the Treasury Department was brought to me. I opened it, recognized Chase's handwriting, read the first sentence, and inferred from its tenor, that this matter was in the way of satisfactory adjustment. I was truly glad of this, and, laying the envelope with its inclosure down upon the desk, went on talking. People were coming and going all the time till three o'clock, and I forgot all about Chase's letter. . . . While I was sitting alone at table my thoughts reverted to Chase's letter, and I determined to answer it just as soon as I should go up stairs again. Well, as soon as I was back here, I took pen and paper and prepared to write; but then it occurred to me that I might as well read the letter before I answered it. I took it out of the envelope for that purpose, and, as I did so, another inclosure fell from it upon the floor. I picked it up, read it, and said to myself, '*Halloo, this is a horse of another color!*' It was his resignation. I put my pen into my mouth, and *grit my teeth* upon it. I did not long reflect. I very soon decided to accept it.[41]

Lincoln moved swiftly to replace Chase with a respected financial expert in the Senate, William P. Fessenden. He was confirmed as the new treasury secretary, even while he was at the White House protesting his ability to serve. About ten weeks later, Lincoln asked for and received the resignation of the conservative Postmaster General Montgomery

Blair, who, unlike the radical Chase, was a Lincoln loyalist. The dismissal of the outspoken Blair was the price the president paid to obtain the reelection support of key Radical Republicans. Many Radicals wanted Chase appointed to replace Supreme Court Chief Justice Roger Taney, who died in October 1864. Lincoln would appoint Chase for his own reasons, but he held up that appointment until the Senate confirmed James Speed, his nominee for attorney general. Neither the Cabinet nor Congress could dictate the president's decisions, or their timing.

A self-righteous moralist, Chase was to Lincoln what the eccentric Stafford Cripps was to Churchill. Both the president and the prime minister made effective use of their would-be successors, so long as they believed them useful. Churchill had appointed Cripps to be the British ambassador to Moscow in 1940, in recognition of Cripps's pro-Russian sympathies and communist associations. As the British envoy there, he failed dismally, but after the Soviet Union fought Germany's attack on Moscow to a standstill in December 1941, his pro-Russian sympathies raised his British profile. Appointed Leader of the House of Commons in February 1942, Cripps proved ineffective. In March, Churchill sent Cripps to India to negotiate a wartime agreement with the independence-minded Congress Party.[42] Again, Cripps failed, satisfying Churchill, who wanted no agreement. Increasingly disenchanted with Churchill's leadership, Cripps finally resigned from the War Cabinet in the fall of 1942.

The mature Lincoln had great confidence in his own intuition and judgment. The mature Churchill had the same gifts of inspired intuition and good judgment; but throughout his life, he was often moved by his emotions. Lincoln's public rhetoric and decision-making were generally logical, his arguments succinct and compelling, but less impassioned than those of the prime minister. The president's speeches often were grounded in constitutional, philosophical, and circumstantial reasoning. Churchill's powerful intellect showed itself not only in his speeches and writings, but also in the clarity of his innumerable private "minutes" to civil and military subordinates, or to foreign colleagues. With these minutes, often labeled with a maroon sticker "ACTION THIS DAY," Churchill directed his staff by rigorous instruction. The prime minister's speeches could be equally straightforward. Lincoln's mature writing, especially after 1854, reflected his preference for monosyllabic Anglo-Saxon language, as in the Gettysburg Address. Churchill's prose, too, often deployed the simpler Anglo-Saxon forms, mixed with Latinate adjectives, adverbs, and nouns. "When his [Lincoln's] judgment, which acted slowly . . . was grasping some subject of importance, the arguments [Lincoln could make] against his own desires seemed uppermost in his mind, and, in conversing upon it, he would present those arguments to see if they could be rebutted," observed House Speaker Schuyler Colfax.[43] A Wisconsin judge testified to President Lincoln's persuasive power during a visit in August 1864: "As I heard a vindication of his [emancipation] policy from his own lips, I could not but feel that his mind grew in stature like his body, & that I stood in the presence of the great guiding intellect of the age."[44] Lincoln consciously ordered his speeches with prose axioms and postulates inspired by the Euclidean logic he embraced. Churchill's prose often reflected the English poetry he had memorized and the robust writing of great English historians he had studied.

Lincoln was a sympathetic and subtle analyst of people. Fellow Illinois attorney Joseph Gillespie recalled:

> Mr. Lincoln was very tenderhearted. I called at the White House and was detained a considerable time in the anteroom, which was filled with persons waiting their turn to be admitted to the President. While there, I met with an old lady who said she had been several days waiting to see Mr. Lincoln; that she wanted to get permission to see her son, who was a soldier lying at the point of death; that she was unable to obtain permission from the Secretary of War. I told her that if I gained admittance before she did, I would speak to the President about her case. She said she had been told that he was a very kindhearted man. Just about this time, Mr. Lincoln's barber, whom I had known in Springfield, Illinois, came out of Mr. Lincoln's room and, seeing me, offered to take me in by a private door, which I accepted. While shaking hands with the President, I mentioned the case of the old lady, and he remarked that his greatest tribulation consisted in the fact that it was impossible for him to give prompt attention to such cases, but he directed the old lady to be shown in, and without hesitation, granted her request. He saw in an instant that she was honest.[45]

Congressman Colfax wrote of a conversation with Lincoln:

[O]ne night in the telegraph office of the War Department, he suddenly turned the subject from campaigns and battles to mental idiosyncrasies, discussing the individualities of [Republican Congressman] Thaddeus Stevens, of [Senator] Charles Sumner, and, last of all, [Senator] Henry Wilson. After discussing the characteristics of others with a keenness of analysis that strikingly illustrated his own mental powers, he added that a peculiarity of his own life from his earliest manhood had been, that he habitually studied the opposite side of every disputed question, of every law case, of every political issue, more exhaustively, if possible, than his own side. He said that the result had been, that in all his long practice at the bar he had never once been surprised in court by the strength of his adversary's case—often finding it much weaker than he had feared.[46]

His habit of argument emboldened Lincoln to concede much of his opponent's case in the presence of the jury, while bringing all his persuasive powers to prevail on the main points at dispute. So, too, would he proceed in politics.

Lincoln did not impulsively or peremptorily fire people—nor did he hold grudges against those who failed him, opposed him, or even insulted him. In place of Secretary of War Simon Cameron, in January 1862 Lincoln appointed Democrat Edwin Stanton, the famous Pittsburgh lawyer who, before the war, had ignored Lincoln in the course of trying a major legal case in Ohio. Stanton would often dispute Lincoln's authority in War Department matters. Still, Lincoln remained Stanton's loyal supporter, and Stanton reciprocated, coming to revere his commander in chief. They came into daily contact at the War Department, where Lincoln read military telegrams, and at the Soldiers' Home, where their families spent summers. The president perceived Stanton to be personally honest and effective, so he patiently put up with his prickly personality.[47] "Stanton would become furious and fly into fits of rage at Lincoln time and time again," wrote historian David Long. But one must not exaggerate their differences. "Their common devotion to the cause of the Union, and their relentless determination to preserve it, created a bond that did not take the form of backslapping humor and thigh-pounding stories amidst relaxed banter that Lincoln shared

Lord Halifax

Alfred Eisenstaedt/The LIFE Picture Collections/Getty Image

with William H. Seward."[48] Stanton was precisely what Cameron had not
been—a talented, no-nonsense administrator who managed the complicated Northern rail system as an efficient weapon of war.[49]

War did concentrate the wide-ranging intellects of Churchill and
Lincoln, causing them to focus on the evidence of each case or decision
before them.[50] When writer George William Curtis visited the White
House, he observed, "Mr. Lincoln received us in his office. . . . He was
dressed in black and wore slippers. On a table at his side were maps and
plans of the seat of war; and pins with blue and gray heads represented
the position of the soldiers on both sides."[51] Churchill visited his map
room in the Annexe to 10 Downing Street every day—as he would his
makeshift map room when shipboard or overseas. Aide Joan Bright
recalled:

> Daily truth belonged to the Map Room. Well equipped, manned
> by retired officers from the three Services, it was our one cen-
> tre of fact, a haven not because any news it gave was good but
> because it represented a peg in a shifting world and because
> its caretakers were informative, helpful, and charming. Here
> we could know the whereabouts and condition of such-and-
> such convoy ploughing the Atlantic Ocean or squirming its way
> through to the encircled island of Malta; we could see where the
> bombs had fallen the previous night, how stood our shipping
> losses, our civil and military casualties.[52]

In December 1941, FDR endeared himself to Churchill by setting up
a map room for the prime minister in the White House during a visit
occasioned by the Japanese attack on Pearl Harbor.[53] On D-Day, 1944,
the prime minister tracked Allied progress all day in his map room, dis-
consolate he could not accompany the invasion. President Lincoln, a self-
trained and practiced surveyor, made much use of his maps—whether
in his office or at the front. Historian Craig L. Symonds noted: "In the
middle of an inspection tour, he would stop, take out his map, spread it
on his knee, and enquire about possible military movements."[54] Churchill used his map room much the way Lincoln used the telegraph office
at the War Department—as a center for gathering and evaluating news
from the war fronts.

Both war leaders had the strength of character to hold together cabinets of former rivals and controversial appointees. Secretary of State

Seward and Postmaster General Blair were special targets of hostile fire, inside and outside the cabinet. Churchill's friends, Minister of Aircraft Production Lord Beaverbrook, and Minister of Information Brendan Bracken, evoked indignation from their senior colleagues, but their skills and loyal friendship gave the prime minister comfort. His tendency to rely on trusted friends for ad hoc advice infuriated senior cabinet members such as Deputy Prime Minister Clement Attlee. Out of government, Beaverbrook was a loose cannon—campaigning in 1942 to open a second front in western Europe to relieve the pressure on Russia long before the Allies were ready. Churchill said of Beaverbrook: "Max is a good friend in foul weather. Then, when things are going well, he will have a bloody row with you over nothing."[55] King George expressed his misgivings about Beaverbrook to Churchill upon becoming prime minister, and then to Roosevelt-envoy Harry Hopkins, who wrote: "He left me with the impression that he did not have a very high opinion of many of [Churchill's ministers], particularly Beaverbrook, who clearly he does not trust, although he recognizes his good qualities."[56] The rich press lord "did as he liked, when he liked," noted one Churchill military aide.[57]

At critical points in World War II, Beaverbrook made major contributions to the war effort, including crucial service in 1940, as Minister of Aircraft Production. He conducted pivotal discussions with both the Russians and the Americans in late 1941. Revisionist historian A. J. P. Taylor wrote that during World War II, Beaverbrook was the "only member of the war cabinet to dispute the basic principles of British strategy against Churchill and the chiefs of staff. He did not believe that independent bombing of Germany would win the war—a view largely, though not entirely, endorsed by official history. Nor did he believe that North Africa and Italy were the shortest road to victory. He advocated the Second Front within the war cabinet and left office in order to advocate it in public."[58] With the benefit of hindsight, and with partial access to Soviet archives, we now know that Beaverbrook underestimated Stalin's treachery, ruthlessness, and intended expansion in Europe and Asia. Still, many British politicians could sympathize with the comment made by novelist H. G. Wells: "If ever Max gets to Heaven, he won't last long. He will be chucked out for trying to pull off a merger between Heaven and Hell."[59]

With a home on Lafayette Park across from the White House, Secretary of State Seward provided Lincoln a welcome refuge from the pressures of the presidency. In Seward's case, his judgment had matured the more he observed the president's character and decision-making. The commander in chief's reliance on Seward unsettled Radical Republicans during the Civil War. Churchill, too, would find comfort before and during World War II in the friendship of Brendan Bracken, who exhibited the same loyalty to the prime minister that Seward showed President Lincoln—a reassuring and humorous presence to relieve the war pressures on the commander in chief. Bracken "had attached himself to Churchill during the worst period of Churchill's eclipse and gave him the most devoted support in the darkest days. . . . He was full of charitable instincts, which he translated in a quiet and unobtrusive way into reality," wrote Harold Macmillan. "But his importance at this stage was his close friendship with Churchill, to whom he would speak with absolute and often outrageous frankness."[60]

The prime minister relied on the data and charts collected and organized by Professor Frederick Lindemann, an ingenious physicist whom Churchill appointed to oversee the government's "S-branch," devoted to statistical work. One senior military critic recalled that "the Prof"—or Baron Cherwell, as he became in 1941—was "as obstinate as a mule, and unwilling to admit that there was any problem under the sun which he was not qualified to solve. He would write a memorandum on high strategy one day, and a thesis on egg production on the next."[61] Military and civilian officials became infuriated by Lindemann's interventions. Churchill nevertheless claimed that "Lindemann could decipher the signals from the experts on the far horizons and explain to me in lucid, homely terms what the issues were."[62] Lindemann was envied and derided; he was clever but fallible. He argued strenuously against the scientific "lunacy" of the German V-2 rocket, which struck terror in England in 1944. Max Hastings wrote: "'The Prof' was widely perceived as a pernicious influence upon the Prime Minister. MPs who did not dare to attack Churchill himself instead vented their frustrations upon his associates. The prime minister defended [Lord] Cherwell, but he bitterly resented being obliged to do so."[63]

The closest that Lincoln had to an in-house scientist was Professor Joseph Henry, a physicist who was also the director of the Smithsonian Institution. An accused Confederate sympathizer, Henry was not so politically reliable as the intensely anti-German Lindemann. Henry, however, had his uses. "My visits to the Smithsonian, to Dr. Henry, and his able lieutenant, Professor Baird," Lincoln reportedly said, "are the chief recreations of my life."[64] Henry presciently advocated the use of balloons for aerial reconnaissance in war—a topic in which the president took a keen interest. "Professor Henry spent many evenings in the family apartments at the White House," noted journalist Charles Carleton Coffin. "It was a great relief to the President, after the personal perplexities of the day, to converse with one of the foremost scientists of the age."[65] The only president to have successfully filed for a patent, Lincoln had long shown an interest in scientific innovation.

The president and the prime minister forced the introduction and use of new technology and transportation to advance their military goals. They wanted to know all they could about potential innovations in warfare.[66] Lincoln confronted hidebound bureaucrats, such as Dr. Robert C. Wood in the army's Medical Bureau, and James Ripley in the army's Ordnance Bureau. Ripley obtusely opposed the purchase of breech-loading rifles to replace antiquated muskets. George Templeton Strong wrote in July 1862 that the Medical Bureau "was by the universal consent of all but its own members, the most narrow, hidebound, fossilized, red-tape-y of all the departments in Washington. It was wholly incapable of caring for the army when the war broke out. It was without influence or weight with Government."[67] The Union's use of railroad experts like Herman Haupt and Thomas A. Scott enabled Lincoln and his generals to mobilize efficiently the transport of Union soldiers and supplies over widespread exterior lines of battle.

Lincoln and Churchill would even shake up military command structures to introduce new weapons. The prime minister had long fostered an interest in military technology. In World War I, Churchill became an early advocate for the tank. In World War II, he helped to conceive and to order construction of the Mulberry Harbours, indispensable for the landings on the Normandy beaches. (The idea for the Mulberry Harbours had originated with Churchill in 1917 during World War I.[68]) Four years before the D-Day landing, the prime minister ordered: "The ships must have a side-flap cut in them, and a drawbridge long enough to overreach the moorings of the piers. Let me have the best solution worked out."[69] President Lincoln usually confined himself to testing the most plausible inventions that were presented to him. He fired and tested new rifles on the White House grounds. As a young man, he had mastered not only the axe, but also the rifle. Scientific innovation and engineering marvels drew his attention. One Illinois friend wrote that Lincoln "was contemplative rather than speculative[.] He wanted something solid to rest upon, and hence his bias for mathematics and the physical sciences[.]"[70]

Both leaders were on the lookout for more than new weapons.[71] Churchill concerned himself with both offensive and defensive techno-logical innovations; he wrote of the "distaste for novel devices so often found in professional soldiers."[72] Churchill's official biographer, Martin Gilbert, observed: "Churchill's ability to find, encourage and sustain individuals who he knew would make a significant contribution to the war effort was an important feature of his war leadership."[73] The prime minister, for example, protected Percy Hobart, a tank warfare special-ist who designed new motorized vehicles for World War II. Hobart had been isolated as an eccentric inventor, but Churchill recruited him in the face of conventional army opposition, arguing it was necessary "to try men of force and vision and not to be exclusively confined to those who are judged thoroughly safe by conventional standards."[74] Geoffrey Best wrote: "No other conceivable Prime Minister would have paid so much personal attention to the military uses of science and technology, and no other could have had the same earlier experience of inventing, making and using munitions of war. He had an instinctive feel for the qualities of weaponry."[75]

Lincoln developed a close relationship with an inventive naval offi-cer, John A. Dahlgren, creator of the "Dahlgren gun" and commandant of the Washington Navy Yard. After the battle between the Confeder-ate *Merrimack* and the Union *Monitor* on March 8–9, 1862, the presi-dent developed an inordinate faith in the ironclad monitors, which he believed could recapture the key Confederate port of Charleston. Early in World War II, Churchill exhibited a similar faith in battleships, which he believed were immune to attack from the air. Max Hastings wrote that optimistic battleship "deployment reflected his personal decision, their loss an indictment of his misplaced faith in 'castles of steel' amid oceans now dominated by air and submarine power."[76] The Japanese would disabuse the prime minister of his battleship conceit during the naval war in the Pacific.

Churchill would preoccupy himself with the capture of symboli-cally and strategically important Rome in 1943 and 1944, and Berlin in 1945. Lincoln focused on retaking Charleston, South Carolina, for sim-ilar reasons in the first half of 1863. Reluctantly, the president finally resigned himself to the fact that his admirals and generals could not bring it off, but military assaults on Charleston would continue unsuc-cessfully through 1864. Union troops surrounded the city in early 1865;

Charleston finally surrendered on February 18. Taking Rome from a superior German army would prove even harder, but Churchill pressed his generals to capture the city by the end of 1943. "It would be impossible for us to forgo the capture of Rome," Churchill declared at the Teheran conference. "To do so would be regarded on all sides as a crushing defeat, and the British Parliament would not tolerate the idea for a moment."[77] He and Brooke insisted upon its capture prior to any invasion of southern France. Allied forces landed in Italy in September 1943, but they did not take Rome until June 4, 1944, two days before D-Day. It was U.S. General Mark Clark who opted to capture Rome, rather than to pursue the fleeing German army. But Generals Eisenhower and Marshall had agreed to "forget Rome" as strategically superfluous.[78] The slow-moving Clark later admitted he had been moved by the same political symbolism that sometimes influenced Churchill's judgment: "I and all my commanders were always thinking that 'if we could just capture Rome because it's such a big milestone' . . . there was always the feeling that Rome was certainly a great prize and that the sooner we stepped out and got it, then we were in a new and final phase of the war."[79] In defense of the Brooke and Churchill strategy, the airfields north of Rome could be used to bomb southern Germany, and the Italian campaign did tie up crack German troops that could not be used on other critical fronts.

Lincoln and Churchill grappled with fundamentally different historical, economic, and demographic situations, but they used similar problem-solving techniques. "Facts are better than dreams," said Churchill in his memoirs of World War II.[80] "Lincoln knew that numbers, material resources, and sea power were on his side," noted historian T. Harry Williams. "He grasped immediately the advantage that numbers gave the North and urged his generals to keep up a constant pressure on the whole strategic line of the Confederacy until a weak spot was found—and a break-through could be made."[81] Only this war strategy could deny the rebels their defensive advantage of interior lines, by using railroad mobility to move reserves to threatened rebel battlefields.[82] Lincoln's strategy of attacking the rebels all along the entire battlefront would become General Grant's strategy in the spring of 1864. General Lee's unconditional surrender at Appomattox followed one year later. As military historian Correlli Barnett observed, Grant's final strategy had "more in common with Lincoln's thinking than with Grant's own earlier ideas."[83]

Neither Lincoln nor Churchill deferred to conventional wisdom. Innovative strategies appealed to them. Both seized upon information, statistics, and opinions from unorthodox sources. Lincoln quizzed most military visitors—regardless of rank—about their experiences and observations. "Lindemann's Statistical Department," wrote Geoffrey Best, "was central to Churchill's ambition that he should be able to keep an eye on the workings of every part of the war machine: he needed an overview of its week-by-week functioning, all the way from the blunt base where men and women and raw materials were poured into it to the sharp end where the fighting went on."[84] Most historians now agree with Eliot Cohen that "Churchill's war leadership rested in part on his broad strategic vision, and in part on the effect of his probing questions and efforts to animate each of the many parts of the war effort."[85] Churchill's detractors focus on his impulsiveness and his alleged strategic and tactical errors at the Dardanelles in World War I, as well as in Norway, Greece, Libya, and Italy during World War II.[86] After Britain broke Germany's Enigma code, the prime minister knew more about Nazi strategy, troop movements, and submarines than his generals and admirals on the line. Such intelligence could not always be used in battle, lest systematic Allied success tip off the Germans that their encrypted codes had been broken.[87] (Lincoln had nothing resembling Churchill's vast intelligence apparatus.)

Lincoln once confessed to a Republican governor that if he told Jefferson Davis "all I know, I couldn't give him much information that would be useful to him."[88] But Lincoln often masked his confident use of well-placed sources, spies, and informed intuition to guide Union strategy. At the onset of the Civil War, the president had discovered a tiny Union army and navy. In fact, much of the Union officer corps had betrayed their sworn oaths of allegiance to the Constitution and the Union, resigning to join the rebel insurrection in full knowledge that such action was treason. Moreover, Lincoln's Union commanders had little experience leading military operations, as most were junior officers in the army's most recent war, which had been fought in 1846, by a mix of ragtag and regular troops, to conquer Mexico.

With the doubtful exception of the Royal Air Force, Britain's military had not been adequately prepared for war by the government of Neville Chamberlain. The British army and navy had a very long, generally successful history of imperial engagements, but their total effort in World War I had been an exhausting stalemate. At the beginning of World

War II, the British army's strategy, equipment, command structure, and organization were surprisingly antiquated, given the hostile actions initiated by Mussolini, Hitler, and Stalin in the 1920s and 1930s. The intense pacifism of the interwar years had undermined preparations for hostilities. Equally important, the fantasy of perpetual peace persisted under the Kellogg-Briand Pact and the League of Nations. Outdated weapons stayed in production as World War II began. There was too little time and too little initiative to put more modern weapons into production. Historian Raymond Callahan described the "cult of gentlemanly amateurism" that characterized British army leadership. He wrote: "The British officer corps came almost literally from a different nation [the aristocracy] than the other ranks."[89] In Britain, the wellborn had always dominated the officer class and permanent civil service. Since the end of the Napoleonic Wars in 1815, small imperial wars had shaped Britain, the largest being the Crimean War of the 1850s, or the Boer Wars at the end of the nineteenth century. In contrast, during the American Civil War, many Union officers and generals were recruited from a more classless society, army generals often coming from the influential political class. Indeed, at the beginning of the Civil War, many officers were literally elected by Union enlisted men. Neither the elitism of the traditional British military system nor the democracy of American army customs would prove adequate to the challenges faced by Churchill and Lincoln.

Your despatches complaining that you are not properly sustained, while they do not offend me, do pain me very much. . . . I beg to assure you that I have never written you, or spoken to you, in greater kindness of feeling than now, nor with a fuller purpose to sustain you, so far as in my most anxious judgment, I consistently can. But you must act.[1]

ABRAHAM LINCOLN
to George B. McClellan
April 9, 1862

My attitude has always been that if the P.M. has lost confidence in you he should at once replace you. I have told him this several times because I felt he was losing confidence in you; and yet in spite of that I am sure, as I have already said twice, it would be disastrous for you to go now. It is odd how difficult it is to apply simple principles, such as trust or sack.[2]

CHIEF OF THE IMPERIAL GENERAL STAFF JOHN DILL
to General Archibald Wavell
May 21, 1941

VII.

Finding and Managing Generals

Abraham Lincoln and Winston Churchill knew they must have sound military advice; even more important, they required fighting generals with good judgment. Neither the president nor the prime minister expected deferential agreement from their generals, although Churchill could browbeat some, and Lincoln would become impatient with others. "Churchill considered that unless commanders had the stomach to fight him," wrote Max Hastings, "they were unlikely to fight the enemy."[3] But the prime minister often exhausted his Chiefs of Staff (COS) in argument, even late into the night, the Chiefs knowing they must rise early in the morning. Churchill's probing questions provoked British generals, admirals, and their civilian counterparts. David Lloyd George had once told Clement Attlee: "There's Winston—he has half a dozen solutions to it and one of them is right, but the trouble is he does not know which it is." Attlee commented in his memoirs that "Churchill does need men around him who, while ready to support a good idea, however novel, are prepared on occasions to take an emphatic line against a bad one."[4]

Marshal of the Royal Air Force Charles Portal made the same point about his relations with the prime minister: "I had to disagree very forcibly with some proposal of his and used language which would have been more polite if I had had more time to choose my words. During my tirade he fixed me with a glassy stare and at the end when I said I was sorry if I had seemed rude, a broad smile appeared across his face and he said: 'You know, in war you don't have to be nice, you only have to be right.'"[5] Portal was often right. The American chiefs admired him. Historian Geoffrey Best wrote: "It was an admirable feat of Churchill's to have picked winning teams of warriors and ministers and to have presided over them and a cohesive national war-effort, despite having to work with less than ideal materials: for example, industrial obsolescence, a bankrupted economy, awkward allies, an army that had to be built up almost from scratch, and an Empire less united and enthusiastic than he liked to think."[6]

Churchill had been impatient to build a coherent military team. General Edmund Ironside was Chief of the Imperial General Staff (CIGS) when Churchill became prime minister on May 10. Shortly thereafter, Ironside was named Commander of the Home Forces; John Dill replaced Ironside as CIGS.[7] "It is difficult to tackle Winston when he is in one of his go-getter humours," Ironside wrote on July 9, 1940. Ten days later, Ironside was called to see Secretary of War Anthony Eden, who "told me that the Cabinet wished to have someone with late experience of the war" as commander in chief for Home Forces—namely General Alan Brooke, whose views about a mobile defense strategy were in accord with Churchill's own. In his diary, Ironside wrote: "Cabinets have to make decisions in times of stress. I don't suppose that Winston liked doing it, for he is always loyal to his friends."[8]

"[P]erhaps [Churchill's] greatest weakness was not intellectual but emotional," wrote historian Raymond Callahan. "He was a confrontational and aggressive person who obviously had struggled in his youth with concerns about his own physical toughness and courage."[9] The prime minister's boyhood letters confirm this observation. He would fulfill his ambition for glory in war as a cavalry officer, proving his courage in battle. His confidence grew rapidly as he mastered the fear of death in battle that must seize every soldier in war. The taller, muscular, tougher Lincoln had been one of the strongest men in every frontier community in which he lived. As he matured, he learned to persuade opponents rather than to intimidate them. Later, the president "skillfully managed both his cabinet and his generals, and even Congress, where he had to maintain a working majority if the war was to be won," wrote historian Mackubin T. Owens. "He did not hesitate to overrule his advisers, both military and civilian."[10] As head of government, head of state, and commander in chief, the president's inherent Constitutional authority was greater than that of the prime minister, whose force of personality strengthened his military powers.

Despite his military education at Sandhurst, Churchill did not respect many British generals; often they reciprocated. "God knows where we would be without him," noted General Brooke, "but God knows where we shall go with him!"[11] Brooke, who was appointed to replace Dill as Chief of the Imperial General Staff in December 1941, came from an aristocratic clan of fighting Ulstermen who had served as army officers of the Empire for twelve generations. He and Churchill often clashed because, as the prime minister complained, there was "no give" in Brooke.[12] Churchill needed Brooke's self-confident strength, because the prime minister intimidated lesser men. In July 1940, a contentious military staff meeting transpired at Chequers during a weekend dubbed "The Mad Hatter's Dinner Party" by one senior general. Churchill declared: "You soldiers are all alike: you have no imagination."[13] The evening "included remarkable [Churchillian] rudeness . . . to the Chief of the Imperial General Staff, General Sir John Dill; and an ostentatious display of [the prime minister's] confidence in the judgement of the civilians present . . . the purpose of which could only have been to humiliate the professional soldiers," wrote historian Geoffrey Best. The generals accepted their lot, but they chafed under the rough treatment from the prime minister.[14] Correlli Barnett wrote: "Churchill's treatment of close colleagues could oscillate between a thoughtful kindness and, on occasion, a curiously brutal insensitivity to their feelings."[15] His faithful military aide, General Hastings Ismay, wrote: "He made a practice of bombarding commanders with telegrams on every kind of topic, many of which might seem irrelevant and superfluous."[16]

Lincoln had little of Churchill's choleric temperament, nor his occasional imperious insensitivity, but he proved himself Churchill's equal in managing a war of national survival. Though firm and often critical of his generals, Lincoln almost never treated them with contempt. He was a better listener, rarely emotional in their presence. Most of Lincoln's new generals came either from civilian life or from an army in which few had ranked above major before the Civil War. Most professional officers had little experience with civilian oversight or wartime operations. Union General George B. McClellan, a star at West Point and a success as a railroad executive, was as haughty toward Lincoln as Churchill could be with General Dill. Shortly after he was named to command the Army of the Potomac in August 1861, McClellan wrote his wife: "I almost think that were I to win some small success now I could become Dictator or anything else that might please me—but nothing of that kind would please me—I *won't* be Dictator. Admirable self denial!"[17]

Churchill's self-absorption paled by comparison with the self-centered arrogance of McClellan. By the end of October 1862, President Lincoln more than once prompted McClellan to attack the Confederate army. Patiently, the commander in chief wrote McClellan: "Your despatches of night before last, yesterday, & last night, all received. I am much pleased with the movement of the Army. When you get entirely across the river let me know. What do you know of the enemy?"[18] The same day, McClellan wrote his wife:

> It will not do for me to visit Washn now—the tone of the telegrams I receive from the authorities is such as to show that they will take advantage of anything possible to do me all the harm they can & if I went down I should at once be accused by the Presdt of purposely delaying the movement. . . . [19]

John Dill had no such paranoia, nor did he indulge in the delusions of grandeur characteristic of McClellan. Indeed, Dill was too quiet and reserved for the pugnacious prime minister. "I live a very hectic life," Dill wrote, adding philosophically, "Most of it is spent trying to prevent stupid things being done rather than in doing clever things! However that is rather the normal life of a Chief of Staff."[20] General Leslie Hollis recalled that Dill

> was a man of extreme sensitivity, and in 1941, after a year of disasters to British arms, he was so tired mentally that sometimes he could not concentrate on the business in hand at the Chiefs of Staff meetings, and would sit asking totally irrelevant questions. In his reaction to the grave situation, Dill stood in contrast to the other Chiefs of Staff. Admiral of the Fleet Dudley Pound, for instance, who all this time had to contend with the seriousness of the war at sea, was imperturbable; Air Marshal Sir Charles Portal, too, seemed well on top of the job, and never showed any outward sign of disturbance although he was acutely aware of the urgency of the situation.[21]

Historian Reginald W. Thompson observed that "Dill bore the brunt of Churchill's tirades, but very soon he began to show signs of great weariness and strain. In 1940–41 nothing could be squandered, nothing could be irresponsibly committed to any venture unless absolutely vital to the security of the nation, and it was General Dill's job to preserve Britain's slender resources."[22]

Thus, conflict was inevitable between Churchill, who wanted action with Britain's slender resources, and Dill, who would conserve them for a long struggle. With France defeated in June 1940, Great Britain faced Nazi Germany alone. Eden recalled that in July 1940:

> My discussions with the Prime Minister were embarrassed at this time by what I feared was his increasingly critical attitude towards the C.I.G.S., of whom I thought highly. Sir John Dill had an exceptionally fine mind, but he could also be tense. While he was always correct in his attitude to the Prime Minister, he was not so ready to adapt his moods to those of Churchill, which could change with bewildering if engaging rapidity. Dill never lacked personal charm, but it was not in his character to be aware of it, still less to employ it to ease any discussion about which he cared.[23]

Dill was already afflicted in 1940–1941 with the exhausting anemia that eventually cost him his life in 1944. Dill became further distracted by the deteriorating condition of his wife, who suffered a number of strokes before her death in December 1940.[24] In July, John Colville wrote in his diary:

> Winston is displeased with the War Office. In a letter to [then Secretary of War] Eden complaining of a number of things, he says: "I do not think we are having the help from General Dill which we hoped for at the time of his appointment, and he strikes me as being very tired, disheartened and over-impressed with the might of Germany." It is a pity, because no man has greater charm or was expected to give greater confidence.[25]

About two weeks earlier, Clementine Churchill had written her husband:

> My Darling Winston. I must confess that I have noticed a deterioration in your manner; & you are not so kind as you used to be.
> It is for you to give the Orders & if they are bungled—except for the King, the Archbishop of Canterbury & the Speaker, you can sack anyone & everyone—Therefore with this terrific power

you must combine urbanity, kindness and if possible Olympic [sic] calm. You used to quote:—'*On ne règne sur les âmes que par le calme*' [One rules the souls of men only by calm]—I cannot bear that those who serve the Country and yourself should not love as well as admire and respect you—

Besides you won't get the best results by irascibility & rudeness. They *will* breed either dislike or a slave mentality—(Rebellion in War time being out of the question!)[26]

The tension between Dill and Churchill came to a head in November 1941. "The world is upside-down for me," Dill told General John Kennedy. "I am to go. The Prime Minister told me last night. Brooke is to be C.I.G.S."[27] General Brooke, who had skillfully commanded an army corps with the British Expeditionary Force during the fall of France, was a tested battle commander. He would skirmish with Churchill until 1945. Dill had proved insufficiently aggressive at war and in council with Churchill. The tough, tactless, abrupt, straightforward, fast-talking, obstinate, cerebral, energetic Brooke would prove almost *too* pugnacious for Churchill's taste.[28] One military aide wrote that Brooke "would speak so quickly that Churchill sometimes said he couldn't follow what he did say. From my experience it was usually something he didn't want to hear!"[29] Nevertheless, Churchill now had his military team in place. Dr. Charles Wilson admired Brooke, but noted: "It was soon plain that they were not designed by nature to work together in double harness."[30] But they did so until victory—a testimony to Churchill's character and his recognition of merit. After the war, the relationship waned.

In October 1940, while he was still commanding the Home Forces, Brooke recorded Churchill's actions and words at a military conference:

When we were all assembled he shoved his chin out in his aggressive way and, staring hard at me, said: "I had instructed you to prepare a detailed plan for the capture of Trondheim, with a commander appointed and ready in every detail. What have you done? You have instead submitted a masterly treatise on all the difficulties and on all the reasons why this operation should not be carried out." He then proceeded to cross-question me for nearly two hours on most of the minor points of appreciation. I repeatedly tried to bring him back to the main reason—the lack of air-support. He avoided this issue and selected arguments such as: "You state that you will be confronted by frosts and thaws which will render mobility difficult. How can you account for such a statement?"

Brooke called it a "very unpleasant gruelling to stand up to in a full room, but excellent training for what I had to stand up to on many occasions in later years."[31]

Early in the Civil War, Union naval officer David D. Porter observed how McClellan rudely caused Lincoln to wait when the president had come to the general's headquarters. When Porter protested the delay, McClellan shot back: "Well, let the Commander-in-chief wait, he has no business to know what is going on."[32] McClellan's vanity had been inflated after he had been appointed to command the Army of the Potomac in August 1861. Historian Allen C. Guelzo wrote: "McClellan had at first been flattered by the attention paid to him by official Washington, but the more he listened and believed the complimentary nonsense heaped upon him by the press, the bureaucrats, and the politicians, the more he began to believe himself superior to all three."[33] The president was willing that McClellan should become a military hero—so long as he earned it through decisive action.[34] When McClellan failed to act during the next five months, discontent in official Washington grew rapidly. McClellan's contempt for his superiors grew as well. "All quiet on the Potomac" became a derisive metaphor for McClellan's inaction. Historian Donald Stoker wrote: "The longer McClellan delayed, the more he became a political liability to an administration that had far too many of these already."[35] The general's arrogance masked his fear of failure. He had no clear plan of action, nor did he have the will to attack. The president proved he could be patient, even with insubordination, if only McClellan would engage the rebels in battle. (His refusal to share his plans with the president was military conduct that Churchill would never tolerate. McClellan would have been cashiered at once.) As military historian John Keegan concluded, "McClellan was psychologically deterred from pushing action to the point of result. Fearing failure, he did not try to win."[36]

When McClellan would not fight, Lincoln's patience ran out. McClellan would ultimately be removed in November 1862, not least because Lincoln's strategic objective was the destruction of the Confederate army, and thereby the rebellion; McClellan saw his objective as

Richmond.[37] The commander in chief had written McClellan on February 3: "You and I have distinct, and different plans for a movement of the Army of the Potomac—yours to be down the Chesapeake, up the Rappahannock to Urbana, and across land to the terminus of the Railroad on the York River—, mine to move directly to a point on the Railroad South West of Manassas." Lincoln then systematically interrogated McClellan about the relative wisdom of his plan.[38] The president insisted that to gain territory or capture a particular location was not the strategic goal of the Union army. The goal was to engage the rebel army, then destroy it in battle. Without its army, the Confederacy must yield.

Lincoln's effort to anticipate the opponent's next move defined him as a natural strategist—a skill he had developed as a professional litigator and in political debates. By hard study and analysis of the geography of battle, Lincoln became a practiced strategist in war. "With no knowledge of the theory of war, no experience in war, and no technical training, Lincoln, by the power of his mind, became a fine strategist," wrote military historian T. Harry Williams. "He was a better natural strategist than were most of the trained soldiers. He saw the big picture of the war from the start. The policy of the government was to restore the Union by force; the strategy perforce had to be offensive. Lincoln knew that numbers, material resources, and sea power were on his side, so he called for 400,000 troops and proclaimed a naval blockade of the Confederacy. These were bold and imaginative moves for a man dealing with military questions for the first time."[39] President Lincoln confronted a rebel army better prepared for war; the rebels had for years been planning for war. Indeed, at the outset of the Civil War, according to the rebel General P. G. T. Beauregard, the Confederacy had every reason to expect to win the war. "No people ever warred for independence with more relative advantage than the Confederates," commented Beauregard.[40]

Based on his role in World War I and his pre–World War II experience in parliamentary opposition, Churchill had become an acknowledged expert on war mobilization—expertise cited by those who supported his elevation to prime minister. President Lincoln, by contrast, was an amateur at war—especially compared to Confederate President Jefferson Davis, who had been educated at West Point, led troops in the Mexican-American War, and served as secretary of war under President Franklin Pierce in the mid-1850s. Lincoln would master the skills of a strategist, in part by borrowing the best military books from the Library

Winfield Scott, 1862

Gilder Lehrman Collection, GLC00559.12

of Congress. By study of military strategy and warfare, Lincoln "worked hard to master this subject, just as he had done to become a lawyer," wrote historian James McPherson.[41]

The more Lincoln studied key military classics in 1861, the more confident he grew in his own strategy for victory—even as his doubts about specific generals increased. He concluded early that the Union war strategy required unified and coordinated military action. "It has been said that one bad general is better than two good ones; and the saying is true, if taken to mean no more than that an army is better directed by a single mind, though inferior, than by two superior ones, at variance, and cross-purposes with each other," argued Lincoln in his First Annual Message to Congress in December 1861. "And the same is true, in all joint operations where those engaged, *can* have none but a common end in view, and *can* differ only as to the choice of means. In a storm at sea, no one on board *can* wish the ship to sink; and yet, not unfrequently, all go down together, because too many will direct, and no single mind can be allowed to control."[42] The commander in chief became the guiding mind of Union war strategy. In March 1864, based on Grant's winning performance at Vicksburg on the Mississippi and earlier in Tennessee, Lincoln would delegate supreme command to Grant. Grant would embrace Lincoln's strategy of attacking on all rebel fronts at once. It was a winning strategy, based in part on overwhelming brute force. (Churchill could not implement such a brute force strategy until FDR and Stalin joined the Grand Alliance.)

The outnumbered rebels—having shorter interior lines than those of the extended Union front—were finally denied the opportunity to move troops from a quiet theater to an embattled front. Under the Lincoln-Grant strategy, all rebel armies on the entire battlefront would be simultaneously engaged and pinned down. But at the end of December 1861, implementation of Lincoln's war strategy awaited new leadership in the field. General McClellan had taken to bed with typhoid fever. The president, already doubtful of McClellan, grew anxious that his supreme commander had no strategy for victory. Lincoln himself had been forced by circumstances to direct military operations in the west. The hesitant General Henry W. Halleck, commander of troops along the Mississippi River, would receive his orders and strategic objectives from the commander in chief.[43]

In January 1862, Lincoln summarized his military strategy in a letter to General Don Carlos Buell, stating his

> general idea of this war to be that we have the *greater* numbers, and the enemy has the *greater facility* of concentrating forces upon points of collision; that we must fail, unless we can find some way of making *our* advantage an over-match for *his*; and that this can only be done by menacing him with superior forces at *different* points, at the *same* time; so that we can safely attack, one, or both, if he makes no change; and if he *weakens* one to *strengthen* the other, forbear to attack the strengthened one, but seize, and hold the weakened one, gaining so much. To illustrate, suppose last summer, when Winchester ran away to re-inforce Mannassas [sic], we had forborne to attack Mannassas, but had seized and held Winchester. I mention this to illustrate, and not to criticise. I did not lose confidence in McDowell, and I think less harshly of [Robert] Patterson than some others seem to. In application of the general rule I am suggesting, every particular case will have its modifying circumstances, among which the most constantly present, and most difficult to meet, will be the want of perfect knowledge of the enemies' movements. This had its part in the Bull-Run case; but worse, in that case, was the expiration of the terms of the three months men. Applying the principle to your case, my idea is that Halleck shall menace Columbus, and "down river" generally; while you menace Bowling-Green, and East Tennessee. If the enemy shall concentrate at Bowling-Green [Kentucky], do not retire from his front; yet do not fight him there, either, but seize Columbus and East Tennessee, one or both, left exposed by the concentration at Bowling-Green. It is matter of no small anxiety to me and one which I am sure you will not over-look, that the East Tennessee line, is so long, and over so bad a road.[44]

Still, Lincoln delegated tactical decisions to his local commanders: "I am very anxious that, in case of General [Don Carlos] Buell's moving toward Nashville, the enemy shall not be greatly reenforced, and I think there is danger he will be, from Columbus," Lincoln wrote Halleck. "It seems to me that a real or feigned attack upon Columbus from up-river at the same time would either prevent this or compensate for it by throwing Columbus into our hands. I wrote General Buell a letter similar to this, meaning that he and you shall communicate and act in concert, unless it be your judgment and his that there is no necessity for it. You and he will understand much better than I how to do it. Please do not lose time in this matter."[45] Lincoln believed he knew what his generals should do. Moreover, he knew the geography of the West. But the commander in chief rarely presumed to tell them how to implement his general strategy, believing that generals on the spot, in the field, were better equipped to decide tactics.

President Lincoln's sense of urgency—especially about when to engage the enemy in battle—was greater than that of his generals. His strategic goal was to disable completely the rebel army. So he would press his generals into battle. If successful, a shattered Confederate rebellion might temporarily retain its defenseless capital, but the Civil War should come to an end. Still, Lincoln rarely acted precipitously, even when aggravated by dilatory and refractory generals in the field. In contrast to Churchill's impatience to sack commanders he deemed inadequate, Lincoln gave generals more chances to succeed, not least because competent Union officers were so few. In November 1862, the president made this point when he wrote General Carl Schurz, a German-born politician:

> I certainly have been dissatisfied with the slowness of Buell and McClellan; but before I relieved them I had great fears I should not find successors to them, who would do better; and I am sorry to add, that I have seen little since to relieve those fears. I do not clearly see the prospect of any more rapid movements. I fear we shall at last find out that the difficulty is in our case, rather than in particular generals. I wish to disparage no one—certainly not those who sympathize with me; but I must say I need success more than I need sympathy, and that I have not seen the so much greater evidence of getting success from my sympathizers, than from those who are denounced as the contrary. It does seem to me that in the field the two classes have been very much alike, in what they have done, and what they have failed to do.[46]

Lincoln would cut to the heart of McClellan's weakness when he wrote him on April 9, 1862: "By delay the enemy will relatively gain on you—that is he will gain faster by *fortifications* and *reinforcements* than you will by reinforcements alone." He concluded: "The country will not fail to note—is now noting—that the present hesitation to move upon an intrenched enemy, is but the story of Manassas repeated."[47] Both McClellan and Buell were not only slow to act, but they were slow to enforce the increasingly strict antislavery laws passed by Congress and implemented by the president.[48]

Both Lincoln and Churchill would try to base their judgments on facts, as well as on what they believed was their superior understanding of military reality. Historian Ronald Lewin wrote that the prime minister "made it a matter of principle that he should be supplied with such intelligence 'raw'—that is, not in the doctored precis of staff assessment but as it had come to hand. Thus he felt, often with good reason, that in his central position he was exceptionally equipped for keeping himself 'in the know'" and for making military judgments.[49] Like Lincoln, who visited the telegraph office in the neighboring War Department at least once a day for up-to-date military information from the field, Churchill, too, was obsessed with news from the war fronts. Historian Carlo D'Este wrote: "Unlike Hitler and Stalin, Churchill insisted on being informed of everything that took place regardless of whether the information was positive or negative."[50]

Resourceful action, based on perceived opportunities, was the common imperative of both the president and the prime minister. Churchill was confident, perhaps too confident, in his expertise in military affairs, never more so than at the outset of the war. He would yield quickly to no one—not even to accomplished generals and admirals. From Churchill streamed detailed "minutes," which often drove his subordinates to distraction (and bitter complaints in their diaries). The search for the right generals and implementation of his strategy preoccupied Lincoln. The experienced Churchill had managed the Admiralty at the beginning of the First World War, and again as the Second World War broke out. He had even been secretary of war at the end of World War I. Given his background and temperament, the prime minister was tempted to micromanage the army generals, not least because he had little respect for some, no faith in others, confidence in few.

Churchill and Lincoln labored mightily to find generals and admirals with strategic understanding and tactical initiative—fighting men with vision. The prime minister preferred those who were articulate and could not be intimidated. Both leaders inherited an officer corps whose quality they deemed a problem to solve. In peace, America had maintained a very small officer corps. In the decade before the Civil War, many West Point officers had left the peacetime military for private enterprise. Much of Britain's officer corps had been killed or wounded in World War I. Early in the war the prime minister rightly worried that neither British officers nor British soldiers were ready to fight the well-trained German army. As a British officer on the Belgian-French border in 1915–1916, he had observed firsthand the professional training and discipline of the German army. Now he observed it in action again. Humiliating British defeats early in World War II—in France, in Greece, in Libya, in Southeast Asia—suggested that British soldiers might never measure up in battle to German soldiers, the leadership of German officers, or to their ruthless Japanese counterparts. Similarly, Confederate victories and bravado at the beginning of the war not only demoralized the Union political class; Union defeats also convinced some European onlookers that Confederate independence was inevitable. The astonishing Nazi blitzkrieg in France and in eastern Europe suggested to some that German arms were invincible. The bold Nazi remilitarization of the Rhineland, the *Anschluss* with Austria, and the dismemberment of Czechoslovakia intimidated much of the English political class.

Lincoln and Churchill would establish a special bond with their soldiers. Both warlords respected their fighting men. Samuel Beckwith, General Grant's personal telegraph operator, recalled: "The President was . . . immensely popular with the soldiers everywhere. All of them, from the generals down to privates, knew that in him they had a sympathetic friend, a kind and wise protector. The names bestowed upon him, 'Uncle Abe,' 'Father Abraham,' 'Old Abe,' and the like, were terms of genuine affection. The boys felt that he was with them and of them. Stories of his great tenderness of heart were common property of the camp, and the human side of this tall, ungainly, homely man brought him very close to us all."[51] In October 1862, after the president reviewed McClellan's troops, one soldier reported that Lincoln's smile "touched the hearts of the bronzed, rough-looking men more than one can express. It was like an electric shock. It fled from elbow to elbow; and, with one loud cheer which made the air ring, the suppressed feeling gave vent, conveying to the good President that his smile had gone home, and found a ready response."[52] Civil War historian Bell Wiley reviewed thousands of Union soldier letters, and concluded that "it is doubtful if any war president in American history ever elicited as pervasive and as enthusiastic admiration among the fighting forces as did the railsplitter from Illinois."[53] The fighting men knew Lincoln's reputation as a just and merciful commander in chief, who generally vetoed the death penalty for soldiers whom their officers had recommended for desertion.[54]

Once President Lincoln had promulgated the Emancipation Proclamation on January 1, 1863, blacks became eligible to enlist. They, too, bonded with the commander in chief. Soldiers in the First Arkansas Colored Regiment composed lyrics to be sung to the tune of "John Brown's Body":

> We heard the Proclamation, master hush it as he will.
> The bird he sing it to us, hoppin' on the cotton hill.
> And the possum up the gum tree, he couldn't keep it still,
> As he went climbing on. (Chorus)
> They said, "Now colored brethren, you shall be forever free
> From the first of January, eighteen hundred, sixty-three"
> We heard it in the river going rushing to the sea.
> As it went sounding on. (Chorus)
> Father Abraham has spoken and the message has been sent.
> The prison doors he opened, and out the pris'ners went,
> To join the sable army of the "African Descent."
> As we go marching on. (Chorus).[55]

Soldier loyalty and devotion to Lincoln decisively influenced the president's reelection in 1864. Almost 80 percent of the soldiers cast their vote for President Lincoln, although the conditions under which they voted discouraged ballots for his Democratic opponent—General McClellan.[56]

In 1942, British troops—like Union troops in 1862—were desperate for military success. The early British success in late 1940 of Operation COMPASS in North Africa would soon be reversed by German advances. In February 1941, German General Erwin Rommel and the "Afrika Korps" had landed in North Africa. The "Desert Fox" would prove a formidable threat to the Allies in North Africa from 1941 to 1943, just as the intrepid tactics of Robert E. Lee and Stonewall Jackson threatened the Union in 1862–1863. Like the fast-moving Confederate generals, Rommel could hit quickly and hard. Rommel "brought a fresh set of rules to desert fighting," wrote historian John Strawson. "With a combination of speed, daring, surprise and great tactical skill, together with a penchant, not shared by his British counterparts, for leading from the front, Rommel succeeded in bundling the British right out of Cyrenaica and back to Egypt, leaving only the garrison of the port of Tobruk, isolated and besieged."[57]

Churchill himself later wrote: "Rommel proved himself a master in handling mobile formations, especially in regrouping rapidly after an operation and following up success. He was a splendid military gambler, dominating the problems of supply and scornful of opposition." Rommel's "ardour and daring inflicted grievous disasters upon us, but he deserves the salute which I made him—and not without some reproaches from the public—in the House of Commons in January 1942, when I said of him, 'We have a very daring and skillful opponent against us, and may I say across the havoc of war, a great general.'"[58] Superior British leadership had defeated the Italians in Libya in the winter of 1940–1941, but superior German tanks, strategy, and leadership overcame the British in the spring of 1941.

With his smashing victories, Rommel had foreclosed the early and "unique opportunity" for Britain to inflict a major defeat on the Axis. According to Correlli Barnett, "The Prime Minister was to spend eighteen months attempting to retrieve it by egging on his commanders-in-chief in the Middle East to premature desert offensives. The cool reaction of [Archibald] Wavell and later [Claude] Auchinleck to these demands lost both generals their reputations with him; to Churchill their closely reasoned replies proclaimed tiredness and defeatism."[59] Many of Lincoln's generals lost their reputations with the president for similar reasons. He tired of repeated excuses. Even when shocked by the negative turn of events, neither Lincoln nor Churchill allowed themselves to indulge defeatism. The unrelenting pressure of war challenged the resilient president and prime minister to the limit. They recovered quickly from setbacks.

For Lincoln and Churchill, military breakthroughs would come in the autumn of 1862 and the autumn of 1942. For the president, one turning point was the Union's bloody victory at the Battle of Antietam on September 17, 1862, after which the invading Confederates under Robert E. Lee retreated from Maryland across the Potomac River into Virginia. Antietam—the bloodiest single day of the war—was crucial. There, Union forces turned back the invasion of Maryland by an aggressive rebel army. It was the last battle in which General McClellan would command Union forces. When "Little Mac" failed to follow up the Antietam victory and to engage the smaller Confederate army, as it retreated across the Potomac into Virginia, Lincoln's patience ran out. He replaced the "Little Napoleon" immediately after the congressional and state elections of November 1862.

During the second half of 1942, fortune smiled on Churchill. He had finally found his two primary commanders in North Africa—Generals Harold Alexander and Bernard Montgomery. They would later become the top British generals for European operations. "Everybody said what a change there was since Montgomery had taken command," wrote the prime minister of the new commander of the Eighth Army in the summer of 1942. "I could feel the truth of this with joy and comfort." Churchill described the situation in Egypt when "Monty" first arrived in August: "The Army was reduced to bits and pieces and oppressed by a sense of bafflement and uncertainty."[60] Intimately familiar with U.S. Civil War battles, Churchill compared Montgomery to Stonewall Jackson, saying of the British general: "Either on the eve of a great battle, or while the struggle was actually in progress, always I have found the same buoyant, vigorous, efficient personality with every aspect of the vast operation in his mind, and every unit of mighty armies in his grip."[61] Unlike Stonewall Jackson, Montgomery was often cautious to a fault, but he would give Churchill a desperately needed victory.

The turning point came for Britain in the Second Battle of El Alamein of late October and early November 1942, in which the Eighth army under Montgomery drove the Germans out of Egypt and Libya, toward Tunisia.[62] Churchill rejoiced: "This noble Desert Army, which has never doubted its power to beat the enemy, and whose pride had suffered cruelly from retreats and disasters which they could not understand, regained in a week its ardour and self-confidence. Historians may explain Tobruk. The Eighth Army has done better; it has avenged it."[63] Victories at Antietam in Maryland and at El Alamein in Libya demonstrated that Union and British armies could fight bravely—and win. The prime minister explained in February 1943: "The Desert Army is the product of three years of trial and error and the continued perfecting of transport, communications, supplies and signals, and the rapid moving forward of airfields and the like"—not to mention three years of field training for the men-in-arms.[64] For Lincoln, Churchill, and their generals, mobile war on such a scale was unique in their national experience.

In the fall of 1942, Allied Operation TORCH in western North Africa followed the successful British attack against El Alamein to the east. General Eisenhower commanded the Anglo-American amphibious invasion of Vichy-held Morocco and Algeria. Coordinated and hard-fought military operations would eventually eliminate all Axis military power across North Africa by the spring of 1943. Victory opened wide the strategic Mediterranean and the Suez Canal—the vital link to the British Empire in the Middle East and Asia. Churchill had used his influence on President Franklin Roosevelt, mobilizing all his persuasive powers to get American agreement to focus on North Africa before invading northwestern Europe. In 1942, Churchill and Brooke believed the Allies unready to mount a cross-channel invasion of France.[65] The American military chiefs, led by Marshall, strongly disagreed. Persuaded by Churchill, FDR overruled Marshall. On July 25, 1942, the Allies agreed to invade northwestern Africa in the autumn. Churchill aimed to keep the Germans occupied in North Africa—in part to relieve German pressure on Russia by diverting German troops from the Eastern front. In 1942–1943, American fighting units in England had not yet attained sufficient numbers, nor were they adequately trained for an invasion of France. Adequate shipping and landing craft were not yet available for the invasion of Normandy. Allied command of the Mediterranean, however, enabled convoys previously sailing the very long route around Africa by way of the Cape of Good Hope, to resupply military forces in the Middle East directly through the Mediterranean. Thus would scarce shipping become more available.

FDR did agree, against General Marshall's opposition, to Churchill's commonsense notion that if the Allies were not ready to fight the Germans in France, they must fight them somewhere else. In early September 1942, Roosevelt and Churchill agreed on a British-American division of labor for Operation TORCH. The prime minister had aimed to commit American war leadership to the defeat of Germany ahead of the defeat of imperial Japan. Churchill believed that the Russian armies might escape destruction by the *Wehrmacht* if the Allies could force Hitler to keep enough German divisions in the Mediterranean. It was in 1943 that the Allies would directly challenge major German arms in Italy.

The worldwide geographic scale of the strategic problems faced by Churchill dwarfed the continental scale of those encountered by Lincoln. Churchill's was truly a *world war*. Engaging multiple enemies was a *worldwide* exercise. Lincoln's was an immense continental war extending even beyond the Mississippi River, but the shortest road to victory remained the destruction of Robert E. Lee's rebel army on a line between Washington and Richmond—a distance of fewer than 100 miles. Still, the scope of intense Civil War operations extended from the Gulf of Mexico to the Ohio River, theaters where Union arms would prevail before Lee's surrender at Appomattox in April 1865. For the Allies in World War II, the path to victory over the Nazis in Western Europe stretched across the English Channel and from Russia on a not very straight line to Berlin—and across the vast Pacific Ocean to Tokyo. Churchill and Brooke—understanding in 1942 Allied insufficiency of troops, training, and landing craft—opposed a cross-channel invasion from 1940 to 1943. In the early days of the war, Churchill believed almost any military campaign was preferable to a direct assault on Germany through occupied France. Churchill decided wisely in this case.[66] The prime minister preferred to fight in Norway and Greece, or in Egypt and North Africa, or in Sicily and Italy.[67] He advocated flexibility; he chose to be opportunistic in his approach to strategy.[68] He would not waste opportunities as he saw them. "By the middle of 1942," wrote Geoffrey Best, "this had become a mantra in his arguments about operations in the Mediterranean theatre, to the increasing annoyance of his American allies who had one big idea [the cross-channel assault on German arms] and wanted to stick to it."[69] There was more of the zigzag fox in Churchill, much of the single-minded hedgehog in U.S. Generals Marshall and Eisenhower. The prime minister convinced himself the Mediterranean was the "soft underbelly" of Hitler's Europe. Italy would prove instead to be a hard torso. Still, Churchill and Brooke argued that there was little sense to head prematurely into the jaws of well-trained, experienced German armies astride France. Both believed correctly that the German army was then superior, and that insufficient resources were available to establish, maintain, and advance through a German-entrenched position in France on a long, heavily fortified line to Berlin.

The prime minister's military subordinates often disputed the wisdom of his projects, but his senior military staff agreed with him and would not rush Operation OVERLORD. Churchill's focus on invading Sicily and Italy made strategic sense if D-Day were to be postponed until mid-1944. The Balkans were essentially a military sideshow controlled by Marshal Josip Broz Tito. Greece, an ally that Britain ineffectively helped in 1941, became a distraction. American commanders would hold to their focus through 1942. "We were largely [in 1942] trying to get the president to stand pat on what he had previously agreed to," complained Marshall. "The President was always willing to do any sideshow and Churchill was always prodding him."[70] Temperamentally, FDR was more like Churchill—impulsive, loving the bold, unexpected stroke. However, Roosevelt was less organized, less informed, and less experienced in military affairs. In the early war years, FDR, often unprepared, was an easy target for the heroic, persuasive prime minister.

"I remember very well," wrote Eleanor Roosevelt of FDR, "his irritation at Mr. Churchill's determination that we should attack through Greece and the Balkans. Franklin said that would mean the loss of many men, though strategically it might be a help to Great Britain and might get us to Berlin before the Russians. However, he did not think that important and he was not going to risk so many men."[71] Secretary of War Henry L. Stimson recalled President Roosevelt explaining "what his views were in regard to the Balkans. He said he could not think of touching the Balkans unless the Russians got to a position in their invasion of Germany where they wanted us to join and act side by side with them."[72] In the latter part of the war, FDR would be keen to collaborate with Stalin, less with Churchill. By that time, FDR seemed more anti–British Empire, his ally by treaty, than he was wary of the expanding Soviet empire.

There was also in Roosevelt much of the shifty fox as he manipulated Stalin's demands to relieve the massive Nazi assault on Russia with a second front in Western Europe. (In England the popular call to "Start the Second Front Now" was much like the "On to Richmond" campaign at the beginning of the Civil War. It is now hard to appreciate how pro-Russian much of the British people were at that time. Churchill's response to the outcry for a second front was "Yes, we'll start—when we are ready."[73]) Marshall and Eisenhower would make ready. "For Churchill," wrote historian Geoffrey Best, "the purpose of the Italian

John Dill, 1941

© National Portrait Gallery, London

campaign was, first, to form a surrogate Second Front, engaging German divisions that might otherwise be fighting the Red Army; secondly, to facilitate assistance to the guerrilla armies engaging many German divisions in the Balkans; and, thirdly, less explicit but coming into clearer focus with every passing month, to drive on in due course from the north Italian plain towards Vienna."[74] The geography of Italy and the well-led German army stymied the Allied advance south of Rome under U.S. General Mark Clark, who was no match for General Kesselring and the difficult terrain.

Churchill's military leadership suffered sometimes from his unwillingness to recognize the logistical requirements of major operations and the limitations on available equipment for global warfare. In 1940–1941, Churchill had risked the security of Britain by sending tanks to the Middle East. But he did not then appreciate the problems of operating tanks in the deep sand of desert conditions, nor did he know the relative inferiority of British tanks to the German tanks—supported by their mobile antitank guns. Historian Raymond Callahan wrote that Churchill "was impatient with the logistic problems whose solution is the foundation of strategy, and this impatience produced the endless arguments over the ratio between 'teeth and tail' (that is, combat versus support formations)."[75] The prime minister's personal experience in the 1890s as a subaltern consisted of service in cavalry and rifle units, but his World War I experience prepared him for the logistics of large-scale operations, which in the abstract he well understood. General Ismay "also endured many lectures on the size of the 'tail' in the various theatres of war; but once, at least, he [Ismay] was able to hoist Churchill with his own petard, when in 1942 the latter was protesting about the huge quantity of vehicles being shipped to the Middle East," wrote historian Ronald Lewin. "Ismay quietly reminded the Prime Minister of what he himself had written long ago, in [Churchill's book] *The River War*: 'Victory is the beautiful bright-colored flower: Transport is the stem without which it would never have blossomed.'"[76]

There are further remarkable similarities between World War II during 1941–1945 and the Civil War during 1861–1865. Analogies are apparent in larger issues, and the similarities are striking in small but important details such as geography—once adjustments are made for scale and technology. For example, the Balkans were to Churchill as the mountains of eastern Tennessee were to Lincoln—preferred tactical objectives, even if preoccupation with these intractable areas infuriated and confounded their colleagues. The prime minister had a special interest in the Balkans, a bulwark of anti-Nazi sentiment, where his son Randolph fought bravely. Lincoln remained loyal to the latent Union sentiment in the South, especially to the antislavery yeomanry of the mountains of eastern Tennessee near Knoxville. In January 1862, Lincoln wrote to a Union general that "my distress is that our friends in East Tennessee are being hanged and driven to despair, and even now I fear, are thinking of taking rebel arms for the sake of personal protection. In this we lose the most valuable stake we have in the South."[77]

In August 1863, President Lincoln responded to a petition: "I do as much for East Tennessee as I would, or could, if my own home, and family were in Knoxville. The difficulties of getting a Union army into that region, and of keeping it there, are so apparant [sic]—so obvious—that none can fail to see them, unless it may be those who are driven mad and blind by their sufferings. Start by whatever route they may, their lines of supply are broken before they get half way."[78] In October 1863, Lincoln wrote two Knoxville residents worried that Union troops would be withdrawn: "You do not estimate the holding of East Tennessee more highly than I do. There is no *absolute* purpose of withdrawing our forces from it; and only a *contingent* one to withdraw them temporarily, for the purpose of not losing the position *permanently*. I am in great hope of not finding it necessary to withdraw them at all—particularly if you raise new troops rapidly for us there."[79]

Politically, Churchill had a distinct advantage as the parliamentary leader of a coalition government unencumbered by elections. No British general election would be held from November 1935 to July 1945, although by-elections for vacant seats occurred occasionally. Churchill commanded the bully pulpit of the House of Commons and the use of BBC radio. To his annoyance, the House refused him permission to use his parliamentary speeches directly on the radio, so the prime minister sometimes repeated his speeches later in the day. A major difference between the United Kingdom and the United States was that elections in the loyal North were not postponed because of the war—an important consideration for Lincoln. Local, state, and federal votes proceeded as scheduled throughout the war. "It was astonishing," wrote Churchill "that in the height of the ruthless [American] civil war all the process of election should be rigidly maintained."[80] President Lincoln held this fact to be proof of the strength of the American democracy. Rather than let the rebels overturn the Constitution, the commander in chief insisted that the Constitution required elections in peace and war. He set a precedent that would be followed by FDR in World War II.

Lincoln managed the uncertainty of two national elections (1862, 1864)—the telegraph his only electronic communications. John Hay reported on the president's response to a serenade on the day after his reelection in November 1864. Lincoln "wrote [it] late in the evening and read it from the window. 'Not very graceful' he said 'but I am growing old enough not to care much for the manner of doing things.'"[81] The president had declared: "We can not have free government without elections, and if the rebellion could force us to forgo, or postpone a national election, it might fairly claim to have already conquered and ruined us."[82]

A member of Parliament during four decades, Churchill would dominate the House of Commons throughout the war. He wrote that his government operated under "extraordinary powers" granted by act of Parliament in May 1940. In general terms of law, the powers granted by Parliament were absolute. The Act was to "include power by Order in Council to make such Defence Regulations making provision for requiring persons to place themselves, their services and their property at the disposal of His Majesty as appear to him to be necessary or expedient for securing the public safety, the defence of the Realm, the maintenance of public order, or the efficient prosecution of any war in which His Majesty may be engaged, or for maintaining supplies or services essential to the life of the community."[83] The prime minister's war leadership, argued historian Paul Johnson, was enabled in part by "the concentration of power in Churchill's person, with the backing of all parties, [and it] meant that there were never any practical or constitutional obstacles to the right decisions being taken."[84]

Both Lincoln and Churchill were effectively commanders in chief with full powers to control the war effort. Major General Hastings "Pug" Ismay, "a man of unfailing tact and good sense," served as Churchill's staff chief and liaison to the British Chiefs of Staff.[85] Ismay's "chief cleverness lay in knowing just how to treat the Prime Minister; how to bring him round to a necessary decision which he didn't like, how to break bad news to him, how to get his agreement when the Chiefs of Staff most wanted it," observed one Churchill secretary.[86] Ismay "provided an aura of personal attraction and unchallenged reliability which never palled," wrote John Colville. "Pug Ismay could be counted on, without appeasing either side beyond what was reasonable, to pour exactly the right measure of oil on the waters, to soothe and to explain." The even-tempered Ismay was a shrewd go-between. "As Churchill's staff officer, he was a functionary; as a member of the Chiefs of Staff, he could influence executive decisions; he never confused the two positions," wrote John Keegan.[87] As Ismay aide Leslie Hollis observed, Ismay "could easily have fallen foul of the Chiefs of Staff, but he never did; in fact, they would have been lost without him and his amazing gift for smoothing over clashes of temperaments. He got on equally well with Ministers, Service Chiefs, Civil Officials, Americans—everyone, in fact. He knew everything and he said little. As one who served as Ismay's No. 2 for thirteen years, I think I can say I knew him pretty well; he was indeed the wisest of old owls."[88]

Lincoln neither inherited nor created any of the elaborate command infrastructure with which Churchill surrounded himself. According to Leslie Hollis, the prime minister's military staff included "the Joint Planning Staff which consisted of the Directors of Plans of each of the Services, plus such groups as Strategical Planning Staff, the Executive Planning Staff, the Future Operational Planning Staff and, later on in the war, the Post-Hostilities Planning Staff, together with the Joint Intelligence Staff."[89] The president had no one comparable to Ismay; Lincoln never appointed a chief of staff as Roosevelt reluctantly did in World War II. Attorney General Edward Bates proposed to Lincoln in early 1862 that the president should have his own military staff. On January 10, 1862, Bates wrote in his diary: "I renewed formally, and asked that it be made a question before the Cabinet,—my proposition, often made heretofore—that the President as 'comm[an]der in Chief of the Army and Navy' do organize a *Staff* of his own, and assume to be in fact, what he is in law, the *Chief Commander*. His aid[e]s could save him a world of trouble and anxiety—collect and report to him all needed information, and keep him constantly informed, at a moment's warning—keep his military and naval books and papers—conduct his military correspondence,—and do his bidding generally 'in all the works of war[.]'" Bates believed that Lincoln could assume a broader role to "take and act out the powers of his place."[90] Lincoln may have needed such assistance, but he never took steps to establish such a structure. There was something in Lincoln's genius for command that preferred uncluttered

autonomy to consult whenever and whomever he pleased of whatever
rank, whenever he pleased. Staffs do help, but they also constrain. The
self-sufficient president did not shed the habits of the gifted loner on the
frontier. The resourceful prime minister, head of an empire, encompass-
ing one-quarter of the earth's landmass, embraced and consolidated the
procedures and powers of the "King's First Minister" at war.

As both defense minister and prime minister, Churchill, by act of
Parliament, wielded unprecedented wartime powers. Despite criticism inside and outside the War Cabinet, he insisted on keeping both
positions.[91] Churchill listened to his military chiefs and took the opinions of the War Cabinet into serious consideration. By tradition he was
required to bring issues and decisions before the cabinet. The prime
minister "was not a dictatorial leader, although he could be emphatic in
his requests and suggestions. If the Chiefs of Staff opposed any initiative
he proposed, it was abandoned. He had no power to overrule their col-
lective will. But on most occasions there was no such stark dichotomy,"
wrote Martin Gilbert.[92] In early November 1940, Churchill attached a
plaintive memo to an earlier "minute": "Although I bowed before the difficulties so industriously assembled by the Joint Planners in their report
of August 31st, and the general attitude of negation, I should be very
much obliged to the C.O.S. Committee if they would kindly read my
minute and see if there was not something in it after all."[93] The prime
minister respected his staff. Still, it took a very strong general to oppose
Churchill's will and arguments.

Both Lincoln and Churchill used cabinet meetings as sounding
boards for discussion of strategy. In the case of very controversial decisions, each leader could play devil's advocate in cabinet for the position
he actually doubted. Lincoln often read aloud important papers to the
cabinet. Navy Secretary Welles described a typical cabinet meeting in
January 1864: "At the Cabinet council only a portion were present. The
President in discussion narrated some stories, very apt, exhibiting wisdom and sense. He requested me to read an article in the *North American Review* [by James Russell Lowell], just received, on the policy of the
Administration, which he thought very excellent, except that it gave him
over-much credit."[94] The prime minister could use any meeting or meal
as a springboard for lectures and debates. He dominated most gatherings in which he participated—sometimes frustrating colleagues like
Anthony Eden. South African Prime Minister Jan Smuts, a longtime

friend of the prime minister, once said that under Churchill, British "Cabinet meetings are good stuff, but they are monologues."[95]

In the summer of 1944, First Sea Lord Andrew Cunningham complained of Churchill's obstinacy: "The trouble is the PM can never give way gracefully. He must always be right and if forced to give way gets vindictive and tries by almost any means to get his own back."[96] Churchill was not always realistic. A demanding, sometimes unreasonable taskmaster, the prime minister dismissed obstacles to his proposed offensive and defensive strategies. Robert Menzies, prime minister of Australia at the outbreak of the conflict, wrote that Churchill "does not seem to realise that men without proper equipment, and with nothing but rifles, do not count in modern war."[97] British military officials acknowledged other drawbacks in Churchill's leadership skills. They deplored his interference in and supervision of military operations.[98]

Above all, Churchill was a military activist. He drove commanders in battle; he drove them, too, in strategic discussion. "My personal authority even seemed to be enhanced by the uncertainties affecting several of my colleagues or would-be colleagues. I did not suffer from any desire to be relieved of my responsibilities," Churchill wrote in his memoirs. "All I wanted was compliance with my wishes after reasonable discussion."[99] The "uncertainties" of his colleagues could stem from intimidation. Labour Leader Clement Attlee defended Churchill as "a great War Minister. No one else could have done the job he did. But there was quite a lot of discussion at the Defence Committee. We surveyed the whole strategic field." Attlee recalled that Churchill did not always get his way. "He'd get some idea he wanted to press, and after we had considered it the rest of us would have to tell him there was no value in it. But you needed someone to prod the Chiefs of Staff. Winston was sometimes an awful nuisance . . . but he always accepted the verdict of the Chiefs of Staff."[100] (When the prime minister was away from London and Attlee chaired these meetings, they proceeded with more dispatch and less emotion.)

The Chiefs of Staff keenly felt the point of the prime minister's stick. "I am a prod," Churchill would say.[101] General Kennedy recalled an incident when "the Prime Minister summoned the Chiefs of Staff to discuss the plans we had drawn up for raids on the coast of Italy. The First Sea Lord said that these raids could not be carried out because the Admiralty was preoccupied with Japan. Churchill thereupon banged his papers on the table and walked out, saying, 'You frustrate me in all my offensive projects.'"[102] Friction between Churchill and the country's military leadership was ongoing. As historian Reginald Thompson observed, "Churchill did not like Dill, and with Churchill that was always fatal."[103] Dill's successor as CIGS, Alan Brooke, "was often charmed by the prime minister's puckish wit, and did not doubt his greatness, [but] he and Churchill never achieved full mutual understanding," Max Hastings wrote. "The new CIGS [Brooke] was a harsh and ruthless man. These qualities equipped him to fulfil his role far more effectively than the mild-mannered Dill."[104]

Churchill's incompatibility with Dill would prove an unforeseen blessing to his government. Sent off to Washington, Dill developed a strong relationship with the U.S. Army Chief of Staff, George Marshall. Leonard Moseley wrote that Dill's "quiet, almost supercilious manner had . . . grated on the more flamboyant premier, who always used to feel that Dill was sneering at him ('Dill's veinegar,' he called it), and he had demanded his resignation and posted him to Washington, just to be rid of him. It turned out that quite inadvertently he had made a brilliant appointment." Alex Danchev wrote: "Dill's appeal was rooted in his personality; his 'high character', to use Marshall's phrase. What Dill himself called 'the relationships between man and man' bulk large in what follows, for Anglo-American experience fully bore out his assertion of their essentiality to the business of war. In the same context Dill highlighted perhaps the primordial element in such relationships, the winning and keeping of confidence."[105] The disdain with which Marshall and Brooke held each other magnified Dill's importance. Dill proved crucial in informing Marshall confidentially about what FDR was saying to Churchill. The prime minister shared such correspondence with Brooke, who shared it with Dill, who very, very quietly read it privately to Marshall.[106] Dill and Marshall trusted each other—so did Brooke and Dill. Dill was diplomatic, though his friends Marshall and Brooke sometimes were not. One American general observed that American

> military people were at a marked disadvantage compared with the British. You see, Mr. Churchill was not only the prime minister, but also he was minister of defense, and, as you know, he was in intimate touch with his staff officers at all hours of the day and night. And he was vitally interested. But the prime minister of England is not the same as the President of the United States.

You don't just casually see the President—it isn't that kind of thing. The British knew what was on Churchill's mind. We didn't know what was on the President's. So at times the only way we could find out what the prime minister and the President were up to was through Sir John [Dill].[107]

More so than Churchill, Lincoln had early in life developed a vital leadership virtue—patient listening—often scarce among supreme political and military leaders. During the Civil War, the president would listen to each person he engaged—to generals and admirals, to ordinary soldiers and sailors, to civilians and politicians. California Congressman Cornelius Cole recalled: "Always in consultation he was argumentative, but not dictatorial. He was one of the best of listeners and was always open to conviction, yet if his own reasons were well founded, and no one had a better reason to offer, he could not be moved. But he was never offensively opinionated."[108] The president knew when to listen carefully. "Knowing he was not an expert," wrote Craig Symonds, "Lincoln was conscientious in soliciting the views of those who were. He let them play the role of teacher while he adopted that of the student. In the end, he graduated with honors."[109]

As politicians and national leaders, Lincoln consistently played himself, but Churchill would play many different roles. Early in his governmental career, a London reporter observed that Churchill "is always unconsciously playing a part—a heroic part. And he is his most astonished spectator. He sees himself moving through the smoke of battle—triumphant, terrible, his brow clothed in thunder, his legions looking to him for victory, and not looking in vain. He thinks of Napoleon; he thinks of his great ancestor [the first Duke of Marlborough, John Churchill]. Thus did they bear themselves; thus, in this rugged and most awful crisis, will he bear himself. It is not makebelieve, it is not insincerity."[110] The prime minister would adjust his behavior to the situation—commanding, charming, or churlish as necessary.

Lincoln exhibited a wise and paternal attitude toward many of those around him. As constitutional head of state, Lincoln possessed full authority to appoint his cabinet—but he governed them lightly. The president's shrewd letters to his commanders were paragons of paternal advice, not always understood by subordinates. In April 1862, he wrote General McClellan that "it is indispensable to you that you strike a blow.

I am powerless to help you. You will do me the justice to remember I always insisted that going down the Bay in search of a field instead of fighting at or near Manassas, was only shifting, and not surmounting, a difficulty—that we should find the same enemy, and the same, or equal entrenchments, at either place. The country will not fail to note—is now noting—that the present hesitation to move upon an entrenched enemy is but the story of Manassas repeated."[111]

Churchill, as a member of the House of Commons, had direct access to MPs on the floor of Parliament. As a nonlegislative leader, Lincoln's power was more circumscribed by the constitutionally independent Congress. Listening, then persuading, were his decisive talents. Outside of Congress, President Lincoln's authority was more unfettered than Churchill's, but he exercised a calm restraint in using it. Even with generals, the president would persuade rather than order. "If possible I would be very glad of another movement early enough to give us some benefit from the fact of the enemies communications being broken, but neither for this reason, or any other, do I wish anything done in desperation or rashness," the president wrote the commander of the Army of the Potomac, Joseph Hooker, in May 1863. "An early movement would also help to supersede the bad moral effect of the recent one, which is sure to be considerably injurious. Have you already in your mind a plan wholly, or partially formed? If you have, prossecute [sic] it without interference from me. If you have not, please inform me, so that I, incompetent as I may be, can try [to] assist in the formation of some plan for the Army."[112] Lincoln's modesty in this case was a virtue acting in the service of persuasion toward his goal—even though the president had the authority to give summary orders. When faced with great decisions—such as the Emancipation Proclamation—the president would seek advice, but not consent, from the Cabinet. If a general ignored Lincoln's measured advice and repeatedly failed, he would be replaced.

The full execution of the U.S. Constitution's war power, as Lincoln would define it, sustained the commander in chief. In July 1862, Lincoln aide Stoddard wrote: "The President is almost a mystery. Men no longer query whether such or such a General or statesman directs his [Lincoln's] actions, but 'what will he do with' this statesman or that General. He is the most perfect representative of the purely American character now in public life, perhaps the most perfect that ever has existed. This is why the mutual understanding between him and the people is so perfect. This it is which enables him to exercise powers which would never by any possibility be entrusted to another man, though his equal in other respects."[113] A Labour minister wrote of Churchill at a secret session of the Commons in July 1940: "Winston in grand form, both before and during. He now leads the whole House, unquestioned and ascendant."[114] In January 1941, late in the Battle of Britain, Harry Hopkins wrote President Roosevelt from London: "*Churchill* is the gov't. in every sense of the word—he controls the grand strategy and often the details—labor trusts him—the army, navy, air force are behind him. The politicians and upper crust pretend to like him. I cannot emphasize too strongly that he is the one and only person over here with whom you need to have a full meeting of the minds."[115]

Through their arguments, their decisions, their victories, both the Civil War president and the World War II prime minister would broaden the theory and application of the constitutional powers of the executive in war.

I said I would remove him if [Union General George B. McClellan] let Lee's army get away from him, and I must do so. He has got the "slows," Mr. Blair.[1]

ABRAHAM LINCOLN
Speaking to Francis P. Blair Sr. about the president's decision
to dismiss General George B. McClellan
November 6, 1862

It was a terrible thing to have to do. [Claude Auchinleck] took it like a gentleman. But it was a terrible thing. It is difficult to remove a bad General at the height of a campaign: it is atrocious to remove a good General. We must use Auchinleck again. We cannot afford to lose such a man from the fighting line.[2]

WINSTON S. CHURCHILL
November 6, 1942

VIII.

Army Leadership

Voters, writers, opponents wondered aloud and in print whether the Union army in the Civil War, the British army in World War II, and their leaders would measure up to the unprecedented military challenges they faced. "During Churchill's first months as warlord he began the process of ruthlessly weeding out and replacing deadwood military officers, reshaping the three armed services into the most cohesive force in British history," wrote military historian Carlo D'Este. Churchill was not slow to decision. Equally important, both supreme warlords understood that their armed forces must be rebuilt on the slim foundation they inherited; and despite the urgency, their military strategy must be informed by political purpose. "War is the continuation of politics by other means," wrote Carl von Clausewitz, the Prussian theorist of war.[3] For Lincoln and Churchill, military strategy could, when necessary, be subordinated to tactical political issues.

As supreme commanders the president and prime minister pushed for speedy action. "I am certainly not one of those who need to be prodded. In fact, if anything, I am a prod," Churchill told the House on November 11, 1942. "My difficulties rather lie in finding the patience and self-restraint to wait through many anxious weeks for the results to be achieved."[4] A few weeks earlier, Churchill had admitted: "I myself find waiting more trying than action."[5] General Brooke wrote in his diary at about the same time: "It is a regular disease that he suffers from, this frightful impatience to get an attack launched!"[6]

At the outset of World War II, Chief of the Imperial Staff John Dill represented for Churchill what General-in-Chief Winfield Scott had been for Abraham Lincoln in the Civil War. In 1861, most loyal Union officers remaining at their posts had experienced limited roles in the

Mexican-American War, 1846–1848. The exception was the 75-year-old Scott, the hero of the war, who had served in the army nearly five decades. Scott's slow and deliberate approach to military operations in 1861 grated against the demands from newspapers and the public that Union soldiers immediately march "On to Richmond."[7] Scott did make a very important contribution to war strategy—the "Anaconda Plan," whereby the South should be surrounded by land and sea and then blockaded and strangled by armed forces.[8] (Undermined by the ambitious George McClellan, Scott would resign in November 1861.) Historian Donald Stoker wrote of Lincoln in the summer of 1861: "He was beginning to see the broad sweep of the war, not just defaulting to a single campaign against Richmond or down the Mississippi. He established strategic goals—blockades, securing Union possessions—as well as operational objectives, and envisioned campaigns in the East and West . . . Lincoln designated the objectives but advised 'the military men to find the way' of reaching them."[9]

Churchill had his own anaconda strategy of sorts: "forging a ring around Germany, by naval blockade in the North Sea and eastern Atlantic, and on land from French North Africa, east to Cairo and north through Baghdad to the Caucasus, the eastern perimeter of the ring delineated [after June 1941] by the 1,800-mile Soviet front," noted Manchester and Reid. They wrote of Churchill in 1943–1944: "In wanting to attack everywhere, Churchill manifested two abiding traits: impatience and flexibility in the face of changing fortunes. His belief in an opportunistic strategic approach—attack the weaker of two enemies if the stronger could not be engaged—had not diminished since the 1941 Greek debacle, nor since 1915 and the Dardanelles, for that matter. Now Italy was weak, and getting weaker."[10] Moreover, wrote historian John Keegan, "Churchill's restless search for means to hit back at least had the effect of sustaining his own fierce resolve to achieve eventual victory, even at the lowest points of the war. In 1940 it yielded a priceless dividend, when he decided, though Britain lay under threat of imminent invasion, to reinforce its tiny army in the Middle East."[11] Churchill had suffered through disaster at the Dardanelles in World War I, as well as in Greece and Norway early in World War II, but these reverses did not suppress his will to take the offensive.

Churchill's own history of the U.S. Civil War criticized Lincoln's appointment of political generals, writing that Lincoln's "appointments were too often made on purely political grounds."[12] But Churchill did not recognize that one-third of the trained Union officer corps quit or betrayed their sworn oath to the Union—giving their allegiance to the Confederacy at the onset of secession. At the beginning of the Civil War, the Union army, and its surviving officer corps, was a puny thing to behold. By the time the commander in chief was assassinated in 1865, over 2.2 million men, including a whole new generation of officers, had served in the Union armed forces.[13]

Lincoln's war strategy included appointing "political" generals from both parties, with the express purpose of consolidating bipartisan Northern Democrat and Republican war leadership behind his strategic goal of national reunion, directed as it was by the first Republican Party administration in American history. Historian James M. McPherson argued that criticism of political generals was "grounded in a narrow concept of *military* strategy. But Lincoln made . . . [these] appointments for reasons of *national* strategy. Each of the political generals represented an important ethnic, regional, or political constituency in the North. The support of these constituencies for the war effort was crucial."[14] Though political war aims influenced Lincoln's strategy, failed "political" generals did encumber his strategic goals. Churchill argued that Lincoln "was too ready, especially at first, to yield to the popular clamour which demanded the recall of an unsuccessful General."[15] Churchill as an historian erred on that point; Lincoln gave most generals several chances—McClellan's unsuccessful command effectively lasting fifteen months. After the Second Battle of Bull Run in August 1862, Lincoln resisted strong pressure from members of his own cabinet to discharge McClellan promptly. Even after the president had removed generals from command of the Army of the Potomac, he would often try to find alternative uses for their leadership.

Churchill's leadership dilemma was similar to Lincoln's with Winfield Scott. John Dill did not measure up to the challenges he confronted. The prime minister literally wore out Dill during the nineteen months in which he served as Chief of the Imperial General Staff. Shortly after he arrived at the War Office in April 1940, when Churchill was the aggressive First Lord of the Admiralty, Dill wrote: "The War Office is, as far as I can see, in complete chaos and the situation in Norway as bad as I expected . . . I'm not sure that Winston isn't the greatest menace. No-one seems able to control him. He is full of ideas, many brilliant, but most of them impracticable. He has such drive and personality that no-one seems able to stand up to him."[16]

Historian Alex Danchev would summarize the problem that would develop: "Catapulted into the daily circus surrounding the Prime Minister, Dill's relationship with Churchill, intimate yet uncomprehending, interdependent yet adversarial, necessary yet unsatisfactory, was both rich in paradox and deeply flawed."[17] Dill was an experienced, capable, thoughtful general who was not prepared to do battle with the prime minister. Historian John Connell observed: "Churchill used every weapon of aggressive debate—mordant sarcasm, prosecuting counsel's bullying, extravagant rhetorical flourishes, urchin abuse, Ciceronian irony and sledgehammer brutality—and Dill had to bear it all and suppress his anger and anguish."[18] Few men could bear the battering that the prime minister could bring to his arguments.

In October 1941, Brooke had written in his diary: "Winston had never been fond of Dill. They were entirely different types of character and types that could never have worked harmoniously together. Dill was the essence of straightforwardness, blessed with the highest principles and an unassailable integrity of character. I do not believe that any of these characteristics appeal to Winston."[19] In fact, Churchill did respect those characteristics in fighting generals. Dill would resign in December 1941. Churchill had demanded action and victories that Dill, with very limited resources, could not deliver. Churchill needed confident, aggressive, thick-skinned field generals who could recruit and train fighting troops and lead them into battle. He searched until he found them. He accepted little without "a continuous audit of the military's judgement," wrote political scientist Eliot Cohen. "Churchill's manner of dealing with his subordinates [was] a relentless querying of their assumptions and arguments, not just once but in successive iterations of a debate."[20] Verging sometimes on harassment, he could be exhausting.

Like Churchill, Lincoln "was sometimes critical and even sarcastic when events moved slowly," noted a telegraph operator in the War Department.[21] In May 1862, the president wrote General McClellan, then just beginning his protracted peninsula campaign in Virginia: "Your call for Parrott guns from Washington alarms me—chiefly because it argues indefinite procrastination. Is anything to be done?"[22] Lincoln did not confine such comments to quarrelsome generals; he also used them on political allies. In September 1863, he reacted to a patronage request by two longtime Illinois friends and political colleagues: "What nation do you desire Gen. [Robert] Allen to be made Quarter-Master-General of? This nation already has a Quarter-Master-General."[23]

As heads of government, Lincoln and Churchill concentrated on their executive duty to command the war effort. They delegated most other executive functions to appropriate cabinet members. As both president and head of the Republican Party, Lincoln insisted that cabinet members handle patronage such that it would not undermine the war effort by agitating his contentious Northern political base, divided as it was between Union Democrats and Republicans. Nor could he risk alienating members of Congress. Indeed, patronage was the political glue that held the new Republican Party together—and thus also the Union. Patronage was perhaps as important to some Union men as loyalty to the Stars and Stripes.

As head of a coalition government, Churchill presided over a comparable situation. Cabinet offices went to Labour as well as Tory leaders—even a few token Liberals. He made a special effort to attract Labour support by nominating Ernest Bevin to be Minister of Labour and National Service, even though Bevin was not then a member of Parliament.[24] Lincoln tried to unify the Republican Party in his 1861 selection of the cabinet—and in 1862, by adding War Democrat Edwin M. Stanton as secretary of war. The prime minister tried to unify the anti-Churchill and anti-Chamberlain wings of the Conservative Party, even as he brought Labour and Liberal representatives into the cabinet. As in the first weeks of Lincoln's administration, political patronage played an important role in Churchill's first weeks of office. In his case, lesser posts were allocated not only to Churchill loyalist Brendan Bracken, but also to House Chief Whip David Margesson, a Chamberlain supporter. "The spoils were divided in such a way as to leave every group, if not content, at least unable to complain overmuch," wrote historian Andrew Roberts. "Most important for Churchill's survival, it accorded the Chamberlainites just enough senior places to remove their immediate discontent, yet not enough to give them overall control of the ministry."[25] J. M. Lee noted that Churchill's "ministerial appointments in the War Cabinet itself were designed primarily to keep a party balance and to hold together the principal co-ordinating posts."[26] The prime minister preferred congenial people around him, but he needed a broad cross-section of British politicians to support him in parliament. Like

Lincoln, he gathered a War Cabinet consisting of a team of rivals, two of whom would later occupy 10 Downing Street.[27]

Lincoln and Churchill understood that war required victories to maintain public support and sacrifice. Over the objections of Union commanders in the early summer of 1861, Lincoln pushed them to fight the rebels in Virginia. "On to Richmond" was the battle cry in the North as troops mobilized near Washington. Nicolay and Hay, Lincoln's senior staff, wrote:

> When Lincoln, on June 29, assembled his council of war, the commanders, as military experts, correctly decided that the existing armies—properly handled—could win a victory at Manassas and a victory at Winchester, at or near the same time. General Scott correctly objected that these victories, if won, would not be decisive; and that in a military point of view it would be wiser to defer any offensive campaign until the following autumn. Here the President and the Cabinet, as political experts, intervened, and on their part decided, correctly, that the public temper would not admit of such a delay. Thus the Administration was responsible for the forward movement, Scott for the combined strategy of the two armies, McDowell for the conduct of the Bull Run battle, [Robert] Patterson for the escape of [Joseph] Johnston, and Fate for the panic; for the opposing forces were equally raw, equally undisciplined, and as a whole fought the battle with equal courage and gallantry.[28]

After the battle of Bull Run (Manassas), the defeated Union troops streamed into nearby Washington, where, for consolation, there was "a licensed bar for about every seventy-five of the fixed population, and a large number of unlicensed drinking places."[29]

An Illinois friend queried the president how the Bull Run battle had gone. Lincoln replied that "it was contrary to Army Regulations to give military information to parties not in military service. I said to him [Lincoln] then, I don't ask for the news, but you tell me the quality of the news,—is it good, or is it bad. Placing his mouth near my ear he said in a sharp, shrill voice, '*damned bad.*'"[30] An aide to General Winfield Scott remembered: "The entire night of that 21st of July was spent by the President and Cabinet, and some military officers, at General Scott's quarters.

The telegraph-office in the War Department, a short distance off, was in momentary receipt of dispatches from the field. At first, the success of the Union arms seemed assured. Then came tidings of a reverse; then of a panic, and *rout*. Then followed in quick succession details of the disaster, and rumors, with earnest appeals to guard the capital."[31] So close was Manassas to Washington that fear of rebel assault on the capital was not unreasonable.

The British counterpart to Lincoln's First Battle of Bull Run in 1861 was the Battle of Norway in April 1940. Churchill, then First Lord of the Admiralty, had pressed for an attack. Narvik, the gateway for Swedish iron ore on the way to Germany, was the target. Historian Carlo D'Este wrote: "Norway was an example of everything a military operation should *not* be." The British operations revealed a fatal lack of coordination among air, sea, and ground forces—resulting in "easily one of Britain's worst military performances of the war." Indecision and shifting operational targets doomed British efforts. Churchill bore some, but not all responsibility for the debacle. "Britain had not the power to mount and to sustain the assaults on the Norwegian coastline," wrote Reginald W. Thompson. "There seemed to be no idea in Whitehall of the geography of Norway, of the weather conditions, of the deep snow."[32] D'Este blamed Churchill, writing that he "seems to have learned little from the Norway venture; particularly, he did not learn that large-scale military operations cannot suddenly be altered on an impulse without serious consequences."[33] Norway would fall to a well-planned, well-executed German attack, forcing a hasty British retreat.

World War II differed from Churchill's youthful war experiences involving imperial skirmishes and victories in India and the Sudan, and in a larger winning war in South Africa. The failures of World War I, and his experience at the Dardanelles, did prepare him for more deliberate leadership in World War II. Though his impulsiveness remained a lifelong problem, the same temperament often led to swift, effective decisions. Norway would demonstrate Churchill's good and bad leadership qualities. "The best showed in his quickness to respond to unexpected bad news, the characteristic energy and resolution with which he sought to catch up after being wrong-footed, and the readiness to take responsibility," wrote historian Geoffrey Best. "The worst showed in the extent of his interference with the way the professionals went about their work, whether in the Admiralty itself or at their command posts off the Norwegian coast."[34] Ironically, the Norwegian failure led to a no-confidence vote in the House of Commons, where Chamberlain's war policy would be defended and scrutinized. The government's conduct was debated on May 7–8, 1940—just before the German invasion of Belgium, Holland, and Luxembourg on the morning of May 10. Prime Minister Neville Chamberlain won the vote, but he had clearly lost the confidence of the House of Commons. For the Labour Party, Churchill became the only acceptable alternative, although he still had many opponents and skeptics among Conservatives. Lord Halifax, the Conservative favorite, withdrew because his title did not allow him to serve in the House of Commons, the ultimate locus of the parliamentary war power. As Germany launched its well-planned May 10 invasion into France, one of the authors of the Norwegian fiasco would become prime minister.

Ambitious, strong, inspired statesmen such as Lincoln and Churchill were forces of nature, some of whose military and civilian subordinates often bristled under the self-confident leadership of their chiefs. "I think that no idea is so outlandish that it should not be considered with a searching, but at the same time, I hope, with a steady eye," said Churchill shortly after he took office.[35] Some ideas were better than others, and Churchill himself would decide. In December 1941, General Brooke took over as CIGS. From that moment, Brooke would give the prime minister stubborn counsel, strategic advice, and operational support. (Lincoln needed the very same counsel in 1861, but he never received it during the first three years of the Civil War from his commanding generals—Winfield Scott, George B. McClellan, and Henry W. Halleck.) Brooke frequently disagreed with Churchill, but their arguments rarely interfered with the advice Brooke gave. Nor did the prime minister intimidate Brooke. "When I thump the table and push my face towards him," said Churchill of Brooke, "what does he do? Thumps the table harder and glares back at me."[36] The prime minister, equipped with decades of knowledge of Britain's historic officer corps, chose the right man in Brooke. In the gritty Ulsterman, the prime minister found a worthy military adviser—an equally worthy adversary in debate. Stubborn as Churchill, Brooke often disagreed on strategy. Loyal to and more knowledgeable about the British officers corps, Brooke disagreed equally often with his American counterparts. "Brooke almost never fought Churchill out of pride or pugnacity or perversity," wrote historian Andrew Roberts, "but did so because of the effect of their decisions on the services."[37]

Henry W. Halleck, ca. 1860–1865
Gilder Lehrman Collection, GLC05111.02.0443

Brooke resisted Churchill's relentless, sometimes impetuous criticism of army leadership, while helping to resist premature American pressure to invade France in 1942–1943.

Churchill would exercise authority over all wartime strategy and tactics. But war and politics bring the irony of unintended consequences. Churchill was 65 when he became prime minister. Under the stress of war, Churchill's energy ran down as he approached seventy years of age. Fortunately, Brooke's did not. In July 1944, Foreign Minister Anthony Eden recorded in his diary a confrontation at "a really ghastly Defence Committee." He wrote: "Winston hadn't read the paper and was perhaps rather tight. Anyway we opened with a reference from Winston to American criticism of Monty [Bernard Montgomery] for over-caution which Winston appeared to endorse. This brought explosion from CIGS [Brooke], 'If you would keep your confidence in your generals for even a few days I think we should do much better.' [Winston puzzled or feigns to be so. Brooke spells it out.] 'You asked me questions, I gave you answers. You didn't accept them and telegraphed to Alexander who gave the same answers,' and more in the same vein."[38]

Lincoln adopted a different approach to his generals. British historian Correlli Barnett argued that "while Lincoln's interventions with McClellan in 1862 were fully justified by military realities, Churchill's interventions in 1940–42 were not. There is a further contrast between the two war leaders; whereas Lincoln was patient and supportive with McClellan, as indeed with other generals, Churchill was too often a relentless harasser of commanders already under stress."[39] McClellan had maneuvered to win promotion in November 1861, to the position of General-in-Chief in place of Winfield Scott. Soon it became clear— contrary to McClellan's statement that "I can do it all"—that he could not do it all. Indeed, he could not even lead the Army of the Potomac. He did train the army well, but McClellan hesitated to take his army into battle. Lincoln abruptly relieved him of overall army command in March 1862, but kept him in charge of the campaign in Virginia—finally to fire him in November.

General Brooke, who had served courageously as corps commander with the British Expeditionary Force in France during 1939–1940, had the training advantage of moving steadily up the chain of British command until, as CIGS, it was his job to see the broad picture of British military needs. He had an intimate, albeit argumentative relationship with the prime minister, who admired and promoted him. President Lincoln's relationship with his victorious Union commander, Ulysses S. Grant, was one of mutual respect. Before he appointed Grant as General-in-Chief, Lincoln had developed great confidence in him—without even meeting him. Lincoln had gained confidence in Grant not only as a result of Grant's victories throughout the western theater of war, but especially because of the extraordinary siege and capture of the Mississippi River stronghold of Vicksburg on July 4, 1863. After this victory, the president was moved to exclaim in his creative idiom: "Now, the Father of Waters again goes unvexed to the sea."[40] After the fall of Vicksburg, the Union controlled the vital Mississippi River on the west, the Gulf to the south, the Atlantic coast to the east. The Confederacy had been split in two, its heartland surrounded by Union waters.

"With this honor devolves upon you also, a corresponding responsibility. As the country herein trusts you, so under God, it will sustain you," said Lincoln in March 1864, when appointing Grant the first lieutenant general since George Washington to lead the Union armies.[41] The taciturn Grant would retain the cautious George Meade as commander of the Army of the Potomac, but he wisely made his headquarters with Meade at the Virginia front, instead of Washington. The top Union civilian and military leaders had relatively little interaction until March–April 1865, when Lincoln spent several weeks near Richmond conferring with Grant. The president told a journalist: "Grant is the first General I have had. You know how it has been with all the rest. As soon as I put a man in command of the Army, he'd come to me with a plan of campaign and about as much as to say, 'Now, I don't believe I can do it, but if you say so, I'll try it on,' and so put the responsibility of success or failure on me. They all wanted me to be the general. . . . I am glad to find a man that can go ahead without me."[42] Lincoln's search for a winning commander was simple in its purpose. "What Lincoln looked for in his generals," wrote John Keegan, "was the ability to achieve results without constantly requiring guidance from Washington or reinforcement by additional troops."[43]

Henry W. Halleck, Grant's predecessor as General-in-Chief, had "scratched his elbows" but gave little direction to the war effort. In June 1862, Lincoln had appointed Halleck, then commanding Union troops along the Mississippi River, to the post formerly held by McClellan and Scott. It proved an unsuccessful decision. Halleck did not provide firm advice, nor did he attempt to make important decisions. Although a former West Point instructor and author of a book on military strategy, Halleck would not give direction to military commanders in the field who, he rationalized, were better able to understand local battlefield conditions. In July 1862, Halleck's first chore was to harness Generals McClellan and John Pope to engage the rebels in northern Virginia. Halleck did not have the force of personality to coordinate McClellan's Army of the Potomac with the new Army of Virginia commanded by Pope, who exhibited more bravado than brains. Historian Michael Burlingame wrote: "Lincoln . . . wanted Halleck to formulate strategic plans and coordinate the movement of all Union armies. When asked what would be done with McClellan's army, Lincoln replied: 'You forget we have a general who commands all the armies and makes all the plans to suit himself—ask him!'" In Burlingame's words, "Halleck, unable or unwilling to lead, had failed in his assignment to produce victory. McClellan had outmaneuvered him as sure-footedly as he had outmaneuvered Scott."[44] McClellan would be replaced sooner than Halleck.

Until 1864, Lincoln continued to hire and fire Union generals, hoping he could find the one to whom he could entrust an all-out military struggle for victory. McClellan's successor and his successor's successor experienced overwhelming defeats in Virginia at Fredericksburg in December 1862, and at Chancellorsville in May 1863. Lincoln and Secretary of War Stanton would effectively become overall commanders of the Union military effort until March 1864, when Lincoln chose Grant for the unified command post. The new general-in-chief came to a White House reception on the night of March 8. There for the first time, Grant met the president. The next day, he received from Lincoln his commission as the Union's sole lieutenant general, commander of all the Union armies. (It is unlikely that Churchill would have made such an appointment without more intimate personal contact. Lincoln, it is true, had received reports from several confidantes he sent to visit and evaluate the general.)

Lincoln's most serious leadership problems developed in the eastern theater threatening Washington. Churchill grappled with the geographically widespread problem of British military leadership and coordination in the Near East, India, and Southeast Asia. In North Africa at the beginning of World War II, Churchill had to manage the talented but taciturn General Archibald Wavell. Wavell would serve as the British commander in Egypt from July 1939 to June 1941. Whereas Lincoln overestimated

McClellan, Churchill underestimated Wavell—although the prime minister admitted in February 1941 that Wavell "has proved himself a master of war, sage, painstaking, daring, and tireless."[45] Wavell's Cairo colleague, Admiral Andrew Cunningham, recalled that Wavell "was cool and imperturbable when things went wrong, and steadfastly refused to be riled by the prodding messages to which he, like myself, was at times subject from the authorities at home, and which were, it must be confessed, singularly unhelpful and irritating in times of stress. Wavell was always ready to take a chance. Never once did he have the good fortune to fight with all the resources he really needed."[46] Resources were very scarce in 1941. Britain was insolvent; Lend-Lease did not get in full swing until 1942, galvanized by Pearl Harbor.

A fatal difference in the personalities of Churchill and Wavell surfaced when they first met in the summer of 1940. "Churchill, apt on impulse to be over-enthusiastic about a new relationship, and to his credit, as tenacious in these sudden loyalties as in his dislikes, found it impossible to like Wavell," wrote Wavell biographer John Connell. "One who was present at the latter's first meeting with the War Cabinet and the Chiefs of Staff has described as 'disastrous' the way in which the emotional temperature dropped in the face of Wavell's taciturnity."[47] Wavell resembled McClellan in his reluctance to discuss his war plans with Churchill, despite Dill's plaintive request: "Talk to him, Archie."[48] Wavell further angered Churchill by insisting on cautious planning for the worst. Churchill preferred articulate generals. The soldierly, intellectual Wavell was a man of few words.[49] It was Anthony Eden who had persuaded Churchill to bring Wavell home for consultation at the beginning of August 1940. On August 8, "we had a meeting of the Middle East Committee and the Chiefs of Staff," recalled Eden. "I thought then that Wavell's account was masterly and it is even more so in retrospect. He admitted that if the Italians were to bring up a large force, some withdrawal would be necessary for a while. The real danger would not arise until German armour and motorized units appeared. The outcome of this meeting was a strong recommendation by our Committee and the Chiefs of Staff that the despatch of convoys taking reinforcements to the Middle East should be hastened."[50] Churchill still doubted Wavell. On August 13, 1940, Churchill wrote Eden: "I am favourably impressed with General Wavell in many ways, but I do not feel in him that sense of mental rigour and resolve to overcome obstacles which is indispensable to successful war. I find, instead, tame acceptance of a variety of local circumstances in different theatres, which is leading to a lamentable lack of concentration upon the decisive point."[51]

In his friends and colleagues, Churchill valued dash and argument—not Wavell's strengths. John Martin, Churchill's private secretary, remembered that Wavell "seemed strangely unforthcoming and negative. He seemed to make no attempt to 'get across,' though it was important for him to have the Prime Minister's confidence at a time when his Command was making such large demands on scarce resources of men and materials and receiving such generous support from the Prime Minister and the Chiefs of Staff."[52] Reginald W. Thompson wrote: "Two more dissimilar or more incompatible men would be difficult to imagine. . . . Churchill was exuberant, rhetorical weaving words; Wavell was quiet, a dedicated soldier, a master of his command and its problems."[53] Their communication gap proved impossible to bridge. Wavell himself wrote:

> I do not think Winston quite knew what to make of me and whether I was fit to command or not. He was determined that something must be done to put the defence of Egypt on a sound basis; and in providing reinforcement of tanks and sending a convoy through the Mediterranean was bold in overriding the views both of those who wish to keep all armoured forces for home defence—[Nazi] invasion [of Britain] was very much a possibility at the time—and of the First Sea Lord, who stressed the dangers of sending merchant ships through the Mediterranean.[54]

Wavell "was tough, self-confident, and given to long and intimidating silences," wrote historian Raymond Callahan. "Wavell was outwardly a stolid and conventional, if highly capable, professional soldier, but there were other currents running deep in his character. He had a gambler's streak, a penchant for believing that things would work out."[55] Churchill's exuberance was matched by Wavell's reticence. Carlo D'Este wrote: "Wavell's guarded emotions and inability to see the necessity of keeping Churchill happy—and thus off his back—were fatal to satisfying a warlord prone to run roughshod over others, particularly generals whom he distrusted."[56] Unlike Lincoln, Churchill had at times an overbearing personality. He wanted to know everything possible about the theaters of war. Wavell preferred to develop his plans without interference.[57] But he had none of McClellan's arrogance and contempt for civilian superiors. Military historian Harold E. Raugh wrote: "Wavell . . . was severely distressed by the curt interrogations to which the Prime Minister subjected him, and by Churchill's attempts to usurp the prerogatives of the military commander in the field."[58]

Churchill had a brief burst of confidence in Wavell in November 1940, when Secretary of War Eden brought back to London the Mideast commander's plans for Operation COMPASS, a bold desert attack on numerically superior Italian forces. Eden disclosed to the Defence Committee:

> Wavell had decided not to await [Rodolfo] Graziani's attack at Mersa Matruh, but to take the offensive himself at an early date; and he followed up this startling announcement with an explanation of Wavell's plans. Every one of us could have jumped for joy, but Churchill could have jumped twice as high as the rest. He has said that he "purred like six cats." That is putting it mildly. He was rapturously happy. "At long last we are going to throw off the intolerable shackles of the defensive," he declaimed. "Wars are won by superior will-power. Now we will wrest the initiative from the enemy and impose our will on him."[59]

Churchill's euphoria did not last long. Eden wrote in his diary of a Defence Committee meeting on December 4, 1940: "W. asked for news of 'Compass' and was indignant that I had not asked date. He was also critical of army and generals. 'High time army did something,' etc. I made it plain that I did not believe in fussing Wavell with questions. I knew his plan, he knew our view, he had best be left to get on with it. This did not suit W."[60] Chasing the Italian army out of Egypt in December 1940, Operation COMPASS proved a rare victory for Britain during the early years of World War II. Although heavily outnumbered in both weapons and personnel, the British captured the Libyan port of Tobruk in January, along with thousands of Italian soldiers. In early February, Australian troops captured Benghazi and thousands more Italians. Tripoli was probably open to British capture as well, but Wavell chose not to give the orders to advance.[61]

In late October 1940, Italian troops had invaded Greece. Greek troops successfully resisted, but in early 1941, well-prepared German divisions massed along the Yugoslav and Bulgarian borders to finish what the Italians could not. Churchill had first favored and then doubted British action in Greece, but Anthony Eden, on the scene, supported the prime minister's original decision.[62] Wavell suggested in January 1941 that Germany might be engaged in an elaborate bluff to draw Britain into Greece. "We expect and require prompt and active compliance with our decisions for which we bear full responsibility," responded Churchill on January 10. He had added: "Nothing must hamper capture of Tobruk, but thereafter all operations in Libya are subordinated to aiding Greece."[63] The prime minister had been influenced by Britain's previous commitment to help defend Greece. In January, however, during a Wavell visit to Athens, the Greek government rejected British help—probably to the general's relief. In February 1941, Churchill dispatched Dill and Secretary of War Anthony Eden to the eastern Mediterranean to review the situation. After visiting Greece, the delegation returned to Cairo in March, recalled Eden:

> Here we receive telegrams from Mr. Churchill and the Chiefs of Staff expressing grave doubts about the wisdom of our decision to go on with the despatch of our troops to the Aliakmon line [in Greece]. . . . We discussed these with the three British Commanders-in-Chief. Although both [Air Chief Marshal Arthur] Longmore and [Admiral Andrew] Cunningham were unhappy about the risk they foresaw of losing most of the convoy ships and most of our air forces in Greece, all three agreed that, despite the dangers involved, the decision taken in Athens was the only possible one and that we should go ahead. Dill said that the situation was grimmer than we had thought. All the same, he saw no alternative but to persist with our plans.[64]

Although Churchill's support for a Greek intervention had wavered in the early months of 1941, Dill, Eden, and Wavell proved persuasive. British operations in Greece would go forward.

Wavell, like McClellan, was a student of warfare. McClellan made a study of the Crimean War, which pitted Russia against an alliance that included Britain and France. The intellectual Wavell had observed the Russian army for a year in 1911. He had even translated from the Russian a book about Czar Nicholas II. Churchill granted the modest Wavell less latitude than he had earned. The prime minister, usually quick to judgment, had doubts about Wavell from the beginning. Lincoln had confidence in McClellan at the outset. The president steadily lost confidence in 1862, as McClellan refused to engage the enemy on Lincoln's timetable, and he insisted on moving the Army of the Potomac from Manassas to the Virginia Peninsula. Both generals were diverted by tactical initiatives that undermined their military advantages. In Wavell's case, it would be military assistance to Greece, decided (and then doubted) by the prime minister, and approved in the end by Wavell, February 1941. The transfer of Commonwealth troops from North Africa to Greece began in early March.

Generals can only win victories on battlefields. Tactical defeats and triumphs often occasion the rise and fall of generals. In the winter of 1940–1941, British victories against the Italians in Libya would convince Hitler to send German armies to reinforce the Italians. Germany then conquered the Balkans and threatened to invade Greece. As ever, Churchill wanted action. It was on February 11, 1941, that the War Cabinet decided to send assistance to Greece, but not without a bitter argument between Churchill and Dill. "I gave it as my view that all the troops in [the] Middle East are fully employed and that none are available for Greece," reported Dill. "The Prime Minister lost his temper with me. I could see the blood coming up his great neck and his eyes began to flash. He said: 'What you need out there is a Court Martial and a firing squad. Wavell has 300,000 men, etc. etc.' I [Dill] should have said, 'Whom do you want to shoot exactly?' but I did not think of it till afterwards."[65]

Ultimately Wavell supported the Greek diversion. It proved fatal to his efforts to hold off Rommel in North Africa. On April 27, 1941, the prime minister would defend his hesitant decision to help Greece: "By solemn guarantee given before the war, Great Britain had promised them [Greece] her help. They declared they would fight for their native soil even if neither of their neighbors made common cause with them, and even if we left them to their fate. But we could not do that. There are rules against that kind of thing; and to break those rules would be fatal to the honor of the British Empire, without which we could neither hope nor deserve to win this hard war."[66] Churchill had rationalized his Greek decision.

To respond to the Greek emergency, some Commonwealth forces had been diverted from North Africa, where they had the Italians on the run. Churchill's "mixed feelings about the [Greek] venture had replaced his initial enthusiasm by the time 'the men on the spot,' Eden, Wavell and Dill, made the decision delegated to them," wrote Geoffrey Best. He blamed Churchill, who "failed to balance certain loss (the near certainty of eliminating the Italians from Libya before the Germans could arrive in strength) against such speculative gains as a Greek redoubt or leverage on Turkey."[67] Carlo D'Este blamed Wavell and Anthony Eden for the British intervention. "What was out of character was Churchill's failure to subject the decision to his usual scrutiny. Instead, he and the War Cabinet wholly bought in to the recommendations of Eden and Wavell to intervene."[68] John Colville wrote in his diary that British support for Greece "was thrust upon us partly because, in the first place, the PM felt that our prestige, in France, in Spain and in the US, could not stand our desertion of Greece [an ally]; partly because Eden, Dill, Wavell and Cunningham (who has now telegraphed to point out the extreme length to which his resources are stretched) recommended it so strongly."[69] Britain, it should be remembered, stood alone against the German war machine. The risk was clear.

With the passage of time, the risk of diversion of British forces to Greece would be linked to the defeat of British forces in the Libyan Desert. Perhaps the British expedition to Greece did assist the eventual Allied effort in one important if unintended way. Some argue it may have delayed the German invasion of Russia by diverting Nazi resources to Greece. Thus, in the judgment of Churchill, British intervention in Greece helped to cause the German invasion of Russia to be put off a few weeks until mid-June 1941.[70] Historians such as John Keegan have argued on the contrary that it was muddy, bad weather, and necessary German logistical planning, not the Greek diversion, that determined the timing of the Nazi attack on the Soviet Union.[71] Churchill and others, however, have contended that one of the unintended consequences of the Greek diversion—and the delay of the German invasion—was that Nazi troops were stopped just outside Moscow by the early onset of a most bitter Russian winter in October–November 1941. Still, no matter the arguments, the Greek diversion has been widely considered a setback for Britain and a tactical misstep by Churchill.[72]

With the success of the German invasion of Greece, some British troops had been evacuated to Crete. There, the British commander expected a German invasion by sea. Instead, the *Wehrmacht* attacked by

Alan Brooke, 1943

© Yousuf Karsh

air—a brilliant parachute assault onto the island, capturing an airfield, and thus enabling German reinforcements to arrive. Germany ran Britain out of Greece, taking 9,000 prisoners in the process. (The defeats in Greece and then in Crete during the spring of 1941 resembled Lincoln's abject defeat at the First Battle of Bull Run in July 1861. They were avoidable defeats that undermined public confidence.) The Greek intervention might have stemmed more from Churchill's political objectives than his military tactics.[73] Like Churchill, Lincoln understood the centrality of politics and political aims in war, which might even cause premature action. The president's assistants, Hay and Nicolay, would write:

> Historical judgment of war is subject to an inflexible law, either very imperfectly understood or very constantly lost sight of. Military writers love to fight over the campaigns of history exclusively by the rules of the professional chess-board, always subordinating, often totally ignoring, the element of politics. This is a radical error. Every war is begun, dominated, and ended by political considerations; without a nation, without a Government, without money or credit, without popular enthusiasm which furnishes volunteers, or public support which endures conscription, there could be no army and no war—neither beginning nor end of methodical hostilities. War and politics, campaign and statecraft, are Siamese twins, inseparable and interdependent; and to talk of military operations without the direction and interference of an Administration is as absurd as to plan a campaign without recruits, pay, or rations.[74]

Nicolay and Hay thus summarized Clausewitz, perhaps unaware of the Prussian strategist. Above all, war implies hope of victory, dread of defeat. Battle setbacks bring blame and rationalization; battle victories know only competing authors.

As a consequence of the decision to intervene in Greece, Wavell had diverted badly needed troops and resources from the North Africa campaign. There, German General Erwin Rommel's Panzers would charge across the Libyan desert toward Egypt, besieging the British garrison at Tobruk for the next eight months. Churchill's original North African strategy foundered with the arrival of Rommel and the intervention in Greece. North Africa had been Churchill's battlefield of choice. By defeating the Italians there at the beginning of 1941, Britain had inadvertently tempted Hitler to intervene in North Africa. At one crucial moment, British tanks had returned to Cairo for maintenance just as Rommel's tanks were about to arrive, compounding the problem that British tanks neither performed as well as German tanks, nor were they as ready for desert battle as Churchill thought them to be.[75]

In the spring of 1941, the prime minister's opinion of Wavell steadily deteriorated as Greece and Crete fell to the Germans. Historian Ian Beckett wrote: "Already alarmed by the discovery that Wavell had contingency plans for the evacuation of Egypt—Wavell's belief in planning for the 'worst possible case' was often interpreted as defeatism—Churchill found Wavell's preparations for Crete lacking in drive."[76] The prime minister also found unacceptable Wavell's delay in getting new British tanks into battle. Beckett wrote: "Churchill had rushed the 'Tiger' convoy through the Mediterranean, a total of 238 new tanks for Wavell reaching Alexandria on 12 May. The Prime Minister expected his 'Cubs' to be used immediately, especially as Ultra [decryption technology] had revealed the parlous state of Rommel's logistics." Unlike Churchill, Wavell faced the mechanical realities of making the Cubs ready for desert battles for which they were structurally unsuited.[77] The prime minister wrote in his memoirs that "on May 31st General Wavell reported the technical difficulties which he was having with the re-formation of the 7th Armoured Division." In fact, on May 30 and 31, Wavell sent Dill and Churchill telegrams about the need to repair the tanks before engaging in battle. Operation BATTLEAXE would thus be postponed until June 15. John Connell wrote: "The strategist and the tactician alike were powerless in the oil-blackened hands of the garage mechanic; and this was a factor whose effect Winston Churchill—who had, as a younger man, done so much to bring about the mechanical and technical revolution in war—admitted too seldom in the years 1940–45."[78]

Wavell launched partial offensives first in mid-May, and then with the new tanks in mid-June. Both failed. Beckett wrote: "There were severe mechanical defects in many of the new tanks and Ultra could not reveal either the qualitative superiority of the Germans nor how Rommel would deploy 88mm [mobile] anti-aircraft guns in an anti-tank role to blunt the offensives."[79] By June 1941, wrote Churchill in his memoirs, the British government "had the feeling that Wavell was a tired man. It might well be said that we had ridden the willing horse to a standstill.

The extraordinary convergence of five or six different theatres, with their ups and downs, especially downs, upon a single Commander-in-Chief constituted a strain to which few soldiers have been subjected. I was discontented with Wavell's provision for the defence of Crete, and especially that a few more tanks had not been sent."[80] Churchill would order his dismissal on June 21, just as the massive German invasion of Russia began. After his dismissal, Wavell commented: "The Prime Minister is quite right. There ought to be a new eye and a new hand in this theatre."[81]

Churchill would mitigate his responsibility for the intervention in Greece. In September 1941, Colville reported in his diary: "The P.M. talked to me while he was dressing for dinner. He said that so far the Government had only made one error of judgment: Greece. He had instinctively had doubts. We could and should have defended Crete and advised the Greek Government to make the best terms it could. But the campaign, and the Yugoslav volte-face which it entailed, had delayed Germany and might after all prove to have been an advantage." The Churchill aide "was surprised at the P.M.'s assertion that he had doubted the wisdom of going to Greece. I seem to remember his influencing the decision in favour of an expedition and Dill being against it. Incidentally he has now got his knife right into Dill and frequently disparages him."[82] Dill would be replaced in December 1941.

Max Beaverbrook observed that the prime minister "was intensely pugnacious and never bore rancour."[83] Churchill interfered because he believed he knew better than the generals, as he sometimes did. His nature and his office compelled him to prod, suggest, and interfere. Historian Christopher Bell argued "that Churchill's strategic judgement was, at best, inconsistent . . . he possessed a brilliant and fertile imagination, tremendous courage, and unbounded optimism, but . . . these qualities were marred by his restlessness and offensive spirit, which sometimes led him to champion reckless and impracticable schemes."[84] In 1940–1942, the Prime Minister had focused on those who commanded the North African theater. "Churchill," wrote Carlo D'Este, "interfered with every aspect of operations in the Middle East." This was especially true early in the war, when there were fewer constraints on the prime minister from effective British military leaders; or, as occurred later, from U.S. military commanders.[85] "Every effort is to be made to reinforce General Wavell with military and Air forces, and if Admiral Cunningham requires more ships, the Admiralty will make proposals for supplying them," Churchill wrote on April 28, 1941, emphasizing the importance of his Middle East strategy: "It is to be impressed upon all ranks, especially the highest, that the life and honour of Great Britain depends upon the successful defence of Egypt."[86] In principle, the honor and preservation of the British Empire ranked high for Churchill. The strategic and tactical importance of the Suez Canal and the oil-rich Middle East ranked just as high. Eventually, the British military chiefs, and later the American military chiefs, would impose an external discipline on the prime minister's freedom of action. But honor and empire were not abandoned.

To achieve a British victory in northern Africa, Churchill would shuffle commanders until Rommel's Afrika Corps was defeated. Eden recalled that on May 10, 1941, at a meeting of top cabinet ministers, Churchill had been "in favour of changing Auchinleck and Wavell about. Max [Beaverbrook] agreed as [Leo] Amery had already done. The other three of us were more doubtful. As I knew the men best, I found the advice not easy to give. I have no doubt that Archie [Wavell] has the better mind, but one does not know how he is bearing the strain and one cannot tell, though some of his recent reactions seem to indicate that he is flagging. In the end I weakly counseled delay and asked to wait for Crete result. Winston agreed there was not unanimity."[87]

About a month later, Wavell's Operation BATTLEAXE failed. It had been undertaken to relieve the British garrison at the port of Tobruk by attacking Axis forces in North Africa. Churchill had decided on a change in command. Eden wrote that "when I realized that a decision was near, I talked to Dill about it and asked his opinion. Reluctantly he had to admit that a change could not be resisted. He thought the Commander-in-Chief [Wavell] tired and that he knew it himself. I accepted this judgment as final so far as I was concerned."[88] On June 21, 1941, Churchill wrote Wavell: "I have come to the conclusion that public interest will best be served by appointment of General Auchinleck to relieve you in command and conduct of these armies both in success and adversity, and victories which are associated with your name will be famous in the story of the British Army and are an important contribution to our final success in this obstinate war. I feel however that after the long strain you have borne[,] a new eye and a new hand are required in this most seriously menaced theatre." Wavell, ever the gentleman, answered the prime minister: "I think you are wise to make change and get new ideas and action on the many problems in Middle East and am sure Auchinleck will be [a] successful choice. I appreciate your generous references to my work and am honoured that you should consider me fitted to fill post of C.-in-C. in India."[89]

Churchill had chosen, as Middle East commander, General Claude John Eyre Auchinleck, a quiet but careful planner—not unlike Wavell himself. The prime minister preferred generals who could challenge him as well as the Germans. General Ismay wrote of Auchinleck: "Only those who knew him well realised that he was shy and sensitive. He was as much an introvert as his political chief was an extrovert, and there were likely to be misunderstandings between them unless they [Churchill and Auchinleck] got to understand each other."[90] Air Marshal Arthur Tedder, who served in Cairo with both Wavell and Auchinleck, thought much more highly of Auchinleck. Tedder described Auchinleck: "Calm, determined and confident, without indulging in the wishful thinking which has been so much a weakness of some of the senior soldiers (when they are not in the depths of equally unjustifiable pessimism!) A. [Auchinleck] is balanced—which is worth anything!"[91] Churchill continued to gamble on victory in the Middle East. Now he wagered that Auchinleck could deliver it.

The new commander was soon recalled from Cairo to Britain for consultations—as Wavell had been one year earlier. At Chequers, General Ismay tried to help Auchinleck understand Churchill, arguing that

> Churchill could not be judged by ordinary standards; he was different from anyone we had ever met before, or were ever likely to meet again. As a war leader, he was head and shoulders above anyone that the British or any other nation could produce. He was indispensable and completely irreplaceable. The idea that he was rude, arrogant and self-seeking was entirely wrong. He was none of these things. He was certainly frank in speech and writing, but he expected others to be equally frank with him. To a young brigadier from Middle East Headquarters, who had asked if he might speak freely, he replied, "Of course. We are not here to pay each other compliments." He was a child of nature.[92]

Historians William L. Langer and S. Everett Gleason summed up the prime minister's plans for General Auchinleck: "Churchill, ever disposed to think in offensive rather than defensive terms, was eager to take advantage of the respite provided by the Nazi-Soviet conflict to rush reinforcements to Egypt and launch an attack on Rommel in the hope of driving him out of North Africa before Hitler could make more troops, tanks and planes available to the Libyan theater."[93]

The prime minister brought pressure to bear on Auchinleck. "On 8th August Auchinleck came to see me to say good-bye—he was to fly back that night," General Kennedy recalled the meeting:

> It was impossible not to like and admire Auchinleck. He had great charm, a strong personality, and a fine presence. Had he been a little more fortunate, he might well have been one of the great figures of the war. But three things were to bring him down. He had got his command at the wrong time, before we were very strong in Egypt; he was a "frontier" soldier, one of the very best we ever had—but he knew little of European war; and we felt in the War Office he was not a good picker of men, nor would he take advice in selecting his subordinates. Probably this last fault was the most serious of the three. But with this criticism he would never agree, because if ever there was a man who was loyal to his subordinates it was Auchinleck.[94]

Wavell had been fortunate that his campaign against the Italians was led by the very able General Richard O'Connor. Subsequent British efforts would suffer after the Germans captured O'Connor in April 1941.[95] Auchinleck could have used him.

Auchinleck's army command in India was taken up by Wavell. At the time, the switch seemed a propitious move. Churchill would press Auchinleck to continue on the offensive before the situation in the Middle East might deteriorate further. The general insisted on several months to prepare for an offensive and to get the necessary tank reinforcements. Historian Richard Lamb wrote that in the summer of 1941, "Churchill felt it was intolerable for the Eighth Army to stand idle while fierce battles raged between Russia and Germany in the East; he also feared an autumn attack on the Middle East by the Germans from the north, through Anatolia or the Caucasus, which would oblige Auchinleck to divide his forces."[96] As Churchill wired Auchinleck in October: "It is impossible to explain to Parliament and the nation how it is our Middle East armies had to stand for 4½ months without engaging the enemy while all the time Russia is being battered to pieces. I have hitherto managed to prevent public discussion, but at any time it may break out. Moreover, the few precious weeks that remain to us for the exploitation of any success are passing."[97] Eventually, Auchinleck launched the British attack on his own timetable and achieved striking success, relieving the siege of Tobruk and retaking Benghazi. The British Eighth army under Auchinleck drove Axis forces back to El Agheila in December 1941. In part, hampered by ineffective subordinates, Auchinleck would not achieve the decisive victory Churchill craved.

In February 1942, the Germans began retaking the established British positions. Churchill demanded speedy action, not least because the British-held island of Malta, the naval key to the eastern Mediterranean, had become increasingly precarious. Hitler did not fully grasp the strategic importance of Malta, which was essential to resupply the Middle East, to control North Africa, and to protect the Suez Canal. Churchill "was anxious to help the island by an attack in force on Rommel, but Auchinleck persisted that he was not ready to give battle," wrote the prime minister's doctor. "And then early in May he [Auchinleck] offered to send strong forces to India. This was the last straw. It was decided to send him definite orders for an early offensive, which he must obey, or in default be relieved of his command."[98] Thus, by the spring of 1942, Auchinleck had lost the support of his London masters, who aimed for an immediate offensive—partly to protect Malta. "The manner in which he [Auchinleck] had conducted the long discussions [over strategy] had lost him the confidence of both the Cabinet and the Chiefs of Staffs," wrote General Kennedy. "We were now in a very tricky situation. On the one hand, it was dangerous that the Cabinet should direct the operations, and overrule the advice of their Commander-in-Chief [Auchinleck]. On the other hand time was short, and the delay inseparable from a change of command might well entail the loss of Malta. It could be argued with some reason that an exceptional situation had arisen, in which the Cabinet would be bound to assume a greater degree of military responsibility than would be normally justified."[99]

Like the strategic island of Malta, Tobruk, a strategic Libyan port near the border with Egypt, would preoccupy Churchill and it would eventually lead to Auchinleck's dismissal. Martin Gilbert wrote: "Intent on following the defence of Tobruk as closely as possible, Churchill asked Ismay to prepare both a large-scale plan and a model for him, and, meanwhile, 'the best photographs available, both from the air and from the ground.'"[100] In the spring of both 1941 and 1942, Churchill made clear his decision to hold Tobruk. "You should surely be able to hold Tobruk, with its permanent Italian defences, at least until or unless the enemy brings up strong artillery forces," the prime minister had earlier written General Wavell on April 7, 1941. "Tobruk therefore seems to be a place to be held to the death without thought of retirement. I should be glad to hear of your intentions."[101] Churchill's attitude would not change in 1942 with Auchinleck in charge.

Far away from London, control of Tobruk would change hands four times in World War II. By comparison, President Lincoln's worries about strategic threats arose much closer to the American capital—at a crucial border town on the Potomac River. Harpers Ferry, Virginia, changed hands fourteen times during the Civil War. Failure to secure the strategically sited transportation hub at the confluence of the Shenandoah and Potomac Rivers repeatedly irritated President Lincoln. It was first abandoned by Union troops on April 18, 1861—just three days after the Confederate attack on Fort Sumter. "I intend to give blows," said Lincoln. "The only question at present is, whether I should first retake Fort Sumter or Harper's Ferry."[102] In 1862, after a three-day siege by Confederates under Stonewall Jackson, the Union garrison of 12,400 surrendered on September 15. The capture of Harpers Ferry allowed Jackson to join the main body of Robert E. Lee's troops for the Battle of Antietam.

Tobruk and Harpers Ferry never failed to agitate both Lincoln and Churchill. Their geographical grasp of strategic chokepoints would always focus their attention.

I shall not do more than I can, and I shall do all I can to save the government, which is my sworn duty as well as my personal inclination. I shall do nothing in malice. What I deal with is too vast for malicious dealing.[1]

ABRAHAM LINCOLN
to Cuthbert Bullitt
July 28, 1862

When I survey and compute the power of the United States and its vast resources and feel they are now in it with us, with the British Commonwealth of Nations all together, however long it lasts, till death or victory, I cannot believe there is any other fact in the whole world which can compare with that. That is what I have dreamed of, aimed at, and worked for, and now it has come to pass.[2]

WINSTON S. CHURCHILL
February 15, 1942

IX.

1862/1942

For both political and military reasons, Abraham Lincoln in 1862 and Winston S. Churchill in 1942 desperately needed an impressive, quick victory. Like President Franklin D. Roosevelt, Lincoln was never far from a contested election. For FDR, national elections in 1940, 1942, and 1944 influenced what he believed politically and militarily possible—or desirable. For Lincoln, state and congressional elections extended over a comparatively broad time frame, affecting political decisions throughout the Civil War. After the Fort Sumter attack, Lincoln did not call Congress into session during the spring of 1861, because of pending congressional elections in some states. At the time congressional elections did not have uniform dates in all states.

In need of home front support, the Civil War president and the World War II prime minister each pressed their military leaders relentlessly—giving rise to resentment among the generals. In 1862, Lincoln needed a military triumph in Virginia, the most newspaper-accessible battlefront. In 1942, Churchill needed a victory in North Africa to shore up parliamentary support. "Papa is at a very low ebb. He is not too well physically—and is worn down by the continuous crushing pressure of events," wrote Churchill's daughter Mary in February 1942.[3] General Ismay recalled:

> 1942 was a year of extraordinary contrasts. It opened on a scene of hideous calamity. The American fleet had been crippled at Pearl Harbor. The *Prince of Wales* and *Repulse* [British battleship and battlecruiser] were at the bottom of the China Sea. The *Ark Royal* and *Barham* had been sunk in the Mediterranean. The *Valiant* and *Queen Elizabeth* had been put out of action for several

months by one-man submarines in Alexandria harbour. The light forces based on Malta had been practically annihilated in a minefield. The German armies were on the outskirts of Leningrad, and only twenty miles from Moscow. Hong Kong had fallen. Even worse was to follow in the early months of the New Year [1942]. Singapore, the Dutch East Indies, Burma and the Philippines, all passed into Japanese hands. India, Ceylon, Australia and New Zealand were wide open to invasion.[4]

In January 1862, a series of major problems afflicted Lincoln. Missteps by Treasury Secretary Salmon P. Chase compounded the straitened financial circumstances of the government. Convertibility of the currency to gold had been suspended in December 1861. The Union government was insolvent, financed by the controversial issue of paper "greenbacks." The Army of the Potomac had settled into winter camp. Its commander, George B. McClellan, was laid up in bed with typhoid. Plaintively, Lincoln asked Quartermaster General Montgomery Meigs: "General what shall I do? The people are impatient; Chase has no money and he tells me he can raise no more; the General of the Army has typhoid fever. The bottom is out of the tub. What shall I do?"[5] After reverses in June 1862, during McClellan's Peninsula Campaign, Lincoln wrote him:

Save your Army at all events. Will send reinforcements as fast as we can. Of course they can not reach you today, tomorrow, or next day. I have not said you were ungenerous for saying you needed reinforcements. I thought you were ungenerous in assuming that I did not send them as fast as I could. I feel any misfortune to you and your Army quite as keenly as you feel it yourself. If you have had a drawn battle, or a repulse, it is the price we pay for the enemy not being in Washington. We protected Washington, and the enemy concentrated on you; had we stripped Washington, he would have been upon us before the troops sent could have got to you. Less than a week ago you notified us that reinforcements were leaving Richmond to come in front of us. It is the nature of the case, and neither you or the government that is to blame. Please tell at once the present condition and aspect of things.[6]

The first two years of warfare generally went badly—both in the 1860s and in the 1940s. In April 1942, Churchill's wife wrote FDR aide Harry Hopkins that "we are indeed walking through the Valley of Humiliation."[7] In his memoirs, Churchill described the "cataract of disasters" endured by Britain in the first 28 months of his leadership: "The fiasco of Dakar, the loss of all our Desert conquests from the Italians, the tragedy of Greece, the loss of Crete, the unrelieved reverses of the Japanese war, the loss of Hong Kong, the overrunning of the A.B.D.A. [American-British-Dutch-Australian] Command and all its territories, the catastrophe of Singapore, the Japanese conquest of Burma, Auchinleck's defeat in the Desert, the surrender of Tobruk, the failure, as it was judged, at Dieppe—all these were galling links in a chain of misfortune and frustration to which no parallel could be found in our history."[8] Early in the war during the winter of 1940–1941, Operation COMPASS had provided a rare victory for the British. (Likewise, early in the Civil War during February 1862, the capture of Fort Henry and Fort Donelson in Tennessee by troops under General Grant represented rare Union triumphs.)

Lincoln and Churchill endured the consequences of military errors of judgment in early 1862 and early 1942. In February 1862, Union strategy would emphasize a Union attack down the Shenandoah Valley of Virginia. It was not to be a success. Lincoln aide John G. Nicolay reported how, on February 27, the president, already distraught over the recent death of his young son Willie, reacted to news of the operation's failure. That evening, Secretary of War Edwin M. Stanton entered the president's office,

> and after locking the door read the President two dispatches from the Gen [McClellan]. The first one reported that the bridge (pontoon, at Harper's [sic] Ferry) had been thrown in splendid style. . . . That a portion of the troops had crossed—that although it was raining; the troops were in splendid spirits and apparently ready to fight anything. The President seemed highly pleased at this. "The next is not so good," remarked the Sec. [of] War. It ran to the effect that the "lift lock" had turned out to be too narrow to admit the passage of the canal boats through to the river (as one of the facilities and precautions, arrangements had been made to build a permanent bridge of canal-boats across the Potomac, and a large number of canal-boats had

been fathered for that purpose.) That in consequence of this, he [McClellan] had changed the plan and had determined merely to protect the building of the bridges and the opening of the road. (Leaving the obvious inference that he proposed to abandon the movement on Winchester [Virginia]. In fact he so stated [because] the impossibility of building the permanent bridge as he had expected would delay him so that Winchester would be reinforced from Manassas, &c.).

"What does this mean?" asked the President.

"It means," said the Sec. War, "that it is a d—d fizzle. It means that he doesn't intend to do anything."

Later that night, Lincoln confronted General Randolph B. Marcy, father-in-law and chief of staff to McClellan, over the failure to assure that the boats would fit through locks in the Potomac Canal. The president asked: "Why . . . couldn't the Gen. have known whether a boat would go through that lock, before spending a million dollars getting them there? I am no engineer, but it seems to me that if I wished to know whether a boat would go through a hole, or a lock, common sense would teach me to go and measure it. I am almost despairing at these results. Everything seems to fail. The general impression is daily gaining ground that the Gen[eral] does not intend to do anything. By a failure like this we lose all the prestige we gained by the capture of Ft Donelson [Tennessee, by General Grant]. I am grievously disappointed—grievously disappointed and almost in despair."[9]

Churchill had a similar moment when in January 1942, he learned that Singapore, with 100,000 Commonwealth troops, might fall to a smaller force of Japanese attacking inland from British Malaya. His physician wrote that "one day in the middle of January I found him in a positively spectacular temper. He had just learnt from Wavell [now commander of Allied forces in Southeast Asia] that the defences of Singapore—the work of many years—were built only to meet attacks from the sea. Many of the guns could only fire seaward. It had never entered his head, he complained, that the rear of the fortress was quite unprotected against an attack from the land." Churchill asked: "Why didn't they tell me about this? Oh no, it is my own fault. I ought to have known. I could have asked. I cannot understand it. Did no one realize the position?"[10] Churchill had not been well-served by the information from military and civilian leaders in Singapore. (But "Churchill was almost culpably ignorant of the weakness of the British Army,"[11] wrote historian Richard Lamb. Perhaps, but the prime minister and General Brooke did focus on the general army weakness they inherited.)

In the wake of Churchill's mild heart attack in the White House of December 1941, and setbacks in the Far East, the prime minister appeared physically debilitated and mentally depressed in January and February 1942. Churchill might even have suffered a minor stroke. Loyalist Brendan Bracken had doubts about Churchill's stamina to handle the strain of his position. After talking to Churchill's worried physician, Bracken told Anthony Eden that Churchill might have suffered an occasional "blackout." Eden wrote that "this sounds very alarming & more like a stroke. Anyway, B[racken] maintained that Winston must give up more work or he would not be able to carry on. He was most depressed now, sat with his head in his hand, talked of lasting only a few weeks, etc. Only way out was to get him to shed greater part of his Defence duties & only person to whom he might shed them was me."[12] Churchill would recover and resume his punishing schedule.

Other ambitious men were at work in the London of February 1942. Eden and Beaverbrook, both Churchill allies, seemed to have sensed an opportunity to replace the weakened prime minister as he sought to reorganize his cabinet in the wake of the humiliating loss of Singapore. On February 12, Eden aide Oliver Harvey reported on a conversation he had with Eden: "A.E. feels he [Churchill] is more and more obstinate and at the same time losing his grip. I spoke of the rising of public opinion at successive disasters and failures which we both agreed was entirely justifiable. There might be an explosion which would sweep the whole Government out. The War Cabinet is now quite ineffective and so is the Defence Committee. A most disturbing situation which can't last. A.E. hesitates to say more to the PM who knows his views well enough."[13] Eden would even talk to the ambitious socialist, Stafford Cripps, about the need for change, but Churchill outmaneuvered both. First, he appointed Clement Attlee as deputy prime minister, thus pinning down the Labour Party. Then he offered Eden the additional powerful post of "Leader of the House."

When Eden hesitated, he swiftly gave the post to Cripps without first telling Eden. Harvey wrote in his diary: "A.E. rather annoyed at PM offering it to Cripps before he had had A.E.'s views and rather bitten now with leading H of C [House of Commons] as a stepping stone to being

PM later. He doesn't want Cripps to groom himself for PM."[14] Churchill had demonstrated that he was still boss, still prime minister, still minister of defence. Meanwhile, he had put Cripps into a position in which he was likely to fail. Eventually, Cripps would be moved aside for Eden—and Eden himself would struggle to handle the House leadership in addition to his Foreign Office duties. Indeed, when Eden became very sick in the spring of 1944 and 1945, it was Churchill who would take on the Foreign Office. It was always premature, even in sickness, to count out the indomitable prime minister.[15]

Lord Beaverbrook proved to be a greater problem for Churchill. Beaverbrook had been very effective in expanding aircraft production. He had been useful in developing warm relations with Roosevelt and Stalin, but the overbearing Beaverbrook created animosity and friction within the Churchill government. Beaverbrook and Churchill came to loggerheads on February 9 and 10, over a "White Paper" on war production that Churchill intended to send to Parliament, inciting Beaverbrook to threaten resignation. Churchill then sent the paper to Beaverbrook with a challenge: "I am sure it is your duty to undertake this work and try your best to make a success of it, and that you have ample powers for the purpose."[16] Beaverbrook blinked, using the occasion to support Churchill's policy with a speech in the House of Lords. The mercurial Beaverbrook would again change his position over the next week, his attitude toward Cripps also having changed. "We are in the midst of a political crisis. The newspapers made it. But the Prime Minister keeps it alive," Beaverbrook wrote on February 17.[17] That same day, he wrote to Churchill, expressly undermining Cripps and advocating a reorganization of the War Cabinet.[18] Curiously, among Beaverbrook's candidates to continue in the War Cabinet were Attlee and Bevin. But when Churchill proposed a tentative new War Cabinet with Attlee as deputy prime minister, Cripps as leader of the House, and Beaverbrook as minister of production, Beaverbrook protested against the posts for Cripps and Attlee.[19] The conflict intensified when the blunt Beaverbrook personally confronted Attlee with a distinctly negative assessment of the Labour leader's value to the government.[20]

Cripps, too, caused problems for the prime minister. He had made it clear that he would not take the job of Minister of Supply without getting a seat in the War Cabinet. In his letter to Churchill, he wrote: "From this you will see that I should not feel myself justified in taking on the task under the conditions suggested, as I do not feel I could make a success of the post, and I should only disappoint both you and the public. I am sorry that I feel myself compelled, after the most careful and anxious consideration, to come to this negative conclusion, as I had hoped that I might be able to give you some small help with the heavy burden you are bearing."[21] Churchill replied with a tortured explanation as to why the War Cabinet could not be expanded. By later bringing Cripps into the cabinet as leader of the House of Commons, Churchill effectively tried to construct a team of rivals around him. Better to keep them close by inside the cabinet than as hostiles outside in Parliament.

Beaverbrook had maneuvered himself out of the Cabinet—refusing the new posts the prime minister offered him. It was finally agreed that Beaverbrook would resign on grounds of bad health. Churchill commented: "He needn't have gone. He could have had any one of three or four offices. . . . I didn't want him to go. He was good for me! Any number of times, if things were going badly, he would encourage me saying, 'Look at all the things on your side. Look what you've accomplished. Be of good courage!' and he put courage and pep into me!"[22] On February 26, 1942, Beaverbrook resigned, gracefully stating: "All the time, everything that has been done by men has been due to your holding me up. You took a great chance in putting me in and you stood to be shot at by a section of members for keeping me here."[23] Churchill replied: "We have lived & fought side by side through terrible days, & I am sure our comradeship & public work will undergo no break. All I want you to do now is to recover yr strength & poise, so as to be able to come to my aid when I shall v[er]y greatly need you."[24] Such struggles among ambitious, successful men in high office had been summarized by a cynical Lloyd George: "No friends at the top."[25] In his speech to the House, the prime minister explained: "After nearly two years of strain and struggle, it was right and necessary that a Government called into being in the crash of the battle of France should undergo both change and reinvigoration."[26]

In early April 1942, Harry Hopkins and George Marshall posed another challenge for Churchill when they led an American delegation to London to present American war plans for Europe. They proposed three related operations—first, an American buildup in the United Kingdom called BOLERO; then a limited cross-channel strike against German-occupied France in 1942 called SLEDGEHAMMER; followed by a larger cross-channel invasion in 1943 of Northwest France, called ROUNDUP. Though outwardly polite and encouraging, Churchill and his military associates thought the invasion plans naive, premature, and unrealistic. The British believed that a massive buildup of American troops and materiel would be necessary for the invasion, and that much more training of green American soldiers would be required.[27] (As it would turn out, the needed experience in complex, multiservice amphibious landings—such as that to be gained in the preparations and execution of combined Anglo-American operations in North Africa and Italy—would prove vital.) British officials were reluctant to tell the American military planners that their preliminary invasion ideas of 1942 were premature. (The British were diplomatic, not least because they were becoming substantial debtors to the United States for necessary supplies obtained under the expanding Lend-Lease program.) General Kennedy confided in his diary:

> *If* we could be sure that the Germans might be knocked out by a maximum effort this spring [of 1942] we could of course do enough to make them divert considerable forces [from the eastern front] to France. But the fundamental difficulty is that we cannot be sure. We had to carry on this war for over a year [1940–1941] without the Russians. We may have to carry it on again without them [if Russia were defeated]. It would be the most colossal gamble in history to stake everything on this spring offensive [a cross-channel invasion of France]. It could mean the sacrifice of the means of defence of the UK both at sea and on land, the sacrifice of everything in the Indian Ocean and the Middle East. For nothing less would provide the naval, military and shipping resources for a big European effort. In fact the gamble for us could be far bigger than it ever was for Hitler to attempt invasion of this country. We are not prepared to risk everything—and it would be everything—on this one throw.[28]

General Kennedy's considered view would prevail, supported by Brooke, Churchill, and finally, Roosevelt.

The British carefully communicated their attitude toward U.S. military plans in France. Churchill and Brooke fully supported the buildup of American forces in the United Kingdom preparatory to an invasion (BOLERO). They concluded, however, that the proposed 1942 cross-channel invasion (SLEDGEHAMMER) would not only be premature, but a doomed effort, thus doing little to aid the Russians, who did insist on a Second Front. The Americans came to London

George B. McClellan, ca. 1861–1864
Gilder Lehrman Collection, GLC05135.028

looking for agreement to their plans. The British aimed to show support for a future invasion plan in principle, but that they thought the timing wrong. The prime minister did want the Americans to focus on Europe (not Japan)—but he would not rush plans even for a 1942 limited invasion of France that he believed sure to fail. Nevertheless, the Americans departed thinking their arguments had been successful; the British allowed them to think so. Historian Andrew Roberts suggested that Churchill misled Roosevelt when the prime minister wired him: "We wholeheartedly agree with your conception of concentration against the main enemy, and we cordially accept your plan with one broad qualification . . . prevent[ing] a junction of the Germans and the Japanese." Churchill further told FDR of the necessity

> to act this year. Your [American] plan visualised this, but put mid-September as the earlier date. Things may easily come to a head before then. Marshall explained that you had been reluctant to press for an enterprise that was fraught with such grave risks and dire consequences until you could make a substantial air contribution; but he left us in no doubt that if it were found necessary to act earlier, you, Mr President, would earnestly wish to throw in every available scrap of human and material resources. We are proceeding with plans and arrangements on that basis. Broadly speaking, our agreed programme is a crescendo of activity on the Continent.[29]

Churchill's fertile brain continued to hatch ideas for prosecuting the war. A few were impractical—but, as he often implied, far better to have impractical ideas than, out of irresolution, none at all. Military strategist Kennedy recalled that in June 1942, "before he left for Washington, Churchill had given us, in considerable detail, plans of campaign for the reconquest of Burma, for the occupation of the northern end of Norway, for rolling up the Germans by an advance from Northern Europe, and for an invasion of Germany from the West." Kennedy concluded: "The project for Burma was impracticable because the means were lacking, especially naval and air forces. The Norwegian idea was impracticable for all three Services; so were the proposals for the invasion of Germany. We consumed a great deal of time and energy in pointing out these facts."[30] The prime minister's habit was to propose plans and to question the expert opinions of his military and civilian staff and colleagues. It was a mark of his leadership, as commander in chief, often resented by subordinates.

When Union generals early in the Civil War had objected to a premature battle in the summer of 1861 with Confederate forces in Virginia—because Union soldiers were "green"—Lincoln had pointed out that so, too, were the Confederate soldiers. In World War II, green American soldiers landing on the European continent would meet well-trained, battle-hardened German troops occupying northern France. To convince Churchill that the Americans were ready, General Marshall arranged for the prime minister in June 1942 to view American military maneuvers in South Carolina. Churchill might have been struck more by the stifling southern humidity than the readiness of American troops for battle. General Ismay told Churchill that "to put these [American] troops against continental [German] troops would be murder." He responded that the American soldiers were "wonderful material and will learn very quickly." The prime minister believed, however, that training alone did not prepare a soldier for war, especially against the hardened Germans.[31]

In the spring of 1942, the reality governing Allied war plans became clear. The Americans wanted to open a second front in Europe, but they were not yet equipped or prepared to lead it. The British knew that they alone could not undertake the invasion. Indeed, the required shipping and landing craft were unavailable. Furthermore, some senior American officials such as Admiral Ernest King resented efforts to put operations in the European theater before his preferred Pacific operations against Japan. For the Russians, the most misleading development occurred when Soviet Foreign Minister Vyacheslav Molotov visited Washington in May 1942. President Roosevelt tried to mollify Molotov in order to ensure Stalin's continued resistance to Germany—by promising a second front before the end of 1942.[32] The U.S. ambassador to Russia, William H. Standley, wrote FDR on June 22 of the consequences of his dissimulation: "In view of the manner in which the Soviet government and people have accepted what would appear here to be a solemn obligation on the part of the United States and Great Britain to create a second front in 1942, I feel convinced that if such a front does not materialize quickly and on a large scale, these people [the Russian authorities] will be so deluded in their belief in our sincerity of purpose and will for concerted action that inestimable harm will be done to the cause of the United Nations."[33] FDR's empty promise would become an embarrassment, thereby reducing American credibility in the alliance, especially with Stalin.

More shocks would greet Churchill when he visited Washington in June 1942. His worst moment came with news of the surrender of the British garrison in Tobruk, Libya—overrun by General Rommel—threatening all British positions in the Middle East. In silent humiliation on June 21, Churchill received the news while in conference with Roosevelt at the White House. "Neither Winston nor I had contemplated such an eventuality and it was a staggering blow," wrote Alan Brooke. "I cannot remember what the individual words were that the President used to convey his sympathy, but I remember vividly being impressed by the tact and real heartfelt sympathy that lay behind these words,"[34] The prime minister had previously issued orders that Tobruk should not be evacuated, but Auchinleck even earlier had made clear that if necessary, it should be. "What matters is that it should happen when I am here," Churchill told his physician. "I am ashamed. I cannot understand why Tobruk gave in. More than 30,000 of our men put their hands up."[35] Churchill, ever resilient, would recover quickly. Two days later, Dr. Wilson noted in his diary that "before I left his bedroom on Sunday, Winston had refused to take the count; he got up a little dazed, but full of fight. I sat up on the night of Tobruk and last night till he went to bed, thinking he might want me. But he isn't made like that. There is never any danger of his folding up in dirty weather. My heart goes out to him. I do like a really fullsized man. With our military prestige at zero here, he has dominated the discussions."[36] The prime minister himself often would speak of his "black dog" of melancholy. But the dog could vanish as swiftly as it appeared.

Ironically, the fall of Tobruk, according to some historians, may have been the unfortunate result of Churchill's interventions. Auchinleck had made it clear on January 19: "It is NOT my intention to try to hold permanently Tobruk or any other locality west of the frontier."[37] Neither Churchill nor Brooke commented on Auchinleck's intended tactics at the time. Auchinleck repeated his intention one month later when he wrote: "If for any reason, we should be forced at some future date to withdraw from our present forward positions, every effort will still be made to prevent Tobruk being lost to the enemy, but it is not my intention to continue to hold it once the enemy is in a position to invest it effectively." The prime minister had written Auchinleck to emphasize the importance of keeping sufficient soldiers at Tobruk "to hold the place for certain." Richard Lamb contended: "Churchill's insistence on Tobruk being defended pushed his general into a gross tactical mistake against his better judgement at the eleventh hour."[38] Correlli Barnett wrote that Churchill had effectively ordered Auchinleck to hold Tobruk, writing the general on June 15: "We are glad to have your assurance that you have no intention of giving up Tobruk. War Cabinet interpret your telegram to mean that, if the need arises, General [Neil M.] Ritchie would leave as many troops in Tobruk as are necessary to hold the place for certain." Barnett wrote: "This of course was an order, and Auchinleck obeyed it," paving "the way for one of the greatest single disasters ever suffered by the British in the Middle East and Mediterranean in the Second World War."[39] The strategic disaster also consisted of the capture of thirty thousand British soldiers and officers, and huge stores of war materials. Churchill himself did not accept responsibility, writing in his memoirs: "We did not however know the conditions prevailing in Tobruk. Considering that Auchinleck's plan had been to await an attack, and remembering all the months that had passed, it was inconceivable that the already well-proved fortifications of Tobruk should not have been maintained in the highest efficiency, and indeed strengthened."[40] He did acknowledge that the surrender of Tobruk "was one of the heaviest blows I can recall during the war."[41]

Tobruk's capture reinforced Churchill's determination to focus Allied military plans on North Africa. Before going to Washington on June 21, the prime minister spent several days in private discussions with President Roosevelt at Hyde Park. While American and British military officials in Washington were discussing an invasion of Europe, Churchill tried to persuade Roosevelt that a joint operation in North Africa was the optimum strategy of practical opportunity. The prime minister was convinced that the overwhelming armed force and the necessary shipping, then unavailable, must first be produced and assembled to mount an effective invasion of France. He presented well-prepared, sound military reasons to delay the cross-channel invasion. Roosevelt, however, wanted to put American troops into battle before the 1942 mid-term congressional elections (much as Lincoln had political reasons for pressing a battle with the rebels in Virginia in October 1862).

Churchill had outlined his strategy in a memo he gave to FDR in New York: "We strongly hold to the view that there should be no substantial landing in France this year unless we are going to stay. No responsible British military authority has so far been able to make a plan for September 1942 which had any chance of success unless the Germans became utterly demoralized, of which there is no likelihood."[42] "The

British," wrote historian Andrew Roberts, "effectively used their own vulnerability as a trump card, somehow trading on their very weakness after
the fall of Tobruk to get what they wanted." Roberts noted that even
Marshall, skeptical of political considerations, later observed that "the
leader in a democracy has to keep the people entertained. . . . People
demand action. We couldn't wait to be completely ready."[43] Operation
GYMNAST, as the North Africa invasion was initially named, satisfied
several military objectives—putting American soldiers into real combat,
training them for battle in amphibious operation, testing cooperation
between American and British invasion forces, engaging the French
forces stationed in North Africa, and showing Stalin that a diversion-
ary western front had been opened against Hitler. This second front in
North Africa would give some relief to the beleaguered Russian army
fighting for survival along more than a thousand-mile front from Leningrad in the north to Stalingrad in the south.[44]

Alarmed by defeats and anxious for a victory, Churchill relentlessly
pressed Auchinleck in the early summer of 1942. "It is such a pity that
Winston's fine courage and drive cannot be harnessed to the war effort
in a more rational way," wrote General Kennedy of the prime minister's
telegraphed advice.[45] (Like Lincoln's McClellan, Auchinleck wanted
more troops.) The prime minister told his general none was available.[46]
In the "first" Battle of El Alamein during July, British and German forces
fought each other to a stalemate. There, the incompetence of Auchinleck's subordinates became clear. Rommel blocked every British break-
through attempt. Auchinleck halted the offensive to rest his exhausted
troops. That would not do for Churchill. (Similarly, McClellan's lack of
follow-through in September 1862 after the Battle of Antietam would not
do for Lincoln.)

In early August 1942, at great personal risk, Churchill flew to Cairo
to investigate. "I saw that Army," he wrote. "It was a broken, baffled
Army, a miserable Army. I felt for them with all my heart."[47] Still, he
was reluctant to replace the commander. "The PM hates the thought of
removing one of his commanders," wrote Dr. Wilson in his diary.[48] None-
theless on August 8, Churchill named General Harold Alexander to
replace Auchinleck.[49] A veteran of the Dunkirk evacuation, in June 1940,
Alexander had in early 1942 been named commander of British forces
in Burma; he had overseen the withdrawal of those troops to India.
Brooke supported the prime minister's decision to cashier Auchinleck,

but critics like historian Reginald W. Thompson have argued that Churchill exceeded his authority in dismissing the commander's subordinates. "Auchinleck's position of strength and his plans (fully adopted by his inheritors) made no difference to the prime minister's attitude. His mind was fully made up, not only to get rid of Auchinleck but to sweep the whole command structure out of his way."[50] But according to General Brooke, it was Auchinleck's subordinates, such as Ritchie, who had been the problem. They "had so dispersed our forces in the desert that Rommel, with his more effective tanks and guns, had little difficulty in defeating the scattered fragments piece-meal," wrote Dr. Wilson. He added: "There is another reason [for his dismissal]: the Auk does not understand Winston."[51] The order Churchill delivered to Alexander was simple: "Your prime and main duty will be take or destroy at the earliest opportunity the German-Italian Army commanded by Field Marshal Rommel, together with all its supplies and establishments in Egypt and Libya."[52] It was a tall order.

From 1940 to 1942, the British army consistently disappointed the harried Churchill. Max Hastings wrote that the British army "was much less effective a military institution [than the U.S. army]. For every clever officer such as Brooke, Ismay or Jacob, there were a hundred others lacking skill, energy, and imagination." Indeed, for much of 1941–1942, the British army outside of the Middle East was, as the prime minister suggested, underemployed. But it was also undersupplied. "Of some twenty-five infantry and four armoured divisions at home, only perhaps ten were battleworthy," wrote Hastings.[53]

Though Churchill's relations with his generals often proved unsatisfactory, his interactions with admirals were sometimes worse.[54] Despite two stints as First Lord of the Admiralty, Churchill's naval strategy could be strikingly flawed, such as ordering the battleship *Prince of Wales* and the battlecruiser *Repulse* to South Asia under his headstrong friend Admiral Tom Phillips. In Churchill's defense, American diplomat Averell Harriman observed that the prime minister would try "to do his share in the Pacific. He knew it would be mostly the United States, but he wanted Great Britain to do its share."[55] In fact, the prime minister had sent the British ships in an effort to deter conflict with Japan, not to encourage it. At the time, Churchill underestimated the vulnerability of the unprotected fleet to attacks from the air. On the whole, he well-understood, from long experience and study, the vital role of the navy and merchant marines, as he would write: "The Battle of the Atlantic was the dominating factor all through the war," and moreover, "Never for one moment could we forget that everything happening elsewhere, on land, at sea, or in the air, depended ultimately on its outcome, and amid all other cares we viewed its changing fortunes day by day with hope or apprehension."[56]

"[N]avies and naval matters were utterly foreign to Lincoln," wrote military historian Craig Symonds. "Yet as president he would preside over the development and deployment of the largest naval force in American history to date."[57] Lincoln's general relations with the leadership of the Union navy were good, especially with Admirals John A. Dahlgren, David G. Farragut, and David Dixon Porter. Destruction of the rebel armies, however, remained the president's dominant military focus. Still, Lincoln's naval strategy sought control of the rivers and the coast, believing that Union supremacy on the water could cut off Confederate exports and supply lines.

Delay and defeat tried Lincoln and Churchill to the quick. In October 1863, journalist Noah Brooks, a Lincoln confidante, wrote: "Two years ago, when Governor [Richard] Yates, of Illinois, urged upon the president the confiscation of rebel property, emancipation and the enlistment of a million black soldiers, Old Abe telegraphed: 'Hold fast, Dick, and see the salvation of the Lord.' I believe that Dick begins to 'see it.'"[58] Yates grasped the president's strategy, but the governor's timing was premature. Lincoln's inner drive for action rarely overcame his patience.

Churchill's sense of urgency was legendary. He questioned. He challenged. "[H]e pushed and pushed and pushed, which was all to the good," said General Ian Jacob.[59] But the prime minister needed colleagues and subordinates such as General Brooke to oppose ill-conceived plans.[60] General Kennedy wrote: "It had become a well-known idiosyncrasy of the Prime Minister's to talk of shooting generals. But, of course, nobody took it literally, or as other than a vent for his feelings of exasperation."[61] Harold Macmillan, who spent much of the war as a diplomat in the Mediterranean, recalled that in November 1943, "Somebody rashly remarked that Services were better coordinated in this war than in the last. The Chiefs of Staff system was a good one. 'Not at all,' said Winston. 'Not at all. It leads to weak and faltering decisions—or rather indecisions. Why, you may take the most gallant sailor, the most intrepid airman, or the most audacious soldier, put them at a table together—what do you get? *The sum total of their fears!*"[62] President Lincoln also worried when a council of war had been called in the Army of the Potomac; he believed that such councils too often erred on the side of caution. He became much distressed by the one called by General George Meade, after the Battle of Gettysburg in July 1863; the generals decided that an aggressive pursuit of the Confederates was not immediately possible.[63] (The father of General Douglas MacArthur had once told his son: "Doug, councils of war breed timidity and defeatism."[64])

Churchill motivated his military commanders even when his advice was not the best. Colville wrote that the prime minister "was not just a critic of their deliberations and an instigator of decisions. He would dictate 'directives' for them to consider. These were masterly documents, well thought out, original in content, clear and to the point. Like papal encyclicals they were known in central government circles by their opening words. Thus a long and detailed one which began, 'Renown awaits the Commander who first . . . ' was in frequent demand and was simply called 'Renown Awaits.' They were the instruments by which Churchill sought to direct the conduct and strategy of the war."[65] At the end of the war in Europe, the prime minster would gather the Chiefs of Staff at Downing Street for a toast and a photo. To the embarrassment of aides, the COS did not reciprocate Churchill's praise of the generals as "architects of victory."[66]

President Lincoln, too, could occasionally become impatient, writing George McClellan on October 13, 1862, a few days after he visited the general: "You remember my speaking to you of what I called your overcautiousness. Are you not over-cautious when you assume that you can not do what the enemy is constantly doing? Should you not claim to be at least his equal in prowess, and act upon the claim?"[67] In September 1863, the president reached the limit of his frustration with General Ambrose E. Burnside, then operating in eastern Tennessee: "Yours of the 23rd. is just received, and it makes me doubt whether I am awake or dreaming. I have been struggling for ten days, first through Gen. Halleck, and then directly, to get you to go to assist Gen. [William] Rosecrans in an extremity, and you have repeatedly declared you would do it, and yet you steadily move the contrary way."[68] Lincoln marked the telegram: "Not sent." This, the president did when he concluded that his words would not be constructive under the strain of present facts and circumstances. His prudence often trumped his impatience.

Inactive armies in the field bedeviled both President Lincoln and Prime Minister Churchill. In a parliamentary debate on May 7, 1941, Churchill responded to criticism by David Lloyd George, Britain's former prime minister in whose World War I cabinet Churchill had served:

> My right hon. Friend [Lloyd George] spoke of the great importance of my being surrounded by people who would stand up to me and say, "No, No, No." Why, good gracious, has he no idea how strong the negative principle is in the constitution and working of the British war-making machine? The difficulty is not, I assure him, to have more brakes put on the wheels; the difficulty is to get more impetus and speed behind it. At one moment we are asked to emulate the Germans in their audacity and vigour, and the next moment the Prime Minister is to be assisted by being surrounded by a number of "No-men" to resist me at every point and prevent me from making anything in the nature of a speedy, rapid and, above all, positive constructive decision.[69]

Such were Lincoln's thoughts after McClellan's failure to follow and destroy General Lee's army after Antietam. The president despaired again when General Meade failed, after victory at Gettysburg, to chase Lee's army to destruction. "I have no faith that Meade will attack Lee; nothing looks like it to me," the president told Gideon Welles. "I believe he can never have another as good opportunity as that which he trifled away. Everything since has dragged with him."[70]

In 1942, British leaders were more realistic than their American counterparts about a premature, underequipped, overmatched Allied invasion of France. The British knew from hard experience the skill and bravery of the German armies and their officer corps. William Manchester and Paul Reid observed of the prime minister's discussions with General Marshall in April 1942 that "Churchill had done to Marshall what Brooke and the British chiefs regularly did to him when he proposed a scheme not to their liking: voiced enthusiasm and then studied the proposal to death." They wrote that "in Churchill, Marshall believed he had found a true statesman, a man he could trust. And in Marshall, Churchill had found a man he could respect, a man who told the truth, whatever the political costs. Thus, Churchill felt regret when Marshall, a few weeks after departing [London], realized the British had no intention of landing in France, in force, in 1942."[71] Unlike U.S. military leaders, the prime minister recognized that America was simply unprepared for such an invasion. He then deftly managed American leaders, especially FDR, to support his goal of deferring the cross-channel invasion until ready.[72] Still, the Americans would press their case. The British evaded them quietly, unwilling to broadcast their military inadequacies. "The universal cry to start a second front is going to be hard to compete with, and yet what can we do with some 10 divisions against the German masses?" wrote Alan Brooke.

In effect, Churchill spent much of 1942 telling both the Americans and the Russians what they wanted to hear—that opening a second front was planned—while he bought time for a more effective strategy in North Africa with a greater probability of success. The Anglo-Americans hoped the Russian army could keep Hitler pinned down in the east. Even as the prime minister desired to keep American attention focused on Europe, he would not allow American generals to act precipitously. Instead, the British chose to bomb Germany itself, where area bombing had more limited military impact than the English or Americans believed, not least because the bombs often missed their targets.[73]

Churchill had also focused on organizing special operations within enemy-held territory to "set Europe ablaze," but the prime minister underestimated the gruesome brutality of German reprisals that limited local assistance for such guerilla warfare.[74] John Keegan wrote: "Churchill's belief that the defeated peoples of Europe could be brought to wear down Germany's control from within was to prove, almost everywhere, one of his most ill-judged ideas. On July [22], 1940, he instructed Hugh Dalton, head of the new created Special Operations Executive (SOE), to 'set Europe ablaze.' . . . The result was that in urbanized, law-abiding Western Europe most citizens were, understandably, too frightened to resist; they were discouraged from doing so, in any case, by the domestic bureaucracies that the Germans left in place."[75] When local residents did resist or commit sabotage, Nazi brutality discouraged future efforts that would invite even more reprisals.

Churchill confidently advocated Operation TORCH, his contemplated invasion of North Africa in 1942, as the primary way to divert German arms from the Russian front. Such was the message that the prime minister took to the United States in June 1942. American military officials felt betrayed by their British counterparts—whom they thought had supported the cross-channel operation during the joint meeting in London in April. Roosevelt shared both the prime minister's doubts about an invasion of France, and his desire to launch a major operation as soon as possible. Despite the spirited opposition of top officials of the U.S. Department of War, including Secretary Stimson and General Marshall, Roosevelt in late July 1942 agreed with Churchill to undertake Operation TORCH (originally named GYMNAST) as the first major Allied initiative.[76] FDR wanted the American-led landings in French-occupied North Africa to take place under an American commander before the November 1942 elections. The prime minister wanted the joint landings to reinforce British operations against Rommel on the Egyptian-Libyan frontier.[77] Better than Roosevelt, Churchill understood the difficulties that the untested American soldiers would encounter when up against German arms.

From early 1941, the prime minister and his generals had focused on their Mediterranean strategy. From 1942 on, the American military leaders would campaign for a cross-channel strategy. "The American Chiefs of Staff did not believe that the conquest of Italy would threaten Germany, and they also feared that the Germans would withdraw and that we should find ourselves hitting the air," wrote Winston Churchill in his memoirs. "They did not think there was much to be gained by bombing Southern Germany from airfields in Southern Italy and they wanted all efforts against Germany to be concentrated on the shortest route across the English Channel."[78] Churchill resisted because "[t]he last thing the British government wanted was a premature cross-Channel attack," noted historian Jean Edward Smith. "The enormous battlefield losses of World War I, Churchill's own unfortunate experience with the amphibious landing at Gallipoli in 1915, and an awareness of how ill prepared and unready the Western Allies, particularly the United States, were to take on the Wehrmacht made London doubly cautious about launching an invasion of the Continent."[79] The prime minister grasped the strategic fact that a massive, waterborne invasion of France could only be tried once, and that it must be done right and successfully. Ultimately, his invasion timing prevailed in the Allied councils of war.

The Tobruk disaster in June 1942 had prompted a second parliamentary crisis in London. In the House of Commons, MP John Wardlaw-Milne moved: "That this House, while paying tribute to the heroism and endurance of the Armed Forces of the Crown in circumstances of exceptional difficulty, has no confidence in the central direction of the war."[80] MP Harold Nicolson wrote at the time:

Claude Auchinleck, 1945

Wardlaw-Milne is an imposing man with a calm manner which gives the impression of solidity. He is in fact rather an ass, and the position he has acquired as one of the leaders of the backbenches has caused his head to swell badly. He begins well enough, but then suddenly suggests that the Duke of Gloucester [the younger brother of King George VI] should be made Commander-in-Chief. A wave of panic-embarrassment passes over the House. For a full minute the buzz goes round, "But the man must be an ass." Milne pulls himself together and recaptures the attention of the House, but his idiotic suggestion has shaken the validity of his position and his influence is shattered.[81]

Churchill stood on shaky ground because he had consistently maintained that British tanks were the equal of German tanks. In fact, inferior British tanks helped to cause continuing setbacks for Middle East commanders. Fortunately for the prime minister, his parliamentary antagonists also proved inferior.[82]

Churchill used the crisis to praise the House of Commons: "This long Debate has now reached its final stage. What a remarkable example it has been of the unbridled freedom of our Parliamentary Institution in time of war!" The prime minister concluded:

The mover of this Vote of Censure has proposed that I should be stripped of my responsibilities for Defence in order that some military figure or some other unnamed personage should assume the general conduct of the war, that he should have complete control of the Armed Forces of the Crown, that he should be the Chief of the Chiefs of the Staff, that he should nominate or dismiss the generals or the admirals, that he should always be ready to resign, that is to say, to match himself against his political colleagues, if colleagues they could be considered, if he did not get all he wanted, that he should have under him a Royal Duke as Commander-in-Chief of the Army, and finally, I presume, though this was not mentioned, that his unnamed personage should find an appendage in the Prime Minister to make the necessary explanations, excuses, and apologies to Parliament when things go wrong, as they often do, and often will. That is at any rate a policy. It is a system very different from the Parliamentary system under which we live. It might easily amount to or be converted into a dictatorship. I wish to make it clear that as far as I am concerned I shall take no part in such a system.[83]

Churchill's opponents proved more inept in debate than did British soldiers in some recent battles. Still, the prime minister's margin of support on the confidence motion, 476–25, with more than three dozen abstentions, was not so overwhelming as the January vote of confidence had been. He would later express his abiding contempt for the actions and views of Aneurin Bevan, his most persistent and articulate opponent in the House. "I should think it was hardly possible to state the opposite of the truth with more precision," Churchill responded to his Welsh critic in a Commons debate in December 1944. "I back up those who seek to establish democracy and civilization. The Hon. Member [Bevan] must learn to take as well as to give. There is no one more free with interruptions, taunts, and jibes than he is. I saw him—I heard him, not saw him—almost assailing some of the venerable figures on the bench immediately below him. He need not get so angry because the House laughs at him; he ought to be pleased when they only laugh at him."[84]

The prime minister's tactical position in 1942 was complicated by his desire to contribute enough tanks, bombers, and supplies to Russia, while not depriving Britain of the American food and supplies it desperately needed. Moreover, he could not allow the United States to make the Pacific, rather than Europe, its primary theater of operations.[85] His position in 1942 was further complicated by his relationship with the French. Most Vichy French military leaders hated the English in general and Churchill in particular, inaccurately blaming the prime minister for insufficient support as France was collapsing in June 1940—and they resented the subsequent scuttling of the French fleet in July. Churchill had also successfully argued for an Allied invasion of Vichy-held North Africa and would urge his military commanders to strike across Libya toward French territory.

After flying to Moscow for his first meeting with Soviet dictator Joseph Stalin, the prime minister's impatience with operations in the Mediterranean quickly returned. On September 17, 1942, he wrote General Alexander, his newly appointed commander in the Mediterranean: "I am anxiously awaiting some account of your intentions [to attack]. My understanding with you was the fourth week in September. Since then you have stated that the recent battle, which greatly weakened the enemy, has caused delay in regrouping, etc. I do not wish to know either your plan or the exact date, but I must know which week it falls in, otherwise I cannot form the necessary judgments affecting the general war."[86] Brooke wrote that on September 23, Churchill complained about Alexander and "started all his worst arguments about generals only thinking about themselves and their reputations and never attacking until matters were a certainty, and never prepared to take risks, etc., etc.," wrote the CIGS. Much later that night, Brooke and Churchill "had a hammer and tongs argument which ended on friendly terms."[87]

The fall of 1942 proved a turning point for the Allied command in North Africa. Churchill pressed General Montgomery for more aggressive action in Libya.[88] He refused to be bullied or rushed. As the day for Montgomery's offensive grew closer in late October, the prime minister wrote Alexander that "all our hopes are centred upon the battle you and Montgomery are going to fight. It may well be the key to the future."[89] On October 29, Brooke wrote in his diary: "When I went to see Winston, having been sent for from the COS meeting, I was met by a flow of abuse of Monty. What was *my* Monty doing now, allowing the battle to peter out (Monty was always *my* Monty when he was out of favour!) He had done nothing now for the last three days, and now he was withdrawing troops from the front. Why had he told us he would be through in seven days if all he intended to do was to fight a half-hearted battle?"[90] General Bernard Montgomery would soon show the prime minister that he could defeat Rommel in desert warfare.

Fortunately for the British, General Rommel was absent from the desert front when on October 23, the battle for El Alamein commenced, for which Montgomery had carefully prepared.[91] Then, on November 8, the Allies launched Operation TORCH, invading North Africa. (Unfortunately for President Roosevelt, the invasion came five days after the mid-term elections in which the Republicans gained 45 seats in the House; the Democrats maintained only a 13-vote margin.) On November 7, Sarah Churchill had visited her father at Chequers. "Do you know at this moment six hundred forty-two ships are approaching the coast of North Africa?" the prime minister asked. His daughter, an intelligence analyst, corrected her father, "Six hundred forty-*three*." When her father inquired why she had not told him she had been working on the invasion, she replied: "I believe there is such a thing as security." Sarah recalled: "He looked at me with what I feared would be a blaze of anger at my impudence. Instead, he chuckled, and we went down to dinner."[92]

TORCH operations became politically complicated because Western

North Africa was controlled by the Vichy government, dominated by the Nazis. In response to the Allied invasion, Vichy Admiral François Darlan commented: "I have known for a long time that the British were stupid, but I always believed that the Americans were more intelligent. I begin to believe that you make as many mistakes as they do."[93] Darlan was in North Africa by chance—his presence disrupting Allied plans to deal with other Vichy military leaders. The Allies distrusted and despised Darlan, but the Vichy admiral controlled the fate of the French fleet (as he had since 1939), which could not be allowed to fall into Nazi hands. Eventually, the French scuttled their ships at Toulon before the Germans could seize them. On December 24, 1942, Darlan was assassinated under mysterious and suspicious circumstances.[94] His death provided an opening for Free French leader de Gaulle, considered a traitor by many Vichy officers.

After Montgomery's triumph at El Alamein, Churchill announced on November 10, 1942: "I have never promised anything but blood, tears, toil and sweat. Now, however, we have a new experience. We have victory—a remarkable and definite victory. The bright gleam has caught the helmets of our soldiers, and warmed and cheered all our hearts. . . . I have, I trust, a human disposition, but I must say I could not help feeling that what was happening, however grievous, was only justice grimly reclaiming her rights."[95] By February 1943, Churchill would say: "Let me also pay my tribute to this vehement and formidable General Montgomery, a Cromwellian figure, austere, severe, accomplished, tireless, his life given to the study of war, who has attracted to himself in extraordinary measure the confidence and devotion of his Army."[96]

If El Alamein at the end of 1942 was a turning point for Winston Churchill, the end of 1862 was a crucial moment for Abraham Lincoln's political and military strategy. In the summer of 1862, Secretary of State Seward had convinced the president that he should look for an appropriate Union victory as the moment to issue his draft Emancipation Proclamation.[97] Union setbacks—first in the Peninsula campaign in the spring, and then at the Second Battle of Bull Run in August—delayed the president. The Union victory at the Battle of Antietam on September 17, 1862, gave Lincoln the occasion he needed to issue the draft Emancipation Proclamation on September 22. Similarly, by November 1942, observed historian Maxwell Philip Schoenfeld, "Churchill had been waiting a long time for the tide of victory to serve as a vehicle on which he could launch the wave of emotion long building inside him."[98] Churchill would issue a ringing call of affirmation of the British empire in his Mansion House speech on November 9: "I have not become the King's First Minister in order to preside over the liquidation of the British Empire."[99] His sincere words were designed for British listeners, but they would prove poison to FDR and his anticolonial American ears, ever suspicious of Churchill's devotion to the historic empire to which he had given four decades of military and political service.

As 1942 almost undid Churchill, the setbacks of 1862 had demoralized Abraham Lincoln. He began the year with a sick military commander, George B. McClellan, who could not leave his bed. His treasury secretary, Salmon P. Chase, could not get sufficient loans to finance the war. In February, Lincoln's beloved son Willie died at the White House, at the same time as the Congressional Committee on the Conduct of the War pressed him for action by the stalled Army of the Potomac. In March, the president had to deal with the panic in Washington when a Confederate ironclad wrought havoc in the nearby Hampton Roads area of Virginia. Then in May, frustrated by the absence of military leadership and movement in Virginia, Lincoln would personally command the Union capture of nearby Norfolk. Lincoln's simmering conflict with General McClellan continued for virtually the entire year. First came the disappointing Peninsula campaign, then the disastrous Second Battle of Bull Run, and finally victory but lost opportunity at Antietam. To the president's chagrin, Lee's army escaped intact to Virginia. Tried beyond his patience, the president felt a moment of despair. Although he had been encouraged by General Grant's capture of two important Tennessee forts in February, Grant's near-defeat at the bloody Battle of Shiloh in April gave rise to caution. After substantial political losses in the midterm elections in November 1862, Lincoln received news of the bloody Union defeat at the Battle of Fredericksburg on December 11–15. A few days later, Republican members of the Senate staged a revolt. At the same time, Lincoln had to put down a cabinet crisis set in motion by criticism and gossip spread by Secretary of the Treasury Chase. January 1, 1863, the appointed day to issue the Emancipation Proclamation, drew near.

Winston Churchill's defeats of early 1942 had been similarly disappointing. He had to keep Parliament behind him after staggering defeats at Singapore and Tobruk. In February, he reorganized his War Cabinet, even as his longtime ally Beaverbrook undermined him, his colleague Anthony Eden contemplated replacing him, and erstwhile Labourite Stafford Cripps rode a wave of popular approval as a possible successor to Churchill. Defeats abroad and opposition intrigue at home would unnerve the prime minister. "I'm fed up," he said repeatedly when his loyal friend, Violet Bonham Carter, visited him on February 11. "He said he was urged to add talent to his Govt—'but where is the galaxy?' He became sombre again—& my heart went out to him when he said to me again & again 'I can't get the victories. It's the victories that are so hard to get.'"[100] His personal courage all recognized, but now success depended upon his soldiers, sailors, and airmen.

At the same time, the prime minister aspired to coordinate Anglo-American war planning. Just as he was fending off domestic critics, Churchill found himself negotiating very divergent views of how to achieve Allied victory. He knew he must keep the United States focused on the agreed "Germany First" strategy, while not ignoring Japan and the Pacific, simultaneously reassuring Joseph Stalin that a "Second Front" was in the plan. Moreover, the prime minister would replace British commanders in the Middle East. In the first half of 1942, Britain was beset in the Battle of the Atlantic by disastrous losses of Allied shipping caused by German U-Boats. These losses threatened Britain's lifeline for food and military supplies. In the summer of 1942, Churchill would also help to coordinate the complicated plans for the seaborne Allied invasion of western North Africa, at the same time driving his generals for an all-British attack on Rommel in eastern North Africa. Politically, he had to negotiate the conflicts over which Frenchmen to recognize as leaders of the new French government-in-exile.

The prime minister's tireless efforts to bring the United States into the war meant that eventually the United States, with its immense resources, would soon dominate the war effort in the West. The prime minister's strength of character, his physical constitution, his stamina, his public optimism, his leadership skills—all were tested in 1942, to the limits of his endurance. His example in adversity was not fully appreciated by FDR and Stalin.

My last attempt upon Richmond was to get McClellan, when he was nearer there than the enemy was, to run in ahead of him. Since then I have constantly desired the Army of the Potomac to make Lee's army and not Richmond, its object point.[1]

ABRAHAM LINCOLN
Letter to Henry W. Halleck
September 19, 1863

I have no fear of the future. Let us go forward into its mysteries, let us tear aside the veils which hide it from our eyes, and let us move onward with confidence and courage. All the problems of the post-war world, some of which seem so baffling now, will be easier of solution once decisive victory won in arms has been gained.[2]

WINSTON S. CHURCHILL
Royal Albert Hall
September 29, 1943

X.

1863/1943

Winston Churchill had successfully insisted upon his strategic priority to open up a North Africa front in 1942 and, upon victory there, a Mediterranean front in Sicily and Italy in 1943. His strategy proved to be sound. Despite General Marshall's skepticism, backed up by opposition from some American military and political leaders, the prime minister convinced General Eisenhower to invade Italy.[3] Both the Americans and the Russians resented Churchill's crucial efforts to delay a cross-channel invasion of France. The prime minister's persuasive arguments, combined with FDR's assent to postpone the invasion of France, was surely one of Churchill's major contributions to victory in the West. Aide Norman Brook argued that Churchill deserved "full marks for his long struggle to postpone the invasion of France until the American infantry was seasoned. His stubborn resistance, when the Americans wanted to get at the Germans, was quite wonderful."[4]

Lincoln's difficulties stemmed primarily from domestic problems, but Churchill's challenges were largely international. In January 1943, the Anglo-American conference at Casablanca decided the future framework for Anglo-American strategy in Europe. There the British leadership and senior staff mobilized in force. At Casablanca, they overwhelmed their American counterparts with a huge organization and thorough preparation. "When the Combined Chiefs met, it was apparent that the British were more united than the Americans," wrote Churchill biographer Henry Pelling. "The British were clear that the most favourable theatre for operations was the Mediterranean, with the object of knocking Italy out of the war and perhaps bringing Turkey in. Of the Americans, Admiral King's interest was, very understandably, largely focused on the Pacific, and it was only General Marshall who doggedly maintained the idea of a cross-Channel operation in 1943."[5] These were hard discussions at Casablanca—physically so for the 68-year-old Churchill, given his previous exertions, leading to pneumonia in mid-February after he returned to London. By sustained argument and goodwill, the prime minister had delayed the American plans to open up a second front in France. At the same time, he would assure Stalin that such a front was being planned. It was President Roosevelt who had made the disingenuous promise of a second front to Russian Foreign Minister Molotov in May 1942; but it was Churchill who took responsibility to travel to Moscow in August 1942 to explain the delay to Stalin. Churchill and the British COS would emphasize that because German U-boats had been decimating the Atlantic convoys supplying England and bringing across American troops, additional time and preparation would be necessary. The prime minister did not oppose the invasion of Western Europe in principle, but he argued that once begun, it must be a success. Hastings Ismay believed that "ultimately the deathblow to Germany must be delivered across the Channel."[6] Still, destruction of German arms would be accomplished mainly by Russian armies in the East. The Anglo-Americans would make sure that the Germans were tied down in the West after their June 1944 invasion of northern France.

During 1942–1943, the Anglo-American disagreements on strategy led to confusion of purpose, enabling the resourceful prime minister to advocate and launch military operations that drew resources away from Operation OVERLORD. Churchill's seaborne North African and Italian expeditions would give Allied forces the necessary military experience to prepare for the cross-channel invasion. But some Allied operations in World War II were not allied. Eisenhower wrote in his diary at the beginning of 1943: "Conversations with the British grow wearisome. They're difficult to talk to, apparently afraid that someone is trying to tell them what to do and how to do it. Their practice of war is dilatory."[7] British military diplomacy was self-consciously "dilatory," delaying the Normandy invasion but deploying Allied arms elsewhere, in order to relieve the embattled Russians by diluting somewhat the concentration of German arms on the eastern front.

Each major member of the Alliance played a crucial domestic game of politics. For example, "just as Churchill in 1940–41 prompted in

Britain much higher expectations of American belligerence than the facts merited, so Stalin wished to trumpet to the Russian people Roosevelt's and Churchill's assurances that a Second Front was coming, even though he did not himself believe them," wrote Max Hastings.[8] After the astonishing German onslaught of Operation Barbarossa in June 1941, Stalin would demand a second front—even as his spies inside the British government informed Stalin that it was unlikely. In April–May 1943, Churchill descended on Washington for the third time in two years. On May 19, he addressed Congress for the second time—six weeks before the 80th anniversary of "the decisive battle of the American Civil War," as Churchill then observed. "No one after Gettysburg doubted which way the dread balance of war would incline, yet far more blood was shed after the Union victory at Gettysburg than in all the fighting wars which went before. It behooves us, therefore, to search our hearts and brace our sinews and take the most earnest counsel one with another, in order that the favourable position which has already been reached both against Japan and against Hitler and Mussolini in Europe shall not be let slip."[9]

Supreme command for Churchill and Lincoln required resourcefulness to muster public opinion to surmount the setbacks of war. To sustain the will to victory was not only a matter of brute force. "In the absence of news the President strives to feel encouraged and to inspire others, but I can perceive he has doubts and misgivings, though he does not express them," wrote Gideon Welles in his diary of May 1863.[10] Both the president and the prime minister understood that victory would not come quickly. Their honesty would discipline public expectations. In 1943, when prominent military colleagues thought victory might come before the end of the year, Churchill despite success would disagree. Lincoln, in remarks composed for a September 1863 Union rally in Springfield, Illinois, despite victories at Gettysburg and Vicksburg, concluded: "Still let us not be over-sanguine of a speedy final triumph. Let us be quite sober. Let us diligently apply the means, never doubting that a just God, in his own good time, will give us the rightful result."[11]

In the first three years of the war, the president had dismissed one general after another. His resilience and tenacity revealed themselves in his positive attitude toward each new commanding general. General Ambrose Burnside survived only three months as commander of the

Army of the Potomac in 1862–1863. The ambitious and scheming General Joseph Hooker succeeded Burnside, whom Hooker had undermined. In appointing Hooker, Lincoln admonished his new man: "Beware of rashness, but with energy, and sleepless vigilance, go forward, and give us victories."[12] Hooker thought well of himself, but he gave no victories. Hooker's disastrous defeat at Chancellorsville in early May 1863 alarmed the president. A month before the battle, the president had reviewed the Army of the Potomac. One soldier observed how "care-worn and anxious" Lincoln looked, adding that "we thought there must be a '*heap of trouble on the old man's mind.*'"[13] But Lincoln held on to Hooker, calculating him the lesser evil of the moment. Hooker, literally shell-shocked at Chancellorsville, should have been replaced. But the question always arose: With whom? After Chancellorsville, relations between Hooker and General-in-Chief Halleck became increasingly strained. Hooker submitted his resignation in late June, as General Lee's Army of Northern Virginia crossed into Maryland on the way to central Pennsylvania. Lee would pose a mortal threat to Washington, DC. On June 28, Lincoln appointed George C. Meade the new commander of the Army of the Potomac.

General Robert E. Lee's invasion of Maryland and Pennsylvania created general panic throughout the North, his targets believed to be the national capital and the capital of Pennsylvania, Harrisburg. Lee's advance culminated with Union victory in a three-day battle at Gettysburg, Pennsylvania, July 1–3, 1863. On the final day of battle, Union artillery and soldiers, 30 percent Pennsylvanians, decimated the rebel ranks mobilized for "Pickett's Charge"—mounted against the Union army holding Cemetery Ridge. Lee retreated, recrossed the Potomac into Virginia, there to prepare his surviving troops for renewed battle. On July 4, the Confederate garrison at the Vicksburg fortress surrendered to General Grant, opening up the Mississippi River, the indispensable transportation artery through the heart of the continent.

In October 1862, Lincoln had been astounded that McClellan failed to follow up his near victory at the Battle of Antietam. Nine months later, after the Battle of Gettysburg, Lincoln again reacted with anguish, caused by the victorious but dilatory Union commander, General George Meade. "I was deeply mortified by the escape of Lee across the Potomac, because the substantial destruction of his army would have ended the war," Lincoln confided to General Oliver Howard.[14] Lincoln's son,

Robert Todd Lincoln, had come home from his studies at Harvard: "I went into my father's office at the time in the afternoon at which he was accustomed to leave his office to go to the Soldiers Home, and found him in [much] distress, his head leaning upon the desk in front of him, and when he raised his head there were evidences of tears upon his face. Upon my asking the cause of his distress he told me that he had just received the information that Gen. Lee had succeeded in escaping across the Potomac river at Williamsport without serious molestation by Gen. Meade's army."[15] Although he was deeply aggravated, Lincoln had learned a discipline which Churchill would emulate: The president wrote a harsh letter of reproach to Meade, but he did not send it, knowing that the touchy Meade had already reacted badly to a message sent by General Halleck.[16] Lincoln would not demoralize the victorious general. Nor would he indulge Meade with false praise.

In contrast to his disappointment after Gettysburg, Lincoln lavished fulsome praise on General Grant, after a long and successful siege of the Confederate fortress on the Mississippi River at Vicksburg. The president knew the challenging geography of the battle. Lincoln wrote the Union commander:

> I do not remember that you and I ever met personally. I write this now as a grateful acknowledgement for the almost inestimable service you have done the country. I wish to say a word further. When you first reached the vicinity of Vicksburg, I thought you should do, what you finally did—march the troops across the neck, run the batteries with the transports, and thus go below; and I never had any faith, except a general hope that you knew better than I, that the Yazoo Pass expedition, and the like, could succeed. When you got below, and took Port-Gibson, Grand Gulf, and vicinity, I thought you should go down the river and join Gen. [Nathaniel P.] Banks; and when you turned Northward East of the Big Black, I feared it was a mistake. I now wish to make the personal acknowledgement that you were right, and I was wrong.[17]

Eight decades later, on July 9, 1943, American and British soldiers would launch Operation HUSKY—the invasion of Sicily—the ultimate purpose of which was to drive the Axis from Italy, liberate Rome, and use the airfields north of Rome to bomb Germany. General Eisenhower showed little enthusiasm for HUSKY, so Churchill proposed an all-British operation. Instead, the Anglo-American allies would agree to undertake the invasion together. The prime minister pressed for a prompt invasion of the Italian mainland as a follow-up to HUSKY. General Eisenhower would later write of the Casablanca conference in January 1943: "The British were confident that a quick attack on the lower part of Italy would further our war aims materially. The Americans, agreeing that we should attempt anything that offered results, urged that we not forget that the next year—or certainly by the spring of '44—we were all committed to the OVERLORD campaign, the invasion of northwest Europe. It developed that General Brooke . . . had never really liked the OVERLORD idea. At times during the two-day conference, he seemed to be reflecting the Prime Minister's thoughts." Eisenhower wrote that Brooke

> came to see me privately and argued that all Allied ground troops should stay in the Mediterranean, chipping away at the periphery of the Axis empire. But we should avoid any commitment of major ground forces. His idea was that we would be doing our part by building up our navies to kill off the Nazi submarines, while our bombers flew concentric attacks on the Axis and pounded Germany and Italy. The Russians coming in from the east, according to General Brooke, would carry on the ground battle. Of course this would have meant the complete abandonment of the OVERLORD plan. I believe that the British Chief of Staff [Brooke] was badly underestimating Allied strength and efficiency and overestimating Nazi power in Western Europe.[18]

Indeed, with the benefit of hindsight, General Brooke was too cautious about OVERLORD. While he was not opposed in principle to the cross-channel invasion, he focused primarily on its timing and preparation—and elsewhere.

Churchill used 1943 to prepare for the D-Day invasion of France. He had tried to explain the delay to the impatient Joseph Stalin, who persistently demanded a second front in northern Europe. The prime

George Meade, ca. 1865
Gilder Lehrman Collection, GLC05135.030

minister's diplomatic maneuvering, even more his evasions, infuriated Stalin and his Russian sympathizers in England and America, who clamored for a second front to relieve the pressure on the Soviet Union. Churchill reminded Stalin that England had faced Hitler alone, when the cynical Stalin found it convenient in 1939 to make a nonaggression pact with his mortal enemy, Nazi Germany—with an equally cynical agreement to partition Poland. The prime minister would not be intimidated by Stalin, who in November 1943 was finally reassured at Teheran by FDR of a second front. Meanwhile, Churchill's diplomacy and FDR's Lend-Lease aid had knit the three-nation Alliance together. By air and sea, the prime minister would attend war conferences, make military inspections, and focus on the adherence of Russia to the Anglo-American alliance. In August 1943, Churchill and Roosevelt would meet in Québec to make plans for 1944.

The prime minister had successfully postponed plans for an Anglo-American invasion of France in 1943, but his caution had irritated American military and political leaders. "He does not fully understand the suspicions that exist on the American side regarding the British determination to cross the Channel," wrote Churchill's friend, Averell Harriman, after a discussion with the prime minister.[19] "From the Quebec conference onward," wrote John Keegan, "Churchill was increasingly to find himself the odd man out among the Big Three. The change of status was demeaning, however successfully he disguised it in public and from himself."[20] In 1941, the prime minister had rejoiced over American entry into the war. American industrial might, money, and manpower led inexorably to Britain's military and diplomatic eclipse. By mid-1943, Churchill's influence on the Allied war effort had diminished. Full of strategic and tactical ideas as always, he faced American, even British military authorities, unwilling to yield to his arguments. With immense Russian sacrifice, Stalin had survived the massive German invasion. His generals, led by Marshal Georgy Zhukov, had successfully counterattacked in early 1943. At Kursk in July, the Soviets won a pivotal victory, the greatest tank battle in military history.[21] By 1944, the Russian army would drive the Germans out of the Soviet Union and into Poland.

Churchill's declining influence became noticeable in late 1943. The prime minister enthused over a potential attack on Rhodes and the Dodecanese Islands in the eastern Aegean off the coast of Turkey.[22] Americans opposed what they viewed as a diversion, even one that might mean further British reservations about a cross-channel invasion.[23] "The surrender of Italy gave us the chance of gaining important prizes in the Ægean at very small cost and effort," wrote Churchill.[24] His enthusiasm for additional operations in Greece and the Balkans undermined his credibility with the Americans, even compromising his effectiveness with some British advisers. Churchill would write in his memoirs of the "painful" failure of U.S. officials to support the Dodecanese campaign. He titled the chapter in his memoirs (on the October 1943 campaign) "Island Prizes Lost."[25] In his diary, Brooke wrote: "He has worked himself into a frenzy about the Rhodes attack, had magnified its importance so that he can no longer see anything else and has set himself on capturing this one island even at the expense of endangering his relations with the President and the Americans and the future of the Italian campaign."[26] Still, Brooke did sympathize with Churchill's overall goals, writing a few weeks later: "If only I had had sufficient force of character to swing those American Chiefs of Staff and make them see daylight, how different the war might be. We should have been in a position to force the Dardanelles by the capture of Crete and Rhodes, we should have the whole Balkans ablaze by now, and the war might have been finished by 1943!"[27] General Marshall dismissed the idea.

The Rhodes initiative stemmed from Churchill's strategy for postwar control of the Mediterranean and the Middle East, the key to the Suez Canal and India, as well as his wartime preoccupation with bringing neutral Turkey into the war against Germany. It was not the prime minister's finest hour. Correlli Barnett observed of the inadequate plans for the Aegean campaign, whose code name was SLAPSTICK, that it "makes a dismal contrast with the carefully prepared and completely successful Anglo-American landings in Sicily and Italy that same year."[28] On another occasion, General Brooke, with exaggeration, suggested the heart of the problem: Churchill "preferred to work by intuition and impulse. . . . He was never good at looking at all the implications of any course he favoured."[29] Nor did he fully appreciate the logistics necessary to implement his ideas. The Americans stood fast, refusing to participate in the Aegean operation. Arthur Tedder recalled: "Roosevelt, in effect, refused Churchill's suggestion of a high-level conference. It seemed to Alan Brooke that Churchill had worked himself into a frenzy of excitement about an attack on Rhodes, even at the expense of endangering his relations with Roosevelt and the Americans; certainly Churchill pressed upon 'Jumbo' Wilson the need to claim extra support for 'Accolade' [the name of the Dodecanese campaign]. But the issue had now become largely academic."[30]

In September 1943, without American support, Britain would launch an offensive in the Dodecanese Islands off the southern coast of Turkey. Handicapped by bad planning, bad coordination, and bad execution, the British were crushed by a well-coordinated German air, sea, and ground operation. The result was not unlike the Norwegian defeat in 1940. Max Hastings wrote: "Britain's Aegean commitment was trifling in the grand scheme of the war, but represented a blow to national pride and prestige, precipitated by the personal decisions of the prime minister."[31]

Churchill's obsessions of 1943 had impeached his credibility with Stalin. The prime minister insisted from the outset of World War II that Turkey must be forced into the war. At the Teheran summit in November 1943, Stalin doubted and Roosevelt equivocated about Turkey joining the Allies. Italy remained another Churchill priority. When American and British leaders met in Cairo in November 1943, prior to the summit conference with Stalin in Teheran, even Hopkins was impatient with Churchill's talk about "his bloody Italian war." Hopkins said: "Winston said he was a hundred per cent for OVERLORD. But it was very important to capture Rome, and then we ought to take Rhodes." Hopkins warned that unless Churchill changed his tune at Teheran, "You will find us lining up with the Russians."[32]

The prime minister preferred military operations he could control —opportunistic, small-scale operations that could be launched quickly: "Because the Americans want to invade France in six months' time," he argued, "that is no reason why we should throw away these shining, gleaming opportunities in the Mediterranean."[33] The prime minister continued to play the zigzagging fox to the focused American hedgehog. Indeed, the American hedgehog, by late 1943, had "lost faith in his strategic judgment," wrote Max Hastings. Until then, Churchill's "strategic judgement had been superior to that of America's Chiefs of Staff. Hereafter, however, as the balance of war changed, his vision became increasingly clouded and the influence of his country waned."[34] General Brooke neatly summarized the poker game the prime minister played with the president: "He is inclined to say to the Americans, all right, you won't play with us in the Mediterranean, we won't play with you in the English Channel. And they will say all right, well, then we shall direct our main effort to the Pacific, to reply you are welcome to do so if you wish!"[35] An American campaign in the Pacific was well under way, but Churchill had successfully fought for two years to make the campaign against Germany the top priority of the Allies.

By the time he arrived for conferences at Cairo and Teheran in November 1943, his personal energy and political influence had waned in proportion to his exhausting schedule and the preeminence of Stalin and Roosevelt in making Allied strategy. Along the way, he stayed two days in Malta to recover from a serious cold. Roosevelt had self-consciously determined that in order to coordinate with Stalin: (1) He would give no excuse to Stalin to think that he and Churchill would combine against him; (2) his personal relationship with Stalin was the principal goal of the conference; (3) he would promote no formal agenda that would get in the way of a free-form discussion in which FDR could charm and co-opt Stalin; and (4) he would include China in the "Big Four" policemen who would in the future secure world peace. The depth of some American leaders' worries about Churchill came through in a diary entry by Henry Stimson after the Teheran conference: "I thank the Lord that Stalin was there." Fearful of Churchill's influence over FDR, Stimson wrote: "Up to the time of [Stalin's] arrival, our side was at a disadvantage because of the president's rather haphazard grasp of the situation. But when Stalin came in with his General [Kliment] Voroshilov, they completely changed the situation and took the offensive for 'Overlord.'"[36] In the Allied troika, the prime minister had become the third man. In FDR's judgment, the British Empire belonged to the past and the Soviet Empire to the future. "Roosevelt was growing tired of Churchill playing Marlborough at their meetings," wrote historian John Pearson. "There were also signs that he was impatient with Churchill's taking him and the massive efforts of the great United States for granted."[37]

In late November 1943, Churchill and FDR met Stalin in Teheran, the only site outside Russia where the Soviet leader would agree to go.

The prime minister, now almost 69, had exhausted himself. FDR concentrated on accommodating Stalin—even if he alienated and demoralized Churchill in the process. The American president even refused to meet separately with the British prime minister for lunch. Asked his opinion of Anglo-American strategy, Stalin insisted on the invasion of France: "If we are here in order to discuss military matters, then Russia is only interested in OVERLORD." FDR concurred: "We are all agreed that OVERLORD is the dominating operation, and that any operation which might delay OVERLORD cannot be considered." Hopkins recalled: "Stalin looked at Winston as much as to say: 'Well, what about that?'"[38] Hopkins then took personal responsibility for informing the prime minister that Operation OVERLORD must go forward without delay.[39] FDR and Stalin overruled Churchill's reservations.[40]

The British chiefs of staff were as aggrieved as the prime minister. Brooke said to Dr. Wilson: "I shall come to you to send me to a lunatic asylum. I cannot stand much more of this." Churchill was distraught, telling his physician: "I believe man might destroy man and wipe out civilization. Europe would be desolate and I may be held responsible." He then added: "Why do I plague my mind with these things? I never used to worry about anything."[41] The Teheran conference was a painful lesson for Churchill. His declining influence embarrassed him. FDR wounded him with gratuitous slights. Believing he could charm the Russian dictator, Roosevelt naively sought a relationship of trust with Stalin, no matter the impact on British interests, even if Churchill was demeaned in the process. On November 30, FDR later would tell a member of his cabinet: "I had scarcely seen Churchill alone during the conference. I had a feeling that the Russians did not feel right about seeing us conferring together in a language which we understood and they didn't." Roosevelt continued:

> On my way to the conference that morning, we caught up with Winston, and I had just a moment to say to him, "Winston, I hope you won't be sore at me for what I am going to do."
>
> Winston shifted his cigar and grunted. I must say he behaved very decently afterward.
>
> I began almost as soon as we went into the conference room. I talked privately with Stalin. I didn't say anything I hadn't said

Harold Alexander, 1945

before, but it appeared quite chummy and confidential, enough so that the other Russians joined us to listen. Still no smile. Then I said, lifting my hand to cover a whisper (which of course had to be interpreted), "Winston is cranky this morning, he got up on the wrong side of the bed."

A vague smile passed over Stalin's eyes, and I decided I was on the right track. As soon as I sat down at the conference table I began to tease Churchill about his Britishness, about John Bull, about his cigars, about his habits. Winston got red and scowled, and the more he did so, the more Stalin smiled. Finally Stalin broke into a deep, hearty guffaw, and for the first time in three days I saw the light. The ice was broken and we talked like men and brothers.[42]

FDR was willing to make a fool of the prime minister for the purpose of soliciting Stalin's goodwill. With immense global stakes in play, Roosevelt displayed a self-absorbed vanity, the celebration of his own charm, and his willingness to wound his friend and ally. In the curt judgment of Clementine Churchill, Roosevelt's "personal vanity was inordinate."[43] Before Teheran Roosevelt had sought Stalin's agreement to a bilateral or trilateral conference. FDR had only received Russia's agreement to the Teheran meeting on the very day that he left Washington for the Middle East.[44] At Teheran, Roosevelt and Stalin would occasionally mock Churchill with cavalier comments. "Churchill used every trick in his oratorical bag, assisted by illustrative and emphasizing gestures, to put over his point," wrote an American general. "At times he was smooth and suave, pleasant and humorous and then he would clamp down on his cigar, growl, and complain."[45] Stalin remained focused, aiming to drive the Russian border westward, while Roosevelt aimed to make the Soviet dictator relax, agreeing with Stalin on strategy.[46] With FDR's soft support, Churchill tried to stand up for the future integrity and freedom of France and Poland. "The discussions on the Polish frontiers became increasingly academic on the American side," wrote historian Robert Rhodes James, "and when the Russians realized this, harder on the Soviet" side.[47]

Stalin's rudeness might have been characteristic, but Churchill had considered Roosevelt, his fellow "Former Naval Person," a comrade in arms. The prime minister felt betrayed, wounded in the house of his friend. With FDR's help, Stalin had effectively hijacked the conference. The American president repeatedly asked Stalin's opinion about Anglo-American military strategy, thereby giving Stalin more of a voice than Churchill in Allied affairs. Until then, the British prime minister had counted on two devoted friends at Roosevelt's court—Harry Hopkins and Averell Harriman—a devotion Churchill had reciprocated when Britain stood alone. The Americans under President Roosevelt, however, were now less reliable allies for Britain. "I realized at Teheran for the first time, what a small nation we are," Churchill remarked. "There I sat with the great Russian bear on one side of me, with paws outstretched, and on the other side the great American buffalo, and between the two sat the poor little English donkey who was the only one, the one of the three, who knew the right way home."[48] In his memoirs, Churchill, a very clever, experienced, and confident donkey, summarized one vital conclusion reached at the conference: "The cross-Channel invasion was fixed for May, subject naturally to tides and the moon."[49]

Churchill's self-esteem had been hurt. In early December in North Africa upon his return from Teheran, the prime minister collapsed—suffering pneumonia and two mild heart attacks. Churchill was so tired that after bathing, he could not dry himself. He would fall on the bed still wet. Dried by the open air, the prime minister told his bodyguard, "I am tired out in body, soul and spirit."[50] His condition was so grave that Dr. Wilson ordered a pathologist and two nurses from Cairo. On December 12, Churchill wired his wife: "I am laid up here at Carthage with temperature of 101 and rather violent neuralgic sore throat, due, I think, to a draught in the airplane . . . I am sure I had better try to get well here rather than hurry home."[51] Two days later, the prime minister was diagnosed with pneumonia. Awakening briefly from sleep, Churchill told his daughter Sarah: "Don't worry, it doesn't matter if I die now, the plans of victory have been laid, and it is only a matter of time."[52] On December 16, Clementine flew to his side. After her arrival, Churchill wired his daughter Mary: "Your mother is here. All is joyful. No need to worry."[53] On December 20, Clementine wrote home: "Papa very refractory and naughty this morning and wants to leave this place at once."[54] Churchill's aides controlled the flow of news so that the British public would not be notified of his condition until he began to recover. Even then, they greatly downplayed his health problems. The prime minister spent much of the rest of the month recuperating. He roused himself for a war conference on December 25, worried as he was about the effect on the Italian campaign of the transfer of landing craft from the Mediterranean to Britain for use in the OVERLORD invasion. He spent the next month resting at his beloved resort in Marrakech, Morocco. He cherished the sun, as well as the luxury and ease of life at La Mamounia. Churchill found walking to be difficult, however: "I never remember such extreme fatigue and weakness in body."[55]

Despite the self-discipline and sheer willpower exerted by the war leaders, conflict and anxiety would debilitate them. Lincoln, too, would experience a comparable medical crisis in late 1863. After giving the Gettysburg Address on November 19, the feverish president returned to Washington with variloid, a mild form of smallpox that confined him to bed and isolation for weeks. Fortune spared him, but it did not spare William Johnson, the president's black valet, who died of smallpox. While recuperating, Lincoln stayed focused on three goals: conclusive military victory, widening of emancipation, and beginning the reconstruction of the slave states in rebellion. In his Annual Message to Congress at the end of 1863, he concluded:

> In the midst of other cares, however important, we must not lose sight of the fact that the war power is still our main reliance. To that power alone can we look, yet for a time, to give confidence to the people in the contested regions, that the insurgent power will not again overrun them. Until that confidence shall be established, little can be done anywhere for what is called reconstruction. Hence our chiefest care must still be directed to the army and navy, who have thus far borne their harder part so nobly and well. And it may be esteemed fortunate that in giving the greatest efficiency to these indispensable arms, we do also honorably recognize the gallant men, from commander to sentinel, who compose them, and to whom, more than to others, the world must stand indebted for the home of freedom disenthralled, regenerated, enlarged, and perpetuated.[56]

Not unlike this Lincoln tribute to his soldiers in December 1863, Churchill had said of British airmen in August 1940 during the Battle of Britain: "Never in the field of human conflict was so much owed by so many to so few."[57]

Not expecting to see you again before the Spring campaign opens, I wish to express, in this way, my entire satisfaction with what you have done up to this time, so far as I understand it. The particulars of your plans I neither know, or seek to know. You are vigilant and self-reliant; and, pleased with this, I wish not to obtrude any constraints or restraints upon you. While I am very anxious that any great disaster, or the capture of our men in great numbers, shall be avoided, I know that these points are less likely to escape your attention than they would be mine. If there is anything wanting which is within my power to give, do not fail to let me know it.[1]

ABRAHAM LINCOLN
to Ulysses S. Grant
April 30, 1864

[D]uring the night and the early hours of this morning the first of the series of landings in force upon the European Continent has taken place. In this case the liberating assault fell upon the coast of France. An immense armada of upwards of 4,000 ships, together with several thousand smaller craft, crossed the Channel. . . . This vast operation . . . involves tides, wind, waves, visibility, both from the air, and the sea standpoint, and the combined employment of land, air, and sea forces in the highest degree of intimacy and in contact with conditions which could not and cannot be fully foreseen.[2]

WINSTON S. CHURCHILL
Speech to House of Commons
June 6, 1944

XI.

1864/1944

At the beginning of 1944, Winston Churchill held the conquest of Italy to be the uppermost Allied priority. The prime minister had embraced Operation OVERLORD, but he became implacably opposed to Operation ANVIL, the proposed Allied landing on the south coast of France. The prime minister feared diversion of resources from the beleaguered Italian front, where well-led German armies and difficult terrain had immobilized Allied troops. President Roosevelt differed, writing Churchill in June 1944: "My interests and hopes centre on defeating the Germans in front of Eisenhower and driving on into Germany, rather than on limiting this action for the purpose of staging a full major effort in Italy."[3] Churchill summed up his own argument: "A second condition also governed 'Anvil's' usefulness. Many of the forces needed for the operation—that is to say, for the full-scale invasion as opposed to a feint or threat—would have to come from our armies in Italy. But these had first to accomplish the arduous and important task of seizing Rome and the airfields. Until this was done little could be spared or taken from [General Harold] Alexander's forces. Rome must fall before 'Anvil' could start."[4]

From a political point of view, Churchill's emphasis on Italy's total defeat made sense. However, in his strategy for Italy and the Balkans, Churchill underestimated the physical impediments in Italy in the way of a northeast Allied thrust through the mountainous terrain of the Balkans toward Vienna—likely to bog down in winter in the Ljubljana Gap. The Americans saw "the Balkans as a political jungle and they weren't going to have their troops in there," recalled a British strategist.[5] In a letter to Harry Hopkins on August 6, Churchill made the case against ANVIL:

The decision to undertake Anzio and the delays at Cassino forced us to continue putting off "Anvil," until its successor "Dragoon" bears no relation to the original conception. However, out of evil came good, and the operations in Italy being persevered in drew not fewer than twelve divisions from the German reserves in North Italy and elsewhere, and they have been largely destroyed. The coincidence that the defeat of [German General Albert] Kesselring's army and the capture of Rome occurred at the exact time of launching "Overlord" more than achieved all that was ever foreseen from "Anvil", and, to those who do not know the inner history, wears the aspect of a great design. Thus I contend that what "Anvil" was meant for is already gained.[6]

Churchill's disappointment with FDR's dismissive attitude toward his analysis of Anvil did not diminish the prime minister's self-confidence, nor did it inhibit his assertiveness when he believed himself right. In fact, Roosevelt's focus at the time was not on Europe. Preparing for a tough reelection campaign for an unprecedented fourth term, despite his grave heart condition, the president would spend much of July and August on a long trip to the West Coast, Hawaii, and Alaska—meeting at Honolulu with his Pacific commanders, full-scale war in the Pacific now under way.

Political strategy often preoccupied Churchill, who believed its importance crucial. In 1943, he had focused on the capture of Rome, a political and military symbol of Allied war success. The possession of airfields north of Rome—from which to bomb Germany—seemed of great tactical importance. The prime minister hoped to liberate Rome by January 1944—a goal not to be realized until June 4, two days before D-Day. By 1945, the prime minister's focus would shift to the German capital. On March 31, 1945, Churchill wrote that "General Eisenhower may be wrong in supposing Berlin to be largely devoid of military and political importance. . . . The idea of neglecting Berlin and leaving it to the Russians to take at a later stage does not appear to me correct. As long as Berlin holds out and withstands a siege in the ruins, as it may easily do, German resistance will be stimulated. The fall of Berlin might cause nearly all Germans to despair."[7] The same day, he wrote Eisenhower directly: "If we deliberately leave Berlin to them, even if it should be in our grasp, the double event may strengthen their [Russian] conviction, already apparent, that they have done everything."[8] Two days later, he wrote again to Eisenhower: "I am . . . all the more impressed with the importance of entering Berlin."[9]

On the way to the Teheran summit in November 1943, Roosevelt himself had speculated about a "race to Berlin," but the American high command determined that the German capital was not worth the American lives it would cost; it would be more convenient to let Russian lives be lost in its capture.[10] General Marshall "resisted protests from Churchill and the British that a great propaganda victory had been thrown away for the West by the abandonment of Berlin," wrote Marshall biographer Leonard Moseley. "For him [Marshall] it had been a purely military decision" that recognized "that Russia was still the ally of the West."[11] Marshall wrote of the Russians: "At that time, toward the close of the struggle, they were exceedingly sensitive, looking all the time for something that would indicate that the British and the Americans were preparing to go off alone and settle the thing, . . . So we were very careful about this, the Americans more so than the British, because Mr. Churchill was quite positive in the matter, and events have rather proved that he was possibly more nearly right [about Berlin] than the American position."[12] The American high command could ignore the prime minister more easily, because by late 1943, FDR would defer to Stalin. Moreover, the Russian occupation zone, by agreement, included Berlin.

The prime minister believed that only if the Anglo-Americans were in possession of conquered German territory could they resist the grasping imperial reach of the expansive Soviet empire, as its armies advanced into central Europe in 1945. Churchill feared this westward advance; FDR seemed indifferent. In April 1945, Churchill telegraphed FDR that "nothing will exert a psychological effect of despair upon all German forces of resistance equal to that of the fall of Berlin. It will be the supreme signal of defeat to the German people."[13] He also pressed General Eisenhower: "I do not consider myself that Berlin has yet lost its military and certainly not its political significance. The fall of Berlin would have a profound psychological effect on German resistance in every part of the Reich."[14] The prime minister advocated greater American efforts to take the German capital, wrote Marshall biographer Ed Cray, but Roosevelt had reduced Churchill to "a decidedly junior partner raising feeble protest. Moreover, any arguments the prime minister might make were undercut by the immediate success of the Eisenhower tactical plan. On Easter Sunday, April 1, elements of two American armies closed a pincers around the Ruhr, trapping more than 317,000 German troops."[15] To capture Axis-held capitals would remain both a political and a strategic British goal, as Russian armies moved farther into Central Europe. To that end, Churchill also urged General Eisenhower to move on Prague. But the prime minister would emphasize that Berlin was "the most decisive point in Germany."[16] As Churchill had worried about the cost of Allied lives in a premature cross-channel invasion, so did Eisenhower focus on the high cost of Allied lives in a race for the German capital. Stalin and Marshal Zhukov had no such worries. Eisenhower did not yield to the prime minister's arguments.

Churchill (like Lincoln) integrated military and political strategy. Both statesmen believed political war aims with long-term consequences should trump short-term military strategy and tactics. General Eisenhower's strategy, as he acknowledged, had been formulated on military grounds, concluding that Berlin was "no longer a particularly important objective." For Eisenhower, Anglo-American capture of Berlin was not necessary militarily to win the war, and would be very costly in Anglo-American lives.[17] Fearing Soviet domination of Eastern and Central Europe, Churchill's strategy was to take Berlin and other central European political targets in 1945. To Eisenhower, Churchill's Berlin objective was not realistic—especially because the boundaries of post-surrender zones of occupation had already been spelled out. Moreover, historian Maxwell Philip Schoenfeld emphasized that Eisenhower "saw vast Russian armies on the Oder only 40 miles from Berlin, while the Western Allies were still almost 200 miles away across country broken by lakes and waterways. He concluded that a thrust to Berlin was thus much more likely to be completed from the east than from the west."[18]

Eisenhower did, in fact, embrace Lincoln's strategy to destroy the enemy's army, not to focus on capturing the enemy capital. By April 1865, Lincoln's strategy to preserve the Union had been achieved by trapping the rebel army near Richmond. After General Lee's surrender at Appomattox Court House on April 9, only minor military actions continued in the South and West. One of Churchill's political postwar goals was to enlarge and secure the area of freedom in all of Europe. He foresaw that the Soviet Union was an imperial power on the march westward with Stalin's conquering armies. Moreover, the prime minister foresaw that no major armed power would stand between Stalin and the English Channel, if as FDR promised, the American soldiers would go home at war's end.

At the beginning of World War II, Churchill had successfully flattered and courted the president of the United States in order to create a winning Anglo-American alliance. Toward the end of the war, FDR launched his own courtship of Stalin. Thus in 1944–1945, Roosevelt would ignore much of Churchill's advice and counsel. Needing Stalin's armies to crush German forces, the prime minister would waffle too in his opposition to Soviet advances—agreeing in 1944 to Stalin's demands to shift the Polish-Russian border west to the Curzon line. Churchill did understand that without serious Anglo-American resistance, much of Central and Eastern Europe would fall under Soviet control. Given the strength of the French and Italian communist parties in 1945, even Western Europe would be threatened. From such a strategic position, Soviet arms could intimidate France and Britain. Alone at Moscow with Stalin in 1944, Churchill tried to reduce Soviet and increase British influence in Eastern Europe, bargaining with Stalin for relative influence there. To some of his entreaties, Stalin tactically agreed, especially in the case of Greece. Indeed, Stalin would adhere to his agreement on Greece with the prime minister. However, Stalin's armies proceeded to commandeer Eastern Europe.

When communists threatened to take over Greece in December 1944, the intrepid prime minister, now 70, decided to intervene. Abruptly, he left a family Christmas Eve celebration at Chequers, flying with Anthony Eden to Athens to negotiate an agreement among the warring anti-Nazi Greek parties. "I was looking forward to a quiet family Christmas," complained Eden in his diary.[19] On December 26, Churchill wrote Clementine from Athens: "Conference at Greek Foreign Office was intensely dramatic. All these haggard Greek faces round the table and Archbishop with enormous hat making him I should think 7 feet high, whom we got to preside. The American[,] Russian[,] and French ambassadors were all very glad to be invited."[20] As quixotic as some at first thought Churchill's mission to the gunfire-ridden Greek capital, historian Maxwell Philip Schoenfeld argued it demonstrated "[t]he sweep of Churchill's historic vision, the depth of his compassionate concern for the values of western civilization, and the greatness of his courage and fortitude."[21] Churchill's rush to the rescue of Greece was reminiscent of his bold endeavors in the British cavalry five decades earlier, and of his efforts in World War I to hold Antwerp. He would castigate his private secretary for neglecting to carry a pistol on the Athens mission.

The prime minister certainly carried his. When John Colville borrowed a tommy gun from their driver, Churchill demanded to know what the driver could then use for protection.[22] The communist insurgency in Athens was armed to the teeth, aiming at a coup.

The prime minister believed Greece a test for postwar reconstruction in western Europe. He acted in Greece without the support of his American partners. Still oblivious to the strategic importance of preventing a communist takeover of Greece, FDR had served Churchill notice he would not keep American armies in Western Europe. "The Arnold-King-Marshall combination [the American high command] is one of the stupidest strategic teams ever seen," the prime minister remarked in 1944.[23] Strategy involved not only armies in battle, but strategic political planning for the future to ensure the fruits of victory. On January 23, 1945, Churchill privately predicted to Colville: "Make no mistake, all the Balkans, except Greece, are going to be Bolshevized; and there is nothing I can do to prevent it. There is nothing I can do for poor Poland either."[24] Perhaps the prime minister himself regretted his October 1944 meeting in Moscow with Stalin. There, he had accommodated Stalin's acquisitive attitude because of the commanding position and thrust of Soviet armies in Eastern Europe. Churchill and Stalin had carved up the countries of Eastern Europe into spheres of influence—Greece reserved for Britain. With Russian armies already conquering Romania, Bulgaria, and much of Poland, Churchill had little practical alternative.

Polish leaders in London would refuse to recognize Russian-imposed borders. Stalin had decided to allow no strong political alternative to his Polish puppet in Moscow, the Lublin leadership. The prime minister remained a principled realist in dealing with the Russian bear through 1944. The powerless Polish government-in-exile in London rejected the "Curzon line," which the Russians insisted upon as their advancing western border. The Russians would ruthlessly ignore the Warsaw uprising against the Germans in the summer of 1944, during which one in five Polish residents died fighting. Russian troops were but 20 miles distant.[25] They could have helped. Instead, Soviet soldiers stayed in place while the Nazis destroyed the Warsaw rebellion, easing thereby the subsequent Soviet occupation.

Frustrated by American indifference and the London Poles' intransigence, Churchill had gone to Moscow in October 1944, to negotiate directly with Stalin. Polish exile leaders opposed Stalin's plans for

Ulysses S. Grant, 1864
Gilder Lehrman Collection, GLC05111.02.0409

their country. To agree to Stalin's proposed borders would cost them all credibility with fellow Poles. "I am absolutely convinced that it is in the profound future interest of the Polish nation that they should reach agreement with the Soviet Government about their disputed frontiers in the east before the march of the Russian armies through the main part of Poland takes place," concluded Churchill in December.[26] The Soviet dictator would ignore the London Poles, frustrating Anglo-American attempts at the 1945 Yalta summit to form a true Polish coalition government. The Yalta promise of free elections in Poland and Eastern Europe proved an illusion. Stalin's armies of occupation would determine the outcome—violating the Yalta agreements with impunity.

Churchill did not cease his diplomacy on behalf of Poland. (Similarly, Lincoln never stopped trying to help Union loyalists in eastern Tennessee break away from the Confederacy.) After trying to broker an agreement between the London Poles and Stalin's Lublin Poles, the prime minister argued in a letter to Stalin in early March 1945: "Force can achieve much but force supported by the goodwill of the world can achieve more. I earnestly hope that you will not close the door finally to a working arrangement with the Poles which will help the common cause during the war and give you all you require at the peace."[27] Churchill persisted, writing the Russian dictator late in April 1945, after FDR's death, that the British people "can never feel this war will have ended rightly unless Poland has a fair deal in the full sense of sovereignty, independence, and freedom, on the basis of friendship with Russia." Churchill warned Stalin: "There is not much comfort in looking into a future where you and the countries you dominate, plus the Communist parties in many other States, are all drawn up on one side, and those who rally to the English-speaking nations and their associates or Dominions are on the other. It is quite obvious that their quarrel would tear the world to pieces and that all of us leading men on either side who had anything to do with that would be shamed before history."[28]

The Soviet dictator could not be shamed by Churchill's appeal to peace and honor. For the prime minister, support of a free Poland had been a matter of principle—the very principle that had brought Britain into the war in September 1939—after Hitler's invasion of Poland. For Stalin, the Poles were pawns in a deadly game of Bolshevik *real politik*. Stalin's geopolitical strategy aimed to close off the historic invasion path to Russia through Poland and the Ukraine. As Averell Harriman, the U.S. ambassador to Moscow, acknowledged to Churchill: "The Russian bear is demanding much and yet biting the hands that are feeding him."[29] Indeed, Russia was a great beneficiary of U.S. Lend-Lease support. Moreover, the prime minister himself did have a long history of opposing the Russian Revolution. Stalin had not forgotten Churchill's support for British intervention against the Bolsheviks in 1918–1920.[30] By the Potsdam Conference of July 1945, the prime minister had lost patience with the Polish issue: "I'm sick of the bloody Poles. I don't want to see them. Why can't Anthony [Eden] talk to them? If I have to see them I shall tell them there is no support in western Europe for a puppet Polish state, the tool of Russia."[31]

Churchill's war against Bolshevism after World War I had begun in 1919, with a very limited British army intervention in Russia to stem the tide of communist revolution. No statesman of the twentieth century perceived so early the threat to the free world of Soviet totalitarianism. No statesman was more committed, when armed intervention failed in 1920, to the peaceful extinction of communism. Especially in principle but also in grand strategy, Churchill opposed the Bolsheviks, but he would embrace and support the alliance with Stalin in order to defeat Hitler. In June 1941, the prime minister would say: "I have only one purpose, the destruction of Hitler, and my life is much simplified thereby." This he declared on the eve of the German invasion of Russia: "If Hitler invaded hell I would make at least a favourable reference to the devil in the House of Commons."[32]

Lincoln hated slavery, but he embraced the loyal border slave states that fought for the Union against the Confederacy. Though Lincoln and Churchill were war leaders of principle, under pressure they would make tactical compromises to survive and to win. But the emphasis of Lincoln's military strategy differed from Churchill's, not least because the facts and circumstances were so different. Lincoln insisted that the destruction of the Confederate army must be the strategic goal of the Union armies, whereupon, he believed, the defenseless rebel government in Richmond would collapse. In October 1862, Lincoln spelled out to General McClellan his strategy to fight the Confederate enemy on a broad front wherever it appeared: "In coming to us, he [the rebel commander] tenders us an advantage which we should not waive. We should not so operate as to merely drive him away. As we must beat him somewhere, or fail finally, we can do it, if at all, easier near to us, than far away. If we can not beat the enemy where he now is [i.e., nearby], we never can, he again being within the entrenchments of Richmond."[33]

In September 1863, Lincoln would again define, this time, for General Halleck his strategy for the Army of the Potomac:

> To avoid misunderstanding, let me say that to attempt to fight the enemy slowly back into his intrenchments at Richmond, and there to capture him, is an idea I have been trying to repudiate for quite a year. My judgment is so clear against it, that I would scarcely allow the attempt to be made, if the general in command should desire to make it. My last attempt upon Richmond was to get McClellan, when he was nearer there than the enemy was, to run in ahead of him. Since then I have constantly desired the Army of the Potomac, to make Lee's army, and not Richmond, its objective point. If our army can not fall upon the enemy and hurt him where he is, it is plain to me it can gain nothing by attempting to follow him over a succession of intrenched lines into a fortified city.[34]

Lincoln proved correct. Grant had Lee's army on the run—away from Richmond. With the final surrender of rebel armies, the entire South would fall under Union control. During the war, the president's war aims had expanded. Restoration of the Union *with emancipation* of the slaves had become Lincoln's integrated war aim. The Thirteenth Amendment, abolishing slavery, passed Congress in January 1865. Lincoln would call it the "king's cure" for ending slavery in America permanently. The Thirteenth Amendment was a constitutional remedy, not a war proclamation based on the military authority of the commander in chief. On the day of Lincoln's assassination in April, it was clear that the Union had been restored and that the slaves would be free.

Churchill's power and influence in the "Grand Alliance" had diminished during the last years of war, 1943–1945. But Lincoln's domestic authority and preeminence grew during 1863–1865. The president's self-confidence would rise after the victories at Gettysburg and Vicksburg, and especially after reelection in November 1864. Churchill himself would write of the American Civil War: "By the end of 1863 all illusions had vanished [in America]. The South knew they had lost the war, and would be conquered and flattened. It is one of the enduring glories of the American nation that this made no difference to the Confederate resistance. In the North, where success was certain, they could afford to have bitter division. On the beaten side, the departure of hope left only the resolve to perish arms in hand."[35] This Churchillian notion—not his alone—of an already victorious but divided North in 1863, and an already vanquished but united South, is not supported by the evidence. First, the North was divided, but not sure of victory. Second, the South was not yet resigned to defeat. Third, the South was not united; in Georgia, politicians led by Governor Joseph Brown and Confederate Vice President Alexander Stephens were openly critical of the Confederate government under Jefferson Davis. Stephens wanted the South to cooperate with Copperhead Democrats in the Union presidential election of 1864, in order to bring about a negotiated peace—far from wanting to "perish arms in hand."

By 1863, Lincoln had no internal competition so strong as Churchill did with Stalin and FDR. The Civil War president did face a jealous Treasury Secretary, Salmon P. Chase, and the ambitious but feckless General George McClellan, each of whom longed to replace him. Both were dispatched—Republican Chase to the U.S. Supreme Court and Democrat McClellan to retirement (after the general lost the November 1864 presidential election). In June 1864, Lincoln had been renominated by his Republican Party (temporarily renamed the "Union Party"). Serious opposition had dissipated. Despite the hard challenges of August 1864, by September Lincoln had tightened his military and political grip. Rear Admiral David G. Farragut's victory at Mobile Bay, Alabama, in early August completed the encirclement of the rebel South. General William T. Sherman's capture of Atlanta four weeks later proved even more decisive in Lincoln's reelection victory of November.

Unlike Churchill, Lincoln at war did not early on desire to direct field military strategy. Such a role fell to the president not only as constitutional commander in chief, but also by the circumstances created by defeats of failed Union generals. Indeed, for three long years, the president did not find the right military commanders to implement the "Anaconda Plan" by which he hoped to encircle the Confederacy and end the rebellion. Eliot A. Cohen wrote: "The most efficacious means of achieving the destruction of the Confederate armies was by a concerted offensive around the circumference of the South, thereby allowing the numerical and material superiority of the Union to come into play."[36] Such an opportunity would elude Lincoln after the Battle of Gettysburg when General Meade stalled out in northern Virginia, and, as a result, the noose failed to tighten around the Confederacy.

Decisive action finally materialized in western Tennessee in the fall of 1863. (Much as Churchill hoped that partisan warfare in the remote Balkans could support an Allied military drive to Vienna.) Lincoln hoped to restore Tennessee to the Union in his drive to isolate Confederate armed forces south and west of the Appalachian Mountains. Ominously, Union forces holding Chattanooga and Knoxville, Tennessee, were almost enveloped by the rebel armies. Secretary of War Stanton utilized the superiority of Union rail transportation to launch an unprecedented movement of Union troops by rail from Virginia to the Tennessee front. "The effective teamwork that had developed between Lincoln and Stanton was fully on display," wrote historian Matthew Pinsker.[37] Western Tennessee was secured when Generals Grant and Sherman won a major victory at the Battle of Missionary Ridge at Chattanooga, on November 23. Above all, Lincoln now had identified the battle-ready field commanders for whom he had been searching. They had not emerged from the prewar officer class. Indeed, Grant and Sherman, two army castoffs, had resigned their commissions in the 1850s, struggling thereafter in middle-class civilian life. They did not resemble the aristocratic senior officers of the British army, like General Harold Alexander, nor the plantation gentlemen of the South, such as General Robert E. Lee.

Churchill's power and influence had declined as early as late 1943. "I see that the Ministry of Negation has successfully marshaled bellyaches as usual," the prime minister responded on one disappointing occasion. After 1943, the diminution of his central role in the alliance went hand-in-hand with his physical and mental weariness. On taking office at 65 in 1940, the prime minister was 13 years older than Lincoln—52 at his 1861 inauguration. But the prime minister was made ready by his hard experience in the Great War. Still, his crucial World War I role may have hobbled him somewhat. Carlo D'Este argued that "Churchill's thinking [in World War II] sprang directly from his experience and knowledge of the Great War. He did not fully realise the change that had taken place since then in large-scale warfare."[38] With no substantial military experience, Lincoln's genius would enable him to adapt quickly, learning from failure and success, always dealing with present realities, unencumbered by past military experience.

Churchill and Lincoln would embrace generals such as Bernard Montgomery and Ulysses S. Grant, because they gave battle and won. Churchill's argumentative nature inclined him toward clever, articulate soldiers such as Harold Alexander, given command of British forces in the Middle East during the summer of 1942. Alexander looked like a general—and he knew how to handle Churchill.[39] John Colville wrote of General Alexander: "Widely respected for his gallant First War record as an officer of the Irish Guards, Alexander had commanded, with cool efficiency, first the rearguard on the Dunkirk beaches, and the fighting retreat of the British Army in Burma. . . . [H]e had a personal charm which enabled him to allay discord. He explained his plans with a quiet confidence that won immediate attention without seeming to demand it; and he stuck to his guns with as much courage in the Council Chamber as on the field of battle."[40] Alexander subsequently commanded the successful invasion of Sicily, later the Allied forces in Italy.

General Montgomery was in some ways a cross between Union Generals Sherman and Philip H. Sheridan—both able, aggressive warriors. After Lincoln met "Little Phil" in 1864, the president said: "General Sheridan, when this particular war began, I thought a cavalryman should be at least six feet four inches high, but I have changed my mind. Five feet four will do in a pinch."[41] Montgomery could be as impudent and arrogant in his relations with Churchill and Eisenhower as McClellan had been with Lincoln and Stanton. Though critical in his private correspondence, Sherman maintained a correct public relationship with his superiors. Montgomery was less respectful. When he prevented the prime minister from visiting his battlefront in July 1944, Churchill demanded: "Who was Monty to stop him?"[42] General Brooke observed that American generals did not like Montgomery. "It is most distressing that the Americans do not like him . . . and it will always be a difficult matter to have him fighting in close proximity to them."[43] General George S. Patton detested Monty. Patton thought Montgomery too cautious in battle, referred to him as "that cocky little limey fart." Montgomery said of Patton that he was a "foulmouthed lover of war."[44] Churchill wrote Clementine that Montgomery was "a highly competent, daring and energetic soldier, well-acquainted with desert warfare. If he is disagreeable to those about him, he is also disagreeable to the enemy."[45] In Montgomery, Churchill had met his personality match. D'Este wrote: "Their first meeting was an occasion of two very stubborn, strong-willed pugnacious men testing and eyeing each other much like prizefighters before a bout. Despite his experience with outspoken men . . . Churchill had never met anyone quite like Bernard Montgomery, a man who both stimulated and impressed with his knowledge and forceful command presence, yet who was irreverent, obnoxious, and dictatorial, and who stirred Churchill's combative juices."[46]

Montgomery was vain and self-important. By contrast, General Grant was casual and modest, a man of few words but a master of clear written orders in the midst of battle. Grant's friend Sherman would write: "Grant's whole character was a mystery even to himself."[47] Grant avoided drawing attention to his rank—generally wearing a private's blouse or coat with shoulder stars. The president's great confidence in his new lieutenant general was born of Grant's battlefield victories in Tennessee and the Mississippi River valley in 1862 and 1863. When the long-anticipated Union offensive in Virginia got underway in May 1864, the president encouraged his new general-in-chief. On May 1, former Illinois Senator Browning wrote in his diary: "In conversation with the President last night he expressed great solicitude about the coming struggle with the Army of the Potomac. Said he had no fault to find with Genl Grant—believed he had done, and was doing all that was possible, but Lee would select his own ground, and await an attack, which would give him great advantages. Furthermore he had doubts of the fidelity of some of the officers under Grant, but had directed that they be watched & superceded on the first indication of faltering."[48]

Soon came news of bloody Union defeats of May–June 1864—at the battles of the Wilderness, Spotsylvania, and Cold Harbor. Lee's Army of Northern Virginia kept retreating, with Grant doggedly pursuing. John Keegan wrote: "Grant had a philosophy of war, which was to keep the enemy under relentless pressure at all points and to fight whenever opportunity offered. This style of generalship tried his men very hard."[49] Despite setbacks, Grant moved inexorably to surround General Lee's army, arrayed outside Richmond. To the public, however, the Union effort had stalled. In the summer of 1864, Lincoln had to deal with unmet expectations of military victory, revulsion at Union casualty numbers, and Northern demoralization (much the same as Churchill experienced when V-1 and V-2 rockets rained terror and death on Britain in 1944).

Churchill's personality from his early years exhibited a special character trait, observable in the many different roles he played as soldier, MP, writer, and war leader. The actor in Churchill never strayed far from the scene. In his major biography of his father, Lord Randolph, published in 1906, Churchill, only 31, had used a rare Latin quotation:

Bernard Montgomery, 1946

© Yousuf Karsh

"*Omnium quae dixerat, feceratque arte quadam ostenator*" ("He had the showman's knack of drawing attention to everything he said or did").[50] Writer H. G. Wells once observed: "Before all things, he desires a dramatic world with villains—and one hero."[51] A British cabinet member recalled: "In an expansive moment [at a cabinet meeting] Winston told us his apprehensions about the 'Overlord' policy [the timing] which the Americans have forced upon us . . . when we might have gone on more effectively in Italy and the Balkans."[52] The prime minister had continued to raise timing objections that undermined his credibility with American and Russian allies intent on a cross-channel invasion of France. They accused him of focusing too much on strategies to protect the British Empire. In the spring of 1944, the prime minister would try to stop the so-called Transportation Plan of Operation OVERLORD, citing French casutalities to be expected. The invasion plan called for bombing French railroad facilities, among other targets, to impede Germany's ability to reinforce its battlefront after the D-Day landing. The Americans pushed ahead successfully despite his opposition.

Churchill was uncharacteristically pessimistic about the obstacles facing OVERLORD, obsessed as he was by the stalled Italian campaign and the memories of bloody trench warfare in Belgium during World War I. He championed smaller-scale, opportunistic operations, such as the landings at Dieppe in France and Anzio in Italy. Both turned into disasters, poorly planned and poorly managed. The prime minister summoned too little faith in the risky but well-planned amphibious invasion of Europe; but he did support it and made early innovative contributions to its success. The necessary energy for OVERLORD was driven by the fixed purpose of the American hedgehogs, Generals Marshall and Eisenhower. On D-Day, Churchill reported to Parliament on OVERLORD: "This vast operation is undoubtedly the most complicated and difficult that has ever taken place."[53] Despite his doubts, and the danger, Churchill had planned to go with the fleet crossing the English Channel when OVERLORD launched.

Lincoln did not generally seek recognition and celebrity by defying danger, but on July 11–12, 1864, the president risked his life by observing firsthand Confederate General Jubal Early's invasion near Washington. At Fort Stevens Lincoln would witness military operations. Standing upon the parapet of the fort, he presented a target nearly seven feet tall in his top hat, while bullets buzzed about him. A nearby officer ordered him to get down. After the rebels retreated, Lincoln would be disappointed by the failure of the Union army to pursue the rebels to destruction. Journalist Noah Brooks observed: "If Lincoln was the meddlesome marplot in military affairs which some have represented him to be, he would have peremptorily ordered a sortie of the Union forces, then numerously massed inside the defenses of Washington; but although he was 'agonized' (as he said) over the evident failure of all attempts at pursuit, he kept his hands off. . . . Lincoln frequently referred to the escape of Early as one of the distressing features of his experience in the city of Washington."[54]

Living dangerously was standard operating procedure for Churchill. Indeed, as a young subaltern in the cavalry, he had cheated death recklessly on the way to world fame and a seat in Parliament at age 25. In 1944, General Eisenhower and King George VI would veto the prime minister's plan to accompany the D-Day invasion. The King wrote the prime minister:

> I have been thinking a great deal of our conversation yesterday, and I have come to the conclusion that it would not be right for either you or I to be where we planned to be on D Day. I don't think I need emphasise what it would mean to me personally, and to the whole Allied cause, if at this juncture a chance bomb, torpedo, or even a mine, should remove you from the scene; equally a change of Sovereign at this moment would be a serious matter for the country and Empire. We should both, I know, love to be there, but in all seriousness I would ask you to reconsider your plan. Our presence, I feel, would be an embarrassment to those responsible for fighting the ship or ships in which we were stationed.[55]

After more exchanges, Churchill finally responded: "I must defer to Your Majesty's wishes, and indeed commands. It is a great comfort to me to know that they arise from Your Majesty's desire to continue me in your service."[56]

Operation OVERLORD had been originally scheduled for May 1944. Churchill still worried about disaster. So did Brooke. Writing later about the plan, General Eisenhower observed:

> It became quickly obvious that the Prime Minister was not oversold on its value, at least in the early spring of 1944. He felt that it

would be far better for the Western Allies to wait for more significant signs of German collapse. Sometimes, in his contemplation of the possibilities before us, he spoke as if he were addressing a multitude. He would say, "When I think of the beaches of Normandy choked with the flower of American and British youth, and when, in my mind's eye, I see the tides running red with their blood, I have my doubts . . . I have my doubts."[57]

General Eisenhower, dealing with forbidding weather conditions, would carefully choose the risky moment for D-Day on June 6, 1944. Allied planes commanded the airspace, but Normandy beaches were well-defended by General Rommel's preparations. Allied troops bravely fought their way onto bloody beachheads. (Soviet arms were resurgent on the eastern front, pinning down three million German soldiers, vast stores of German field weapons, and Luftwaffe fighter and bomber squadrons.) The Allies had carefully planned feints and deceptions which convinced key German officers that the main invasion force would come later to the northeast—and that D-Day itself was a feint. The Anglo-American armies would struggle to establish a front in northwest France—contested there by about ten German battle-ready infantry and Panzer divisions. They were commanded by General Rommel, who had rushed back to his command in France from his wife's birthday celebration in Germany.

On June 12, six days after the Allied landings, Churchill walked onto the Normandy beach. At one point, he proclaimed he could smell Germans. He turned out to be right. Two stranded German soldiers were hiding nearby in the bushes. In March 1945, the prime minister returned to the western front in France. Amidst the danger of nearby combat he relished every moment. "Prime Minister, there are snipers in front of you; they are shelling both sides of the bridge; and now they have started shelling the road behind you," an American general told him. "I cannot accept responsibility for your being here and must ask you to come away."[58]

Both Churchill and Lincoln tempted fate, Lincoln less rashly. Throughout their lives, both had proven their moral and physical courage. The prime minister's inward drive stemmed from the ambition and bravery of a lifelong military and political entrepreneur, whereas Lincoln had aspired from the beginning of his political career (at 23) to no ambition "so great as that of being truly esteemed of my fellow men."[59]

By the summer of 1864, the Union Army of the Potomac under General Grant had stalled outside Richmond. Renewed discussion got underway of a peace initiative. Democrats in the North would make peace their dominant campaign issue. Radical Republicans, furious over the president's veto of the Wade-Davis reconstruction bill, decided that President Lincoln could not be reelected. On August 25, Lincoln aide Nicolay wrote a colleague:

Hell is to pay. The N.Y. politicians have got a stampede on that is about to swamp everything. [Henry G. Raymond, editor of the *New York Times*] and the National Committee are here today. R[aymond] thinks a commission to Richmond is about the only salt to save us—while the Tycoon [Lincoln] sees and says it would be utter ruination. The matter is now undergoing consultation. Weak-kneed d—d fools like [Massachusetts Senator] Chas. Sumner are in the movement for a new candidate—to supplant the Tycoon. Everything is darkness and doubt and discouragement. Our men see giants in the airy and unsubstantial shadows of the opposition, and are about to surrender without a fight.[60]

From Illinois, John Hay wrote Nicolay of the disaffection of Lincoln's longtime allies: "I found among my letters here, sent by you, one from Joe Medill [a Chicago journalist] inconceivably impudent, in which he informs me that on the Fourth of next March thanks to Mr. Lincoln's blunders & follies we will be kicked out of the White House. The damned scoundrel needs a day's hanging. . . . Old Uncle Jesse [K. Dubois] is talking like an ass—says if the Chicago nominee is a good man, he don't know &c &c."[61] After visiting New York Republicans in August, Lincoln ally Leonard Swett wrote his wife: "Unless material changes can be wrought, Lincoln's election is beyond any possible hope. It is probably clean gone now."[62] On September 8, Swett wrote her from Washington: "There was not a man doing anything except mischief. . . . We are in the midst of conspiracies equal to the French Revolution."[63] Lincoln's prospects would depend on military success.

From the early days of the Civil War, William T. Sherman had doubted the president's competence. In early September 1864, General Sherman captured Atlanta, helping to save Lincoln's faltering reelection campaign. Sherman won high praise from Lincoln. Thereafter, the general mellowed toward the president. Later that fall, the general wrote of his astonishing advance through the heartland of plantation slavery: "This may seem a hard species of warfare, but it brings the sad realities of war home to those who have been directly and indirectly instrumental in involving us in its attendant calamities."[64] With little news during the next few months about Sherman's progress through Georgia, Lincoln grew concerned. In November 1864, New York Governor-Elect Reuben Fenton went to the White House, where political etiquette required the president to greet the hundreds of New Yorkers who had accompanied Fenton: "After one or two sentences, rather commonplace, the President farther said he had no war news other than was known to all, and he supposed his ignorance in regard to General Sherman was the ignorance of all; that 'we all knew where Sherman went in, but none of us knew where he would come out.'"[65]

On December 26, Sherman would announce the location where he "came out." writing the president: "I beg to present you as a Christmas gift the City of Savannah, with 150 heavy guns & plenty of ammunition & also about 25000 bales of cotton."[66] Lincoln promptly responded: "Many, many, thanks for your Christmas-gift—the capture of Savannah. When you were about leaving Atlanta for the Atlantic coast, I was *anxious*, if not fearful; but feeling that you were the better judge, and remembering that 'nothing risked, nothing gained' I did not interfere. Now, the undertaking being a success, the honor is all yours."[67] This response was not unlike that of the president to Grant after Vicksburg. Lincoln consistently rewarded the loyalty and enterprise of victorious generals. Of his final meeting with Lincoln in early April 1865, Sherman wrote that he was "more than ever impressed by his kindly nature, his deep and earnest sympathy with the afflictions of the whole people, resulting from the war, and by the march of hostile armies through the South; and that his earnest desire seemed to be to end the war speedily, without more bloodshed or devastation, and to restore all the men of both sections to their homes."[68]

Although Churchill's influence over Allied war strategy had declined between 1943 and 1945, the prime minister continued hard travel on crucial diplomatic missions. He went to Quebec again in September 1944 to meet with Roosevelt to confer about postwar planning. There, the prime minister dictated a summary memo in response to FDR's initiative: "At a conference between the President and the Prime Minister upon the best measures to prevent renewed rearmament by Germany, it was felt that an essential feature was the future disposition of the Ruhr and the Saar. . . .

This programme for eliminating the war-making industries in the Ruhr and in the Saar is looking forward to converting Germany into a country primarily agricultural and pastoral in its character."[69] This shortsighted document had stemmed from a plan prepared by Treasury Secretary Henry Morgenthau Jr. (agreed to by FDR)—largely written by Morgenthau's primary deputy, Harry Dexter White (later revealed to be a Soviet spy). The prime minister would at first reject the so-called Morgenthau Plan as inhumane and impractical, then tentatively accept it. By the time Churchill returned from the Quebec summit with FDR, he had resigned himself to American dominance of strategy and the sidelining of his Mediterranean tactics: "Stalin will get what he wants. The Americans have seen to that. They haven't given Alex [General Alexander] a dog's chance [in Italy]," Dr. Wilson wrote in his diary. "He will do his best, but the cream of his army has been skimmed off" for deployment elsewhere.[70]

Indeed, the September 1944 Quebec conference proved contentious for British-American military strategists. The pugnacious U.S. Admiral Ernest King insulted the British by calling their navy a "liability" in the Pacific. Admiral King wanted the American navy to do it all. The prime minister would soldier on—traveling in October to Moscow for a meeting with Stalin regarding Eastern Europe. Churchill "cannot decide whether to make one last attempt to enlist Roosevelt's sympathy for a firmer line with Stalin, in the hope that he has learnt from the course of events, or whether to make his peace with Stalin and save what he can from the wreck of Allied hopes," wrote Dr. Wilson. "At one moment he will be pleased with the President for a common front against Communism and the next he will make a bid for Stalin's friendship."[71]

After a few public speeches in the spring of 1864, President Lincoln restricted his travels and public comments. He did not make his customary visits to the headquarters of the Army of the Potomac. He did work behind the scenes to support his presidential campaign—especially in negotiations that led to the withdrawal of independent candidate John C. Frémont. He would make no speeches nor issue public letters—with the exception of a bold letter to a Kentucky editor in which he explained his position on slavery: "I am naturally antislavery. If slavery is not wrong, nothing is wrong. I can not remember when I did not so think, and feel. And yet I have never understood that the Presidency conferred upon me an unrestricted right to act officially upon this judgment and feeling. It was in the oath I took that I would, to the best of my ability, preserve, protect, and defend the Constitution of the United States." Lincoln concluded the letter: "Now, at the end of three years struggle the nation's condition is not what either party, or any man devised, or expected. God alone can claim it. Whither it is tending seems plain. If God now wills the removal of a great wrong, and wills also that we of the North as well as you of the South, shall pay fairly for our complicity in that wrong, impartial history will find therein new cause to attest and revere the justice and goodness of God."[72] The president foreshadowed, in these words, the sublime Second Inaugural Address.

That autumn, Lincoln urged support for a Maryland referendum to emancipate their slaves voluntarily. Lincoln had come to believe that his presidential reelection and his continued prosecution of the war until military victory were the necessary conditions to restore the Union and abolish slavery. Emancipation had acquired political appeal as well as moral power. "By July 1864, then, Republicans had come together to frame the issue of slavery as an institution that should be abolished everywhere by law, preferably by a constitutional amendment," wrote historian Michael Vorenberg. "The party was thus ready to make the election a referendum on the law question. This issue had a moral appeal, because it established the Republicans' commitment to emancipation everywhere, even in the [loyal] Border States, which so far had been immune (in theory at least) from the operation of federal emancipation policy."[73]

To attain political victory, Lincoln could not afford to alienate those Northerners who wanted restoration of the Union, but did not favor emancipation as a precondition for peace. He was caught between Radical Republicans, who wanted abolition and a hard peace, and Union Democrats and moderate Republicans, who wanted Union victory and peace as soon as possible. After Lincoln had vetoed the radical Wade-Davis reconstruction bill in July, its congressional sponsors, Ohio Senator Benjamin Wade and Maryland Congressman Henry Winter Davis, issued the "Wade-Davis Manifesto." It declared that President Lincoln "must understand that our support is of a cause and not of a man; that the authority of Congress is paramount and must be respected; that the whole body of the Union men of Congress will not submit to be impeached by him of rash and unconstitutional legislation; and if he wishes our support, he must confine himself to his executive duties—to obey and execute, not make the laws—to suppress by arms armed Rebellion, and leave political reorganization to Congress."[74]

Thus did Lincoln's opponents try to box him in. Because of these political issues and the upcoming election in November 1864, Lincoln had to pay some attention to an assortment of peace feelers—even though he believed that Jefferson Davis would never accept peace if reunion were required. In August 1864, when his political support had slipped badly and his reelection was in doubt, Lincoln tried to compose a message to satisfy northern War Democrats. Ultimately, he decided not to release either of the two drafts he had drawn up in response to a Wisconsin editor. He was influenced by black abolitionist Frederick Douglass, to whom he had shown the letters. Douglass contended that Lincoln's proposed letters "would be given a broader meaning than you intend to convey; it would be taken as a complete surrender of your anti-slavery policy, and do you serious damage. In answer to your Copperhead accusers, your friends can make the argument of your want of power, but you cannot wisely say a word on that point."[75]

In September, Lincoln again wrote a draft letter, this time to Isaac M. Schemerhorn, who had invited the president to a Union rally in Buffalo:

I am yet unprepared to give up the Union for a peace which, so achieved, could not be of much duration. The preservation of our Union was not the sole avowed object for which the war was commenced. It was commenced [by the rebels] for precisely the reverse object—*to destroy our Union*. The insurgents commenced it by firing upon the Star of the West, and on Fort Sumpter [sic], and by other similar acts. It is true, however, that the administration accepted the war thus commenced, for the sole avowed object of preserving our Union; and it is not true that it has since been, or will be, prossecuted [sic] by this administration, for any other object. In declaring this, I only declare what I can know, and do know to be true, and what no other man can know to be false.[76]

Lincoln never finished the letter—perhaps deciding, as he had in the election of 1860, that any public communication by him would be misinterpreted and that his commitment to slavery's abolition could not be equivocated.

You owe me no thanks for what I have been able to do for you. If I may be permitted to say it, I owe you no thanks for what you have so excellently done for the country and for me; we are both alike working in the same cause, and it is because of the fact of its being a just one which gives us our mutual joy and reward in its service.[1]

ABRAHAM LINCOLN
Remarks to Christian Commission
January 27, 1865

I say that in the long years to come not only will the people of this island but of the world . . . look back to what we've done and they will say "do not despair, do not yield to violence and tyranny, march straight forward and die if need be—unconquered."[2]

WINSTON S. CHURCHILL
May 8, 1945

XII.

1865/1945

Abraham Lincoln did not shy away from controversy. His decision to meet with Confederate peace commissioners at Hampton Roads in February 1865 caused consternation among Radicals in Congress. In order to avoid creating road blocks to passage of the Thirteenth Amendment by the House of Representatives on January 31, the president had issued a carefully worded statement that no such talks would be held in Washington. Hampton Roads was not Washington. Lincoln knew nothing would come of the talks, but he felt it necessary to go through the motions of testing the intentions of the Confederate government. Journalist Noah Brooks, a Lincoln confidante, wrote that editor "J. W. Forney, in his eagerness to be considered as the oracle of the President (rushing to the conclusion that Lincoln was going to obtain peace by compromise) . . . telegraphed [articles] all over the country, indorsed by [Horace] Greeley, as the outgivings of the President, read by astonished and indignant thousands, scouted by the Wade-and-Davisites, debauching public sentiment, and filling the minds of vast multitudes, who did not know all the facts, with alarm and dejection."[3] In the end, nothing came of the Hampton Roads conference.

As the president approached his second term and the likely defeat of the Confederacy, he would focus on the permanent solution to the problem of slavery, restoration of the Union, and reconstruction of the rebel South. Lincoln could concentrate on these issues because he finally had a winning military team to manage the battlefield. He had the strength of character to shun publicity and to give credit to others. When necessary, the president had intervened in military operations. However, he took care not to interfere when visiting the military headquarters of the Army of the Potomac. He respected General Grant and his judgment. Lincoln bodyguard William H. Crook wrote:

As March 31, 1865, drew near, the president (then at City Point, Virginia) knew that Grant was to make a general attack upon Petersburg, and grew depressed. The fact that his own son was with Grant was one source of anxiety. But the knowledge of the loss of life that must follow hung about him until he could think of nothing else. On the 31st there was, of course, no news. Most of the first day of April Mr. Lincoln spent in the telegraph-office, receiving telegrams and sending them on to Washington. Toward evening he came back to the *River Queen*, on which we had sailed from Washington to City Point.[4]

After observing combat on Sunday, April 2, 1865, the president met General Grant in the conquered city of Petersburg. The same day, the Confederates abandoned Richmond. Two days later, Lincoln would casually walk into the rebel capital, accompanied by twelve sailors from his boat. Only eleven days before his assassination, he seemed completely indifferent to any lurking danger in the Confederate capital, where freed slaves greeted him enthusiastically.

Churchill, like Lincoln, appreciated military demonstrations. When in June 1944 Churchill toured the D-Day landing beaches aboard the destroyer HMS *Kelvin*, the "*Kelvin* fired a few salvos toward the German lines for Churchill's benefit." South African Prime Minister Jan Smuts mentioned to Churchill that the ship's captain was annoyed by Churchill's request for the shelling because "the destroyer was well within range of the German guns and they might have fired at us." Churchill responded: "That's what I did it for. I wanted them to fire."[5] In April 1865, a similar incident had occurred shortly before Richmond surrendered. Admiral David Dixon Porter recalled a conversation with President Lincoln,

> sitting on the Malvern's upper deck, enjoying the evening air. The president, who had been some time quiet, turned to me and said, "Can't the navy do something at this particular moment to make history?"
>
> "Not much," I replied; "the navy is doing its best just now holding in utter uselessness the rebel navy, consisting of four heavy ironclads. If those should get down to City Point they would commit great havoc—as they came near doing while I was away at Fort Fisher. In consequence, we filled up the river with

stones so that no vessels can pass either way. It enables us to 'hold the fort' with a very small force, but quite sufficient to prevent any one from removing obstructions. Therefore the rebels' iron-clads are useless to them."

"But can't we make a noise?" asked the President; "that would be refreshing."

"Yes," I replied, "we can make a noise; and, if you desire it, I will commence."

"Well, make a noise," he said.[6]

The final months of these great wars of national survival found Lincoln and Churchill exhausted. The president was "certainly growing feeble," observed one Lincoln administration official after a visit. "He wrote a note while I was present, and his hand trembled as I never saw it before, and he looked worn & haggard."[7] After his Second Inauguration of March 1865, the president became very sick. Lincoln's longtime Kentucky friend, Joshua Speed, visited the White House to see Lincoln "worn down in health & spirits." After watching the president deal with a constant stream of visitors, Speed said: "Lincoln with my knowledge of your nervous sensibility it is a wonder that such scenes as this don't kill you." The president responded: "I am . . . very unwell—my feet & hands are always cold—I suppose I ought to be in bed."[8] Julia Grant suggested her husband invite the debilitated president for a restorative visit to Union army headquarters near Richmond. Lincoln arrived at Grant's headquarters on March 24, and stayed nearby until April 8.

Churchill, too, went often to the battlefront—but the global travel and the stress of events would overtake the prime minister as victory approached. "I was very tired and physically so feeble that I had to be carried upstairs in a chair by the Marines from Cabinet meetings under the Annexe," wrote Churchill.[9] Both he and Lincoln aged dramatically during wartime. Both grew desperately weary. After visiting the front in April 1863, Lincoln commented that he did indeed "feel some better, I think; but, somehow, it don't [sic] appear to touch the tired spot, which can't be got at."[10] In March 1865, the president declared: "I am a tired man. Sometimes I think I am the tiredest man on earth."[11] Churchill often became exhausted. In March 1942, after a series of British reverses, Ivan Maisky, the Soviet ambassador to Britain, observed: "Churchill is in a 'twilight mood.' He even let slip the remark: 'I'm not long for this world . . . I'll be ashes soon.'" Maisky concluded: "My general impression is that

Churchill has an acute sense of being on the wane and is harnessing his remaining strength and energy in pursuit of one fundamental and all-exclusive goal—to win the war. He looks and thinks no further than that."[12] Two years later in March 1944, General Brooke observed Churchill "in a desperately tired mood."[13] A few weeks later, John Colville remarked that he was "[s]truck by how very tired and worn out the PM looks now."[14] Lincoln and Churchill had a melancholy sense of their own mortality, well aware of the toll of war on their bodies.

Both leaders did possess a morbid streak. When in early 1864, Lincoln visited terminally ill Congressman Owen Lovejoy, the president confided: "This war is eating my life out. I have a strong impression that I shall not live to see the end."[15] William Manchester and Paul Reid noted that in 1944, Churchill "began telling friends . . . he had not long to live."[16] At the end of war, the prime minister tended toward pessimism; Lincoln toward optimism. "I consider *this day*, the war has come to a close," Lincoln told his wife as they drove together in a carriage on the afternoon before he was assassinated: "We must *both*, be more cheerful in the future—between the war & the loss of our darling Willie—we have both, been very miserable."[17] Churchill's pessimism stemmed largely from the military advances of the Russian bear and FDR's indifference. War had taken its toll on Churchill's partner, President Roosevelt. FDR's health was failing during the war. In 1945 it would fail completely—obvious to all at Yalta. He died in Warm Springs, Georgia, on April 12—only 3 days short of the 80th anniversary of Lincoln's death on April 15, 1864. The prime minister heard the news of Roosevelt's death about midnight. A secretary recalled: "I was hurried into the study for dictation. Mr Churchill was sitting crumpled up in his chair, his face white. When he dictated he was gentle as a lamb, but his voice sounded quite dead."[18]

Roosevelt had accommodated Stalin's demand to meet on isolated Yalta for the February 1945 summit. To FDR Churchill had telegraphed: "I shall be waiting on the quay. No more let us falter! From Malta to Yalta! Let nobody alter!"[19] But FDR did falter when Churchill asked for a pre-Yalta meeting at Malta. Roosevelt at first refused, relenting one month before the Yalta summit with the prime minister. FDR would avoid substantive discussions there once he arrived.

After Germany surrendered in May, Churchill wrote that American help "will forever stir the hearts of Britons in all quarters of the world in which they dwell, and will I am certain lead to even closer affections and ties than those that have been fanned into flame by the two world wars

Abraham Lincoln, 1865
Gilder Lehrman Collection, GLC05111.02.0028

through which we have passed with harmony and elevation of mind."[20] This he wrote despite the fact that Roosevelt and the American government had become more peremptory with the British as the war moved toward its conclusion. At the Teheran summit in November 1943, and at the Yalta summit in February 1945, Churchill reacted with disappointment when Roosevelt froze him out of some meetings and agreements with Stalin. "The President is behaving very badly," Churchill admitted at the Yalta conference.[21] By then, even Harry Hopkins, a Churchill ally early in the war, supported Stalin's contentious demand for exorbitant war reparations.[22] FDR would have been better advised had he included the prime minister in every meeting with Stalin at both summits. Churchill's understanding of Soviet Imperialism and the threat to postwar Europe would ultimately prove correct. At Yalta, Roosevelt was dying, Stalin in top form, Churchill frustrated.[23] All three aimed to negotiate the shape of the postwar world. FDR aimed to get out of Europe, to create the United Nations, and to bring Russia into the war against Japan. Churchill and Stalin focused primarily on the control of Europe and the balance of power.

On May 7, 1945, Churchill learned of the German surrender from the chief of his map room. "For five years you've brought me bad news, sometimes worse than others. Now you've redeemed yourself," he told Navy Captain Richard P. Pim.[24] On May 8, the prime minister announced the Allied victory on radio, declaring that the British should celebrate "today and tomorrow as Victory in Europe days." Then, the British prime minister left for Parliament. "The house rose as a man, and yelled and yelled and waved their Order Papers," wrote MP Harold Nicolson. "He responded, not with a bow exactly, but with an odd shy jerk of the head and with a wide grin."[25] Churchill would reminisce: "We have all of us made our mistakes, but the strength of the Parliamentary institution has been shown to enable it at the same moment to preserve all the title-deeds of democracy while waging war in the most stern and protracted form." The prime minister, leader of a coalition government throughout the war, told his parliamentary colleagues: "I wish to give my hearty thanks to men of all Parties, to everyone in every part of the House where they sit, for the way in which the liveliness of Parliamentary institutions has been maintained under the fire of the enemy, and for the way in which we have been able to persevere—and we could have persevered much longer if need had been—till all the objectives which we set before us for the procuring of the unlimited and unconditional surrender of the enemy had been achieved."[26] Nicolson reported that "the Serjeant at Arms put the mace on his shoulder and, following the Speaker, we all strode out. Through the Central Lobby we streamed, through St Stephen's Chapel, and out into the sunshine of Parliament Square."[27] After a service of thanksgiving at nearby St. Margaret's Church (where Churchill had been married in 1908), the prime minister appeared on the balcony of Buckingham Palace, flanked by King George VI and Queen Elizabeth. Cheering crowds of joyous Londoners greeted the prime minister and the king. From Moscow, where Clementine Churchill had gone on a goodwill mission, she telegraphed: "My darling. Here in the British Embassy we have all been listening to your solemn words. God bless you."[28]

On May 9, the prime minister spoke to London from the balcony of the Ministry of Health—for Britain and the world to hear:

Happy days are what we have worked for, but happy days are not easily worked for. By discipline, by morale, by industry, by good laws, by fair institutions—by those ways we have won through to happy days for millions and millions of people. You have been attacked by a monstrous enemy—but you never flinched or wavered. . . . London, like a great rhinoceros, a great hippopotamus, saying: "Let them do their worst. London can take it." London can take anything. My heart goes out to the Cockneys. . . . God bless you all. You long remain as citizens of a great and splendid city. May you long remain as the heart of the British Empire.[29]

In a BBC broadcast four days later, Churchill declared: "In July, August and September 1940, forty or fifty squadrons of British fighter aircraft in the Battle of Britain broke the teeth of the German air fleet at odds of seven or eight to one. May I repeat again the words I used at that momentous hour: 'Never in the field of human conflict was so much owed by so many to so few.'"[30]

President Lincoln spoke on April 11, 1865, to the citizens of Washington, whose windows were illuminated by candles to celebrate the Confederate surrender at Appomattox. "We meet this evening, not in sorrow, but in gladness of heart," he said from a second floor window of the White House. "The evacuation of Petersburg and Richmond, and the surrender of the principal insurgent army, give hope of a righteous and speedy peace whose joyous expression can not be restrained. In the midst of this, however, He, from Whom all blessings flow, must not be forgotten. A call for a national thanksgiving is being prepared, and will be duly promulgated." Lincoln felt greater optimism for the future of America than Churchill could for the future of ravaged Europe or the weakened British Empire. John Colville wrote that during the trip to Quebec in 1944: "The P.M. produced many sombre verdicts about the future, saying that old England was in for dark days ahead, that he no longer felt he had a 'message' to deliver, and that all that he could now do was to finish the war, to get the soldiers home and to see that they had houses to which to return."[31] Churchill surely sensed, in the words of the military historian Correlli Barnett, that the audit of World War II would entail the collapse of British power.[32]

Separated by a mere four score years, two of the gravest wars of the English-speaking peoples came to an end. So, too, did two presidencies and a prime ministry. On Good Friday at Ford's Theater, April 14, 1865, Abraham Lincoln was assassinated. Vice President Andrew Johnson succeeded Lincoln on April 15. On April 12, 1945, Franklin D. Roosevelt died of a stroke at Warm Springs, Georgia. Vice President Harry Truman immediately succeeded Roosevelt. In July 1945, Churchill was defeated in a general election. On July 26, Clement Attlee succeeded Churchill. Unlike Churchill, Lincoln had anticipated possible defeat by George McClellan in the November election of 1864. Indeed, he had written a memorandum in August on how the administration should handle such a political reverse.[33] As early as September 1863, Lincoln had urged Tennessee Governor Johnson to press ahead with reconstruction. John Hay wrote in his diary that "the President cannot tell who will be the next occupant of his place or what he will do. Present action is therefore important."[34] Churchill, more confident, expected to be vindicated by voters in July 1945. He was stunned and depressed by the magnitude of his rejection. Labour overwhelmed the Tories in Parliament, 393 to 213 seats, in the first British general election since 1935. On the day after her husband's defeat, Clementine suggested that his defeat "may well be a blessing in disguise." He responded: "Well, at the moment it's certainly very well disguised."[35]

In his memoirs, Churchill wrote of "the deadly hiatus which existed between the fading strength of President Roosevelt's hold on presidential responsibilities and the growth of President Truman's grip on the world issues. In this melancholy void, one president could not act and the other could not know. Neither the military chiefs nor the State

Winston S. Churchill, 1940
© National Portrait Gallery, London

Department diplomats received the guidance they required. The former confined themselves to their professional sphere; the latter did not comprehend the issues involved. The indispensable political direction was lacking at the moment when it was most needed."[36] The truth was that the sickened FDR's "hold on presidential responsibilities" had been failing since late 1944.

Marshal Stalin was alive with plans. After FDR's death, Churchill would fix his charm on Truman—but found him less susceptible to flattery than Roosevelt, and more understanding of Churchill's logic. After first meeting Churchill in July 1945, the blunt Truman said that he thought they would have a good relationship if Churchill did not "soft soap" him too much.[37] By the time the Potsdam conference concluded, Truman described Churchill as a "likable person."[38] Years later, the former president would remark: "Churchill was a man who didn't listen very often." Truman recalled that the prime minister "liked to talk, and he was one of the best."[39] Dr. Wilson reported that: "Winston has fallen for the President. Truman's modesty and simple ways are certainly disarming."[40] Churchill's daughter declared: "Papa is relieved and confident. He likes the President immensely."[41] Although his influence and stamina waned during the war, Churchill's strategic vision did not weaken. In his postwar memoirs, Churchill summarized what he thought in 1945 were the key points of his Allied strategy:

First, that Soviet Russia had become a mortal danger to the free world.

Secondly, that a new front must be immediately created against her onward sweep.

Thirdly, that this front in Europe should be as far east as possible.

Fourthly, that Berlin was the prime and true objective of the Anglo-American armies.

Fifthly, that the liberation of Czechoslovakia and the entry into Prague of American troops was of high consequence.

Sixthly, that Vienna, and indeed Austria, must be regulated by the Western Powers, at least upon an equality with the Russian Soviets.

Seventhly, that Marshal Tito's aggressive pretensions against Italy must be curbed.

> *Finally*, and above all, that a settlement must be reached on all major issues between the West and the East in Europe *before the armies of democracy melted*, or the Western Allies yielded any part of the German territories they had conquered, or, as it could soon be written, liberated from totalitarian tyranny.[42]

The prime minister often said that he would be well regarded by history because he intended to write it. His memoirs are the evidence.

Lincoln and Churchill were magnanimous in victory—statesmen at war who had fought for unconditional surrender. Both had overcome hardships, reversals, and failures to attain the highest offices of the land. The precedents set by Lincoln and Grant had not gone unnoticed by Prime Minister Churchill and President Roosevelt. At a Casablanca news conference in January 1943, FDR announced unconditional surrender as the Allied war aim: "The elimination of German, Japanese and Italian war power means the unconditional surrender of Germany, Italy and Japan. . . . It does not mean the destruction of the population of Germany, Italy, or Japan, but it does mean the destruction of the philosophies in those countries which are based on conquest and the subjugation of other peoples."[43] The American president and the British prime minister reserved unto themselves the power to negotiate enemy surrender. "In no event," wrote FDR to Churchill in July 1943, "should our officers in the field fix on any general terms without your approval and mine."[44] FDR may have had in mind the victorious General Sherman negotiating in North Carolina with the defeated Confederate General Joseph Johnston in late April 1865—on very generous terms, which were summarily rejected by Secretary of War Stanton.

Churchill had declared in May 1940: "[V]ictory at all costs, victory in spite of all terror, victory, however long and hard the road may be; for without victory there is no survival."[45] Such a victory would have to be unconditional: "Negotiation with Hitler was impossible. He was a maniac with supreme power to play his hand out to the end, which he did, and so did we," declared the prime minister after the war.[46] Churchill aimed to reconstruct a free Europe. Only unconditional elimination of Nazism could pave the way. The Allies would destroy the Nazi armies, but some of FDR's key advisers, led by Secretary of the Treasury Henry Morgenthau Jr. and his deputy, Harry Dexter White, aimed to pastoralize and deindustrialize postwar Germany. Unlike Roosevelt and Stalin,

Churchill, in the end, opposed emasculating Germany. "I'm all for disarming Germany, but we ought not to prevent her living decently," Churchill had said after the Quebec Conference in 1944, where Morgenthau made his proposals for German deindustrialization. "There are bonds between the working classes of all countries, and the English people will not stand for the policy you are advocating."[47] The prime minister saw Germany as a buffer, with a restored France, against the expansion of Soviet imperialism. "We are no extirpators of nations," Churchill contended in his parliamentary speech of January 1945. Still, he demanded unconditional surrender. "We make no bargain with you," he said in radio remarks directed to the German people. "We accord you nothing as a right. Abandon your resistance unconditionally."[48]

In late 1864, President Lincoln had three main political objectives. The first was passage by the House of Representatives of the Thirteenth Amendment to the Constitution abolishing slavery. With uncharacteristic personal intervention in Congress, he achieved this aim on January 31, 1865. The second goal was reconstruction of the Southern states to be occupied by Union soldiers. The test case was Louisiana, but Republican Radicals in the Senate would block some of his efforts. The third objective was the restoration of the Union by military victory and unconditional rebel surrender. Union victory seemed only a matter of time, but pressure would continue to end hostilities through negotiation. Neither President Lincoln nor Confederate President Davis embraced peace negotiations, but neither could appear to rule them out. As a result, a three-man delegation was dispatched from Richmond at the end of January 1865, to meet with Union representatives. At first, Lincoln intended to rebuff the delegation. Then, he decided to send Secretary of State Seward to meet with them. After Seward departed for the meeting, Lincoln decided to go himself to Hampton Roads. As expected, Lincoln refused to discuss peace without reunion and emancipation. The Confederates were not willing to discuss peace if Union and emancipation were required conditions. One Confederate commissioner introduced the example of Britain's King Charles I—in the English Civil War two centuries earlier—as a precedent for negotiating. Confederate Vice President Alexander Stephens recalled: "Allusion having been made to Charles I of England, and his treating with men whom he called 'rebels,' Lincoln laughed and said we must talk with Seward about that matter; all he remembered about Charles was that he lost his head."[49] After a few hours, the conference ended.

Lincoln would lose neither his head nor control of negotiations. On March 3, 1865, Secretary of War Edwin Stanton telegraphed General Grant: "The President directs me to say to you that he wishes you to have no conference with General Lee unless it be for the capitulation of Gen. Lee's army, or on some minor, and purely, military matter. He instructs me to say that you are not to decide, discuss, or confer upon any political question. Such questions the President holds in his own hands; and will submit them to no military conferences or conventions. Meantime you are to press to the utmost, your military advantages."[50] Lincoln had earlier admonished Grant by telegram: "Let the *thing* be pressed."[51] With no mistrustful allies to restrain him, the president was at the height of his political and military powers in the final month of his life. (Churchill's mental self-discipline partially deserted him in his last months of office—exhaustion itself leading to tactical mistakes such as an intemperate campaign speech against the Labour Party.) Lincoln made an important mistake as the war ended—a well-intentioned move to call the Confederate legislature of Virginia back into session, at the beginning of April, after the fall of Richmond. Chastened, he quickly reversed that error.

The president had resolved to keep in his own hands political negotiations to end the Civil War. Under the pressure of public opinion, he had toyed briefly with peace feelers in the summer of 1864. Lincoln clearly defined his position at the end of his Fourth Annual Message to Congress in December 1864:

> In presenting the abandonment of armed resistance to the national authority on the part of the insurgents, as the only indispensable condition to ending the war on the part of the government, I retract nothing heretofore said as to slavery. I repeat the declaration made a year ago, that "while I remain in my present position I shall not attempt to retract or modify the emancipation proclamation, nor shall I return to slavery any person who is free by the terms of that proclamation, or by any of the Acts of Congress." If the people should, by whatever mode or means, make it an Executive duty to re-enslave such persons, another, and not I, must be their instrument to perform it. In stating a single condition of peace, I mean simply to say that the war will cease on the part of the government, whenever it shall have ceased on the part of those who began it.[52]

It has long been a grave question whether any government, not too strong for the liberties of its people, can be strong enough to maintain its own existence, in great emergencies.[1]

ABRAHAM LINCOLN
November 10, 1864

I acquired the chief power in the State, which henceforth I wielded in ever-growing measure for five years and three months of world war, at the end of which time, all our enemies having surrendered unconditionally or being about to do so, I was immediately dismissed by the British electorate from all further conduct of their affairs.[2]

WINSTON S. CHURCHILL
The Gathering Storm: The Second World War, 1948

XIII.

Reelection and Reconstruction

President Lincoln claimed not to have controlled events, but to have been controlled by them.[3] In this disavowal, one observes Lincoln's modesty and realism. But it was also the useful deceit of a disciplined statesman, who *did* control major events, but whose ego felt no need for self-congratulation. It was sufficient for him to fasten his iron grip on Union strategy and policy. James M. McPherson summed up Lincoln's wartime leadership: "As president of the nation and leader of his party as well as commander in chief, Lincoln was principally responsible for shaping and defining national policy. From first to last, that policy was preservation of the United States as one nation, indivisible, and as a republic based on majority rule."[4] The president had emphasized that there would be neither peace, nor reunion, without emancipation. Moreover, it was Lincoln's original military strategy, brought to fulfillment by General Grant, which led to the unconditional surrender of the Confederacy. Without this victory, North America could have been riven with a free republic in the North, a slave-based republic in the South, and never-ending discord and conflict between them.

Churchill dominated Britain's strategy. Even as First Lord of the Admiralty in the fall of 1939, he had become the inspiration of his countrymen. One Admiralty aide said of him: "He practically killed people with overwork, and at the same time inspired people to extreme devotion."[5] The prime minister was more of a micromanager than Lincoln, who intervened when necessary, not as a routine.[6] Churchill's secretary Elizabeth Layton, whose night duty sometimes ended around 5 A.M., noted:

As the Prime Minister read through the telegrams each day . . . he would often pick out some slight decision or circumstance which he felt was wrong, and would instantly address a Minute inquiring into it. In this way he kept his finger on all aspects, both great and small, of the prosecution of the war. He was always roused to anger by any suspicion of slackness, lethargy or red-tape delay, and would dispatch a stinging Minute, which he would not forget to follow up if he did not at once receive a report in reply. His memory of what he had read and written was excellent, and he acted as a constant spur to those under him.[7]

Churchill detested delay. Eliot Cohen argued: "Churchill believed that the formulation of strategy in war did not consist merely in drawing up state documents sketching out a comprehensive view of how the war would be won, but also in a host of detailed activities which, when united and dominated by a central conception, would form a comprehensive picture."[8] The "detailed activities" would include the Ultra code-breaking operation, which enabled the prime minister to know more about the day-to-day movement of German land and sea forces than did his commanders in the field and on the ocean.

At the onset of the Civil War, President Lincoln grasped its global significance for the future of free people and democratic government. In 1861, almost all countries of the world were governed by royal families or despotic rulers, with limited popular participation. In May 1861, President Lincoln confided to John Hay: "For my part, I consider the central idea pervading this struggle is the necessity that is upon us of proving that popular government is not an absurdity. We must settle this question now, whether in a free government the minority have the right to break up the government whenever they choose. If we fail, it will go far to prove the incapability of the people to govern themselves."[9] By March 1864, the perceptive *Harpers Weekly* editorialized:

From the beginning of his term the President has evidently been persuaded that this was a people's war: that, if the people were wise and brave enough, they would save the Union and the Government; and if they were not, then that no leader could or ought to save them. Twenty months ago he was without a party. The Copperheads hated him; the "Conservative Republicans" thought him too fast; the "Radical Republicans" thought him too slow; the War Democrats were looking for the chance of a return to political power. He held steadily upon his way. As he thought the country ready he took each advancing step. He issued the preparatory [Emancipation] proclamation. He followed it with the New Year's decree [of the Final Emancipation Proclamation]. He wrote the Greeley [in response to Horace Greeley's "Prayer of 20 Millions" urging emancipation], the [Clement] Vallandigham letter, the Springfield letter, simple, plain, direct; letters which the heart of every man in the land interpreted, and unlike any other instance in our political annals, every letter he wrote, every speech he made, brought him nearer to the popular heart; so that now it is a little too late to call him "well-meaning," "incompetent," "a mere joker," because it is the general conviction that he is no man's puppet; that he listens respectfully to his Cabinet and then acts from his own convictions; that by his calm and cheerful temperament, by his shrewd insight, his practical sagacity, his undaunted patience, his profound faith in the people and their cause, he is peculiarly fitted for his solemn and responsible office. Nor is it likely that the people who elected him when he was comparatively unknown will discard him because, in the fierce light of war which tries every quality and exposes every defect, he has steadily grown in popular love and confidence.[10]

After his second inauguration in March 1865, the president told Treasury Secretary Hugh McCulloch, "I am here by the blunders of the [Northern] Democrats. If, instead of resolving that the war was a failure, they had resolved that I was a failure and denounced me for not more vigorously prosecuting it, I should not have been reelected, and I reckon that you would not have been Secretary of the Treasury."[11] Lincoln's modesty was again at work, this time to reinforce his strategy to prosecute war to victory.

The American president was a frontier lawyer born into poverty. The English prime minister was a well-born grandson of the Duke of Marlborough. They came by different routes to deep belief in the rule of law and democratic institutions. Both had felt the pain of losing elections. On October 31, 1944, Churchill told the House of Commons: "The foundation of all democracy is that the people have the right to vote. To deprive them of that right is to make a mockery of all the high-sounding phrases which are so often used. . . . The people have the right to choose representatives in accordance with their wishes and feelings."[12]

Lincoln's wartime reelection in November 1864 fortified his will to fight for unconditional surrender of the slave power. John Hay wrote that on election night, he and the president left for the War Department about 7 P.M. Major Thomas Eckert

> came in shaking the rain from his cloak, with trousers very disreputably muddy. We sternly demanded an explanation. He had slipped, he said, & tumbled prone, crossing the street. . . . The President said, "For such an awkward fellow, I am pretty sure-footed. It used to take a pretty dexterous man to throw me. I remember, the evening of the day in 1858, that decided the contest for the Senate between Mr Douglas and myself, was something like this, dark, rainy & gloomy. I had been reading the returns, and had ascertained that we had lost the Legislature [and the Senate election] and started to go home. The path had been worn hog-backed & was slippering [sic]. My foot slipped from under me, knocking the other one out of the way, but I recovered myself & lit square, and I said to myself, *'It's a slip and not a fall.'*"[13]

The president might have thought of the agony of his first two years in office, one slip after another, in each case righting himself, proceeding with his strategy, step by step to victory, reunion, and the abolition of slavery. In November 1861, Radical Republican Senator Zachariah Chandler had complained: "Lincoln means well but has no force of character. He is surrounded by Old Fogy Army officers more than half of whom are downright traitors and other one half sympathize with the South."[14] Events had proved that Lincoln's character was sufficient for the greatest national challenge since the founding of the republic.

Lincoln, in mid-conflict, had received from the voters a national mandate to direct the war government for another term of four years. Regular congressional and local elections generally came off on schedule during the Civil War. Lincoln needed to be a practicing politician during the war—winning renomination and reelection, adept not only at managing Northern War Democrats and Congress, but also building an effective patronage machine in the loyal states to support the new Republican Party, of which he was a founder and its first president.[15] Churchill was not free of political pressure. He held office, to some extent, at the sufferance of the Labour Party, and with the ambivalence of much of the Conservative Party. There would be no mid-war election to liberate Churchill from the constraints of his coalition government. During World War II, he did not face in a general election the public discontent that grew as mortal threat to British survival dissipated. Lincoln maintained his base of Republican strength, even against strong Union Democrats in the North. Tory strength in Britain fell precipitously during the war, as voter desire for postwar social change intensified. As the leader of the Conservative Party, Churchill turned sharply partisan in the month before the 1945 parliamentary election. Until then, he had focused on unifying the nation at war, resisting partisan diversion on the issues of domestic reconstruction and reform.

In contrast to severe British rationing and deprivation in World War II, the free economy of the American North boomed during the Civil War—despite the relatively massive debt the Union government assumed to finance war purchases in an inflationary market. No matter the circumstances, both Lincoln and Churchill maintained a laser-like focus on victory. British citizens supported Churchill as a war leader, but they grew increasingly tired of price controls, rationing, and poverty. The privations of the Civil War were concentrated in the Confederate South much more than in the Union North. Those conditions were made worse by the ineffective financial policies of the Confederate government. Allen Guelzo wrote that "the collapse of Southern bonds and notes wiped out any fiscal leverage the Confederates might have had on the Northern financial markets in 1861, the uncertainty made worse by the Confederate decision to sequester loans owed by Southerners to Northern finance for the duration of the war."[16] The Confederates hoarded cotton at the beginning of the war when there existed a glut in England. Hoarding cotton would not help the South. Prices fell and the South also lost leverage in international trade because new sources for cotton were developed in Egypt and India.

On May 21, 1945, the Labour Party Conference decided to withdraw from the British coalition government. Churchill thus must face the voters. In 1940, he had become a coalition prime minister as a leader of the Conservative Party. (Neville Chamberlain remained the party's official leader until October 1940.) On May 23, 1945, after five years of coalition government, Churchill asked King George to call new parliamentary elections. He would not remain in power to see the surrender of Japan on August 15, 1945. His powers of insight and inspiration often failed him during the highly charged politics of the election campaign wherein postwar domestic policy became paramount. Far-sighted in international affairs, Churchill did not fully grasp the decisive shift in Britain toward cradle-to-grave security and socialism. Voters became indifferent to the glories of the British Empire. Britain was poor and insolvent.

Churchill's vital interests still remained global. The Communist expansion in Europe preoccupied Churchill, whereas Lincoln could concentrate domestically on how best to reintegrate the country. Lincoln, the superior grassroots politician, knew he could only be so strong in the Union as he was in the loyal North—his voter base, as well as the source of national wealth and the sustenance of his two-million-man army. Sheltered behind the vast Atlantic and Pacific Oceans, and the dominant British navy, there were no major external threats to the Union. Thus, Lincoln could focus on his domestic base. Churchill's single-minded war efforts had forged the Alliance, but his indifference to domestic issues allowed the Conservative Party's popularity to fall as peace approached.

President Lincoln wrote to Congress at the end of 1863 that "our chiefest care must still be directed to the army and navy, who have thus far borne their harder part so nobly and well."[17] The prosecution of the war remained his top priority, just as it would for Churchill. As the Civil War and World War II gradually moved to their conclusions, reconstruction at home would preoccupy Lincoln. But the prime minister's vision encompassed the whole world. Indeed his political aims were further complicated by his commitment to the preservation of the weakened British Empire.

Victory could bring not only peace, the president believed, but also a gradual reconstruction of social attitudes as well. The abolitionist author of *Uncle Tom's Cabin*, Harriet Beecher Stowe, wrote in February 1864 that "Almighty God has granted to him [Lincoln] that clearness of vision which he gives to the true-hearted, and enabled him to set his honest foot in that promised land of freedom which is to be the patrimony of all men, black and white—and from henceforth nations shall rise up to call him blessed."[18] Addressing a victory serenade on April 11, 1865, Lincoln would say: "Nor must those [the soldiers, both white and black] whose harder part gives us the cause of rejoicing, be overlooked. Their honors must not be parcelled out with others. I myself, was near the front, and had the high pleasure of transmitting much of the good news to you; but no part of the honor, for plan or execution, is mine."[19]

Before that speech, Lincoln told friendly journalist Noah Brooks: "It

***Harpers Weekly,* November 26, 1864**

Gilder Lehrman Collection, GLC00623, pg. 168.

is true that I don't usually read a speech, but I am going to say something to-night that may be important. I am going to talk about reconstruction, and sometimes I am betrayed into saying things that other people don't like." Brooks wrote that there was "something terrible about the enthusiasm with which the beloved Chief Magistrate was received—cheers upon cheers, wave after wave of applause rolled up, the President modestly standing quiet until it was over."[20] Present that night was an actor who had a very different reaction to Lincoln's reconstruction hopes for emancipated slaves. "That is the last speech he will ever make," declared John Wilkes Booth, who was repulsed by Lincoln's support for black suffrage.[21] Speaking of the reconstruction of Louisiana, Lincoln had said: "It is also unsatisfactory to some that the elective franchise is not given to the colored man. I would myself prefer that it were now conferred on the very intelligent, and on those who serve our cause as soldiers."[22] This would be the president's last public speech.

Churchill had the chance to reset Britain's domestic priorities, but he was no socialist. "The Prime Minister was in no hurry to take advantage of the opportunities presented by mobilization for total war in order to introduce permanent measures of social reform," wrote historian J. M. Lee. "He quite deliberately left as much as possible of 'home front' business to the Lord President's Committee."[23] Under Labour auspices, Sir William Beveridge prepared an ambitious report on postwar Britain in December 1942.[24] Because Britain was insolvent, the prime minister and his aides focused on the fiscal implications of the Beveridge recommendations, worried as they were at the same time about the political costs of opposing the reforms. Moreover, Churchill wanted no distractions from his focus on Allied victory, but he was loath to appear unsympathetic to the aspirations of Britain's laboring classes, the source of Churchill's fighting men abroad. On March 21, 1943, he declared in a BBC broadcast: "Nothing would be easier for me than to make any number of promises and to get the immediate response of cheap cheers and glowing leading articles. I am not in any need to go about making promises in order to win political support or to be allowed to continue in office." The prime minister added that he would not "make all kinds of promises and tell all kinds of fairy tales to you who have trusted me, and gone with me so far, and marched through the valley of the shadow, till we have reached the upland regions on which we now stand with firmly planted feet."[25] Unlike Lincoln, Churchill in 1943 faced no immediate general election in which Conservatives would have to defend not only war policies, but also future domestic policies. In fact, the Republican-controlled Congress passed important domestic legislation during the Civil War, providing for cheap homesteading, a transcontinental railroad, land-grant universities, and a national banking act—among other reform initiatives that had previously been blocked by southern Democrats.

For Lincoln and Churchill, victory in war had been inextricably linked to the preservation of democratic freedoms. Addressing a London crowd from the Ministry of Health on VE-Day, May 8, 1945, the prime minister declared: "The lights went out and the bombs came down. But every man, woman and child in the country had no thought of quitting the struggle. London can take it. So we came back after long months from the jaws of death, out of the mouth of hell, while all the world wondered."[26] None knew better than Churchill that his was a war of national survival wherein not only British liberty was at stake. Speaking to a Sanitary Fair in Baltimore in April 1864, Lincoln would shrewdly analyze the meaning of liberty:

> We all declare for liberty; but in using the same *word* we do not all mean the same *thing*. With some the word liberty may mean for each man to do as he pleases with himself, and the product of his labor; while with others the same word may mean for some men to do as they please with other men, and the product of other men's labor. Here are two, not only different, but incompatable [sic] things, called by the same name—liberty. And it follows that each of the things is, by the respective parties, called by two different and incompatable [sic] names—liberty and tyranny.[27]

Before and throughout the war, the president emphasized the irony that slavemasters insisted upon the liberty to take by force the value of the labor of another man and woman.

However large their visions, the monumental tasks of reconstruction confounded Lincoln and Churchill. Post–Civil War reconstruction would be an immense, continental undertaking. "We can't undertake to run state governments in all these southern states," said the president at a cabinet meeting on the day he was assassinated. "Their people must do that, though I reckon that at first, they may do it badly."[28] Lincoln prepared himself to take his chances with the least imperfect arrangements acceptable to the victorious North and the congress. Long before victory, he laid out his vision in December 1863, in a document that was first universally praised and later criticized by Radical Republicans who wanted, root and branch, to destroy the slave-based plantation culture of the South. Thus, they would oppose Lincoln's drive for wartime reconstruction.

As World War II came to an end, Churchill's vision of reconstruction continued to focus on global peace, the balance of power with the Soviet Union, and the interests of the British Empire. "'Victory' for the [British] people meant more than it did for Churchill," wrote Geoffrey Best. "He was so obsessed with winning a victory in military terms that only grudgingly did he turn part of his mind to the people's more comprehensive aim of a victory that would inaugurate the construction of a better Britain, a victory that would justify all wartime's sacrifices and be a 'glory' of its own kind."[29] For the Labour Party, a better Britain meant a cradle-to-grave system of government subsidies in health, housing, and social security—a "New Jerusalem." Churchill failed to devise a compelling vision for postwar Britain at home, leading to his decisive defeat in the parliamentary elections of July 1945. The chronicler of *The Collapse of British Power*, Correlli Barnett, has dated the discussion of postwar reconstruction to an article, entitled "A Plan for Britain," published in the *Picture Post* of January 1941. In an accompanying editorial, the magazine referred to the lack of change that followed World War I: "This time we can be better prepared if we think now. This is not the time for putting off thinking 'till we see how things are' . . . More than that, our plan for a new Britain is not something outside the war, or something *after* the war. It is an essential part of our war aims. It is, indeed, our most positive war aim. The new Britain is the country we are fighting for." Barnett noted: "From [then] on the Cabinet would come under ever increasing public pressure to commit itself to a blueprint for this better Britain, however much the War Premier might try to stonewall pressure too from Labour members of his own government."[30]

Churchill resisted this pressure. Speaking to Parliament on October 31, 1944, he warned: "I have no hesitation in declaring that it would be a wrongful act, unworthy of our country's fame, to break up the present governing instrument before we know where we are with Hitler's Germany. Those who forced such a disaster, even thoughtlessly, would take on themselves a measureless responsibility, and their action would be fiercely resented by the nation at large." Churchill, sensing the desire for reform, added: "The prolongation of the life of the existing Parliament by another two or three years would be a very serious constitutional lapse. Even now, no one under thirty has ever cast a vote at a General Election, or even at a by-election, since the registers fell out of action at the beginning of the war."[31] By 1945, many foresaw that the Tories were losing the electorate to the Labour Party and its socialist blueprint for the future.

Reconstruction of the homeland would become the soft underbelly of Churchill's prime ministership. The Tories tried to contain Labour pressure for social and economic reform—buried as it was under paperwork and reports. "I regard it as a definite part of the duty and responsibility of this National Government," said the prime minister in a November 1943 speech, "to have its plans perfected in a vast and practical scheme to make sure that in the years immediately following the war food, work and homes are found for all. No airy visions, no party doctrines, no party prejudices, no political appetites, no vested interest, must stand in the way of the simple duty of providing beforehand for food, work, and homes." With this bromide, Churchill would turn again to war. But much of the electorate—the soldiers and the homefront that had sacrificed life and well-being—had their eyes on a "New Britain." The prime minister resisted. "The Conservative Party," said Churchill in March 1945, "had far better go down telling the truth and acting in accordance with the verities of our position than gain a span of shabbily bought office by easy and fickle froth and chatter."[32] Whenever his colleagues sought to engage Churchill in postwar domestic planning, he resisted. He concentrated his mind on battlefield maps and the global geography of the postwar world. "For all Churchill's continued personal misgivings about saddling a postwar government with vast commitments," wrote Barnett, "his only recourse in these last two years of the war lay in trying to slow up the Whitehall machinery by judiciously shoving wedges into the cogs, in the form of referring schemes agreed by the Labour-dominated home-front ministries and committees to [his loyal friends] Lord Beaverbrook (the Lord Privy Seal) and Brendan Bracken (Minister of Information)."[33] Labour leader Clement Attlee lost his patience with Churchill's policy delays and rhetorical detours at cabinet meetings. To preserve the confidentiality of his complaints, Attlee in January 1945 personally pecked out a 2,000-word memo on his own typewriter. "This should have given the missive more and not less force. It showed the trouble Attlee had taken to avoid even his personal staff knowing of the exasperation with which he had written," concluded Churchill biographer Roy Jenkins (himself a cabinet member in several Labour governments).[34] Writing of the work of the reconstruction committees, Attlee complained about their treatment to Churchill:

What happens then? Frequently a long delay before they [the reform proposals] can be considered. When they do come before the cabinet it is very exceptional for you to have read them. More and more often you have not read even the note prepared for your guidance. Often half an hour or more is wasted in explaining what could have been grasped by two or three minutes reading of the document. Not infrequently a phrase catches your eye which gives rise to a disquisition on an interesting point only slightly connected with the subject matter. The result is long delays and unnecessarily long Cabinets.

Attlee went on to deliver a strong critique of Churchill's annoying deference to the opinions of Beaverbrook and Bracken, "neither of whom has given any serious attention to the subject."[35] Churchill bridled at Attlee's critique when he received it. He was in bed with a cold. "Outraged," recalled a Churchill aide, "Churchill sought a denial of the distasteful [Atlee] thesis first from Lord Beaverbrook and then from Brendan Bracken. Both said they thought Attlee quite right. He had then turned to Mrs Churchill . . . only to be met with the reply that she admired Mr Attlee for having the courage to put into writing what everybody else was thinking. . . . Suddenly, at about 4 p.m., he threw back the bedclothes, [smiled and said]: 'Let us think no more of Hitlee or of Attler; let us go and see a film.'"[36]

Such criticism annoyed Churchill.[37] His political intuition was failing him. Churchill would patronize Attlee, writing: "You may be sure I shall always endeavor to profit by your counsels." Obtuse to Attlee's feelings, his superficial and dismissive response may explain Attlee's refusal to postpone elections that spring. Churchill's failure to grasp the national mood, as Attlee certainly did, was a primary cause of Churchill's defeat at the polls in July 1945. Even Clementine Churchill viewed Attlee's arguments as "both true and wholesome."[38] Moreover, Churchill's work habits increasingly grated on his colleagues. Permanent Under-Secretary of Foreign Affairs Alexander Cadogan often complained about the prime minister in his diary. In April 1944, he wrote: "Altogether he kept me away from my work for three hours today on matters which shouldn't have taken more than twenty mins. How does he get through his work? Between 11 P.M. and 3 A.M., I suppose." About six weeks later, Cadogan complained of the cabinet meeting—"the shorter the agenda the longer the ramble."[39]

Daily Express, June 8, 1940

© *Strube/*Daily Express*/N&S Syndication*

Churchill was stubborn but not so thick-skinned as Lincoln. No president has been more vilified in the press than the sixteenth. He generally ignored the more sustained, vicious, and personal venom of his critics—except when newspapers published malicious mistruths intended to incite treason and desertion—or to spread economic or political disorder. Journalist James Russell Lowell wrote: "The peddlers of rumor in the North were the most active allies of the rebellion. A nation can be liable to no more insidious treachery than that of the telegraph, sending hourly its electric thrill of panic along the remotest nerves of the community, till the excited imagination makes every real danger loom heightened with its unreal double."[40] Lincoln had fewer tools to control the press than did Churchill, who took his complaints directly to the press barons. The prime minister would suppress news when he thought it might undermine public confidence in the war effort.[41] The Lincoln administration did suppress some disloyal or treasonous newspapers, but often Lincoln would quickly lift the restrictions.

Churchill's most important political tool was his ability to communicate through speeches, especially in Parliament, but the 1945 election campaign, given British sentiment, would on June 4 get off on the wrong foot. "Socialism is," declared Churchill, "in its essence, an attack not only upon British enterprise, but upon the right of the ordinary man or woman to breathe freely without having a harsh, clumsy, tyrannical hand clapped across their mouths and nostrils. A Free Parliament—look at that—a Free Parliament is odious to the Socialist doctrinaire." Churchill added: "No Socialist Government conducting the entire life and industry of the country could afford to allow free, sharp, or violently-worded expressions of public discontent. They would have to fall back on some form of Gestapo, no doubt very humanely directed in the first instance. And this would nip opinion in the bud; it would stop criticism as it reared its head, and it would gather all the power to the supreme party and the party leaders, rising like stately pinnacles above their vast bureaucracies of Civil Servants, no longer servants and no longer civil."[42] True enough of Soviet communism, but his inept association of Atlee and the British Labour Party with the Gestapo suggested that Churchill the politician seemed tone-deaf. The next evening, Attlee deftly outlined "the difference between Winston Churchill, the great leader in war of a united nation, and Mr. Churchill, the Party Leader of Conservatives."[43] Even Churchill's doctor admitted: "[A]s I listened, it became plain that one ounce of [William Ewart] Gladstone's moral fervour was worth a ton of skilled invective. It is clear that the P.M. is on the wrong tack."[44]

The writing had literally been on the wall concerning Churchill's fate—especially with British soldiers. In February 1944, MP Harold Nicolson had written in his diary:

> I fear that Winston has become an electoral liability now rather than an asset. This makes me sick with human nature. Once the open sea is reached, we forget how we clung to the pilot in the storm. Poor Winston, who is so sensitive although so pugnacious, will feel all this. In the [rail] station lavatory at Blackheath last week I found scrawled up, "Winston Churchill is a bastard." I pointed it out to the [RAF] Wing Commander who was with me. "Yes," he said, "the tide has turned. We find it everywhere." "But how foul," I said. "How bloody foul!" "Well, you see, if I may say so, the men [soldiers] hate politicians."[45]

Public applause would mask underlying trends. Harold Macmillan noted that: "Vast crowds, who had hardly seen him in person since the beginning of the war and had only heard his voice through those famous broadcasts, by which they had been sustained in times of disaster and inspired at moments of success, turned out in flocks to see and applaud him." Conservative MP Macmillan further wrote in his memoirs that: "They wished to thank him for what he had done for them; and in that all were sincere. But this did not mean that they wished to entrust him and his Tory colleagues with the conduct of their lives in the years that were to follow."[46] The *Times* declared that Churchill's campaign "indulged in accusations, imputations and even personal abuse against his wartime colleagues which shocked his hearers—even his friends—and embittered his opponents."[47] Churchill's daughter Mary Soames recalled: "The Socialists cleverly and effectively presented two images of Winston to the public: one was 'Churchill the Great War-time Leader,' who had led the nation to victory; the other was 'Churchill the Party Leader,' irresponsible, out of touch with ordinary people, subject to the malign influence of Lord Beaverbrook, and not to be trusted in peacetime."[48] Eden observed that "while there is much gratitude to W[inston] as a war leader, there is not the same enthusiasm for him as P.M.

of the peace. We should, I think, have probably been beaten anyway, but Labour majority should have been smaller."[49] The British public wanted Atlee socialism.

The British electorate voted at the beginning of July 1945, but the results were not announced until the end of the month—after the far-flung soldier vote had been tallied. Churchill had hoped to keep the coalition in place until the end of the war with Japan. Attlee had countered with a proposal to keep the coalition government in place until October. Churchill and his advisers thereupon decided upon an immediate election.[50] Harold Macmillan wrote: "Attlee naturally complained that we were rushing the election, to which Churchill equally naturally replied that so far from rushing it he was prepared not only to grant the normal twenty days between dissolution and polling, but an additional three weeks' notice."[51]

On the afternoon of July 26, the prime minister went to Buckingham Palace to give up the seals of office. In what King George VI called "a very sad meeting," he told Churchill, "I thought the people were very ungrateful after the way they had been led in the War. He [Churchill] was very calm & said that with the majority the Socialists had got . . . they could remain in power for years."[52] Labour had captured nearly twice as many seats as the Conservatives in the House of Commons. "The decision of the British people has been recorded in the votes counted to-day," announced Churchill. "It only remains for me to express to the British people for whom I have acted in these perilous years, my profound gratitude for the unflinching, unswerving support which they have given me during my task, and for the many expressions of kindness which they have shown towards their servant."[53]

Dr. Wilson wrote that in defeat, the ousted prime minister "blamed no one. He was very sad as he talked quietly about what had happened." Churchill himself thought that: "The public will be staggered when they hear tonight at nine o'clock that I've resigned. Labour will be in for four years at least. They may make it difficult for the Conservatives to come in again. But I think the financial consequences of their [Labour's] policy will be their undoing. This is not necessarily the end." The next day, Wilson wrote that Churchill admitted being "stunned by the result" and that he felt "some disgrace in the size of the majority." He acknowledged that the soldier vote went for Labour. He said: "I had made all my plans; I feel I could have dealt with things better than anyone else. This is Labour's opportunity to bring in socialism, and they will take it. They will go very far."[54] Churchill counseled one of his private secretaries: "You must not think of me any more; your duty is now to serve Attlee, if he wishes you to do so. You must therefore go to him, for you must think also of your future."[55]

The Labour victory should not have come as a surprise; polls had signaled Labour's rise over the previous three years. Labour had consistently led the Tories in the Gallup Poll published in the *News Chronicle*. The Conservatives actually did somewhat better in the 1945 election results than in surveys, losing the popular vote by 8 percent.[56] Labour leader Aneurin Bevan, a longtime thorn in Churchill's side in Parliament, wrote in the *Tribune*: "The significance of the election is that the British people have voted deliberately and consciously for a new world, both at home and abroad. In fact they have proved more courageous and far-sighted than their leaders. They had turned their backs on the wartime prime minister and his Tory values before their national leaders had realized that they had done so."[57] When a visitor told Churchill "while you held the reins, you managed to win the race," the defeated prime minister responded: "Yes, I won the race—and now they have warned me off the turf."[58]

Lincoln took criticism and political setbacks better than Churchill. The president was less inclined to emotional extremes. Though brave and aggressive, the prime minister was more thin-skinned. But Lincoln did not have to face directly the fierce barbs of the House of Commons. However, he regularly endured the poisonous criticism of a partisan press and the leaders of the Congressional Committee on the Conduct of the War, controlled as it was by the Radicals of Lincoln's own party. Lincoln said he had not read the vicious Wade-Davis manifesto, written by two powerful Radical Republican critics in the summer of 1864, but he confessed: "To be wounded in the house of one's friends is perhaps the most grievous affliction that can befall a man."[59] The president dwelt not on the wound, but moved promptly to the political consequences.[60] He wondered if Wade and Davis "intend openly to oppose my election—the document looks that way."[61] Wade and Davis would reluctantly fall in behind Lincoln's reelection.[62] Lincoln dispatched his worst critics in a few words: "If I were to try to read, much less to answer all the attacks made upon me this shop might as well be closed for any other business."[63] The president would be vindicated by reelection in November 1864. So beloved was the commander in chief by his men in arms that about four in five soldiers voted for his reelection.[64]

This extraordinary war in which we are engaged falls heavily upon all classes of people, but the most heavily upon the soldier. For it has been said, all that a man hath will he give for his life; and while all contribute of their substance the soldier puts his life at stake, and often yields it up in his country's cause. The highest merit, then is due to the soldier.[1]

ABRAHAM LINCOLN
Sanitary Fair, Washington, DC
March 18, 1864

Some people assume too readily that, because a Government keeps cool and has steady nerves under reverses, its members do not feel the public misfortunes as keenly as do independent critics. On the contrary, I doubt whether anyone feels greater sorrow or pain than those who are responsible for the general conduct of our affairs.[2]

WINSTON S. CHURCHILL
Remarks to House of Commons
July 2, 1942

XIV.

Managing Men at War—Lincoln Style

On election day, 1864, President Lincoln reflected: "It is a little singular that I who am not a vindictive man, should have always been before the people for election in canvasses marked for their bitterness: always but once: When I came to Congress it was a quiet time: but always besides that the contests in which I have been prominent have been marked with great rancor."[3] In these contests the slavery issue—the most contentious in American history—preoccupied the voters of Illinois and the nation. Lincoln the candidate, and as president, despite the rancor, was generally even-tempered. On rare occasions during the war, Lincoln's frustration with military leaders and their excuses gave rise to sarcasm. On November 11, 1864, the president wrote Secretary of War Stanton to complain about the interrogation by prospective white officers of black troops: "I personally wish Jacob R. Freese, of New-Jersey to be appointed a Colonel for a colored regiment—and this regardless of whether he can tell the exact shade of Julius Caesar's hair."[4] Stanton frequently proved to the president that he could be a convenient "no" or "yes" man. In fact, Lincoln sometimes drafted memos to generals for Stanton or General Henry W. Halleck to sign.

For escape from the dissension in his senior team, some of them his rivals in 1860, the president would surround himself privately with able and congenial people with whom he could relax. That meant spending nights at the nearby home of Secretary of State Seward, or taking rides with John Dahlgren, a Washington-based naval officer. Lincoln found it easier to deal with Assistant Secretary of the Navy Gustavus V. Fox than Fox's stuffy boss, Gideon Welles. Stanton, once a bitter critic of Lincoln, became a congenial companion as they shared summer cottages on the grounds of the Soldiers' Home in northeast Washington. At night, Lincoln sometimes relaxed with old Illinois friends in his office, or walked into the bedroom of his aides to exchange a joke or news. Lincoln loved both telling and listening to jokes. He admired quick wit of the kind exemplified by his clever aide John Hay. One night, Lincoln walked in on Hay telling a long joke to his colleagues. The president waited until the end of the story and ordered: "Now, John, just tell that thing again." When Hay concluded the second telling, "the President's foot [came down] from across his knee, with a heavy stamp on the floor, and out through the hall went an uproarious peal of fun."[5] On another occasion Hay recorded in his diary:

> A little after midnight as I was writing those last lines, the President came into the office laughing, with a volume of Hood's works in his hand, to show Nicolay & me the little Caricature "An unfortunate Bee-ing," seemingly utterly unconscious that he with his short shirt hanging above his long legs & setting out behind like the tail feathers of an enormous ostrich was infinitely funnier than anything in the book he was laughing at. What a man it is! Occupied all day with matters of vast moment, deeply anxious about the fate of the greatest army of the world, with his own fame & future hanging on the events of the passing hour, he yet has such a wealth of simple bonhommie & good fellowship that he gets out of bed and perambulates the house in his shirt to find us that we may share with him the fun of one of poor Hoods queer little conceits.[6]

Edward D. Neill, another aide who worked at the White House toward the end of the war, observed: "Every month my impression of the greatness of President Lincoln increased. He was above a life of mere routine. In his bearing there was nothing artificial or mechanical." Neill wrote that Lincoln "was independent of all cliques. Willing to be convinced, with a wonderful patience he listened to the opinions and criticisms of others."[7] In August 1863, one month after the Union victories at Gettysburg and Vicksburg, Hay recorded his own personal observations of Lincoln's mastery of his administration:

> The Tycoon is in fine whack. I have rarely seen him more serene & busy. He is managing this war, the draft, foreign relations,

and planning a reconstruction of the Union, all at once. I never knew with what tyrannous authority he rules the Cabinet, till now. The most important things he decides & there is no cavil. I am growing more and more firmly convinced that the good of the country absolutely demands that he should be kept where he is till this thing is over. There is no man in the country, so wise, so gentle and so firm. I believe the hand of God placed him where he is.[8]

Nearly a week later, Hay wrote a New York friend: "The trash you read every day about wrangles in the Cabinet about measures of state policy looks very silly from an inside view, where Abraham Rex is the central figure continually. I wish you could see as I do, that he is devilish near an autocrat in this Administration."[9] The president proved to be a master of men, master of events, not least because he was master of himself.

Lincoln's secretaries did complain that the president had no conventional system for administration. Generally, he held cabinet meetings on Tuesdays and Fridays, but the most important cabinet members—Seward and Stanton (both a bit self-important)—occasionally did not attend or failed to participate when they did. During the summer, important meetings sometimes were held at night at the cooler Soldiers' Home, where Lincoln and Stanton maintained seasonal residences. The president "was extremely unmethodical: it was a four-years struggle on Nicolay's part and mine to get him to adopt some systematic rules," wrote Hay. "He would break through every regulation as fast as it was made. Anything that kept the people themselves away from him he disapproved—although they nearly annoyed the life out of him by unreasonable complaints & requests."[10] Hay wrote a fellow White House aide in July 1864: "I leave matters in your hands till my return. There will probably be little to do. Refer as little to the President as possible. Keep visitors out of the house when you can. Inhospitable, but prudent."[11] The president did have his own inner-directed management system: (1) rigorously measure success and failure; (2) find the causes of success; (3) eliminate the cause of failure.

Lincoln had earned the fervent admiration of his few young aides. Still, they lacked the president's stamina. During the Civil War, principal secretary John Nicolay wandered as far as Colorado, often to Illinois and the Midwest; John Hay went north to Providence, Rhode Island, south to Florida and South Carolina. William O. Stoddard visited New York to play the stock and gold markets. Seeking respite, each was often gone for months at a time. In the late summer of 1863, with Nicolay gone, Hay also wanted some time off, so he recalled Stoddard from New York. Stoddard wrote on his return: "The White House is deserted, save by our faithful and untiring Chief Magistrate, who, alone of all our public men, is *always* at his post. He looks less careworn and emaciated than in the spring, as if, living only for his country, he found his vigor keeping pace with the returning health of the nation."[12] It is easy to underestimate Lincoln's powerful physique, the strength of an axeman, the conditioning of a lifetime free of the corrupting excess of fine food, alcohol, or tobacco. Even when sick and worn, he recuperated quickly and kept to his demanding schedule.

After Lincoln's death, John Hay wrote of his boss: "It is absurd to call him a modest man. No great man was ever modest. It is his intellectual arrogance and unconscious assumption of superiority that men like Chase and Sumner never could forgive."[13] Lincoln was rarely overbearing, but he could be sharp and decisive. Moving from Springfield to Washington did not change him. Henry J. Raymond, the *New York Times* editor who also served as chairman of the Republican National Committee, marveled that: "Mr. Lincoln never seemed to be aware that his place or his business were essentially different from those in which he had always been engaged. He brought to every question,—the loftiest and most imposing,—the same patient inquiry into details, the same eager longing to know and do exactly what was just and right, and the same working-day, plodding, laborious devotion, which characterized his management of a client's case at his law office in Springfield."[14] It was not only for others that he pressed his famous dictum: "Work, work, work is the main thing."[15]

Lincoln stuck to his post—even while his far younger aides required vacations. Edward Neill recalled: "The President's capacity for work was wonderful. While other men were taking recreation through the sultry months of summer, he remained in his office attending to the wants of the nation."[16] Although he often visited the battlefront in Virginia, Lincoln seldom ventured far north—once to New York in 1862, once to Gettysburg, Pennsylvania, in 1863, and to Baltimore and Philadelphia in 1864. The president would relax a little in the summer at the Soldiers'

Home. In March 1865, a beleaguered president visited the war front near Richmond, after General Grant and his wife invited Lincoln to take a break from Washington. Asked how long he would remain at City Point, he responded with a typical, homespun Lincoln story: "Well, I am like the western pioneer who built a log cabin. When he commenced he didn't know how much timber he would need, and when he had finished, he didn't care how much he had used up. So you see I came down among you without any definite plans, and when I go home I shan't regret a moment I have spent with you."[17]

The grim reality of war and death shadowed the president's work. Lincoln's frustration with military outcomes sometimes depressed him—particularly after the Union victories at Antietam and Gettysburg when the president thought that Union generals should have vigorously pursued the Confederates. Strangely, Churchill, as historian, did not fully appreciate President Lincoln's problems with McClellan. According to Churchill, "Ill-treatment was meted out to General McClellan by the Washington politicians and Cabinet, with the cautious, pliant General Halleck as their tool. For this Lincoln cannot escape responsibility. The president wanted an aggressive general who would energetically seek out Lee's army and destroy it. McClellan, for all his qualities of leadership, lacked the final ounces of fighting spirit. Lincoln knew this. But he also knew that McClellan was probably the ablest trainer of troops and best commander available to him."[18] Lincoln's patience with the arrogant McClellan, Churchill did not understand. In letters to the general, such as one of early May 1862, the president attempted to school the general on the intersection of political and military affairs. The letter typified the president's method of command—direct but not harsh:

I have just assisted the Secretary of War in framing the part of a despatch to you, relating to Army Corps, which despatch of course will have reached you long before this will. I wish to say a few words to you privately on this subject. I ordered the Army Corps organization not only on the unanimous opinion of the twelve Generals whom you had selected and assigned as Generals of Division, but also on the unanimous opinion of every *military man* I could get an opinion from, and every modern military book, yourself only excepted. Of course, I did not, on my own judgment, pretend to understand the subject. I now think it indispensable for you to know how your struggle against it [the reorganization] is received in quarters which we cannot entirely disregard. It [McClellan's resistance] is looked upon as merely an effort to pamper one or two pets, and to persecute and degrade their supposed rivals. I have had no word from [Edwin] Sumner, [Samuel] Heintzelman, or [Erasmus] Keyes. The commanders of these Corps are of course the three highest officers with you, but I am constantly told that you consult and communicate with nobody but General Fitz John Porter, and perhaps General [William] Franklin. I do not say these complaints are true or just; but at all events it is proper you should know of their existence. Do the Commanders of Corps disobey your orders in any thing?

When you relieved General [Charles] Hamilton of his command the other day, you thereby lost the confidence of at least one of your best friends in the Senate. And here let me say, not as applicable to you personally, that Senators and Representatives speak of me in their places as they please, without question; and that officers of the army must cease addressing insulting letters to them for taking no greater liberty with them.[19]

Tolerance for abuse was a job requirement for Lincoln and Churchill. So, too, was an ability to cajole subordinates to act appropriately. In his letters to army generals, Lincoln could be alternately paternal and prodding. In July 1863, the president admonished Adjutant General Lorenzo Thomas about the dilatory pursuit of Confederate General Robert E. Lee after the Battle of Gettysburg earlier in the month:

Your despatch of this morning to the Sec. of War is before me. The forces you speak of, will be of no immagineable [sic] service, if they can not go forward with a little more expedition. Lee is now passing the Potomac faster than the forces you mention are passing Carlyle [sic]. Forces now beyon[d] Carlyle, to be joined by regiments still at Harrisburg, and the united force again to join [Lewis B.] Pierce somewhere, and the whole to move down the Cumberland Valley, will, in my unprofessional opinion, be quite as likely to capture the Man-in-the-Moon, as any part of Lee's Army.[20]

Abraham Lincoln, 1864

Gilder Lehrman Collection, GLC05111.02.0018

Increasingly frustrated by the failure to pursue the retreating Confederates, President Lincoln addressed a long and important letter to General
Meade, then commander of the Army of the Potomac:

> I have just seen your despatch to Gen. Halleck, asking to be
> relieved of your command, because of a supposed censure of
> mine. I am very—*very*—grateful to you for the magnificent suc-
> cess you gave the cause of the country at Gettysburg; and I am
> sorry now to be the author of the slightest pain to you. But I
> was in such deep distress myself that I could not restrain some
> expression of it. I had been oppressed nearly ever since the bat-
> tles of Gettysburg, by what appeared to be evidences that your-
> self, and Gen. [Darius] Couch, and Gen. [William F.] Smith,
> were not seeking a collision with the enemy, but were trying to
> get him across the river without another battle. What these evi-
> dences were, if you please, I hope to tell you at some time, when
> we shall both feel better. The case, summarily stated is this. You
> fought and beat the enemy at Gettysburg; and, of course, to say
> the least, his loss was as great as yours. He retreated; and you
> did not, as it seemed to me, pressingly pursue him, but a flood
> in the river detained him, till, by slow degrees, you were again
> upon him. You had at least twenty thousand veteran troops
> directly with you, and as many more raw ones within supporting
> distance, all in addition to those who fought with you at Gettys-
> burg; while it was not possible that he [Lee] had received a single
> recruit; and yet you stood and let the flood run down, bridges
> be built, and the enemy move away at his leisure, without attack-
> ing him. And Couch and Smith! The latter left Carlisle in time,
> upon all ordinary calculation, to have aided you in the last battle
> at Gettysburg; but he did not arrive. At the end of more than ten
> days, I believe twelve, under constant urging, he reached Hagers-
> town from Carlisle, which is not an inch over fifty-five miles, if so
> much. And Couch's movement was very little different.
>   Again, my dear general, I do not believe you appreciate the
> magnitude of the misfortune involved in Lee's escape. He was
> within your easy grasp, and to have closed upon him would, in
> connection with our other late successes, have ended the war. As
> it is, the war will be prolonged indefinitely. If you could not safely

attack Lee last Monday, how can you possibly do so South of
the river, when you take with you very few more than two thirds
of the force you then had in hand? It would be unreasonable
to expect, and I do not expect you can now effect much. Your
golden opportunity is gone, and I am distressed immeasureably
because of it.

I beg you will not consider this a prossecution [sic], or persecution of you. As you had learned that I was dissatisfied, I have
thought it best to kindly tell you why.[21]

Sensitivity to his relationship with Meade caused the commander in
chief *not* to send the letter. The president's deliberate judgment caused
him to forbear criticism when he believed the results would be counter-
productive. He would not plant a thorn in any man's bosom, much less
that of a top military commander. Still, Lincoln, like Churchill, wanted
"Action This Day." His mood in July 1863 swung sharply from elation
over victory at Gettysburg, to frustration with the bungled follow up.
John Hay wrote in his diary on July 19, 1863: "The President was in very
good humour. . . . In the afternoon, he & I were talking about the position at Williamsport the other day. He said 'Our Army held the war in
the hollow of their hand & they would not close it.' [A]gain he said, 'We
had gone through all the labor of tilling & planting an enormous crop &
when it was ripe we did not harvest it. Still,' he added, 'I am very grateful
to Meade for the great service he did at Gettysburg.'"[22] Though disappointed, he could maintain balanced judgment.

The commander in chief demonstrated unusual sensitivity to
the feelings of subordinates. Late in July, he wrote General Robert C.
Schenck, the Union commander in Maryland who was close to Radical
Republicans: "Returning to the Executive Room yesterday, I was mortified to find you were gone, leaving no word of explanation. I went
down stairs, as I understood, on a perfect understanding with you
that you would remain till my return. I got this impression distinctly
from 'Edward' [a White House doorkeeper] whom I believe you know.
Possibly I misunderstood him. I had been very unwell in the morning, and had scarcely tasted food during the day, till the time you saw
me go down. I beg you will not believe I have treated you with inten-
tional discourtesy." Two days later, Schenck responded: "I did not for
a moment suppose there was any discourtesy intended me. But I left

your anteroom without waiting longer, because I was hurried by the approach of the hour when I was to take a little dinner with a friend, & get ready for the train by which I was to return to Baltimore."[23] Even in small matters, the president focused on maintaining the morale of Union soldiers and officers.

Like Churchill, Lincoln found ways to make use of failed generals. Defeated commanders of the Army of the Potomac, like Irvin McDowell, Ambrose Burnside, and Joseph Hooker, were recycled to other duties. Even if it took a year—as it did in the case of General Benjamin F. Butler—Lincoln searched for alternative assignments that would employ the talents of his generals without exposing their defects. Two exceptions were George B. McClellan, who languished without deployment for two years before he resigned in November 1864; and General John C. Frémont, who stayed in limbo after he was dismissed for cause in 1862. (Churchill reused his generals, too, but he could also "write off a man for good simply because he had refused a job."[24])

President Lincoln would try to make use of Meade's predecessor, Joseph Hooker, after his disastrous defeat at Chancellorsville in early May 1863. But Hooker had become increasingly unresponsive to orders from Washington after he had been dismissed from command of the Army of the Potomac in late June, in favor of the reluctant Meade. "I have not thrown Gen. Hooker away; and therefore I would like to know whether, it would be agreeable to you, all things considered, for him to take a corps under you, if he himself is willing to do so," the president wrote Meade. "Write me, in perfect freedom, with the assurance that I will not subject you to any embarrassment, by making your letter, or its contents, known to any one. I wish to know your wishes before I decide whether to break the subject to him. Do not lean a hair's breadth against your own feelings, or your judgment of the public service, on the idea of gratifying me."[25] On a more urgent matter, two days later on the morning of July 29, 1863, Lincoln sent a note to General-in-Chief Halleck, who promptly sent it to Meade: "Seeing General Meade's dispatch of yesterday to yourself, causes me to fear that he supposes the government here is demanding of him to bring on a general engagement with Lee as soon as possible. I am claiming no such thing of him. In fact, my judgment is against it; which judgment, of course, I will yield if yours and his are the contrary."[26] Impatience with Meade after Gettysburg would not rush the deliberate president into an untimely battle with General Lee.

That same summer, the commander in chief would patiently endure the insolent behavior and prickly sensitivity of Generals William Rosecrans and Ambrose Burnside, serving in Kentucky and Tennessee. Lincoln wanted them to act in concert against Confederate forces. In early August 1863, the president patiently reviewed for General Rosecrans his communications with General Halleck:

> I am sure you, as a reasonable man, would not have been wounded, could you have heard all my words and seen all my thoughts, in regard to you. I have not abated in my kind feeling for and confidence in you. I have seen most of your despatches to General Halleck—probably all of them. After Grant invested Vicksburg, I was very anxious lest Johnston should overwhelm him from the outside, and when it appeared certain that part of [Confederate General] Bragg's force had gone, and was going to Johnson, it did seem to me, it was the exactly proper time for you to attack Bragg with what force he had left. In all kindness, let me say it so seems to me yet.

The president then suggested what he thought Rosecrans should do.[27] Lincoln concluded the letter with a truly Lincolnian touch: "And now, be assured once more, that I think of you in all kindness and confidence; and that I am not watching you with an evil-eye."[28] But watching Rosecrans, Lincoln surely was.

He continued to prod Rosecrans in order to get him to attack Confederate General Braxton Bragg in eastern Tennessee. On September 19–20, 1863, Rosecrans was defeated at the Battle of Chickamauga. On September 21, John Hay wrote that Lincoln "came into my bedroom before I was up, & sitting down on my bed said, 'Well, Rosecrans has been whipped, as I feared. I have feared it for several days. I believe I feel trouble in the air before it comes. Rosecrans says we have met with a serious disaster—extent not ascertained. Burnside instead of obeying the orders which were given him on the 14th and going to Rosecrans has gone up on foolish affair to Jonesboro to capture a party of guerillas who are there.'"[29] Still, Lincoln would encourage Rosecrans: "Be of good cheer. We have unabated confidence in you, and in your sold⸱ and officers." He added: "In the main you must be the judge ⸱ is to be done."[30] Despite victories at Gettysburg and Vicksb

1863, almost two more years of vexation would plague the commander in chief.

During the Civil War, Lincoln observed that even long military experience was no guarantee of military wisdom.[31] Thus, his own communications with generals tended to be more advisory than peremptory. He understood that he could not know local conditions. The president would urge and cajole, but he seldom ordered his generals. Lincoln's respect for their judgment in the theater of battle did not always gain the support of his cabinet members, many of whom wanted more aggressive action from the generals and more direct orders from the president. On July 7, 1863, shortly after Union victories at Gettysburg and Vicksburg, Navy Secretary Welles acidly observed: "This is the President's error. His own convictions and conclusions are infinitely superior to Halleck's; even in military operations more sensible and more correct always,— but yet he says, 'It being strictly a military question, it is proper I should defer to Halleck, whom I have called here to counsel, advise, and direct in these matters, where he is an expert.' I question whether he should be considered an expert. I look upon Halleck as a pretty good scholarly critic of other men's deeds and acts, but as incapable of originating or directing military operations."[32] Like others in Washington, Welles was particularly critical of Halleck: "The army is still at rest. Halleck stays here in Washington, within four hours of the army, smoking his cigar, doing as little as the army. If he gives orders for an onward movement and is not obeyed, why does he not remove to headquarters in the field? If this [Confederate] army is permitted to escape across the Potomac, woe be to those who permit it!"[33] In their diaries, Secretary Welles and Attorney General Edward Bates often questioned Lincoln's judgment and his methods.

At last the president would find his fighting general in Ulysses Grant, who had led successful campaigns in Mississippi and Tennessee in 1863. John Hay was not in Washington when Grant was appointed General-in-Chief in 1864. When Hay returned to the White House on March 24, President Lincoln told him that Grant "is Commander in Chief & Halleck is now nothing but a staff officer. In fact says the President 'when McClellan seemed incompetent to the work of handling an army & we sent for Halleck to take command he stipulated that it should be with the full power and responsibility of Commander in Chief. He ran it on that basis till [General] Pope's defeat; but ever since that event, he has

John G. Nicolay, Abraham Lincoln, John Hay, 1863

Gilder Lehrman Collection, GLC08565

shrunk from responsibility whenever it was possible.'"[34] Grant's strategic thinking coincided with Lincoln's. Five weeks later, Hay wrote:

> The President has been powerfully reminded, by General Grant's present movements and plans, of his (President's) old suggestion so constantly made and as constantly neglected, to Buell & Halleck, et al to move at once upon the enemy's whole line so as to bring into action to our advantage our great superiority in numbers. Otherwise by interior lines & control of interior railroad system the enemy can shift their men rapidly from one point to another as they may be required. In this concerted movement, however, great superiority of numbers must tell: as the enemy, however successful where he concentrates must necessarily weaken other portions of his line and lose important position. This idea of his own, the Prest recognized with especial pleasure when Grant said it was his intention to make all the line useful—those not fighting could help the fighting. Lincoln added: "Those not skinning can hold a leg."[35]

Secretary of the Interior John Palmer Usher recalled President Lincoln declaring: "Grant is the most extraordinary man in command that I know of. I heard nothing direct from him and wrote him to know why, and whether I could do anything to promote his success, and Grant replied that he had tried to do the best he could with what he had, that he believed that if he had more men and arms he could use them to good advantage, and do more than he had done; but he supposed I had done and was doing all I could, and if I could do more he felt that I would do it."[36] Still, the gruesome battles of spring 1864 did shake Lincoln's confidence. House Speaker Schuyler Colfax remembered:

> The morning after the bloody battle of the Wilderness, I saw him walk up and down the Executive Chamber, his long arms behind his back, his dark features contracted still more with gloom; and as he looked up, I thought his face the saddest one I had ever seen. He exclaimed: "Why do we suffer reverses after reverses! Could we have avoided this terrible, bloody war! Was it not forced upon us! Is it ever to end!" But he quickly recovered, and told me the sad aggregate of those days of bloodshed. Of course it is

perfectly well known that the battle of the Wilderness, however, then claimed as a drawn battle, was, on the contrary, a bloody reverse to our arms, our loss in killed and wounded alone being fifteen thousand more than the Confederates. Hope beamed on his face as he said, "Grant will not fail us now; he says he will fight it out on that line, and this is now the hope of our country." An hour afterward, he was telling story after story to congressional visitors at the White House, to hide his saddened heart from their keen and anxious scrutiny.[37]

Lincoln's cabinet members often disagreed with his policies. The president would listen but still did what he thought best regardless of their opposition. More than a decade later, Gideon Welles tellingly observed: "The individuals composing his cabinet had but slight previous personal intimacy with Mr Lincoln, or with each other."[38] The president was not constrained by personal friendship to rely on his cabinet, as he alone had the constitutional responsibility for executive decisions. "That Lincoln did not use his Cabinet efficiently is clear," argued historian Allen Nevins.

> He went to the War Office daily, and saw Seward frequently, for Seward was a "comfort" to him; the others he neglected. Chase, though a leader of one of the two great wings of the party, fell into the role of mere financial specialist, and resented the fact. Stanton complained that in important military matters the President took counsel of none but army officers, thought he ought to be consulted, or at least be kept informed. Yet Stanton himself in Cabinet meetings imparted little information, and had a way of drawing Lincoln into a corner and talking with him in a low voice.[39]

Given the peculiar and jealous personalities of some self-important cabinet members, Lincoln may not have been able to deal with them in any other way. With hard experience, he came to trust his own judgments and decisions.

Failing to gain a special relationship with the president early in the war, Chase attempted to enlarge his power first through relations with generals, then with relations with congressmen, and lastly through the network of 15,000 Treasury agents he appointed to collect taxes. Gideon Welles wrote in May 1864 that "the Secretary of the Treasury has enough to do attend to the finances without going into the cotton trade. But Chase is very ambitious and very fond of power. He has, moreover, the fault of most of our politicians, who believe that the patronage of office, or bestowment of public favors, is a source of popularity."[40] Chase put his own picture on the new dollar bill. When questioned, he explained: "I had put the President's head on the higher priced notes, and my own, as was becoming, on the smaller ones."[41] Of Lincoln's original cabinet, only Secretary of the Navy Welles and Secretary of State Seward would serve until Lincoln's death. The two often quarreled over naval, admiralty, and diplomatic issues. Welles, who filled his diary with these disputes, resented Seward's influence. At the beginning of Lincoln's first term, Seward had tried to take the reins of the Lincoln government. By April 1861, he knew he had failed. By June, a changed Seward wrote his wife: "The President is the best of us, but he needs constant and assiduous cooperation."[42]

Having appointed Grant to command the Union army, Lincoln gave him full authority to pursue military victory with their agreed-upon strategy. Lincoln continued to advise, but seldom gave direct orders to the general, except on political matters. Orville H. Browning observed in his diary in June 1864:

> During the past week, the President visited Grants army, and returned only a day or two ago — He told me last night that Grant said, when he left him, that "you Mr President, need be under no apprehension. You will never hear of me farther from Richmond than now, till I have taken it. I am just as sure of going into Richmond as I am of any future event. It may take a long summer day, but I will go in." The President added that Grant told him that in the Wilderness he had completely routed Lee, but did not know it at the time—and that had he known it, he could have ruined him, and ended the campaign.[43]

The Civil War, like most battlefield conflicts, consisted largely of tactics and ad hoc strategy. (Unlike Churchill, Lincoln had not spent years experiencing and contemplating the military implications of a major conflict like World War I. Neither did he attend a military academy, nor study and write the history of war before he became president, as Churchill did.) As president, Lincoln had no grand planning staff in Washington. "The fundamental problem for the historian attempting to understand and describe the grand strategy for the American Civil War is that it was nowhere written down at the time," noted historian Mark E. Neely Jr. "In an era without military war 'colleges' and a peacetime general staff, there were no contingency plans or white papers laying out strategic doctrine. There were only ad hoc responses to pressing military problems of war as it raged."[44] Lincoln would respond to events as they happened, and take advantage of opportunities as they presented themselves. But the president did have a grand strategy from early in the war, clearly set forth in his writings.

Near the end of the war, Lincoln's original strategy had become Grant's strategy—to pursue and defeat Lee's army in Virginia, while other Union armies, reporting to him, destroyed resistance elsewhere. Lincoln never hesitated to communicate with Union commanders. He simply walked next door to the Telegraph Office in the War Department and spelled out his message. Unlike Churchill with his War Cabinet and Chiefs of Staff, President Lincoln did not have to check with anyone— although, prudently, he did consult often with Stanton, Halleck, some other generals, trusted junior advisers, and anyone else he thought useful. As with Churchill, Lincoln's challenge was not only to define war aims, but also to set strategy, then to find the commanders who could fulfill the strategy on the battlefield. "As he grew comfortable in holding the reins of power, Lincoln became more assertive as commander in chief," wrote Craig L. Symonds. "[B]y 1862 he was beginning to exercise hands-on management, even issuing operational orders to division commanders; and by 1863 he was hitting his full stride as an activist commander in chief."[45]

Lincoln's firmness was ever touched with mercy when he dealt with Union soldiers.[46] He made every effort to find reasons to cancel military executions. Illinois Congressman Isaac N. Arnold recalled: "One summer's day, walking along the shaded path leading from the Executive mansion to the War office, I saw the tall, awkward form of the President seated on the grass under a tree. A wounded soldier, seeking backpay and a pension, had met the President, and, having recognized him, asked his counsel. Lincoln sat down, examined the papers of the soldier, and told him what to do, sent him to the proper bureau with a note, which secured prompt attention."[47] According to painter Francis B. Carpenter, at a White House reception in winter of 1864, President Lincoln

> had been standing for some time, bowing his acknowledgments
> to the thronging multitude, when his eye fell upon a couple who
> had entered unobserved,—a wounded soldier, and his plainly
> dressed mother. Before they could pass out, he made his way
> to where they stood, and taking each of them by the hand, with
> a delicacy and cordiality which brought tears to many eyes, he
> assured them of his interest and welcome. Governors, senators,
> diplomats, passed with simply a nod; but that pale young face
> he might never see again. To him, and to others like him, did
> the nation owe its life; and Abraham Lincoln was not the man
> to forget this, even in the crowded and brilliant assembly of the
> distinguished of the land.[48]

In June 1863, Lincoln responded eloquently to those protesting his decisive handling of those who had abused civil liberties in the North during wartime:

> Must I shoot the simpleminded soldier boy who deserts, while I
> must not touch a hair of a wiley [sic] agitator who induces him to
> desert? This is none the less injurious when effected by getting
> a father, or brother, or friend, into a public meeting, and there
> working upon his feelings, till he is persuaded to write the sol-
> dier boy, that he is fighting in a bad cause, for a wicked admin-
> istration of a contemptable [sic] government, too weak to arrest
> and punish him if he shall desert. I think that in such a case, to
> silence the agitator, and save the boy, is not only constitutional,
> but, withal, a great mercy.[49]

President Lincoln worked without respite to be worthy of the sacrifices of Union soldiers. Replying to an invitation to speak at Cooper Institute on December 2, 1863, the president wrote: "Honor to the Soldier, and Sailor everywhere, who bravely bear his country's cause. Honor also to the citizen who cares for his brother in the field, and serves, as he best can, the same cause—honor to him, only less than to him, who braves, for the common good, the storms of heaven and the storms of battle."[50] A few weeks later, John Hay wrote: "The President tonight had a dream. He was in a party of plain people and as it became known who he was they began to comment on his appearance. One of them said, 'He is a very common-looking man.'" Lincoln replied: "The Lord prefers Common-looking people: that is the reason he makes so many of them."[51]

*I did not like having unharnessed Ministers around me.
I preferred to deal with chiefs of organisations rather than
counsellors. Everyone should do a good day's work and be
accountable for some definite task; and they do not make
trouble for trouble's sake or to cut a figure.*[1]

WINSTON CHURCHILL
The Gathering Storm: The Second World War, **1948**

*Prime Ministers need luck as well as Generals; Prime
Ministers who usurp the role of Commanders-in-Chief
need a double dose of it. His boldness had certainly been
justified on several occasions, and had strengthened his
position vis-a-vis the Chiefs of Staff.*[2]

GENERAL JOHN KENNEDY
The Business of War, **1957**

XV.

Managing Men at War—Churchill Style

Abraham Lincoln and Winston Churchill, not surprisingly, set up surrogate families at work, with whom they were familiar and with whom they made war. A social animal, the prime minister liked familiar, congenial faces. The president treasured his solitude even as he sought relief among friends. Whereas President Lincoln shined his own boots, Churchill was almost never without a valet and servants.[3] The prime minister was appalled one night in November 1940, when he found himself completely alone. He exclaimed "that no one was looking after him & that he had been deserted!!!" wrote a private secretary. "He really is fond of congenial companions."[4] By the time he became prime minister, he had served four decades in national public life, in which he had met most everyone who was anybody. His official family was often beset by intense arguments. Alan Brooke stood up to him. So did Clementine and his contemporary from World War I, Max Beaverbrook, whom both Brooke and Clementine despised. Others were more accommodating.

Churchill was taken aback when aides sought time off. "When the generals, who in many cases were still geared to the regular hours of peace-time soldiering, with leaves at stated intervals, and week-ends free, explained to him that he would have to run the war without them for a few days while they went on leave, salmon-fishing, shooting, or bird watching, his amazement left him temporarily speechless," recalled Leslie Hollis. "He would look at them with astonishment from across his desk. At his most Pickwickian—spectacles down on his nose, mouth agape with amazement, cigar clamped between the first two fingers of his right hand on the desk in front of him, he stared with incredulity at this pronouncement." Churchill asked: "Leave? Aren't you *enjoying* the war? H'm, h'm, don't you want to *win* this war?"[5] The prime minister left London not only for weeks at a time for meetings; he also had to take time to recover from illness. Churchill would take short vacations in Pompano Beach in January 1942, and at Quebec in August 1943. He would relax as he recovered from sickness, in the sun and sea of North Africa and the Middle East. In July 1945, he took a holiday in southwest France.[6] Churchill understandably applied a different standard to himself, at 65–70 years of age, than he did to younger generals or civil servants. Still he would match his military and civilian staff in his sustained work effort.

Both the World War II prime minister and the Civil War president shouldered enormous burdens, well aware of the ultimate stakes inherent in wars of national survival. When Foreign Secretary Eden needed a forced rest in March 1944 to recover his health, Churchill became interim foreign minister, in addition to his continuing responsibilities as defence minister and prime minister. No wonder aides described how exhausted Churchill appeared. "P.M., I fear, is breaking down," wrote Alexander Cadogan on April 19, 1944. "I really am fussed about the P.M. He is not the man he was 12 months ago, and I really don't know if he can carry on."[7] Churchill's working hours would begin in bed in the morning, where he received ministers and military officers. Revived by his afternoon nap, he would get his nighttime sleep sometimes as late as 3 A.M. or later.[8] Under the pressure of military affairs, Churchill would stay up even later—to the detriment of his health and, to the detriment of the health of those who worked with him. Even Churchill's bodyguard Walter Thompson had a breakdown.

Marian Holmes recalled how the prime minister insisted on the highest standards from his secretaries. He could be impatient with anything less than full commitment. "But in all his moods—totally absorbed in the serious matter of the moment, agonised over some piece of wartime bad news, suffused with compassion, sentimental and in tears, truculent, bitingly sarcastic, mischievous or hilariously funny—he was at all times splendidly entertaining, humane and lovable."[9] Churchill's character and his personality proved one of Britain's great wartime resources. He could be mercurial with plans and people. But like Lincoln, he was steadfast in important objectives. In conflict and crisis, the prime minister was virtually indomitable. "Churchill's courage, and the charisma he won by it, was matched by his extraordinary boldness in adversity," wrote John Keegan. "A lesser man would have husbanded every resource to defend his homeland under the threat of invasion. Under such threat, Churchill nevertheless sought means to strike back."[10]

The prime minister respected the British Chiefs of Staff even as he argued with them, but he did develop other sources of ideas. "The new machinery for the conduct of the war owed much to Churchill's thinking and proved highly successful in preventing the rifts between the 'frocks' [politicians] and 'brasshats' [Generals] which had occurred in the First World War," wrote historian Paul Addison.[11] General Bernard Paget, who worked on preparations for D-Day, wrote: "Often I wondered during the war where Churchill got some of his more outrageous strategic ideas from. He much preferred to seek and take advice from people like Cherwell [Frederick Lindemann] . . . than of the C. of S. Fortunately for us, unlike Hitler, he did not in the last resort go against the advice of the C. of S."[12] Churchill would argue and bully, but ultimately he respected lines of authority. In the spring of 1944, the COS engaged in a particularly bitter battle with the prime minister. As John Dill wrote Brooke: "It is a thousand pities that Winston should be so confident that his knowledge of the military art is profound when it is so lacking in strategical and logistical understanding and judgment."[13]

In the face of stiff criticism, Lincoln and Churchill developed the ability to concentrate on what was truly important. This faculty frustrated Cabinet members because Lincoln would effectively ignore them and their problems—confident that they must handle their own responsibilities. "Winston had an extraordinary capacity for seizing on things that mattered, concentrating on them and mastering them," wrote British civil servant Norman Brook. "Of course, he liked to pretend that he was looking after everything. It wasn't true. All the same, no one knew when this searchlight, sweeping round, would settle on them, so everyone worked like blazes."[14] Indeed, recalled secretary Elizabeth Layton Nel, "Through all of this I perceived an inner kindness and appreciation." She added that "yes, he was difficult, yes, he was impatient, yes, he was demanding—but never impossible."[15] With his military chiefs, the prime minister could be difficult, as when he frequently told CIGS Brooke: "I do not want any of your long term projects, they cripple initiative."[16] In politics and war, Churchill considered himself a ready and bold opportunist, but he underestimated the monumental planning and logistics required to prepare for the major military operations of World War II.

Churchill's war organization followed a more precise structure than did Lincoln's. The British structure was imposed as much by attentive aides as by the prime minister.[17] In June 1941, John Colville wrote in his diary: "John Peck and I agreed that P.M. does not help the Government machine to run smoothly and his inconsiderate treatment of the service departments would cause trouble were it not for the great personal loyalty of the service Ministers to himself. He supplies drive and initiative, but he often meddles where he would better leave things alone and the operational side of the war might profit if he gave it a respite and turned to grapple with labour and production."[18] Military leaders did complain. General Kennedy described the "heavy strain . . . being imposed upon the Chiefs of Staff by the prime minister's habits. He worked in bed in the morning, slept in the afternoon, kept the Chiefs of Staff up at night, and went off to the country for long weekends. This system suited him, if nobody else; and it certainly enabled him to remain fresh. . . . The usual hour for meeting the Chiefs of Staff was 9:30 p.m. and he often kept them up until one or two in the morning." Kennedy added: "Everybody realized and appreciated Churchill's great qualities. But there were few who did not sometimes doubt whether these were adequate compensation for his methods of handling the war machine, and the immense additional effort they imposed upon the Service Staffs."[19]

In early 1941, Kennedy and then-CIGS John Dill had a talk about Churchill: "We discussed the prime minister's methods of conducting the war and we agreed that his great qualities made up for the vast amount of work, often useless as we thought, which he imposed upon the staffs. Dill said that if he ever wrote his memoirs he would put him down as the greatest leader we could possibly have had, but certainly no one could describe him as the greatest strategist."[20] Andrew Roberts noted that Dill "regarded Churchill as an arch-meddler whose interventions had to be borne with as much patience as he could muster."[21] Dill's successor shared that opinion. Despite Alan Brooke's authority, the prime minister felt free to communicate with whomever he pleased. Roberts wrote: "Churchill would occasionally address questions to British Staff officers besides Brooke, but they automatically sent the answer to the CIGS first for approval." When Churchill confronted Brooke about the arrangement, the CIGS told the prime minister "that even if he chose to ignore the chain of responsibility he would still get replies from me!"[22] Brooke was tough; Churchill needed him.

"Churchill was too much of an individualist to be a tidy administrator," wrote aide John Martin. "But, even if he is allowed no credit for the general efficiency of the official machine over which he presided, it is remembered by those who served in it that from the moment when he assumed control a new drive and energy pulsed through it. He established the structure at the summit which endured, almost unchanged, to the end."[23] Military aide Ian Jacob wrote: "Organisation did not loom large in Churchill's mind, and he cared little whether others were disgruntled, as long as he got his way."[24] The order of Churchill's office did not originate with the prime minister. Jacob credited General Ismay with opposing the ad hoc approach to government that the prime minister outlined in an early memo: Ismay "sat on the Minute and set to work to bring Churchill to realise that, on military matters at any rate, he had at his elbow an official and responsible organism, and that there would be no scope in the military field for the operations of irregular advisers and links."

Ismay would assert the influence and effectiveness of the Chiefs of Staff.[25] Sometimes called an "Appeaser!" (meaning diplomatic), "Pug" Ismay would absorb Churchill's abuse. The modest general admitted: "If someone with sounder and stronger judgment could hold his job it would doubtless be better, but the chances are that such a person would soon be thrown out."[26] In 1941, Ismay told General Auchinleck:

> Churchill could not be judged by ordinary standards; he was different from anyone we have ever met before, or would ever meet again. As a war leader, he was head and shoulders above anyone the British or any other nation could produce. He was indispensable and completely irreplaceable. . . . He was a child of nature. He venerated tradition, but ridiculed convention. When the occasion demanded, he could be the personification of dignity; when the spirit moved him, he could be a gamin. His courage, enthusiasm and industry were boundless, and his loyalty was absolute. No commander who engaged the enemy need ever fear that he would not be supported.[27]

Staff and ministers grumbled. Civilian aide Norman Brook noted that Churchill "showed from the start that he intended to take personal charge of all matters affecting the strategic direction of the war. . . .

[The prime minister] worked through the existing Departments and agencies of Government, military and civil. But he brought the Chiefs of Staff Committee under his own control [as Minister of Defence] and made it directly responsible to him for all matters affecting the strategy of the war. He thus established a clear chain of command, and set himself to dominate it."[28] He did benefit from the contrast with the lack of direction and control of the government by Neville Chamberlain. He inherited the defined structure of the British Chiefs of Staff (first established in 1923)—which General George Marshall would convince a reluctant President Roosevelt to copy. And finally, Churchill benefited from the dedication of his staff. "There were no frontiers between home and office, between work hours and the rest of the day: work went on everywhere, in his study, in the dining-room, in his bedroom," recalled Edward Bridges, secretary to the War Cabinet. "A summons would come at almost any hour of the day or night to help with some job. Minutes would be dictated, corrected, redictated. One might find oneself unexpectedly sitting in the family circle or sharing a meal while one took his orders."[29] A key to Churchill's control was the tsunami of "ACTION THIS DAY" minutes that rolled out to key government officials. "The long meetings in the Cabinet room drew heavily on his mental and emotional energy," wrote John Martin. "In office work he did not spare himself, dictating not only his own speeches but also (with few exceptions) his letters, other than most formal ones, and his personal Minutes."[30] (Virtually all of Lincoln's correspondence was written in his own clear hand—with copies made by secretaries on occasion.)

In 1911, Churchill and his close friend, F. E. Smith, had founded their own Other Club "for men with whom it was agreeable to dine." During the war he carried on the same way. Edward Bridges noted that Churchill "liked to have about him a group of those whom he saw frequently. Chief of these, of course, were the senior Ministers, with some of whom he was in almost day-to-day consultation. On a different level were those who were called upon to provide him with help and services of various kinds. This group included his Private Secretaries, the senior Staff Officers in the War Cabinet Office . . . As Secretary of the War Cabinet I found myself in this group, which he sometimes called his 'Secret Circle.'"[31] To be included in the Secret Circle was a signal honor. Martin wrote that after about a month of work with Churchill, "The PM gave me such a kind and human goodnight when he went up to bed at one

Winston S. Churchill, 1941

© National Portrait Gallery, London

o'clock this morning—put his hand on my arm and said he was sorry there had been no time in all the rush of these days to get to know me."[32] The bursts of Churchillian charm made bearable his bouts of petulance.

The prime minister's secretaries often worked into the wee hours of the night. Secretary Elizabeth Layton, a native Canadian, recalled: "Sometimes by the time bed was announced I would be feeling nervously worn out, especially if I'd made a few mistakes and come under the hammer that evening. But so often, Mr. Churchill would give a beaming 'Good night,' sometimes accompanied by a small remark intended to convey 'Sorry I was cross,' so that, far from resenting his previous displeasure, one would feel honored to have been a sort of safety-valve for his feelings."[33] The members of his Secret Circle treasured their association with the prime minister in time of crisis. Clearly, the excitement of the war, the gravity of the tasks at hand, and the charisma of the prime minister stayed in the memories of his colleagues. According to Secretary Marian Holmes, her work with Winston Churchill and his successor, Clement Attlee, was "the difference between champagne and water."[34] No contrast might have pleased the prime minister more, as he was a daily champagne man.

Despite the demands of working with the prime minister, Leslie Rowan observed that Churchill's aides "felt, rightly, that we were serving a real leader; such a person as is only produced once in a century, even if that often. It would surely be enough for anyone merely to serve, and ask or receive no more. But we received from him, and, let me add, from Mrs Churchill, the most precious gift of all, his friendship for us as individuals, irrespective of our jobs and duties."[35] Still, noted Dr. Wilson, the prime minister did not "know much about those with whom he works."[36] It was the threat to national survival that enabled the grinding sacrifice of men and women on the home front. Rationing, scarcity, unreasonable working hours in wartime hardly compared with the hardships endured by soldiers risking violent death in battle. The prime minister knew this, and his staff felt it.

Churchill's secretaries endured a variety of airborne threats. When Nazi bombs damaged secretary Mary Shearburn's bedroom at No. 10 Downing Street, dropping the ceiling onto her bed, Churchill remarked: "You would have been all right, Miss Shearburn. The bed is still there."[37] Typist Marian Holmes recalled preparing to leave the room when the prime minister was not yet finished dictating. "Dammit, don't go," he snapped. "I've only just started." Then he added: "I'm so sorry. I thought it was Miss Layton. What is your name?" Told it was "Miss Holmes," the prime minister mispronounced her name—a perverse Churchillian custom. He then resumed dictation before announcing with a smile: "That is all for the moment. You know you must never be frightened of me when I snap. I'm not snapping at you but thinking of the work."[38]

President Lincoln cleverly gave nicknames to Secretary of War Stanton ("Mars") and Secretary of the Navy Welles ("Neptune"). The Union navy was "Uncle Sam's webbed feet." Churchill carried the practice much further, including friends and opponents—the pious fox-hunting Lord Halifax ("The Holy Fox"), the vegetarian Stafford Cripps ("Christ and Carrots"), the insufficiently aggressive Field Marshall John Dill ("Dilly-Dally"). For Churchill, the *New Yorker* magazine was "The New York Porker." FDR friend Harry Hopkins was "Lord Root of the Matter."[39]

Both leaders used language as a weapon. As a young politician, Lincoln's fierce barbs had stung many fellow politicians, sometimes bringing opponents to tears—one to the verge of a duel. After this episode, Lincoln's rhetoric mellowed. His outlook also changed after he broke off his engagement to Mary Todd—according to Douglas L. Wilson: "Lincoln may, for the first time, have understood 'honor' and honorable behavior as all-important, as necessary as a matter of life and death."[40] As president, he said of himself that he intended to plant no thorn in any man's bosom.[41] A frequent White House visitor said of President Lincoln: "I never heard him speak unkindly of any man; even the rebels received no word of anger from him."[42] But he did not spare the word *treason* when referring to the rebel leaders such as Robert E. Lee.

Churchill dominated his staff with great expectations. Martin observed: "He was an alarming master. For a newcomer it was often difficult to understand his instructions. His speech was hard to follow. Only after months did one acquire skill to interpret what at first seemed inarticulate grunts or single words thrown out without explanation. One had to learn his private allusions as when he referred to 'that moon-faced man in the Foreign Office' or identified one of his own Minutes by its opening words like a Papal encyclical."[43] One assistant recalled the morning in 1944, when Churchill phoned a private secretary and abruptly demanded: "Gimme the moon." A fast-thinking John Peck came back with a chart of the moon for the month of the intended invasion of France.[44]

The prime minister did not spare human sensibilities. Churchill's relationships with generals and admirals were as problematic as those with his personal staff. On October 12, 1941, after successive military defeats, he complained: "I sometimes think some of my generals don't want to fight the Germans!"[45] His generals, it is true, did not always agree to fight Germans the Churchill way. "The charges of defeatism which Churchill hurled at us all continually and which were so fiercely resented at first, came to be regarded as time went on as a matter of course, and were even taken lightheartedly," recalled General Kennedy. "But, though we would probably have denied this hotly then, there is no doubt that his taunts and exhortations and his criticism of every detail of our work, kept us continuously on our toes."[46]

The prime minister did not always see clearly the occasional demoralization he engendered. The British Chiefs of Staff and the prime minister "worked together in perfect harmony," he would say in 1944.[47] Historian Maxwell Philip Schoenfeld wrote: "There is no doubt that Churchill meant this. To him the strains and turmoil, the controversy and conflict which preceded the achievement of harmony, were secondary."[48] One way that Brooke managed the prime minister was to limit the information he received. The CIGS once admonished General Kennedy: "The more you tell that man about the war, the more you hinder the winning of it." Kennedy observed that Brooke's remark was half-serious, "but we were all nervous at all times of feeding a new idea into that fertile brain in case it might lead us away from the main stream into irrelevant back waters."[49] Churchill was fortunate that Alan Brooke stood up to him and gave him good advice. Brooke, Ismay, and others worked hard to help the prime minister steady the ship of state.

Most of Churchill's staff, no matter the trouble he caused, thought him unique. On May 27, 1941, General Brooke wrote: "It is surprising how he maintains a light-hearted exterior in spite of the vast burden he is bearing. He is quite the most wonderful man I have ever met, and it is a source of never-ending interest, studying him and getting to realise that occasionally such human beings make their appearance on this earth—human beings who stand out head and shoulders above all others."[50] Several months later, Brooke described a discussion with the prime minister: "PM very dissatisfied with our appreciation [i.e. memo]! Told me that he was expecting a detailed plan for the operation [against Trondheim in Norway] and instead I had submitted a masterly treatise on all the difficulties! He then proceeded to cross-question me for nearly 2 hours on various items of the appreciation, trying to make out that I had unnecessarily increased the difficulties on most of the minor points of the appreciation." Brooke added later:

> I repeatedly tried to bring him back to the main reason—the lack of air-support. He avoided this issue and selected arguments such as: "You state that you will be confronted by frosts and thaws which will render mobility difficult. How can you account for such a statement?" I replied that this was a trivial matter and that the statement came from the "Climate Book." He at once sent for this book, from which it became evident that this extract had been copied straight out of the book. His next attack was: "You state that it will take you some twenty-four hours to cover the ground between A and B. . . . [E]xplain to me exactly how every hour of those twenty-four will be occupied!" As this time had been allowed for overcoming enemy resistance on the road, removal of road-blocks and probably reparation to demolition of bridges and culverts, it was not an easy matter to paint this detailed picture of every hour of those twenty-four. This led to a series of more questions, interspersed with sarcasm and criticism. A very unpleasant gruelling to stand up to in a full room, but excellent training for what I had to stand up to on many occasions in later years.[51]

Brooke's diaries alternate between marvel and despair at Churchill's leadership, his virtues, and his vices. Nearly two years later in August 1943, Brooke wrote of Churchill: "He is quite the most difficult man to work with . . . but I would not have missed the chance of working with him for anything on earth."[52] Brooke himself was impatient, curt, articulate, and fast-talking—a match for the prime minister.[53] His impatience with Churchill and American commanders boiled over in December 1944:

> At 6 pm met Ike and Tedder with PM in the latter's Map Room, with the whole COS [Chiefs of Staff]. Ike explained his plan, which contemplates a double advance into Germany, north of Rhine, and by Frankfurt. I disagreed flatly with it, accused Ike of

violating principles of concentration of force, which had resulted in his present failures. I criticised his future plans and pointed out impossibility of double invasion with the limited forces he has got. I stressed the importance of concentrating on one thrust. I drew attention to the fact that with his limited forces any thought of attack on both fronts could only lead to dispersal of effort. Quite impossible to get the P.M. to understand the importance of the principles involved. Half the time his attention was concentrated on the possibility of floating mines down the Rhine!!! He *cannot* understand a large strategical concept and must get down to detail.[54]

Despite Churchill's obstinate confidence in his opportunistic tactics, he did not override his military chiefs, no matter how much he might argue with them.

Still, "Churchill displayed a consistency he held to throughout the war. He deferred (often with great reluctance) to his Chiefs of Staff in military matters, and he deferred (again, often with reluctance) to the War Cabinet in strictly political matters," noted William Manchester and Paul Reid. "As a believer in the 'Parl' [Parliament] he could not do otherwise."[55] Sentimentality would often undergird his relationships. In August 1943, as he relaxed in his bath while on vacation in Canada, Churchill told Anthony Eden: "I don't know what I should do if I lost you all. I'd have to cut my throat. It isn't just love, though there is much of that in it, but you are my war machine. Brookie, Portal, you and Dickie [Mountbatten], I simply couldn't replace you."[56] The prime minister had a clubby attitude toward intimate colleagues. Still, he often drove these same men to exhaustion, sometimes to the hospital. Colville wrote:

Whatever the P.M.'s shortcomings may be, there is no doubt that he does provide guidance and purpose for the Chiefs of Staff and the F.O. [Foreign Office] on matters which, without him, would often be lost in the maze of inter-departmentalism or frittered away by caution and compromise. Moreover he has two qualities, imagination and resolution, which are conspicuously lacking among other Ministers and among the Chiefs of Staff. I hear him much criticized, often by people in close contact with him, but I think much of the criticism is due to the inability to see people and their actions in the right perspective when one examines them at quarters too close.[57]

Close quarters with Churchill could be uncomfortable.

To survive, Churchill's subordinates needed to engage in energetic but exhausting dialogue with the prime minister. Norman Brook argued: "It was almost impossible to change his mind once it was made up. The only chance was to go to him with the news, and put your view before he had made up his mind."[58] In comparison with the sensitivity with which Lincoln often treated his generals, Churchill could be remarkably insensitive to the feelings and ambitions of his military leaders. In mid-August 1943, while walking along the heights of Quebec, Churchill bluntly told General Brooke that an American, not Brooke, would be commanding the Allied invasion of France—casually ignoring several previous promises of the command to the CIGS. "Not for one moment did he realize what this meant to me," wrote Brooke. "He offered no sympathy, no regrets at having had to change his mind, and dealt with the matter as if it were one of minor importance!"[59] For Brooke, the news was particularly galling because he had little respect for the strategic judgment of Marshall and Eisenhower, the leading American generals who might command Operation OVERLORD. (FDR insisted on an American commander for OVERLORD.) General Brooke was not alone among experienced British generals in his opinion of American military leaders, but as Charles de Gaulle later astutely observed: "By choosing reasonable plans, by sticking firmly to them, by respecting logistics, General Eisenhower led to victory the complicated and prejudicial machinery of the armies of the free world."[60]

Both Lincoln and Churchill concentrated on strategy and war aims, but the World War II prime minister focused in a different way from the Civil War president. "When his mind was occupied with any particular problem it was relentlessly focused upon it and would not be turned aside," wrote General Ian Jacob.

His usual method was to decide at the start what he wanted to do, and then to beat down opposition and drive through his course of action to the last point at which the conduct of the affair had finally to pass into other hands. In the course of this process it frequently happened that his proposed action was shown to be unsound, or quite impracticable with the resources available—or seemed to be so at first sight. This did not deter him in the least. He drove on regardless, until either he had his way or additional resources had been found from somewhere, or until at length he had to recognise that his proposal, was no good, or could be replaced by a better. It often happened that it was the Chiefs of Staff who had to examine his proposals and who had to fight against them. Sometimes he prevailed, and sometimes he gave way; but only after having driven them to the limit in the process.[61]

In his diary, General Brooke detailed his perception of Churchill's waning faculties in the last year of his prime ministership. He later wrote of the Quebec conference in September 1944, "I was in for a series of the most difficult conferences with Winston on this journey. Conferences where he repudiated everything he had agreed to up to date. I do not think that he had thoroughly recovered from his go of pneumonia and he was still suffering from the after effects of the heavy doses of M and B [a sulfonamide manufactured by May and Baker] which he had been given. He was quite impossible to argue with."[62] On September 8, aboard the *Queen Mary*, Brooke wrote that Churchill "looked old, unwell, and depressed."[63] Two days later, Brooke wrote: "He was again in a most unpleasant mood. Produced the most ridiculous arguments to prove that operations could be speeded up. . . . He knows no details, has only got half the picture in his mind, talks absurdities and makes my blood boil to listen to his nonsense. I find it hard to remain civil. And the wonderful thing is that 3/4 of the population of the world imagine that Winston Churchill is one of the Strategists of History, a second Marlborough."[64] In Quebec on September 13, a COS meeting was interrupted by the prime minister's call for the chiefs to meet with him. Brooke wrote that "we found he had nothing special to see us about! I would have given a great deal to tell him what I thought of him."[65] The prime minister suggested the British must present a united strategic front to the Americans, but he would follow his own agenda.

By September 14, General Ismay was "at the end of his tether." Brooke wrote: "Winston had accused us all to Ismay of purposely concealing changes of plan from him to keep him in the dark. That we were

Front Row: John Colville, Winston Churchill, John Martin, Tony Bevir
Back Row: Leslie Rowan, John Peck, E. M.Watson,
"Tommy" Thompson, Charles Barker
British Official Photograph

all against him, and heaven knows what not!" Ismay was ready to submit his resignation. Brooke later wrote that "poor old Pug always got the worst of it, but he was always so patient, and made so many allowances for all Winston's whims, that I felt it would take a climax to make him hand in his papers. I believe he did hand in his resignation and that Winston refused to take any notice of it."[66] At the end of the Quebec conference on September 16, Britain's leading military leaders prepared to fly off on a fishing vacation to Hudson Bay in mid-afternoon, and were upset when Churchill called a meeting with them for 5 P.M. "We told him that planes were ordered and all plans made," wrote Brooke. "He said that we should not be seeing each other for 10 days and must have a meeting!"[67] Then, by noon, the prime minister reversed himself and released his chiefs for their fishing. Several weeks later in London, Brooke met with Churchill, who was still in bed. The prime minister suddenly revealed animosity toward General Montgomery. Churchill asked why King George had not presented Montgomery with his baton as a new field marshal when the king visited France. The prime minister asserted: "Monty wants to fill the Mall [in London] when he gets his baton!. . . . Yes, he will fill the Mall because he is Monty, and I will not have him filling the Mall!"[68] Such was the churlish behavior that Churchill could exhibit from time to time.

The prime minister was a restless manager. "He was not a *calm* thinker whose attention was naturally directed to grand strategy, a student of campaigns in their academic aspect, a [B. H. Liddell] Hart or a [Carl von] Clausewitz," wrote military aide Ian Jacob. Churchill was

> a man who required to push away at some concrete project, not a cold, aloof strategist. He had studied battles, and by instinct tended to think of life as a series of conflicts, with barriers to overcome, opposition to be borne down. He hated those periods which are inevitable in a war when operations have come to a conclusion, and there must be a pause for planning and preparation, for regrouping and organization. His mind chafed, and he always turned to any project however minor, or however irrelevant to the main theme, in the hope that it would fill the gap. His frequent efforts to get the Chiefs of Staff and the planning staffs to work out an operation in Norway sprang not so much

from a desire to free that country or to close German access to the oceans, but from his wish to have something happen before the next major operation was due to start.[69]

The prime minister did not believe fighting men should sit idle.

Brooke's struggles with the prime minister continued until the end of the war. At one meeting, the CIGS was so rude that Churchill later told Ismay: "I have decided to get rid of Brooke. He hates me. You can see the hate in his eyes." Ismay defended Brooke: "I think that he behaved very badly at the meeting but he is under terrific strain. He is bone honest and whatever else his views may be, he doesn't hate you." When Ismay relayed the conversation to Brooke, he responded: "I don't hate [him]: I adore him tremendously; I do love him, but the day that I say that I agree with him when I don't, is the day he must get rid of me because I am no use to him any more."[70] The prime minister bridled at opposition to his ideas, but he needed debate. Indeed, he desired it. Fortunately for the prime minister, the CIGS met the challenge. Brooke wrote on July 6, 1944:

At 10 pm we had a frightful meeting with Winston which lasted til 2 am!! It was quite the worst we have had with him. He was very tired as a result of his speech in the House concerning the flying bombs, he had tried to recuperate with drink. As a result he was in a maudlin, bad tempered, drunken mood, ready to take offence at anything, suspicious of everybody, and in a highly vindictive mood against the Americans. In fact so vindictive that his whole outlook on strategy was warped. I began by having a bad row with him. He began to abuse Monty because operations were not going faster, and apparently Eisenhower had said he was over cautious. I flared up and asked him if he could not trust his generals for 5 minutes instead of continuously abusing them and belittling them. He said that he never did such a thing. I then reminded him that during two whole Monday Cabinets in front of a large gathering of Ministers, he had torn [Harold] Alexander to shreds for his lack of imagination and leadership in continually attacking at Cassino. He was furious with me, but I hope may do some good in the future.

Brooke observed that Churchill picked more fights as the next day began. The prime minister "became ruder and ruder. Fortunately he finished by falling out with Attlee and having a real good row with him concerning the future of India! We withdrew under cover of this smokescreen just on 2 am, having accomplished nothing beyond losing our tempers and valuable sleep!!" Years later, Brooke remembered "that ghastly evening as if it were yesterday."[71] Brooke resisted Churchill's micromanagement and his focus on secondary issues. On September 9, 1944, Brooke wrote: "We received 2 minutes from the PM today which show clearly that he is a sick man. His arguments are again centred on one point Istria [a peninsula in the Adriatic which bordered Italy and Yugoslavia]. We have come for one purpose only—to secure landing craft for an operation against Istria!! All else of importance fades into the shade of second considerations."[72]

Harold Alexander was much less inclined to provoke the prime minister. Churchill held Alexander to represent the ideal British general —a gentleman and brave soldier who generally agreed with him. The Mediterranean-based commander comported himself very differently from the pugnacious Brooke, who had only limited respect for Alexander. In August 1944, Churchill met with Alexander in Naples. Dr. Wilson wrote:

If Winston came to Italy eager to see Alex, Alex is even more eager to see Winston. He has found that the preoccupation of the Americans with the invasion of France and their indifference towards the Italian campaign is wrecking his command. He knows that only Winston can stop the rot. While I have been busy exploring the side streets of Siena, Winston had spent the sunny days working in bed. But at night Alex comes into the picture. Tonight he turned to me and said: "The Prime Minister knows so much about our job that he was the first to see that we should soon be well on our way to Vienna if only the Americans would be sensible." P.M.: "Glittering possibilities are opening up." Alex: "There is still time to set things right. I am not at all pessimistic." A clock struck two, but the P.M. had no intention of going to bed. It is not what Alex says that wins the day. He is not so foolish as to suppose that anyone has ever got his way with Winston

by argument. Winston likes a good listener; he is always ready
to do the talking. And Alex seems to wait on his words. He will
listen attentively until half the night is over . . . when Alex does
open his mouth he is always so reassuring, always so sure that
the P.M.'s plans are right, and that there will be no difficulty at
all in carrying them out. That is what Winston wants; he dislikes
people who are forever making trouble. "Anyone can do that," he
snorts impatiently. Soon he found himself confiding to Alex his
most intimate thoughts. "I envy you," he said, "the command of
armies in the field. That is what I should have liked."[73]

Shocked and depressed in private by battlefield reverses, Lincoln
and Churchill would hide their disappointments from public view. They
needed to sustain the morale of their generals, their soldiers, their cabinet members, and their peoples. "If there is a worse place than Hell,
I am in it," said the president after the carnage of Fredericksburg in
December 1862. "I am the most miserable Englishman in America—
since [General John] Burgoyne," said Churchill in June 1942, after he
received news at the White House of the fall of Tobruk.[74] Australian
Prime Minister Robert Menzies found Churchill steeped "in gloom," but
the next day observed: "There is no defeat in his heart."[75] In July 1942,
just days after learning the disastrous news of Tobruk's surrender, Churchill would reveal his private feeling: "Some people assume too readily that, because a Government keeps cool and has steady nerves under
reverses, its members do not feel the public misfortunes as keenly as
do independent critics. On the contrary, I doubt whether anyone feels
greater sorrow or pain than those who are responsible for the general
conduct of our affairs."[76]

The Union rout at Chancellorsville at the beginning of May 1863
depressed Lincoln. On May 26, an aide to New York Governor Horatio
Seymour delivered a message to him at the Soldiers' Home:

After the servant returned and announced that the President
would receive us, we sat for some time in painful silence. At
length we heard slow, shuffling steps come down the carpeted
stairs, and the President entered the room as we respectfully rose
from our seats. That pathetic figure has ever remained indelible

in my memory. His tall form was bowed, his hair disheveled; he wore no necktie or collar, and his large feet were partly incased in very loose, heelless slippers. It was very evident that he had got up from his bed or had been very nearly ready to get into it when we were announced, and had hastily put on some clothing and those slippers that made the *flip-flap* sounds on the stairs.[77]

At brief moments, the president would despair of a Union victory.

In both ways, the president and the prime minister managed a revolving door of generals in and out of key theaters. Churchill went through four commanders in the Middle East. Lincoln appointed and dismissed five commanders of the Army of the Potomac. In late August 1862, General Halleck complained: "The government seems determined to apply the guillotine to all unsuccessful generals. It seems rather hard to do this where the general is not in fault, but perhaps with us now, as in the French Revolution, some harsh measures are required."[78] In their military strategy, the Mediterranean and the Atlantic were to Churchill as the Mississippi and the Gulf were to Lincoln. For both far-seeing war leaders, control of strategic waterways was indispensable for victory. As Halleck wrote Grant in March 1862, "In my opinion the opening of the Mississippi River will be to us of more advantage than the capture of forty Richmonds."[79] For this very reason, the president would celebrate the July 1863 capture of Vicksburg. Churchill's preoccupation with the Mediterranean proved effective, because it provided an alternate theater in which to engage first the Italians, later the Germans in North Africa, Sicily, Italy, and southern France. The prime minister's Mediterranean campaign diverted German infantry and armored divisions desperately needed on the embattled Russian front, and it reopened the Suez Canal, eliminating the long route around the Cape of Good Hope. As a result, indispensable shipping could be released to other vital theaters.

Lincoln and Churchill have often been criticized for interference with the military plans and operations of their generals. They were, however, often right in their key strategic insights. The prime minister's leadership style was more overtly aggressive toward his generals. Lincoln discussed strategy with his generals, made suggestions, and attempted to persuade them. Churchill would try to intimidate his generals and admirals—much of the time unsuccessfully. Noel Annan, who served with the Joint Intelligence Staff in the War Cabinet Office, wrote: "Unlike Napoleon or Hitler, Churchill in the end nearly always gave way to his marshals and admirals—and they in turn gave way on the matter of appointments or decorations. But in Germany no battalion, let alone army group, could move without Hitler's agreement. . . . Brooke once said that Hitler was 'worth forty divisions to us.'"[80]

I retract nothing heretofore said as to slavery. I repeat the declaration made a year ago, that "while I remain in my present position I shall not attempt to retract or modify the emancipation proclamation, nor shall I return to slavery any person who is free by the terms of that proclamation, or by any of the Acts of Congress." If the people should, by whatever mode or means, make it an Executive duty to re-enslave such persons, another, and not I, must be their instrument to perform it.[1]

ABRAHAM LINCOLN
Fourth Annual Message to Congress
December 6, 1864

It is not given to human beings, happily for them, for otherwise life would be intolerable, to foresee or to predict to any large extent the unfolding course of events. In one phase men seem to have been right, in another they seem to have been wrong. Then again, a few years later, when the perspective of time has lengthened, all stands in a different setting. There is a new proportion. There is another scale of values. History with its flickering lamp stumbles along the trail of the past, trying to reconstruct its scenes, to revive its echoes, and kindle with pale gleams the passions of former days.[2]

WINSTON S. CHURCHILL
Eulogy for Neville Chamberlain
November 12, 1940

XVI.

Legacies

"All his life he was a man of extraordinary personal courage," wrote biographer William Manchester of Winston Churchill. "During raids he would dart out after close hits to see the damage. Sometimes he climbed up to the roof and squatted there on a hot-air vent, counting the Heinkel 11's as the searchlights picked them up. He wanted to be wherever the bombs were falling."[3] The prime minister refused to let German explosives impede his mobility in moving about London. Geoffrey Best wrote that Churchill "had repeatedly risked death with the same insouciance as when he was a young cavalry lieutenant and a middle-aged colonel, and he would have come really close to it on several occasions if strong-minded companions had not restrained him."[4] Churchill became annoyed when Allied generals would not let him cross the Rhine River with the troops in March 1945. His loyal aide, Jock Colville, did cross the Rhine as part of Operation PLUNDER. "You succeeded where I failed," Churchill said. "Tomorrow nothing shall stop me."[5] Indeed, nothing did. Sometimes there was in Churchill's conduct a rash tempting of death, even a staging of his bravado—as when he urinated on Nazi rubble.[6] From early years as a cavalry officer, Churchill believed in his star. It may have been either a virtue or a vanity, but he would often cheat death bravely on the field of battle.

Lincoln's courage—developed from boyhood on the frontier—was steadfast, unselfconscious, rarely staged. In a speech on the floor of the U.S. House of Representatives in 1848, Congressman Lincoln even mocked his own courage as a "military hero," a captain during the Black Hawk War with Indians in Northwest Illinois: "I had a good many bloody struggles with the musquetoes [sic]; and, although I never fainted from loss of blood, I can truly say I was often very hungry."[7] Captain Lincoln did not feel the need to portray himself as a fearless leader, remarking, "I who am not a specially brave man have had to sustain the sinking courage of these professional fighters in critical times."[8] However, Lincoln did not flinch when challenged. As a young man in 1831, he had taken on the bullies in New Salem, an act that made him a local hero. In Washington, three decades later as president, he brushed off attempts on his life—paying little attention when a bullet knocked off his hat. He would review Union troops in sight of well-equipped enemy snipers. In May 1862, as commander *in situ*, he personally directed operations to capture Norfolk, Virginia. Nor did he hesitate in July 1864 to mount the battlements of Fort Stevens to observe the attack going on directly before him.

The president's distinctive silhouette, over seven feet with top hat, put him in danger when he visited soldiers in the field (and elsewhere). He once asked General Benjamin Butler to "ride along your lines and see them, and see the boys and how they are situated in camp." Butler recalled:

When we got to the line of intrenchment, from which the line of rebel pickets was not more than 300 yards, he towered high above the works, and as we came to the several encampments the boys all turned out and cheered him lustily. Of course the enemy's attention was wholly directed to this performance, and with the glass it could be plainly seen that the eyes of their officers were fastened upon Lincoln; and a personage riding down the lines cheered by the soldiers was a very unusual thing, so that the enemy must have known that he was there. Both [Assistant Secretary of the Navy Gustavus] Fox and myself said to him, "Let us ride on the side next to the enemy, Mr. President. You are in fair rifle-shot of them, and they may open fire; and they must know you, being the only person not in uniform, and the cheering of the troops directs their attention to you." "Oh, no," he said laughing, "the commander-in-chief of the army must not show any cowardice in the presence of his soldiers, whatever he may feel." And he insisted upon riding the whole six miles, which was about the length of my intrenchments.[9]

Force of will, joined to the bravery of both commanders in chief, proved vital to their victories. In 1940–1941, Churchill's Britain alone kept the fight against Hitler alive after France had surrendered, and Bolshevik Russia had sidelined itself by its cynical nonaggression pact with its ideological enemy, fascist Germany. Isolationist America remained aloof. During the 1944 Quebec summit, the prime minister told Roosevelt "quite frankly that if Britain had not fought as she did at the start, while others were getting under way, America would have had to fight for her existence. If Hitler had got into Britain and some Quisling government had given them possession of the British Navy, along with what they had of the French fleet, nothing would have saved this [North American] continent."[10] Churchill's own feelings went deeper: America could have been more generous to Britain, fighting alone; Lend-Lease had provided little help in 1941; France could have sustained the fight longer; Stalin's Russia might not have made a cynical deal with Hitler, if the Nazis had been challenged in the mid- or late 1930s. The prime minister believed the challenge could have succeeded.

Churchill and Lincoln made war rather than submit to aggression and insurrection. They led their nations along a perilous road, having repudiated appeasement of dictators and slavemasters. Upon victory, after the exhausting war efforts in Europe, Churchill spoke to his elated countrymen on May 13, 1945: "I told you hard things at the beginning of these last five years; you did not shrink, and I should be unworthy of your confidence and generosity if I did not still cry: Forward, unflinching, unswerving, indomitable, till the whole task is done and the whole world is safe and clean."[11] Japan had not yet surrendered.

The president and the prime minister grieved for their wounded, the dead, the widows, and the orphans. Churchill observed that "the British and Empire sacrifice in loss of life was even greater than that of our valiant [American] Ally. The British total dead, and missing, presumed dead, of the armed forces amounted to 303,240, to which should be added over 109,000 from Dominions, India, and the Colonies, a total of over 412,240. This figure does not include 60,500 civilians killed in the air raids on the United Kingdom, nor the losses of our Merchant Navy and fishermen, which amounted to about 30,000."[12] But Britain's sacrifice did pale in comparison to that of the Soviet Union, which lost 8.7 million dead and missing soldiers, plus another 19 million civilians who died as a result of battles, genocide, famine, and incarceration.[13] In the American Civil War, it was estimated then that death and disease took about 360,000 Union soldiers and about 258,000 Confederate soldiers. Newer estimates by British historian David Packer suggest that the death toll was about 752,000—greater than Britain's losses in World War II.[14] Measured as a percentage of population, American soldiers lost in the Civil War were the catastrophic equivalent of more than six million dead American soldiers today, not unlike the Russian losses of World War II.

The prime minister and the president mourned these losses—still forbearing revenge after victory. Each was by instinct and judgment magnanimous to defeated foes. "Churchill had his faults," wrote historian John Lukacs. "He had his sycophants, and opportunists rallied to his side when that seemed timely. His greatest virtue was his magnanimity. 'Bygones are bygones,' he said, again and again. He forgave many, much, and easily. He was often moved to public emotion, the tears of which he was not ashamed. His daughter wrote to him in 1951: 'It is hardly in the nature of things that your descendants should inherit your genius—but I earnestly hope that they may share in some way the qualities of your heart.'"[15] Churchill's generous and shrewd political strategy could be seen in his treatment of erstwhile antagonists after he became prime minister in 1940. He kept in his cabinet adversaries such as Foreign Secretary Edward Halifax and Prime Minister Neville Chamberlain. He insisted on bringing into his government—over the strong objections of King George VI—Max Beaverbrook, a friend, a former appeaser, and a longtime press lord who had savaged Churchill as a warmonger in the late 1930s. Tory rebels who brought down the Chamberlain government and brought Churchill to Downing Street—such as Churchill's former Harrow schoolmate Leo Amery—received less generous treatment. Curiously, "Churchill did indeed seem to mistrust and resent Amery and the other Tory rebels who had helped bring him to power," noted historian Lynne Olson. "It was one of the many paradoxes of Winston Churchill that although he himself had been viewed as a rebel for years, he was, as Robert Rhodes James pointed out, 'fundamentally a very conservative man.' Throughout his career he had longed to be part of the power structure, not to bring it down."[16] As prime minister he had arrived. He was no longer a rebel.

Lincoln's way was easier on staff and coworkers in war and peace. Lincoln "never chided, never censured, never criticized my conduct," said law partner William H. Herndon, whom Lincoln occasionally had to rescue from drunken binges.[17] Churchill, born to the aristocracy, could act harshly with *droit de seigneur*, but just as generously with *noblesse oblige*. Lincoln, born poor, would by self-discipline mold his character, which came to exemplify the virtues of the gentleman, the statesman, and a relentless war leader. Neither Churchill nor Lincoln was vindictive. In his First Inaugural, the president earnestly pleaded with the angry secessionists: "We are not enemies but friends."[18] In the days after Lee's surrender at Appomattox, Lincoln sincerely hoped Confederate President Davis would evade Union capture, trial for treason, and possible execution.

Lincoln's longtime friend and sometime bodyguard, Ward Hill Lamon, recalled that as victory approached:

> General Grant asked for special instructions of Mr. Lincoln, — whether he should try to capture Jefferson Davis, or let him escape from the country if he wanted to do so. Mr. Lincoln replied by relating the story of an Irishman who had taken the pledge of Father Matthew, and having become terribly thirsty applied to a bar-tender for a lemonade; and while it was being prepared he whispered to the bar-tender, 'And couldn't you put a little brandy in it all unbeknownst to myself?' Mr. Lincoln told the general he would like to let Jeff Davis escape all unbeknown to himself: he had no use for him.[19]

Presidential aide Edward Duffield Neill, a pastor and educator, recalled that on April 13, 1865, "those persons always ready to give advice began to call, and tell what they thought should be done with Mr. Jefferson Davis. Wearied and annoyed, he said to [William] Slade his mulatto doorkeeper: 'This talk of Mr. Davis tires me. I hope he will mount a fleet horse, reach the shores of the Gulf of Mexico, and drive so far into its waters that we shall never see him again.'"[20] Churchill himself wrote of Lincoln: "To those who spoke of hanging Jefferson Davis he replied, 'Judge not that ye be not judged.' On April 11, [1865] he proclaimed the need of a broad and generous temper and urged the conciliation of the vanquished."[21] At the request of Alexander H. Stephens of Georgia in February 1865, Lincoln would pardon the imprisoned officer-nephew of the Confederate vice president; he received Stephens's nephew at the White House, and then sent the former rebel South to his family.

Churchill hated Hitler, whom he called "the mainspring of evil."[22] But the prime minister did not hate the German people, though when embattled, he could exhort his warriors to kill the Hun. He once said: "I hate nobody except Hitler—and that is professional."[23] On another occasion, Churchill told an aide: "You know, I may seem to be very fierce, but I am fierce with only one man, Hitler."[24] Asked in July 1940 if he wanted to reply to a speech that Hitler had made to the Reichstag, the prime minister responded: "I do not propose to say anything in reply to Herr Hitler's speech, not being on speaking terms with him."[25] Although Churchill and Lincoln were not vengeful in victory, this virtue did not diminish the prime minister's determination to crush Germany. Speaking to Parliament in January 1943, after the Royal Air Force unleashed a massive bombing campaign against Germany, Churchill declared his goal was "to make the enemy burn and bleed in every way that is physically and reasonably possible, in the same way as he is being made to bleed and burn along the vast Russian front."[26] Churchill's war strategy aimed at unqualified German surrender. Long before World War II, Churchill had written: "I have always urged fighting wars and other contentions with might and main till overwhelming victory, and then offering the hand of friendship to the vanquished. Thus I have always been against the Pacificists during the quarrel, and the Jingoes at its close."[27] Churchill recalled as he made his way through bombed-out Berlin in July 1945 that: "When I got out of the car and walked about among them, except for one old man who shook his head disapprovingly, they all began to cheer. My hate had died with surrender and I was much moved by their demonstrations, and also by their haggard looks and threadbare clothes."[28]

At war, the prime minister was all-in, all the time. But his code of honor excluded the excess of the vengeful victor: "Nothing is more costly, nothing is more sterile, than vengeance."[29] Paul Johnson wrote that Churchill "was relieved by Hitler's suicide. He had not relished the prospective task of hanging him."[30] Bodyguard Walter Thompson

Abraham Lincoln and staff of General George B. McClellan, 1862

Gilder Lehrman Collection, GLC04346

recalled that after the prime minister heard the news, he "went to a window and looked out at the lawns for a long time." Asked if he thought Hitler had taken his own life, Churchill replied: "That is the way I should have expected him to have died."[31] Stalin's reaction was more direct: "So that's the end of the bastard."[32] Historian Norman Davies noted that earlier, "Churchill [had] proposed shooting the Nazi leaders as bandits, instead of putting them on trial."[33] He would later prove to be more balanced toward Germany's military officers. At the Teheran summit, an indignant prime minister had walked out of a cavalier discussion between Russian and American leaders about Stalin's proposal to execute 50,000 German officers.[34]

In the warlords of both nations, hardness and tenderness cohabited. Lincoln confided to his oldest friend, Joshua F. Speed: "Speed, die when I may, I want it said of me by those who know me best that I always plucked a thistle and planted a flower where I thought a flower would grow."[35] The president's political genius stemmed in part from his intuitive sense for the feelings of others. "Lincoln's abhorrence of hurting another was born of a more than simple compassion," wrote historian Doris Kearns Goodwin. "He possessed extraordinary empathy—the gift or curse of putting himself in the place of another, to experience what they were feeling, to understand their motives and desires."[36] Lincoln might have failed without his self-confident intelligence, his intense ambition, and a thick public skin, no matter his private sensitivity. His was a "laudable" ambition, as General Washington said of Alexander Hamilton.[37] Lincoln "was always a most ambitious man," recalled friend Orville Browning. "I think his ambition was to fit himself properly for what he considered some important predestined labor or work."[38] Illinois Governor Richard Yates recalled that Lincoln's "was an unselfish ambition, to serve his country and to be a benefactor of his race. He never sought glory. There was none of the vain gloriousness, of ostentation, of the noise and glare about him which men call glory."[39]

As a young cavalry officer, Churchill did seek the glory and fame he believed necessary to enter Parliament, where he intended to vindicate his father's controversial legacy as a failed Tory leader. The young MP would say of himself: "We are all worms, but I do believe that I am a glow-worm."[40] Churchill's self-absorption was mitigated by his self-deprecating puckishness. At 22, he had confessed that it was not his "intention to become a mere professional soldier. I only wish to gain some experience. Some day I shall be a statesman as my father was before me."[41] Three years later, he wrote: "I am 25 today. It is terrible to think how little time remains."[42] (His father, Randolph, had died at 45; his son Randolph would die at 57.) As a young man in the Illinois state legislature, Lincoln too wistfully yearned for public recognition. At age 33, in a very melancholy moment, he mused that his death might be easily forgotten because he "had done nothing to make any human being remember that he had lived."[43]

Churchill could be irascible and intemperate—Lincoln, in maturity, rarely so. Churchill may have been the more imaginative, but such a faculty does not always make for steady management and leadership. After consulting others, both relied upon their own judgment for decisions. The prime minister "always retained unswerving independence of thought," one of Churchill's secretaries observed. "He approached a problem as he himself saw it and of all the men I have ever known he was the least liable to be swayed by the views of even his most intimate counsellors."[44] Even in maturity, Churchill was not only quick to decision; he could also be impetuous. President Lincoln was more deliberate, careful, contemplative. Both stood firmly behind their decisions once made. Massachusetts Senator Henry Wilson, an abolitionist, observed that Lincoln was "a firm man when he clearly saw duty. His most earnest, devoted and ablest friends in and out of congress pressed him for months to issue a declaration of Emancipation, but he could not be coaxed nor driven into action till he saw the time had come to do it."[45] Lincoln's wife, Mary Todd, observed that "no man nor woman Could rule him after he had made up his mind. I told him about Seward[']s intention to rule him— he said—'I shall rule myself—shall obey my own Conscience and follow God in it.'"[46] Michigan Senator Chandler, a frequent adversary, reported that the president was "stubborn as a mule when he gets his back up."[47] Journalist and friend Horace White observed, "There is no backdown in Old Abe."[48] Nor was there backdown in the bulldog prime minister, dubbed the "Old Boss" by some subordinates.[49]

Deeply patriotic, Churchill and Lincoln loved their countries with unapologetic loyalty. They cherished the common culture of their inheritance. Alexander Stephens remarked that for the president, "the Union . . . rose to the sublimity of a religious mysticism."[50] Both war leaders revered free, democratic institutions, which inspired their love of country. Lincoln believed the United States the "last best hope of earth."[51] In his 1852 eulogy for Henry Clay, Lincoln emphasized that the Kentucky Senator "loved his country partly because it was his own country, but mostly because it was a free country."[52] At Gettysburg in 1863, the president declared, "[T]his nation shall, under God, have a new birth of freedom; and that government of the people, by the people, and for the people, shall not perish from the earth."[53] As Lincoln had written a decade earlier in resolutions prepared for the visit by Hungarian freedom fighter Lajos Kossuth, "the sympathies of the country, and the benefits of its position, should be exerted in favor of the people of every nation struggling to be free."[54]

Churchill was both English aristocrat and, like his father, Tory democrat. "The preservation and enhancement of democracy was an integral part of Churchill's war leadership, a vision of the world that would follow an Allied victory," wrote Martin Gilbert.[55] Lincoln's genealogy, too, was ancient Anglo-Saxon; his ancestors came from East Anglia, home to Oliver Cromwell, who had successfully challenged the monarchy during the English Civil War of the seventeenth century. In the December 1944 debate in the House of Commons over Britain's intervention in the Greek Civil War, Churchill declared: "Democracy is not based on violence or terrorism, but on reason, on fair play, on freedom, on respecting the rights of other people. Democracy is no harlot to be picked up in the street by a man with a tommy gun. I trust the people, the mass of the people, in almost any country, but I like to make sure that it is the people and not a gang of bandits [the Bolsheviks] who think, by violence, they can overturn the constituted authority."[56]

Meeting Churchill in 1899, a British naval captain had remarked: "I feel certain that I shall some day shake hands with you as prime minister of England. You possess the two necessary qualifications, genius and plod."[57] General Brooke cited Churchill's "most marvelous qualities of superhuman genius mixed with an astonishing lack of vision at times, and an impetuosity which if not guided must inevitably bring him into trouble again and again."[58] Genius and plod: Prime Minister Churchill and President Lincoln would exhibit both character traits in peace and in war. Rarely did they waver in prosecuting their wars of national survival. Victory, they understood, could only come at great pains. As the prime minister had announced, without victory against the Nazis, there would be no survival. "Churchill," wrote Carlo D'Este, "refused to be ruled by what may be termed the culture of failure: a fear of innovation and boldness that might induce blame or defeat."[59] His boldness in war was surely one of his most important contributions to the Allied victory. The prime minister would not accept defeat. Nor could Lincoln accept anything less than victory in war. He would say in his Second Inaugural Address in March 1865: "The progress of our arms, upon which all else chiefly depends, is as well known to the public as to myself."[60]

Lincoln, better than Churchill, knew his countrymen from the poorest to the most powerful. Lincoln's law partner observed that "the strongest point in his make-up was the knowledge he had of himself; he comprehended and understood his own capacity—what he did and why he did it—better perhaps than any man of his day. He had a wider and deeper comprehension of his environments, of the political conditions especially, than men who were more learned or had the benefits of a more thorough training."[61] The president's arguments before trial courts, during political debates, and in his decision-making at war were shorn of romance. Churchill was brave and enterprising—occasionally to the point of recklessness. If he had not mastered his ego in the manner of Lincoln, the prime minister surely had mastered the history of the English-speaking peoples. With courage, discipline, and hard work, he, too, would bend its history to his statecraft.

More clearly than Franklin Roosevelt, Winston Churchill correctly foresaw the threat of postwar Soviet power in Europe. FDR and his advisers did not heed the prime minister's pleas to cooperate on postwar strategy in Europe. FDR wanted to bring the troops home. Indeed, the prime minister sometimes did not heed his own warnings, so desperately did the Allies need Russian armies to defeat the vast Nazi military machine in the east. Still, it was he who had joined foresight to force of personality by fighting Hitler alone, in order to hold Britain together in 1940–1941. It might be said that Churchill's "Gettysburg Address" came three years after the war in Europe had ended. Speaking on May 28, 1948, at the Westminster Abbey dedication of a memorial to British commandos, Churchill said in his eulogy: "Today we unveil a memorial to the brave who gave their lives for what we believe future generations of the world will pronounce a righteous and noble cause. In this ancient

Abbey, so deeply wrought into the record, the life and message of the British race and nation—here where every inch of space is devoted to the monuments of the past and to the inspiration of the future—there will remain this cloister now consecrated to those who gave their lives in what they hoped would be a final war against the grosser forms of tyranny." Churchill concluded: "Above all, we have our faith that the universe is ruled by a Supreme Being and in fulfilment of a sublime moral purpose, according to which all our actions are judged. This faith enshrines, not only in bronze but forever the impulse of these young men, when they gave all they had in order that Britain's honour might still shine forth and that justice and decency might dwell among men in this troubled world."[62] Churchill knew well Lincoln's Gettysburg Address; its echoes resounded at Westminster Abbey.

Lincoln and Churchill saw their struggles through the magnifying glass of a principled moral framework. Philosopher Isaiah Berlin wrote that "the single, central organizing principle of his [Churchill's] moral and intellectual universe, is an historical imagination so strong, so comprehensive, as to encase the whole of the present and the whole of the future in a framework of a rich and multicolored past. Such an approach is dominated by a desire—and a capacity—to find fixed moral and intellectual bearings to give shape and character, color and direction, to the stream of events."[63] Lincoln, too, had fixed his bearings in maturity. In his last public speech on April 11, 1865, President Lincoln declared without equivocation: "Important principles may, and must, be inflexible."[64] In this terse rule of conduct, there was no room for moral relativism; there existed no romance with words, only objective standards to guide actions. Historian John Lukacs observed that Churchill "had an extraordinarily quick mind, and these traits of his were not only inseparable from his temperament and character but inseparable, too, from the visionary capacity of his mind."[65] Lincoln—animated by his own tenacious vision and personal experience of the American dream—became "one of the foremost hedgehogs in American history," wrote James M. McPherson. "More than any of his Civil War contemporaries, he pursued policies that were governed by a central vision, expressed in the Gettysburg Address, that this 'nation, conceived in Liberty, and dedicated to the proposition that all men are created equal . . . shall not perish from the earth.' Lincoln was surrounded by foxes who considered themselves

**General Alan Brooke, Winston S. Churchill,
General Bernard Montgomery, General William Simpson, 1945**

Pictoral Press Ltd / Alamy Stock Photo

smarter than he but who lacked his depth of vision and therefore sometimes pursued unrelated and contradictory ends."[66]

Massachusetts Congressman George Boutwell summed up the president's war leadership and its consequences: "The policy of Mr. Lincoln
and those who acted with him secured the reign of justice ultimately in
our domestic affairs."[67] Lincoln's sense of justice would prompt rare exhi-
bitions of anger. In early 1864, a longtime friend brought him a petition
from a woman in Union-occupied Mississippi who wanted permission to
use former slaves to work her plantation. Lincoln responded aggressively
that he "would rather take a rope and hang myself than to do it."[68] A
few months earlier in his eulogy for the fallen soldiers at Gettysburg, the
president had explained "the cause for which they gave the last full measure of devotion . . . that this nation, under God, shall have a new birth
of freedom."[69] So, too, would Mississippi slaves.

"War is terrible, but slavery is worse," wrote Churchill in January
1939. Only 75 years earlier, Lincoln in his seminal, antislavery speech at
Peoria of October 16, 1854, insisted "that no man is good enough to govern another man without that other's consent." There Lincoln declared:
"Slavery is founded in the selfishness of man's nature—opposition to it,
[in] his love of justice."[70] It was at Peoria that Lincoln declared the moral
proposition that Churchill, too, would embrace: "Slavery is a monstrous
injustice."[71] Speaking to the nation as First Lord of the Admiralty in
1939, Churchill remarked:

> Of all the wars that men have fought in their hard pilgrimage,
> none was more noble than the great Civil War in America nearly
> eighty years ago. Both sides fought with high conviction, and the
> war was long and hard. All the heroism of the South could not
> redeem their cause from the stain of slavery, just as all the cour-
> age and skill which the Germans show in war will not free them
> from the reproach of Nazism, with its intolerance and its brutal-
> ity. We may take good heart from what happened in America in
> those famous days of the nineteenth century.[72]

A certain fatalism inhabited the minds of both men. "I am like a
bomber pilot. I go out night after night, and I know that one night I
shall not return," Churchill remarked at lunch in April 1942.[73] "Lincoln's

whole life was a calculation of the law of forces and ultimate results. The world to him was a question of cause and effect," observed fellow attorney Leonard Swett. "He believed the result to which certain causes tended, would surely follow; he did not believe that those results could be materially hastened, or impeded," wrote Swett. "His tactics were to get himself in the right place and remain there still, until events would find him in that place."[74] His antislavery campaign of the 1850s would find him in the right place.

In January 1862, Britain's Prince Albert died at 42 after a short illness. President Lincoln wrote to Albert's widow, Queen Victoria:

[Y]ou are honored on this side of the Atlantic as a friend of the American People. The late Prince Consort was with sufficient evidence regarded as your counsellor in the same friendly relation. The American People, therefore, deplore his death and sympathize in Your Majesty's irreparable bereavement with an unaffected sorrow. . . . I do not dwell upon it, however, because I know that the Divine hand that has wounded, is the only one that can heal: And so, commending Your Majesty and the Prince Royal, the Heir Apparent, and all your afflicted family to the tender mercies of God.[75]

After the president was assassinated on April 14, 1865, Queen Victoria wrote Lincoln's widow about how "terrible a calamity has fallen upon you and your country" and the "shocking circumstances of your present—dreadful misfortune. No one can better appreciate, than I can, who am myself utterly broken hearted by the loss of my own beloved husband, who was the light of my life, my stay, my all,—what your own sufferings must be, and I earnestly pray that you may be supported by Him, to whom alone the sorely stricken can look for comfort in their hour of heavy afflication [sic]."[76] Mary Todd Lincoln would remain inconsolable.

President Roosevelt's death in April 1945 likewise deeply affected Prime Minister Churchill. "No one realises what he meant to this country and to the world," he said to his bodyguard.[77] "I am much weakened by this loss," Churchill told a military subordinate. Publicly, the prime minister said: "It is, indeed, a loss, a bitter loss to humanity that those heart beats are stilled for ever."[78] Churchill first decided to attend FDR's funeral, reversing himself at the last minute because too many British cabinet officials were out of the country, preoccupying him with political decisions at war's end. The prime minister had often gone to see FDR in life, but he would not see him in death. To Eleanor Roosevelt, Churchill wrote: "Accept my most profound sympathy in your grievous loss, which is also the loss of the British nation and of the cause of freedom in every land. I feel so deeply for you all. As for myself, I have lost a dear and cherished friendship which was forged in the fire of war."[79]

The saga of the Civil War and the life of Lincoln ended together. From the outset of the conflict, President Lincoln had understood the ultimate stakes at issue in the war. In a letter drafted for Wisconsin leaders in August 1864, Lincoln had said that if he reversed his emancipation pledge to black slaves, as he had been asked many times to do, "I should be damned in time & in eternity for so doing."[80] As Churchill himself would write: "Lincoln's political foes, gazing upon him, did not know vigour when they saw it. These were hard conditions under which to wage a war to the death."[81]

For Churchill, victorious in war but vanquished at the ballot box, life went on. Speaking to the House of Commons, after electoral defeat in July 1945, Churchill declared:

> I have great hopes of this Parliament, and I shall do my utmost to make its work fruitful. It may heal the wounds of war, and turn to good account the new conceptions and powers which we have gathered amid the storm. I do not underrate the difficult and intricate complications of the task which lies before us; I know too much about it to cherish vain illusions; but the morrow of such a victory as we have gained is a splendid moment both in our small lives and in our great history. It is a time not only of rejoicing but even more of resolve. When we look back on all the perils through which we have passed and at the mighty foes we have laid low and all the dark and deadly designs we have frustrated, why should we fear for our future? We have come safely through the worst.[82]

At the end of the Civil War, President Lincoln could not have said it better.

Winston S. Churchill, 1942

© BBC Photo Library

*Fellow citizens, we cannot escape history. We of this Con-
gress and this administration, will be remembered in spite
of ourselves. No personal significance, or insignificance,
can spare one or another of us. The fiery trial through
which we pass, will light us down, in honor or dishonor,
to the latest generation. We say we are for the Union. The
world will not forget that we say this. We know how to save
the Union. The world knows we do know how to save it.
We—even we here—hold the power, and bear the responsibility. In giving freedom to the slave, we assure freedom
to the free—honorable alike in what we give, and what
we preserve. We shall nobly save, or meanly lose, the last
best, hope of earth. Other means may succeed; this could
not fail. The way is plain, peaceful, generous, just—a
way which, if followed, the world will forever applaud,
and God must forever bless.*[1]

ABRAHAM LINCOLN
Second Annual Message to Congress
December 1, 1862

*The people of the United States cannot escape world respon-
sibility. . . . Not only are the responsibilities of this great
Republic growing, but the world over which they range is
itself contracting in retaliation to our powers of locomo-
tion at a positively alarming rate. . . . But to the youth
of America, as to the youth of Britain, I say "You cannot
stop." There is no halting place at this point. We have now
reached a stage in the journey where there can be no pause.
We must go on. It must be world anarchy or world order.*[2]

WINSTON S. CHURCHILL
Speech at Harvard
September 6, 1943

XVII.

Epilogue

When in May 1940, Winston Churchill entered 10 Downing Street as prime minister, his name had been a household word in Britain for four decades. At 25, after his spectacular escape from prison in the Boer War, he became one of the most famous men in England. When in 1860 Abraham Lincoln ran for president, he was, except in Illinois, a virtual unknown. London in 1940 was the cosmopolitan center of the world. Washington in 1861 was a small southern town dominated socially by the slavemasters. The capital's major thoroughfare was either a dust bowl or a muddy mess. In war, the capital quickly transformed itself into a vast military and hospital encampment. Great battles would be fought nearby in Virginia.

The prime minister had inherited the huge government bureaucracy of the British Empire. By contrast, President Lincoln inherited a small bureaucracy, a 16,000-man army shrunken further by the defection of Confederate sympathizers. President Lincoln could walk to the nearby government buildings—War, Navy, and Treasury. The public thought the Executive Mansion a public place that might be entered at any hour of the day or night. Nevertheless, the president's office on the second floor "was a remarkably silent workshop, considering how much was going on there," according to William Stoddard. "The very air seemed heavy with the pressure of the times, centering toward that place. There was only now and then a day bright enough to send any great amount of sunshine into the house, especially upstairs. It was not so much that coming events cast their shadows before, although they may have done so, as that the shadows, the ghosts, if you will, of all sorts of events, past, present and to come, trooped in and flitted around the halls and lurked in the corners of the rooms."[3] The volume of traffic varied, however. The White House

371

overflowed with supplicants when Congress was in session, but sat virtually vacant in the sizzling days of summer, when Lincoln himself would
escape to the relative cool of the more elevated Soldiers' Cottage. Civil
War General Carl Schurz wrote:

> Those who visited the White House—and the White House
> appeared to be open to whosoever wished to enter—saw there
> a man of unconventional manners, who, without the slightest
> effort to put on dignity, treated all men alike, much like old
> neighbors; whose speech had not seldom a rustic flavor about it;
> who always seemed to have time for a homely talk and never to
> be in a hurry to press business, and who occasionally spoke about
> important affairs of State with the same nonchalance—I might
> almost say, irreverence—with which he might have discussed an
> every-day law case in his office at Springfield, Illinois. People
> were puzzled. Some interesting stories circulated about Lincoln's
> wit, his quaint sayings, and also about his kindness of heart and
> the sympathetic loveliness of his character; but, as to his qualities
> as a statesman, serious people who did not intimately know him
> were inclined to reserve their judgment.[4]

New York businessman James R. Gilmore observed: "As he leaned
back in his chair, he had an air of unstudied ease, a kind of careless
dignity, that well became his station; and yet there was not a trace of
self-consciousness about him. He seemed altogether forgetful of himself
and his position, and entirely engrossed in the subject that was under
discussion."[5] Soldiers of all ranks were welcome at the White House, and
likely to be quizzed on military matters. When scientist Louis Agassiz visited the White House, Lincoln whispered to a friend, "Now sit still and
see what we can pick up that's new."[6]

A student of people, Lincoln evaluated their character, analyzed
their useful knowledge. The president called his weekly receptions at the
White House—to which any American in Washington might attend—his
"public-opinion baths."[7] These exhausting receptions could be monoto-
nous, but, noted Chicago activist Mary Livermore, "when he was met by
a warm grasp of the hand, a look of genuine friendliness, the President's
look and manner answered the expression entirely. To the lowly and
humble he was especially kind; his worn face took on a look of exquisite

tenderness, as he shook hands with soldiers who carried an empty coat sleeve, or swung themselves on crutches; and not a child was allowed to pass him by without a kind word from him."[8]

Churchill once told the American ambassador that whereas Americans valued success, "we English rather like a man who hasn't come off . . . if he is staunch and uncomplaining in adversity. You see, it's a man's character that counts with us, not his achievements."[9] Luck—in the form of weather, intelligence, or serendipity—does play a strong role in war. Early in both wars, the prime minister and the president were conspicuously lacking in good fortune. General John Kennedy observed of Churchill: "Prime Ministers need luck as well as Generals; Prime Ministers who usurp the role of Commanders-in-Chief need a double dose of it."[10] At the outset of the war, both leaders lacked the generals they needed. Their armies suffered a string of battlefield reverses, sometimes compounded by political errors. The president and the prime minister would substitute grit and pluck for luck—counting on time and patience for success.

Fortunately, both Lincoln and Churchill were students of history. The prime minister had been writing it for four decades. Both were shrewd students of their national traditions, which they put to effective use. "Churchill believed that customs and laws and traditions, the entire body of historical memory for a people, were a living guide which man badly needed as he attempted to chart the course of his life amid the disorder of the modern world," wrote Maxwell Philip Schoenfeld.[11] Lincoln reminded the defenders of the Union that the charter of their liberties and independence, the Declaration of Independence in 1776, defined the American proposition "that all men are created equal." At war, the president would never overlook the crucial importance of the Declaration.

John Hay described Lincoln's routine:

The President rose early, as his sleep was light and capricious. In the summer, when he lived at the Soldiers' Home, he would take his frugal breakfast and ride into town in time to be at his desk at eight o'clock. He began to receive visits nominally at ten o'clock, but long before that hour struck the doors were besieged by anxious crowds, through whom the people of importance, Senators and members of Congress, elbowed their way after the fashion which still survives. On days when the Cabinet met, Tuesdays and Fridays, the hour of noon closed the interviews of the morning. On other days it was the President's custom, at about that hour, to order the doors to be opened and all who were waiting, to be admitted. The crowd would rush in, thronging the narrow room, and one by one, would make their wants known. Some came merely to shake hands, to wish him Godspeed; their errand was soon done. Others came asking help or mercy; they usually pressed forward, careless, in their pain, as to what ears should overhear their prayer. But there were many who lingered in the rear and leaned against the wall, hoping each to be the last, that they might in tete a tete unfold their schemes for their own advantage or their neighbor's hurt. These were often disconcerted by the President's loud and hearty, "Well, friend, what can I do for you?" which compelled them to speak, or retire and wait [for] a more convenient season.[12]

Lincoln's usual candor contrasted with his evasiveness when the president would say: "That reminds me of a story." These stories enabled the president to move swiftly away from the topic pursued by his visitor. The prime minister tended to disagree bluntly—sometimes disagreeably. Given the unrelenting pressures they faced, the health of Churchill and Lincoln would deteriorate in office. The contaminated water from the Potomac River and the swampy areas near the White House bred disease and sickened its residents.

"Everybody who spends much time in the White House is certain to suffer more or less," wrote William Stoddard. "To be sure, the President has had only the smallpox, but he was well seasoned before he came, and he is too full of anxiety, all the while, for a different kind of fever to get into him. Mrs. Lincoln has suffered in ways which have no chronicle, and little Tad has undoubtedly been injured so that his constitution will not recover. Willie Wallace Lincoln died of it. The private secretaries were all tough, healthy fellows, pretty well seasoned, but they have had sharp down-turns to wrestle with."[13]

In order to recover their health, aides departed for vacations—a privilege in war the president denied himself but that his wife and his aides would indulge.

White House, Washington, DC

Sketch from Obsequies of Abraham Lincoln

The informal president preferred that his friends call him "Lincoln," not the more ostentatious "Mr. President." He remained oblivious to his safety. Although two aides worked and lived down the hall, they were not on twenty-four-hour call. Stoddard recalled working late one night, in the aftermath of the Union disaster at Chancellorsville in May 1863. All night, he heard the heavy tread of the president pacing back and forth in his office.

> Two o'clock came, for I again looked at my watch, and Lincoln was walking still. It was a vigil with God and with the future, and a long wrestle with disaster and, it may be, with himself—for he was weary of delays and sore with defeats. It was almost three o'clock when my own long task was done and I arose to go. . . . At the top of the stairway, however, I paused and listened before going down, and the last sound that I heard and that seemed to go out of the house with me was the sentry-like tread with which the President was marching on into the coming day.[14]

Amid the carnage of war, neither Lincoln nor Churchill would lose his sensitive nature. The pain caused by the bloodshed of others never left them. After nearby battles in the Civil War, the dead and maimed were often brought to Washington. Lincoln was never far from the wounds of war, visiting the hospitals regularly. One of the first casualties of the conflict was a bright young man, Ephraim Ellsworth, who was virtually a member of the Lincoln family. A few months later, a longtime Lincoln friend and former Illinois political colleague, Oregon Senator Edward D. Baker, died in battle while serving as a Union officer. These deaths distressed the president—as did the death of his son Willie in February 1862. "When the [funeral] ceremony was about concluded and President Lincoln stood by the bier of his dead boy, with tear-drops, falling from his face, surrounded by Seward, Chase, Bates, and others, I thought I never beheld a nobler-looking man," wrote a Springfield colleague.[15]

Prominent detractors severely criticized the strategic and tactical war leadership of Lincoln and Churchill. McClellan wrote his wife: "Honest A has again fallen into the hands of my enemies & is no longer a cordial friend of mine!"[16] But generals who served well and long enough with Lincoln changed their minds about Lincoln's military leadership. In their multivolume biography of the president, John G. Nicolay and John Hay wrote: "General W[illiam] F. Smith says: 'I have long held to the opinion that at the close of the war Mr. Lincoln was the superior of his generals in his comprehension of the effect of strategic movements and the proper method of following up victories to their legitimate conclusions.' General J[ames] H. Wilson holds the same opinion; and Colonel Robert N. Scott, in whose lamented death the army lost one of its most vigorous and best-trained intellects, frequently called Mr. Lincoln 'the ablest strategist of the war.'"[17]

Even harsh critics of Lincoln and Churchill would admit their grudging admiration. Rivals of the president and the prime minister came to admire them. General Brooke sometimes damned the prime minister in his diary, but after the war he wrote: "Throughout all these troublesome times I always retained the same unbounded admiration, and gratitude for what he had done in the early years of the war. One could not help also being filled with the deepest admiration for such a genius and super man."[18] General Ismay, Churchill's embattled military aide, wrote that "a nation which is so fortunate as to produce a Winston Churchill at the critical moment would surely be insane if it did not give the fullest rein to his unrivalled experience and qualifications. He was a 'war man' if ever there was one, and his whole life had been a preparation for the task which now confronted him."[19] The pompous Massachusetts Senator Charles Sumner often made himself a thorn in President Lincoln's side on issues like emancipation and reconstruction. After Lincoln was assassinated, the intellectual Sumner delivered a long eulogy in which he compared the deceased president to Saint Louis, the thirteenth-century king of France.

Ultimately, Lincoln and Churchill were their own severest critics. "Each night, I try myself by Court Martial to see if I have done anything effective during the day. I don't mean just pawing the ground, anyone can go through the motions, but something really effective," the prime minister told John Colville.[20] The president and the prime minister were well aware they had achieved their nations' highest political offices under the most unlikely of grave circumstances. In August 1940, just three months after becoming prime minister, Churchill observed that "in this war he had had no success, and had received nothing but praise, whereas in the last war [World War I] he had done several things which he thought were good, and had got nothing but abuse."[21]

The more patient of the two, Lincoln exemplified the cardinal virtue of prudence.[22] When possible, he tended to make revolutionary change in evolutionary steps. The president knew when to be bold, when to exercise restraint. He could be bold in resisting unwise counsel to attack when unready. Along the way, he knew how to solicit—and to reject—advice. When he was advised not to give the "radical" "House Divided" speech at the 1858 Illinois Republican Convention, he delivered it anyway. When *Chicago Tribune* editor Joseph Medill and others begged Lincoln not to raise questions about the controversial Lecompton Constitution of Kansas at the Freeport debate, he did so anyway. When he presented the Emancipation Proclamation to the cabinet in the summer of 1862, he made it clear that he was not asking for the cabinet's advice, although he welcomed comments. When it counted and the timing was right, Lincoln was bold, not passive—the essence of prudence. Timing would determine his actions. He directed events, with great stakes at risk, much as a good director might direct a play—allowing talented, proven actors the freedom to interpret their roles, giving firmer instructions to those who needed his advice on means as well as ends, replacing those who failed to play their assigned parts.

Churchill governed a relatively united Britain beset by financial insolvency, wartime frugality, severe rationing, poverty, and aerial bombing. Lincoln's America had been divided by the secessionists into North and South, free and slave. Even in the booming North, there were serious divisions—such as the violent disputes among Unionists in Missouri and other loyal border slave-states. Some disloyal Democrats in the North collaborated with the rebels. In late September 1863, Lincoln met with a large delegation of Radicals from Missouri. Their leader, Enos Clarke, recalled:

> Toward the close of the conference he went on to speak of his great office, of its burdens, of its responsibilities and duties. Among other things he said that in the administration of the government he wanted to be the president of the whole people and of no section. He thought we, possibly, failed to comprehend the enormous stress that rested upon him. "It is my ambition and desire," he said with considerable feeling, "to so administer the affairs of the government while I remain president that if at the end I shall have lost every other friend on

earth I shall at least have one friend remaining and that one shall be down inside of me."[23]

Both Lincoln and Churchill were historians—Lincoln as an amateur doing research for his great speeches of the 1850s, Churchill as a professional. At war they could not help but think about their place in history. The prime minister remarked in December 1940 that he "would retire to Chartwell and write a book on the war, which he had already mapped out in his mind chapter by chapter. This was the moment for him; he was determined not to prolong his career into the period of reconstruction," recalled John Colville.[24] "The verdict of history," wrote historian David Reynolds, "was the subject of one of Churchill's favorite aphorisms. 'History will say,' declared Churchill in an exchange with [Prime Minister Stanley] Baldwin in the Commons in the 1930s, 'that the Right Honourable Gentleman was wrong in this matter.' Pause. Broad grin. 'I know it will, because I shall write that history.' He adopted a similar line with Stalin in 1944, after a vigorous exchange of telegrams about whether Britain could have secured a separate peace in 1940. 'I agree that we had better leave the past to history,' he wrote in a draft reply, 'but remember if I live long enough I may be one of the historians.'"[25]

After his 1945 defeat, Churchill remained evasive about future book projects until he got in place a very favorable, perhaps unique, legal and tax ruling to govern his negotiations with publishers.[26] Churchill's estate and his heirs would grow rich from the proceeds of his writings. Doctor Charles Wilson suggests that after the war Churchill became obsessed about his place in "posterity," leading to depression. The doctor wrote that Churchill "must have known that he had a tired mind, but he would not be turned from his purpose. In 1949 [at 75]—it may have been about the turn of the year—when he was halfway through the third volume of *The Second World War* it became plain that he no longer had the energy of mind to do the job properly. I tried to argue with him. Surely he had done enough, had not the time come to take in sail? 'You do not understand,' he said sadly. He could not bring himself to talk of it."[27] With the inspired help of his large and sophisticated research team, he would live to complete his six-volume memoir of the war, each volume with its own pithy title, detailed narrative, and supporting documents.

Both statesmen at war would battle for "unconditional surrender" of their opponents. General Grant popularized the phrase when he besieged Fort Donelson on the Tennessee River in February 1862: "No terms except unconditional surrender can be accepted. I propose to move immediately upon your works."[28] Great pressure was brought to bear on Lincoln to negotiate a conditional peace with the Confederates, but he took pains to avoid such an outcome to the very end. As he had written in December 1860 to Illinois Senator Lyman Trumbull, "The tug has to come, & better now, than any time hereafter." The president would allow several peace missions to go forward in 1864 and 1865. He did so primarily to emphasize his two preconditions—reunion and emancipation. Fractious Northern politics and growing casualties forced the president to appear ready to discuss an end to hostilities with the South, but Lincoln consistently repeated conditions for negotiation that he knew would be unacceptable to Confederate leaders. No peace without reunion and emancipation.

In World War II, Winston Churchill himself made the first reference to "unconditional surrender" in a telegram to the War Cabinet in January 1943. Later in the month, President Roosevelt used the term at Casablanca at a press conference. FDR's notes for the conference stated:

> The President and the Prime Minister, after a complete survey of the world war situation, are more than ever determined that peace can come to the world only by a total elimination of German and Japanese war power. This involves the simple formula of placing the objective of this war in terms of an unconditional surrender by Germany, Italy and Japan. Unconditional surrender by them means a reasonable assurance of world peace, for generations. Unconditional surrender means not the destruction of the German populace, nor of the Italian or Japanese populace, but does mean the destruction of a philosophy in Germany, Italy and Japan which is based on the conquest and subjugation of other peoples.[29]

Churchill at Casablanca reacted testily to Roosevelt's declaration, according to Averell Harriman—not only because "Roosevelt had proclaimed it on his own," but also because he had doubts about its wisdom.[30] By the nature of alliance, the prime minister felt it desirable that both parties should agree on major policies. But FDR had peremptorily ruled out negotiations with the Nazis—a position earlier taken by the

10 Downing Street, London

Photo: Sergeant Tom Robinson RLC/MOD

prime minister himself. General Kennedy wrote in his diary in 1942 that Churchill "has only one interest in life at this moment, and that is to win the war. Every waking moment is devoted to that."[31] The prime minister, however, understood the negative ramifications within Germany caused by trumpeting unconditional surrender in August 1942:

> We certainly do not want, if we can help it, to get them all fused together in a solid desperate block for whom there is no hope. I am sure you will agree with me that a gradual break-up in Germany must mean a weakening of their resistance, and consequently the saving of hundreds of thousands of British and American lives.[32]

Lincoln spelled out his war aims in subtle, simple terms—now often misinterpreted. In an August 1862 public letter to Horace Greeley, he wrote:

> I would save the Union. I would save it the shortest way under the Constitution. The sooner the national authority can be restored; the nearer the Union will be "the Union as it was." If there be those who would not save the Union, unless they could at the same time *save* slavery, I do not agree with them. If there be those who would not save the Union unless they could at the same time *destroy* slavery, I do not agree with them. My paramount object in this struggle *is* to save the Union, and is not either to save or to destroy slavery. If I could save the Union without freeing any slave I would do it, and if I could save it by freeing all the slaves I would do it; and if I could save it by freeing some and leaving others alone I would also do that. What I do about slavery, and the colored race, I do because I believe it helps to save the Union; and what I forbear, I forbear because I do *not* believe it would help to save the Union.[33]

This letter was the President's clever tactical deception. Lincoln had prepared the Greeley letter at the same time he made ready to issue the preliminary Emancipation Proclamation. Read carefully, the president's letter would address all constituencies of the Northern coalition, including those who backed the Union but not emancipation. But what he had carefully written to gain Northern support did not foreclose the Proclamation, which he was then preparing.

With time, both Lincoln and Churchill had broadened their objectives. Victory would come first, but other issues—like permanent emancipation of all American slaves—would gain equal rhetorical status. "Without slavery the rebellion could never have existed; without slavery it could not continue," Abraham Lincoln wrote in his Second Annual Message to Congress in December 1862, shortly before he would issue the Emancipation Proclamation on January 1, 1863.[34] In December 1942, Churchill declared that "we are all of us defending something which is, I won't say dearer, but greater than a country, namely, a cause. That cause is the cause of freedom and justice; that cause is the cause of the weak against the strong; it is the cause of law against violence, of mercy and tolerance against brutality and iron-bound tyranny. That is the cause that we are fighting for."[35] In this cause, Churchill would see clearly the irony that Stalin was a murderous dictator—but a necessary member of the grand alliance to defeat Hitler.

John Keegan wrote: "Famously, Charles de Gaulle begins his memoirs with the declaration: 'I have always had a particular idea of France.' Churchill, similarly, had a particular view of Britain."[36] For the prime minister, Britain and the British Empire, no matter their imperfections, had been the vanguard of liberty, progress, justice, and human well-being the world over. So too might it be said that Lincoln had a particular idea of America. To him, America was the "last best hope on earth."

In these two statesmen—one born well, the other born poor—the genius, the virtue, and the hope of the human race had expressed themselves so as to be studied, admired, and emulated for all time to come.

**Abraham Lincoln with Allan Pinkerton and
General John McClernand, 1862**

Library of Congress

Winston Churchill, 1940

© Imperial War Museum

HISTORIOGRAPHY AND ACKNOWLEDGMENTS

Every work of history depends on the scholarship of historians who have gone before. Lincoln's friends and colleagues—William H. Herndon, Isaac N. Arnold, Edward Bates, Gideon Welles, Noah Brooks, Francis B. Carpenter, Elizabeth Keckley, William O. Stoddard, John G. Nicolay, and John Hay—were among the first to contribute to the record of Lincoln's life. Over the decades, historians such as Ida Tarbell, Albert Beveridge, Lord Charnwood, Benjamin Thomas, Allan Nevins, Hary Jaffa, David Herbert Donald, James McPherson, Doris Kearns Goodwin, Philip Shaw Paludan, Harold Holzer, Kenneth Winkle, Doug Wilson, Allen Guelzo, Richard Carwardine, and Michael Burlingame, among many others, have contributed to the impressive canon of Lincoln's life.

In the late 1940s and early 1950s, Roy P. Basler and his team assembled *The Collected Works of Abraham Lincoln* into eight volumes and two later supplements—using the Robert Todd Lincoln Collection at the Library of Congress. Letters and documents left in other hands have been gathered in major repositories like the Abraham Lincoln Museum and Library in Springfield, Illinois. Lincoln's legal papers were not included in the *Collected Works*, but were gathered in the *Lincoln Legal Papers* in the 1990s. "The Papers of Abraham Lincoln" project under Daniel W. Stowell continues the process of collecting the Lincoln archive into a new compilation of both incoming and outgoing correspondence. Professor Don E. Fehrenbacher and his wife, Virginia, did a special service in sifting through the many quotes attributed to Lincoln, in order to distinguish the authentic from the spurious. Thankfully, many contemporaries who interacted with Lincoln recorded their remembrances in newspaper and magazine articles, or interviews with would-be biographers like Herndon, determined, as Lincoln's law partner would be, to elicit the truth from contemporaries.

Regrettably, with few exceptions, those who knew and worked with
Abraham Lincoln were not as diligent diarists as those around Winston
Churchill. Union Treasury official Maunsell B. Field recalled: "Upon
one occasion, I remarked to the Secretary [Salmon P. Chase] that I supposed he had kept a diary, or at least memoranda, of everything that had
occurred at Cabinet meetings since the incoming of the Administration.
He told me, in reply, that during several months in the beginning he had
very faithfully done so; but that very soon the personal relations between
some of his colleagues became so inharmonious, and so much unworthy
bickering, and even quarreling, was indulged in upon these occasions,
that he discontinued making a record, and destroyed the notes which
he had already taken."[1] Chase nevertheless made sporadic diary entries.
Secretary of State Seward kept a diary for a single day at the beginning
of the war. He told his son: "One day's record satisfies me that if I should
every day set down my hasty impressions, based on half information, I
should do injustice to everybody around me, and to none more than my
most intimate friends."[2] Historians must be grateful that Gideon Welles
scrupulously kept a detailed record of events in the Navy Department,
and discussions of Cabinet meetings, intra-cabinet feuds, and the shortcomings of other officials. Thanks to the late Harvard Professor William
Gienapp and his wife, Erica, the inscrutable handwriting of Secretary
Welles has been deciphered. General Edward Bates kept a diary, but his
entries were skimpy and reflected his rather distant relationship with
President Lincoln.

Both Lincoln and Churchill looked back nostalgically to a time in
the histories of their countries when democracy seemed more vigorous.
In *My Early Life*, Churchill wrote of his childhood: "Politics seemed very
important and vivid to my eyes in those days. They were directed by
statesmen of commanding intellect and personality. The upper classes
in their various stations took part in them as a habit and as a duty. The
working men whether they had votes or not followed them as a sport."[3]
In 1856, Lincoln bemoaned the track on which he found America moving away from the vision of the Founders—"the fourth of July has not
quite dwindled away; it is still a great day—*for burning firecrackers!*"[4]

Lincoln himself had little faith in biographies. He once refused to
read a biography of Edmund Burke, telling his law partner: "I do not
wish to read his life, nor any man's life as now written. You and I have
talked over lifewriting . . . many times, and you know that biographies

are eulogistic, one-sided, colored, and false. The dead man's glories are painted hugely, brightly, and falsely; his successes are held up to eulogy, but his failures, his shortcomings, his negatives, his errors, slips, and foibles, and the like are kept in the dark. You don't get a peep at them."[5] Churchill, himself a biographer, had no inhibitions about writing his own story. In young adulthood he began defining his historical legacy. His five-volume memoir of World War I, *The World Crisis*, would be followed by his six volumes on World War II. No one should miss reading *My Early Life*, surely the master's writing at his most imaginative, perhaps his best.

Churchill's colleagues were constrained by law, custom, and self-restraint not to publish memoirs that might reflect badly on the once and future prime minister. Among the most unrestrained were the diaries of General Alan Brooke, who used his diary as a release from the pressures of his office and as a way of conveying his feelings and activities to his wife—he called them "my nightly talk with you on paper." Those diaries were used by much-criticized Arthur Bryant to write *The Turn of the Tide, 1939–1943*, published in 1957, and *The Triumph of the West*, published in 1959. The books tarnished the reputation of both Brooke and Churchill. Historian Andrew Roberts observed: "Brooke seems to have taken a strangely inconsistent attitude towards security; he would severely admonish anyone giving classified information over non-scrambler telephones, yet he posted his diaries to his wife by Royal Mail."[6] Brooke biographer David Fraser noted: "A diary entry is evidence of the state of mind of the writer on a particular evening. It is imperfect evidence of the facts it records and can imperfectly reflect the writer's true self. A man's irritations when exhausted are atypical of him, and of none more than Brooke. When there is passion felt on vital subjects, dispute can turn men savage."[7] Brooke later regretted some of his most intemperate comments in the diary as published by Bryant. Historian David Reynolds noted: "Privately, several of Churchill's wartime contemporaries believed that the portrait in [Bryant's] *Turn of the Tide* was apt and essentially fair. Clement Attlee told Bryant, 'We who worked with him know how quickly he could change from the great man to the naughty child.'"[8] Bryant had selectively edited Brooke's diaries—which were published in their entirety in 2001 by Alex Danchev and Daniel Todman. The editors wove into the diaries some mitigating "Notes for my memoirs" that Brooke had written in 1951–1956,[9] during Churchill's second premiership.

In the case of Dr. Wilson and General Brooke, their critical analysis and published comments about Churchill caused consternation among Churchill loyalists, called his Secret Circle during the war. When published in 1966, shortly after Churchill's death, his physician's edited diaries were considered a serious breach of professional ethics between doctor and patient. They were much criticized. A collection of essays by other Churchill aides was developed by John Wheeler-Bennett as a counternarrative to the critical comments recorded by Wilson. Danchev criticized *Action This Day* as "the authorized inner circle version, in which Churchill achieves almost mythic status . . . The loyalty evoked in such circumstances—at once privileged and parasitic—is, of course, both understandable and praiseworthy; but, as Roskill noted of *Action This Day*, 'how restricted was the outlook of those who came most closely under Churchill's influence. There is scarcely a hint in the whole book that the great prime minister's judgement was ever at fault.'"[10] In a more recent publication of the diaries edited by Dr. Wilson's son, the introduction states that "the manuscripts amount not to a 'diary' . . . but rather the notes for the book on Churchill Moran always intended to write, in a near-constant state of flux and revision."[11] Other Churchill colleagues, such as Leslie Hollis and Commander Charles R. "Tommy" Thompson, used third-party writers to compile their memories in book form.

The doubtful nature of recollections was suggested by Anthony Eden in his memoirs. He recalled conversation and drinks he had with Harry Hopkins in March 1943. Eden did not record the event in his diary, but Hopkins wrote a memo about it that found its way into Robert E. Sherwood's *The White House Papers*, published in 1948. Churchill called Eden about the Sherwood book "because there are some things in them put down to me which I shall question. You may have to do the same." Eden was "relieved to read its relative discretion" in Hopkins's report of their discussion over oysters at a Washington restaurant. Eden continued: "The moral of this is that a true friend can be trusted to report even one's indiscretions discreetly, but it is quite a risk to take. Diplomacy is never off the record. The only advantage of pretending that it can be is to pursue diplomatic ends by undiplomatic means."[12]

Churchill's civilian and military friends and subordinates from the war—such as Joan Astley Bright, Violet Bonham Carter, John Colville, John Martin, Leslie Hollis, Hastings Ismay, Alexander Cadogan, and

Abraham Lincoln, 1861

Gilder Lehrman Collection, GLC05111.02.0002

John Kennedy—later published invaluable diaries or memoirs. A surprising number of British public servants disobeyed official regulations against such diaries. John Colville observed of Private Secretary John Martin that "he was too law-abiding to keep a diary. That is a pity as his writing is as agreeable as his conversation."[13] Martin actually did occasionally keep a journal, but it was much briefer than the detailed notes of Colville.[14] Explicit pressure and self-censorship prevented some of these memoirs from appearing before Churchill's death in 1965. Bodyguard Walter H. Thompson's memoirs were suppressed by Scotland Yard officials, who threatened him with loss of his pension. Thompson's full manuscript remained unpublished until well after his death in 1978. It was published as *Beside the Bulldog: The Intimate Memoirs of Churchill's Bodyguard*. Key parliamentary and diplomatic colleagues, such as Harold Macmillan, Harold Nicolson, and Leo Amery, added their own diaries and memoirs.

Churchill cabinet member Oliver Lyttleton forecast correctly that he "will, I expect, prove to be the best documented prime minister that ever held the post."[15] Robert Sherwood noted "that British officials, Churchill included, considered it their sacred duty always to make such notes, or 'minutes,' of conversations as important as this one, not for their own personal diaries, but for the official records. A few Americans, principally those who had rigorous training in the Foreign Service, also did this. Hopkins made such notes whenever he could find time to do so, but Roosevelt seldom wrote or dictated any record of a conversation in which he had been involved."[16] Some of FDR's most illuminating comments were made in chatty letters to his worshipful distant cousin, Margaret "Daisy" Suckley. Americans, less constrained by official regulations, could be more diligent in keeping diaries. Secretary of the Treasury Henry Morgenthau and Interior Secretary Harold Ickes dictated or wrote large volumes. Secretary of Labor Frances Perkins published brief memoirs, as did many top generals and admirals. On the military side, Secretary of War Henry Stimson kept a diary, but Chief of Staff George C. Marshall disdained diaries as self-serving. Historian David Kaiser wrote that Stimson "took everything he did very seriously and kept a thorough diary, earning the everlasting thanks of several generations of future historians."[17] American perspectives were amplified by Averell Harriman. The collected papers of Harry Hopkins were edited by fellow White House aide Sherwood.

Dwight D. Eisenhower's personal interactions with Churchill were detailed by his public relations aide, Harry "Butch" Butcher, in diaries he published after the war; and memoirs written by Ike's driver, assistant, and perhaps his lover, Kate Summersby Morgan, three decades later, just before her death. Eisenhower enjoyed Churchill's company, but like the general's British colleagues, Ike did not enjoy it late at night when he sought sleep. Painfully for Churchill, Butcher published his truncated diary in 1946 as *My Three Years with Eisenhower.* Butcher recalled a dinner in May 1943 in Algiers, at which "the question of diaries came up. The prime minister said that it was foolish to keep a day-by-day diary because it would simply reflect the change of opinion or decision of the writer, which, when and if published, makes one appear indecisive and foolish. . . . For his part, the Prime Minister said, he would much prefer to wait until the war is over and then write impressions, so that, if necessary, he could correct or bury his mistakes."[18] Churchill had decided to write the history of World War II himself, unhampered by American amateurs like Butcher who mangled history. Butcher's book was both a gossipy best seller and an embarrassment to Churchill and Eisenhower—though Butcher had many kind things to say about the relationship between the two leaders. Eisenhower biographer Geoffrey Perret wrote: "The worst offense Butcher committed was to hold Churchill up to ridicule and make Montgomery seem stupid."[19]

Churchill had also been disturbed by *As He Saw It* (1946), a critical book by FDR's son, Elliott Roosevelt. After an incident at the Teheran Conference in November 1943, when Elliott had interjected himself to support comments by Joseph Stalin about executing 50,000 German officers, Churchill had taken offense. "Are you interested in damaging relations between the Allies?" Elliott recalled Churchill saying. "Do you know what you are saying? How can you dare say such a thing?" The younger Roosevelt said he tried to apologize to his father, who declared: "Winston just lost his head when everybody refused to take the subject seriously." FDR said that Churchill would forget it, but Elliott wrote: "I don't think he ever did forget it. All the months I was to be stationed in England, later on, I was never again invited to spend the night at Chequers."[20]

Winston Churchill was determined to be the most influential chronicler of his World War II record. His defeat in July 1945, at age 70, gave him and his staff the time to start to assemble the mountain of material from which to write *his story*, his memoirs, which even he did not equate with history. Churchill would use official documents of the war to write of his five years as wartime prime minister. Historian Walter Reid contended: "Churchill's approach to these papers was very simple: 'they are mine. I can publish them.' The constitutional position was much more opaque, and all that can be said with certainty is that Churchill was quite wrong."[21] Churchill wrote in his World War II memoirs:

> I rely upon the series of my directives, telegrams, and minutes, which owe their importance and interest to the moment in which they were written, and which I could not write in better words now. These original documents were dictated by me as events broke upon us. As they are my own composition, set forth at the time, it is by these that I prefer to be judged. It would be easier to produce a series of after-thoughts, when the answers to all the riddles were known, but I must leave this to the historians who will in due course be able to pronounce their considered judgments.[22]

The quantity of material now available to Churchill researchers defies imagination. His own pen (or his dictated words transcribed on the typewriters of his stenographers) produced about 15–20 million words.[23] According to Martin Gilbert, "When Randolph Churchill began work on his father's biography in 1961, he had at his disposal an estimated 15 tons of paper—his father's personal archive, now at Churchill College, Cambridge."[24] More has been revealed since. And that does not include vast official British government materials at Whitehall and elsewhere, regarding Churchill's government—documents that were forbidden for historical use until several decades after their origin. There are voluminous papers related to his nine cabinet positions.

After the war, Churchill carefully cultivated Cabinet Secretary Edward Bridges in order to ensure extraordinarily favorable tax and ownership treatment of his wartime papers by the British government. (Clement Attlee blocked the use of other government papers from the war.[25]) "I feel I have a right, if I so decide to tell my tale and I am convinced it would be to the advantage of our country to have it told, as perhaps I alone can tell it."[26] When in 1946 Churchill pressed Bridges for use of government documents, the former prime minister wrote: "I should like to tell the story so far as possible in my own words written at the time. As you know, a great part of my work was done in writing (dictated typescript) and I should scarcely need to publish any documents other than those I have composed myself. . . . In telling a tale [in] the words written in the circumstances of the moment are of far greater significance than any paraphrase of them or subsequent composition."[27] In early October 1946, Churchill was granted permission by the Labour government to use and quote from his papers. His wartime papers remained under his control until a few years before his death in 1965—giving Churchill a head start in establishing the reigning narrative of World War II, one in which he undeniably played a central role on the Allied side with FDR and Stalin.

It is his own written record that formed the heart of Churchill's memoirs. Historian Elisabeth Barker observed: "To read these minutes today is to be tempted to think that Churchill, in writing them, felt that he was doing two creative acts at one time: dictating the course of future historical events by making them happen, and also dictating the history of the Second World War as it would eventually be written."[28] In the view of Tuvia Ben-Moshe, the memoirs' "strength lies in the felicity of its author's special style, which is captivating and replete with stirring rhetoric. Indeed, the power of its language occasionally conceals logical and other weaknesses of some of its arguments." Ben-Moshe added: "When rereading his papers, he did not simply attempt to reconstruct his thoughts and actions at the time of the composition. He also often looked for what he ought to have thought and done."[29]

As Churchill historian Larry Arnn observed, the prime minister had a heroic view of history: "Churchill wrote as much as he acted, and he wrote about every action."[30] Churchill "saw history as a pageant, a colourful drama," wrote historians Robert Blake and William Roger Louis. "His attitude was highly personal, and his memoirs of both world wars have to be read in the light of what he said to one of his helpers, Sir William Deakin: 'this is not history, this is my case.' Like other prominent statesmen he was liable to claim a greater degree of foresight, consistency, and single-mindedness than the facts warrant."[31] Churchill was painting on a big canvas. David Dilks noted that for Churchill, writing history "was a means of expressing a vision of men and events seen through what [William] Deakin called the 'prism of a superb historical imagination.' Thus history was not a 'subject,' like geography or physics; rather, it was to WSC 'the sum of things.'"[32]

Among Churchill's biographers have been his son Randolph, Martin Gilbert, Paul Addison, Correlli Barnett, Geoffrey Best, John Charmley, Carlo D'Este, Max Hastings, Roy Jenkins, John Keegan, William Manchester, Paul Reid, Maxwell Philip Schoenfeld, and A. J. P. Taylor. Not all of the eminent historians who have chronicled Churchill's war leadership have been uncritical. Some historians—such as Correlli Barnett, John Connell, and Alex Danchev, who studied the roles of Generals Auchinleck, Brooke, and Wavell—have been particularly critical of Churchill's strategic leadership, especially in 1940–1942. Barnett, in his remarkable quadrilogy on *The Pride and Fall of Britain* and in his military histories, has contributed much not only to the understanding of the British Empire, but also to the analysis of Churchill's relationships with his generals and admirals. Andrew Roberts, who integrated Churchill's leadership with that of the Allies in several volumes on World War II, has begun work on a major Churchill biography. Richard M. Langworth, who edited *Finest Hour* for years, has compiled the most important Churchill quotations in *Churchill by Himself.* The prime minister's monumental, multivolume official biography was begun by Randolph Churchill and continued by Martin Gilbert, who also presided over the publication of Churchill's papers. Their work continues at Hillsdale College, under the supervision of its president, Larry Arnn, and of Richard Langworth.

No participant's recollection is infallible. The recollections of both Roosevelt and Churchill about the introduction of "unconditional surrender" at the press conference at the end of the Casablanca conference is a case in point. FDR's recollection that it was an ad hoc comment was wrong. The recollection of Churchill that he had never been consulted was also wrong. Much criticism and revisionism has been directed at Churchill since 1965, but it is well to remember the words of Lord Carrington: "There is a fashion now to judge people of a different generation by the standards and customs and thoughts of the present generation. Now I think that is a very difficult and wrong thing to do. How can you really judge what people felt like when they were born 130 or 140 years ago and were brought up in totally different circumstances and totally different customs than those which you find today. I think those critics of Winston Churchill sometimes seem to ignore that."[33] A late Victorian, Churchill was born in 1874. At maturity, he was an Edwardian. In World War II, he was an elderly but vigorous prime minister.

Winston S. Churchill, ca. 1941

© National Portrait Gallery, London

For much of his life, he earned a handsome living as a writer and speaker, becoming rich in the last two decades of his life. Indeed, Churchill once quipped: "I lived in fact from mouth to hand."[34] Abraham Lincoln tried and failed as a paid speaker in the late 1850s, because he was uninterested in speeches or writing without legal or political purpose. The future president's speeches, all with political purpose, generally fell into clearly defined areas. In the 1840s, for example, he was known for his expertise on trade, banking, and other economic issues. His best-known (and uniquely remunerated) speaking engagement was the anti-slavery Cooper Union speech of February 1860.[35] Lincoln earned a good living as a lawyer. His public documents reflect his legal training, his study of classic English literature, as well as his mastery of the English language itself and its lawyerly derivatives. He had received fewer than twelve months of formal education. Lincoln was not unaware of the influence of nineteenth-century historians such as George Bancroft. A century later, historian Richard Current wrote: "In 1864 the relations between the two grew increasingly cordial and, indeed, almost close."[36] Bancroft, a Democrat who had served in the cabinet of President James Polk, reported his attendance at a White House reception in February: "Last night I went to the President's reception. He took me by one of his hands, and trying to recall my name, he waved the other a foot and a half above his head, and cried out, greatly to the amusement of the bystanders: 'Hold on—know you: you are—History, History of the United States—Mr.—Mr. Bancroft, Mr. George Bancroft,' and seemed disposed to give me a hearty welcome—expressing a wish to see me some day apart from the crowd." Lincoln subsequently fulfilled Bancroft's request for a copy of the Gettysburg Address in his own hand.[37] During the war, Bancroft was critical of Lincoln. After the war, Bancroft wrote: "The measure by which Abraham Lincoln takes his place, not in American history only, but in universal history, is his Proclamation of January 1, 1863, emancipating all slaves within the insurgent States. It was, indeed, a military necessity, and it decided the result of the war. It took from the public enemy one or two millions of bondmen, and placed between one and two hundred thousand brave and gallant troops in arms on the side of the Union."[38]

In Lincoln's case, the bulk of his written output was owned by Robert Todd Lincoln, who maintained strict control of the papers—allowing only his friends John G. Nicolay and John Hay to use the papers in their still relevant ten-volume biography of the late nineteenth century. (Given this special access, Nicolay and Hay, like Churchill after World War II, could dominate the interpretation of Lincoln and the Civil War.) Eventually, Robert gave his father's documents to the Library of Congress, but forbade publication until 1947. A Knox College team led by Douglas L. Wilson and Rodney O. Davis did a monumental service to historians by digitizing much of the collection, including important incoming correspondence to President Lincoln. I was gratified to assist their project. Much Lincoln correspondence was destroyed—some by Lincoln when he left Springfield in 1861, and some after his death by his distraught widow. Important documents and letters were dispersed by friends and family.

Over the years, I have cherished the opportunity to get to know many distinguished American and British historians of the Civil War and World War II periods. I concluded long ago that there must be much to learn from the juxtaposition of the greatest elected English-speaking war leaders of the nineteenth and twentieth centuries. To my knowledge, the subject had never before received book-length attention. Undoubtedly, much remains to be examined concerning the way that Abraham Lincoln and Winston S. Churchill led their countries to victory in terrible wars wherein the stakes were no less than national survival.

My Readers

For help with the publication of this manuscript, I acknowledge with gratitude my outstanding readers—Larry Arnn, James Basker, Michael Burlingame, Allen Guelzo, Doris Kearns Goodwin, Richard Langworth, Thomas Lehrman, Nicole Seary, and Frank Trotta. The reach of their scholarship, the clarity of their advice, and their recommendations have proved invaluable. Arnn carries forward the monumental work of Randolph Churchill and Martin Gilbert on the multivolume, authorized Churchill biography. He was also the director of research for Martin Gilbert. Now president of Hillsdale College, Arnn and the college have assumed responsibility for finishing the task of publishing of *The Churchill Documents* and to archive the papers of Martin Gilbert. It was through Arnn that I came to know Gilbert, a biographer and historian with few peers. Professor James Basker, president of the Gilder Lehrman Institute, a master of the English language, has combed this book with the well-tutored eye of an accomplished writer and editor. Professor Burlingame is held by many scholars to be one of the outstanding Lincoln biographers of all time, certainly the most comprehensive. His *Abraham Lincoln: A Life* consists of more than 2,000 octavo pages, wherein he reveals the life and times of Mr. Lincoln as never before. Allen Guelzo is a multiple prize–winning American historian of the Civil War, Abraham Lincoln, and Reconstruction. His original research has even won for him a major prize in military history. Doris Kearns Goodwin is a Pulitzer Prize–winning American historian whose work includes celebrated studies of Presidents Lincoln and Lyndon Johnson, as well as of Theodore, Franklin, and Eleanor Roosevelt—among others. Her work has been featured in major movies and documentaries. Richard Langworth is a master of the primary sources of Mr. Churchill's life and times. His Churchill research is available to students of history worldwide. He is the founder of the International Churchill Society and of its journal, *Finest Hour*, and its newsletter, *The Chartwell Bulletin*. He now supervises the encyclopedic Hillsdale College Churchill website. Thomas Lehrman, my son, has the eye and the touch of a fact-based historian; he specializes in the history of science and technology, intellectual history, and the history of economic thought; he is a careful reader, with no fear of his father's reaction to his shrewd criticisms.

Nicole Seary is surely one of the best copy editors. Her painstaking preliminary edit was deeply appreciated. At Stackpole Books, Judith Schnell, David Reisch, and Stephanie Otto, publisher and editors, have been indispensable. They are masters of the craft of publishing; Reisch is himself an expert in the historical period of this book. As they surely know, I am grateful for their every effort and support. My copy editor at Stackpole, Amy Rafferty, called my attention to composition errors of all types. Richard Behn, my research associate, was a crucial ally in the plumbing of the vast research material available in primary and secondary sources. His work was invaluable.

For this book, there are others to whom I am grateful, men who were not readers for this volume. Professor Andrew Roberts of King's College London, in the opinion of fellow scholars on both sides of the Atlantic, is one of the great masters of modern and military history; he has a matchless command of the period upon which this book concentrates.

Professor Robin Winks, with whom I long ago studied as a Carnegie Teaching Fellow at Yale, was a scholar of British imperial and commonwealth history at Yale. Correlli Barnett, an outstanding British imperial and military historian, received me at Churchill College, Cambridge, with great generosity. He is the former keeper of the Churchill Archives at Churchill College, Cambridge University. When I was a Woodrow Wilson Fellow at Harvard, Professor Ernest May shared his incomparable research on World War I, and by extension World War II; Professor Merle Fainsod, his mastery of Soviet history in the twentieth century. In one of my previous books, *Lincoln at Peoria* (the history of Mr. Lincoln's antislavery campaign from 1854 until 1865), I did acknowledge many men and women. Their influence carries on into *Lincoln & Churchill: Statesmen at War*. It goes without saying that those named in the bibliography and endnotes of *Lincoln & Churchill: Statesmen at War* are scholars and writers to whom I am also indebted. I must acknowledge those who helped with the preparation of *Churchill, Roosevelt & Company: Studies in Character and Statecraft*, published in early 2017. Both books were researched, written, and edited between 2010 and 2017—even though the reading and study go back to my undergraduate and teaching years long ago.

I am ever grateful to the staff in my business office who carry on when I must disappear to study, write, and edit: Deja Hickcox, Mary MacKenzie, Steve Szymanski, Susan Tang, and Frank Trotta. Deja Hickcox and Susan Tang coordinated my work with the readers and publishers, making my labors on this book the more efficient; they are exacting and disciplined. Deja Hickcox was the master-organizer.

These unstinting efforts of my readers, my friends, and my colleagues, have helped me to avoid many errors of commission and omission. All remaining errors are mine alone.

SELECTED BIBLIOGRAPHY
ON ABRAHAM LINCOLN

NOTE: This bibliography emphasizes books that reflect on the presidency of Abraham Lincoln and the Civil War—necessarily omitting many important works.

Angle, Paul M., ed. *Abraham Lincoln by Some Men Who Knew Him.* Bloomington, IL: Pantagraph Printing & Stationery Company, 1910.

Arnold, Isaac N. *The Life of Abraham Lincoln.* Lincoln, NE: University of Nebraska Press, 1994.

Belz, Herman. *Abraham Lincoln, Constitutionalism, and Equal Rights in the Civil War Era.* New York: Fordham University Press, 1998.

———. *Reconstructing the Union: Theory and Policy during the Civil War.* Ithaca, NY: Cornell University Press, 1969.

Beveridge, Albert. *Abraham Lincoln, 1809–1858*, Volume II. Boston: Houghton Mifflin Co., 1928.

Blumenthal, Sidney. *A Selfmade Man: The Political Life of Abraham Lincoln, 1809–1849.* New York: Simon and Schuster, 2016.

Boritt, Gabor S. *Lincoln and the Economics of the American Dream.* Urbana, IL: University of Illinois Press, 1994.

———. *The Gettysburg Gospel: The Lincoln Speech That Nobody Knows.* New York: Simon & Schuster, 2006.

Briggs, John Channing. *Lincoln's Speeches Reconsidered.* Baltimore: Johns Hopkins University Press, 2005.

Brookhiser, Richard. *Founders' Son.* New York: Basic Books, 2014.

Brooks, Noah. *Abraham Lincoln and the Downfall of Slavery.* New York: G. P. Putnam & Sons, 1894.

———. *Washington, D.C., in Lincoln's Time.* Athens, GA: University of Georgia Press, 1989.

Burlingame, Michael. *Abraham Lincoln: A Life*, Volumes I & II. Baltimore: Johns Hopkins University Press, 2008.

———. *The Inner World of Abraham Lincoln.* Urbana, IL: University of Illinois Press, 1994.

———. *Lincoln and the Civil War.* Carbondale, IL: Southern Illinois University Press, 2011.

———, ed. *At Lincoln's Side: John Hay's Civil War Correspondence and Selected Writings.* Carbondale, IL: Southern Illinois University Press, 2000.

———, ed. *Dispatches from Lincoln's White House: The Anonymous Civil War Journalism of Presidential Secretary William O. Stoddard.* Lincoln, NE: University of Nebraska Press, 2002.

———, ed. *Inside the White House in War Times: Memoirs and Reports of Lincoln's Secretary: William O. Stoddard.* Lincoln, NE: University of Nebraska Press, 2000.

———, ed. *Lincoln's Journalist: John Hay's Anonymous Writings for the Press, 1860–1864.* Carbondale, IL: Southern Illinois University Press, 1998.

———, ed. *An Oral History of Abraham Lincoln: John G. Nicolay's Interviews and Essays.* Carbondale, IL: Southern Illinois University Press, 1996.

———, ed. *With Lincoln in the White House: Letters, Memoranda, and Other Writings of John G. Nicolay, 1860–1865.* Carbondale, IL: Southern Illinois University Press, 2000.

Burlingame, Michael, and John R. Turner Ettlinger, eds. *Inside Lincoln's White House: The Complete Civil War Diary of John Hay.* Carbondale, IL: Southern Illinois University Press, 1997.

Carwardine, Richard. *Abraham Lincoln and the Fourth Estate: The White House and the Press During the American Civil War.* Reading, UK: University of Reading, 2004.

———. *Lincoln: A Life of Purpose and Power.* New York: Alfred A. Knopf, 2006.

Cox, LaWanda. *Lincoln and Black Freedom: A Study in Presidential Leadership.* Columbia: University of South Carolina Press, 1981.

Current, Richard Nelson. *The Lincoln Nobody Knows.* New York: Macmillan, 1958.

———. *Speaking of Abraham Lincoln: The Man and His Meaning for Our Times.* Urbana: University of Illinois Press, 1983.

Dirck, Brian R. *Lincoln & Davis: Imagining America, 1809–1865.* Lawrence, KS: University Press of Kansas, 2001.

Donald, David Herbert. *Lincoln.* New York: Simon & Schuster, 1995.

———. *Lincoln's Herndon.* New York: Alfred A. Knopf, 1948.

———, ed. *Inside Lincoln's Cabinet: The Civil War Diaries of Salmon P. Chase.* New York: Longmans, Green and Co., 1954.

Fehrenbacher, Don E. *The Dred Scott Case: Its Significance in American Law and Politics.* New York: Oxford University Press, 2001.

———. *The Leadership of Abraham Lincoln.* New York: John Wiley & Sons, Inc., 1970.

———. *Lincoln in Text and Context: Collected Essays.* Stanford, CA: Stanford University Press, 1987.

———. *Prelude to Greatness: Lincoln in the 1850s.* Stanford: Stanford University Press, 1962.

———. *Sectional Crisis and Southern Constitutionalism.* Baton Rouge, LA: Louisiana State University Press, 1995.

Fehrenbacher, Don E., and Virginia Fehrenbacher, eds. *Recollected Words of Abraham Lincoln.* Stanford, CA: Stanford University Press, 1996.

Foner, Eric. *The Fiery Trial: Abraham Lincoln and American Slavery.* New York: W. W. Norton, 2010.

———. *Free Soil, Free Labor, Free Men: The Ideology of the Republican Party Before the Civil War.* New York: Oxford University Press, 1970.

———. *Politics and Ideology in the Age of the Civil War.* New York: Oxford University Press, 1980.

Forney, John W. *Anecdotes of Public Men.* New York: Harper & Brothers, 1873.

Fornieri, Joseph R. *Abraham Lincoln's Political Faith*. DeKalb, IL: Northern Illinois University Press, 2003.

———, ed. *The Language of Liberty: The Political Speeches and Writings of Abraham Lincoln*. Washington, DC: Regnery Publishing, 2003.

Franklin, John Hope. *The Emancipation Proclamation*. Wheeling, IL: Harlan Davidson, 1995.

French, Benjamin Brown. *Witness to the Young Republic: A Yankee's Journal, 1828–1870*. Hanover, NH: University Press of New England, 1989.

Gienapp, William. *Abraham Lincoln and Civil War America: A Biography*. New York: Oxford University Press, 2002.

Goodwin, Doris Kearns. *Team of Rivals: The Political Genius of Abraham Lincoln*. New York: Simon & Schuster, 2006.

Grant, Ulysses S. *Personal Memoirs of Ulysses S. Grant and Selected Letters, 1837–1865*. New York: Library of America, 1990.

Grimsted, David. *American Mobbing, 1828–1861, Toward Civil War*. New York: Oxford University Press, 1998.

Guelzo, Allen C. *Abraham Lincoln, Redeemer President*. Grand Rapids, MI: William B. Eerdmans Publishing Co., 1999.

———. *Gettysburg: The Last Invasion*. New York: Knopf, 2013.

———. *Lincoln and Douglas: The Debates That Defined America*. New York: Simon & Schuster, 2008.

———. *Lincoln's Emancipation Proclamation: The End of Slavery in America*. New York: Simon & Schuster, 2004.

Harris, William C. *Lincoln and the Border States: Preserving the Union*. Lawrence, KS: University Press of Kansas, 2011.

———. *Lincoln's Rise to the Presidency*. Lawrence, KS: University Press of Kansas, 2007.

———. *With Charity for All: Lincoln and the Restoration of the Union*. Lexington, KY: University Press of Kentucky, 1999.

Herndon, William H., and Jesse W. Weik. *Herndon's Life of Lincoln*. Cleveland: The World Publishing Company, 1949.

Holzer, Harold, ed. *Lincoln as I Knew Him: Gossip, Tributes and Revelations from His Best Friends and Worst Enemies*. Chapel Hill, NC: Algonquin Books, 1999.

———. *Lincoln at Cooper Union*. New York: Simon & Schuster, 2006.

———. *President-Elect Lincoln: Abraham Lincoln and the Great Secession Winter 1860–1861*. New York: Simon & Schuster, 2008.

Hubbard, Charles M., ed. *Lincoln Reshapes the Presidency*. Macon, GA: Mercer University Press, 2003.

Jaffa, Harry V. *Crisis in the House Divided*. Chicago: University of Chicago Press, 1959.

———. *A New Birth of Freedom: Abraham Lincoln and the Coming of the Civil War*. Lanham, MD: Rowman & Littlefield Publishers, Inc., 2000.

Jaffa, Harry V., and Robert W. Johannsen. *In the Name of the People: Speeches and Writings of Lincoln and Douglas in the Ohio Campaign of 1859*. Columbus, OH: Ohio State University Press, 1959.

Johannsen, Robert W. *Lincoln, the South, and Slavery: The Political Dimension*. Baton Rouge, LA: Louisiana State University Press, 1991.

———. *Stephen A. Douglas*. New York: Oxford University Press, 1973.

Johnson, Allen. *Stephen A. Douglas: A Study in American Politics*. New York: Da Capo Press, 1970.

Keegan, John. *The American Civil War*. New York: Alfred A. Knopf, 2009.

Lehrman, Lewis E. *Lincoln at Peoria.* Mechanicsburg, PA: Stackpole Books, 2008.

———. *Lincoln "by littles."* The Lehrman Institute, 2013.

Manning, Chandra. *What This Cruel War Was Over: Soldiers, Slavery and the Civil War.* New York: Random House, 2007.

McClintock, Russell. *Lincoln and the Decision for War: The Northern Response to Secession.* Chapel Hill, NC: University of North Carolina Press, 2008.

McPherson, James. *Abraham Lincoln and the Second American Revolution.* New York: Oxford University Press, 1990.

———. *Battle Cry of Freedom.* New York: Oxford University Press, 1988.

———. *For Cause and Comrades: Why Men Fought in the Civil War.* New York: Oxford University Press, 1997.

———. *Ordeal by Fire: The Civil War and Reconstruction.* New York: Alfred A. Knopf, 1982.

———. *Tried by War, Abraham Lincoln as Commander in Chief.* New York: Penguin Books, 2009.

McPherson, James, ed., *"We Cannot Escape History": Lincoln and the Last Best Hope of Earth.* Champaign, IL: University of Illinois Press, 2001.

Mearns, David C., ed. *The Lincoln Papers.* Garden City, NY: Doubleday, 1948.

Miller, William Lee. *Lincoln's Virtues: An Ethical Biography.* New York: Alfred A. Knopf, 2002.

———. *President Lincoln: The Duty of a Statesman.* New York: Random House LLC, 2009.

Mitgang, Herbert. *The Fiery Trial: A Life of Abraham Lincoln.* New York: Viking, 1974.

Mitgang, Herbert, ed. *Lincoln as They Saw Him.* Athens, GA: University of Georgia Press, 1956.

Morel, Lucas. *Lincoln's Sacred Effort: Defining Religion's Role in American Self-Government.* Lanham, MD: Lexington Books, 2000.

Neely Jr., Mark E. *The Civil War and the Limits of Destruction.* Cambridge: Harvard University Press, 2007.

———. *The Fate of Liberty: Abraham Lincoln and Civil Liberties.* New York: Oxford University Press, 1991.

———. *Lincoln and the Triumph of the Nation: Constitutional Conflict in the American Civil War.* Chapel Hill: University of North Carolina Press, 2011.

Neill, Edward Duffield. *Reminiscences of the Last Year of President Lincoln's Life.* St. Paul, MN: Pioneer Press Company, 1885.

Nevins, Allan. *The Emergence of Lincoln*, Volumes I & II. New York: Charles Scribner, 1950.

———. *The War for the Union*, Volumes I–IV. New York: Charles Scribner, 1975.

Nevins, Allan, and Irving Stone, eds. *Lincoln: A Contemporary Portrait.* Garden City, NY: Doubleday, 1962.

Nicolay, John G., and John Hay. *Abraham Lincoln: A History*, Volumes I–VIII. New York: The Century Co., 1914.

Niven, John. *The Coming of the Civil War, 1837–1861.* Arlington Heights, IL: Harlan Davidson, 1990.

———. *Salmon P. Chase: A Biography.* New York: Oxford University Press, 1995.

Oakes, James. *Freedom National: The Destruction of Slavery in the United States.* New York: W. W. Norton & Company, 2012.

———. *The Radical and the Republican: Frederick Douglass, Abraham Lincoln and the Triumph of Antislavery Politics.* New York: W. W. Norton and Company, 2007.

Oates, Stephen B. *With Malice Toward None: A Life of Abraham Lincoln.* New York: Harper Perennial, 1984.

Oldroyd, Osborne H. *The Lincoln Memorial: Album Immortelles.* New York: G. W. Carleton & Co., 1883.

Paludan, Phillip Shaw. *The Presidency of Abraham Lincoln.* Lawrence, KS: University Press of Kansas, 1994.

Pease, Theodore Calvin, ed. *The Diary of Orville Hickman Browning,* Volumes I and II. Springfield, IL: Illinois State Historical Library, 1925.

Peck, Graham, "Abraham Lincoln and the Triumph of an Antislavery Nationalism," *Journal of the Abraham Lincoln Association,* Summer 2007.

Pinsker, Matthew. *Lincoln's Sanctuary: Abraham Lincoln and the Soldier's Home.* New York: Oxford University Press, 2005.

Potter, David M. *The Impending Crisis, 1848–1861.* New York: Harper & Row, 1976.

———. *Lincoln and His Party in the Secession Crisis.* Baton Rouge, LA: Louisiana State University Press, 1995.

Quarles, Benjamin. *Lincoln and the Negro.* New York: Da Capo, 1991.

Randall, James G. *Lincoln the President: From Springfield to Gettysburg.* New York: Dodd, Mead & Company, 1945.

Rawley, James A. *Abraham Lincoln and a Nation Worth Fighting For.* Wheeling, IL: Harland Davidson, Inc., 1996.

Raymond, Henry J. *History of the Administration of President Lincoln: Including His Speeches, Letters, Addresses, Proclamations, and Messages.* New York: J.C. Derby & N.C. Miller, 1864.

Rice, Allen Thorndike, ed. *Reminiscences of Abraham Lincoln by Distinguished Men of His Time.* New York: North American Publishing Co., 1866.

Sandburg, Carl. *Abraham Lincoln: The War Years.* New York: Harcourt, Brace & World, 1939.

Scripps, John Locke. *Life of Abraham Lincoln.* Peoria, IL: 1860.

Simon, Paul. *Lincoln's Preparation for Greatness: The Illinois Legislative Years.* Urbana, IL: University of Illinois Press, 1989.

Stampp, Kenneth M. *And the War Came: The North and the Secession Crisis, 1860–61.* Baton Rouge, LA: Louisiana State University Press, 1950.

———. *The Peculiar Institution: Slavery in the Antebellum South.* New York: Vintage Books, 1989.

Stevens, Walter B. *A Reporter's Lincoln.* Michael Burlingame, ed. Lincoln, NE: University of Nebraska Press, 1998.

Stoddard, William O. *Abraham Lincoln: The True Story of a Great Life.* New York: Fords, Howard & Hulbert, 1884.

Stowell, Daniel W., ed. *Papers of Abraham Lincoln: Legal Documents and Cases.* Charlottesville, VA: University of Virginia Press, 2008.

Striner, Richard. *Lincoln and Race.* Carbondale, IL: Southern Illinois University Press, 2012.

Symonds, Craig L. *Lincoln and His Admirals: Abraham Lincoln, the U.S. Navy and the Civil War.* New York: Oxford University Press, 2008.

Tap, Bruce. *Over Lincoln's Shoulder: The Committee on the Conduct of the War.* Lawrence, KS: University Press of Kansas, 1998.

Thomas, Benjamin. *Abraham Lincoln.* New York: Alfred K. Knopf, Inc., 1973.

Vorenberg, Michael. *Final Freedom: The Civil War, the Abolition of Slavery, and the Thirteenth Amendment.* Cambridge, UK: Cambridge University Press, 2001.

Weed, Thurlow. *The Life of Thurlow Weed Including His Autobiography and a Memoir.* Boston: Houghton, Mifflin and Company, 1884.

Welles, Gideon. *The Diary of Gideon Welles,* Volumes I & II. Boston: Houghton Mifflin, 1911.

Wert, Jeffrey D. *The Sword of Lincoln.* New York: Simon and Schuster, 2005.

White Jr., Ronald C. *A. Lincoln: A Biography.* New York: Random House, 2009.

———. *The Eloquent President: A Portrait of Lincoln Through His Words.* New York: Random House, 2005.

Whitney, Henry Clay. *Life on the Circuit with Abraham Lincoln.* Caldwell, ID: Caxton Printers, 1940.

Williams, Frank J., William D. Pederson, and Vincent J. Marsala, eds. *Abraham Lincoln: Sources and Style of Leadership.* Westport, CT: Greenwood Press, 1994.

Wilson, Douglas L. *Honor's Voice: The Transformation of Abraham Lincoln.* New York: Knopf, 1998.

———. *Lincoln Before Washington.* Urbana, IL: University of Illinois Press, 1997.

———. *Lincoln's Sword: The Presidency and the Power of Words.* New York: Random House, 2011.

Wilson, Douglas L., and Rodney O. Davis, eds. *Herndon's Informants.* Urbana, IL: University of Illinois Press, 1998.

———. *Herndon's Lincoln.* Urbana, IL: University of Illinois Press, 2006.

———. *Lincoln Douglas Debates.* Urbana, IL: University of Illinois Press, 2008.

Wilson, Rufus Rockwell, ed. *Intimate Memories of Lincoln.* Elmira, NY: The Primavera Press, Inc., 1945.

———. *Lincoln Among His Friends.* Caldwell, ID: Caxton Printers, Ltd., 1942.

Winkle, Kenneth J. *The Young Eagle: The Rise of Abraham Lincoln.* Dallas, TX: Taylor Trade Publishing, 2001.

SELECTED BIBLIOGRAPHY
ON WINSTON S. CHURCHILL

Addison, Paul. *Churchill on the Home Front, 1900–1955*. London: Pimlico, 1993.
———. *Churchill: The Unexpected Hero*. New York: Oxford University Press, 2005.
Arnn, Larry. *Churchill's Trial: Winston Churchill and the Salvation of Free Government.* Nashville: Nelson Books, 2015.
Astley, Joan Bright. *The Inner Circle: A View of War at the Top*. Boston: Little, Brown and Company, 1971.
Barnett, Correlli. *The Audit of War*. London: Faber & Faber, Limited, 2011.
———. *The Collapse of British Power*. New York: William Morrow, 1972.
———. *The Desert Generals*. London: Orion, 2011.
———. *The Lords of War: From Lincoln to Churchill*. Barnsley, UK: Pen & Sword Books Limited, 2013.
Bell, Christopher M. *Churchill and Seapower*. Oxford: Oxford University Press, 2012.
Ben-Moshe, Tuvia. *Churchill: Strategy and History*. Boulder, CO: Lynne Rienner Publishers, 1991.
Bercuson, David, and Holger Herwig. *The Secret Meeting Between Roosevelt and Churchill That Changed the World*. Toronto: McArthur & Company, 2006.
Best, Geoffrey. *Churchill and War*. New York: Continuum International Publishing Group, 2006.
———. *Churchill: A Study in Greatness*. New York: Oxford University Press, 2003.
Blake, Robert, and William Roger Louis, eds. *Churchill*. Oxford: Oxford University Press, 1993.
Broad, Charles Lewis. *The War That Churchill Waged*. London: Hutchinson, 1960.
———. *Winston Churchill, 1874–1951*. New York: Philosophical Library, 1952.
Callahan, Raymond. *Churchill and His Generals*. Lawrence, KS: University Press of Kansas, 2007.
Charmley, John. *Churchill: The End of Glory, a Political Biography*. New York: Harcourt Brace & Company, 1993.
Churchill, Winston S. *Closing the Ring*, Volume V. New York: Houghton Mifflin, 1951.
———. *The Gathering Storm*, Volume I. New York: Houghton Mifflin, 1948.
———. *The Grand Alliance*, Volume III. New York: Houghton Mifflin, 1950.
———. *Great Contemporaries*. London: Octopus Publishing Group, 1990.
———. *The Great Republic*. New York: Modern Library, 2001.
———. *The Hinge of Fate*, Volume IV. New York: Houghton Mifflin, 1950.
———. *My Early Years*. New York: Charles Scribner's Sons, 1973.
———. *Their Finest Hour*, Volume II. New York: Houghton Mifflin, 1949.
———. *Thoughts and Adventures*. Wilmington, DE: ISI Books, 2009.

————. *Triumph and Tragedy*, Volume VI. New York: Houghton Mifflin, 1953.

Cohen, Eliot. *Supreme Command: Soldiers, Statesmen, and Leadership in Wartime*. New York: Simon and Schuster, 2012.

Colville, Jack. *Footprints in Time: Memories*. London: Collins, 1976.

————. *The Fringes of Power: The Incredible Inside Story of Winston Churchill During World War II*. Guilford, CT: Globe Pequot Press, 1985.

————. *Winston Churchill and His Inner Circle*. New York: Wyndham Books, 1981.

Connell, John [John Henry Robertson]. *Wavell, Scholar and Soldier*. New York: Harcourt, Brace & World, Inc., 1964.

Cunningham, Andrew. *A Sailor's Odyssey: The Autobiography of Admiral of the Fleet Viscount Cunningham of Hyndhope*. New York: Dutton, 1951.

Dallek, Robert. *Franklin D. Roosevelt and American Foreign Policy, 1932–1945*. New York: Oxford University Press, 1995.

Dalton, Baron Hugh. *The Second World War Diary of Hugh Dalton 1940–45*. London: Cape in association with the London School of Economics and Political Science, 1986.

Danchev, Alex, "'Dilly-Dally,' or Having the Last Word: Field Marshall Sir John Dill and Prime Minister Churchill," *Journal of Contemporary History*, Volume 22, 1987.

————. *Very Special Relationship: Field Marshal Sir John Dill and the Anglo-American Alliance 1941–44*. London: Brassey's Defence Publishers, 1986.

Danchev, Alex, and Daniel Todman, eds. *Field Marshal Lord Alanbrooke: War Diaries, 1939–1945*. London: Phoenix Press, 2002.

Dilks, David. *Churchill and Company*. London: I. B. Tauris, 2012.

————, ed. *The Diaries of Sir Alexander Cadogan, O.M., 1938–1945*. New York: G. P. Putnam's Sons, 1972.

Eade, Charles. *Churchill by His Contemporaries*. New York: Simon and Schuster, 1954.

Eden, Anthony. *Memoirs: The Reckoning*. Boston: Houghton Mifflin Co., 1965.

Eisenhower, Dwight D. *At Ease: Stories I Tell to Friends*. Philadelphia: Eastern Acorn Press, June 1981.

————. *The Eisenhower Diaries*. New York: Norton, 1981.

D'Este, Carlo. *Warlord: A Life of Winston Churchill at War, 1874–1945*. New York: Harper Perennial, 2009.

Fergusson, Bernard, ed. *The Business of War: The War Narrative of Major-General Sir John Kennedy*. London: Hutchinson of London, 1957.

Fraser, David. *Alanbrooke*. London: Hamlyn Paperback, 1983.

Gilbert, Martin. *Churchill and America*. New York: Simon and Schuster, 2008.

————. *Churchill, Finest Hour, 1939–1941*, Volume VI. Boston: Houghton Mifflin Company, 1983.

————. *Churchill: A Life*. New York: Henry Holt and Company, Inc., 1991.

————. *Churchill: The Power of Words*. Cambridge, MA: DaCapo Press, 2012.

————. *Churchill: Road to Victory, 1942–1945*, Volume VII. Boston: Houghton Mifflin Company, 1986.

————. *Churchill, War Leadership*. Knopf Doubleday Publishing Group, 2004.

————. *Churchill's Political Philosophy*. New York: Oxford University Press, 1981.

Harriman, William Averell, and Elie Able. *Special Envoy to Churchill and Stalin, 1941–1946*. New York: Random House, 1975.

Hastings, Max. *Winston's War: Churchill, 1940–1945*. New York: Vintage, 2011.

Hough, Richard. *Winston and Clementine: The Triumphs & Tragedies of the Churchills*. New York: Bantam Books, 1991.

Hull, Cordell. *The Memoirs of Cordell Hull.* New York: The Macmillan Company, 1948.

Ironside, Edmund. *Ironside Diaries, 1937–1940.* New York: David McKay Co., 1962.

Ismay, Hastings Lionel. *Memoirs of General Lord Ismay.* New York: Viking Press, 1960.

Jenkins, Roy. *Churchill.* New York: Plume, 2002.

Johnson, Paul. *Churchill.* New York: Viking, 2009.

Lamb, Richard. *Churchill as War Leader.* New York: Carroll & Graff Publisher, 1991.

Langworth, Richard. *Churchill by Himself: The Definitive Collection of Quotations.* New York: Public Affairs, 2008.

———. *Churchill in His Own Words.* London: Ebury Press, 2012.

———. *The Definitive Wit of Winston Churchill.* New York: Public Affairs, 2009.

———. *The Patriot's Churchill: An Inspiring Collection of Churchill's Finest Words.* London: Ebury Press, 2011.

Leasor, James, ed. *War at the Top: Based on the Experiences of General Sir Leslie Hollis.* London: Michael Joseph, 1959.

Lee, Celia, and John Lee. *The Churchills: A Family Portrait.* London: Palgrave Macmillan, 2010.

Lee, J. M. *The Churchill Coalition, 1940–1945.* Hamden, CT: Archon Books, 1980.

Lehrman, Lewis. *Churchill, Roosevelt & Company: Studies in Character and Statecraft.* Guilford, CT: Stackpole Books, 2017.

Lewin, Ronald. *Churchill as Warlord.* New York: Stein and Day, 1982.

Lukacs, John. *Churchill: Visionary, Statesman, Historian.* New Haven: Yale University Press, 2002.

———. *The Duel: 10 May–31 July 1940: The Eighty-Day Struggle Between Churchill and Hitler.* New York: Ticknor & Fields, 1991.

———. *Five Days in London, May 1940.* New Haven: Yale Note Bene, 1999.

Macmillan, Harold. *War Diaries, 1943–1945.* London: Macmillan, 1945.

Manchester, William. *The Last Lion: Visions of Glory, 1874–1932.* Boston: Little, Brown & Co, 1983.

———. *The Last Lion: Winston Spencer Churchill: Alone, 1932–1940.* Boston: Little, Brown & Co., 1988.

Manchester, William, and Paul Reid. *The Last Lion: Winston Spencer Churchill, Defender of the Realm, 1940–1965.* New York: Little, Brown and Company, 2012.

Martin, John. *Downing Street: The War Years.* London: Bloomsbury Publishing Limited, 1991.

Moran, Baron Charles McMoran Wilson. *Churchill Taken from the Diaries of Lord Moran: The Struggle for Survival, 1940–1965.* Boston: Houghton Mifflin, 1966.

Moseley, Leonard. *Marshall: Hero for Our Times.* New York: Hearst Books, 1982.

Nel, Elizabeth. *Winston Churchill by His Personal Secretary.* Lincoln, NE: iUniverse, 2007.

Nicolson, Nigel, ed. *Diaries and Letters of Sir Harold Nicolson.* London: Collins, 1967.

Norwich, John Julius, ed. *The Duff Cooper Diaries.* London: Weidenfeld & Nicolson, 2005.

Olson, Lynne. *Citizens of London: The Americans Who Stood with Britain in Its Darkest, Finest Hour.* New York: Random House Trade Paperbacks, 2011.

———. *Troublesome Young Men: The Rebels Who Brought Churchill to Power and Helped Save England.* New York: Farrar, Straus and Giroux, 2008.

Pawle, Gerald. *The War and Colonel Warden.* London: George G. Harrap, 1963.

Pearson, John. *The Private Lives of Winston Churchill.* New York: Touchstone Books, 1992.

Pelling, Henry. *Winston Churchill.* New York: E. P. Dutton & Co., Inc., 1974.

Pilpel, Robert H. *Churchill in America, 1895–1961: An Affectionate Portrait.* New York: Harcourt Brace Jovanovich, 1976.

Pogue, Forrest C. *George C. Marshall.* New York: Viking, 1966.

———. *George C. Marshall: Ordeal and Hope, 1939–1942.* New York: Viking, 1965.

Mark Pottle, ed. *Champion Redoubtable: The Diaries and Letters of Violet Bonham-Carter, 1914–1945.* London: Phoenix, 1999.

Reynolds, David. *In Command of History: Churchill Fighting and Writing the Second World War.* New York: Random House, 2005.

Rhodes James, Robert. *Churchill: A Study in Failure, 1900–1939.* London: Weidenfeld & Nicolson, 1990.

———, ed. *Churchill Speaks: Winston S. Churchill in Peace and War: Collected Speeches, 1897–1963.* London: Chelsea House, 1980.

Roberts, Andrew. *Eminent Churchillians.* New York: Simon & Schuster, 1994.

———. *A History of the English-Speaking Peoples Since 1900.* New York: Harper Perennial, 2008.

———. *Hitler and Churchill: Secrets of Leadership.* London: Weidenfeld & Nicolson, 2003.

———. *"The Holy Fox": A Biography of Lord Halifax.* London: Phoenix Giant, 1991.

———. *Masters and Commanders: How Four Titans Won the War in the West, 1941–1945.* New York: Harper, 2009.

———. *The Storm of War.* New York: Harper, 2011.

Roosevelt, Eleanor. *This I Remember.* New York: Harper & Brothers, 1949.

Rose, Jonathan. *The Literary Churchill: Author, Reader, Actor.* New Haven, CT: Yale University Press, 2015.

Rose, Norman. *Churchill: An Unruly Life.* New York: Simon & Schuster, 1994.

Schoenfeld, Maxwell Philip. *The War Ministry of Winston Churchill.* Ames, IA: Iowa State University Press, 1972.

Sherwood, Robert E. *Roosevelt and Hopkins: An Intimate History.* New York: Harper & Brothers, 1948.

Singer, Barry. *Churchill Style: The Art of Being Winston Churchill.* New York: Abrams, 2012.

Smith, Jean Edward. *FDR.* New York: Random House, 2007.

Soames, Mary. *Clementine Churchill: The Biography of a Marriage.* Boston: Houghton Mifflin Company, 1979.

———. *A Daughter's Tale.* New York: Random House, 2012.

———, ed. *Winston and Clementine: The Personal Letters of the Churchills.* Boston: Houghton-Mifflin Company, 1999.

Spears, Edward. *Assignment to Catastrophe: Prelude to Dunkirk, July 1939–May 1940.* New York: A. A. Wyn, 1954.

Stafford, David. *Roosevelt and Churchill: Men of Secrets.* Woodstock, NY: Overlook Press, 1999.

Stelzer, Cita. *Dinner with Churchill.* New York: Pegasus, 2012.

Taylor, A. J. P. *Beaverbrook: A Biography.* New York: Simon and Schuster, 1972.

———. *English History, 1914–1945.* New York: Oxford University Press, 1965.

Taylor, A. J. P., Robert Rhodes James, J. H. Plumb, Basil Liddell Hart, and Anthony Storr. *Churchill Revised.* New York: Dial Press, 1969.

Thompson, Reginald W. *Generalissimo Churchill.* New York: Charles Scribner's Sons, 1973.

————. *The Yankee Marlborough.* London: George Allen & Unwin, 1963.

Thompson, Walter H. *Assignment: Churchill.* New York: Farrar, Straus and Young, 1955.

————. *Beside the Bulldog: The Intimate Memoirs of Churchill's Bodyguard.* London: Apollo, 2003.

————. *Sixty Minutes with Winston Churchill.* London: C. Johnson, 1953.

Toye, Richard. *Churchill's Empire: The World That Made Him and the World He Made.* New York: Henry Holt and Co., 2010.

Wheeler-Bennett, John, ed. *Action This Day: Working with Churchill.* London: Macmillan, 1969.

Weisbrode, Kenneth. *Churchill and the King: The Wartime Alliance of Winston Churchill and George VI.* New York: Viking, 2013.

ENDNOTES

PREFACE: WARS OF NATIONAL SURVIVAL

1. Jonathan Rose, *The Literary Churchill: Author, Reader, Actor*, pp. 21–23.
2. Charles Winslow Elliott, *Winfield Scott: The Soldier and the Man*, p. 703.
3. John G. Nicolay and John Hay, *Abraham Lincoln*, Volume III, p. 394.
4. Roy P. Basler, ed., *The Collected Works of Abraham Lincoln (CWAL)*, Volume IV, p. 280.
5. Elizabeth Barker, *Churchill and Eden at War*, p. 143.
6. Norman Rose, *Churchill*, p. 325.
7. Winston S. Churchill, *Their Finest Hour: The Second World War*, Volume II, p. 88.
8. Winston S. Churchill, *The Great Democracies: A History of the English-Speaking Peoples*, p. 165.
9. Winston S. Churchill, *The Grand Alliance*, p. 551.
10. Winston S. Churchill, *The Great Republic: History of the English-Speaking Peoples*, Volume IV, p. 165.
11. *CWAL*, Volume VIII, p. 399 (April 11, 1865).
12. Winston S. Churchill, *Triumph and Tragedy: The Second World War*, Volume 6, p. 479.

PROLOGUE

1. Roy P. Basler, ed., *CWAL*, Volume VII, p. 512 (Speech to 166th Ohio, August 22, 1864).
2. Robert Rhodes James, ed., *Churchill Speaks*, p. 787 (Speech to Canadian Parliament, December 30, 1941).
3. John Colville, *The Fringes of Power: The Incredible Inside Story of Winston Churchill*, p. 170 (June 25, 1940).
4. Rufus Rockwell Wilson, ed., *Intimate Memories of Lincoln*, p. 131.
5. Eleanor Roosevelt, *This I Remember*, pp. 242–243.
6. Andrew Roberts, *Masters and Commanders: How Four Titans Won the War in the West, 1941–1945*, p. 59.
7. Winston S. Churchill, *Triumph and Tragedy: The Second World War*, Volume V, p. 342.

8. Michael Burlingame and John R. Turner Ettlinger, eds., *Inside Lincoln's White House: The Complete Civil War Diary of John Hay*, p. 289.

9. Dwight D. Eisenhower, *Crusade in Europe*, p. 105.

10. Correlli Barnett, *The Lords of War: From Lincoln to Churchill*, p. 13.

11. Michael Burlingame, ed., *Lincoln's Journalist: John Hay's Anonymous Writings for the Press, 1860–1864*, p. 130 (November 2, 1861).

12. R. Crosby Kemper II, ed., *Winston Churchill: Resolution, Defiance, Magnanimity, Good Will*, p. 134 (Robert Rhodes James, "Churchill, the Man").

13. Hastings Lionel Ismay, *Memoirs of General Lord Ismay*, p. 177.

14. Andrew Roberts, *Masters and Commanders: How Four Titans Won the War in the West, 1941–1945*, p. 106.

15. Geoffrey Best, *Churchill: A Study in Greatness*, p. 180.

16. *CWAL*, Volume II, p. 506 (Speech at Springfield, July 17, 1858).

17. Roy Jenkins, *Churchill: A Biography*, p. 511.

18. Roderick Macleod and Denis Kelly, eds., *Time Unguarded: The Ironside Diaries, 1937–1940*, p. 293 (May 3, 1940).

19. Robert Blake and William Roger, eds., *Churchill*, p. 28.

20. Isaiah Berlin, *Personal Impressions*, p. 7.

A COMPARISON

1. *CWAL*, Volume VI, p. 288 (Lincoln to Cadet Quintin Campbell, June 28, 1862).

2. Martin Gilbert, ed., *Churchill Speaks*, p. 288 (October 29, 1941).

3. Martin Gilbert, *Continue to Pester, Nag and Bite: Churchill's War Leadership*, p. 3.

4. Raymond Callahan, *Churchill and His Generals*, p. 9.

5. John Wheeler-Bennett, ed., *Action This Day: Working with Churchill*, pp. 225–226, 231.

6. Lincoln biographer Michael Burlingame observed: "Lack of egotism, a quality at the core of Lincoln's personality, won over many juries, colleagues, and judges. Judge [John M.] Scott noted, 'No lawyer on the circuit was more unassuming than was Mr. Lincoln. He arrogated to himself no superiority over any one—not even the most obscure member of the bar.'" Michael Burlingame, *Abraham Lincoln: A Life*, Volume I, p. 317.

7. Leslie Hollis, *One Mariner's Tale*, p. 141.

8. Lincoln was a principled but ambitious realist. There is a pragmatism even to Abraham Lincoln's selection of a wife. Lincoln's ambition was reflected in his courtship. He was not satisfied to marry those his father had married—women without education. Whether he courted Ann Rutledge, Mary Owens, or Mary Todd, he demonstrated a distinct ambition toward social advancement. Mary Todd was the product of Lexington's French finishing school and its first family.

9. Martin Gilbert, ed., *The Churchill War Papers: The Ever-Widening War, 1941*, p. 784 (June 10, 1941).

10. *CWAL*, Volume I, p. 8 (March 9, 1832).

11. The Soviet ambassador in London, Ivan Maisky, saw many sides of Churchill's personality and remarked on his boyishness. "Apropos Churchill's boyishness. He described to me in great detail the measures he took to prevent an attempt upon his life during the journey," wrote Maisky after a long meeting in February 1943. "He had everything you could think of: armoured cars, bullet-proof windows, automatic pistols and revolvers, secret buildings surrounded by armed guards, a sudden change of route, and much more besides. Sounded a bit like vaudeville. Of course, Churchill does have to take security measures. Yet, judging by the way he recounted his adventures, he got quite carried away by all this and approached it with quite boyish exaggeration." Gabriel Gorodetsky, ed., *Maisky Diaries: Red Ambassador to the Court of St. James's 1932–1943*, pp. 480–482 (February 9, 1945).

12. Robert Rhodes James, ed., *Winston S. Churchill: His Complete Speeches, 1897–1963: 1897–1908*, Volume I, p. 110.

13. Charles McMoran Wilson Moran, *Churchill, Taken from the Diaries of Lord Moran: The Struggle for Survival, 1940–1965*, p. 132 (October 29, 1943).

14. Robert Rhodes James, *Churchill: A Study in Failure, 1900–1939*, pp. 17–18.

15. Carlo D'Este, *Warlord*, p. 382.

16. *CWAL*, Volume III, p. 323 (Seventh and Last Debate with Stephen A. Douglas at Alton, Illinois, October 15, 1858).

17. Steven E. Woolworth and Kenneth J. Winkle, *Atlas of the Civil War*, p. 52. Estimates of the number of soldiers who served in the Union army range from about 1.5 to 2.4 million.

18. Correlli Barnett, *The Lords of War: From Lincoln to Churchill*, p. 286. John Colville wrote: "Churchill was essentially a romantic, and although he only once wrote a poem—as a boy of fifteen—he was a poet at heart. Describing the scene in 1940, he wrote of 'a white glow, overpowering, sublime, which ran through our island from end to end.' None but a poet could have written that; and listening as I did, usually in the House of Commons, to all those famous 1940 speeches, I was conscious of an unquenchable fire that burned within him, of a bright flame that gave a blaze to his eloquence." R. Crosby Kemper II, ed., *Winston Churchill: Resolution, Defiance, Magnanimity, Good Will*, p. 121 (John R. Colville, "The Personality of Winston Churchill"). John Keegan wrote: "Churchill the aristocrat was also Churchill the populist: in either guise he was always, close beneath the skin, Churchill the romantic. He romanticized the history of his country and, in so doing, easily romanticized its people." John Keegan, *Winston Churchill: A Life*, p. 8.

19. Baron Charles McMoran Wilson Moran, *Churchill: Taken from the Diaries of Lord Moran: The Struggle for Survival, 1940–1965*, p. 273 (June 22, 1945).

20. Winston S. Churchill, *Their Finest Hour: The Second World War*, Volume II, p. 315.

21. Winston S. Churchill, *The Great Republic: A History of America*, p. 182.

22. *CWAL*, Volume V, p. 292 (Lincoln to William H. Seward, June 28, 1862).

23. Don Fehrenbacher and Virginia Fehrenbacher, eds., *Recollected Words of Abraham Lincoln*, p. 249 (William H. Herndon to Jesse Weik, December 22, 1988).

24. Allen Thorndike Rice, ed., *Reminiscences of Abraham Lincoln*, p. 577 (John B. Alley).

25. Noah Brooks, *Abraham Lincoln: The Nation's Leader in the Great Struggle Through Which Was Maintained the Existence of the United States*, p. 426.

26. Richard Toye, *Lloyd George & Churchill: Rivals for Greatness*, p. 1.

27. Henry Clay Whitney, *Life on the Circuit with Lincoln*, pp. 112–113.

28. Harold Holzer, ed., *Lincoln As I Knew Him*, p. 130 (Marquis de Chambrun).

29. *CWAL*, Volume IV, pp. 268–269 (First Inaugural Address, March 4, 1861).

30. *CWAL*, Volume VIII, p. 332 (Second Inaugural Address, March 4, 1865).

31. Martin Gilbert, *Churchill: A Life*, p. 623 (Speech in House of Commons, September 3, 1939).

32. Winston S. Churchill, *Great Contemporaries*, p. 131.

33. John Kennedy, *The Business of War*, p. 249.

34. Saul Kussiel Padover, ed., *Karl Marx on America and the Civil War*, p. xxvi.

35. Henry Clay Whitney, *Life on the Circuit with Lincoln*, p. 147. William H. Herndon wrote: "The convolutions of his brain were long; they did not snap off quickly like a short, thick man's brain. . . . The enduring power of Mr. Lincoln's thought and brain was wonderful. He could sit and think without food or rest longer than any man I ever saw." William E. Barton, *The Soul of Abraham Lincoln*, p. 266 (William H. Herndon to Truman H. Bartlett).

36. Biographer Norman Rose wrote: "Patrician by birth, outlook, and behaviour, those around him were left little option but to subordinate their wants to his whims. Nor did he find this strange; it was simply the natural order of things. His super-ego would allow nothing else." Norman Rose, *Churchill: An Unruly Life*, p. 344. Historian John Charmley wrote: "That he was a great man cannot be doubted, but his flaws too were on the same heroic scale as the rest of men." John Charmley, *The End of Glory*, p. 648.

37. Paul Addison, *Churchill: The Unexpected Hero*, p. 173.

I. MEN OF CHARACTER: QUINTESSENTIAL LEADERS WITH DIFFERENT PERSONALITIES

1. *CWAL*, Volume IV, p. 109 (Address Before the Young Men's Lyceum of Springfield, Illinois, January 27, 1838).
2. Martin Gilbert, *Winston S. Churchill: Finest Hour, 1939–1941*, p. 665.
3. Roy Jenkins, *Churchill*, p. 300.
4. Walter Thompson, *Beside the Bulldog: The Intimate Memoirs of Churchill's Bodyguard*, p. 86.
5. John Keegan, *Winston Churchill: A Life*, p. 153.
6. Martin Gilbert, *Winston S. Churchill: Finest Hour 1939–1941*, Volume VI, p. 336.
7. Allen Thorndike Rice, ed., *Reminiscences of Abraham Lincoln*, p. 175 (Charles Carlton Coffin).
8. Osborn H. Oldroyd, ed., *The Lincoln Memorial: Album-Immortelles*, p. 462 (Joseph Gillespie).
9. Churchill's family was aristocratic but not distinguished. Historian David Cannadine noted that many fellow aristocrats viewed the family with disdain. To a large extent, they were a collection of aristocratic misfits whose behavior was occasionally scandalous. Cannadine wrote: "In some sense, young Winston may indeed have been a self-made man. But he was also, by birth and by connection, a member of Britain's charmed 'inner circle,' and he early on learned how to pull its strings to his own advantage." Robert Blake and William Roger Louis, eds., *Churchill: A Major New Assessment of His Life in Peace and War*, p. 10 (David Cannadine, "The Pitfalls of Family Piety").
10. Richard Langworth, ed., *Churchill by Himself*, p. 579. Churchill was elaborating on a comment originally made by his friend F. E. Smith, who had said: "Churchill is easily satisfied with the best." Langworth wrote: "Churchill with his great memory could quite easily have repeated and embroidered on Birkenhead's remark when he visited the Plaza Hotel in New York shortly after Birkenhead's death, in 1931, as is sometimes recorded." Churchill admitted to his mother that, like her, he was "spendthrift and extravagant." David Lough, *No More Champagne: Churchill and His Money*, p. 46 (Letter from Churchill to Jennie Churchill, January 1897).
11. David Davis recalled that Lincoln "was the most simple and unostentatious of men in his habits, having few wants, and those easily supplied." Rufus Rockwell Wilson, ed., *Intimate Memories of Lincoln*, p. 69 (David Davis). Michael Burlingame wrote that Lincoln once "told a potential client to seek out John Todd Stuart [Lincoln's former law partner], explaining that 'he's a better lawyer than I am.'" Michael Burlingame, *Abraham Lincoln: A Life*, Volume I, p. 351. Joseph Gillespie wrote: "It required no effort on his part to admit another man's superiority."

Douglas Lawson Wilson and Rodney O. Davis, eds., *Herndon's Informants: Letters, Interviews, and Statements about Abraham Lincoln*, p. 187 (Joseph Gillespie to William H. Herndon, January 31, 1866).

12. John Pearson, *The Private Lives of Winston Churchill*, p. 282.

13. William Manchester, *The Last Lion: Visions of Glory, 1874–1932*, p. 26.

14. David Reynolds, *In Command of History: Churchill Fighting and Writing the Second World War*, p. 40.

15. Douglas L. Wilson and Rodney O. Davis, eds., *Herndon's Informants: Letters, Interviews, and Statements about Abraham Lincoln*, p. 331 (John Hay to William H. Herndon, September 5, 1866).

16. John Kennedy, *The Business of War*, p. 275.

17. William Manchester, *Last Lion: Visions of Glory, 1874–1932*, p. 6.

18. Historian Ronald Lewin argued that Churchill "was excessive in emotion; in egocentricity; in physical and mental energy; excessive in his single-minded concentration on selected objectives. ('Excessive' is here used not in a pejorative sense, but to mean 'far above the average.') For a war leader these traits were at once a strength and a weakness, but they had been evident in Churchill's character since his earliest days and by 1940 nothing could change him." He added: "During the Second World War . . . his egomania was far from being diminished: if anything it was intensified." Ronald Lewin, *Churchill as Warlord*, p. 3.

19. William O. Stoddard, *Abraham Lincoln: The True Story of a Great Life*, p. 403.

20. John Colville, *The Fringes of Power*, p. 126.

21. The devotion of Churchill's staff would become legendary. Chef Georgina Landemare worked virtually around the clock to make sure that Churchill could eat whenever he wanted. Barry Singer, *Churchill Style: The Art of Becoming Winston Churchill*, pp. 152–153.

22. Max Hastings, *Winston's War: Churchill 1940–1945*, p. 190.

23. Lincoln secretary John Nicolay claimed that this was the sole occasion when he heard President Lincoln swear. Michael Burlingame, ed., *With Lincoln in the White House: Letters, Memoranda, and Other Writings of John G. Nicolay*, p. 217.

24. *CWAL*, Volume V, p. 474 (Lincoln to George B. McClellan, October 25, 1862).

25. After a rare wartime visit to his Chartwell home in April 1942, Churchill wrote his son Randolph: "The goose I called naval aide-de-camp and the male black swan have both fallen victims to the fox. The Yellow Cat however made me sensible of his continuing friendship, although I had not been there for eight months." Martin Gilbert, *Winston S. Churchill: Road to Victory 1941–1945*, p. 99 (Churchill to Randolph Churchill, May 2, 1942). Three years later, on April 6, 1945, Churchill wrote his wife: "One big goldfish was retrieved from the bottom of the pool at Chartwell. All the rest have been stolen, or else eaten by an otter. I have

put Scotland Yard on the work of finding the thief. I fear we shall never see our poor fish any more." Mary Soames, ed., *Winston and Clementine: The Personal Letters of the Churchills*, p. 523.

26. See https://www.nationalchurchillmuseum.org/winston-churchill -biography.html.

27. Cita Stelzer, *Dinner with Churchill*, p. 237.

28. By 1937, Churchill's extravagant lifestyle had effectively bankrupted him; his creditors and tax authorities were demanding money that he did not have. Churchill even put Chartwell on the market in the spring of 1938; he was saved only by a bailout by industrialist Henry Strakosch. Churchill badly needed the money that his writing paid him; he was hard at work on his *History of the English-Speaking Peoples* when Germany invaded Poland; his appointment to the cabinet closed down his paid writing options but provided him with government-paid accommodations. David Lough, *No More Champagne: Churchill and His Money*, pp. 256–265, 281–284.

29. In 1858, future Secretary of War Edwin M. Stanton described Lincoln: "A long, lank creature from Illinois, wearing a dirty linen duster for a coat." James G. Randall, *Lincoln the President: Springfield to Gettysburg*, p. 27.

30. "Lincoln's dress was always, both by compulsion and choice, of that commonplace respectability equally free from shabbiness on the one hand, and pretentious effort at display of gentility on the other." John G. Nicolay, "Lincoln's Personal Appearance," *Century Illustrated Monthly Magazine*, October 1891, Volume 42, p. 936. In contrast, Stephen Douglas clothed himself in a pretentious display of gentility. Biographer Damon Wells described Douglas in the 1858 debates as "turned out in what was in those days known as plantation style, complete with ruffled shirt, dark blue coat with shiny buttons, and a broad-brimmed felt hat." Damon Wells, *Stephen Douglas: The Last Years, 1857–1861*, p. 86.

31. Barry Singer wrote: "By far Churchill's favorite uniform was not a uniform at all but a garment he designed himself—his 'siren suit,' a zip-up all-in-one that his children referred to as his 'rompers.' Though ideally suited to hurried dressing at the sound of an air raid siren, the siren-suit had, in fact, been conceived and designed by Churchill before the war in imitation of the boiler suits worn by his fellow bricklayers at Chartwell." Barry Singer, *Churchill Style: The Art of Being Winston Churchill*, p. 172. Churchill sometimes combined his siren suit with his red, green, and gold dressing gown. Geoffrey Best, *Churchill and War*, p. 119.

32. Churchill used his own American ancestry when convenient. "My mother was American and my ancestors were officers in Washington's army, I am myself an English-Speaking Union," Churchill observed after the war. Dwight D. Eisenhower, "The Churchill I Knew," *National Geographic*, Volume 128, No. 2 (August 1965), pp. 153–157.

33. In an interview with a University of Michigan law student in 1901, Churchill observed: "I was lucky enough to start with a name very well known in England, and as you know, a name counts a great deal with us. In your country it is somewhat of a handicap to have a great father—few of your great men have had great sons." Gustavus A. Ohlinger, "WSC: A Midnight Interview," *Finest Hour,* Summer 2013, p. 35 (First published in *Michigan Quarterly Review,* February 1966).

34. Max Hastings, *Winston's War, Churchill 1940–1945,* p. 481.

35. Lincoln was very close to his youngest sons, but maintained an uneven relationship with his oldest son, Robert, who complained that he seldom had a lengthy conversation with his father in the White House. Jason Emerson, *The Life of Robert Todd Lincoln,* p. 81. Until 1865, Robert was thwarted in his desire to serve in the army by his mother's morbid fear of losing him after she lost son Willie in February 1862. Churchill's relations with his pampered only son, Randolph, who served honorably in special forces during World War II, was far more contentious. "I love Randolph, but I don't like him." Max Hastings, *Winston's War,* p. 225.

36. Celia and John Lee refuted the standard contentions that Randolph Churchill died of syphilis. Celia Lee and John Lee, *The Churchills: A Family Portrait,* pp. 230–235.

37. Winston S. Churchill, *The Gathering Storm: The Second World War,* Volume I, p. 66 (May 13, 1932).

38. Martin Gilbert, ed., *Churchill: The Power of Words: His Remarkable Life Recounted Through His Writings and Speeches,* pp. 189–191 (March 23, 1933).

39. Martin Gilbert, ed., *Churchill: The Power of Words: His Remarkable Life Recounted Through His Writings and Speeches,* p. 197 (September 1, 1935).

40. *CWAL,* Volume II, p. 355 (Speech at Galena, Illinois, July 23, 1856).

41. *CWAL,* Volume IV, p. 150 (Lincoln to Lyman Trumbull, December 10, 1860). Questioned by the New York delegation before his inauguration about his intentions as president, Lincoln responded: "If I shall ever come to the great office of President of the United States, I shall take an oath. I shall swear that I will faithfully execute the office of President of the United States, of all the United States, and that I will, to the best of my ability, preserve, protect, and defend the Constitution of the United States. This is a great and solemn duty. With the support of the people and the assistance of the Almighty I shall undertake to perform it. I have full faith that I shall perform it. It is not the Constitution as I would like to have it, but as it is, that is to be defended. The Constitution will not be preserved and defended until it is enforced and obeyed in every part of every one of the United States. It must be so respected, obeyed, enforced, and defended, let the grass grow where it may." Lucius Eugene Chittenden, *Recollections of President Lincoln and His Administration,* p. 75.

42. *CWAL*, Volume IV, p. 159 (Lincoln to David Hunter, December 22, 1860).

43. *CWAL*, Volume IV, p. 237 (Speech to New Jersey State Assembly, February 21, 1861).

44. *CWAL*, Volume IV, pp. 252, 269 (First Inaugural Address, March 4, 1861).

45. *CWAL*, Volume IV, p. 332 (Proclamation Calling the Militia and Convening Congress, April 15, 1861).

46. *CWAL*, Volume IV, p. 341 (Remarks to a delegation from Baltimore, April 22, 1861).

47. *CWAL*, Volume IV, p. 426 (Special Message to Congress, July 4, 1861).

48. *CWAL*, Volume V, p. 51 (First Annual Message to Congress, December 3, 1861).

49. Winston S. Churchill, *Blood, Sweat and Tears*, pp. 58–59. (Speech at House of Commons, October 5, 1938).

50. Historian Robert Blake wrote of Churchill's Munich speech: "When he uttered the words 'we have sustained a total and unmitigated defeat,' he had to pause for some moments in face of the angry storm of protest which followed. His peroration was heard in silence but it was to be remembered later: 'And do not suppose that this is the end. This is only the beginning of the reckoning. This is only the first sip, the first foretaste of a bitter cup which will be proffered to us year by year unless by a supreme recovery of moral health and martial vigour, we rise again and take our stand for freedom as in the olden time." Robert Blake and William Roger Louis, eds., *Churchill: A Major New Assessment of His Life in Peace and War*, p. 260 (Robert Blake, "How Churchill Became Prime Minister").

51. Martin Gilbert, *Churchill: The Power of Words: His Remarkable Life Recounted Through His Writings and Speeches*, p. 203 (Speech at the House of Commons, October 5, 1938).

52. A hero requires a worthy antagonist. Stephen A. Douglas was that antagonist for more than two decades. "I have often thought of the characters of the two great rivals, Lincoln and Douglas," recalled Lincoln's longtime friend Joshua F. Speed. "They seemed to have been pitted against each other from 1836 till Lincoln reached the Presidency. They were the respective leaders of their parties in the State. They were as opposite in character as they were unlike in their persons. Lincoln was long and ungainly. Douglas, short and compact. Douglas, in all elections, was the moving spirit in the conduct and management of an election, he was not content without a blind submission to himself. He could not tolerate opposition to his will within his party organization. He held the reins and controlled the movement of the Democratic chariot. With a large State majority, with many able and ambitious men in it, he stepped to the front in his youth and held it till his death."

Joshua Fry Speed, *Reminiscences of Abraham Lincoln and Notes of a Visit to California*, p. 35 (J. P. Morton and Company, 1884).

53.   *CWAL*, Volume II, p. 274 (Speech at Peoria, October 16, 1854).

54.   *CWAL*, Volume III, p. 315 (Alton Debate, October 15, 1858).

55.   *CWAL*, Volume VII, p. 281 (Letter to Albert Hodges, April 4, 1864).

56.   *CWAL*, Volume II, p. 482 (ca. July, 1858).

57.   John Colville, *The Fringes of Power*, pp. 125, 127.

58.   Michael Burlingame, *Abraham Lincoln: A Life*, Volume I, p. 356.

59.   Michael Burlingame, ed., *An Oral History of Abraham Lincoln, John G. Nicolay's Interviews and Essays*, p. 6 (Conversation with Orville H. Browning, June 17, 1875).

60.   Michael Burlingame and John R. Turner Ettlinger, eds., *Inside Lincoln's White House: The Complete Civil War Diary of John Hay*, p. 219 (July 4, 1864).

61.   Douglas L. Wilson and Rodney O. Davis, eds., *Herndon's Informants*, p. 499 (Joshua F. Speed to William H. Herndon, December 6, 1866).

62.   Andrew Roberts, *A History of the English-Speaking Peoples Since 1900*, p. 280.

63.   In 1942 British Admiral Andrew B. Cunningham wrote about "a lunch at 10 Downing Street with two American Generals, and the Prime Minister being full of new ideas for confounding our enemies. The conversation switched to the battles of the American Civil War, about which Mr. Churchill's knowledge was amazing. I confided to my relative that I thought him 'an extraordinary man!'" Andrew B. Cunningham, *Sailor's Odyssey: The Autobiography of Admiral of the Fleet, Viscount Cunningham of Hyndhope*, p. 476.

64.   At Harrow School, recalled Churchill, "I got into my bones the essential structure of the ordinary British sentence—which is a noble thing." Martin Gilbert, *Churchill: A Life*, p. 24.

65.   William H. Herndon and Jesse W. Weik, *Herndon's Lincoln*, p. 15.

66.   Isaac N. Arnold, *The Life of Abraham Lincoln*, p. 443.

67.   Gerald Pawle, *The War and Colonel Warden*, p. 204.

68.   Joshua Speed recalled: "The Bible, Esop's Fables, Weems's Life of Washington, and Bunyan's Pilgrim's Progress. These he almost committed to memory. From these I suppose he got his style. His mind was not quick, but solid and retentive. It was like polished steel, a mark once made upon it was never erased. His memory of events, of facts, dates, faces, and names, surprised every one." Joshua Fry Speed, *Reminiscences of Abraham Lincoln and Notes of a Visit to California*, pp. 38–39.

69.   Roy Jenkins, *Churchill: A Biography*, p. 466.

70.   John Colville, *The Fringes of Power: The Incredible Inside Story of Winston Churchill*, p. 285 (November 3, 1940).

71.   Martin Gilbert, *Continue to Pester, Nag and Bite: Churchill's War Leadership*, p. 12.

72. Winston S. Churchill, *The Grand Alliance, The Second World War*, p. 602. Speaking to the House of Commons in March 1938 after the German Anschluss, Churchill said: "For five years I have talked to the House on these matters—not with very great success. I have watched this famous island descending incontinently, fecklessly, the stairway which leads to a dark gulf. It is a fine broad stairway at the beginning, but after a bit the carpet ends. A little further on there are only flagstones, and a little farther on still these break beneath your feet." Martin Gilbert, *Winston Churchill*, Volume V, p. 927.

73. Martin Gilbert, *Churchill and America*, p. 226.

74. *CWAL*, Volume VII, p. 499 (Lincoln to Ulysses S. Grant, August 17, 1864).

75. Francis B. Carpenter, *The Inner Life of Abraham Lincoln: Six Months at the White House*, p. 283.

76. John Colville, *The Fringes of Power*, p. 476. Both liked animal metaphors. After the Battle of Chickamauga, Lincoln described Union General William S. Rosecrans as "confused and stunned like a duck hit on the head." Michael Burlingame and John R. Turner Ettlinger, eds., *The Complete Civil War Diary of John Hay*, p. 99 (October 24, 1863).

77. Winston S. Churchill, *The Great Republic*, p. 214.

78. Winston S. Churchill, *The Great Republic*, p. 149.

79. Winston S. Churchill, *The Great Republic*, p. 159.

80. *CWAL*, Volume VIII, p. 405 (Last Public Address, April 11, 1865).

81. Carlo D'Este, *Warlord*, pp. 307–308 (November 23, 1932).

82. *CWAL*, Volume II, pp. 461–462 (House Divided Speech at Springfield, June 16, 1858).

83. Charles Eade, *Churchill—by His Contemporaries*, pp. 271–272 (Leslie Hore-Belisha, "How Churchill Influences and Persuades").

II. THE UNLIKELY EMERGENCE OF LINCOLN AND CHURCHILL

1. *CWAL*, Volume IV, p. 376 (Lincoln to Henry L. Pierce, April 6, 1859).

2. Martin Gilbert, *Churchill: The Power of Words: His Remarkable Life Recounted Through His Writings and Speeches*, p. 195 (June 7, 1935).

3. Carlo D'Este wrote that "Chamberlain was hopelessly ill prepared and lacked the state of mind and the resolve necessary to be an effective war leader." Carlo D'Este, *Warlord: A Life of Winston Churchill at War, 1874–1945*, p. 347.

4. Baron Hugh Dalton, *Memoirs: The Fateful Years, 1931–1945*, p. 198.

5. Jonathan Schneer, *Ministers at War: Winston Churchill and His War Cabinet*, p. 37.

6. Winston S. Churchill, *The Gathering Storm: The Second World War*, Volume I, p. 597.

7. Andrew Roberts, *"The Holy Fox": The Life of Lord Halifax*, p. 205.

8. Adam Kirsch, *Benjamin Disraeli*, p. 188 (New York: Knopf Doubleday Publishing Group, 2008).

9. Walter Thompson recalled: "As he turned away he muttered something to himself. Then he set his jaw and with a look of determination, mastering all emotion, he began to climb the stairs of the Admiralty." Walter Thompson, *I Was Churchill's Bodyguard*, p. 37.

10. Martin Gilbert, *Churchill: The Power of Words: His Remarkable Life Recounted Through His Writings and Speeches*, p. 249 (June 17, 1940).

11. Seward had delivered a number of speeches that highlighted his opposition to slavery and its incompatibility with American democracy. Opposing the Compromise of 1850 on the Senate floor, Seward declared that "a higher law than the Constitution" existed. On August 26, 1852, Seward had delivered a speech "Freedom National; Slavery Sectional." On October 27, 1858, Seward delivered a similar speech in Rochester, New York. Lincoln had said comparable things, but Seward was perceived as more radical.

12. John Wheeler-Bennett, ed., *Action This Day: Working with Churchill*, pp. 48–49 (John Colville).

13. John Wheeler-Bennett, ed., *Action This Day: Working with Churchill*, p. 162 (Ian Jacob).

14. Lord Chandos, *The Memoirs of Lord Chandos*, p. 181.

15. Allan Nevins, *The Emergence of Lincoln: Douglas, Buchanan, and Party Chaos, 1857–1859*, Volume I, pp. 354–355.

16. Douglas Wilson and Roderick Davis, eds., *Herndon's Informants*, p. 348 (Interview with David Davis, September 20, 1866).

17. Winston S. Churchill, *Thoughts and Adventures*, pp. 11–12.

18. *Abraham Lincoln: Tributes from His Associates*, p. 45 (William O. Stoddard, "Lincoln's Vigil").

19. *CWAL*, Volume V, pp. 535, 537 (Second Annual Message to Congress, December 1, 1862).

20. Winston S. Churchill, *The Gathering Storm: The Second World War*, Volume I, p. 601.

21. *CWAL*, Volume IV, p. 423 (Message to Congress, July 4, 1861).

22. Correlli Barnett, *The Collapse of British Power*, p. 583.

23. John Lukacs, *Five Days in London*, May 1940, p. 67.

24. Martin Gilbert, *Continue to Pester, Nag and Bite: Winston Churchill's War Leadership*, p. 21.

25. Roy Jenkins, *Churchill*, p. 608.

26. John Lukacs, *The Duel: The Eighty-Day Struggle Between Churchill and Hitler*, p. 97.

27. Geoffrey Best, *Churchill and War*, p. 115.

28. William Manchester and Paul Reid, *The Last Lion: Winston Spencer Churchill, Defender of the Realm, 1940–1965*, p. 82.

29. *CWAL*, Volume IV, p. 265 (First Inaugural Address, March 4, 1861). The law as principle was very important to Lincoln. Nearly seven decades after he first heard Abraham Lincoln speak in 1859, an Indiana journalist recalled: "The part of the speech . . . which most strongly impressed

me, at the time, and has remained the longest in my memory is what he said about reverence for the law. I noticed that he never used the term obedience to the law, but always reverence, seeming to regard that term higher and more comprehensive than the other." Rufus Rockwell Wilson, ed., *Intimate Memories of Lincoln*, p. 269 (William H. Smith).

30.   British civil servant Norman Brook observed: "His general method of work was to concentrate his personal attention on the two or three things that mattered most at any given moment, and to give to each of these all the time and attention that it merited. He had a remarkable intuitive capacity for picking out the questions on which he could most usefully concentrate his effort." John Wheeler-Bennett, ed., *Action This Day: Working with Churchill*, p. 21.

31.   Winston S. Churchill, *Their Finest Hour: The Second World War*, Volume II, p. 24.

32.   Winston S. Churchill, *Their Finest Hour: The Second World War*, Volume II, p. 154.

33.   Churchill remarked about Dunkirk to his bodyguard: "Thompson, I thought we should be lucky if we got away safely twenty thousand, but now, thank God, ninety thousand are already back in England, and we hope for many more to come." Walter Thompson, *Sixty Minutes with Winston Churchill*, p. 52. Although Britain was able to evacuate much of its personnel at Dunkirk through Operation DYNAMO, it lost over 60,000 motor vehicles and 475 tanks, tons of ammunition, and thousands of rifles. Manchester and Reid wrote: "Altogether, Dynamo had rescued 338,226 Allied soldiers, 112,000 of them French, although a greater number of French troops turned and went home, to take their chances." William Manchester and Paul Reid, *The Last Lion: Winston Spencer Churchill: Defender of the Realm, 1940–1965*, p. 86.

34.   Winston S. Churchill, *Their Finest Hour: The Second World War*, Volume II, p. 205.

35.   Viscount Andrew Browne Cunningham, *A Sailor's Odyssey: The Autobiography of Admiral of the Fleet, Viscount Cunningham of Hyndhope*, p. 244. The Confederate capture of the Union fleet at Norfolk in the spring of 1861 was Lincoln's Oran, but the Union commander failed to follow orders to destroy the fleet at that Virginia naval base rather than allow it to fall into Confederate control.

36.   Historian Norman Davies wrote: "Britain's victory in the air was crucial on three scores. It gave the Allied cause an impregnable base, where the vastly superior land forces of the Continent could never be brought to bear. Secondly, by turning Britain into 'the world's most unsinkable aircraft carrier,' it secured a platform for the sensational growth of Allied air power—the decisive element of the war in the West. Thirdly, on the diplomatic front, it gained a breathing-space within which the latent alliance of the English-Speaking world could mature." Norman Davies, *A History of Europe*, p. 1008.

37. Winston Churchill, *Their Finest Hour: The Second World War*, Volume II, p. 297.

38. Lord Ismay, *The Memoirs of General Lord Ismay*, pp. 181–182.

39. Martin Gilbert, *Churchill: The Power of Words: His Remarkable Life Recounted Through His Writings and Speeches*, p. 275.

40. Paul Johnson, *Churchill*, p. 113.

41. *CWAL*, Volume IV, p. 121 (Lincoln to John M. Brockman, September 25, 1860).

42. *CWAL*, Volume IV, p. 556 (Lincoln to George Ramsay, October 17, 1861).

43. *Abraham Lincoln: Tributes from His Associates*, p. 45 (William O. Stoddard, "Lincoln's Vigil").

44. George Yeaman, "Abraham Lincoln: An address before the Commandery of the State of Colorado, Military Order of the Loyal Legion of the United States," February 13, 1899, pp. 7–8.

45. Charles A. Dana, *Recollections of the Civil War*, p. 173.

46. Churchill had ordered on July 19, 1940 "that all directions emanating from me are made in writing, or should be immediately afterwards confirmed in writing." Winston S. Churchill, *Their Finest Hour*, p. 17.

47. William Manchester and Paul Reid, *The Last Lion: Winston Spencer Churchill, Defender of the Realm, 1940–1965*, p. 207.

48. John Colville, *Footprints in Time: Memories*, p. 78.

49. Harold Macmillan, *War Diaries, 1943–1945*, p. 339.

50. General Scott's memorandum to the president read: "It is doubtful, according to recent information from the South, whether the voluntary evacuation of Fort Sumter alone would have a decisive effect upon the States now wavering between adherence to the Union and secession. It is known, indeed, that it would be charged to necessity, and the holding of Fort Pickens would be adduced in support of that view. Our Southern friends, however, are clear that the evacuation of both the forts would instantly soothe and give confidence to the eight remaining slave-holding States, and render their cordial adherence to this Union perpetual." John G. Nicolay and John Hay, *Abraham Lincoln: A History*, Volume III, p. 394. President Lincoln did not accept this advice. "I am directed by the President," wrote Secretary of War Simon Cameron to Scott, "to say that he desires you to exercise all vigilance for the maintenance of all the places within the military department of the United States." *CWAL*, Volume IV, p. 280 (March 9, 1861).

51. John G. Nicolay and John Hay, *Abraham Lincoln: A History*, Volume III, p. 395.

52. Gideon Welles, *Diary of Gideon Welles*, Volume II, pp. 515–516. (May 29, 1866).

53. President Lincoln has sometimes been accused of maneuvering the Confederacy into triggering the Civil War with its attack on Fort Sumter. Historian Russell McClintock wrote: "Lincoln's decision on Sumter

was consistent with his stance throughout the crisis in that he leaned as far toward conciliation as he could without sacrificing federal authority. That is to say, as circumstances at Charleston grew dire, the need for firmness became paramount; it was now the appearance of magnanimity that counted." Russell McClintock, *Lincoln and the Decision for War: The Northern Response to Secession*, p. 248.

54.   Robert S. Eckley, *Lincoln's Forgotten Friend, Leonard Swett*, pp. 239–240.

55.   Guy Gugliotta, "New Estimate Raises Civil War Death Toll," *New York Times*, April 2, 2012. The 700,000 Civil War deaths would be equivalent to six million mortalities in the United States in 2016. See http://www.nytimes.com/2012/04/03/science/civil-war-toll-up-by-20-percent-in-new-estimate.html?_r=0.

III. THE RHETORIC OF LEADERSHIP

1.   *CWAL*, Volume VIII, pp. 332–333 (Second Inaugural Address, March 4, 1865).

2.   Martin Gilbert, ed., *The Churchill War Papers: The Ever-Widening War 1941*, p. 941 (July 14, 1941).

3.   "I am so conceited," cavalryman Churchill, then 24, wrote his mother from India in 1898, that "I do not believe that the gods would create so potent a being as myself for so prosaic an ending." Martin Gilbert, *Churchill: A Life*, p. 82.

4.   Nigel Nicolson, ed., *Harold Nicolson: Diaries and Letters, 1939–1945*, p. 93 (June 5, 1940) (London: William Collins Sons & Co., 1967).

5.   R. Crosby Kemper II, ed., *Winston Churchill: Resolution, Defiance, Magnanimity, Good Will*, p. 113 (John R. Colville, "The Personality of Winston Churchill").

6.   William Manchester and Paul Reid, *The Last Lion: Winston Spencer Churchill, Defender of the Realm, 1940–1965*, p. 295.

7.   Correlli Barnett, *The Lords of War: From Lincoln to Churchill*, p. 280.

8.   Charles McMoran Wilson Moran, *Churchill, Taken from the Diaries of Lord Moran: The Struggle for Survival, 1940–1965*, p. 772 (June 23, 1957).

9.   Churchill colleague Oliver Lyttleton recalled: "As an orator Winston strictly rationed his powers of improvisation, and hardly ever set sail upon uncharted seas. He trusted himself with no more than a few impromptu remarks at the beginning of a speech, or some bridges to link his arguments with those that had preceded him." Lord Chandos, *The Memoirs of Lord Chandos*, p. 182.

10.   Lincoln celebrated Independence Day as well as Union victories at Gettysburg and Vicksburg when he said: "Eighty odd years—since on the Fourth of July for the first time in the history of the world a nation by its representatives, assembled and declared as a self-evident truth that 'all men are created equal.' That was the birthday of the United States of America." *CWAL*, Volume VI, p. 319 (Response to serenade, July 7, 1863).

11. Andrew Roberts, *Masters and Commanders: How Four Titans Won the War in the West, 1941–1945*, p. 295.

12. Michael Burlingame, ed., *William O. Stoddard: Inside the White House in War Times*, pp. 129–130. Lincoln well understood the power of words. From Lincoln's experiences as a young politician, he understood that words could hurt; they could be abused, especially when emotions were aroused.

13. Samuel John Gurney Hoare Templewood, *Nine Troubled Years*, pp. 431–432 (London: Collins, 1954).

14. Winston S. Churchill, Speech to House of Commons, May 19, 1940. Churchill's words suggested those of Oliver Cromwell in a 1646 letter: "His is our comfort, God is in heaven, and He doth what pleaseth Him; His, and only His counsel shall stand, whatsoever the designs of men, and the fury of the people be."

15. John Wheeler-Bennett, ed., *Action This Day: Working with Churchill*, p. 156.

16. Dean Acheson, *Present at the Creation*, p. 596.

17. Robert Blake and William Roger Louis, eds., *Churchill: A Major New Assessment of His Life in Peace and War*, p. 221 (D. J. Wenden, "Churchill, Radio and Cinema").

18. Geoffrey Best, *Churchill and War*, p. 123. Much of the impact of Churchill and his words came not on the BBC, but with his image in movie house newsreels. D. J. Wenden wrote: "Newsreels show how an Edwardian Parliamentary figure became, partly fortuitously, the hero of the British people. He appeared, undaunted, with a bulldog air, in a variety of costumes and hats, stomping around with a cigar and walking stick, raising the morale of cinema audiences. . . . Newsreels projected this image to at least half the British people almost every week." Robert Blake and William Roger Louis, eds., *Churchill: A Major New Assessment of His Life in Peace and War*, p. 236 (D. J. Wenden, "Churchill, Radio and Cinema").

19. Mark Pottle, ed., *Champion Redoubtable: The Diaries and Letters of Violet Bonham Carter, 1914–1945*, p. 222 (June 11, 1940).

20. Mark Pottle, ed., *Champion Redoubtable: The Diaries and Letters of Violet Bonham Carter, 1914–1945*, p. 297 (March 26, 1944).

21. David Mearns, *The Lincoln Papers: The Story of the Collection, with Selections to July 4, 1861*, Volume II, p. 463 (Joseph Holt and Winfield Scott to Abraham Lincoln, March 5, 1861).

22. *CWAL*, Volume IV, p. 275 (Reply to Massachusetts Delegation, March 5, 1861).

23. Its closest competitor, the Mongol Empire in the eleventh century, was almost the same size and encompassed one-quarter of the world's population at that time.

24. Winston S. Churchill, *Their Finest Hour: The Second World War*, Volume II, p. 14.

25. Geoffrey Best, *Churchill: A Study in Greatness*, p. 167.

26. BBC Broadcast, April 27, 1941, Arthur Hugh Clough's poem, "Say Not the Struggle Nought Availeth."

27. Winston Churchill, *Their Finest Hour: The Second World War*, Volume II, p. 198 (June 14, 1940).

28. Historian Simon Schama noted that world-weary cynics like Lord Halifax "sniggered when they heard Winston do yet another impersonation of Henry V before Agincourt. Churchill, Halifax told a friend rather grandly, was talking 'the most frightful rot' and he didn't know how long he could continue working with him." Simon Schama, *A History of Britain: The Fate of Empire, 1776–2000*, Volume II, pp. 515–516.

29. *CWAL*, Volume V, p. 537 (Annual Message to Congress, December 1, 1862).

30. Paul M. Angle, "Lincoln's Power with Words," *Journal of the Abraham Lincoln Association*, 1981, p. 27.

31. Martin Gilbert, ed., *Churchill: The Power of Words*, p. 293 (Speech to U.S. Congress, December 26, 1941).

32. Martin Gilbert, *Winston S. Churchill, 1916–1922*, Volume IV, p. 404.

33. Winston S. Churchill, *Their Finest Hour: The Second World War*, Volume II, p. 104 (Speech to House of Commons, June 4, 1940).

34. William Safire, ed., *Lend Me Your Ears: Great Speeches in History*, p. 147.

35. Nigel Nicolson, ed., *Harold Nicolson: Diaries and Letters, 1939–1945*, p. 125 (November 5, 1940).

36. Martin Gilbert, *Churchill: A Life*, p. 633.

37. Martin Gilbert, ed., *Churchill: The Power of Words: His Remarkable Life Recounted Through His Writings and Speeches*, p. 292 (December 26, 1941).

38. Martin Gilbert, *Churchill: The Power of Words: His Remarkable Life Recounted Through His Writings and Speeches*, p. 328 (May 19, 1943).

39. Richard Langworth, ed., *Churchill by Himself*, p. 271.

40. Don E. and Virginia Fehrenbacher, eds., *The Recollected Words of Abraham Lincoln*, p. 32 (Albert Blair).

41. Laura Wood Roper, *FLO: A Biography of Frederick Law Olmsted*, p. 176 (Letter from Frederick Law Olmsted to Mary Cleveland Bryant Olmsted, October 1861).

42. Max Hastings, *Winston's War, Churchill 1940–1945*, p. 354 (January 2, 1944).

43. Don E. and Virginia Fehrenbacher, *Recollected Words of Abraham Lincoln*, p. 166 (James B. Fry).

44. Michael Burlingame and John R. Turner Ettlinger, eds., *Inside Lincoln's White House: The Complete Civil War Diary of John Hay*, p. 62 (July 14, 1863).

45. *CWAL*, Volume V, p. 535 (Annual Message to Congress, December 1, 1862).

46. Richard Langworth, ed., *Churchill by Himself*, p. 54 (May 15, 1938).

47. John Wheeler-Bennett, ed., *Action This Day: Working with Churchill*, p. 147 (John Martin).

48. James Leasor, *War at the Top: The Experiences of General Leslie Hollis*, p. 249.

49. Elizabeth Nel, *Winston Churchill by His Personal Secretary*, pp. 73–74.

50. Robert A. Ferguson, "Hearing Lincoln and the Making of Eloquence," *American Literary History*, Winter 2009, p. 691.

51. James G. Randall, *Lincoln the President, Springfield to Gettysburg*, Volume I, p. 49.

52. Churchill liked to use strong language to describe Nazis. In one letter to Tito, he referred to the "filthy Nazi-Fascist taint." In another, he called them "filthy Hitlerite murderers." Winston S. Churchill, *Closing the Ring: The Second World War*, Volume V, pp. 416, 423.

53. Richard Langworth, ed., *Churchill by Himself*, pp. 170–171 (radio broadcasts, December 23, 1940, November 29, 1942).

54. John Wheeler-Bennett, ed., *Action This Day: Working with Churchill*, p. 256.

55. Paul Selby, *Lincoln's Life, Stories, and Speeches*, pp. 141–142.

56. General Hastings Ismay wrote of accompanying the prime minister on a tour of the London docks in September 1940: "Our first stop was at an air-raid shelter in which about forty persons had been killed and many more wounded by a direct hit, and we found a big crowd, male and female, young and old, but all seemingly very poor. One might have expected them to be resentful against the authorities responsible for their protection; but, as Churchill got out of his car, they literally mobbed him. 'Good old Winnie,' they cried. 'We thought you'd come and see us. We can take it. Give it 'em back.' Churchill broke down, and as I was struggling to get him through the crowd, I heard an old woman say, 'You see, he really cares; he's crying.'" Ismay wrote: "On and on we went until darkness began to fall. The dock authorities were anxious that Churchill should leave for home at once, but he was in one of his most obstinate moods and insisted that he wanted to see everything. Consequently, we were still within the brightly-lit target when the Luftwaffe arrived on the scene and the fireworks started. It was difficult to get a large car out of the area, owing to many of the streets being completely blocked by fallen houses, and as we were trying to turn in a very narrow space, a shower of incendiary bombs fell just in front of us. Churchill, feigning innocence, asked what they were. I replied that they were incendiaries, and that we were evidently in the middle of the bull's eye!" Hastings Ismay, *The Memoirs of General Lord Ismay*, pp. 185–186.

57. *CWAL*, Volume IV, p. 441 (Special Address to Congress, July 4, 1861).

58. Edward Davis Townsend, *Anecdotes of the Civil War in the United States*, pp. 91–92.

59. Richard Langworth, ed., *Churchill by Himself: The Definitive Collection of Quotations*, p. 271 (BBC Broadcast, October 1, 1939).

60. Edward Spears, *Assignment to Catastrophe: Prelude to Dunkirk*, July 1939– May 1940, Volume I, p. 293.

61. Hastings Lionel Ismay, *Memoirs of General Lord Ismay*, p. 158 (New York: The Viking Press, 1960).

IV. ANGLO-AMERICAN RELATIONS

1. *CWAL*, Volume VI, p. 64 (Letter to Workingmen of Manchester, January 19, 1863).

2. Winston S. Churchill, *The Grand Alliance: The Second World War*, Volume III, p. 596 (Speech to Congress, December 26, 1941).

3. Robert E. Sherwood, *Roosevelt and Churchill: An Intimate History*, p. 257. Historian Ronald Lewin wrote: "It was an enormous achievement on Churchill's part to have convinced this shrewd and sceptical spy [Harry Hopkins], nor was it done without conscious and dexterous diplomacy." Ronald Lewin, *Churchill as Warlord*, p. 63.

4. William Manchester and Paul Reid, *The Last Lion: Winston Spencer Churchill, Defender of the Realm, 1940–1965*, p. 382.

5. William Manchester and Paul Reid, *The Last Lion: Winston Spencer Churchill, Defender of the Realm, 1940–1965*, p. 292.

6. Robert E. Sherwood, ed., *The White House Papers of Harry L. Hopkins*, Volume II, p. 374.

7. Martin Gilbert, *Finest Hour, 1939–1941*, p. 1267.

8. Winston S. Churchill, *The Grand Alliance: The Second World War*, Volume III, p. 538.

9. Norman Rose, *Churchill: An Unruly Life*, p. 290.

10. Warren F. Kimball, ed., *Churchill & Roosevelt: The Complete Correspondence*, Volume I, p. 24 (Roosevelt to Churchill, September 1, 1939).

11. Dr. Wilson recalled Churchill telling him: "We were at dinner at Chequers on Sunday when I lifted the lid of the pocket wireless which Harriman gave me. The nine o'clock news had started. At the end there was something about the Japanese attacking American shipping. It wasn't very clear, and I didn't realize what had happened when Sawyers came into the room. He said: 'It's quite true. We heard it ourselves outside. The Japs have attacked the Americans.'" Charles McMoran Wilson Moran, *Churchill, Taken from the Diaries of Lord Moran*, p. 10 (December 20, 1941).

12. Gerald Pawle, *The War and Colonel Warden*, p. 145.

13. Jean Edward Smith, *FDR*, p. 543.

14. Jean Edward Smith, *FDR*, p. 544.

15. Martin Gilbert, *Winston S. Churchill: The Finest Hour, 1939–1941*, Volume VI, p. 358.

16. Warren F. Kimball, ed., *Churchill & Roosevelt: The Complete Correspondence*, Volume I, p. 50 (Churchill to Roosevelt, June 15, 1940).

17. Warren F. Kimball, ed., *Churchill & Roosevelt: The Complete Correspondence*, Volume 1, p. 190 (Churchill to Roosevelt, May 19, 1941).

18. Churchill's relationship with Harriman became complicated when the American began an affair with Churchill's daughter-in-law, Pamela Digby Churchill, who married Harriman in 1971. The World War II liaison strained the Churchills' father-son relationship and led to Randolph's divorce.

19. One February weekend at Ditchley Park, John Kennedy watched as Churchill held up his hand with the fingers spread out, and said, "Do you play poker? Here is the hand that is going to win the war: A Royal Flush—Great Britain, the Sea, the Air, the Middle East, American aid." Richard Langworth, ed., *Churchill by Himself: The Definitive Collection of Quotations*, p. 505 (February 16, 1941).

20. For example, Churchill's trip to Hyde Park in July 1942.

21. Doris Kearns Goodwin, *No Ordinary Time*, p. 408.

22. Richard Toye, *Churchill's Empire: The World That Made Him and the World He Made*, p. 204.

23. Richard Toye, *Churchill's Empire: The World That Made Him and the World He Made*, p. 253 (December 31, 1944).

24. Warren F. Kimball, ed., *Churchill & Roosevelt: The Complete Correspondence*, Volume I, p. 446 (April 11, 1942).

25. Simon Berthon and Joanna Potts, *Warlords: An Extraordinary Re-creation of World War II Through the Eyes and Minds of Hitler, Churchill*, p. 141 (Diary of Henry Stimson, April 22, 1942).

26. Gerald Pawle, *The War and Colonel Warden*, p. 250 (London: George G. Harrap & Co., 1963).

27. Alex Danchev and Daniel Todman, eds., *Alanbrooke War Diaries 1939–1945: Field Marshall Lord Alanbrooke*, p. 473.

28. William Manchester and Paul Reid, *The Last Lion: Winston Spencer Churchill*, p. 507.

29. Francis B. Carpenter, *The Inner Life of Abraham Lincoln: Six Months at the White House*, p. 245. One Illinois contemporary recalled: "It was a rather dangerous operation to try to get a laugh at Mr. Lincoln's expense. I have known some very sharp men to try the experiment, and it never failed to secure a hearty laugh at their own expense." Rufus Rockwell Wilson, ed., *Intimate Memories of Lincoln*, p. 95 (Thomas W. S. Kidd).

30. Winston S. Churchill, *The Great Republic*, p. 183.

31. Rufus Rockwell Wilson, ed., *Intimate Memories of Lincoln*, p. 604 (Edward Duffield Neill).

32. Ralph Gary, *Following in Lincoln's Footsteps*, p. 371.

33. Martin Gilbert, *Winston S. Churchill: Road to Victory 1941–1945*, p. 28.

34. Don E. and Virginia Fehrenbacher, eds., *Recollected Words of Abraham Lincoln*, p. 308 (Agnes Harrison MacDonell).

35. The South overestimated the leverage of their cotton in Europe. Historian Roger G. Kennedy wrote: "By the 1850s, the planters of South

Carolina, led by James Henry Hammond, came to believe that by with-holding their cotton they could force British intervention in American politics on Southern terms. In his 'King Cotton' speech in 1858, Hammond posed his famous rhetorical question: 'What would happen if no cotton was furnished for three years?' and offered his famously foolish answer: 'Britain would topple headlong.'" Roger G. Kennedy, *Mr. Jefferson's Lost Cause: Land, Farmers, Slavery, and the Louisiana Purchase*, p. 237. Lack of cotton did hurt British industry and workers early in the war but, encouraged by high prices, alternatives were eventually found. Historian Donald Stoker wrote: "By 1863, cotton was flowing from Egypt, Brazil, India, and the West Indies, while British and French munitions makers, iron and steel firms, manufacturers of wool and linen products, and producers of many other items did brisk business in war-related matériel." Donald Stoker, *The Grand Design: Strategy and the U.S. Civil War*, p. 30.

36. *The Times* disdained Lincoln, who shared that distinction with Churchill. Ronald Lewin wrote of the latter in 1940: "The *Times* could not stomach him." Ronald Lewin, *Churchill as Warlord*, p. 10.

37. Historian Colin R. Ballard wrote of Charles Francis Adams: "This gentleman, elderly, calm, and honest, soon won the respect of Lord John Russell, the British Foreign Minister, and though there were moments of severe tension he always received a polite if not sympathetic hearing. It seems to have been due to the patience and wisdom of Adams that Great Britain never gave official recognition to the South, and yet accepted the blockade as a fact." Colin R. Ballard, *The Military Genius of Abraham Lincoln*, p. 63.

38. Charles Francis Adams, *An Address on the Life, Character and Services of William Henry Seward*, p. 30.

39. Kevin Peraino, *Lincoln in the World*, passim.

40. Craig L. Symonds, *Lincoln and His Admirals*, p. 40.

41. Gordon H. Warren, *Fountain of Discontent: The Trent Affair and Freedom of the Seas*, pp. 53–55.

42. William Howard Russell, *My Diary, North and South*, pp. 42–43.

43. Frederick W. Seward, *Seward at Washington, as Senator and Secretary of State: 1861–1872*, p. 26.

44. The situation threatened to result in hostilities between the United States and Britain. Colin R. Ballard wrote: "In 1863 there were three ships in the yard of Laird & Sons. Ostensibly they were built to the order of a French purchaser, but there was little doubt at the time . . . that the French sheepskin was a thin disguise for the Confederate wolf. The ships were powerful ironclads: they would be a serious menace to commerce: they might be strong enough to raise the blockade: they might even threaten the ports of the North. The American Minister in London, C. F. Adams, sent in very strong representations to the British Foreign Minister, Lord John Russell, asking that the vessels might be

detained: in one letter (dated September 5th), after referring to the refusal of the Government to take action, he said—'It would be superfluous in me to point out to your lordship that this is war.'" Colin R. Ballard, *The Military Genius of Abraham Lincoln*, p. 233.

45. Burton J. Hendrick, *Lincoln's War Cabinet*, pp. 253–255.

46. Frederick W. Seward, *Seward at Washington, as Senator and Secretary of State: 1861–1872*, p. 186.

47. Martin Gilbert, *Churchill: The Power of Words: His Remarkable Life Recounted Through His Writings and Speeches*, p. 284 (June 16, 1941).

48. Martin Gilbert, *Winston S. Churchill: Road to Victory, 1941–1945*, p. 524 (Marian Holmes diary, October 7, 1943).

49. Martin Gilbert, *Churchill: The Power of Words: His Remarkable Life Recounted Through His Writings and Speeches*, p. 243 (Speech to Parliament, May 13, 1940).

50. Martin Gilbert, ed., *Churchill: The Power of Words: His Remarkable Life Recounted Through His Writings and Speeches*, p. 330 (September 6, 1943).

51. Martin Gilbert, *Churchill and America*, p. 77.

52. Winston S. Churchill, *The Grand Alliance: The Second World War*, Volume III, pp. 539–540.

53. Winston Churchill, *Their Finest Hour: The Second World War*, Volume II, p. 22.

54. FDR speech writer Robert E. Sherwood wrote: "In many meetings that were to follow [Placentia Bay summit in August 1941], Churchill's respect for Roosevelt may have wavered at times but it never ceased. Nor did Churchill ever lose sight of the fact that Roosevelt was his superior in rank—the President being the Head of State, on the level with the King, whereas the Prime Minister is Head of Government." Robert E. Sherwood, *Roosevelt and Hopkins: An Intimate History*, p. 351. Historian Keith Sainsbury wrote: "Churchill's attitude to Roosevelt was less complicated, and more trustful. He had watched with admiration Roosevelt's gradual conquest of the deep-seated American isolationist tradition, and remembered with gratitude the successive acts of practical assistance—the Destroyers-Bases deal, Lend-Lease, the increasing participation in the Atlantic battle—which Roosevelt had coaxed out of a reluctant Congress, even before Pearl Harbour brought the United States into the war. His attitude to Roosevelt personally was cordial, loyal, and understanding and he showed uncharacteristic patience for the most part, with what he regarded as Roosevelt's sometimes uninformed comments and proposals for Europe and the Empire. Privately he thought that Roosevelt and the Americans generally knew very little and understood less about India and other imperial problems: nor did he think the President particularly knowledgeable about Europe." Keith Sainsbury, *The Turning Point: Roosevelt, Stalin, Churchill, and Chiang-Kai-Shek*, 1943, p. 142. Some critics believe that Churchill erred in his preoccupation with FDR. John Keegan wrote that "Churchill . . .

undoubtedly invested too large a hope in the likelihood of American entry. This is a ticklish subject, around which the establishment historians on both sides of the Atlantic continue to pussyfoot. Roosevelt's whole-hearted endorsement of the war against Hitler, once he was in, seems retrospectively to justify Churchill's faith that the President's commitment to United States entry matched his own in strength and date of conception." Robert Blake and William Roger Louis, eds., *Churchill: A Major New Assessment of His Life in Peace and War*, pp. 338–339 (John Keegan, "Churchill's Strategy").

55. Max Hastings, *Winston's War: Churchill 1940–1945*, p. 152.

56. Winston S. Churchill, *The Grand Alliance, The Second World War*, p. 596 (Speech to U.S. Congress, December 26, 1941).

57. David Cannadine, *In Churchill's Shadow: Confronting the Past in Modern Britain*, p. 107.

58. Churchill's physician, Dr. Wilson, wrote of Churchill's meetings in Washington in late December 1941: "I have seen Winston content to listen. You could almost feel the importance he attaches to bringing the President along with him, and in that good cause he has become a very model of restraint and self-discipline; it is surely a new Winston who is sitting there quite silent. And when he does say anything it is always something likely to fall pleasantly on the President's ear." Baron Charles McMoran Wilson Moran, *Churchill: Taken from the Diaries of Lord Moran: The Struggle for Survival, 1940–1965*, p. 21 (December 31, 1941). Churchill's top military aide, General Hastings Ismay, wrote of the June 1942 session in Washington: "It had been intensely interesting to see Roosevelt and Churchill together at close quarters. There was something so intimate in their friendship. They used to stroll in and out of each other's rooms in the White House, as two subalterns occupying adjacent quarters might have done. Both of them had the spirit of eternal youth." Hastings Lionel Ismay, *Memoirs of General Lord Ismay*, p. 256.

59. Eleanor Roosevelt, *This I Remember*, pp. 252–253. (New York: Harper & Brothers, 1949).

60. Charles McMoran Wilson Moran, *Churchill, Taken from the Diaries of Lord Moran: The Struggle for Survival, 1940–1965*, p. 153 (November 30, 1943).

61. FDR's antagonism to de Gaulle was echoed by other members of his administration, especially in the State and War Departments. Historian Robert Dallek wrote: "'Arrogant' and even 'vicious' in his defense of what he considered legitimate French rights, de Gaulle provoked other Americans as well. Hull, Stimson recorded in June, 'hated de Gaulle so fiercely that he was almost incoherent on the subject.' De Gaulle's refusal to broadcast his support of the invasion as it began, to endorse the supplemental currency, or to send more than a handful of French liaison officers with the invading forces put Marshall in 'a white fury.' If the American public learned what de Gaulle had been doing to hamper the invasion, Marshall declared, it would demand a break with

the French National Committee." Robert Dallek, *Franklin Roosevelt and American Foreign Policy, 1932–1945*, p. 459.

62. Winston S. Churchill, *Their Finest Hour: The Second World War*, Volume II, p. 192.

63. Winston S. Churchill, *Their Finest Hour: The Second World War*, Volume II, p. 189.

64. Historian Walter Reid wrote that de Gaulle "was not indispensable, and America would have been delighted to see him go. Churchill felt attached to him, but that attachment could wear thin. British public opinion helped de Gaulle. So repeatedly did Eden. So did the War Cabinet: in May 1943 in Washington Churchill was ready to let the Frenchman go, and it was only a rebellion by the War Cabinet that saved him." *Walter Reid, Churchill: 1940–1945, Under Friendly Fire*, p. 226.

65. Eleanor Roosevelt, *This I Remember*, p. 281.

66. Martin Gilbert, *Winston S. Churchill: Road to Victory, 1941–1945*, p. 646.

67. Elizabeth Nel, *Winston Churchill by His Personal Secretary*, p. 140.

68. James Leasor, *War at the Top: The Experiences of General Leslie Hollis*, p. 14. De Gaulle was briefed on Operation OVERLORD shortly before it took place in June 1944. He and Churchill quarreled about de Gaulle's reluctance to deliver a speech to the French people. Churchill became so incensed with the general that he declared that de Gaulle should be returned to Algiers, "in chains if necessary. He must not be allowed to enter France." Walter Reid, *Churchill 1940–1945: Under Friendly Fire*, p. 301.

69. William Manchester and Paul Reid, *The Last Lion: Winston Spencer Churchill, Defender of the Realm, 1940–1965*, p. 808.

70. Charles Eade, *Churchill—by his Contemporaries*, p. 221 (Paul Reynaud, "Churchill and France").

71. Speaking in a secret session of the House, Churchill said that "the House must not be led to believe that General de Gaulle is an unfaltering friend of Britain. On the contrary, I think he is one of those good Frenchmen who have a traditional antagonism engrained in French hearts by centuries of war against the English. On his way back from Syria in the summer of 1941 through the French Central and West African Colonies he left a trail of anglophobia behind him. On August 25, 1941, he gave an interview to the correspondent of the 'Chicago Daily News' at Brazzaville in which he suggested that England coveted the African colonies of France, and said: 'England is afraid of the French Fleet. What in effect England is carrying out is a war-time deal with Hitler in which Vichy served as a go-between.'" Martin Gilbert, *Road to Victory: Winston S. Churchill, 1941–1945*, p. 277. As D-Day approached, de Gaulle balked at broadcasting a message to France requested by Anglo-American leaders. "It is an odious example of his malice," complained Churchill. De Gaulle "has no regard for common causes—I may have to exhibit him in his true light, as a false and puffed up

personality." Andrew Roberts, *Masters and Commanders: How Four Titans Won the War in the West, 1941–1945*, p. 487.

72.   Baron Charles McMoran Wilson Moran, *Churchill: Taken from the Diaries of Lord Moran: The Struggle for Survival, 1940–1965*, p. 88 (January 22, 1943). In his memoirs de Gaulle showed better understanding of Churchill's problems: "The British, whatever their self-control, did not conceal their gloom at no longer being masters in their own country and at finding themselves dispossessed of the leading role they had played— and so deservingly!—for the last two years." Charles de Gaulle, *War Memoirs: Unity*, Volume II, p. 4 (New York: Simon & Schuster, 1959).

73.   FDR had virtually no use for de Gaulle or de Gaulle's vision of a postwar French colonial empire. But Eisenhower wanted recognition of the Free French (FCNL). FDR strongly resisted, writing: "You are not to recognise the Committee under any condition without full consultation and approval of the President." Elisabeth Barker, *Churchill and Eden at War*, p. 81 (July 8, 1943).

V. VIRTUES OF GREAT WAR LEADERS

1.   *CWAL*, Volume V, p. 537 (Second Annual Message to Congress, December 1, 1862).

2.   Martin Gilbert, *Churchill: The Power of Words: His Remarkable Life Recounted Through His Writings and Speeches*, p. 300 (December 30, 1941).

3.   Lincoln, Churchill, and Roosevelt had different and similar reasons to tell stories. Lincoln used stories to avoid conflict with guests or to make a point. Churchill used stories to dominate conversation and to make a point. Roosevelt used stories to avoid confrontation and decisions.

4.   Osborn H. Oldroyd, ed., *The Lincoln Memorial: Album-Immortelles*, p. 428.

5.   Joshua Fry Speed, *Reminiscences of Abraham Lincoln and Notes of a Visit to California*, p. 38.

6.   Harry V. Jaffa, *Crisis in the House Divided*, p. 386.

7.   Philip Shaw Paludan, ed., *Lincoln's Legacy: Ethics and Politics*, p. 10.

8.   Historian William C. Harris wrote: "By the 1850s Lincoln had become a 'lawyer's lawyer.' In 1860, a correspondent of the *New York Herald* interviewed separately 'three of the ablest jurists in the State' regarding Lincoln's standing with the bar in Illinois and his qualities as a lawyer. Two of the judges were political opponents of Lincoln. All of them indicated, according to this reporter, that Lincoln 'has been among the leading practitioners of the State for many years, and probably not a judge or a member of the bar can be found . . . who will express a doubt as to his being a superior man. While he is exceedingly well informed upon all general subjects, he cannot be considered a learned man. . . . The learning which is applicable to the case in hand he understands,' they said, and had acquired in 'a practical way.'" William C. Harris, *Lincoln's Rise to the Presidency*, p. 33.

9.   *CWAL*, Volume III, p. 27 (Debate with Stephen A. Douglas at Ottawa, Illinois, August 21, 1858).

10. Celia Sandys, *Churchill Wanted Dead or Alive*, p. 9.

11. Carlo D'Este, *Warlord: A Life of Winston Churchill at War, 1874–1945*, p. 427.

12. When aide John G. Nicolay met with Lincoln on October 2, 1861, he listed a balance sheet of national woes under headings for political, financial, and military problems. Under "political," Nicolay wrote:

>   "Frémont ready to rebel
>   Chase despairing
>   Cameron utterly ignorant and regardless of the course of things, and the probable result.
>   Cameron
>   Selfish and openly discourteous to the President
>   Obnoxious to the Country
>   Incapable either of organizing details or conceiving and advising general plans."

Michael Burlingame, ed., *With Lincoln in the White House: Letters, Memoranda, and Other Writings of John G. Nicolay*, p. 59 (October 2, 1861).

13. John Kennedy, *The Business of War*, p. 156.

14. Dwight D. Eisenhower, *At Ease: Stories I Tell to Friends*, pp. 273–274.

15. William McNeill, *America, Britain and Russia: Their Co-operation and Conflict, 1941–1946*, p. 187.

16. Alex Danchev and Daniel Todman, eds., *Lord Alanbrooke War Diaries, 1939–1945*, p. 231 (February 18, 1942).

17. W. H. Thompson, *Sixty Minutes with Winston Churchill*, p. 65.

18. Max Hastings, *Winston's War: Churchill 1940–1945*, p. 225.

19. Martin Gilbert, *Churchill: The Power of Words: His Remarkable Life Recounted Through His Writings and Speeches*, p. 312 (February 15, 1942).

20. Martin Gilbert, *Churchill: The Power of Words: His Remarkable Life Recounted Through His Writings and Speeches*, p. 277 (Speech on BBC, February 9, 1941).

21. Churchill would say: "I have got a black dog on my back today." Martin Gilbert, *In Search of Churchill: A Historian's Journey*, p. 210.

22. Charles McMoran Wilson Moran, *Churchill, Taken from the Diaries of Lord Moran: The Struggle for Survival, 1940–1965*, p. 195. Historian Ronald Lewin wrote: "Churchill appears to have been one of those mental types known as cyclothymic—oscillating periodically from a state of angst, gloom and uncertainty to one of an exhilaration sometimes euphoric." Ronald Lewin, *Churchill as Warlord*, p. 5.

23. Paul Johnson, *Churchill*, p. 165.

24. David Reynolds, *In Command of History: Churchill Fighting and Writing the Second World War*, pp. 520–521.

25. William Manchester and Paul Reid, *The Last Lion: Winston Spencer Churchill, Defender of the Realm, 1940–1965*, p. 463.

26. Lord Moran, *Churchill: The Struggle for Survival, 1940–1965*, p. 198 (September 21, 1944). Biographer Norman Rose wrote: "Whenever Churchill gave offence, a sixth sense alerted him that he had overstepped the mark. A winning smile, some appropriate words, a touching gesture, and he would swiftly make amends, repairing the damage, appeasing the aggrieved party. In a curious way, he was respected and loved all the more for these transgressions, for his wayward behaviour was cushioned by a disarming naïveté." Norman Rose, *Churchill: An Unruly Life*, p. 344.

27. Richard Langworth, ed., *Churchill by Himself: The Definitive Collection of Quotations*, p. 322.

28. Churchill also possessed an impressive scriptural knowledge. He sometimes used Bible verses as shorthand to communicate with others. Churchill wrote General Archibald Wavell in December 1940: "St. Matthew, Chapter 7, Verse 7." That verse declared: "Ask, and it shall be given you; seek, and ye shall find; knock, and it shall be opened unto you." Martin Gilbert, *Winston S. Churchill: Finest Hour, 1939–1941*, p. 947. Wavell replied: "St. James, Chapter 1, Verse 17, first part." ("Every good endowment and every perfect gift is from above, coming down from the Father of lights with whom there is no variation or shadow due to change.") Harold E. Raugh Jr., *Wavell in the Middle East, 1939–1941*, p. 105.

29. John Wheeler-Bennett, ed., *Action This Day: Working with Churchill*, p. 148 (John Martin). Martin wrote of a weekend at Chequers in October 1940: "The talk at dinner here is quite the best entertainment I know. I feel peeved that I haven't the sort of memory that could treasure up the PM's obiter dicta to chuckle over afterwards." John Martin, *Downing Street: The War Years*, p. 32 (October 27, 1940).

30. John Wheeler-Bennett, ed., *Action This Day: Working with Churchill*, p. 67. Similar in John Colville, *The Fringes of Power*, p. 461 (January 2, 1944). FDR often used his stories to divert attention from the subject at hand and to avoid making decisions he preferred to postpone.

31. John Wheeler-Bennett, ed., *Action This Day: Working with Churchill*, p. 148 (John Martin).

32. Dean Acheson, *Present at the Creation*, p. 596.

33. Martin Gilbert, *Churchill: The Power of Words: His Remarkable Life Recounted Through His Writings and Speeches*, p. 233 (October 1, 1939).

34. Winston S. Churchill, *Their Finest Hour: The Second World War*, Volume II, p. 211.

35. Winston S. Churchill, *Their Finest Hour: The Second World War*, Volume II, p. 136.

36. Geoffrey Best, *Churchill: A Study in Greatness*, p. 180. Churchill's optimism was not always an asset. Best wrote that Francophile Churchill "was confident that the French army would be able to deal with the invader and, although his own country's readiness for war fell far below the ideal, he never doubted that in the long run the combined strength

of France, Britain and their respective empires would sooner or later prevail over a Germany unfitted (so the government believed) for a long war and undermined (so he expected) by the resistance of the peoples it oppressed." Geoffrey Best, *Churchill and War*, p. 113.

37. *CWAL*, Volume I, p. 279 (Speech to Springfield Washington Temperance Society, February 22, 1842).

38. *CWAL*, Volume VII, p. 395 (Remarks at Central Sanitary Fair, June 16, 1864).

39. *CWAL*, Volume VI, p. 267 (Lincoln to Erastus Corning et al., June 12, 1863).

40. *CWAL*, Volume VII, p. 528 (Remarks to One Hundred Forty-eighth Ohio Regiment, August 31, 1864).

41. *CWAL*, Volume VI, p. 306 (Lincoln to Matthew Birchard et al., June 29, 1863).

42. Allan Nevins, *The War for the Union: The Organized War to Victory, 1864–1865*, Volume IV, p. 132.

43. Don E. and Virginia Fehrenbacher, eds., *The Recollected Words of Abraham Lincoln*, p. 261.

44. Ronald C. White, *A. Lincoln: A Biography*, p. 449.

45. Winston S. Churchill, *Their Finest Hour: The Second World War*, Volume II, p. 198 (June 18, 1940).

46. *CWAL*, Volume V, p. 537 (Second Annual Message to Congress, December 1, 1862).

47. *CWAL*, Volume VIII, p. 333 (Second Inaugural Address, March 4, 1865).

48. General Douglas MacArthur wrote that "though foreign and hostile lands may be the duty of young pilots, but for a Statesman burdened by the world's cares, it is an act of inspiring gallantry and valor." William Manchester and Paul Reid, *The Last Lion: Winston Spencer Churchill: Defender of the Realm, 1940–1965*, p. 596.

49. Hastings Lionel Ismay, *Memoirs of General Lord Ismay*, pp. 177–178.

50. Alex Danchev and Daniel Todman, eds., *Lord Alanbrooke War Diaries, 1939–1945*, p. 589 (September 8, 1944).

51. John Colville, *The Fringes of Power*, p. 511 (September 9, 1944).

52. Martin Gilbert, *Road to Victory: Winston S. Churchill 1941–1945*, p. 922 (August 29, 1944).

53. Joan Bright Astley, *The Inner Circle: A View of War at the Top*, p. 153.

54. Gideon Welles, *Diary of Gideon Welles*, Volume I, p. 157 (October 1, 1861).

55. Warren F. Kimball, ed., *Churchill & Roosevelt: The Complete Correspondence*, Volume III, p. 34 (September 29, 1944).

56. John Colville wrote: "Clementine Churchill thought that her husband's least admirable characteristic was a yearning for luxury so pronounced that he would accept hospitality from anybody able to offer the surroundings and the amenities he enjoyed. Lord Birkenhead had made

the much-quoted quip: 'Mr. Churchill is easily satisfied with the best.' It was a side of him abhorrent to Clementine's principles, and there was undeniably an element of truth in her criticism." John Colville, *Winston Churchill and His Inner Circle*, p. 271. Clementine, who grew up poor, was by nature austere but genteel.

57. John Keegan, *Winston Churchill*, p. 153.

58. Alex Danchev and Daniel Todman, eds., *Lord Alanbrooke War Diaries, 1939–1945*, p. 369 (January 25, 1943).

59. Winston S. Churchill, *Hinge of Fate: The Second World War*, Volume IV, p. 412.

60. Winston S. Churchill, *Closing the Ring: The Second World War*, Volume V, p. 547 (King George to Churchill, May 31, 1944).

61. Winston S. Churchill, *Closing the Ring: The Second World War*, Volume V, p. 551.

62. Mary Soames. *Clementine Churchill: The Biography of a Marriage*, p. 392.

63. Winston S. Churchill, *Triumph and Tragedy: The Second World War*, Volume V, p. 13.

64. David Dixon Porter, *Incidents and Anecdotes of the Civil War*, p. 294.

65. *CWAL*, Volume VIII, pp. 384–385 (Edwin M. Stanton to Abraham Lincoln, April 3, 1865).

66. *CWAL*, Volume VIII, p. 385 (Lincoln to Edwin M. Stanton, April 3, 1865).

67. John S. Barnes, "With Lincoln from Washington to Richmond in 1865," *Appleton's Magazine*, May 1907, pp. 747–748.

68. Don E. and Virginia E. Fehrenbacher, eds., *Recollected Words of Abraham Lincoln*, p. 115 (Schuyler Colfax).

69. *CWAL*, Volume IV, p. 240 (Speech at Independence Hall, Philadelphia, February 22, 1861).

70. Margarita Spalding Gerry, *Through Five Administrations: Reminiscences of Colonel William H. Crook*, p. 3.

71. Noah Brooks, *Abraham Lincoln*, p. 424.

72. Roy Jenkins, *Churchill*, p. 751.

73. *CWAL*, Volume VIII, p. 151 (Fourth Message to Congress, December 6, 1864). Lincoln was fortunate that his Confederate counterpart, Jefferson Davis, was unwilling to negotiate on the key issues of Union and emancipation. A more flexible opponent would have caused Lincoln more difficulties.

VI. MANAGING MINISTERS AND LEGISLATORS

1. *CWAL*, Volume VII, p. 419 (Lincoln to Salmon Chase, June 30, 1864).

2. Martin Gilbert, *Continue to Pester, Nag and Bite: Churchill's War Leadership*, p. 23.

3. Allen Thorndike Rice, ed., *Reminiscences of Abraham Lincoln*, pp. 74–75 (Schuyler Colfax).

4. *CWAL*, Volume V, p. 95 (Lincoln to Simon Cameron, January 10, 1862).

5. "General M. C. Meigs on the Conduct of the Civil War," *American Historical Review*, Volume XXVI, 1921, pp. 292–293.

6. Churchill expressed his doubts when his private secretary suggested bringing Cripps home from Moscow, saying Cripps "is a lunatic in a country of lunatics, and it would be a pity to move him." John Colville, *Fringes of Power: The Incredible Inside Story of Winston Churchill during World War II*, p. 309 (December 12, 1940). Cripps infuriated Churchill in early 1941 by refusing to pass on to Stalin Churchill's warning about an impending German attack. Winston S. Churchill, *The Grand Alliance: The Second World War*, Volume III, pp. 321–323.

7. Jonathan Schneer, *Ministers at War: Winston Churchill and His War Cabinet*, pp. 117–118.

8. Raymond Callahan, *Churchill and His Generals*, p. 29.

9. Martin Gilbert, ed., *Churchill: The Power of Words: His Remarkable Life Recounted Through His Writings and Speeches*, p. 216 (August 2, 1939).

10. Martin Gilbert, ed., *Churchill: The Power of Words: His Remarkable Life Recounted Through His Writings and Speeches*, p. 316 (April 23, 1942).

11. Martin Gilbert, ed., *Churchill: The Power of Words: His Remarkable Life Recounted Through His Writings and Speeches*, p. 348 (Speech to House of Commons, May 8, 1945).

12. Ethan S. Rafuse, *McClellan's War: The Failure of Moderation in the Struggle for the Union*, p. 137 (Benjamin Wade to Zachariah Chandler, October 8, 1861).

13. Hans Louis Trefousse, *Benjamin Franklin Wade: Radical Republican from Ohio*, p. 205.

14. Howard K. Beale, ed., *The Diary of Edward Bates*, p. 333 (February 13, 1864).

15. David E. Long, *The Jewel of Liberty*, p. 25.

16. David Reynolds, *In Command of History: Churchill Fighting and Writing the Second World War*, p. 38.

17. William Manchester and Paul Reid, *The Last Lion: Winston Spencer Churchill*, p. 519. Mountbatten was a great favorite of Churchill's. He was not a favorite of the COS, who denigrated his ideas. Brooke asserted that the admiral "frequently wasted both his time and ours." Andrew Roberts, *Masters and Commanders: How Four Titans Won the War in the West, 1941–1945*, p. 103. Historian David Cannadine wrote that "there was about almost everything Mountbatten did an element of the makeshift, the insubstantial, the incomplete and disingenuous." David Cannadine, *The Pleasures of the Past*, p. 64.

18. Nigel Nicolson, ed., *Harold Nicolson: Diaries and Letters, 1939–1945*, pp. 207–208 (January 27, 1942).

19. Brian Gardner, *Churchill in Power: As Seen by His Contemporaries*, p. 147.

20. Nigel Nicolson, ed., *Harold Nicolson: Diaries and Letters 1930–1964*, p. 209 (January 29, 1942).

21. Charles McMoran Wilson Moran, *Churchill, Taken from the Diaries of Lord Moran: The Struggle for Survival, 1940–1965*, p. 27 (January 29, 1942).

22. Simon Berthon and Joanna Potts, *Warlords*, p. 138.

23. Charles McMoran Wilson Moran, *Churchill, Taken from the Diaries of Lord Moran: The Struggle for Survival, 1940–1965*, pp. 26–27 (January 27, 1942).

24. Winston S. Churchill, *The Hinge of Fate: The Second World War*, Volume V, pp. 498–502.

25. Michael Foot, *Aneurin Bevan: A Biography, Volume One: 1897–1945*, p. 401. Churchill wrote Cripps in October: "You are an honest man. If you had been Lloyd-George, you would have resigned on the issue of a second front," rather than on the war's conduct and direction. J. M. Lee, *The Churchill Coalition, 1940–1945*, p. 43 (Churchill to Stafford Cripps, October 2, 1942).

26. Mr. Lincoln knew otherwise. A correspondent for the *New York Herald*, owned by James Gordon Bennett, asked President Lincoln on the night of his inauguration if he wanted to send a message to Bennett. "Yes," said Lincoln, "you may tell him that Thurlow Weed has found out that Seward was not nominated at Chicago." Don E. and Virginia Fehrenbacher, eds., *Recollected Words of Abraham Lincoln*, p. 160 (Stephen R. Fiske). Lincoln biographer William E. Barton observed: "Not for some time did the correspondent understand that this was one of Lincoln's jokes. It was a very serious joke; it was Lincoln's declaration that he was master of the situation. Thurlow Weed, who had been endeavoring to crowd [Salmon P.] Chase out of the Cabinet, and Seward, who had declined a secretaryship on the very eve of the nomination, had both discovered that Weed had not succeeded either in the nomination or in the control of the executive." William E. Barton, *The Life of Abraham Lincoln*, Volume II, p. 38.

27. *CWAL*, Volume IV, p. 317 (Lincoln to William H. Seward, April 1, 1861).

28. Michael Burlingame, ed., *An Oral History of Abraham Lincoln: John G. Nicolay's Interviews and Essays*, p. 84 (Conversation with Henry Wilson, November 16, 1875).

29. Ivor Jennings, *Cabinet Government*, p. 196.

30. Andrew Roberts, *Masters and Commanders: How Four Titans Won the War in the West, 1941–1945*, p. 302.

31. Mary S. Lovell, *The Churchills: In Love and War*, p. 344.

32. Norman Rose, *Churchill: An Unruly Life*, p. 315.

33. Peter J. Laugharne, ed., *Aneurin Bevan: Speeches at Westminster, 1929–1944*, p. 101.

34. Julia Perkins Cutler and Ephraim Cutler Dawes, *Life and Times of Ephraim Cutler: Prepared from His Journals and Correspondence*, p. 297.

35. Attorney Bates wrote in his diary of the confrontation with Senate Republicans: "To use the P[r]est's quaint language, while they believed

in the Prest's honesty, they seemed to think that when he had in him any good purposes, Mr. S.[eward] contrived to suck them out of him unperceived." Howard K. Beale, ed., *The Diary of Edward Bates*, p. 269 (December 19, 1862).

36. Michael Burlingame and John R. Turner Ettlinger, ed., *Inside Lincoln's White House: The Complete Civil War Diary of John Hay*, p. 104 (October 30, 1863).

37. Frederick W. Seward, *Seward at Washington, as Senator and Secretary of State: 1861–1872*, p. 147.

38. Don Fehrenbacher and Virginia Fehrenbacher, eds., *Recollected Words of Abraham Lincoln*, p. 200.

39. Allen Thorndike Rice, ed., *Reminiscences of Abraham Lincoln*, p. 582 (John B. Alley).

40. Michael Burlingame, *The Inner World of Abraham Lincoln*, p. 172.

41. Maunsell B. Field, *Personal Recollections: Memories of Many Men and Some Women*, pp. 301–302.

42. Paul Addison wrote: "There was a vacancy in British politics for a politician ready and able to capitalize on the popularity of Russia, and Cripps had the additional advantage of freedom from party ties. Having been expelled from the Labour Party in 1939 for advocating a Popular Front, he posed no party political risk to the Conservatives, who were inclined to flatter him at Labour's expense." Paul Addison, *Churchill: The Unexpected Hero*, p. 189.

43. Francis B. Carpenter, *The Inner Life of Abraham Lincoln: Six Months at the White House*, p. 85.

44. *CWAL*, Volume VII, p. 507 (Interview with Alexander W. Randall and Joseph T. Mills, August 19, 1864).

45. Osborn H. Oldroyd, ed., *The Lincoln Memorial: Album-Immortelles*, pp. 462–463.

46. Allen Thorndike Rice, ed., *Reminiscences of Abraham Lincoln*, pp. 333–334 (Schuyler Colfax).

47. Michael Burlingame, *Abraham Lincoln: A Life*, Volume II, pp. 245–248.

48. David E. Long, "A Time for Lincoln," *Lincoln Lore*, Spring 2006, p.16.

49. Allen C. Guelzo, *Fateful Lightning: A New History of the Civil War & Reconstruction*, p. 317.

50. "It is safe to say that no general in the army studied his maps . . . with half the industry" of Lincoln. John G. Nicolay and John Hay, *Abraham Lincoln*, Volume VI, p. 114.

51. "Abraham Lincoln: The Thirtieth Anniversary of His Assassination," pp. 107–108 (George William Curtis to R.R. Wright, undated).

52. Joan Bright Astley, *The Inner Circle: A View of War at the Top*, p. 62.

53. In December 1941, Churchill wrote in the war plan he prepared for FDR, "War is a constant struggle and must be waged from day to day. It is only with some difficulty and within limits that provision can be made for the future. Experience shows that forecasts are usually

falsified and preparations always in arrears. Nevertheless, there must be a design and theme for bringing the war to a victorious end in a reasonable period." Winston S. Churchill, *The Grand Alliance: The Second World War*, Volume III, p. 583 (December 18, 1941).

54.   Craig L. Symonds, *Lincoln and His Admirals*, p. 360.

55.   Baron Charles McMoran Wilson Moran, *Churchill, Taken from the Diaries of Lord Moran: The Struggle for Survival, 1940–1965*, p. 199 (September 22, 1944). "For Beaverbrook," noted historian Richard Toye, "intrigue sprang eternal." In October 1940, Beaverbrook sent an emissary to David Lloyd George to convince the former prime minister "that I should concoct some plan for saving this country from the doom in which it is heading with its accustomed blind fury." Richard Toye, *Lloyd George & Churchill*, p. 375.

56.   Thomas Parrish, *To Keep the British Isles Afloat: FDR's Men in Churchill's London, 1941*, p. 178.

57.   James Leasor, *War at the Top: The Experiences of General Leslie Hollis*, p. 102.

58.   A. J. P. Taylor, *Beaverbrook: A Biography*, p. xiii. Harold Macmillan, who served in the Ministry of Supply early in the war, wrote of Beaverbrook's resignation in 1942: "Beaverbrook had undergone tremendous strain for twenty arduous months. His exertions at the Ministry of Aircraft Production were almost superhuman. His recent journeys to Washington and Moscow, under the harsh conditions of travelling in war-time, had affected him severely. His asthma had grown daily worse. The frame had become too weak to sustain the flame of his spirit. I am sure that if he had been in full health he would have carried on, partly from his devotion to Churchill and partly from his sense of duty." Harold Macmillan, *The Blast of War*, p. 144.

59.   David Low, *Autobiography*, p. 175.

60.   Harold Macmillan, *The Blast of War*, p. 186.

61.   *The Memoirs of General Lord Ismay*, p. 174. Frederick Lindemann's prodigious memory and unquestioned brilliance were matched by his pet hatreds and unresolved quarrels—even with Churchill's son-in-law, Duncan Sandys. See John Colville, *Winston Churchill and His Inner Circle*, pp. 55–59. General Ismay wrote: "Churchill used to say that the Prof's brain was a beautiful piece of mechanism, and the prof did not dissent from that judgment. He seemed to have a poor opinion of the intellect of everyone with the exception of Lord Birkenhead, Mr Churchill and Professor Lindemann; and he had a special contempt for the bureaucrat and all his ways." Hastings Lionel Ismay, *Memoirs of General Lord Ismay*, p. 174. Military historian John Keegan wrote of Lindemann: "He was not a likeable man. Although John Colville found that 'it was impossible not to be fond of him,' he also observed that Lindemann 'demonstrated an implacable, almost ludicrous dislike of anybody who had ever thwarted or opposed him,' which comprised a large group.

Yet, if he aroused dislike in return, few denied that Lindemann had an eclectic scientific mind and a brilliant gift of exposition, precisely the qualities Churchill valued." Robert Blake and William Roger Louis, eds., *Churchill: A Major New Assessment of His Life in Peace and War*, p. 345 (John Keegan, "Churchill's Strategy").

62. Winston S. Churchill, *Their Finest Hour: The Second World War*, Volume II, p. 338.

63. Max Hastings, *Winston's War: Churchill 1940–1945*, p. 177.

64. Lucius E. Chittenden, *Recollections of President Lincoln and His Administration*, p. 238.

65. Charles Carleton Coffin, *Abraham Lincoln*, p. 278.

66. William Manchester and Paul Reid, *The Last Lion: Winston Spencer Churchill, Defender of the Realm, 1940–1965*, p. 306.

67. Allan Nevins, ed., *The Diary of George Templeton Strong, 1860–1865*, p. 603 (George Templeton Strong to Francis Lieber, July 12, 1862).

68. William Manchester and Paul Reid, *The Last Lion: Winston Spencer Churchill, Defender of the Realm, 1940–1965*, p. 844. Churchill's fertile mind focused on how to develop technology for both defense and offense. Churchill wrote in his memoirs of his emphasis early in the war on the need to develop landing craft, writing "from the very beginning I provided a great deal of the impulse and authority for creating the immense apparatus and armada for the landing of armour on the beaches, without which it is now universally recognized that all such major operations would have been impossible." Winston S. Churchill, *Their Finest Hour: The Second World War*, Volume II, p. 224.

69. Richard Langworth, ed., *Churchill by Himself*, p. 284 (May 30, 1941). Churchill added: "Don't argue the matter. The difficulties will argue for themselves."

70. Douglas L. Wilson and Rodney O. Davis, eds., *Herndon's Informants*, pp. 505–506 (Joseph Gillespie to William H. Herndon, December 8, 1866).

71. Churchill had been tested in war as a young subaltern cavalry officer—in Northwest India, the Sudan, and South Africa. There, his bravery approached recklessness. Historian Ronald Lewin wrote that Churchill's bravery in wartime conditions helps "explain why he was both respected by the seasoned men of war who surrounded him and revered by millions to whom he appeared to be not so much a remote War Lord as a larger and more heroic version of themselves." Ronald Lewin, *Churchill as Warlord*, p. 131.

72. Winston S. Churchill, *Their Finest Hour: The Second World War*, Volume II, p. 348.

73. Martin Gilbert, *Continue to Pester, Nag and Bite: Winston Churchill's War Leadership*, p. 79.

74. Geoffrey Best, *Churchill: A Study in Greatness*, p. 203.

75. Geoffrey Best, *Churchill: A Study in Greatness*, p. 199.

76. Max Hastings, *Winston's War: Churchill 1940–1945*, p. 183.

77. Winston S. Churchill, *Closing the Ring: The Second World War*, Volume V, p. 314.

78. Harry C. Butcher wrote that the British chiefs agreed with Eisenhower "that no particular geographical location, including Rome, has in itself any significance from a military viewpoint as compared with the principal mission of the Supreme commander of the Mediterranean forces, which as already given him by the Combined Chiefs, is to carry on operations which will give maximum support to the cross-Channel invasion of France. The Prime Minister was not present and he likely will favour the capture of Rome for the psychological effect." Harry C. Butcher, *Three Years with Eisenhower: The Personal Diary of Captain Harry C. Butcher, USNR, Naval Aide to General Eisenhower, 1942–1945*, p. 509 (March 27, 1944). London: William Heinemann LTD, 1946.

79. Robert Katz, *The Battle for Rome: The Germans, the Allies, the Partisans, and the Pope*, p. 140.

80. Winston Churchill. *The Gathering Storm: The Second World War*, Volume I, p. 601.

81. T. Harry Williams, *Lincoln and His Generals*, p. 7.

82. In World War II, it was Germany that had the advantage of interior lines and the ability to transport troops from one theater of the conflict to another. The Nazis had another advantage, noted historian William H. McNeill: "Despite the sullen discontent of most of Europe, the Germans found themselves in a position to use the population and resources of the continent as a whole to support their war machine." William McNeill, *America, Britain and Russia: Their Co-operation and Conflict, 1941–1946*, p. 34. General William T. Sherman would make similar use of a sullen South in 1864–1865 by feeding his army with local foodstuffs.

83. Correlli Barnett, *The Lords of War: From Lincoln to Churchill*, p. 22.

84. Geoffrey Best, *Churchill and War*, p. 179.

85. Eliot Cohen, *Supreme Command: Soldiers, Statesmen, and Leadership in Wartime*, p. 114.

86. Churchill had been chastened by his experiences in World War I. "[I]t was precisely because of the Dardanelles débâcle that Churchill behaved in so relatively restrained a manner towards his General Staff when he became prime minister. He railed, ranted, wept sometimes, often cajoled and relentlessly pressurized, but the Dardanelles had been the defining crisis of his life so far, and he had genuinely learned from it," wrote historian Andrew Roberts. Andrew Roberts, *Masters and Commanders: How Four Titans Won the War in the West, 1941–1945*, p. 236.

87. In the Battle of the Atlantic, a change in the German enigma codes caused a major intelligence crisis and a greater crisis regarding the convoys supplying food and equipment to Britain.

88. Michael Burlingame, *Abraham Lincoln: A Life*, Volume II, p. 213.

89. Raymond Callahan, *Churchill and His Generals*, pp. 18–21. Attacking Churchill in July 1943, Aneurin Bevan also attacked the class structure

of the British army. "The Prime Minister must realise that in this country there is a taunt on everyone's lips that if Rommel [a middle-class German] had been in the British Army he would still have been a sergeant." Winston S. Churchill, *The Hinge of Fate: The Second World War,* Volume IV, p. 359. Notable World War II generals such as Claude Auchinleck, Alan Brooke, Richard O'Connor, Archibald Wavell, and Henry Maitland Wilson were sons of British army officers.

VII. FINDING AND MANAGING GENERALS

1. *CWAL,* Volume V, pp. 184–185 (Lincoln to George B. McClellan, April 9, 1862).
2. John Connell, *Wavell, Scholar and Soldier,* p. 463 (John Dill to Archibald Wavell, May 21, 1941).
3. Max Hastings, *Winston's War: Churchill 1940–1945,* p. 123.
4. Clement Attlee, *As It Happened,* p. 198.
5. Denis Richards, *Portal of Hungerford: The Life of Marshal of the Royal Air Force, Viscount Portal of Hungerford,* p. 185. Historian Geoffrey Best wrote of the COS: "Churchill was not gentle in argument when determined to get his way. Sometimes he was not even gentlemanly. The men who served on that committee had to be tough, but, once the professionally defensive and overcautious Field Marshal Sir John Dill had been replaced as CIGS by General Sir Alan Brooke, they all were so." Geoffrey Best, *Churchill: A Study in Greatness,* p. 210.
6. Geoffrey Best, *Churchill: A Study in Greatness,* p. 207.
7. Churchill wrote in his memoirs: "There was a very strong feeling in Cabinet and high military circles that the abilities and strategic knowledge of Sir John Dill, who had been since April 23 Vice-Chief of the Imperial Staff, should find their full scope in his appointment as our principal Army adviser. No one could doubt that his professional standing was in many ways superior to that of Ironside." Dill was appointed CIGS on May 27 while Ironside stepped down to serve as commander of British Home Forces. Then in July, Anthony Eden recommended that General Alan Brooke succeed Ironside as chief of the Home Forces." Winston S. Churchill, *Their Finest Hour: The Second World War,* Volume II, p. 64.
8. Roderick Macleod and Denis Kelly, eds., *Time Unguarded: The Ironside Diaries, 1937–1940,* pp. 383, 387 (July 10 and 19, 1940).
9. Raymond Callahan, *Churchill and His Generals,* p. 11.
10. Mackubin T. Owens, "Lincoln as Commander-in-Chief," August 6, 2007, John M. Ashbrook Center for Public Affairs. www.ashbrook.org/tools/printerpage.asp.
11. Alex Danchev and Daniel Todman, eds., *War Diaries 1939–1945: Field Marshal Lord Alanbrooke,* p. 207 (December 4, 1941).
12. Charles McMoran Wilson Moran, *Churchill, Taken from the Diaries of Lord Moran: The Struggle for Survival, 1940–1965,* p. 758.

13. Martin Gilbert, *Winston S. Churchill: Finest Hour, 1939–1941*, pp. 683–685 (General James Marshall-Cornwall).

14. Geoffrey Best, *Churchill: A Study in Greatness*, p. 181.

15. Correlli Barnett, *The Lords of War: From Lincoln to Churchill*, p. 284.

16. Hastings Lionel Ismay, *Memoirs of General Lord Ismay*, p. 270.

17. Stephen W. Sears, ed., *The Civil War Papers of George B. McClellan: Selected Correspondence, 1860–1865*, p. 70 (George B. McClellan to Mary Ellen McClellan, July 27, 1861).

18. *CWAL*, Volume V, p. 481 (Lincoln to George McClellan, October 29, 1862).

19. George B. McClellan, *McClellan's Own Story: The War for the Union, the Soldiers Who Fought It*, pp. 657–658 (George McClellan to his wife, October 29, 1862).

20. John Keegan, ed., *Churchill's Generals*, p. 60 (Alex Danchev, "Field-Marshal Sir John Dill").

21. James Leasor, *War at the Top: The Experiences of General Sir Leslie Hollis, KCB KBE*, pp. 148–149.

22. Reginald W. Thompson, *Generalissimo Churchill*, p. 92.

23. Anthony Eden, *The Reckoning; the Memoirs of Anthony Eden, Earl of Avon*, p. 147.

24. Alex Danchev, "The Strange Case of Field Marshall Sir John Dill," *Medical History*, July 1991, p. 354.

25. John Colville, *The Fringes of Power*, p. 188 (July 10, 1940).

26. Mary Soames, *Clementine Churchill: The Biography of a Marriage*, p. 383.

27. John Kennedy, *The Business of War*, p. 178. Kennedy wrote: "Dill was regarded by many as being completely worn out. They said his brain was anyhow not agile enough for his job, that he had no drive, and that he was always half asleep at meetings of the Defence Committee and of the Chiefs of Staff. Beaverbrook had remarked that Dill, although no doubt a very sound soldier, was the sort of man who made no impression when he came into a room; but that, in any case, there were no outstanding soldiers in this war such as there had been in the last." John Kennedy, *The Business of War: The War Narrative of Major-General Sir John Kennedy*, p. 161. Dill we know was sick with anemia.

28. After the war, Churchill told David Margesson, who had been Secretary of State for War in 1941, "Brooke was the right man—the only man." Andrew Roberts, *Masters and Commanders: How Four Titans Won the War in the West, 1941–1945*, p. 56. After the war, Churchill would see little of Brooke. He did not suit Churchill's taste in men. Brooke was a noted bird-watcher, a master of ornithology.

29. James Leasor, *War at the Top: The Experiences of General Leslie Hollis*, p. 11. Historian Keith Sainsbury wrote that Brooke's "obvious ability and decisive, rather forbidding manner enabled him to command the respect of all his military subordinates, including the difficult and obstreperous [Bernard] Montgomery. He was not afraid to stand up to Churchill,

and frequently did so. On Brooke, indeed, fell the principal burden of checking the Prime Minister's wilder flights of fancy." Keith Sainsbury, *The Turning Point: Roosevelt, Stalin, Churchill, and Chiang-Kai-Shek,* 1943, p. 155.

30.   Charles McMoran Wilson Moran, *Churchill, Taken from the Diaries of Lord Moran: The Struggle for Survival, 1940–1965,* p. 758.

31.   Alex Danchev and Daniel Todman, eds., *War Diaries, 1939–1945: Field Marshal Lord Alanbrooke,* pp. 189–190.

32.   Michael Burlingame, *Abraham Lincoln: A Life,* Volume II, p. 197.

33.   Allen C. Guelzo, *Fateful Lightning: A New History of the Civil War and Reconstruction,* p. 160.

34.   Political scientist Waller R. Newell noted that Lincoln "never sought military glory for himself as commander in chief—but he encouraged such ambition in his generals to give them further incentive to win the war and bring justice to the oppressed. His example taught them: All honor through serving the good, with no thought of material benefits for oneself." Waller R. Newell, *The Soul of a Leader, Character, Conviction, and Ten Lessons in Political Greatness,* p. 167.

35.   Donald Stoker, *The Grand Design: Strategy and the U.S. Civil War,* p. 64.

36.   John Keegan, *The American Civil War,* p. 151.

37.   Correlli Barnett wrote that "Lincoln showed that he had learned faster about strategy than his generals, writing to Halleck about Meade's proposal: 'My last attempt upon Richmond was to get McClellan, when he was nearer there than the enemy was, to run in ahead of him. Since then I have constantly desired the Army of the Potomac to make Lee's army and not Richmond, its object point.'" Correlli Barnett, *The Lords of War: From Lincoln to Churchill,* p. 21.

38.   *CWAL,* Volume V, p. 118 (Lincoln to George B. McClellan, February 3, 1862). Some English military historians hold different views of McClellan. Military historian John Keegan wrote that McClellan's "scheme to bypass the region altogether by an amphibious but flanking movement to the Virginia Peninsula was strategically brilliant, and one for which he has never received correct credit." John Keegan, *The American Civil War,* p. 238. McClellan's plan was far better than its execution, however. Military historian Colin R. Ballard wrote that McClellan "has been accused of hesitation, over-caution, timidity, but none of these words really fits. Hesitation is certainly wrong; McClellan never hesitated about anything in his life; it is quite a mistake to picture him trembling on the brink and trying to screw up courage for the plunge. Not a bit of it. The river was impassable—of course, it was—and nobody but a fool would attempt it till to-morrow. Timidity is not the right term; he was physically brave; his assurance is shown by the calm way in which he pursued his own path regardless of suggestions, appeals, or even definite orders; his letters to the Government contain terms which are far from timid, and might be called impertinent. There certainly was

caution, plenty of it, but even this word is not satisfying, because from his point of view the caution was quite justifiable. Perhaps we can get nearest to it by saying that his organizing faculties were overdeveloped, and he was governed by an overwhelming desire to complete his preparations. His victory must be certain and complete." Colin R. Ballard, *The Military Genius of Abraham Lincoln*, pp. 107–108. Ballard's contrary view is plausible but not convincing. Certain and complete victory could not be planned, only won in the fog of war.

39. T. Harry Williams, *Lincoln and His Generals*, p. 7.

40. Michael Burlingame, *Lincoln and the Civil War*, pp. 2–3.

41. James M. McPherson, *Tried by War: Abraham Lincoln as Commander in Chief*, p. 4.

42. *CWAL*, Volume V, p. 51 (Annual Message to Congress, December 1, 1861).

43. *CWAL*, Volume V, pp. 98–99 (Lincoln to Don Carlos Buell, January 13, 1862).

44. *CWAL*, Volume V, pp. 98–99 (Lincoln to Don Carlos Buell, January 13, 1862).

45. *CWAL*, Volume V, p. 87 (Lincoln to Henry W. Halleck, January 1, 1862).

46. *CWAL*, Volume V, pp. 510–511 (Lincoln to Carl Schurz, November 24, 1862).

47. *CWAL*, Volume V, pp. 185–186 (Lincoln to George B. McClellan, April 9, 1862).

48. Historian James Oakes wrote: "Grant was indifferent rather than hostile to emancipation, and Sherman resisted emancipation for legal and practical reasons. General Buell was closer in spirit to McClellan. Both men hated the idea that a war to restore the Union had to be a war against slavery as well. During 1862, Buell's orders regarding slaves were, if anything even more restrictive than Sherman's or Grant's. Oblivious to the shift in federal policy, Buell continued to enforce a rigid exclusion policy that both Grant and Sherman had abandoned." James Oakes, *Freedom National; The Destruction of Slavery in the United States, 1861–1865*, pp. 338–339.

49. Ronald Lewin, *Churchill as Warlord*, p. 75.

50. Carlo D'Este, *Warlord: A Life of Winston Churchill at War, 1874–1945*, p. 339.

51. David L. Wilson and John Y. Simon, *Ulysses S. Grant: Essays and Documents*, p. 127. (E. B. Long, "Ulysses S. Grant for Today.")

52. Michael Burlingame, *Abraham Lincoln: A Life*, Volume II, p. 425.

53. Bell Irvin Wiley, "Billy Yank and Abraham Lincoln," *The Abraham Lincoln Quarterly*, June 1950, Vol. 6, no. 2, p. 103.

54. Historian Richard Carwardine noted of Lincoln: "Quite apart from his offering impromptu remarks to particular units passing by the executive mansion, he [met] very many Union volunteers individually. Early in the war he earnestly promised his troops that he would take care

of them, urging even the lowliest privates to bring their problems and grievances to him. He and his secretaries found themselves bombarded by letters and speculative visitors, as soldiers and their families sought help in cases that most often related to sickness, pay, furlough or military punishment. Lincoln held perhaps two thousand or more private interviews with Union soldiers. This was a tiny proportion of the enlisted men, but it did not take long for the impressions of those who had seen or met the president to be broadcast throughout the close-knit regimental communities that made up the Federal army." Richard J. Carwardine, *Lincoln: A Life of Purpose and Power*, p. 284.

55.   Harold Holzer and Sara Vaughn Gabbard, eds., *Lincoln and Freedom: Slavery, Emancipation, and the Thirteenth Amendment*, p. 114.

56.   James McPherson, *This Mighty Scourge: Perspectives on the Civil War*, p. 165. The true proportions of Lincoln's soldier vote have been questioned by Jonathan W. White in *Emancipation, the Union Army, and the Reelection of Abraham Lincoln*, passim.

57.   John Strawson, *Churchill and Hitler: In Victory and Defeat*, p. 305.

58.   Winston S. Churchill, *The Grand Alliance: The Second World War*, Volume III, p. 177.

59.   Correlli Barnett, *The Desert Generals*, p. 71.

60.   Winston Churchill, *The Hinge of Fate: The Second World War*, Volume V, pp. 464–465.

61.   Richard Langworth, ed., *Churchill by Himself: The Definitive Collection of Quotations*, p. 362 (Speech at October 23, 1945).

62.   Correlli Barnett called this an unnecessary battle. "Had the Eighth Army held its attack until the moment Rommel had left the shelter of his fixed defences and begun to retreat, it could have completely destroyed the Panzerarmee at small cost." Correlli Barnett, *The Desert Generals*, p. 272. Barnett accepted little of the Montgomery myth. Indeed, Barnett exposed Monty's deceptions.

63.   Charles Lewis Broad, *Winston Churchill, 1874–1952*, p. 437 (November 11, 1942).

64.   Charles Eade, ed., *Winston Churchill, War Speeches: From June 25, 1941 to September 6, 1943*, p. 420 (February 11, 1943).

65.   Canadian Prime Minister Mackenzie King recorded that Churchill "said, using the expression 'By God,' nothing would ever induce him to have an attack made upon Europe without sufficient strength and being positively certain that they could win. He said that to go there without a sufficient force would be to incur another Dunkirk, and what would be worse than that, they would have of course to supply the French with arms and cause them to rise when any invasion was made, and that to have to leave them to the Huns would be to have the whole of the French massacred, and none of them left." Nigel Hamilton, *The Mantle of Command: FDR at War, 1941–1942*, p. 314.

66. "It was characteristic of him that he always approved attacks, and seldom retreats, even when . . . failure to withdraw would mean encirclement and annihilation." Correlli Barnett, *The Lords of War: From Lincoln to Churchill*, p. 66.

67. General Ismay wrote that through 1941, Churchill pushed for an invasion of northern Norway. The COS opposed it. "They were almost certainly right. The Prime Minister continued to press them for some time, but did not persist. Not once during the whole war did he overrule his military advisers on a purely military question." Hastings Lionel Ismay, *Memoirs of General Lord Ismay*, pp. 165–166.

68. Historian Maxwell Philip Schoenfeld wrote: "The main impression of Churchill's conduct in Quebec [in 1943] and, subsequently, in Washington is that his approach to strategy was largely opportunistic; he was bent on grabbing prizes cheaply and quickly as Italy fell and the Axis position in the Mediterranean collapsed." Maxwell Philip Schoenfeld, *The War Ministry of Winston Churchill*, p. 198. Less sympathetically, historian Vincent Orange wrote that Churchill's "life-long enthusiasm for 'forlorn endeavour in remote places' cost many men their lives during his years as Prime Minister." Vincent Orange, *Churchill and His Airmen*, p. 117.

69. Geoffrey Best, *Churchill and War*, p. 150.

70. Forrest C. Pogue, *George C. Marshall: Ordeal and Hope*, Volume II, p. 329.

71. Eleanor Roosevelt, *This I Remember*, p. 252.

72. Simon Berthon and Joanna Potts, *Warlords: An Extraordinary Re-creation of World War II Through the Eyes and Minds of Hitler, Churchill, Roosevelt, and Stalin*, p. 210.

73. Walter Thompson, *Beside the Bulldog: The Intimate Memoirs of Churchill's Bodyguard*, p. 123.

74. Geoffrey Best, *Churchill and War*, pp. 156–157.

75. Raymond Callahan, *Churchill and His Generals*, p. 11.

76. Ronald Lewin, *Churchill as Warlord*, p. 14.

77. *CWAL*, Volume V, p. 91 (Lincoln to Don Carlos Buell, January 6, 1862).

78. *CWAL*, Volume VI, p. 373 (Lincoln to John M. Fleming and Robert Morrow, August 9, 1863).

79. *CWAL*, Volume VI, p. 525 (Lincoln to John Williams & N. G. Taylor, October 17, 1863).

80. Winston S. Churchill, *The Great Republic*, p. 214.

81. Michael Burlingame and John R. Tuner Ettlinger, *Inside Lincoln's White House: The Complete Civil War Diary of John Hay*, p. 248 (November 11, 1864).

82. *CWAL*, Volume VIII, p. 101 (Response to Serenade, November 10, 1864).

83. Winston Churchill, *Their Finest Hour: The Second World War*, Volume II, p. 56.

84. Paul Johnson, *Churchill*, p. 110.

85. Geoffrey Best, *Churchill: A Study in Greatness*, p. 175.

86. Elizabeth Layton Nel, *Winston Churchill by His Personal Secretary*, p. 39.

87. Robert Blake and William Roger Louis, eds., *Churchill: A Major New Assessment of His Life in Peace and War*, p. 329 (John Keegan, "Churchill's Strategy").

88. James Leasor, *War at the Top: The Experiences of General Leslie Hollis*, p. 11.

89. James Leasor, *War at the Top: The Experiences of General Leslie Hollis*, p. 14. One general, who served as a Churchill aide, wrote: "The normal mode of operation would be something like this. About 9:30 a.m. Ismay would see the Prime Minister, usually in bed. He would often emerge with one or two Minutes that Churchill had dictated late at night or early that morning addressed to 'General Ismay for Chiefs of Staff Committee.' The Chiefs . . . met at 10.30 a.m. every day, the Agenda having been sent out by Jo Hollis, the Secretary, the afternoon before. . . . The meeting usually lasted until noon or later, and resulted in instructions to the Planning Staff, or to a Commander-in-Chief, or in a report to go forward to the Prime Minister. It was the job of the secretariat to draft the necessary terms of reference, for the Joint Planning Staff, or telegram to the Commander-in-Chief . . . Often the Chiefs would go on to a meeting with the Prime Minister at 12.30 p.m. or later in the day (or night), or there would be meetings of the Defence Committee or Cabinet." John Wheeler-Bennett, *Action This Day; Working with Churchill*, pp. 193–195 (Ian Jacob).

90. Howard K. Beale, ed., *The Diary of Edward Bates*, pp. 223–224 (January 10, 1862).

91. Winston Churchill wrote: "I had never intended to embody the office of Minister of Defence in a department. . . . There was however in existence and activity under the personal direction of the Prime Minister the Military Wing of the War Cabinet Secretariat, which had in pre-war days been the Secretariat of the Committee of Imperial Defence. At the head of this stood General Ismay, with Colonel Hollis and Colonel Jacob as his two principals, and a group of specially-selected younger officers drawn from all three Services. This Secretariat became the staff of the office of the Minister of Defence." Winston Churchill, *Their Finest Hour: The Second World War*, Volume II, p. 19.

92. Martin Gilbert, *Churchill the War Leader: Continue to Pester, Nag and Bite*, p. 6.

93. John Colville, *The Fringes of Power*, p. 289 (November 9, 1940).

94. Gideon Welles, *Diary of Gideon Welles*, Volume II, p. 504 (January 5, 1864).

95. John Kennedy, *The Business of War*, p. 317.

96. Andrew Roberts, *Masters and Commanders: How Four Titans Won the War in the West, 1941–1945*, p. 500.

97. Carlo D'Este, *Warlord: A Life of Winston Churchill at War, 1874–1945*, p. 526.

98. Max Hastings, *Winston's War, Churchill 1940–1945*, p. 362.

99. Winston S. Churchill, *The Hinge of Fate: The Second World War*, Volume V, p. 78.

100. Francis Williams, *A Prime Minister Remembers*, 1961, pp. 45–46.

101. Martin Gilbert, *Churchill the War Leader*, p. 49. Lincoln was less domineering. He generally sought to persuade and prod generals early in the war rather than directly to order them to take action. Still, he reserved to himself the prerogatives of the commander in chief. In August 1861 when John C. Frémont issued orders freeing slaves in Missouri command, Lincoln first suggested that the orders be retracted. When the general did not do so voluntarily, Lincoln ordered him to do so. When Lincoln rejected the emancipation orders of General David Hunter in May 1862, the president noted that the subject was one "I reserve to myself, and I can not feel justified in leaving to the decision of commanders in the field." *CWAL*, Volume V, pp. 222–223 (Proclamation Revoking General Hunter's Order, May 19, 1862).

102. John Kennedy, *The Business of War*, p. 182.

103. Reginald W. Thompson, *Generalissimo Churchill*, p. 92.

104. Max Hastings, *Winston's War: Churchill 1940–1945*, p. 179.

105. Alex Danchev, *Very Special Relationship: Field Marshal Sir John Dill and the Anglo-American Alliance 1941–44*, p. 4.

106. Andrew Roberts, *Masters and Commanders: How Four Titans Won the War in the West, 1941–1945*, pp. 76–78.

107. Leonard Moseley, *Marshall: Hero for Our Times*, p. 274.

108. Rufus Rockwell Wilson, ed., *Intimate Memories of Lincoln*, p. 474 (Cornelius Cole).

109. John Y. Simon, Harold Holzer, and Dawn Vogel, eds., *Lincoln Revisited*, p. 212 (Craig L. Symonds, "Lincoln and His Admirals").

110. David Jablonsky, *Churchill, the Great Game and Total War*, p. 18. Churchill established his heroic image at age 25 when he escaped from imprisonment by South African authorities during the Boer War. He was quickly catapulted to fame.

111. *CWAL*, Volume V, p. 185 (Lincoln to George B. McClellan, April 9. 1862).

112. *CWAL*, Volume VI, p. 201 (Lincoln to Joseph Hooker, May 7, 1863).

113. Michael Burlingame, ed., *Dispatches from Lincoln's White House: The Anonymous Civil War Journalism of William O. Stoddard*, p. 88 (July 21, 1862).

114. Baron Hugh Dalton, *The Second World War Diary of Hugh Dalton 1940–45*, p. 67 (July 30, 1940).

115. Robert E. Sherwood, *Roosevelt and Hopkins, An Intimate History*, p. 243.

VIII. ARMY LEADERSHIP

1. Don E. and Virginia Fehrenbacher, eds., *Recollected Words of Abraham Lincoln*, p. 32.
2. Richard Langworth, ed., *Churchill by Himself*, p. 280.
3. Michael Howard and Peter Paret, ed., *Carl von Clausewitz, On War*, p. 87, in the Princeton University Press translation (1976).
4. Martin Gilbert, *Winston S. Churchill: Road to Victory, 1941–1945*, p. 255.
5. Martin Gilbert, *Winston S. Churchill: Road to Victory, 1941–1945*, p. 234.
6. Martin Gilbert, *Winston S. Churchill: Road to Victory, 1941–1945*, p. 227. Alex Danchev and Daniel Todman, eds., *War Diaries, 1939–1945: Field Marshal Lord Alanbrooke*, p. 319 (September 8, 1942).
7. Charles Winslow Elliott, *Winfield Scott: The Soldier and the Man*, pp. 723–727.
8. "The initial Union strategy involved blockading Confederate ports to cut off cotton exports and prevent the import of manufactured goods; and using ground and naval forces to divide the Confederacy into three distinct theaters," wrote historian David Brion Davis. "Ridiculed in the press as the 'Anaconda Plan,' after the South American snake that crushes its prey to death, this strategy ultimately proved successful." David Brion Davis, *The Boisterous Sea of Liberty*, p. 510.
9. Donald Stoker, *The Grand Design: Strategy and the U.S. Civil War*, p. 43.
10. William Manchester and Paul Reid, *The Last Lion: Winston Spencer Churchill, Defender of the Realm, 1940–1965*, pp. 451, 602.
11. John Keegan, *Winston Churchill*, p. 139.
12. Winston S. Churchill, *The Great Republic*, p. 155.
13. James M. McPherson, *Tried by War*, pp. 35–36.
14. Gabor S. Boritt, ed., *Lincoln, the War President: The Gettysburg Lectures*, p. 37 (James M. McPherson, "Lincoln and the Strategy of Unconditional Surrender").
15. Winston S. Churchill, *The Great Republic*, p. 155.
16. John Keegan, ed., *Churchill's Generals*, p. 55 (Alex Danchev, "Field-Marshal Sir John Dill").
17. John Keegan, ed., *Churchill's Generals*, pp. 51–52 (Alex Danchev, "Field-Marshal Sir John Dill").
18. John Connell, *Wavell, Scholar and Soldier*, p. 256.
19. Alex Danchev and Daniel Todman, eds., *War Diaries, 1939–1945: Field Marshal Lord Alanbrooke*, p. 192 (October 20, 1941).
20. Eliot Cohen, *Supreme Command*, pp. 118, 120.
21. Michael Burlingame, *Abraham Lincoln: A Life*, Volume II, p. 213.
22. *CWAL*, Volume V, p. 203 (Lincoln to George B. McClellan, May 1, 1862).
23. *CWAL*, Volume VI, p. 450 (Lincoln to Jesse K. Dubois and Ozias M. Hatch, September 15, 1863).
24. The initial breakdown of top ministers was fifteen Tories, four Labour, and one Liberal. J. M. Lee, *The Churchill Coalition, 1940–1945*, p. 32.

One must carefully distinguish between Churchill's relationship with Labour leader Ernest Bevin, whom Churchill strongly admired, and Labour leader Aneurin Bevan, whom Churchill deeply detested. Bevan reciprocated Churchill's disdain.

25. Andrew Roberts, *Eminent Churchillians*, p. 147.

26. John M. Lee, *The Churchill Coalition, 1940–1945*, p. 38.

27. "No President ever had a Cabinet of which the members were so independent, had so large individual followings, and were so inharmonious," commented New York Republican Chauncey Depew. Rufus Rockwell Wilson, ed., *Intimate Memories of Lincoln*, p. 503 (from Chauncey M. Depew, *My Memories of Eighty Years*). Doris Kearns Goodwin extensively portrayed Lincoln's Team of Rivals. Churchill's war cabinet contained several members who nurtured dreams of becoming prime minister themselves, such as Atlee, Stafford Cripps, Anthony Eden, and Lord Beaverbrook. Cabinet members did not necessarily like or respect each other. Beaverbrook, for example, disdained Stafford Cripps and Ernest Bevin. Bevin detested Beaverbrook and fellow Labourite Herbert Morrison. Morrison would attempt to prevent Labour leader Clement Attlee from succeeding Churchill in 1945. Jonathan Schneer, *Ministers at War: Winston Churchill and His War Cabinet*, pp. 248–249.

28. John G. Nicolay and John Hay, *Abraham Lincoln: A History*, Volume IV, p. 360.

29. Albert G. Riddle, *Recollections of War Times*, p. 59.

30. Robert Wilson declared this occasion was "the only time I ever heard Mr Lincoln use profane language." Douglas Wilson and Rodney O. Davis, eds., *Herndon's Informants*, p. 207 (Robert L. Wilson to William H. Herndon, February 10, 1866).

31. Edward Davis Townsend, *Anecdotes of the Civil War in the United States*, p. 58.

32. Reginald W. Thompson, *Generalissimo Churchill*, p. 63.

33. Carlo D'Este, *Warlord: A Life of Winston Churchill at War, 1874–1945*, p. 364. David Reynolds wrote: "Churchill undoubtedly unsettled the operational conduct of the Norwegian campaign by changing plans (particularly between Narvik and Trondheim as the main target) and by offering frequent advice to commanders on the spot. He also underestimated the potency of airpower and the capacity of the Germans to invade Western Scandinavia. But in all this, as Arthur Marder has observed, his faults were also those of the Chiefs of Staff and the senior Admiralty officials, including Pound. The First Lord, was 'a main contributor' to the fiasco and not its sole author. As for the larger strategic conception, Churchill was surely misguided in his fixation with Scandinavia." Robert Blake and William Roger Louis, eds., *Churchill: A Major New Assessment of His Life in Peace and War*, p. 245 (David Reynolds, "1940: The Worst and Finest Hour").

34. Geoffrey Best, *Churchill and War,* p. 109.

35. Richard Langworth, ed., *Churchill by Himself: The Definitive Collection of Quotations* (May 23, 1940).

36. Alex Danchev and Daniel Todman, eds., *Lord Alanbrooke War Diaries, 1939–1945,* p. xvi.

37. Andrew Roberts, *Masters and Commanders: How Four Titans Won the War in the West, 1941–1945,* p. 42.

38. Geoffrey Best, *Churchill: A Study in Greatness,* p. 181.

39. Correlli Barnett, *The Lords of War: Supreme Leadership from Lincoln to Churchill,* p. 16.

40. *CWAL,* Volume VI, p. 409 (Lincoln to James C. Conkling, August 26, 1863).

41. *CWAL,* Volume VII, p. 234 (Speech, March 9, 1864).

42. Michael Burlingame, *Abraham Lincoln: A Life,* Volume II, p. 655.

43. John Keegan, "A Brit Rates Our Generals," *Civil War Times,* December 2009, p. 58.

44. Michael Burlingame, *Abraham Lincoln: A Life,* Volume II, pp. 370, 376.

45. Richard Langworth, ed., *Churchill by Himself,* p. 376 (February 9, 1941).

46. Viscount Andrew Browne Cunningham, *A Sailor's Odyssey: The Autobiography of Admiral of the Fleet, Viscount Cunningham of Hyndhope,* p. 402.

47. John Connell, *Wavell, Scholar and Soldier,* p. 255 (New York: Harcourt, Brace & World, 1964). "John Connell" was the pseudonym of John Henry Robertson, who served in the Middle East during World War II, working on British propaganda efforts.

48. John Keegan, ed., *Churchill's Generals,* p. 76 (Ian Beckett, "Field-Marshal Earl Wavell").

49. Historian Gerald Pawle wrote: "On paper he invariably expressed himself with complete clarity, but at the conference table he would often remain silent for an unconscionable period, apparently tongue-tied by indecision." Gerald Pawle, *The War and Colonel Warden,* p. 116.

50. Anthony Eden, *The Reckoning; the Memoirs of Anthony Eden, Earl of Avon,* p. 149.

51. Robert Rhodes James, *Anthony Eden: A Biography,* p. 238 (Eden to Churchill, August 13, 1940).

52. John Martin, *Downing Street: The War Years,* p. 19.

53. Reginald W. Thompson, *Generalissimo,* pp. 94–95.

54. John Connell, *Wavell, Scholar and Soldier,* p. 255.

55. Raymond Callahan, *Churchill and His Generals,* p. 35.

56. Carlo D'Este, *Warlord: A Life of Winston Churchill at War, 1874–1945,* p. 491.

57. Max Hastings, *Winston's War: Churchill 1940–1945,* pp. 112–113.

58. Harold E. Raugh Jr., *Wavell in the Middle East, 1939–1941,* p. 94.

59. Hastings Lionel Ismay, *Memoirs of General Lord Ismay,* p. 197.

60. Anthony Eden, *The Reckoning; the Memoirs of Anthony Eden, Earl of Avon,* pp. 206–207.

61. Military historian Harold E. Raugh wrote: "O'Connor was confident that this composite force could have been in Tripoli in thirty-six hours. Wavell, on the other hand, not having visited the scene of operations since 4 February, was not as familiar as he should have been with the status of captured equipment, unit preparations for a continuance of the advance, and the morale of the soldiers. Or, perhaps, he did not seriously consider an advance to Tripoli, being aware of Churchill's probable intentions in the Balkans." That is, Greece. Harold E. Raugh Jr., *Wavell in the Middle East, 1939–1941*, p. 122.

62. Finger-pointing about the responsibility for the intervention and its later ramifications has continued for decades.

63. Winston Churchill, *The Grand Alliance: The Second World War*, Volume III, p. 17 (Winston S. Churchill to Hastings Ismay, January 10, 1941).

64. Anthony Eden, *The Reckoning*, p. 251.

65. John Kennedy, *The Business of War*, p. 75.

66. Larry Arnn, *Churchill's Trial: Winston Churchill and the Survival of the Free Government*, p. 63.

67. Geoffrey Best, *Churchill and War*, p. 154. Admiral Andrew Cunningham recalled the deliberations regarding Greece: "We, the naval element, thought roughly as follows. We were bound by treaty to help Greece if she were threatened, so there was no question at all that it was, politically, the right thing to do. On the other hand, we had serious misgivings if it was correct from the military point of view. We doubted very much if our Naval, Military and Air resources were equal to it." Viscount Andrew Browne Cunningham, *A Sailor's Odyssey: The Autobiography of Admiral of the Fleet, Viscount Cunningham of Hyndhope*, p. 315. On the other hand, a top aide to Wavell recalled: "All the military evidence . . . was absolutely against the campaign. It was clearly going to be a disaster from the start. But Eden had obviously made up his mind that we had got to do it, and . . . he was quite unscrupulous and tried to make [me] fudge the figures counting rifles as guns and things like that . . . In fact the campaign had not been more of a disaster only because of very good luck and some extremely good generalship." David Dutton, *Anthony Eden: A Life and Reputation*, p. 181.

68. Carlo D'Este, *Warlord: A Life of Winston Churchill at War, 1874–1945*, pp. 511–515.

69. John Colville, *The Fringes of Power: The Incredible Inside Story of Winston Churchill*, p. 367 (March 5, 1941).

70. William Manchester and Paul Reid, *The Last Lion: Winston Spencer Churchill, Defender of the Realm, 1940–1965*, p. 334.

71. Historian John Keegan argued that the weather and logistical problems would have postponed Operation Barbarossa until June and that German operations in Greece had no effect. "The Balkan campaign . . . had been successfully concluded even more rapidly than his [Hitler's] professional military advisers could have anticipated, while the choice

for D-Day for Barbarossa had always depended not on the sequence of contingent events but on the weather and objective military factors. The German army found it more difficult than expected to position the units allocated for Barbarossa in Poland, while the lateness of the spring thaw, which had left the eastern European rivers in spate beyond the predicted date, meant that Barbarossa could not have been begun very much earlier than the third week of June, whatever Hitler's intentions." John Keegan, *The Second World War*, p. 174. Max Hastings wrote: "The British . . . persuaded themselves that their intervention in Greece had imposed a delay upon Operation Barbarossa. In reality, a late thaw and German equipment shortages were the decisive factors in causing the assault to take place later than Hitler had wished." Max Hastings, *Winston's War*, p. 130. Churchill observed that the Greece operation had served a purpose: Without it, "Yugoslavia would not now be an open enemy of Germany. Further, the Greek war had caused a marked change of attitude in the United States." Martin Gilbert, *Winston S. Churchill: Finest Hour, 1939–1941*, p. 1072 (Diary of John Colville, April 29, 1941). Keegan observed: "In the long run, Churchill's fixed belief that the northern shore of the Mediterranean was a theatre which offered wide strategic advance was to be proved correct; without Britain's chivalrous intervention in Greece in 1941, it is unlikely that Churchill could have intervened decisively in the Greek Civil War in 1944; but for Churchill's preference for Tito over [Draza] Mihailovic in 1943, it is unlikely that Yugoslavia would have detached itself from Stalin in 1948." Robert Blake and William Roger Louis, eds., *Churchill: A Major New Assessment of His Life in Peace and War*, p. 335 (John Keegan, "Churchill's Strategy").

72. Carlo D'Este, *Warlord: A Life of Winston Churchill at War, 1874–1945*, p. 514.

73. Churchill's government, especially Wavell, may have also been unduly influenced by advice from Roosevelt's unofficial envoy, William Donovan, who toured the Mediterranean in early 1942. Historian Harold E. Raugh wrote: "Donovan was convinced . . . that the Balkans offered perhaps the only place for a defeat of the Germans, and for that reason the British must retain a foothold there and form a Balkan alliance with Greece, Turkey, and Yugoslavia." Harold E. Raugh Jr., *Wavell in the Middle East, 1939–1941*, pp. 141–142, 148–149. In his memoirs, Under Secretary of State Sumner Welles supported the British decision to aid Greece. Sumner Welles wrote in his memoirs regarding reaction in Washington of Britain's strategy on Greece: "It seemed to me then, as it does now, that this decision, for which I believe Anthony Eden was largely responsible, was one of the wisest taken during the war. In the first place, if Great Britain had not lived up to its obligations to give this assistance to her allies in their moment of desperate peril, particularly after they had made so gallant and successful a resistance against

Italy, she would have incurred the justifiable resentment not only of Greece but of all the smaller powers of Europe as well. . . . It is true that sending aid to Greece made possible the subsequent advance of Rommel's armies and put Alexandria in imminent danger of Axis occupation. But the issues involved warranted the gamble taken." Sumner Welles, *The Time for Decision*, p. 168.

74. John G. Nicolay and John Hay, *Abraham Lincoln: A History*, Volume IV, pp. 359–360.

75. William Manchester and Paul Reid, *The Last Lion: Winston Spencer Churchill, Defender of the Realm, 1940–1965*, p. 288. Churchill admitted, "Not having access to official information for so many years, I did not comprehend the revolution effected since the last war by the incursion of a mass of fast-moving heavy armour." Winston S. Churchill, *Their Finest Hour: The Second World War*, Volume II, p. 39. One British Commonwealth official stationed in the Middle East observed in 1942: "After two and three-quarter years of war we are not making a tank that is any good. Our radio sets can't stand up to the jolting of a car or truck. We do not have amongst our anti-aircraft guns the equivalent of the German 88mm used in an anti-tank role." Reginald W. Thompson, *Generalissimo Churchill*, p. 172.

76. John Keegan, ed., *Churchill's Generals*, p. 79 (Ian Beckett, "Field-Marshal Earl Wavell").

77. Churchill had an "obsession with the belief of the infallibility of his precious 'Tiger Cubs,'" noted military historian Harold E. Raugh. Harold E. Raugh Jr., *Wavell in the Middle East, 1939–1941*, p. 207. Historian Richard Lamb noted that the tanks "were found on arrival at Alexandria [in May 1941] to be in an unsatisfactory condition; they consisted of Crusaders, Matildas (the slow-moving infantry tank) and light tanks. The vehicles had been rushed on to the ships without even elementary mechanical checking. At Alexandria all had to be camouflaged and modified for the desert, and many needed overhauls." Air filters also had to be installed to prevent sand from entering the engines. Richard Lamb, *Churchill as War Leader*, p. 127. Lamb wrote: "Churchill was wrong in ascribing the failure of Battleaxe [in June 1941] to poor generalship: it was a failure of British equipment. Not only were German armoured cars and tanks superior, but Rommel also had an overwhelming advantage in anti-tank guns." Richard Lamb, *Churchill as War Leader*, p. 128.

78. John Connell, *Wavell: Scholar and Soldier*, p. 485.

79. John Keegan, ed., *Churchill's Generals*, p. 80 (Ian Beckett, "Field-Marshal Earl Wavell").

80. Winston S. Churchill, *The Grand Alliance: The Second World War*, Volume III, p. 308.

81. Winston S. Churchill, *The Grand Alliance: The Second World War*, Volume III, p. 310.

82. John Colville, *The Fringes of Power*, p. 443 (September 28, 1941).

83. Jon Meacham, *Franklin and Winston*, p. 30.

84. Christopher M. Bell *Churchill and Seapower*, p. 337.

85. Carlo D'Este, *Warlord: A Life of Winston Churchill at War, 1874–1945*, p. 489.

86. Martin S. Gilbert, *Winston S. Churchill: Finest Hour, 1939–1941*, p. 1072.

87. Anthony Eden, *The Reckoning: The Memoirs of Anthony Eden, Earl of Avon*, p. 291.

88. Anthony Eden, *The Reckoning: The Memoirs of Anthony Eden, Earl of Avon*, pp. 289–293.

89. John Connell, *Wavell: Scholar and Soldier*, pp. 504, 506 (Winston S. Churchill to A. P. Wavell, June 21, 1941, A. P. Wavell to Winston S. Churchill, June 22, 1941). In his memoirs, Rommel had a different analysis of Wavell's leadership: "Wavell's strategic planning of this offensive had been excellent. What distinguished him from other British army commanders was his great and well-balanced strategic courage, which permitted him to concentrate his forces regardless of his opponent's possible moves. He knew very well the necessity of avoiding any operation which would enable his opponent to fight on interior lines and destroy his formations one by one with locally superior concentrations. But he was put at a great disadvantage by the slow speed of his heavy infantry tanks, which prevented him from reacting quickly enough to the moves of our faster vehicles. Hence the slow speed of his armour was his soft spot, which we could seek to exploit tactically." John Connell, *Wavell: Scholar and Soldier*, p. 501.

90. Hastings Lionel Ismay, *Memoirs of General Lord Ismay*, p. 269.

91. Lord Tedder, *With Prejudice: The War Memoirs of Marshal of the Royal Air Force*, p. 200. Tedder recalled that "Auchinleck had had to pay a heavy price for his inability to select his senior staff well, or perhaps for the lack of suitable senior generals from whom to select. I admired the way in which he had taken a grip on a critical situation . . . and recognised to the full how much the Army's attitude toward the exercise of air-power had improved under his regime." Lord Tedder, *With Prejudice: The War Memoirs of Marshal of the Royal Air Force*, p. 326.

92. Hastings Lionel Ismay, *Memoirs of General Lord Ismay*, p. 269 (August 2, 1941).

93. William L. Langer and S. Everett Gleason, *The Undeclared War, 1940–1941*, p. 589. Historian Tuvia Ben-Moshe: "In August 1941 it was impossible to change course. The decision Churchill had made late in 1940 to rush to the Middle East as many forces as shipping could carry, and British entanglements in that region, had become Britain's most effective argument vis-à-vis the Americans in support of its strategy." Tuvia Ben-Moshe, *Churchill: Strategy and History*, p. 171.

94. John Kennedy, *The Business of War: The War Narrative of Major-General Sir John Kennedy*, p. 159.

95. General Richard O'Connor, responsible for the remarkable success of Operation COMPASS in 1940–1941, was captured by the Germans in April 1941.

96. Richard Lamb, *Churchill as War Leader,* pp. 134–135. Historian Tuvia Ben-Moshe wrote that in mid-June 1941 Churchill had pushed "Wavell to launch a premature counteroffensive (Battleaxe), which immediately turned into a resounding failure. Thereafter he began to exert pressure on Auchinleck . . . to bring forward the date of his attack in Libya. But Auchinleck refused to open his offensive before the autumn of 1941. Churchill recalled him to London, where he informed the general that it would be most unpleasant were the Russians to bear the main burden of the war while Britain did nothing at all. Eden added that should the Russians drive back the Germans without Britain having launched any offensive, the former would subsequently claim the credit for Germany's defeat." Tuvia Ben-Moshe, *Churchill: Strategy and History,* p. 169.

97. Winston S. Churchill, *The Grand Alliance, The Second World War,* p. 481 (Churchill to Claude Auchinleck, October 18, 1941).

98. Charles McMoran Wilson Moran, *Churchill, Taken from the Diaries of Lord Moran: The Struggle for Survival, 1940–1965,* p. 52.

99. John Kennedy, *The Business of War,* p. 226.

100. Martin Gilbert, *Winston S. Churchill's Finest Hour, 1939–1941,* p. 1055.

101. Winston S. Churchill, *The Grand Alliance: The Second World War,* Volume III, p. 183 (Churchill to Wavell, April 7, 1941).

102. Michael Burlingame, *Abraham Lincoln: A Life,* Volume II, p. 176.

IX. 1862/1942

1. *CWAL,* Volume V, p. 346 (Lincoln to Cuthbert Bullitt, July 28. 1862).

2. Robert Rhodes James, *Churchill Speaks,* p. 798 (Churchill, February 15, 1942).

3. Martin Gilbert, *Winston S. Churchill: Road to Victory, 1941–1945,* p. 67 (Mary Churchill Diary, February 27, 1862).

4. Hastings Lionel Ismay, *Memoirs of General Lord Ismay,* p. 280.

5. Montgomery Meigs, "General M. C. Meigs on the Conduct of the Civil War," *American Historical Review,* Volume XXVI, 1921, p. 292.

6. *CWAL,* Volume V, pp. 289–290 (Lincoln to George B. McClellan, June 28, 1862).

7. Max Hastings, *Winston's War: Churchill 1940–1945,* p. 205.

8. Winston S. Churchill, *The Hinge of Fate: The Second World War,* Volume V, pp. 493–494.

9. Michael Burlingame, ed., *With Lincoln in the White House: Letters, Memoranda, and Other Writings of John G. Nicolay, 1860–1865,* pp. 72–73 (February 27, 1862).

10. Charles McMoran Wilson Moran, *Churchill, Taken from the Diaries of Lord Moran,* p. 29.

11. Richard Lamb, *Churchill as War Leader*, p. 185.

12. Robert Rhodes Jones, *Anthony Eden*, p. 262.

13. John Harvey, ed., *The War Diaries of Oliver Harvey, 1941–1945*, p. 94 (February 12, 1942).

14. John Harvey, ed., *The War Diaries of Oliver Harvey, 1941–1945*, p. 98 (February 18, 1942).

15. "The strength of his power of persuasion had to be experienced to realize the strength that was required to counter it," wrote Brooke. Alex Danchev and Daniel Todman, eds., *War Diaries, 1939–1945: Field Marshal Lord Alanbrooke*, p. 82.

16. Winston S. Churchill, *The Hinge of Fate: The Second World War*, Volume IV, p. 67 (Churchill to Beaverbrook, February 10, 1942).

17. Kenneth Young, *Churchill and Beaverbrook: A Study in Friendship and Politics*, p. 227.

18. Historian Jonathan Schneer wrote of Churchill's handling of Labour and his dismissal of Greenwood from the War Cabinet: Churchill's "mastery of mollifying them reveals his mastery of the political game: he would sack [Arthur] Greenwood but simultaneously promote Labour Party leader Clement Attlee to become secretary of state for the dominions—and deputy prime minister (which would mollify not only Labour supporters but Attlee himself)." Jonathan Schneer, *Ministers at War: Winston Churchill and His War Cabinet*, p. 132.

19. Beaverbrook despised Bevin, Attlee, and Herbert Morrison, another Labour Minister who served as Home Secretary and who would join the War Cabinet in November 1942. Jonathan Schneer, *Ministers at War: Winston Churchill and His War Cabinet*, pp. 76–77, 107–108.

20. Winston S. Churchill, *The Hinge of Fate: The Second World War*, Volume IV, p. 63.

21. Winston S. Churchill, *The Hinge of Fate: The Second World War*, Volume IV, p. 63 (January 31, 1942).

22. Martin Gilbert, *Winston S. Churchill: Road to Victory, 1941–1945*, p. 64.

23. Winston S. Churchill, *The Hinge of Fate: The Second World War*, Volume IV, p. 74 (February 26, 1942).

24. Martin Gilbert, *Winston S. Churchill: Road to Victory, 1941–1945*, p. 64.

25. Lord Hankey, *The Supreme Command, 1914–1918*, Volume I, p. 5. London: Routledge, 2014.

26. Martin Gilbert, *Winston S. Churchill: Road to Victory 1941–1945*, p. 66 (Speech to House of Commons, February 24, 1942).

27. Union Generals Winfield Scott and Irvin McDowell protested in July 1861 that Union troops needed more training before engaging Confederate forces. "This is not an army. It will take a long time to make an army," said McDowell before the First Battle of Bull Run. Nathaniel W. Stephenson, *Lincoln: An Account of His Personal Life*, p. 173 (Bobbs-Merrill, 1922). After the battle, McDowell observed that the Union army lacked any officer "who had ever manoeuvred troops in large

bodies. There was not one in the Army. I did not believe there was one in the whole country." James A. Rawley, *Turning Points of the Civil War*, p. 54. President Lincoln responded: "You are green, it is true; but they are green, also; you are green alike." Michael Burlingame, *Abraham Lincoln: A Life*, Volume II, p. 181. Lincoln was partially right; the First Battle of Bull Run might have been won under better Union leadership. Lincoln began his presidency without an officer corps schooled in war. Their limited experience came from the Mexican-American War, in which most were junior officers. Many went over to the Confederacy. But the Americans in February 1943 were preparing to fight battle-tested German troops. Again, they lacked an experienced officer corps or battle experience. Robert Nisbet wrote: "The results of insufficient American training and experience showed up immediately in Tunisia; almost disastrously at Kasserine [Pass in February 1943]. Despite superior numbers and military equipment, the Americans were no match for the Germans. The Americans were routed, with over half of their heavy artillery captured by the German forces. Had it not been for the British troops, the battle for North Africa would have been over before it really began." Robert Nisbet, *Roosevelt and Stalin: The Failed Courtship*, p. 37. Lincoln thought the fighting abilities of North and South were equal. "We must not forget that the people of the seceded States, like those of the loyal ones, are American citizens, with essentially the same characteristics and powers," he said after the bombardment of Fort Sumter. "Exceptional advantages on one side are counterbalanced by exceptional advantages on the other. We must make up our minds that man for man the soldier from the South will be a match for the soldier from the North and vice versa." John George Nicolay and John Hay, *Abraham Lincoln, a History*, Volume IV, p. 79.

28. Andrew Roberts, *Masters and Commanders: How Four Titans Won the War in the West, 1941–1945*, p. 132.

29. Andrew Roberts, *Masters and Commanders: How Four Titans Won the War in the West, 1941–1945*, pp. 164–165.

30. John Kennedy, *The Business of War*, p. 245.

31. Winston S. Churchill, *The Hinge of Fate: The Second World War*, Volume IV, p. 347. Before Churchill left for Washington, he was "very firm on limitations of what was possible for us this year: he would not authorize any large-scale operations which didn't offer fair prospect of success, since a failure would not help Russia either." John Harvey, ed., *War Diaries of Oliver Harvey*, pp. 131–132 (June 10, 1942).

32. At the conclusion of the Washington meeting with Molotov, a communiqué declared a "full understanding was reached with regard to the urgent tasks of creating a Second Front in Europe in 1942." General Marshall objected to the reference to 1942 and enlisted Hopkins to push for its deletion, but FDR decided to keep it. A similar statement was signed in London by Churchill. David Roll, *The Hopkins Touch*, p.

198. Thus the president, according to Harriman, "hoped to encourage the Russians to hold out by raising their expectations for Allied action in the west." W. Averell Harriman and Elie Abel, *Special Envoy to Churchill and Stalin, 1941–1946*, p. 138. After Molotov departed, FDR proclaimed the meeting "a real success" in a telegram to Churchill. "[W]e have got on a personal footing of candor and as good friendship as can be acquired through an interpreter. . . . I am especially anxious that he carry back some real results of his mission and that he will give a favorable account to Stalin." Warren F. Kimball, ed., *Churchill & Roosevelt: The Complete Correspondence*, Volume I, pp. 503–504 (May 30, 1942). FDR did not hesitate to dissimulate for short-term gain, risking long-term embarrassment.

33. Herbert Feis, *Churchill-Roosevelt-Stalin: The War They Waged and the Peace They Sought*, p. 71 (William H. Standley to Franklin D. Roosevelt, June 22, 1942).

34. Alex Danchev and Daniel Todman, eds., *Lord Alanbrooke War Diaries, 1939–1945*, p. 269 (June 21, 1942).

35. Baron Charles McMoran Wilson Moran, *Winston Churchill: The Struggle for Survival, 1940–1965*, p. 41 (June 21, 1942).

36. Charles McMoran Wilson Moran, *Churchill, Taken from the Diaries of Lord Moran: The Struggle for Survival, 1940–1965*, pp. 41–42 (June 23, 1942). Churchill had been buoyed when after the shock of Tobruk's fall, Roosevelt had asked: "What can we do to help?" When Churchill asked for Sherman tanks for Egypt, FDR sent them immediately. Churchill recalled "that the Americans were better than their word. Three hundred Sherman tanks with engines not yet installed and a hundred self-propelled guns were put into six of their fastest ships and sent off to the Suez canal. The ship containing the engines for all the tanks was sunk by a submarine off Bermuda. Without a single word from us the President and Marshall put a further supply of engines into another fast ship and dispatched it to overtake the convoy." Winston S. Churchill, *The Hinge of Fate: The Second World War*, Volume IV, p. 344.

37. Correlli Barnett, *The Desert Generals*, p. 161 (Auchinleck to John Kennedy, January 19, 1942).

38. Richard Lamb, *Churchill as War Leader*, pp. 138–139 (Auchinleck to John Kennedy, January 19, 1942). Churchill contended: "Tobruk glared upon us, and, as in the previous year, we had no doubt that it should be held at all costs." Winston S. Churchill, *The Hinge of Fate: The Second World War*, Volume IV, p. 331.

39. Correlli Barnett, *The Desert Generals*, p. 161.

40. Winston S. Churchill, *The Hinge of Fate: The Second World War*, Volume IV, p. 333.

41. Winston S. Churchill, *The Hinge of Fate: The Second World War*, Volume IV, p. 343. Rommel's failure to follow up after his June victories was

attributed to Field Marshal Albert Kesselring, according to Churchill: "Believing that the Axis position in the Desert would never be secure until Malta was captured, he [Kesselring] was alarmed at the change of plan. He pointed out to Rommel the dangers of this 'foolhardy enterprise' of continuing the attack on Egypt." Winston S. Churchill, *The Hinge of Fate: The Second World War*, Volume IV, p. 378.

42. Warren F. Kimball, ed., *Churchill and Roosevelt: The Complete Correspondence*, Volume I, p. 515 (June 20, 1942).

43. Andrew Roberts, *Masters and Commanders: How Four Titans Won the War in the West, 1941–1945*, pp. 201–204.

44. Americans thought they should lead these efforts, in part because of presumed French animosity toward Britain. General Kennedy admitted in his diary: "The truth of the matter is that although the French hate the Germans, I am afraid they hate us more." *Andrew Roberts, Masters and Commanders: How Four Titans Won the War in the West, 1941–1945*, p. 298.

45. John Kennedy, *The Business of War*, p. 242.

46. Correlli Barnett, *The Desert Generals*, p. 219. Churchill had written to Auchinleck: "You . . . no doubt realize that it is practically impossible to send six or even four additional divisions from Home or United States to the northern theatre before the end of October."

47. Nigel Hamilton, *Montgomery: D-Day Commander*, p. 15.

48. Baron Charles McMoran Wilson Moran, *Winston Churchill: The Struggle for Survival, 1940–1965*, p. 55 (August 4, 1942).

49. John Colville called General Alexander "Churchill's beau idéal of a soldier and the admiration was mutual." John Colville, *Fringes of Power*, p. 730.

50. Reginald W. Thompson, *Generalissimo Churchill*, p. 213.

51. Charles McMoran Wilson Moran, *Churchill, Taken from the Diaries of Lord Moran: The Struggle for Survival, 1940–1965*, p. 58 (August 7, 1942).

52. Winston S. Churchill, *The Hinge of Fate: The Second World War*, p. 646 (Churchill to Alexander, August 10, 1942).

53. Max Hastings, *Winston's War: Churchill 1940–1945*, pp. 218, 221, 135.

54. Correlli Barnett, *The Lords of War: From Lincoln to Churchill*, p. 284. Naval historian Stephen Wentworth Roskill wrote: "Between 1939 and 1943 there was not one Admiral in an important sea command—Forbes (Home Fleet), Cunningham (Mediterranean), Somerville (Force H at Gibraltar), Tovey (Home Fleet) and Harwood (Mediterranean)— whom Churchill, sometimes with Pound's support, did not attempt to have relieved." Ronald Lewin, *Churchill as Warlord*, p. 265. Captain S. W. Roskill, *RUSI Journal*, December 1972, p. 50.

55. William Manchester and Paul Reid, *The Last Lion: Winston Spencer Churchill, Defender of the Realm, 1940–1965*, p. 434.

56. Winston S. Churchill, *Closing the Ring: The Second World War*, Volume V, p. 6.

57.   Craig L. Symonds, *Lincoln and His Admirals*, p. x.

58.   Michael Burlingame, ed., *Lincoln Observed: Civil War Dispatches of Noah Brooks*, p. 72 (October 21, 1863).

59.   Martin Gilbert, *Winston S. Churchill: Finest Hour, 1939–1941*, Volume VI, p. 659.

60.   Historian Andrew Roberts concluded that Churchill was "a genius, and the madcap schemes he occasionally came up with were merely the tiny portion of inevitable detritus that floated in the wash of his greatness." Andrew Roberts, *Masters and Commanders: How Four Titans Won the War in the West, 1941–1945*, p. 575.

61.   John Kennedy emphasized: "In spite of this mutual criticism, all worked together loyally, and strained every nerve to achieve the best possible direction of the war. Once decisions were taken, previous disagreements were forgotten." John Kennedy, *The Business of War: The War Narrative of Major-General Sir John Kennedy*, pp. 106, 161.

62.   Harold Macmillan, *War Diaries, 1943–1945*, p. 294 (November 16, 1943). Historian Andrew Roberts wrote of the Chiefs of Staff that each had his own way of handling Churchill: "Brooke was forthright, Pound charming, Portal logical and Admiral Sir Andrew Cunningham—who replaced Pound in the autumn of 1943—uncompromising." To outsiders, Churchill would defend the COS. Admiral Cunningham recalled that the COS "were primarily responsible for the grand strategy of the war. Anything which might affect the running of the war, even in the slightest degree, was referred to them for an opinion, and as a body they had attained a position of considerable importance and independence. This was principally due to Mr. Churchill's close and intimate connection with their work. Anyone criticizing the Chiefs of Staff, no matter how high his position, was likely to find the Prime Minister's heavy guns turned against him." Viscount Andrew Browne Cunningham, *A Sailor's Odyssey: The Autobiography of Admiral of the Fleet, Viscount Cunningham of Hyndhope*, pp. 584–585.

63.   On July 14 at Meade's headquarters, newspaperman Noah Brooks met Vice President Hannibal Hamlin, who "raised his hands and turned away his face with a gesture of despair. Later on, I came across General [James S.] Wadsworth, who almost shed tears while he talked with us about the escape of the rebel Army. He said that it seemed to him that most of those who participated in the council of war had not stomach for the fight. 'If they had,' he added, the rebellion, as one might say, might have been ended then and there." Noah Brooks, *Washington in Lincoln's Time*, p. 95.

64.   Bong Lee, *The Unfinished War: Korea*, p. 135.

65.   John Colville, *Winston Churchill and His Inner Circle*, p. 187.

66.   Martin Gilbert, *Road to Victory: Winston S. Churchill 1941–1945*, p. 1339.

67.   *CWAL*, Volume V, p. 460 (Lincoln to George B. McClellan, October 13, 1862).

68. *CWAL*, Volume VI, pp. 480–481 (Lincoln to Ambrose Burnside, September 25, 1863).

69. Richard Langworth, *Churchill by Himself: The Definitive Collection of Quotations*, p. 293 (May 7, 1941).

70. Gideon Welles, *Diary of Gideon Welles*, Volume I, p. 383 (July 26, 1863). The frustration extended to General-in-Chief Henry W. Halleck.

71. William Manchester and Paul Reid, *The Last Lion: Winston Spencer Churchill*, p. 510.

72. Churchill wrote in a memo to General Ismay on June 8, 1942: "I would ask the Chiefs of staff to consider the following two principles:
      (a) No substantial landing in France unless we are going to stay: and
      (b) No substantial landing in France unless the Germans are demoralised by another failure in Russia." Winston S. Churchill, *The Hinge of Fate: The Second World War*, Volume IV, p. 311.

73. For much of the war, Churchill had an excessive faith in air power. "When I look round to see how we can win the war I see that there is one sure path," Churchill wrote on July 8, 1940: "We have no Continental Army which can defeat the German military power. The blockade is broke and Hitler has Asia and probably Africa to draw from. Should he be repulsed here, or not try invasion, he will recoil Eastward and we have nothing to stop him. But there is one thing that will bring him back and bring him down, and that is an absolutely devastating, exterminating attack by very heavy bombers from this country upon the Nazi homeland. We must be able to overwhelm them by this means, without which I do not see a way through. We cannot accept any lower aim than air mastery. When can it be obtained?" Kenneth Young, *Churchill and Beaverbrook: A Study in Friendship and Politics*, p. 154. B. H. Liddell Hart wrote: "Until 1944 the strategic air offensive had fallen far short of the claims made for it, as an alternative to land invasion, and its effect had been greatly overestimated. The indiscriminate bombing of cities had not seriously diminished munitions production, while failing to break the will of the opposing peoples and compel them to surrender, as expected." B. H. Liddell Hart, *History of the Second World War*, p. 712.

74. Ben Pimlott, ed., *The Second World War Diary of Hugh Dalton 1940–45*, p. 62 (July 22, 1940). Churchill encouraged partisan and nationalist warfare against the Germans. Except for Yugoslavia it had little effect except to trigger horrible reprisals by the German against those uninvolved. "We shall aid and stir the people of every conquered country to resistance and revolt," promised Churchill in June 1941. "We shall break up and derange every effort which Hitler makes to systematize and consolidate his subjugation." Martin Gilbert, *The Churchill War Papers: The Ever-Widening War, 1941*, p. 799. Lincoln sought successfully to encourage the flight to freedom and recruitment to the Union army of former black slaves. But, like Churchill, he ran the risk that the South would retaliate—as they did, for example, when Confederate troops murdered black soldiers at Fort Pillow on April 12, 1864.

75. John Keegan, *Winston Churchill*, pp. 136–137. Ben Pimlott, ed., *The Second World War Diary of Hugh Dalton 1940–45*, p. 62 (July 22, 1940).

76. Roosevelt aide Robert Sherwood contended that Gymnast "was one of the very few major military decisions of the war which Roosevelt made entirely on his own and over the protests of his highest-ranking advisers." In fact, FDR prevailed over Marshall. Churchill himself was an advocate of GYMNAST (TORCH). Sherwood reported that FDR determined that the plan "must be carried through with expedition and vigor." Robert E. Sherwood, *Roosevelt and Hopkins*, p. 615. Historian Elisabeth Barker wrote: "Roosevelt thought of Torch—the plan for landings in French North Africa—as his own especial brain-child. Churchill also had a claim to fatherhood but was perfectly happy to yield it to Roosevelt if that would help to get the U.S. Chiefs of Staff to agree. But they disliked the child at the start and never learned to love it, so Churchill wanted to do his utmost to back up Roosevelt in every way." Elisabeth Barker, *Churchill and Eden at War*, p. 49. Joseph Persico wrote that in June 1942, FDR dictated a memo to his top military commanders, concluding, "'I do not believe we can wait until 1943 to strike at Germany.' That month *Time* magazine noted that six months after Pearl Harbor the United States had 'not taken a single inch of enemy territory, not yet beaten the enemy in a major battle on land, nor yet opened an offensive campaign.' The president then proposed an alternative to his chiefs that would have warmed Churchill's heart. If Sledgehammer could not be carried off, 'then we must attack at another point. Gymnast might not be decisive, but it would hurt Germany.'" Joseph Persico, *Roosevelt's Centurions: FDR and the Commanders He Led to Victory in World War II*, p. 188. Churchill pushed relentlessly for Operation TORCH. In August 1942, he wrote FDR "that you and I should lay down the political data and take this risk upon ourselves." Martin Gilbert, *Winston S. Churchill: Road to Victory, 1941–1945*, p. 219.

77. William Manchester and Paul Reid, *The Last Lion: Winston Spencer Churchill, Defender of the Realm, 1940–1965*, pp. 548–549.

78. Winston S. Churchill, *Closing the Ring: The Second World War*, Volume V, p. 36.

79. Jean Edward Smith, *FDR*, p. 559.

80. William Manchester and Paul Reid, *The Last Lion: Winston Spencer Churchill, Defender of the Realm, 1940–1965*, p. 542.

81. Nigel Nicolson, ed., *Harold Nicolson: Diaries and Letters, 1939–1945*, p. 231 (July 1, 1942).

82. Auchinleck understood that British tanks were inferior to the German tanks. Philip Warner wrote: "Auchinleck was fully aware that unless he had superiority in quantity to overcome his army's deficiencies in quality, any further offensive action was doomed." Warner added: "This eminently sensible policy infuriated Churchill, who was unaware of the facts behind the situation—facts which should have been made clear to

the War Cabinet by technical intelligence. He began to feel that he had made a mistake in appointing Auchinleck, who was not going to be the forceful, adventurous commander he required. Even Auchinleck did not know why his tanks and guns were so inferior to the Germans', but he did know that if he went into battle as Churchill was constantly urging him to do, the result would be catastrophe. Methodically he began to build up an army which would bring victory and satisfy Churchill." John Keegan, ed., *Churchill's Generals*, p. 139 (Philip Warner, "Field Marshall Sir Claude Auchinleck").

83. Winston S. Churchill, *The Hinge of Fate: The Second World War*, Volume IV, p. 365.

84. Richard Langworth, ed., *Churchill by Himself*, p. 325 (December 8, 1944).

85. There were political as well as military reasons to take decisive action in 1942. On July 16, Roosevelt wrote a memo of instructions for the American leaders visiting Britain—Harry Hopkins, George C. Marshal, and Admiral Ernest King. Roosevelt, worried about upcoming congressional elections, wrote his military chiefs to overrule their proposed shift of American focus away from Europe: "I am opposed to an American all-out effort in the Pacific against Japan with the view to her defeat as quickly as possible. It is of the utmost importance that we appreciate that defeat of Japan does not defeat Germany and that American concentration against Japan this year or in 1943 increases the chance of complete German domination of Europe and Africa." Winston S. Churchill, *The Hinge of Fate: The Second World War*, Volume IV, p. 400 (Roosevelt memo to Harry Hopkins, George Marshall, and Ernest King, July 16, 1942). FDR endorsed Churchill's strategy.

86. Winston S. Churchill, *The Hinge of Fate: The Second World War*, Volume IV, p. 527 (Churchill to Harold Alexander, September 17, 1942).

87. Alex Danchev and Daniel Todman, eds., *Lord Alanbrooke War Diaries, 1939–1945*, p. 324 (September 23, 1943).

88. Historian Walter Reid wrote: "From Churchill's perspective, however, the delay before the start of the Second Alamein was exactly the sort of delay that Wavell and Auchinleck had insisted on, and he was as annoyed by it as he had been in the past. But he could not afford to dismiss another desert general, and when Monty hinted at resignation if he were not allowed an adequate gap between Alam Halfa and Second Alamein he admitted he was indulging in pure blackmail." Walter Reid, *Churchill: 1940–1945, Under Friendly Fire*, p. 230.

89. Winston S. Churchill, *The Hinge of Fate: The Second World War*, Volume IV, p. 528 (Churchill to Harold Alexander, October 20, 1942).

90. Alex Danchev, Daniel Todman, eds., *Lord Alanbrooke War Diaries, 1939–1945*, p. 335 (October 30, 1943).

91. Nigel Hamilton, *D-Day Commander*, pp. 20–25.

92. Sarah Churchill and Paul Medlicott, *Keep on Dancing: An Autobiography*, p. 66.

93. Winston S. Churchill, *The Hinge of Fate: The Second World War*, Volume IV, pp. 548–550.

94. Allied agreement with Darlan, approved by General Eisenhower caused a furor in both London and Washington. Churchill stood by the American government during the storm. General Eisenhower wired Churchill on December 5, 1942: "I assure you again that we are not entering a cabal designed to place Darlan at the head of anything except the local organisation. Here he is entirely necessary, for he and he alone is the source of every bit of practical help we have received." Darlan himself understood he was being used, writing an American general: "Information from various sources tends to substantiate the view that I am 'only a lemon which the Americans will drop after they have squeezed it dry.'" Winston S. Churchill, *The Hinge of Fate: The Second World War*, Volume IV, p. 571.

95. Richard Langworth, ed., *Churchill by Himself*, pp. 280–281 (Winston Churchill, speech at Mansion House, November 10, 1942).

96. Richard Langworth, ed., *Churchill by Himself*, p. 362 (February 11, 1943).

97. Churchill the historian sometimes erred in his observations about Lincoln. For example, he wrote that in the late 1850s, Lincoln "made slavery a moral and not a legal issue, and had propounded the disruptive idea of overriding the Supreme Court decision and of outlawing slavery in the new territories." Winston S. Churchill, *The Great Republic*, p. 145. Lincoln did make slavery a moral issue. But it was a moral issue by which he sought to preserve the American legal tradition begun by the Northwest Ordinance of 1787 and reinforced legally by the Missouri Compromise of 1820, both of which limited slavery's spread by law. What Lincoln did not accept was the undoing of those legal restrictions on slavery by the 1857 *Dred Scott* decision of the Supreme Court. Indeed, in June 1862 Congress did override the *Dred Scott* Supreme Court decision by enacting legislation outlawing slavery in U.S. territories.

98. Maxwell Philip Schoenfeld, *The War Ministry of Winston Churchill*, p. 179.

99. Roy Jenkins, *Churchill: A Biography*, p. 702.

100. Mark Pottle, ed., *Champion Redoubtable, The Diaries and Letters of Violet Bonham Carter, 1914–1945*, pp. 235–237 (February 11, 1942).

X. 1863/1943

1. *CWAL*, Volume VI, p. 467 (Lincoln to Henry W. Halleck, September 19. 1863).

2. Richard Langworth, ed., *Churchill by Himself: The Definitive Collection of Quotations*, p. 565 (September 29, 1943).

3. John S. D. Eisenhower, *Allies: Pearl Harbor to D-Day*, pp. 303–305.

4. Charles McMoran Wilson Moran, *Churchill, Taken from the Diaries of Lord Moran: The Struggle for Survival, 1940–1965*, p. 745 (June 24, 1956).

5. Henry Pelling, *Winston Churchill*, p. 499.

6. Hastings Lionel Ismay Baron Ismay, *The Memoirs of General Lord Ismay*, p. 249.

7. Stephen Ambrose, *Eisenhower: Soldier, General of the Army, President-Elect, 1890–1952*, p. 146.

8. Max Hastings, *Winston's War: Churchill 1940–1945*, p. 237.

9. Winston S. Churchill, *The Great Republic: History of America*, p. 356.

10. Gideon Welles, *Diary of Gideon Welles*, Volume I, p. 293 (May 5, 1863).

11. *CWAL*, Volume VI, p. 410 (Letter to James C. Conkling, August 26, 1863).

12. *CWAL*, Volume VI, p. 79 (Lincoln to Joseph Hooker, January 26, 1863).

13. Michael Burlingame, *Abraham Lincoln: A Life*, Volume II, p. 491.

14. *CWAL*, Volume VI, p. 341 (Lincoln to Oliver O. Howard, July 21, 1863).

15. Michael Burlingame, ed., *An Oral History of Abraham Lincoln: John G. Nicolay's Interviews and Essays*, p. 88 (Conversation with Robert Todd Lincoln, January 5, 1885).

16. Lincoln occasionally worked through Secretary of War Stanton or General Halleck. On the same day that Lincoln decided against writing Meade directly, Halleck telegraphed Meade on July 14: "The enemy should be pursued and cut up, wherever he may have gone. This pursuit may or may not be upon the rear or flank, as circumstances may require. The inner flank toward Washington present[s] the greatest advantages. Supply yourself from the country as far as possible. I cannot advise details, as I do not know where Lee's army is, nor where your pontoon bridges are. I need hardly say to you that the escape of Lee's army without another battle has created great dissatisfaction in the mind of the President, and it will require an active and energetic pursuit on your part to remove the impression that it has not been sufficiently active heretofore." Meade responded: "Having performed my duty conscientiously and to the best of my ability, the censure of the President conveyed in your dispatch of 1 p.m. this day, is, in my judgment, so undeserved that I feel compelled most respectfully to ask to be immediately relieved from the command of this army." *CWAL*, Volume VI, p. 328 (July 14, 1863). Lincoln himself pursued the topic with former Secretary of War Simon Cameron, who had attended strategy meetings with Union generals: "I would give much to be relieved of the impression that Meade, Couch, Smith and all, since the battle at Gettysburg, have striven only to get Lee over the river without another fight. Please tell me, if you know, who was the one corps commander who was for fighting, in the council of War on Sunday-night." *CWAL*, Volume VI, pp. 329–330 (Lincoln to Simon Cameron, July 15, 1863).

17. *CWAL*, Volume VI, p. 326 (Lincoln to Ulysses S. Grant, July 13, 1863).

18. Dwight D. Eisenhower, *At Ease: Stories I Tell to Friends*, pp. 263–264.

19. W. Averell Harriman and Elie Abel, *Special Envoy to Churchill and Stalin, 1941–1946*, p. 222.

20. John Keegan, *Winston Churchill*, p. 161.

21. Norman Davies, *No Simple Victory: World War II in Europe, 1939–1945*, pp. 110–112.

22. British Air Marshal Arthur Tedder wrote: "As Mussolini's régime tumbled, the temptation to make a quick bid for possession of the Dodecanese islands became hard to resist." Tedder himself became increasingly doubtful about the operation: "Alexander, Cunningham, and I were of one mind in advising Eisenhower that the operation against Rhodes, at least, should be promptly abandoned." The British were unable to maintain needed air superiority given the proximity of German air bases in Greece. The Allies were in no position to divert resources from operations in Italy. *Lord Tedder, With Prejudice: The War Memoirs of Marshal of the Royal Air Force*, pp. 469, 473.

23. General Eisenhower recalled: "I never at any time heard Mr. Churchill urge or suggest complete abandonment of the Overlord plan. His conviction, so far as I could interpret it, was that at some time in the indefinite future the Allies would have to cross the Channel. But he seemed to believe that our attack should be pushed elsewhere until the day came when the enemy would be forced to withdraw most of his troops from northwest Europe, at which time the Allies could go in easily and safely." Dwight D. Eisenhower, *Crusade in Europe*, p. 199.

24. Winston S. Churchill, *Closing the Ring: The Second World War*, Volume V, p. 180.

25. Winston S. Churchill, *Closing the Ring: The Second World War*, Volume V, p. 194.

26. Alex Danchev and Daniel Todman, eds., *Lord Alanbrooke War Diaries, 1939–1945*, p. 459 (October 8, 1943).

27. Alex Danchev and Daniel Todman, eds., *Lord Alanbrooke War Diaries, 1939–1945*, p. 465 (November 1, 1943).

28. Correlli Barnett, *The Lords of War: From Lincoln to Churchill*, p. 290.

29. Arthur Bryant, *The Turn of the Tide, 1939–1943*, p. 13.

30. Lord Tedder, *With Prejudice: The War Memoirs of Marshal of the Royal Air Force*, p. 483.

31. Max Hastings, *Winston's War, Churchill 1940–1945*, p. 338.

32. Charles McMoran Wilson Moran, *Churchill, Taken from the Diaries of Lord Moran: The Struggle for Survival, 1940–1965*, pp. 140, 142 (November 25, 1943).

33. Charles McMoran Wilson Moran, *Churchill, Taken from the Diaries of Lord Moran: The Struggle for Survival, 1940–1965*, p. 143 (November 28, 1943).

34. Max Hastings, *Winston's War, Churchill 1940–1945*, p. 296. There were other reasons, not least American and Soviet dominance.

35. Alex Danchev and Daniel Todman, eds., *Lord Alanbrooke War Diaries, 1939–1945*, p. 472 (November 18, 1943).

36. Simon Berthon and Joanna Potts, *Warlords: An Extraordinary Re-creation of World War II Through the Eyes and Minds of Hitler, Churchill, Roosevelt*, p. 226 (Diary of Henry L. Stimson, December 5, 1943).

37. John Pearson, *The Private Lives of Winston Churchill*, p. 318.

38. Charles McMoran Wilson Moran, *Churchill, Taken from the Diaries of Lord Moran: The Struggle for Survival, 1940–1965*, p. 147 (November 29, 1943).

39. Charles Bohlen, *Witness to History, 1929–1969*, p. 148.

40. Stalin biographer Simon Sebag Montefiore wrote of the Teheran summit: "Stalin, 'always smoking and doodling wolf heads on a pad with his red pencil,' was never agitated, rarely gestured and seldom consulted Molotov and Voroshilov. But he kept up the pressure on Churchill for the Second Front: 'Do the British really believe in Overlord or are you only saying so to reassure the Russians?'" Simon Sebag Montefiore, *Stalin: The Court of the Red Czar*, p. 469. There was a good deal of verbal jousting between Churchill and Stalin. At a banquet at the Teheran conference, Stalin talked about his "good friend, Mr. Churchill" before adding: "I hope I may call him my good friend." Sotto voce, Churchill said: "Yes, you may call me 'Winston' if you like—I always call you 'Joe' when you aren't there." John Kennedy, *The Business of War*, p. 314.

41. Charles McMoran Wilson Moran, *Churchill, Taken from the Diaries of Lord Moran: The Struggle for Survival, 1940–1965*, pp. 149, 151 (November 29, 1943).

42. Frances Perkins, *The Roosevelt I Knew*, pp. 81–82. (New York: Penguin Books, 2011).

43. William Manchester and Paul Reid, *The Last Lion: Winston Spencer Churchill: Defender of the Realm, 1940–1965*, p. 729.

44. Keith Eubank, *Summit at Teheran: The Untold Story*, p. 135. Stalin had alternately teased and rejected Roosevelt about a meeting since the summer of 1942. Stalin worried that any prolonged absence might weaken his domination of Soviet generals. Eubank wrote: "Stalin had vetoed the kind of meeting so dear to Roosevelt, and instead had suggested sites that would be totally inconvenient. He had hinted for the first time at the possibility of a conference of the three heads of government—a prospect less than pleasing to Roosevelt. If there were to be any meeting, Stalin had indicated that the site had to satisfy him. At the same time, he had opened the way for a meeting on a lower level. But he had lied when he claimed that the war required him to make frequent trips to the front. In truth, he carefully avoided the battlefront, preferring the safety of the Kremlin where elite troops, constantly rotated, protected him not only from the enemy but also from his own people." Keith Eubank, *Summit at Teheran: The Untold Story*, p. 103.

45. John R. Deane, *Strange Alliance*, p. 42.

46. General Brooke remarked to a Foreign Office official: "This conference is over when it has just begun. Stalin has the President in his pocket." David Dilks, ed., *The Diaries of Sir Alexander Cadogan, OM*

1938–45, p. 582 (December 1, 1943). FDR was not alone in trying to please Stalin. Historian Fraser J. Harbutt wrote that at the Teheran summit, Churchill "gave a powerful impression to Stalin of his eagerness to satisfy Soviet desires and of the British government's fundamental indifference to Poland's future." Churchill told Stalin on December 1 that the Poles were "the sort of people who would never be satisfied anyway." Fraser J. Harbutt, *Yalta 1945: Europe and America at the Crossroads*, p. 136.

47. Robert Rhodes James, *Anthony Eden*, p. 280.

48. John Wheeler-Bennett, *Action This Day: Working with Churchill*, p. 96. U.S. General John R. Deane wrote of the Teheran conference that Stalin 'had an advantage over both Roosevelt and Churchill in that he knew he could act without fear of being called to account by Congress, Parliament, or the people." He noted that "President Roosevelt was thinking of winning the war; the others were thinking of their relative positions when the war was won." John R. Deane, *The Strange Alliance: The Story of Our Efforts at Wartime Cooperation with Russia*, p. 43.

49. Winston S. Churchill, *Closing the Ring: The Second World War*, Volume V, p. 358.

50. Walter Thompson, *Sixty Minutes with Churchill*, p. 77.

51. Mary Soames, ed., *Winston and Clementine: The Personal Letters of the Churchills*, p. 492 (Churchill to Clementine Churchill, December 12, 1943).

52. Mary Soames, ed., *Winston and Clementine: The Personal Letters of the Churchills*, pp. 492–493.

53. Mary Soames, ed., *Winston and Clementine: The Personal Letters of the Churchills*, p. 493 (Churchill to Mary Churchill, December 17, 1943).

54. Mary Soames, *Clementine Churchill: Portrait of a Marriage*, p. 454.

55. Winston S. Churchill, *Closing the Ring: The Second World War*, Volume V, p. 398.

56. *CWAL*, Volume VII, pp. 52–53 (Third Annual Message to Congress, December 8, 1863).

57. Robert Rhodes James, ed., *Churchill Speaks*, p. 727 (August 20, 1940).

XI. 1864/1944

1. *CWAL*, Volume VII, p. 324 (Lincoln to Ulysses S. Grant, April 30, 1864).

2. Winston S. Churchill, *Triumph and Tragedy, The Second Word War*, Volume VI, p. 5 (June 6, 1944).

3. Warren F. Kimball, ed., *Churchill & Roosevelt: The Complete Correspondence*, Volume III, p. 222 (Roosevelt to Churchill, June 29, 1944).

4. Winston S. Churchill, *Triumph and Tragedy: The Second World War*, Volume VI, p. 51. After one contentious meeting with his Chiefs of Staff at the end of 1944, Churchill regretfully acceded to their advice to let Operation ANVIL go ahead as the Americans wanted. Brooke

summarized the British position: "All right, if you [Americans] insist on being damned fools, sooner than falling out with you, which would be fatal, we shall be damned fools with you, and we shall see that we performed the role of damned fools damned well!" Alex Danchev and Daniel Todman, eds., *War Diaries, 1939–1945: Field Marshal Lord Alanbrooke*, p. 565 (June 30, 1944).

5. Ian Jacob contended the Americans "regarded the whole war in Europe merely as a problem for a fire brigade. The fire was in Germany, there you sent the fire brigade by the shortest road into Germany." Andrew Roberts, *Masters and Commanders*, p. 517.

6. Winston S. Churchill, *Triumph and Tragedy*, Volume VI, p. 60 (Churchill to Harry Hopkins, August 6, 1944).

7. Winston S. Churchill, *Triumph and Tragedy*, Volume VI, p. 403 (Churchill to Hastings Ismay, March 31, 1945).

8. Winston S. Churchill, *Triumph and Tragedy*, Volume VI, p. 405 (Churchill to Eisenhower, March 31, 1945).

9. Winston S. Churchill, *Triumph and Tragedy*, Volume VI, p. 409 (Churchill to Eisenhower, April 2, 1945).

10. Roosevelt had said in November 1943: "There would definitely be a race for Berlin. We may have to put United States Divisions into Berlin as soon as possible." Carlo D'Este, *Eisenhower: A Soldier's Life*, p. 691.

11. Leonard Moseley, *Marshall: Hero for Our Times*, pp. 329–330.

12. Forrest C. Pogue, *Organizer for Victory, 1943–45*, Volume III, p. 571.

13. Warren F. Kimball, ed., *Churchill & Roosevelt: The Complete Correspondence*, Volume III, p. 605 (April 1, 1945).

14. Winston Churchill, *Triumph and Tragedy*, p. 405 (Churchill to Dwight D. Eisenhower, March 31, 1945).

15. Ed Cray, *General of the Army: George C. Marshall, Soldier and Statesman*, p. 521.

16. Martin Gilbert, *Churchill and America*, p. 338.

17. Carlo D'Este, *Eisenhower: A Soldier's Life*, p. 691.

18. Maxwell Philip Schoenfeld, *The War Ministry of Winston Churchill*, p. 244.

19. Anthony Eden, *The Eden Memoirs: The Reckoning*, p. 501.

20. Mary Soames, ed., *Winston and Clementine: The Personal Letters of the Churchills*, p. 509 (Churchill to Clementine Churchill, December 26, 1944).

21. Maxwell Philip Schoenfeld, *The War Ministry of Winston Churchill*, p. 233.

22. Winston Churchill, *Triumph and Tragedy: The Second World War*, Volume VI, p. 315.

23. Martin Gilbert, *Winston S. Churchill: Road to Victory 1941–1945*, p. 843 (Churchill to Ismay, July 6, 1944).

24. John Colville, *Fringes of Power: The Incredible Inside Story of Winston Churchill during World War II*, p. 555 (January 23, 1945).

25. Norman Davies, *Rising '44*, pp. 260–354.

26. Richard Langworth, ed., *Churchill by Himself*, p. 178 (December 15, 1944). Churchill tried to reason with the Poles. Similarly, Lincoln tried to reason with Border State representatives. Both groups were resistant to new realities created by war. Lincoln met border state representatives in March of 1862 in an attempt to convince them of the wisdom of accepting compensated emancipation of slaves in their states. David Von Drehle wrote: "John Noell of Missouri assured Lincoln that since slavery in his state would soon die out on its own, there was no need to take any action. Maryland's John Crisfield protested that his constituents were ready to end slavery, but that even indirect pressure from outsiders—pressure such as Lincoln's proposal—was unacceptable to them." David Von Drehle, *Rise to Greatness: Abraham Lincoln and America's Most Perilous Year*, p. 105. Another border state presented an even more intractable problem for President Lincoln. Military historian John Keegan wrote: "Missouri was worse afflicted by neighbourly strife than any other state, and guerrilla warfare persisted between partisans of one side and the other even after 1865." John Keegan, *The American Civil War*, p. 100. The strife among pro-Union factions in Missouri proved difficult for President Lincoln to handle.

27. Warren F. Kimball, ed., *Churchill and Roosevelt: The Complete Correspondence*, Volume III, p. 30 (Churchill to Joseph Stalin, March 7, 1945).

28. Winston S. Churchill, *Triumph and Tragedy: The Second World War*, pp. 431–433 (Churchill to Joseph Stalin, April 29, 1945).

29. Herbert Feis, *Churchill-Roosevelt-Stalin: The War They Waged and the Peace They Sought*, p. 279 (Averell Harriman to Winston Churchill, January 20, 1945).

30. Historian David Carlton wrote that Churchill did not expect the Bolshevik Revolution to survive. He supported an anti-Bolshevik force "whom he thought could be relied upon to recreate a Second Front [in WWI] once they were restored to power in Petrograd—which he believed certain to come about, given vigorous Western help." David Carlton, *Churchill and the Soviet Union*, p. 5. British intervention failed. See George Kennan, *The Decision to Intervene: Soviet-American Relations, 1917–1920*, Volumes I and II (Princeton University Press, 1989).

31. Charles McMoran Wilson Moran, *Churchill, Taken from the Diaries of Lord Moran: The Struggle for Survival, 1940–1965*, p. 304 (July 24, 1945).

32. John Colville, *The Fringes of Power*, p. 404 (June 21, 1941). Churchill repeatedly referred to Hitler as "that man." Norman Brook wrote in his diary of Churchill's attitude toward Hitler's fate: "If Hitler falls into our hands we shall certainly put him to death." Churchill added: "Not a sovereign who could be said to be in hands of ministers like Kaiser. This man is the mainspring of evil" (April 12, 1945). (Thomas Vinciguerra, "The Private Thoughts of a Public Man," *New York Times*, January 22, 2006.)

33. *CWAL*, Volume V, p. 461 (Lincoln to George B. McClellan, October 13, 1862).

34. *CWAL*, Volume VI, p. 467 (Lincoln to Henry W. Halleck, September 19, 1863).

35. Winston S. Churchill, *The Great Republic*, p. 207.

36. Eliot A. Cohen, *Supreme Command: Soldiers, Statesmen and Leadership in Wartime*, p. 31.

37. Matthew Pinsker, *Lincoln's Sanctuary: Abraham Lincoln and the Soldier's Home*, p. 122.

38. Carlo D'Este, *Warlord: A Life of Winston Churchill at War, 1874–1945*, pp. 664, 660.

39. Despite the class structure of Britain there was an egalitarian and mer- itocractic streak in Churchill—particularly when it came to military promotions and appointments. He once observed: "If a telegraphist may rise, why not a painter? Apparently there is no difficulty about painters rising in Germany," referring to Hitler as a young man. Gerald Pawle, *The War and Colonel Warden*, p. 39.

40. John Colville, *Footprints in Time: Memories*, p. 191.

41. David Homer Bates, *Lincoln in the Telegraph Office*, p. 67.

42. Alex Danchev and Daniel Todman, eds., *War Diaries, 1939–1945: Field Marshal Lord Alanbrooke*, pp. 572–573 (July 19, 1944).

43. Alex Danchev and Daniel Todman, eds., *War Diaries, 1939–1945: Field Marshal Lord Alanbrooke*, p. 417 (June 3, 1943). John S.D. Eisenhower perhaps reflected his father's difficult relationship with the British gen- eral when he wrote: "Montgomery was a man who, though exhibiting no remarkable intellect, possessed a quality that compelled his superi- ors to be unusually tolerant of his idiosyncrasies: his self-assurance. He made the most of this mystique, and for his own reasons often seemed to go out of his way to be difficult." John S. D. Eisenhower, *Allies: Pearl Harbor to D-Day*, p. 152. John S. D. Eisenhower was not alone in his opin- ion of Monty. Many shared this view.

44. Terry Brighton, *Patton, Montgomery, Rommel: Masters of War*, p. xvii.

45. Martin Gilbert, *Winston S. Churchill: Road to Victory 1941–1945*, p. 168 (Churchill to Clementine Churchill, August 9, 1942).

46. Carlo D'Este, *Warlord: A Life of Winston Churchill at War, 1874–1945*, p. 448.

47. William S. McFeely, *Grant*, p. 495.

48. Theodore Calvin Pease, ed., *Diary of Orville Hickman Browning*, Volume I, p. 668 (May 1, 1864).

49. John Keegan, *The American Civil War*, p. 329. Keegan wrote of Grant's campaign from the Wilderness: "Territorially, it was one of the largest successes of the war. The cost had been appalling. Grant's losses had been about 1,300 men a day, a total of 52,600 in forty days, in human terms a terrible price, though one that the Union could afford as the

Confederacy could not. Lee's 33,000 casualties were a permanent debit." John Keegan, *The American Civil War*, p. 252.

50. In 1909, Churchill's mother, Jennie Churchill, wrote and produced a play, "His Borrowed Plumes." "Is there so much difference between politicians and actors?" she wrote in the play's dialogue. "Both are equally eager for popular applause and both equally doubtful whether they will get it." Jonathan Rose, *The Literary Churchill: Author, Reader, Actor*, pp. 2, 5.

51. John Pearson, *The Private Lives of Winston Churchill*, p. 176. Once friends, Wells split with Churchill during World War I. Nevertheless, Churchill remained a fan. Rose wrote that Churchill and Wells began as friends but fell out in World War I. By 1920, "Wells had become disillusioned with Churchill: he could not forgive the Gallipoli fiasco of 1914–16. They also fell out over Bolshevik Russia, which Churchill regarded as diabolically evil but which Wells considered a deeply flawed but genuine experiment in socialism." Jonathan Rose, *The Literary Churchill: Author, Reader, Actor*, p. 87. Rose wrote: "In 1931 Churchill claimed to have read all of Wells's books twice over: "I could pass an examination in them." Jonathan Rose, *The Literary Churchill: Author, Reader, Actor*, p. 83.

52. John Barnes and David Nicholson, eds., *The Leo Amery Diaries*, Volume II, p. 947.

53. Winston S. Churchill, *Triumph and Tragedy: The Second World War*, Volume VI, p. 5 (Speech to House of Commons, June 6, 1944).

54. Noah Brooks, *Washington in Lincoln's Time*, pp. 177–178.

55. Winston S. Churchill, *Closing the Ring: The Second World War*, Volume V, p. 550 (King George VI to Churchill, May 31, 1944).

56. Winston S. Churchill, *Closing the Ring: The Second World War*, Volume V, p. 550 (Churchill to King George VI, June 3, 1944).

57. Dwight D. Eisenhower, *At Ease: Stories I Tell to Friends*, p. 273.

58. Alex Danchev and Daniel Todman, eds., *War Diaries, 1939–1945: Field Marshal Lord Alanbrooke*, pp. 676–677 (March 25, 1944).

59. *CWAL*, Volume I, p. 8 (Communication to the People of Sangamo County, March 9, 1832).

60. Michael Burlingame, ed., *With Lincoln in the White House: Letters, Memoranda, and Other Writings of John G. Nicolay, 1860–1865*, p. 152 (August 25, 1864).

61. Michael Burlingame, ed., *At Lincoln's Side: John Hay's Civil War Correspondence and Selected Writings*, p. 91 (August 25, 1864).

62. Ida Tarbell, *Life of Abraham Lincoln*, Volume II, p. 201.

63. Robert S. Eckley, *Lincoln's Forgotten Friend, Leonard Swett*, p. 150.

64. Shelby Foote, *The Civil War, a Narrative: Red River to Appomattox*, Volume III, p. 645.

65. Allen Thorndike Rice, ed., *Reminiscences of Abraham Lincoln by Distinguished Men of His Time*, pp. 70–71 (Reuben E. Fenton).

66. *CWAL*, Volume VIII, p. 182 (William T. Sherman to Abraham Lincoln, December 22, 1864).

67. In response to Lincoln's congratulations, Sherman responded in early January: "I am gratified at the receipt of your letter . . . Especially to observe that you appreciate the division I made of my army, and that each part was duly proportioned to its work. The motto, `Nothing ventured Nothing won' which you refer to is most appropriate, and should I venture too much and happen to lose I shall bespeak your charitable influence. I am ready for the Great Next as soon as I can complete certain preliminaries, and learn of Genl Grant his and your preference of intermediate objectives." *CWAL*, Volume VIII, pp. 181–182 (Lincoln to William T. Sherman, December 26, 1864, Sherman to Lincoln, January 6, 1865).

68. William T. Sherman, *Memoirs of General W. T. Sherman*, p. 476.

69. Eleanor Roosevelt, *This I Remember*, p. 333.

70. Lord Moran, *Churchill; the Struggle for Survival, 1940–1965*, p. 204.

71. Lord Moran, *Churchill; the Struggle for Survival, 1940–1965*, p. 221 (October 30, 1944).

72. *CWAL*, Volume VII, p. 281 (Lincoln to Albert Hodges, April 4, 1864).

73. Michael Vorenberg, "'The Deformed Child': Slavery and the Election of 1864, *Civil War History, 47*:3 (2001), pp. 245–246.

74. Michael Burlingame, *Abraham Lincoln: A Life*, Volume II, p. 663.

75. Michael Burlingame, *Abraham Lincoln: A Life*, Volume II, p. 677.

76. *CWAL*, Volume VIII, pp. 1–2 (Lincoln to Isaac M. Schemerhorn, September 12, 1864, unfinished and unsent).

XII. 1865/1945

1. *CWAL*, Volume VIII, p. 241 (Remarks to Christian Commission, January 27, 1865).

2. Martin Gilbert, *Road to Victory: Winston S. Churchill, 1941–1945*, p. 1348.

3. Michael Burlingame, ed., *Lincoln Observed: Civil War Dispatches of Noah Brooks*, pp. 161–162 (February 12, 1865).

4. Margarita Spalding Gerry, ed., *Through Five Administrations: Reminiscences of Colonel William H. Crook*, p. 47.

5. Walter Thompson, *Beside the Bulldog: The Intimate Memoirs of Churchill's Bodyguard*, p. 128. In August, while aboard the HMS *Kimberley*, Churchill witnessed the Allied landing at Marseilles.

6. David Dixon Porter, *Incidents and Anecdotes of the Civil War*, pp. 292–293.

7. Benjamin Brown French, *Witness to a Young Republic: A Yankee's Journal, 1828–1870*, p. 417 (February 18, 1865).

8. Douglas Wilson and Rodney Davis, *Herndon's Informants*, p. 157 (Joshua F. Speed to William H. Herndon, January 12, 1866).

9. Winston S. Churchill, *Triumph and Tragedy: The Second World War*, Volume VI, p. 512.

10. Michael Burlingame, ed., *Lincoln Observed: Civil War Dispatches of Noah Brooks*, p. 213 (April 12, 1863).

11. Francis Fisher Browne, *The Every-day Life of Abraham Lincoln*, p. 474.

12. Gabriel Gorodetsky, ed., *Maisky Diaries: Red Ambassador to the Court of St. James's 1932–1943*, p. 431 (March 16, 1942).

13. Alex Danchev and Daniel Todman, eds., *War Diaries, 1939–1945: Field Marshal Lord Alanbrooke*, p. 535 (March 28, 1944).

14. John Colville, *The Fringes of Power*, p. 484 (April 12, 1944).

15. Francis B. Carpenter, *The Inner Life of Abraham Lincoln: Six Months at the White House*, p. 17.

16. William Manchester and Paul Reid, *The Last Lion: Winston Spencer Churchill, Defender of the Realm, 1940–1965*, p. 813.

17. Ruth Painter Randall, *Mary Lincoln: Biography of a Marriage*, p. 342.

18. Elizabeth Layton Nel, *Winston Churchill by His Personal Secretary*, p. 125.

19. Winston S. Churchill, *Triumph and Tragedy*, p. 295 (Churchill to Roosevelt, January 1, 1945).

20. Martin Gilbert, *Churchill and America*, p. 352.

21. Charles McMoran Wilson Moran, *Churchill, Taken from the Diaries of Lord Moran*, p. 247 (February 11, 1945).

22. Charles McMoran Wilson Moran, *Churchill, Taken from the Diaries of Lord Moran*, p. 246 (February 10, 1945).

23. General Hastings Ismay wrote of Yalta in his memoirs: "From the gastronomical point of view, it was enjoyable: from the social point of view, successful: from the military point of view, unnecessary; and from the political point of view, depressing." Hastings Lionel Ismay, *Memoirs of General Lord Ismay*, p. 387.

24. Richard Langworth, ed., *Churchill by Himself*, p. 287 (May 7, 1945).

25. Nigel Nicolson, ed., *Harold Nicolson: Diaries and Letters, 1939–1945*, p. 457 (May 8, 1945).

26. Martin Gilbert, *Winston S. Churchill: Road to Victory, 1941–1945*, p. 1346 (May 8, 1945).

27. Nigel Nicolson, ed., *Harold Nicolson's Diaries*, p. 457 (May 8, 1945).

28. Mary Soames, ed., *Winston and Clementine: The Personal Letters of the Churchills*, p. 531 (May 8, 1945).

29. Martin Gilbert, *Churchill: The Power of Words*, pp. 349–350 (May 9, 1945).

30. Martin Gilbert, *Churchill: The Power of Words: His Remarkable Life Recounted Through His Writings and Speeches*, p. 351 (May 13, 1945).

31. John Colville, *The Fringes of Power*, p. 510 (September 7, 1944).

32. Two titles of Correlli Barnett's quadrilogy defined the British dilemma: *The Collapse of British Power* and *The Audit of War*.

33. "This morning, as for some days past, it seems exceedingly probable that this Administration will not be re-elected. Then it will be my duty to so co-operate with the President elect, as to save the Union between

the election and the inauguration; as he will have secured his election on such ground that he can not possibly save it afterwards." *CWAL*, Volume VII, p. 514 (August 23, 1864).

34. Michael Burlingame and John R. Tuner Ettlinger, *Inside Lincoln's White House: The Complete Civil War Diary of John Hay*, p. 84 (September 11, 1863).

35. Mary Soames, *Clementine Churchill: The Biography of a Marriage*, p. 424. On July 26, 1945, Churchill issued a graceful and magnanimous statement: "The decision of the British people has been recorded in the votes counted to-day. I have therefore laid down the charge which was placed upon me in darker times. I regret that I have not been permitted to finish the work against Japan. For this however all plans and preparations have been made, and the results may come much quicker than we have hitherto been entitled to expect. Immense responsibilities abroad and at home fall upon the new Government, and we must all hope that they will be successful in bearing them." He added: "It only remains for me to express to the British people, for whom I have acted in these perilous years, my profound gratitude for the unflinching, unswerving support which they have given me during my task, and for the many expressions of kindness which they have shown towards their servant." Winston S. Churchill, *Triumph and Tragedy: The Second World War*, Volume VI, p. 584 (July 26, 1945).

36. Winston S. Churchill, *Triumph and Tragedy: The Second World War*, Volume VI, p. 399.

37. David McCullough, *Truman*, p. 412. Merle Miller, *Plain Speaking: An Oral Biography of Harry S. Truman*, p. 86 (New York: G. P. Putnam's Sons, 1974).

38. Martin Gilbert, *Churchill and America*, p. 361.

39. Merle Miller, *Plain Speaking: An Oral Biography of Harry S. Truman*, p. 86.

40. Charles McMoran Wilson Moran, *Churchill, Taken from the Diaries of Lord Moran: The Struggle for Survival, 1940–1965*, p. 294 (July 18, 1945).

41. Charles McMoran Wilson Moran, *Churchill, Taken from the Diaries of Lord Moran: The Struggle for Survival, 1940–1965*, p. 292 (July 16, 1945).

42. Winston S. Churchill, *Triumph and Tragedy: The Second World War*, Volume VI, p. 400.

43. Jean Edward Smith, *FDR*, p. 567.

44. Winston S. Churchill, *Closing the Ring: The Second World War*, Volume V, p. 51 (Roosevelt to Churchill, July 26, 1945).

45. Winston S. Churchill, *Their Finest Hour: The Second World War*, Volume II, p. 24.

46. Robert E. Sherwood, *The White House Papers of Harry L. Hopkins*, Volume II, pp. 692–693 (January 26, 1943).

47. Baron Charles McMoran Wilson Moran, *Churchill, Taken from the Diaries*, p. 190. (September 13, 1944).

48. Martin Gilbert, *Churchill: A Life*, p. 815.
49. Richard Malcolm Johnston and William Hand Browne, *Life of Alexander H. Stephens*, p. 485.
50. *CWAL*, Volume VIII, p. 330 (Edwin M. Stanton to Ulysses S. Grant, March 3, 1865).
51. *CWAL*, Volume VII, p. 392 (Lincoln to Ulysses S. Grant, April 7, 1865).
52. *CWAL*, Volume VIII, pp. 152–153 (Fourth Annual Message to Congress, December 6, 1864).

XIII. REELECTION AND RECONSTRUCTION

1. *CWAL*, Volume VIII, p. 100 (Response to a Serenade, November 10, 1864).
2. Winston S. Churchill, *The Gathering Storm, The Second World War*, Volume II, p. 601.
3. *CWAL*, Volume VII, p. 282 (Lincoln to Albert Hodges, April 4, 1864).
4. James J. McPherson, *Tried by War: Abraham Lincoln as Commander in Chief*, p. 5.
5. Martin Gilbert, *Winston S Churchill: Finest Hour, 1939–1941*, p. 156.
6. Admiral Andrew B. Cunningham recalled feeling the impact of Churchill's micromanaging in June 1940: "It was in the sort of 'prodding' message received by me on June 5th that Mr. Churchill was often so ungracious and hasty. We realized, of course, the terrible mental and physical strain under which he was labouring; but so were we. Such messages to those who were doing their utmost with straitened resources were not an encouragement, merely an annoyance. Moreover, as they implied that something was lacking in the direction and leadership, they did positive harm. If such messages were really necessary, if Commanders-in-Chief on the spot who knew all the risks and the chances were not prepared to get at the enemy on every possible occasion, the recipients ought not to have been in the position they held." Viscount Andrew Browne Cunningham, *A Sailor's Odyssey: The Autobiography of Admiral of the Fleet, Viscount Cunningham of Hyndhope*, pp. 231–232.
7. Elizabeth Layton Nel, *Winston Churchill by His Personal Secretary*, p. 27.
8. Eliot Cohen, *Supreme Command: Soldiers, Statesmen, and Leadership in Wartime*, p. 110.
9. Michael Burlingame and John R. Turner Ettlinger, eds., *Inside Lincoln's White House: The Complete Civil War Diary of John Hay*, p. 20 (May 7, 1861).
10. Herbert Mitgang, *Lincoln as They Saw Him*, pp. 388–389 (*Harper's Weekly*, March 5, 1864).
11. Hugh McCulloch, *Men and Measures of Half of a Century*, p. 162.
12. Martin Gilbert, *Churchill: A Life*, p. 802.
13. Michael Burlingame and John R. Turner Ettlinger, eds., *Inside Lincoln's White House: The Complete Civil War Diary of John Hay*, p. 244 (November 8, 1864).

14. Hans L. Trefousse, *The Radical Republicans*, p. v (Zachariah Chandler to Henry W. Lord, November 16, 1861).

15. Lincoln kept close tabs on his reelection prospects, according to friend Leonard Swett, who described Lincoln's "account book of how things were progressing . . . [such as] the resolutions of the Legislatures, the instructions of the delegates." Douglas L. Wilson and Rodney O. Davis, *Herndon's Informants: Letters, Interviews, and Statements about Abraham Lincoln*, p. 165 (Leonard Swett to William H. Herndon, January 17, 1866).

16. Allen C. Guelzo, *Fateful Lightning: A New History of the Civil War and Reconstruction*, p. 220.

17. *CWAL*, Volume VII, p. 53 (Third Annual Message to Congress, December 8, 1863).

18. *Littell's Living Age*, p. 284 (February 6, 1864).

19. *CWAL*, Volume VIII, pp. 399–400 (Last Public Address, April 11, 1865).

20. Michael Burlingame, ed., *Lincoln Observed: Civil War Dispatches of Noah Brooks*, p. 273.

21. William C. Harris, *With Charity for All, Lincoln and the Restoration of the Union*, p. 255.

22. *CWAL*, Volume VIII, p. 403 (Last public speech, April 11, 1865).

23. J. M. Lee, *The Churchill Coalition, 1940–1945*, p. 118.

24. Simon Schama noted: "The Beveridge Report sold 635,000 copies, surely a record for a government white paper. A number of Tories, the 'reform group' that included Anthony Eden, Harold Macmillan and R.A. Butler, sensing a big change in public opinion in the country and anxious not to lose postwar elections, promised 'a great programme of social reform.'" Simon Schama, *A History of Britain: The Fate of Empire 1776–2000*, Volume II, p. 530. Jonathan Schneer wrote that Home Secretary Herbert Morrison was the foremost Labour advocate of postwar reform and implementation of the Beveridge Report. At one cabinet meeting in February 1943, Morrison argued: "If this Government leaves its successor with no legislative preparation for postwar period we shall be treacherous to the country." A debate in Parliament on February 16–18 revealed the strong differences between the Conservative and Labour parties. Jonathan Schneer, *Ministers at War: Winston Churchill and His War Cabinet*, pp. 205–209.

25. Richard Langworth, ed., *Churchill by Himself*, pp. 513, 282 (Winston S. Churchill, Broadcast, March 21, 1943).

26. Martin Gilbert, *Road to Victory: Winston S. Churchill, 1941–1945*, p. 1348.

27. *CWAL*, Volume VII, pp. 301–302 (Speech at Sanitary Fair, Baltimore, April 18, 1864).

28. Frederick W. Seward, *Seward at Washington, as Senator and Secretary of State: A Memoir of His Life, with Selections from His Letters, 1861–1872*, p. 275.

29. Geoffrey Best, *Churchill and War*, p. 124.

30. Correlli Barnett, *The Audit of War*, pp. 21–22.

31. Martin Gilbert, *Churchill: The Power of Words: His Remarkable Life Recounted Through His Writings and Speeches*, pp. 338, 341 (October 31, 1944).

32. Martin Gilbert, *Winston S. Churchill: Road to Victory, 1941–1945*, p. 1252 (March 15, 1945).

33. Correlli Barnett, *The Audit of War*, p. 33.

34. Roy Jenkins, *Churchill*, p. 775.

35. Roy Jenkins, *Churchill*, p. 776.

36. Colville himself wrote: "Greatly as I love and admire the P.M. I am afraid there is much in what Attlee says, and I rather admire his courage in saying it." John Colville, *Fringes of Power*, p. 554 (January 20, 1945).

37. Geoffrey Best, *Churchill and War*, p. 172.

38. Martin Gilbert, *Winston S. Churchill: Road to Victory 1941–1945*, p. 1156 (Colville diary, January 21, 1945).

39. David Dilks, *The Diaries of Sir Alexander Cadogan, OM, 1938–1945*, pp. 618, 630 (April 12, 1944, and May 22, 1944).

40. James Russell Lowell, *Political Essays*, p. 222.

41. Historian William McNeill wrote: "Semi-voluntary war-time censorship, not to mention the shortage of newsprint, restricted the traditional freedom of the British press in a negative way by preventing publication of news. But the most significant relationship between the British Government and the press was not embodied in formal law or regulation. It was rather 'unofficial' and 'off the record' a collaboration between representatives of the Government and of the press whereby delicate issues were handled more or less in accordance with official suggestions." William McNeill, *America, Britain and Russia: Their Co-operation and Conflict, 1941–1946*, p. 60. Home Secretary Herbert Morrison enforced press censorship, but had to do so with voluntary press restrictions on critical newspapers like the *Daily Mirror*. Bernard Donoughue and G. W. Jones, Herbert Morrison: *Portrait of a Politician*, pp. 297–300. British and American media policies were very different in World War II. British interpreter A. H. Birse wrote that his sole experience in Washington "revealed what to my mind was the strange attitude of American officials towards their press: there appeared to be no objection to reporters and photographers encumbering the corridors of the State Department. When we came out of our meeting, there was a struggling crowd of them outside the door, pushing each other away to get near Eden, and a babble of voices asking for information with difficulty that we succeeded in making our way through them." A. H. Birse, *Memoirs of an Interpreter*, p. 195.

42. Martin Gilbert, *Churchill: The Power of Words: His Remarkable Life Recounted Through His Writings and Speeches*, p. 360 (June 4, 1945). On June 1, 1945, longtime friend Violet Bonham Carter had written Churchill to challenge his decision to lead the Conservative Party into the

election campaign: "You have never been 'one of them' and the only action of yours (except one) I have ever regretted since you took office was your decision to become their leader. You should have remained a National Leader—above the battle, and then we could all have followed you into the peace." His long-time friend wrote that Churchill "needed no 'machine.'" Mark Pottle, ed., *Champion Redoubtable, The Diaries and Letters of Violet Bonham Carter, 1914–1945*, p. 349 (June 1, 1945).

43. William Manchester and Paul Reid, *The Last Lion*, p. 942.

44. John Colville wrote that Churchill "decided that those opposed should beware of him and he flung himself into the fight with all his natural, not always well-judged pugnacity. I was never sure that his heart was in it, but as the weeks passed he was buoyed up by the vociferous applause with which millions greeted him as he stumped the country." John Colville, *Footprints in Time: Memories*, p. 200. Charles McMoran Wilson Moran, *Churchill, Taken from the Diaries of Lord Moran: The Struggle for Survival, 1940–1965*, pp. 271–272 (June 5, 1945).

45. Nigel Nicolson, ed., *Harold Nicolson: Diaries and Letters, 1939–1945*, p. 347 (February 7, 1944).

46. Harold Macmillan, *Tides of Fortune, 1945–1955*, p. 32 (New York: Harper & Row, 1969).

47. Richard Hough, *Winston and Clementine: The Triumphs & Tragedies of the Churchills*, p. 485.

48. Mary Soames, *Clementine Churchill: Biography of a Marriage*, p. 504.

49. Anthony Eden, *The Reckoning*, p. 639.

50. Anthony Eden wrote of the 1945 election: "In later years Mr. Churchill and I often discussed this exchange of telegrams and he, naturally enough, would probe the question of whether our party would have fared better in an election later in the year. I do not think that it would. Political trends were boxed off by the war, not deflected." Anthony Eden, *The Reckoning*, p. 619.

51. Harold Macmillan, *Tides of Fortune, 1945–1955*, p. 27.

52. Richard Hough, *Winston and Clementine: The Triumphs & Tragedies of the Churchills*, p. 484.

53. Winston S. Churchill, *Triumph and Tragedy: The Second World War* (July 26, 1945), p. 584.

54. Charles McMoran Wilson Moran, *Churchill, Taken from the Diaries of Lord Moran: The Struggle for Survival, 1940–1965*, p. 308 (July 27, 1945).

55. John Wheeler-Bennett, ed., *Action This Day: Working with Churchill*, pp. 262–263.

56. Henry Pelling, *Winston Churchill*, p. 559, and Roy Jenkins, *Churchill*, pp. 806–807.

57. Michael Foot, *Aneurin Bevan: A Biography*, Volume II, p. 18.

58. Nigel Nicolson, ed., *Harold Nicolson: Diaries and Letters, 1939–1945*, p. 479 (August 1, 1945).

59. Michael Burlingame, ed., *Lincoln Observed: The Civil War Dispatches of Noah Brooks*, p. 264.

60. As a mature politician, Lincoln carefully thought about consequences. He foresaw problems and tried to devise solutions to those problems. He could not be an abolitionist because abolitionists were not sufficiently concerned with the Constitution or consequences. He recognized the racism of 19th century America, both North and South. Lincoln's world clearly had limits—but he knew enough not to push those limits to extremes he could not control. He knew he could not abolish slavery overnight but he also knew he could set goals for its ultimate extinction. The president tried to do what was necessary under each set of circumstances, and he expected others to do the same. He believed it necessary, for example, to review military death sentences. He thought it necessary to involve himself in political patronage—so he did it. But unlike Secretary of State William H. Seward or Secretary of the Treasury Salmon P. Chase, he did not meddle. Lincoln's work ethic was fundamental. And the rewards of hard work were important in politics as well—one reason that the appointment of Justin Butterfield to the federal land commissioner's post so disturbed Lincoln in 1849. Butterfield had not worked in the election campaign, and rewarding him for his lethargy and indifference was not only unjust but bad politics.

61. William C. Harris, *With Charity for All, Lincoln and the Restoration of the Union*, pp. 189–190.

62. In a speech on October 26, 1864, Henry Winter Davis claimed that the election was "not between two individuals, not between the personal qualities of Abraham Lincoln and George B. McClellan . . . but an election between the overthrow and the salvation of the Republic." Bernard Christian Steiner, *Life of Henry Winter Davis*, pp. 306–307.

63. Francis B. Carpenter, *The Inner Life of Abraham Lincoln: Six Months at the White House*, pp. 258–259.

64. Historian Jonathan White argued: "Historians often point out that Lincoln won 78 percent of the soldier vote in 1864, but they rarely scratch beneath the surface of that statistic. Clearly, some soldiers were intimidated or coerced into voting for Lincoln. Other Democrats in the army most likely crossed party lines because they believed Lincoln was the best candidate to restore the Union—but they did not necessarily endorse his positions on other political issues, like emancipation. And many others, like those in George Buck's regiment, simply did not vote. Indeed, many Democratic soldiers abstained from voting in 1864 because they saw Lincoln as an 'abolitionist,' while they viewed their own party as 'disloyal' for calling the war a 'failure' in its national platform." Jonathan White, *Emancipation, the Union Army, and the Reelection of Abraham Lincoln*, passim.

XIV. MANAGING MEN AT WAR—LINCOLN STYLE

1. *CWAL*, Volume VII, pp. 253–254 (Sanitary Fair, Washington, DC, March 18, 1864).

2. Winston S. Churchill, *The Hinge of Fate: The Second World War*, Volume IV, p. 361.

3. Michael Burlingame and John R. Turner Ettlinger, eds., *Inside Lincoln's White House: The Complete Civil War Diary of John Hay*, p. 243 (November 8, 1864).

4. *CWAL*, Volume VII, p. 11 (Lincoln to Edwin M. Stanton. November 11, 1863).

5. Michael Burlingame, ed., *Inside the White House in War Times: Memoirs and Reports of Lincoln's Secretary, William O. Stoddard*, pp. 93–94.

6. Michael Burlingame and John R. Turner Ettlinger, eds., *Inside Lincoln's White House: The Complete Civil War Diary of John Hay*, p. 194 (April 30, 1864).

7. Edward D. Neill, "Reminiscences of the Last Year of President Lincoln's Life," paper presented to the Minnesota Commandery of the Military Order of the Loyal Legion, February 1885, p. 3.

8. Michael Burlingame, ed., *At Lincoln's Side: John Hay's Civil War Correspondence and Selected Writings*, p. 49 (Charles G. Halpine, August 14, 1863).

9. Michael Burlingame, ed., *At Lincoln's Side: John Hay's Civil War Correspondence and Selected Writings*, p. 50 (John Hay to John G. Nicolay, August 13, 1863).

10. Michael Burlingame, ed., *At Lincoln's Side: John Hay's Civil War Correspondence and Selected Writings*, p. 109 (John Hay to William H. Herndon, September 5, 1866).

11. Michael Burlingame, ed., *At Lincoln's Side: John Hay's Civil War Correspondence and Selected Writings*, p. 87 (John Hay to Edward D. Neill, July 14, 1864).

12. Michael Burlingame, ed., *Dispatches from Lincoln's White House: The Anonymous Civil War Journalism of Presidential Secretary William O. Stoddard*, p. 166 (August 31, 1863).

13. Michael Burlingame, ed., *At Lincoln's Side: John Hay's Civil War Correspondence and Selected Writings*, p. 110 (John Hay to William H. Herndon, September 5, 1866).

14. Henry Raymond, *The Life, Public Services, and State Papers of Abraham Lincoln*, Volume II, p. 724.

15. *CWAL*, Volume IV, p. 121 (Lincoln to John M. Brockman, September 25, 1860).

16. Edward D. Neill, "Reminiscences of the Last Year of President Lincoln's Life," paper presented to the Minnesota Commandery of the Military Order of the Loyal Legion, February 1885, p. 4.

17. Don E. and Virginia Fehrenbacher, eds., *Recollected Words of Abraham Lincoln*, p. 115 (Septima Collis).

18.   Winston S. Churchill, *The Great Republic*, p. 179.

19.   *CWAL*, Volume V, p. 208 (Lincoln to George B. McClellan, May 9, 1862).

20.   *CWAL*, Volume VI, pp. 321–322 (Lincoln to Lorenzo Thomas, July 8, 1863).

21.   *CWAL*, Volume VI, pp. 327–328 (Lincoln to George Meade, July 14, 1863, unsent).

22.   Michael Burlingame and John R. Turner Ettlinger, eds., *Inside Lincoln's White House: The Complete Civil War Diary of John Hay*, pp. 64–65 (July 19, 1863).

23.   *CWAL*, Volume VI, p. 345 (Lincoln to Robert C. Schenck, July 23, 1863).

24.   Charles McMoran Wilson Moran, *Churchill, Taken from the Diaries of Lord Moran: The Struggle for Survival, 1940–1965*, p. 720.

25.   *CWAL*, Volume VI, p. 350 (Lincoln to George Meade, July 27, 1863).

26.   *CWAL*, Volume VI, p. 354 (Lincoln to Henry W. Halleck, July 29, 1863).

27.   *CWAL*, Volume VI, p. 377 (Lincoln to William Rosecrans, August 10, 1863).

28.   *CWAL*, Volume VI, pp. 377–378 (Lincoln to William Rosecrans, August 10, 1863).

29.   Michael Burlingame and John R. Turner Ettlinger, eds., *Inside Lincoln's White House: The Complete Civil War Diary of John Hay*, p. 85 (September 27, 1863).

30.   *CWAL*, Volume VI, pp. 472–473 (Abraham Lincoln William Rosecrans, September 21, 1863).

31.   In World War II, General George C. Marshall was a very reluctant convert to Churchill's North Africa operation—believing a quick invasion of France, "Sledgehammer," should not be postponed. More wisely (and more experienced from World War I), Churchill understood that such an invasion should only be undertaken after preliminary weakening of the German position, and readiness of the Allies. FDR agreed.

32.   Gideon Welles, *Diary of Gideon Welles*, Volume I, p. 364 (July 7, 1863).

33.   Gideon Welles, *Diary of Gideon Welles*, Volume I, p. 368 (July 11, 1863).

34.   Michael Burlingame and John R. Turner Ettlinger, eds., *Inside Lincoln's White House: The Complete Civil War Diary of John Hay*, p. 183 (March 24, 1864).

35.   Michael Burlingame and John R. Turner Ettlinger, eds., *Inside Lincoln's White House: The Complete Civil War Diary of John Hay*, pp. 193–194 (April 30, 1864).

36.   Grenville M. Dodge, *Personal Recollections of President Abraham Lincoln, General Ulysses S. Grant and General William T. Sherman*, p. 68.

37.   Allen Thorndike Rice, ed., *Reminiscences of Abraham Lincoln by Men of His Time*, pp. 337–338 (Schuyler Colfax).

38.   Muriel Bernitt, ed., "Two Manuscripts of Gideon Welles," *New England Quarterly*, September 1938, Volume 11, No. 3, p. 587.

39. Allan Nevins, *The War for the Union: War Becomes Revolution, 1862–1863*, Volume II, p. 364.

40. Gideon Welles, *Diary of Gideon Welles*, Volume II, p. 34 (May 17, 1864).

41. John G. Nicolay and John Hay, *Life of Abraham Lincoln*, Volume IX, p. 395.

42. Frederick W. Seward, *Autobiography: Seward at Washington, as Senator and Secretary of State: A Memoir of His Life, with Selections from His Letters, 1846–1872*, p. 590 (William H. Seward to Frances A. Seward, June 5, 1861). John Hay wrote on November 28, 1863: "The Secretary of State [William H. Seward] came in this morning and gave me his contribution to the President's Message, relating exclusively to foreign affairs. He then said he had a matter to submit, which was strictly confidential. 'I saw a great while ago that the President was being urged to do many things which were to redound to the benefit of other men, he [Lincoln] taking the responsibility and the risk. I preferred to leave to these men the attitude they coveted, of running before and shouting for the coming events; I preferred to stay behind, to do with and for the President what seemed best, to share with him the criticism and the risk and to leave the glory to him and to God." Michael Burlingame and John R. Turner Ettlinger, eds., *Inside Lincoln's White House: The Complete Civil War Diary of John Hay*, p. 119 (November 28, 1863).

43. Theodore Calvin Pease, ed., *The Diary of Orville Hickman Browning*, Volume I, pp. 673–674 (June 26, 1864).

44. Mark E. Neely Jr., *The Civil War and the Limits of Destruction*, p. 202.

45. Craig L. Symonds, *Lincoln and His Admirals*, p. xii.

46. In June 1863, Lincoln responded to those protesting his handling of civil liberties in the North: "Must I shoot the simple-minded soldier boy who deserts, while I must not touch a hair of a wiley [sic] agitator who induces him to desert? This is none the less injurious when effected by getting a father, or brother, or friend, into a public meeting, and there working upon his feelings, till he is persuaded to write the soldier boy, that he is fighting in a bad cause, for a wicked administration of a contemptable [sic] government, too weak to arrest and punish him if he shall desert. I think that in such a case, to silence the agitator, and save the boy, is not only constitutional, but, withal, a great mercy." *CWAL*, Volume VI, pp. 266–267 (Lincoln to Erastus Corning et al., June 12, 1863).

47. Isaac N. Arnold, "Abraham Lincoln: A Paper Read Before the Royal Historical Society," London, p. 188.

48. Francis B. Carpenter, *The Inner Life of Abraham Lincoln: Six Months at the White House*, p. 170.

49. *CWAL*, Volume VI, pp. 266–267 (Lincoln to Erastus Corning et al., June 12, 1863).

50. *CWAL*, Volume VII, p. 32 (Lincoln to George Opdyke, Joseph Sutherland, Benjamin F. Manierre, Prosper M. Wetmore, and Spencer Kirby, December 2, 1863).

51. Michael Burlingame and John R. Turner Ettlinger, eds., *Inside Lincoln's White House: The Complete Civil War Diary of John Hay*, p. 132 (December 23, 1863).

XV. MANAGING MEN AT WAR—CHURCHILL STYLE

1. Winston S. Churchill, *The Gathering Storm: The Second World War*, Volume I, pp. 373–374.
2. John Kennedy, *The Business of War*, p. 239.
3. Norman Brook observed that Churchill "thinks of those around him only as menials, they do not really count. He is not in the least interested in any of us or in our future. As long as we are devoted to him, and do not make bad mistakes, Winston will not think of anyone else." Brooke later wrote: "Though he seemed to take our work for granted, and might allow some time to pass without showing any special interest on it or in us, he would at intervals find time to say or write a few words of appreciation which showed a quite exceptional generosity and kindness. He was essentially a very human man, and no one who worked closely with him can have failed to be affected by the generosity of his temperament." John Wheeler-Bennett, ed., *Action This Day: Working with Churchill*, p. 25.
4. John Colville wrote: "The list of Churchill's official advisers is a short one, for he was little responsive to advice. However, when he did have confidence in a man, it was wholeheartedly given and seldom withdrawn." John Colville, *Winston Churchill and His Inner Circle*, p. 173.
5. James Leasor, *War at the Top: The Experiences of General Leslie Hollis*, p. 64.
6. Churchill aides managed their schedules so they could get occasional weekends off. Private Secretary John Martin managed two weeks off for his wedding and honeymoon in May 1943.
7. David Dilks, ed., *The Diaries of Sir Alexander Cadogan, OM, 1938–1945*, p. 621 (April 19, 1944).
8. John Colville admitted that Churchill "was inconsiderate. During the war, provided he himself had seven-hours sleep (one of them in the afternoon), he seldom stopped to think how exhausted others, working perhaps eighteen or nineteen hours a day, might be. He often changed his plans on a sudden whim, careless of the grave inconvenience this might cause. His servants would be kept up to all hours, dining at eight o'clock, he might stay in the dining room till after midnight. Stenographers would have to remain on duty till three or four in the morning in case they were wanted; other people's mealtimes were of no consequence; the presence of ministers or chiefs of staff might be required long after they had gone to bed. Yet none of those who worked for him—did more than utter a few grumbles. They all loved him, and they all forgave him; for if you give affection, as he did, you receive it in return." R. Crosby Kemper II, ed., *Winston Churchill: Resolution, Defiance,*

Magnanimity, Good Will, pp. 111–112 (John R. Colville, "The Personality of Winston Churchill").

9. "Marian Holmes," Obituary, *The London Telegraph*, October 10, 2001. http://www.telegraph.co.uk/news/obituaries/4266205/Marian -Holmes.html.

10. John Keegan, "His Finest Hour," *U.S. News & World Report*, May 29, 2000, p. 56.

11. Paul Addison, *Churchill: The Unexpected Hero*, p. 175.

12. Reginald William Thompson, *Generalissimo Churchill*, p. 93.

13. Andrew Roberts, *Masters and Commanders: How Four Titans Won the War in the West, 1941–1945*, p. 471.

14. Charles McMoran Wilson Moran, *Churchill, Taken from the Diaries of Lord Moran: The Struggle for Survival, 1940–1965*, p. 745 (June 24, 1956).

15. Elizabeth Layton Nel, *Winston Churchill by His Personal Secretary*, p. 140.

16. Alex Danchev and Daniel Todman, eds., *Lord Alanbrooke War Diaries, 1939–1945*, p. 445 (August 19, 1943).

17. General Ismay wrote: "Men of genius are unpredictable, and Mr Churchill was never amenable to regular routine." Hastings Lionel Ismay, *Memoirs of General Lord Ismay*, p. 175.

18. John Colville, *The Fringes of Power*, p. 402 (June 19, 1941).

19. John Kennedy, *The Business of War: The War Narrative of Major-General Sir John Kennedy*, pp. 60–61.

20. John Kennedy, *The Business of War: The War Narrative of Major-General Sir John Kennedy*, p. 74.

21. Andrew Roberts, *Masters and Commanders: How Four Titans Won the War in the West, 1941–1945*, p. 55.

22. Andrew Roberts, *Masters and Commanders: How Four Titans Won the War in the West, 1941–1945*, p. 480.

23. John Wheeler-Bennett, ed., *Action This Day: Working with Churchill*, p. 150 (John Martin).

24. John Wheeler-Bennet, ed., *Action This Day: Working with Churchill*, p. 163 (Ian Jacob).

25. John Wheeler-Bennett, ed., *Action This Day: Working with Churchill*, pp. 163–164 (Ian Jacob).

26. Andrew Roberts, *Masters and Commanders: How Four Titans Won the War in the West, 1941–1945*, p. 111.

27. Hastings Lionel Ismay, *Memoirs of General Lord Ismay*, pp. 269–270.

28. John Wheeler-Bennett, ed., *Action This Day: Working with Churchill*, pp. 19–21 (Norman Brook).

29. Paul Addison, *Churchill: The Unexpected Hero*, p. 183.

30. John Wheeler-Bennett, ed., *Action This Day: Working with Churchill*, p. 144.

31. John Wheeler-Bennett, ed., *Action This Day: Working with Churchill*, pp. 220–221 (Edward Bridges).

32. John Martin, *Downing Street: The War Years*, p. 12.

33. Remarking on her first overseas trip with Churchill, she wrote that "I— Elizabeth Layton from British Columbia—I was the luckiest girl in all the world!" Elizabeth Nel, *Winston Churchill by His Personal Secretary*, pp. 21, 72.

34. Cita Stelzer, *Dinner with Churchill*, p. 260. In May 1943, Harold Nicolson wrote of a session of the House of Commons at which Attlee spoke: "I cannot convey to you the absurdity of that small man. As someone remarked afterwards, 'It is difficult to make defeat sound like a victory: but to make such a victory sound like a defeat is a masterpiece in human ingenuity.'" Nigel Nicolson, ed., *Harold Nicolson: Diaries and Letters, 1939–1945*, pp. 295–296 (May 11, 1943).

35. John Wheeler-Bennett, ed., *Action This Day: Working with Churchill*, p. 263 (Leslie Rowan). Those who worked with Churchill felt honored by the opportunity. British interpreter A. H. Birse wrote of Churchill in the 1942–1945 period: "[T]here was never an impatient word or sign of displeasure. I received nothing but courtesy, appreciation and much consideration. Frequently, during the talks at the Kremlin, in Teheran, Yalta, and Potsdam, he would ask how I was doing. I wonder if he realized how encouraging it was to be asked in the middle of a talk: 'Are you feeling tired, Birsey?' I may have felt tired, but he made me forget it. Fate had been kind in placing me in his path." A. H. Birse, *Memoirs of an Interpreter*, p. 224.

36. Charles McMoran Wilson Moran, *Churchill, Taken from the Diaries of Lord Moran: The Struggle for Survival, 1940–1965*, p. 136 (November 16, 1943).

37. Charles Eade, ed., *Churchill—by His Contemporaries*, p. 161 (Mary T. G. Thompson, "Secretary to Churchill").

38. Martin Gilbert, *Winston S. Churchill: Road to Victory, 1941–1945*, p. 372 (Marian Holmes Diary, March 24, 1943).

39. Warren F. Kimball, ed., *Churchill and Roosevelt: The Complete Correspondence*, Volume I, p. 87.

40. Douglas L. Wilson, *Honor's Voice*, p. 304.

41. *CWAL*, Volume VIII, p. 101 (Response to a Serenade, November 10, 1864).

42. Osborn H. Oldroyd, *The Lincoln Memorial: Album-Immortelles*, p. 422 (Alexander Milton Ross).

43. John Wheeler-Bennett, ed., *Action This Day: Working with Churchill*, p. 140 (John Martin).

44. Elizabeth Layton Nel, *Winston Churchill by His Personal Secretary*, p. 94.

45. James Leasor, *War at the Top*, p. 168.

46. John Kennedy, *The Business of War*, p. 146.

47. Winston S. Churchill, *Triumph and Tragedy*, p. 670 (Speech to House of Commons, September 28, 1944).

48. Maxwell Philip Schoenfeld, *The War Ministry of Winston Churchill*, p. 75.

49. John Kennedy, *The Business of War*, p. 108.

50. Alex Danchev and Daniel Todman, eds., *Lord Alanbrooke: War Diaries, 1939–1945*, pp. 160–161 (May 27, 1941).

51. Alex Danchev and Daniel Todman, eds., *Lord Alanbrooke War Diaries, 1939–1945*, pp. 189–190 (October 12, 1941).

52. Alex Danchev and Daniel Todman, eds., *Lord Alanbrooke War Diaries, 1939–1945*, p. 451 (August 30, 1943).

53. Brooke biographer David Fraser wrote: "Both men grew more and more exhausted as the years passed, and with exhaustion irritation increased. But in fact the partnership was admirable, perhaps more admirable than either appreciated. Their personalities clashed at times, but their qualities were complementary. Brooke was, like Churchill (although it was concealed), emotional, but he was a realist, a pragmatist, a calculator. His will was very strong. He was never prepared to accede to an idea—or a campaign—unless he was personally convinced that it was the best way, that it had at least a decent chance of success, and that the fighting men attempting it were being committed to battle in as good order as could be managed." John Keegan, ed., *Churchill's Generals*, p. 92 (David Fraser, "Field-Marshal Viscount Alanbrooke").

54. Alex Danchev and Daniel Todman, eds., *Lord Alanbrooke War Diaries, 1939–1945*, p. 634 (December 12, 1944).

55. William Manchester and Paul Reid, *The Last Lion: Winston Spencer Churchill, Defender of the Realm, 1940–1965*, p. 684.

56. Anthony Eden, *The Reckoning; the Memoirs of Anthony Eden, Earl of Avon*, pp. 468–469.

57. John Colville, *The Fringes of Power*, p. 489 (May 12, 1944).

58. Charles McMoran Wilson Moran, *Churchill, Taken from the Diaries of Lord Moran: The Struggle for Survival, 1940–1965*, p. 746 (June 24, 1956).

59. Alex Danchev and Daniel Todman, eds., *Lord Alanbrooke War Diaries, 1939–1945*, p. 442 (August 15, 1943).

60. Charles de Gaulle, *War Memoirs: Unity*, Volume I, p. 132. (New York: Simon & Schuster, 1959).

61. John Wheeler-Bennett, ed., *Action This Day: Working with Churchill*, p. 176 (Sir Ian Jacob).

62. Alex Danchev and Daniel Todman, eds., *Lord Alanbrooke War Diaries, 1939–1945*, p. 588.

63. Alex Danchev and Daniel Todman, eds., *Lord Alanbrooke War Diaries, 1939–1945*, p. 589 (September 8, 1944).

64. Alex Danchev and Daniel Todman, eds., *Lord Alanbrooke War Diaries, 1939–1945*, p. 590 (September 10, 1944).

65. Alex Danchev and Daniel Todman, eds., *Lord Alanbrooke War Diaries, 1939–1945*, p. 591 (September 13, 1944).

66. Alex Danchev and Daniel Todman, eds., *Lord Alanbrooke War Diaries, 1939–1945*, pp. 592–593.

67. Alex Danchev and Daniel Todman, eds., *Lord Alanbrooke War Diaries, 1939–1945*, p. 594 (September 16, 1944).

68. Alex Danchev and Daniel Todman, eds., *Lord Alanbrooke War Diaries, 1939–1945*, p. 605.

69. Alex Danchev and Daniel Todman, eds., *Lord Alanbrooke: War Diaries, 1939–1945*, pp. xv–xvi.

70. Andrew Roberts, *Masters and Commanders: How Four Titans Won the War in the West*, p. 475

71. Alex Danchev and Daniel Todman, eds., *Lord Alanbrooke: War Diaries, 1939–1945*, pp. 566–567 (July 6, 1944).

72. Alex Danchev and Daniel Todman, eds., *War Diaries, 1939–1945: Field Marshal Lord Alanbrooke*, p. 590 (September 9, 1944).

73. Baron Charles McMoran Wilson Moran, *Churchill, Taken from the Diaries of Lord Moran: The Struggle for Survival, 1940–1965*, pp. 183–184 (August 20, 1944).

74. Kay Halle, *Irrepressible Churchill*, p. 200 (Cleveland: World, 1966).

75. Menzies noted: "Churchill grows on me. He has an astonishing grasp of detail and, by daily contact with the service headquarters, knows of disposition and establishment quite accurately." Robert Menzies, *Dark and Hurrying Days: Menzies' 1941 Diary*, p. 71 (March 2, 1941).

76. Richard M. Langworth, ed., *Churchill by Himself: The Definitive Collection of Quotations*, p. 279 (July 2, 1942).

77. Rufus Rockwell Wilson, ed., *Lincoln among His Friends: A Sheaf of Intimate Memories*, p. 331.

78. Michael Burlingame, *Abraham Lincoln: A Life*, Volume 2, p. 366 (Henry W. Halleck to Horatio Wright, August 25, 1862).

79. John Y. Simon, ed., *The Papers of Ulysses S. Grant*, Volume VII, p. 401 (Henry W. Halleck to Ulysses S. Grant, March 20, 1863).

80. Noel Annan, "How Wrong Was Churchill?" *New York Review of Books*, April 8, 1993. http://www.nybooks.com/articles/1993/04/08/how-wrong-was-churchill/.

XVI. LEGACIES

1. *CWAL*, Volume VIII, pp. 152–153 (Fourth Annual Message to Congress, December 6, 1864).

2. Martin Gilbert, ed., *Churchill: The Power of Words*, p. 273 (November 12, 1940).

3. William Manchester, *The Last Lion: Visions of Glory, 1874–1932*, p. 8.

4. Geoffrey Best, *Churchill and War*, p. 185.

5. Jack Colville, *Footprints in Time: Memories*, p. 187 (March 24, 1945).

6. Omar N. Bradley and Clay Blair, *A General's Life: An Autobiography by General of the Army Omar N. Bradley*, p. 401.

7. *CWAL*, Volume I, p. 510 (Speech in the House of Representatives on Presidential Question, July 27, 1848).

8. Michael E. Burlingame and John R. Turner Ettlinger, eds., *Inside Lincoln's White House: The Complete Civil War Diary of John Hay*, p. 191 (April 28, 1865).

9. Rufus Rockwell Wilson, ed., *Intimate Memories of Lincoln*, pp. 146–147 (Benjamin F. Butler).

10. Andrew Roberts, *Masters and Commanders: How Four Titans Won the War in the West, 1941–1945*, p. 515.

11. Martin Gilbert, *Churchill: The Power of Words: His Remarkable Life Recounted Through His Writings and Speeches*, p. 358 (BBC address, May 13, 1945).

12. Winston S. Churchill, *Their Finest Hour: The Second World War*, Volume II, p. 5.

13. Edwina S. Campbell, *Twentieth Century Wars*, p. 68.

14. J. David Hacker, "A Census-Based Count of the Civil War Dead," *Civil War History*, December 2011, pp. 307–348. Civil War historian Mark E. Neely Jr. notes that the number of nonbattlefield deaths inflates the casualty numbers for the Civil War. Mark E. Neely Jr., *The Civil War and the Limits of Destruction*, pp. 211–214.

15. John Lukacs, *Churchill: Visionary, Statesman, Historian,* p. 154. New Haven: Yale University Press, 2002.

16. Lynne Olson, *Troublesome Young Men: The Rebels Who Brought Churchill to Power and Helped Save England*, p. 341.

17. Jesse Weik, *The Real Lincoln: A Portrait*, p. 301.

18. *CWAL*, Volume IV, p. 271 (First Inaugural Address, March 4, 1861).

19. Ward Hill Lamon, *Recollections of Abraham Lincoln*, p. 241.

20. Edward Duffield Neill, *Reminiscences of the Last Year of President Lincoln's Life*, p. 14.

21. Winston S. Churchill, *History of the English-Speaking Peoples, The Great Democracies*, Volume IV, p. 262.

22. Andrew Roberts, *Masters and Commanders*, p. 225.

23. John Colville, *Winston Churchill and His Inner Circle*, p. 11.

24. John Wheeler-Bennett, ed., *Action This Day: Working with Churchill*, p. 140 (John Martin).

25. John Colville, *Fringes of Power*, p. 200 (July 24, 1940).

26. Martin Gilbert, *Churchill and America*, p. 270.

27. Winston S. Churchill, *My Early Life: A Roving Commission*, pp. 330–331. Similarly, the purpose of Sherman's march through Georgia, South Carolina, and North Carolina had been to destroy the slaveholders' will to maintain the fight. After Sherman signed an armistice with Confederate General Joseph E. Johnston in late April 1865, the agreement was criticized as excessively generous and repudiated by Stanton.

28. Winston S. Churchill, *Triumph and Tragedy: The Second World War*, Volume VI, p. 545.

29. Richard M. Langworth, ed., *Churchill by Himself: The Definitive Collection of Quotations*, p. 28 (June 5, 1946).

30. Paul Johnson, *Churchill*, p. 138.

31. Walter H. Thompson, *Assignment Churchill*, p. 304.

32. Simon Berthon and Joanna Potts, *Warlords: An Extraordinary Re-creation of World War II Through the Eyes and Minds of Hitler, Churchill, Roosevelt, and Stalin,* p. 304.

33. Norman Davies, *No Simple Victory: World War II in Europe, 1939–1945,* p. 312.

34. Winston S. Churchill, *Closing the Ring: The Second World War,* Volume VII, p. 621.

35. Douglas L. Wilson and Rodney O. Davis, eds., *Lincoln's Informants,* pp. 157–158 (Joshua F. Speed to William H. Herndon, January 12, 1866).

36. Doris Kearns Goodwin, *Team of Rivals: The Political Genius of Abraham Lincoln,* p. 104.

37. John Chester Miller, *Alexander Hamilton and the Growth of the New Nation,* p. 477.

38. Michael Burlingame, ed., *An Oral History of Abraham Lincoln, John G. Nicolay's Interviews and Essays,* p. 7 (Conversation with Orville H. Browning, June 17, 1875).

39. John H. Krenkel, *Richard Yates: Civil War Governor,* p. 227.

40. Violet Bonham Carter, *Winston Churchill: An Intimate Portrait,* p. 14.

41. Martin Gilbert, *Churchill and the Jews: A Lifelong Friendship,* p. 3.

42. Martin Gilbert, *Churchill: A Life,* p. 115 (Winston S. Churchill to Jennie Churchill, November 30, 1899).

43. Don E. and Virginia Fehrenbacher, eds., *Recollected Words of Abraham Lincoln,* p. 413 (Joshua F. Speed).

44. John Colville, *Fringes of Power,* p. 125.

45. Douglas L. Wilson and Rodney O. Davis, eds., *Herndon's Informants: Letters, Interviews, and Statements about Abraham Lincoln,* p. 562 (Henry Wilson to William H. Herndon, May 30, 1867).

46. Douglas L. Wilson and Rodney O. Davis, eds., *Herndon's Informants,* p. 360 (Mary Todd Lincoln interview with William H. Herndon, September 1866).

47. Michael Burlingame, *Abraham Lincoln: A Life,* Volume II, p. 531.

48. Allan Nevins, *The Emergence of Lincoln: Prologue to Civil War, 1859–1861,* Volume I, p. 437.

49. James Leasor, *War at the Top: The Experiences of General Leslie Hollis,* p. 10.

50. Harold Holzer, ed., *Lincoln as I Knew Him: Gossip, Tributes, and Revelations from His Best Friends and Worst Enemies,* p. 139.

51. *CWAL,* Volume V, p. 537 (Second Annual Message to Congress, December 1, 1862).

52. *CWAL,* Volume II, p. 126 (Eulogy of Henry Clay, July 6, 1852).

53. *CWAL,* Volume VII, p. 23 (Gettysburg Address, November 19, 1863).

54. *CWAL,* Volume II, p. 116 (Resolutions in Behalf of Hungarian Freedom, January 9, 1852).

55. Martin Gilbert, *Continue to Pester, Nag and Bite: Winston Churchill's War Leadership,* p. 90.

56. Winston S. Churchill, *Triumph and Tragedy: The Second World War*, Volume VI, p. 257 (December 8, 1944).

57. Randolph Churchill and Martin Gilbert, *Winston S. Churchill: Youth, 1874–1900*, Volume 1, p. 510.

58. Alex Danchev and Daniel Todman, eds., *Lord Alanbrooke: War Diaries, 1939–1945*, p. 451 (August 30, 1943).

59. Carlo D'Este, *Warlord: A Life of Winston Churchill at War, 1874–1945*, p. 356.

60. *CWAL*, Volume VIII, p. 332 (Second Inaugural Address, March 4, 1865).

61. William H. Herndon and Jesse W. Weik, *Herndon's Lincoln*, p. 357.

62. Martin Gilbert, *Churchill: The Power of Words: His Remarkable Life Recounted Through His Writings and Speeches*, pp. 387–389 (May 21, 1948).

63. Isaiah Berlin, *Personal Impressions*, p. 4.

64. *CWAL*, Volume VIII, p. 405 (Response to Serenade, April 11, 1865).

65. John Lukacs, *Churchill: Visionary, Statesman, Historian*, pp. 4–5.

66. James M. McPherson, *Abraham Lincoln and the Second American Revolution*, p. 114.

67. Allen Thorndike Rice, ed., *Reminiscences of Abraham Lincoln by Distinguished Men of His Time*, p. 138 (George S. Boutwell).

68. Theodore Calvin Peace, ed., *Diary of Orville Hickman Browning*, Volume I, p. 659 (February 6, 1864).

69. *CWAL*, Volume VII, p. 23 (Gettysburg Address, November 19, 1863).

70. *CWAL*, Volume II, pp. 266, 271 (Speech at Peoria, October 16, 1854).

71. *CWAL*, Volume II, p. 255 (Speech at Peoria, October 16, 1854).

72. Martin Gilbert, ed., *The Churchill War Papers: At the Admiralty, September 1939–May 1940*, p. 195.

73. Nigel Nicolson, ed., *Harold Nicolson: Diaries and Letters: The War Years*, p. 223 (April 22, 1942).

74. Douglas L. Wilson and Rodney O. Davis, eds., *Herndon's Informants*, p. 184 (Leonard Swett to William H. Herndon, January 17, 1866).

75. *CWAL*, Volume V, p. 118 (Lincoln to Queen Victoria, February 1, 1862).

76. Justin G. Turner and Linda Levitt Turner, eds., *Mary Todd Lincoln: Her Life and Letters*, p. 230 (Queen Victoria to Mary Todd Lincoln, April 29, 1865).

77. Walter Thompson, *Beside the Bulldog: The Intimate Memoirs of Churchill's Bodyguard*, p. 130.

78. Martin Gilbert, *Churchill: The Power of Words: His Remarkable Life Recounted Through His Writings and Speeches*, p. 345 (April 17, 1945).

79. Winston S. Churchill, *Triumph and Tragedy*, Volume VI, p. 412 (Churchill to Eleanor Roosevelt, April 13, 1945).

80. *CWAL*, Volume VII, p. 507 (Interview with Alexander W. Randall and Joseph T. Mills, August 19, 1864).

81. Winston S. Churchill, *The Great Republic*, p. 214. Historian Michael Burlingame wrote: "Lincoln's moral sense dictated this bold insistence on

emancipation as a basis for peace. If he had been motivated by political expediency alone, he could simply have avoided mentioning the slavery issue; he knew that the Confederates would reject any peace terms denying them independence." Michael Burlingame, *Abraham Lincoln: A Life*, Volume II, p. 672.

82. Richard Langworth, ed., *Churchill by Himself: The Definitive Collection of Quotations*, p. 9 (Speech to House of Commons, August 16, 1945).

XVII. EPILOGUE

1. *CWAL*, Volume VI, p. 537 (Second Annual Message to Congress, December 1, 1862).
2. Winston S. Churchill, *Onwards to Victory*, p. 182.
3. William Hayes Ward, ed., *Abraham Lincoln: Tributes from His Associates, Reminiscences of Soldiers, Statesmen and Citizens*, p. 44 (William O. Stoddard, "Lincoln's Vigil: The Defeat of Chancellorsville").
4. Carl Schurz, *Reminiscences of Carl Schurz*, Volume II, pp. 239–240.
5. James R. Gilmore, *Personal Recollections of Abraham Lincoln and the Civil War*, p. 14.
6. Michael Burlingame, ed., *Lincoln Observed: Civil War Dispatches of Noah Brooks*, p. 203 ("Personal Recollections of Abraham Lincoln").
7. Michael Burlingame, *Abraham Lincoln: A Life*, Volume II, p. 289.
8. Allen C. Clark, "Abraham Lincoln in the National Capital," *Journal of the Columbia Historical Society*, Volume XXVII, p. 64 (The New Covenant).
9. Charles McMoran Wilson Moran, *Churchill, Taken from the Diaries of Lord Moran: The Struggle for Survival, 1940–1965*, p. 138 (November 17, 1943).
10. John Kennedy, *The Business of War*, p. 239.
11. Maxwell Philip Schoenfeld, *The War Ministry of Winston Churchill*, p. 251.
12. Michael Burlingame, ed., *At Lincoln's Side: John Hay's Civil War Correspondence and Selected Writings*, pp. 133–134. "From early morning till late at night its lobbies and passages were filled with a motley throng of all classes and all nations." Edward Dicey, *Spectator of America*, p. 96.
13. Michael Burlingame, ed., *William O. Stoddard, Inside the White House in War Times: Memoirs and Reports of Lincoln's Secretary*, p. 124.
14. Rufus Rockwell Wilson, ed., *Intimate Memories of Lincoln*, pp. 236–237 (William O. Stoddard, *Atlantic Monthly*, February, March 1925).
15. Shelby M. Cullom, *Fifty Years of Public Service*, pp. 89–90.
16. Stephen W. Sears, *To the Gates of Richmond: The Peninsula Campaign*, p. 157.
17. Michael Burlingame, ed., *Abraham Lincoln: The Observations of John G. Nicolay and John Hay*, p. 140.
18. Brian Lavery, *Churchill Goes to War: Winston's Wartime Journeys*, p. 112.
19. Hastings Lionel Ismay, *Memoirs of General Lord Ismay*, p. 163.
20. John Colville, *The Fringes of Power: The Incredible Inside Story of Winston Churchill*, p. 231 (August 27, 1940).

21. John Colville, *The Fringes of Power: The Incredible Inside Story of Winston Churchill*, p. 234 (August 31, 1940).

22. Prudence was Lincoln's watchword. "When the hour comes for dealing with slavery, I trust I will be willing to act, though it costs my life." Don and Virginia Fehrenbacher, eds., *Recollected Words of Abraham Lincoln*, p. 118 (Moncure Conway).

23. Michael Burlingame, ed., Walter B. Stevens, *A Reporter's Lincoln*, p. 150.

24. John Colville, *Fringes of Power: The Incredible Inside Story of Winston Churchill during World War II*, p. 310 (December 12, 1940).

25. David Reynolds, *In Command of History: Churchill Fighting and Writing the Second World War*, p. 39.

26. David Reynolds, *In Command of History: Churchill Fighting and Writing the Second World War*, passim.

27. Lord Moran, *Churchill: The Struggle for Survival 1940–65*, p. 802 (June 1959).

28. Edward Longacre, *General Ulysses S. Grant: The Soldier and the Man*, p. 118 (Message from Ulysses S. Grant to Simon Bolivar Buckner, February 16, 1862).

29. Martin Gilbert, *Winston S. Churchill: Road to Victory, 1941–1945*, p. 310.

30. W. Averell Harriman and Elie Abel, *Special Envoy to Churchill and Stalin, 1941–1946*, p. 190.

31. John Kennedy, *The Business of War*, p. 256.

32. Winston S. Churchill, *The Closing of the Ring: The Second World War*, Volume V, p. 584 (Churchill to Eden, August 14, 1943).

33. *CWAL*, Volume V, p. 388 (Lincoln to Horace Greeley, August 22, 1862).

34. *CWAL*, Volume V, p. 530 (Second Annual Message to Congress, December 3, 1862).

35. Richard M. Langworth, ed., *Churchill by Himself*, p. 306 (December 5, 1942).

36. John Keegan, *Winston Churchill*, p. 14.

HISTORIOGRAPHY AND ACKNOWLEDGMENTS

1. Maunsell B. Field, *Memories of Many Men and of Some Women*, pp. 263–264.

2. Frederick Seward, *William H. Seward: 1846–1861*, Volume II, p. 521.

3. Winston S. Churchill, *My Early Life*, p. 33.

4. *CWAL*, Volume II, p. 318 (Letter to George Robertson, August 15, 1855).

5. Don E. and Virginia Fehrenbacher, eds., *Recollected Words of Abraham Lincoln*, pp. 246–247 (William Herndon to Jesse Weik, December 1885).

6. Andrew Roberts, *Masters and Commanders*, p. 22.

7. David Fraser, *Alanbrooke*, p. 196.

8. David Reynolds, *In Command of History: Churchill Fighting and Writing the Second World War*, p. 520.

9. Alex Danchev and Daniel Todman, eds., *War Diaries, 1939–1945: Field Marshal Lord Alanbrooke*, pp. xxxi–xxxiv.

10. Alex Danchev, "'Dilly-Dally', or Having the Last Word: Field Marshall Sir John Dill and Prime Minister Winston Churchill," *Journal of Contemporary History*, 1987, p. 30.

11. Lord Moran, *Churchill: The Postwar Years 1945–60*, p. xvi (New York: Carroll & Graf, 2006).

12. Anthony Eden, *The Reckoning*, p. 441.

13. John Colville, *Fringes of Power*, p. 756.

14. John Martin, *Downing Street: The War Years*, passim.

15. Lord Chandos, *The Memoirs of Lord Chandos*, p. 172.

16. Robert E. Sherwood, *Roosevelt and Hopkins: An Intimate History*, p. 421.

17. David Kaiser, *No End Save Victory: How FDR Led the Nation into War*, p. 76.

18. Harry C. Butcher, *Three Years with Eisenhower: The Personal Diary of Captain Harry C. Butcher, USNR, Naval Aide to General Eisenhower, 1942–1945*, p. 170 (May 30, 1943) (London: William Heinemann LTD, 1946).

19. Geoffrey Perret, *Eisenhower*, p. 372.

20. Elliott Roosevelt, *As He Saw It*, pp. 190–191.

21. Walter Reid, *Churchill: 1940–1945, Under Friendly Fire*, p. 4.

22. Winston S. Churchill, *The Hinge of Fate: The Second World War*, Volume IV, p. xiii.

23. A study by Churchill scholar Richard Langworth found about 15 million published words, but when compilation of more documents is completed may approach 20 million words. (Richard Langworth to author, August 2, 2016).

24. http://www.chu.cam.ac.uk/archives/collections/churchill_papers/the_papers/.

25. Jonathan Rose, *The Literary Churchill: Author, Reader, Actor*, p. 416.

26. David Reynolds, *In Command of History: Churchill Fighting and Writing the Second World War*, p. 57.

27. Elisabeth Barker, *Churchill and Eden at War*, p. 15.

28. Elisabeth Barker, *Churchill and Eden at War*, p. 16.

29. Tuvia Ben-Moshe, *Churchill: Strategy and History*, p. 332.

30. Larry Arrn, *Churchill's Trial: Winston Churchill and the Salvation of Free Government*, p. xviii.

31. Robert Blake and William Roger Louis, eds., *Churchill: A Major New Assessment of His Life in Peace and War*, p. 4. John W. Wheeler-Bennett and Anthony Nicholls wrote: "It would, however, be entirely erroneous to convey the impression that Mr Churchill was entirely consistent in his attitude toward the Russians. Indeed consistency had never been among his virtues or his failings. As he himself has admitted, 'During my life I have often had to eat my own words and I have always found them a wholesome diet.'" John W. Wheeler-Bennett and Anthony Nicholls, *The Semblance of Peace; The Political Settlement of the Second World War*, p. 295.

32. David Dilks, *Churchill and Company*, p. 33.

33. Tony Benn, Lord Carrington, Lord Deedes, Mary Soames, and David Cannadine, "Churchill Remembered," Transactions of the Royal Historical Society, Volume 11 (2001), p. 401.

34. Roy Jenkins, *Churchill: A Biography*, p. 466.

35. As he prepared to return home from his speaking tour of New England after the Cooper Union address, Mr. Lincoln wrote his wife: "I have been unable to escape this toil. If I had foreseen it I think I would not have come East at all. The speech at New York, being within my calculation before I started, went off passably well, and gave me no trouble whatever. The difficulty was to make nine others, before reading audiences, who have already seen all my ideas in print." *CWAL*, Volume III, p. 555 (Lincoln to Mary Todd Lincoln, March 4, 1860).

36. Richard N. Current, *Speaking of Abraham Lincoln*, p. 177.

37. Mark Antony De Wolfe Howe, ed., *The Life and Letters of George Bancroft*, Volume II, p. 155.

38. George Bancroft, "The Place of Abraham Lincoln in History," *Atlantic*, June 1865.

INDEX